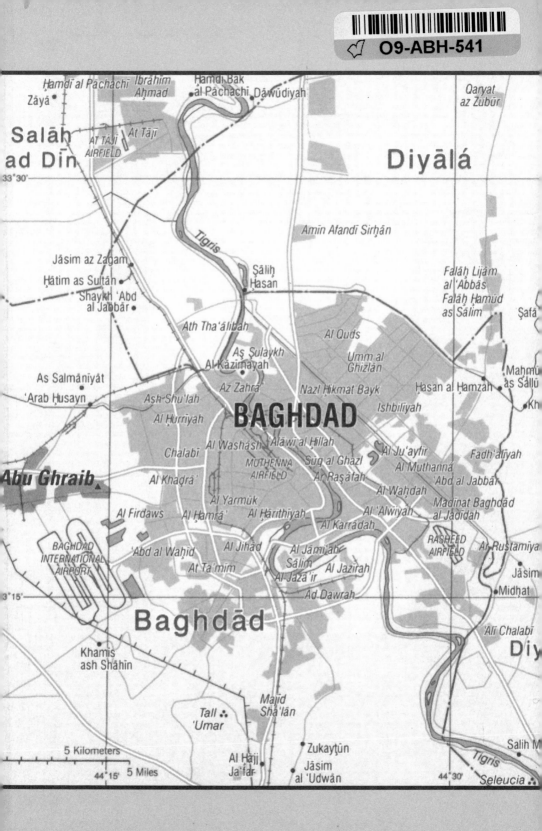

Hamdī al Pāchachī   Ibrāhīm   Hamdī Bak
Zāyā   Ahmad   al Pāchachī   Dāwūdiyah   Qaryat
                                                               az Zubūr

Salāh
ad Dīn   AT TĀJĪ   At Tājī
               AIRFIELD   **Diyālá**
33°30'

                              Tigris   Amīn Afandī Sirhān

Jāsim az Zagam   Sālih   Falāh Lijām
Hātim as Sultān   Hasan   al 'Abbās
  Shaykh 'Abd   Falāh Hamūd
  al Jabbār   Ath Tha'ālibah   as Sālim   Safā

                       Aş Şulaykh   Al Quds
                     Al Kāzimāyah   Umm al   Mahmū
As Salmānīyāt   Az Zahrá'   Ghizlān   as Sāllū
'Arab Husayn   Nazl Hikmat Bayk   Hasan al Hamzah
              Ash Shu'lah   Ishbilīyah   Kh
              Al Hurrīyah   **BAGHDAD**
              Chalabī   Al Washāsh 'Alāwī al Hillah   Al Ju'ayfir   Fadh'alīyah
                              MUTHENNA   Sūq al Ghazl   Al Muthanná
Abu Ghraib   Al Khadrá'   AIRFIELD   Ar Rasāfah   'Abd al Jabbār
                                              Al Wahdah
         Al Firdaws   Al Hamrá' Al Hārithīyah   Al 'Alwīyah   Madīnat Baghdād
            Al Yarmūk   Al Karrādah   al Jādīdah
BAGHDAD   RASHEED   Ar Rustamīya
INTERNATIONAL   'Abd al Wahid   Al Jihād   Al Jāmi'ah   AIRFIELD
AIRPORT   Sālim   Al Jazīrah   Jāsim
         At Ta'mim   Al Jazā'ir   Midhat
3°15'   Ad Dawrah

Baghdād   'Alī Chalabī
                                                              Diy
Khamīs
ash Shāhin

                    Tall   Mājid
                    'Umar   Sha'lān
5 Kilometers   Salih M
                         Zukaytūn   Tigris
44°15'   5 Miles   Al Hājj   Seleucia
                   Ja'far   Jāsim
                           al 'Udwān   44°30'

OUR GOOD NAME

To Toby Field —

A fine reputation is indeed a treasure to defend. We learned what its like to be a 'scape goat' in a world-wide scandal. This book tells our story about that awful time. The quotation on p. 572 say it all.

Always my best)

Jack Hudson '59

June 2010

OUR GOOD NAME

A Company's Fight to Defend Its Honor and
Get the Truth Told About Abu Ghraib

∾

J. Phillip London and the CACI team

Cataloging-in-Publication data on file with the Library of Congress
Our Good Name: A company's fight to defend it's honor and get the truth told about Abu Ghraib/ J. Phillip London and the CACI team
ISBN 978-1-59698-539-1

1. Abu Ghraib Prison — History — U.S. Army use for detainees, 2003 – 2006 — detainee abuse and scandal. 2. CACI International Inc — J. Phillip London, President and CEO, 1984 – 2007. 3. Iraq war — Operation Iraqi Freedom — government contractors. 4. Crisis Management — media abuse — propaganda. I. Title.

Published in the United States by
Regnery Publishing, Inc.
One Massachusetts Avenue, NW
Washington, DC 20001
www.regnery.com

Manufactured in the United States of America

10 9 8 7 6 5 4 3 2 1

Books are available in quantity for promotional, educational or premium use. Write to Director of Special Sales, Regnery Publishing, Inc., One Massachusetts Avenue NW, Washington, DC 20001, for information on discounts and terms or call (202) 216-0600.

This book is dedicated to the noble men and women of
the U.S. military who are fighting the global war on terrorism
and to the loyal people of CACI who support them.

"And you shall know the truth, and the truth shall set you free"

John 8:32
New Testament, Holy Bible, KJV

The Lay of the Last Minstrel
Canto Sixth

Love of Country

BREATHES there the man, with soul so dead,
Who never to himself hath said,
This is my own, my native land!
Whose heart hath ne'er within him burn'd,
As home his footsteps he hath turn'd,
From wandering on a foreign strand!
If such there breathe, go, mark him well;
For him no Minstrel raptures swell;
High though his titles, proud his name,
Boundless his wealth as wish can claim;
Despite those titles, power, and pelf,
The wretch, concentred all in self,
Living, shall forfeit fair renown,
And, doubly dying, shall go down
To the vile dust, from whence he sprung,
Unwept, unhonor'd, and unsung.

by

Sir Walter Scott
1771–1832

In Memoriam

They journeyed nobly

Captain Paul Christopher "Chris" Alaniz, husband of CACI's Thelma Alaniz of San Diego, CA, died on January 26, 2005 when a Marine Corps transport helicopter he was co-piloting crashed in a sandstorm near Rutbah, Iraq. He was with the U.S. Marine Corps, Heavy Helicopter Squadron 361, Marine Aircraft Group 16, 3rd M.A.W., from MCAS in Miramar, CA. Captain Alaniz was 32 years old and originally from Corpus Christi, TX.

~

Corporal Christopher L. Weaver died on January 26, 2005 in hostile combat action in Al Anbar, Iraq. Corporal Weaver, age 24, was the son of CACI's David Weaver, a retired naval officer from Dahlgren, VA. Corporal Weaver, from Fredericksburg, VA, was in the U.S. Marine Corps, 4th Combat Engineer Battalion, 23rd Marine Regiment, 4th Marine Division, Marine Corps Reserve, Lynchburg, VA.

~

First Lieutenant Aaron N. Seesan, from Massilon, OH, died on May 22, 2005 of fatal injuries in a combat IED (Improvised Explosive Device) sweep, near Mosul, Iraq. Lt. Seesan was with the U.S. Army, Combat Engineers, 73rd Engineers Division & 1st Brigade, 25th Infantry Division (Stryker Combat Team), based out of Ft. Lewis, Washington. Seesan, nephew of CACI consultant Dr. Jennifer Burkhart of Arlington, VA, was 24 years old. He was posthumously awarded the Bronze Star.

CONTENTS

"And judgment is turned away backward and justice standeth afar off: for the truth is fallen in the street, and equity cannot enter."

Isaiah 59:14
Old Testament, Holy Bible, KJV

THE TRUTH WILL OUT
A Note to the Reader

IN AUGUST OF 2003, CACI'S LONG-TIME CUSTOMER, THE U.S. ARMY, was in critical need of assistance: could CACI provide intelligence support and logistical services in Iraq — and could the company do it now?

Since its founding in 1962, CACI International Inc has proudly provided information technology (IT) services to government and private sector customers to enhance efficiency and meet mission and project effectiveness. During that time, CACI has worked with the U.S. government and military in a variety of projects through nine U.S. Presidential administrations each with its own policies, agendas and objectives. For over forty-five years, our work for government agencies has played a vital role in protecting America's security, improving the performance of domestic programs and enhancing the country's intelligence capabilities at home and abroad.

Our many offerings have included IT services, systems and support, for both logistics and intelligence efforts. But what the army was asking for was a first for us, to provide this field support for an *immediate wartime* need: intelligence services and interrogator support. CACI's steadfast objective in serving our government clients has always been to provide quality service and dedication in meeting our customers' needs. And, the sense of importance and urgency of the U.S. Army's request was more than obvious. CACI agreed to the job.

Our sense of duty and reputation were soon to come under attack. An *illegally leaked* copy of a classified, preliminary investigative U.S. Army report (SECRET/NO FOREIGN DISSEMINATION), by Major General Antonio M. Taguba came to light in April of 2004 citing details of alleged abuse of Iraqi detainees at Abu Ghraib prison outside Baghdad. The report implicated not only military personnel assigned to the prison, but also civilian contractors. There was an allegation that one CACI employee, another contractor (which the Taguba report mistakenly identified as a CACI employee), and two U.S. Army officers, a colonel and a lieutenant colonel, were "suspected" of having been "either directly or indirectly responsible" for abuses at Abu Ghraib. No direct or specific charges were made, only "suspicions", generalized accusations and allegations. But the infamous photos of the abuses — in which *no* CACI employee appeared — had also just been made public on television on April 28, 2004 setting off a media frenzy all over the world.

Taguba's vague allegations about the CACI employee were not substantiated by any evidence or proof, and not confirmed by any of the subsequent investigations that would soon follow. Nevertheless that one line from the Taguba report about his "suspicions", coupled with the indelible images of the photos would throw CACI into an international spotlight that would continue to glare for well over a year. CACI was put under intense microscopic scrutiny that few other companies have ever faced, including unrelenting media examination and nine extensive government investigations — one even threatening the very existence of the company.

The people of CACI would also face a challenge of conscience. The media, pundits, critics and other bodies and organizations called for accountability by insisting that the company fire the accused, admit guilt, and beg for forgiveness, all before getting to the facts or the truth — to say nothing about proving the allegations. But the CACI team would not give in to such intimidation. At CACI, we took these charges very seriously and no action would be taken without establishing the facts, adhering to the rule of law, including due process and the presumption of innocence until proven guilty. At the same time, with mounting speculation and misstatements of facts, CACI found it necessary to focus considerable effort on correcting egregious statements and false commentary about the company.

One of our first actions was to state our vital position: CACI was requested to assist the U.S. Army in a critical war-time situation that was important to our national defense and saving our soldiers' lives. Furthermore, CACI would not condone, tolerate or endorse any illegal behavior by our employees in any circumstance or at any time. Everyone at CACI was as shocked and disgusted with the apparent abuses as the rest of the world was in watching the images emerge in the global media display. We would act forcefully if the evidence showed that any of our employees acted improperly. But we would not rush to judgment on the basis of speculation, innuendo, partial reports, agenda-driven propaganda, or incomplete investigations. There would be no witch-hunts, no lynch mobs, no kangaroo courts, and no trials by the media. Instead, our motto became: "The Truth Will Out."

While we emphatically condemned the terrible abuses depicted in the Abu Ghraib photos, we had no earlier indication at all of any wrongdoing by any CACI personnel. The army had consistently said that the company was doing a good job. Further, longstanding CACI culture, ethics, and code of conduct all endorsed and emphasized obeying the law, being responsible and accountable, and most important, as a CACI board member would later state, "doing the right thing."

CACI's response and approach throughout the ordeal would be responsible and justifiable. Subsequent in-depth government investigative reports in 2004 and 2005 would neither confirm nor corroborate the allegations made against our CACI employee in the earlier *illegally leaked* Taguba report. And as 2008 approached, not one current or former CACI employee had been be charged with any wrongdoing. But by then, unfortunately, much damage had already been done. Despite all this, the abuse pictures combined with the unsubstantiated mention in the Taguba report of one employee were apparently enough to wrongfully condemn CACI in the court of public opinion. The media's propaganda-like bombardment and distorted portrayal of the allegations about our employee in the Taguba report began a gauntlet of investigations and triggered intense scrutiny of the company — a virtual "wire brushing" — that I dare say few companies could have undergone and survived. Further, publicity-seeking opportunists and self-styled experts with their self-serving opinions became engaged in manipulating the facts to malign the company for their own personal or political gain.

Even as you read this, we routinely find persistent, but critical errors, as well as gross exaggerations and falsehoods about the company regarding Abu Ghraib. And we believe, as our corporate responsibility, it is our obligation to our employees, shareholders, and clients — and the public at large — to address and correct all of these falsehoods.

Yet there has never been any instance that I know of where the media focused a critical and investigative eye on the Taguba report itself, its allegations, or the claims that it got right or that it got wrong. And I also know of no attempt to investigate who *illegally leaked* the report to the public in the first place before the entire investigative process was completed and all of the verified facts were presented.

The tragic events of Abu Ghraib and the obvious abuse of detainees is surely unjustified, regrettable, and a sad moment for our country and our military. The irresponsible acts of a very few at Abu Ghraib have, to a degree, tarnished the reputation and honorable service of all Americans that have ever worn our country's uniform and have saluted and served under our nation's noble flag.

Through all this, CACI faced the allegations by fully cooperating with all government inquiries, and by being forthcoming, thorough, and unyielding to far-fetched speculation, and false and malicious accusations. Throughout CACI's history, our enduring goal has been to support the country's future through quality service achieving the highest ethical standards in doing so.

In all this, I am ever grateful to CACI's employees and supporters. The story you are about to read is how CACI faced this ordeal, how we sought out the truth, and how in the process we upheld *our good name*.

J.P. London

Invictus

OUT of the night that covers me,
Black as the Pit from pole to pole,
I thank whatever gods may be
For my unconquerable soul.

In the fell clutch of circumstance
I have not winced nor cried aloud.
Under the bludgeonings of chance
My head is bloody, but unbowed.

Beyond this place of wrath and tears
Looms but the Horror of the shade,
And yet the menace of the years
Finds, and shall find, me unafraid.

It matters not how strait the gate,
How charged with punishments the scroll,
I am the master of my fate:
I am the captain of my soul.

by

William Ernest Henley
1849–1903

"We will not stand silent when facts
are twisted to debase our good name."
~ JACK LONDON, OP-ED COLUMN,
SEPTEMBER 27, 2004

INTRODUCTION

A company, a crisis, and the fight for the truth

> **"Adversity is the first path to truth"**
> ∼ LORD BYRON

IN LATE APRIL 2004, JUST AS THE ANNUAL EXPLOSION OF WASHINGTON, D.C.'s azalea blossoms heralded the promise of springtime, a heretofore relatively unknown federal government contractor, CACI International Inc., found itself suddenly facing a long dark summer of corporate crisis and external scrutiny.[1] The reason for its travails: an Iraqi prison complex called Abu Ghraib and allegations that a single civilian interrogator employed by CACI at the prison was somehow involved, along with a number of U.S. Army soldiers, in the abuse of prisoners.

Literally overnight CACI's world was turned upside down. CACI and its people would soon be engaged in a modern-day media frenzy, their lives changed irrevocably.

For four decades, CACI had labored quietly outside the spotlight. It had been founded in 1962 by former RAND Corporation colleagues Herb Karr and Harry Markowitz, who put a California park bench and phone booth into service as the company's first "office." From its humble origin marketing a programming language in the nascent computer

---

[1] A public corporation, CACI trades on the New York Stock Exchange as "CAI."

industry, CACI grew by following a simple strategy of watching trends and identifying the most promising technologies and markets. By the 1970s, CACI led efforts in database retrieval programs, software systems and the application of new technologies to U.S. government agency projects. The 1980s would bring new rules and regulations to the government contracting landscape, in which CACI would continue to adapt to the marketplace and build upon its technical knowledge and client relationships.

In the 1990s, under the leadership of its president, chief executive officer, and newly elected chairman of the board, Dr. J. Phillip ("Jack") London, CACI would change from a professional services firm to a full scope information technology (IT) solutions provider. London recognized that IT was shifting from individual software applications to networks and enterprise-wide projects.

London had joined CACI in July of 1972 when the firm had less than 50 employees.[2] By 2004, CACI had grown to a 9,500-person corporation with more than one hundred offices worldwide. The company provided a range of IT and network solutions in defense, intelligence, and e-government, including systems integration and managed network solutions, knowledge management, engineering, simulation, and information assurance.[3] While CACI was an established and well-respected company, it was traditional and low key. Though based in Arlington, Virginia, just across the Potomac River from the power centers of Washington, D.C., CACI operated out of the public spotlight.

Then on April 28, 2004, CBS's *60 Minutes II* aired the now infamous photographs of detainee abuse by American soldiers at Abu Ghraib prison outside Baghdad that set off a media firestorm. Two days later, the media received new fuel for the fire when *The New Yorker* magazine published a story that cited details of a classified army report (based on an investigation of military police), which had been authored by Major

---

[2] London was elected to the Board of Directors in 1981, promoted to President and Chief Executive Officer in 1984, and elected Chairman of the Board in 1990. London is considered by many in the industry to be the founder of the modern day CACI International Inc.

[3] CACI became a Fortune 1000 company in 2006 and had grown to 11,500 employees in over 130 offices by December 2007. In April of 2006, CACI's market capitalization (share price valuation) reached $2 billion.

General Antonio M. Taguba. The Taguba report implicated not only the military units tasked with running Abu Ghraib, but also civilian contractors who were participating in interrogation support and providing translation services at the prison.[4]

For news agencies, the Taguba report became the "second source" that, in effect, confirmed the pictures and added details, suspects, and a story line that seemed to lead from the military police in a single cellblock during the night shift to more senior officers at the prison — and perhaps beyond. Completed in February as one in a series of several ongoing investigations and reports, but not intended for public release, the classified (SECRET/NO FOREIGN DISSEMINATION) report was *illegally leaked* by the ubiquitous "unnamed" source to journalist Seymour Hersh of the *New Yorker* magazine. The magazine posted the story on its website on April 30, two days after the *60 Minutes II* broadcast.[5] The unlawfully released report and the photos were soon available online, on television, and in print all over the world.

Following the initial flurry of follow-on stories, editors, television producers and print reporters began to search for new story ideas, new angles and new potential players in the growing story of the prison scandal. CACI's name was quickly swept into the media spotlight. No CACI employees appeared in any of the Abu Ghraib abuse photos but one sentence in the illegally leaked army report, included the harsh speculation

---

[4] Major General Antonio M. Taguba, *Article 15-6 Investigation of the 800th Military Police Brigade*, March 2004.

[5] The "SECRET/NO FOREIGN DISSEMINATION" government security classification indicated the critical importance of the document and the danger it could pose to the U.S. and the U.S. military if disclosed; the restriction not to release to any foreign national personnel (non U.S. Citizens) clearly established its highly sensitive aspects from the international security relations standpoint. The person or persons who illegally leaked this document would have known the great harm that would ensue. In general, the violation of U.S. government security laws is a criminal offense and felony that is prosecuted under federal statutes. Violations are determined, considered and dealt with under various U.S. government executive orders, codes, and statutes (as may be applicable), such as Executive Order 13292 (classified national security information) of March 25, 2003; U.S. Code Title 18 Crimes and Criminal Procedures (e.g., part I Crimes, Chapter 37 Espionage and Censorship); U.S. Code Title 50, National Security Act of 1947 Amended, and Uniform Code of Military Justice (e.g., Art. 106 Spies, Art 106a. Espionage).

that a single CACI employee was among those soldiers (MPs and MI) with broader responsibility for the misconduct.[6]

The concern of CACI's leadership came down entirely to one paragraph in Taguba's summary report. In only five short lines on page 48, Taguba pointed at a civilian interrogator named Steven Stefanowicz, a former navy intelligence specialist, who was hired by CACI and sent to Iraq in October 2003. A screener who was later promoted to be an interrogator with the agreement of the army, Stefanowicz was never in any position of authority. But without further explanation on the same page, Taguba said he "suspected" Stefanowicz and three others who were not employed by CACI (two military officers and a civilian translator, John Israel, employed by Titan Corporation[7]) were somehow "either directly or indirectly responsible for the abuses."[8]

For CACI, a public company, the photos and the Taguba report produced a corporate life-threatening crisis. While the Taguba Report provided *no* supporting evidence for his "suspicion" about Stefanowicz, the CACI employee's proximity to the incidents at Abu Ghraib exposed the company to months of controversy and unwarranted allegations. More detailed reports later corrected much of the vague and inaccurate information about CACI that the Taguba report initially suggested and, within a few months, official inquiries made clear that none of the company's employees were involved with the photographed abuses. Unfortunately, these reports did not receive the kind of media coverage that the initial Taguba report attracted. The serious damage to CACI was already done.

---

[6] Taguba Report, op. cit. The Taguba investigation and report focused on the Military Police (MPs), not Military Intelligence (MI) units, but did include some MI soldiers. MI, however, was the focus of a later investigation by Major General George W. Fay (unclassified report) published in August 2004.

[7] Titan Corp., a publicly owned company based in San Diego, CA, provided linguistics services to the U.S. Army at Abu Ghraib and also had employees accused in the Taguba report.

[8] Taguba Report, op. cit. "Specifically, I suspect that COL Thomas M. Pappas, LTC Steve L. Jordan, Mr. Steven Stephanowicz [*sic*], and Mr. John Israel were either directly or indirectly responsible for the abuses at Abu Ghraib (BCCF) and strongly recommend immediate disciplinary action as described in the preceding paragraphs as well as the initiation of a Procedure 15 Inquiry to determine the full extent of their culpability."

The images of prisoner abuses at Abu Ghraib ignited an international response and CACI's anonymity disappeared in those two pivotal days in April of 2004. Literally hundreds of editors and reporters from around the world began pursuing the story of Abu Ghraib. For the next several months, the photos were broadcast again and again on television, displayed on the Internet, and printed on the front pages of newspapers around the globe.

As a result of unsupported "suspicions" stated in the Taguba Report, CACI was besieged with a barrage of requests from the news media. CACI faced daily pounding in media stories; two outrageous lawsuits accusing it of a deliberate corporate policy of torture and even murder; a six-week investigation by the government's General Services Administration (GSA) into the manner in which CACI's Iraq contract was issued; the threat of possible suspension by GSA from the government contracts that accounted for nearly a third of CACI's annual revenue (and could affect all of the company's federal work, which totaled 94 percent of revenue); and nine official government investigations of events at Abu Ghraib or related thereto. CACI also experienced a short-term but steep decline in its share price that at one point cost the company 12 percent of its market capitalization (share price valuation) or almost $155 million; public inquiries from California's two state pension funds to explain why they should continue to hold CACI stock; and the prospect of expulsion from the Calvert Group's Social Index for responsible companies.

Stunned by both the shocking photos and the accusation that one of its own might be involved, CACI's leaders were confronted with a major public relations crisis for which they had no guidelines.

One of the company's first actions was to state their position. Everyone at CACI was as shocked and disgusted as the rest of the world with the apparent abuses, as they watched the images emerge in the global media display. CACI stated it would not condone or tolerate any illegal behavior by employees and they would act forcefully if the evidence showed that any employee acted improperly. But the company's leadership would not rush to judgment on the basis of speculation, innuendo, propaganda, or incomplete information. There would be no witch hunts, no lynch mobs, no kangaroo courts, and no trial by the media — only the rule of law. CACI had been asked to assist the army in a critical

wartime situation and they had consistently said that the company was
doing a good job, giving no indication that anything was amiss with
CACI's employees. And so, there would also be no apologies for doing
their job either.

In addition to the normal work of running a business and serving
their customers, the company's leaders had to respond to a wide range
of pressure points from the news media, shareholders, the army, the
U.S. Congress, government agencies, investigative reporters, and Wall
Street. At times, especially in the first weeks, media articles and reports
totaled in the hundreds. Despite the fact that no CACI employee was
ever charged with any abuse or serious misconduct for work at Abu
Ghraib, broadcast outlets, including national network news, reported on
CACI's alleged complicity for days at a time.

CACI International faced some terrible and totally false accusations:
"Torture Profiteers," "Torturers for Hire," "Hired Killers," and "Torture
Conspirators."[9]

Handling the tide of media inquiries alone was almost impossible because of the sheer volume of calls, which early on exceeded a hundred
phone calls and e-mail messages a day. The task was complicated further
because so much of what the media knew came in the form of confused
and conflicting leaks — meaning that CACI's leaders were being asked
to respond to information they hadn't seen or heard and had no way of
verifying. As CACI management learned, the quality of journalism var-
ied widely. The CACI team was forced to spend tremendous amounts of
time correcting media errors and trying to educate reporters about intelligence gathering and the government contracting process.

Compounding the media barrage for CACI was the ensuing avalanche
of "official" investigations and inquiries into the company and its employees that gathered momentum and continued to "pile on" over the

---

9 "Torture Profiteers" is a title given to a reproduction of the Center for Constitutional
Rights' news release announcing their lawsuit against CACI and Titan on a site called
"iwantchange.org." It was also erroneously credited as an Associated Press story. "Torturers for hire" was a slur used in several publications as well as on placards during
demonstrations. An extremist and political activist called the company "Hired Killers"
on a New York-based radio show. "Torture Conspirators" is how CACI et al. are referenced in the lawsuit filed against them in 2004.

following months. The initial negative media onslaught triggered a domino effect by numerous government agencies and sources that put CACI under intense microscopic scrutiny and gave the company a thorough wire brushing that extended, in some cases, into the following year.

Key CACI employees worked night after night and weekend upon weekend, for months, to uncover facts, seek out the truth, respond to the outside audiences and investigations, keep employees informed, and maintain internal morale. Thousands of hours were devoted to a top-to-bottom examination of company records to organize the facts in response to official inquiries, as well as to enable CACI's decision-makers to learn for themselves whether any of the company's people had done any wrong or any of its management systems had failed. From Chairman and CEO Jack London and his Board of Directors down to the senior executives, everyone wanted to know whether the events at Abu Ghraib, and the decisions that had led the company there, involved mistakes that needed correction or were an accident of war that CACI could not have predicted or prevented. Or were these simply reported, but unsubstantiated allegations?

For most Americans, the Hersh story was likely the first time they heard that the army was employing civilian contractors to interrogate detainees. Many probably believed that interrogation was handled exclusively by the military. Hersh's article drew the media to CACI which had provided civilian interrogators in the early fall of 2003 when the army asked for help to make up for the shortage of military interrogator personnel in Iraq. It soon became publicly known that civilian interrogators (though not provided by CACI) had already been employed also in Afghanistan and at Guantanamo Bay, Cuba.

While most Americans are now familiar with the tragic prisoner abuses that occurred at Abu Ghraib, few people are aware of the horrific acts of violence that were inflicted upon the Iraqi people at Abu Ghraib prior to the occupation of Iraq by allied forces. Before the liberation of Baghdad, Abu Ghraib had a horrible reputation as "Hell on Earth" being the dreaded site of Saddam Hussein's "Death Chamber." In 1984 alone, an estimated 4,000 prisoners were executed at Abu Ghraib. Amnesty International reported other mass executions occurring in January of 1994 and in November of 1996 with the slaughter of hundreds of opposition leaders. It was the most notorious prison in Iraq, and that history, in part, established the difficult atmosphere under which American MPs and civilian contractors worked.

The prison's immensity also contributed to its dangerous conditions. The massive prison complex housed twenty-four individual guard towers, which overlooked five walled compounds. Under Saddam Hussein, the prison's population at one time swelled to 15,000 — nearly twice its capacity.

Before the invasion of Iraq, military planners anticipated the massive surrender of large numbers of Iraqi military troops. Instead, many Iraqi soldiers never surrendered. They simply dropped out of their army's ranks, faded back into the fabric of their communities, regrouped and went home to continue a much different kind of insurrectionist and terrorist war against the coalition troops.

Once Baghdad fell to U.S. and coalition forces, the fighting shifted from large-scale combat engagements with well defined troop movements and targets to disparate battles with strong pockets of isolated resistance from terrorist groups or individuals making hit-and-run attacks. U.S. led troops were forced to defend against suicide bombings, sporadic rocket and grenade attacks, remote detonated mines and bombs (Improvised Explosive Devices: IEDs), and other forms of urban guerilla-style tactics. The fighting was often street-to-street, close and deadly.

Consequently, the number of prisoners taken by U.S. forces grew into a volatile mix of Al Qaeda insurgent fighters, Baathists, Sunni and Shia militias, terrorist operatives, common criminals, street thugs and ordinary citizens who were swept up in the violence around them. It was nearly impossible for the coalition ground forces to distinguish between combatants and innocents as they constantly struggled to identify friendly Iraqi citizens while fighting or capturing enemy fighters.

Adding to the challenge was the fact that these prisoners were turned over to an undermanned and relatively inexperienced military police brigade, which became overwhelmed with the task of managing the growing prison population. As the street fighting intensified, the U.S. military and coalition forces captured and detained thousands of Iraqis. All of the Iraq detention facilities were filled to capacity or beyond. Abu Ghraib alone held 7,000 prisoners by the fall of 2003 when the now infamous detainee abuse photos were taken. While army doctrine calls for one full battalion for every 4,000 detainees, the 7,000 prisoners at Abu Ghraib were guarded by a single, under strength battalion — far more prisoners than the army had prepared for or had the facilities or guards to accommodate.

Abu Ghraib was a vulnerable security nightmare. It was also an incredibly dangerous place for everyone there — whether incarcerated or working at the site — as the prison was subjected to almost daily rocket or mortar attacks from insurgent forces, exposing soldiers, contractors, guards and detainees to constant peril. These random attacks created a highly stressful working environment and made it nearly impossible to maintain order. The threat of prison uprisings and riots loomed every day.

Further compounding the problems for troops, contractors, detainees and prisoners were reports that there were differing policies and rules governing prisoner management. Prison facilities at Afghanistan, Guantanamo Bay, Cuba, and Iraq had different concerns and circumstances, and what appeared to be different policies regarding prisoner detention and interrogation. In some cases, soldiers moving from one theater to the other may have brought new policies with them, creating the potential for confused direction in policy.

As this book outlines, later government investigations discovered the U.S. military and contractor personnel reportedly operated under varying policies and rules of engagement regarding interrogation techniques and intelligence gathering. In this complex environment, it was a challenging, difficult and lengthy process for investigators to determine the actual facts regarding detainee abuse at Abu Ghraib. To this day, confusion and misinformation apparently still exists about what took place and who was responsible. But clearly the notorious Abu Ghraib abuse photographs show individuals carrying out abuse, mistreatment and humiliation.

The complexities of prison management policy and the situation at Abu Ghraib also led to media missteps. The media naturally seized on the sensational photos and took advantage of the availability of an illegally leaked classified military document, but this only added to the confusion and resulted in the dissemination of inaccurate and incomplete information which further escalated emotions and reactions to the scandal.[10] The Abu Ghraib situation deserved thorough accurate investigation, not the rush of broadcast and print media aiming to meet deadlines and scoop their media competitors.

News agencies had filed periodic stories about alleged prisoner abuse for several months before the photos surfaced, and these reports passed virtually without notice. The army had announced to the press on January 16, 2004 that an investigation had been initiated into alleged detainee abuses in Iraq. This was followed on February 23, 2004 by a Reuters' report that seventeen soldiers, including two officers, had been suspended pending the outcome of an investigation into detainee abuse. A prison west of Baghdad was mentioned. On March 20, Brigadier General Kimmit held a press conference where he noted that charges had been lodged against six MPs.

But the release of the photos and the illegally leaked army report in late April seared into people's consciousness and moved the story to page one in the newspapers and to the top story on television news. "Abu Ghraib" became shorthand for virtually everything that critics believed was wrong with American war policy. To further complicate the challenge for the CACI team, the company became a convenient example for critics who pointed to Abu Ghraib as evidence that the Department of Defense was relying too heavily on contractors to support military operations in Iraq and Afghanistan.

The Abu Ghraib abuse photographs also unleashed an international cascade of criticism of U.S. policy in Iraq and, in due course, of American treatment of detainees held in Afghanistan and the U.S. military base at Guantanamo Bay, Cuba.

Moreover, the stain of the photos seemed to attach itself to anybody and everybody who worked at Abu Ghraib. The media also seemed all too willing to associate CACI with everything and anything to do with Abu Ghraib. As one researcher noted, "Most observers, even those within professional circles, have unfortunately been influenced by the media's colorful (and artificial) view of interrogation as almost always involving hostility and the employment of force — be it physical or psy-

---

[10] According to commentary during Congressional Hearings on November 17, 2005 attacks on U.S. troops in Iraq doubled following the public revelations and media blitz over the abuses at Abu Ghraib.

chological — by the interrogator against the hapless, often slow-witted subject."[11]

Consequently, the company was derided as "Torturers for Hire," even though no CACI people were in any of the Abu Ghraib abuse photos and none have ever been charged in any jurisdiction. The knee-jerk reaction was that the behavior depicted in the photos had also taken place during interrogations. (Official government investigations would conclude that the abuses depicted in the photos were not linked with interrogations.) The term "torture" was also casually used by both the media and the public, despite the fact that the Taguba report never made that accusation. Sociologist Stjepan Mestrovic, who was an expert witness and observer at the trials of the accused soldiers Javal Davis, Sabrina Harman, and Lynndie England, emphasized that, "The media was obsessed with torture. The word torture was never used in the trials. The reporters would come for an hour or two, leave before lunch, and sensationalize the whole story."[12] Many people simply did not understand the definitional meanings of torture and interrogation or the weight that each carried.[13]

---

[11] Steven M. Kleinmann, "KUBARK Counterintelligence Interrogation Review: Observations of an Interrogator, Lesson Learned and Avenues for Further Research," *Educing Information, Interrogation: Science and Art, Foundations for the Future* (Washington, DC: National Defense Intelligence College, December 2006).

[12] Travis Measley, "Texas A&M professor calls Abu Ghraib trials 'complex human story'," *University Wire*, September 11, 2007.

[13] While this book does not presume to be an authority or claim expertise in the definitions, legal constructions or laws regarding torture, and especially that of torture versus abuse, some operational definitions of these terms and several other related terms are needed for a coherent and objective discussion. The following informal review attempts to establish a viable definitional frame of reference for use in this book.

It should be understood that there is a clear distinction between "interrogation" and "torture." Torture is defined as the "inflicting of severe pain, as to elicit information or force a confession; any [inflicted] severe physical or mental pain, agony." [*Webster's New World Dictionary and Thesaurus*, 2nd Ed., (Wiley Publishing, Inc., Cleveland, 2002)]. (See also Glossary and Terms of Interest) What happened earlier at Abu Ghraib and is recorded under Saddam Hussein's regime fit the definition of "torture" without question.

In contrast, "interrogation" is defined by the same reference source as "to examine by questioning formally or officially." It might also be added that, in most civilized states, interrogation is a formal, legitimate process of questioning, with many rules, procedures, and laws governing it. It is not like the fictional interrogations sometimes

For CACI, having its name connected with the photos in which its employees did not appear was nevertheless tantamount, in the public's eye, to "guilt by association," and would result wrongly in long-term and damaging repercussions. And the company stood alone in getting the media wrongs corrected. Unlike the United Kingdom that has a Press

---

portrayed in television and film, which are often exaggerated and made violent for dramatic purposes. While the CIA's KUBARK Counterintelligence Interrogation Manual produced in 1963 followed a Cold War perspective that supported coercive techniques, those approaches have become discredited. (See also Glossary and Terms of Interest) However, even KUBARK recognized the true nature of interrogation, defining it as a method of obtaining needed, correct and useful information through responses to questions.

In his February 2006 article on interrogation, Steven Kleimann distinguishes two factors unique to interrogation. First, there is a psychological aspect as the interrogator and the source have different — even conflicting — expectations and objectives. The interrogator, obviously, may face some resistance. Second, the interrogator has control over the physical setting, including movement, duration and conditions. While both parties have their advantages in an interrogation situation, the successful interrogator knows the importance of developing a rapport with the source; to understand the source, even make them more cooperative and responsive to interrogation. It is also important to point out that unlike interrogation in law enforcement, intelligence interrogation is typically not meant to coerce a confession or to get the source to self-incriminate, but primarily to acquire useful information

Interrogation is merely a method for gathering information, not unlike traditional investigative or research methods. The information gathering process, including the analysis of information, yields intelligence. For the military, intelligence helps guide policy and action, particularly under exigent, wartime circumstances. Thus there is a significant difference between torture and interrogation. Nonetheless, in the media and political swirl that followed the showing of the Abu Ghraib photographs and the illegally leaked Taguba Article 15-6 report, many would continue to confuse (and at times obfuscate), by using the words "torture" and "interrogation" inaccurately, improperly or interchangeably.

There is also confusion over the meanings of several other important terms that appear frequently in this book. "Abuse" and "humiliation" properly depict certain behaviors that would seem to fall short of "torture." However, the definitions and legal meanings of these terms are crucial. In the research for this book, definitions were sought from authoritative sources, legal documents, and public dictionaries. Also recognized are the definitions and context of these words in treaties and statutes such as the Geneva Conventions, Title 18 of the U.S. Code, the Uniform Code of Military Justice, the War Crimes Act of 1996, the Detainee Treatment Act of 2005, the Military Commissions Act of 2006, the United Nations Convention Against Torture

Complaints Commission (its media's self-regulatory organization) there was nowhere to turn in the U.S. to hold the media directly accountable for their mistakes.

It was a wholly new experience for CACI. It was the first time the company had ever been in the spotlight of media criticism.

In hindsight, Taguba's report with respect to CACI turned out to be wrong in several critical aspects. At the most basic level, Taguba had misidentified one of his four primary suspects, Titan interpreter John Israel, as an employee of CACI. That error, though corrected by CACI and ultimately recognized by most members of the news media, initially enhanced the notion of CACI involvement. A year later, some accounts continued to repeat this mistake, and it also appeared in some legal briefs filed against CACI. The fifty-three-page illegally leaked Taguba report

---

and U.S. Army Counterinsurgency Field Manual No. 3-24. This research lead to the "consensus" definitions, which are presented below and included in the Glossary and Terms of Interest:

Torture — is to intentionally inflict or cause severe, extreme, physical and intense mental pain and suffering, excruciating agony, for inhuman, degrading treatment or coercion or punishment, intimidation, obtaining information or confession, or for intentional cruelty.

Abuse — is the excessive or improper treatment of something or someone; mal-treatment; can be verbal or physical; typically cruel or detrimental in manner, and can be sexual in nature.

Humiliation — is to hurt the pride or dignity of a person or group. While humil-iation can be self-inflicted, humiliation of one person by another is often used as a way of asserting power over others, and is a common form of intimidation, oppression or abuse (as above).

Interrogation — is the methodical, systematic examination of an individual, typically by questioning, in a formal or official manner to obtain specific useful information and intelligence. Interrogations are typically used to derive such information from detained persons, including criminal suspects, prisoners of war, terrorists or insurgents.

Intelligence — is the product resulting from the collection, processing, analysis, evaluation and interpretation of available information; information and knowl-edge obtained through covert or overt observation, investigation, analysis, or understanding; typically gathered and prepared concerning a foreign govern-ment, individual, or organizational adversaries, enemies, combatants or terror-ists; collected from people (i.e., prisoners, informants, or spies) or from a wide variety of technological collection or listening means.

and the thousands of pages of its annexes, which later became (for the most part) publicly available, did *not* provide any specific concrete evidence to support Taguba's suggestion that Stefanowicz or Israel were somehow culpable for the misconduct shown in the photos.

Surprisingly, the Taguba report's statements were not publicly challenged nor validated. However, in August 2004, a more comprehensive army investigation by General Paul J. Kern, Lieutenant General Anthony R. Jones, and Major General George R. Fay (the "Fay report") fully exonerated the Titan employee, John Israel, and significantly scaled back — and did not support — the Taguba allegations against Stefanowicz.

While suggesting that Stefanowicz may have violated some rules, the later Fay report did not link him with the abuses depicted in the photos, nor did it assign him any broad responsibility for the prison abuses. In fact, the Fay report notably detailed a well known incident among those working at the prison in which Stefanowicz himself *reported* abuse.

The Fay report also pointed out: "The events at Abu Ghraib cannot be understood in a vacuum."

"In addition to individual criminal propensities, leadership failures and, multiple policies, many other factors contributed to the abuses occurring at Abu Ghraib," said the Fay report.[14] The Taguba report's initial faulting of Steve Stefanowicz and John Israel clearly was not substantiated by the Fay report. Taguba's allegations in this regard were simply not supported.

In an interview with the *Signal* newspaper in Santa Clarita, California (the hometown paper of John Israel) a year later in April 2005, Taguba himself seemed uncertain about his allegations. He said he cited Israel "only because he was associated with Stefanowicz" with whom Israel served as an interpreter. Noting that Taguba had "suspected" that the civilians involved were either "directly or indirectly" responsible, the newspaper asked which category Israel was in. In a response that could only raise questions concerning his findings, Taguba said: "I wouldn't know that."[15]

---

[14] Major General George R. Fay, Investigating Officer, *AR 15-6 Investigation of the Abu Ghraib Detention Facility and 205th Military Intelligence Brigade*, August 23, 2004.

[15] Leon Worden, "Taguba Interview: Sanchez 'Good Friend," *The Signal*, April 24, 2005.

Moreover, three years after the alleged event in the fall of 2003, neither CACI nor any of its employees had been charged with any wrongdoing in connection with Abu Ghraib.[16] The one and only investigation that focused solely on CACI, a GSA inquiry into whether the interrogation contract complied with government contracting rules, was concluded in the company's favor. The *Washington Post*, writing seven months after Taguba's report became public, conceded that allegations against CACI employees turned out to be "more limited" than initially suggested.[17]

In fact, what emerged from the official military and government investigations into Abu Ghraib, once they were all completed and testified to "under oath," was evidence that the civilian interrogators generally performed their duties well and stayed within the bounds of appropriate conduct. A March 2005 report by Vice Admiral Albert T. Church, III, the navy's Inspector General, concluded that "contractors made a significant contribution to U.S. intelligence efforts," and were often more experienced and more successful than their military counterparts, and provided continuity by serving longer tours than uniformed interrogators.[18]

Looking back over three and a half years after Abu Ghraib became an international incident, it was evident that CACI came through its ordeal with minimal impact on its core business, but with an emotional toll on its people and an undeserved challenge to its reputation. This had been accomplished through the relentless efforts of the company's leadership team to fight back against the media's distortions and activist critics' malicious and false accusations. Despite a growing body of evidence that the heavy focus on CACI in the scandal's early months was unwarranted, the company remained subject to random, unfounded allegations concerning its corporate character fueled on by those who

---

[16] Fay referred all individuals (civilians) suspected of misconduct at the prison to the army General Counsel for determination of whether they should be referred to the Department of Justice for prosecution. As of December 2007, nearly four years after CACI received its Iraq contract, no charges of any kind had been filed against the company or any of its employees, past or present, in connection with any events at Abu Ghraib.

[17] "Changes Behind the Barbed Wire," *Washington Post*, December 13, 2004.

[18] Vice Admiral Albert T. Church, III, "Unclassified executive summary of report by Vice Admiral Albert T. Church, III," March 10, 2005. Also known as the Church Report.

found in CACI a possible scapegoat. While some of the accusations were politically motivated sensationalism, others were malicious and spiteful slurs.

Some news reports suggested ludicrously that CACI's sole task as a corporate entity was prisoner interrogation. This was obviously wrong, but in any case CACI's interrogation support work for the U.S. Army in Iraq amounted to less than 1 percent of the company's total worldwide business.

This misrepresentation of CACI is only one example of the many inaccurate reports discussed in the ensuing pages of this book. The larger story, in many ways, is how the national and international press repeatedly reported inaccurate information and later failed to provide corrections. It was frustrating and infuriating for CACI's leadership and rank-and-file employees to see the company maligned. But they knew better.

CACI's experience illustrates the media's power to inappropriately and wrongfully shape public perception. It also raises important questions about accountability when reporters get facts wrong or when the media's dynamics — including pressures of time and space constraints — produce news stories that contain fact and speculation, and accord equal treatment to reality and theory, but do not make clear which is which. To CACI Chairman and CEO Jack London it felt like his company was the victim of a campaign to besmirch the company. Though not deliberately orchestrated, the daily roll of headlines implicating CACI had the effect of a malicious *propaganda* campaign by firmly implanting untruths about his company in the public's mind — and it seemed, in the minds of some government people as well.[19]

This book provides the view from within CACI as it fought to preserve its business and its reputation. It has been written and prepared by the team at CACI that dealt directly with the company's Abu Ghraib media-driven crisis.[20]

---

[19] Propaganda — is the deliberate (often media-based) dissemination of false or misleading information or ideas with specific intent to further one's cause (most often political in nature) or to damage an opposing cause by attempting to influence or convince with emotional emphasis, promote or oppose opinions, events, organizations or outcomes. See also Glossary and Terms of Interest.

[20] The contributors and participating staff are listed and recognized in Appendix B — Who's Who and in the Acknowledgments at the end of the book.

This book aims to show how the CACI team strived to determine for itself the truth about its employees' conduct at Abu Ghraib; how it responded to media reports that often included errors or misleading context and misinformation; how it pushed back on those who perpetuated falsehoods about CACI; and how it continued to deliver service and gain new business amid the uncertainty of ongoing investigations. This book considers issues of responsibility and accountability on the part of the news media, spokespersons and experts. It also discusses and raises questions about pending lawsuits against CACI, and the actions of certain public institutions and state pension funds toward CACI in response to the news about Abu Ghraib.

This book has several key stories to tell. First, it examines the history of CACI. From the Cold War to the "long war" on global terrorism, CACI has proudly served the U.S. federal government and the nation through nine presidential administrations that have had various policies, agendas and objectives for the American people. The war on terror has been and will be lengthy and challenging. In order to enable the greatest number of soldiers to engage in combat duty, the U.S. military has turned to qualified civilian contractors like CACI to provide a wide range of support. Though CACI personnel do not engage in combat duties, the company's work can be dangerous and on occasion conducted in places where few people would want to work each and every day.

This history includes CACI's involvement in Iraq. The company's employees have acted with integrity, personal sacrifice, bravery and patriotism while carrying out tough duties in extremely dangerous conditions — duties that few companies in America could perform.

Second, this book sets the record straight regarding the realities and the dangers at Abu Ghraib and presents the facts about CACI's work at this now infamous prison. Using publicly available and documented sources, this book aims to correct the misleading picture created by the media's rush to judgment.[21] Hurried and unprofessional reporting created guilt by association, and the American people received a biased,

---

[21] This book draws predominantly from the official government investigative reports and public hearings (and *sworn testimony*) available to the public at large. While the book provides the internal commentary as well as the views of individual CACI people, the research did not include interviewing non-CACI people. The CACI team had learned earlier that individuals being *informally (unofficially) or*

inaccurate and unfair picture of CACI's mission in Iraq and its work at Abu Ghraib. But the CACI team remains proud to have answered the U.S. Army's critical need during an urgent war time situation.

CACI's story, which was essentially a media-driven crisis, would have been practically impossible to tell without referring to the numerous articles, reports, interviews, news releases, books and blogs in which the company was (often unjustly) criticized. But it must also be noted that, as CACI learned, the media often gets things wrong. For example, in this book there are many references to articles and op-eds in the *Washington Post*. Yet the *Post* got many facts about CACI and their work in Iraq wrong. Therefore, this book can only rely on the accuracy of these references insofar as these cited sources have verified their own stories and claims.

The CACI team is also proud to have led the effort to defend the integrity and reputation of a respected company that has been wrongly maligned. The book outlines the crisis response approach and methodology developed by the team and implemented throughout 2004 as it coped with the media challenges.

Furthermore, this book describes the team-focused leadership style of Dr. J. Phillip ("Jack") London, a U.S. Naval Academy graduate (Class of 1959) and a former naval aviator and helicopter pilot, who served on aircraft carriers in the early 1960s hunting down Soviet (U.S.S.R.) Navy submarines throughout the Atlantic, Mediterranean and Caribbean. He had joined CACI in 1972 and quickly rose to the leadership position he would retain for over twenty-five years. London's instinctive impulse

---

privately (or secretly) interviewed, frequently bias or prejudice their commentary to their personal views, agendas, or political opinions, regardless of the facts or the full and complete truth. There is no cross-examination or challenge developed. Books and articles out today about Abu Ghraib, the Iraq War, and the Global War on Terror are often contaminated with "spin" (distortions, exaggerations, omissions, obfuscations, or slant), "off the record," or "anonymous" comments from those interviewed. In this book, CACI has relied on public statements, often made *under oath*, in official government records and publicly available (documented) sources. The threat of perjury in these "sworn testimony" situations while not always compelling, nonetheless tends to impede idle exaggerations and intentional or malicious mischaracterization. Media reports and commentary documented in the public venue were used extensively. This documented foundation is available to the reader through extensive in-text referencing and the footnoting format used in this book (See also the Bibliography).

was to stand firm and push back in driving relentlessly to find the truth. Confident in the fundamental integrity of his employees and a corporate culture of ethical behavior built around CACI's motto "Ever Vigilant," London, a highly principled leader, was driven by a passion to defend the company's good name and a determination to find out the truth and "do the right thing." In both business and personal life, London believes that few things should be guarded more fervently than your name, your honor, and your reputation.

Finally, this book includes appendices that are of particular importance to CACI's story. In addition to key reference information found in many books (e.g., glossary, who's who), the appendices offer an in-depth survey of key perspectives that formed CACI's management approaches, decisions, and responses. For example, Appendix A — Setting the Record Straight is a list of the many fallacies spread about the company with corresponding factual corrections. This list was so informative that an earlier version was posted on the CACI website's section on Iraq. There is also an appendix that details the development and implementation of CACI's crisis communications strategy, which can be used as a model for other organizations to follow. The appendices are a comprehensive supplement that the reader is encouraged to explore.

This book does not address all issues surrounding Abu Ghraib and is not a definitive history of events there. Although the book conducts a thorough and rigorous analysis, it does not seek to draw any final conclusions about the guilt or innocence of any of the men and women, from any military, contractor, or other organization, alleged to have committed (or convicted for committing) abuses there.

Furthermore, it does not delve, at any level, into any other U.S. government or military organizational activity at Abu Ghraib beyond that of U.S. Army personnel and CACI employees. It does not seek to enter or resolve the debate over the relative responsibility of military leaders and government policymakers for the conduct of those assigned to Abu Ghraib. Neither does this book enter the debate about the role of contractors with the government, nor about the government's outsourcing of any of its service requirements. Nor does the book condone any illegal behavior or wrongdoing on the part of any of CACI's employees if they are later charged and convicted of any crime related to these matters. This book, however, does pose proper questions about the *illegal leaking* (unlawful release) of U.S. government classified documents and information, and the inordinate and unnecessary damage leaks can cause to the success of U.S. Armed Services in the field, and ultimately, to the security of the American people.

In particular, this book does provide credible and penetrating analyses of the allegations, the media, and the challenges faced by CACI. From day one (with the initial news of alleged abuse, even before the release of the illegally leaked Taguba report) the company understood the seriousness and importance of the allegations, and thoroughly investigated every aspect of the situation, including through that of its own outside investigative counsel. And the results of all inquiries — government, military and the company's — clearly show from all the information available at the time and to date that no one associated with CACI participated in any behavior that remotely approached the kinds of heinous acts depicted in the Abu Ghraib abuse photos.

Today the detention facility at Abu Ghraib is empty. Associated Press television footage in September of 2006 showed only vacant hallways, rows of unlocked cells with doors swung open. Abu Ghraib's days as a working prison are over, but questions — and misperceptions — about what happened there remain.

As for CACI being at Abu Ghraib, this book is the story — largely from CACI's perspective — of how a company and its people answered the call to serve the U.S. military in time of war. And it is the story of how they responded when, suddenly and without warning, they were swept into a highly publicized international incident, and a media firestorm of distortions and wrongful accusations. It examines the issues and forces they confronted; reviews their successes and failures; and, hopefully, provides some insights into how they steered the company back to its solid footing amid a highly emotion-charged controversy, necessitated by distant events over which they had no control. This is their story.

SECTION ONE

THE CRISIS BEGINS

CHAPTER ONE

THE GATHERING STORM
Abu Ghraib erupts

"This story is too good to check"

~ AN OLD JOURNALISTIC PUNCH LINE[22]

MONDAY, APRIL 26, 2004 WAS A SPECIAL DAY FOR DR. J. PHILLIP ("Jack") London, Chairman of the Board, President, and Chief Executive Officer of CACI International Inc, an Arlington, Virginia-based information technology contractor for the federal government. London had been at the helm of CACI leadership as CEO for twenty of his thirty-two years with the company. His children had grown up with CACI. Now, his daughter was expecting her first child and the family had all assembled at Georgetown University Hospital to await the blessed event. On the morning of Tuesday, April 27, 2004, London's first grand-daughter was born.

But that Monday was also the day he received an ominous call from his Corporate Communications and Public Relations Director, Senior Vice President Jody Brown. She had received an unusual voice message and was very concerned. They were soon to find out that something had

---

[22] Richard Miniter, *Disinformation, 22 Media Myths that Undermine the War on Terror* (Washington, DC: Regnery Publishing, 2005).

been raised about CACI's work for the U.S. Army in Iraq — about a place called Abu Ghraib.

It was Seymour Hersh who was on the phone. More specifically, he was on Jody Brown's voicemail, asking something about a prison in Iraq. There was a question about CACI employees at the site, and she didn't know for sure what Hersh was talking about. But one thing about the tone of his message she knew instinctively: this was not good news.

Except by reputation, Brown did not know Seymour Hersh, a controversial investigative reporter now working for the *New Yorker* magazine. For well over a decade, Brown had been responsible for CACI's public and employee communications. She dealt with reporters all the time — but rarely about page one news or stories with international political implications. As Brown had discovered, like most other lines of work, the news media has a hierarchy. The powerful reporters from national news organizations such as the television networks, the *New York Times*, and the *Washington Post* are in the inner ring. Within the news organizations, their own top rung is occupied by columnists, national news, and political reporters. Local news reporters and business journalists are typically lower down the ladder. Their work is usually featured less prominently inside the paper or later in the broadcast on television (although business writers have been making it to page one with greater frequency in recent years). Many circles further out are the "trade reporters," the hard working, but little known reporters who toil for specialty or trade publications that cover specific industries or economic sectors.

At CACI, Jody Brown's media universe was occupied largely by business and trade reporters. The publications on her call list included respected but limited circulation periodicals such as *Government Executive*, *Washington Technology*, and *Federal Computer Week*. On the broadcast side, she dealt with business-oriented outlets like Bloomberg, MSNBC, and the financial desk at CNN. Contact with major news outlets tended to be sporadic, though *Business Week* and the *Washington Post* were in touch with some regularity. But the *Post* covered CACI, based in Washington's Virginia suburbs, as a "local" business story, which meant Brown didn't work with the paper's inner ring of political or investigative journalists. Her contacts at the paper wrote about government contractors, one of the *Post's* less glamorous beats. Their stories typically ran deep inside the paper and generally involved contract awards and the routine activities of the many government contractors around the Washington beltway.

Seymour Hersh was different altogether. In 1969, at age thirty-two, Hersh made his way into the journalistic spotlight by drawing the world's attention to the infamous My Lai massacre in Vietnam. Tipped off about an army court martial for the murder of civilians in Vietnam, Hersh would win a Pulitzer Prize for his publicity of the killing by an American infantry company of several hundred civilians at the village of My Lai. The exposé helped Hersh get a job at the *New York Times*, where he would later head the newspaper's coverage of the Watergate scandal. Subsequently, he wrote critical and cynical books about American political leaders, winning a National Book Award for *The Price of Power*, an unflattering and disparaging account of Henry Kissinger's service as Secretary of State. He also stirred controversy and became the target of significant criticism for his best-selling condemnation and ridicule of President Kennedy in *The Dark Side of Camelot.*

His focus was to put down those in powerful positions and his style was to confront his subjects and sources. According to some, he deliberately bullied sources. *Time* magazine once called Hersh "a volcanic man . . . who doesn't flinch at shouting through the phone at reluctant sources." *Time* said Hersh once screamed "Bullsh°t! Bullsh°t!" at Charles Peters, the respected editor of *Washington Monthly*, because Peters refused to confirm an accusation about President Kennedy's campaign spending in 1960. The magazine also asserted that, "Hersh is willing to put testimony, hearsay and speculation into close proximity to one another, then declare that they add up to fact."[23] Indeed, there were those in the press who apparently believed Hersh's methods to be disreputable.

According to Hersh, his sources are from among the highest levels of the military and government, (logically those upset by the actions or politics of their bosses or the administration in office at the time). In an

---

[23] Richard Lacayo, "Smashing Camelot; What's Left of the Kennedy Myth Takes a Hit From a Big Bucks Expose," *Time*, November 17, 1997.

interview with the *Daily Californian*, Hersh admitted that the excitement
generated by his reporting of a story like My Lai has kept him working in
the business for more than 40 years.[24] Hersh stated, "Eleven years after
getting out of college, I'm sticking two fingers in a President's eye, with
My Lai and Nixon — Fame, fortune, and glory."[25]

Familiar with his reputation, Jody Brown said later that if not her
worst nightmare, Seymour Hersh calling with questions about her company was high on the list of things she didn't care to deal with.

What Hersh had was an *illegally leaked* copy of an army investigative
report (classified, SECRET/NO FOREIGN DISSEMINATION), written by Major General Antonio M. Taguba. Hersh may have had some or
all of the recently released abuse photos from Abu Ghraib and perhaps
transcripts, testimony, or other documents from the military's legal and
investigative proceedings — in addition to Taguba's report.

Taguba's investigation began in January of 2004 after an army specialist, Sergeant Joseph M. Darby, turned over a computer disc loaded
with photos that showed Iraqi "detainees," many of them nude, in a variety of bizarre, embarrassing, and degrading postures. Some photos
showed detainees in simulated or possibly, actual sexual acts. Others
showed injured Iraqis or detainees shrinking from military dogs. Many
of the photos showed American soldiers giving the thumbs up sign and
smiling at the Iraqis' evident humiliation.

Taguba's report, completed in early March of 2004, stated that the
800th Military Police Brigade "was not adequately trained for a mission
that included operating a prison or penal institution." He said the
brigade was under strength for the task assigned it, and that the quality
of life for the soldiers "was extremely poor." He said the problems were
exacerbated by command failure, and he recommended that Brigadier
General Janis L. Karpinski, commander of the MP Brigade, be relieved
of her command. Karpinski later took issue with the Taguba Report stating, "The Taguba Report is flawed in many ways and [military
spokesman Brigadier General Mark] Kimmit and [Major General Geof-
frey] Miller know it." She also stated that, "He had not even questioned

---

[24] Josh Keller, "Reporter Recounts Years Behind the D.C. Scenes, Seymour Hersh
Wrote on Abu Ghraib Scandal," *The Daily Californian*, October 11, 2004.

[25] Ibid.

me about some of the findings he attributed to me. Yet he recommended that I be reprimanded and relieved of my command."[26]

Taguba's report also included an accusation against CACI employee Steven Stefanowicz, a civilian contractor at the prison, and three other individuals who were *not* CACI employees, two military officers and a contractor employed by another company. The report accused Stefanowicz of making false statements to investigators and said he "allowed and/or instructed" military police to "set conditions" that were not authorized. The Taguba report stated:

"Specifically, I suspect that **COL Thomas M. Pappas, LTC Steve L. Jordan, Mr. Steven Stephanowicz,** and **Mr. John Israel** were either directly or indirectly responsible for the abuses at Abu Ghraib (BCCF) and strongly recommend immediate disciplinary action as described in the preceding paragraphs as well as the initiation of a Procedure 15 Inquiry to determine the full extent of their culpability."[27]

John Israel, an interpreter working for Titan Corporation, was wrongly identified by Taguba as a second CACI employee. The misidentification of Israel's employer was an error in Taguba's report that CACI's CEO Jack London later said helped guide his reaction to the crisis that was about to engulf his company. In addition, Taguba had misidentified another CACI interrogator as an employee of Titan (and consistently misspelled Stefanowicz's name as "Stephanowicz.")[28] Although he didn't

---

[26] Karpinski disagreed with virtually every aspect of Taguba's report. In her book, *One Woman's Army, The Commanding General of Abu Ghraib Tells Her Story*, Janis Karpinski said that Taguba, chief investigator at the time (early 2004) was "a bureaucrat at the Coalition Forces Land Component Command (CFLCC) in Camp Doha, Kuwait." She further noted, "When he later wrote in his report that I had been 'extremely emotional' during much of my testimony, he was not reflecting reality; he was merely using code language for his unspoken subtheme: that discipline at Abu Ghraib had deteriorated under the command of an excitable woman who had lost control" (pp. 223–224). Karpinski was demoted to colonel in May of 2005 under orders from President Bush. The Army found her guilty of dereliction of duty and accused her of concealing a past arrest. Karpinski insisted she had been made a scapegoat for decisions sanctioned above her and that she did not have final authority over the prison. She maintained her innocence on the past arrest accusation.

[27] Taguba Report, op. cit.

[28] In a section noting sources for written confessions and witness statements, Taguba lists Torin Nelson, a former CACI interrogator, as a contractor with Titan Corp.

know it at the time of Hersh's call, London ultimately would learn that, beyond the sweeping allegations appearing on page 48, the 53-page Taguba report *did not provide any specific evidence* to back up its conclusions about Stefanowicz or Israel.[29]

However, the most shocking inconsistency was that Taguba assigned the same level of responsibility to the two lower level contractors as he did to two senior level army leaders located at Abu Ghraib. CACI's team knew it was impossible that two civilian project-level contractors had the authority or influence that the two colonels had. There was much about the report to question.

"If the report got that much wrong, maybe all this isn't quite what Taguba's report had asserted in other respects, and had concluded overall," London explained later. "So from the beginning I was determined not to rush to judgment."

London may have preferred time for calmer deliberation and also to gather basic facts, but Hersh was on the phone and wanted answers immediately.

Upon returning Hersh's call, Jody Brown learned for the first time of the Taguba report. She also learned that Hersh's story was nearly complete and scheduled for publication in the *New Yorker's* next edition, which would be available on the Internet on April 30 (2004) and on the newsstands soon after. That was only days away. Hersh (presuming that Taguba was right about Israel's affiliation with CACI) told her that two CACI employees were about to be publicly cited for prisoner abuse and he demanded to know what she had to say about it.

"He was rude and condescending and essentially chastised me for not knowing what was going on in my company because he had something that I did not — an *illegally leaked* report — which, by virtue of the fact that I was following the law, I could not have possessed," Brown said. "He had an *illegally leaked*, classified government document and was reading me selected passages." Hersh couldn't seem to understand that Brown really didn't have knowledge of a text to which she didn't have legal access.

---

[29] Israel was later exonerated by a subsequent and more detailed report by Major General George R. Fay, wherein he was noted as "Civilian-10." The Fay report also discarded Taguba's suggestion that Stefanowicz was in any way "responsible" for the abuses by military police at Abu Ghraib.

Brown was at a professional disadvantage, a position that became uncomfortably common for her and London in the months ahead. "The reporters kept getting leaks and then calling to ask about things we didn't know about. It was miserable for us, and in some cases, the reporters actually seemed to enjoy our difficulties," she stated. London noted that over time the reporters became less focused on fact-finding than on playing the "gotcha" game in an effort to embarrass him and the company.

The conversation with Hersh also kindled Brown's dismay at reporters' disregard for the proper handling and treatment of classified government documents. In CACI's world, the classification stamp is fully respected and adhered to. But apparently most reporters regard classified documents as fair game for news reporting. London and Brown, who believed that protecting classified national security information was a matter of duty and professionalism, were shocked by the mishandling and ready availability of the classified documents on the Internet that had been opened up to the public through the media.[30]

---

[30] While the media may take improper advantage of unearthing and revealing classified documents, government contractors must respect and comply with the government's classification system. According to the Department of Defense, classification is "the determination that official information requires, in the interests of national security, a specific degree of protection against unauthorized disclosure, coupled with a designation signifying that such a determination has been made." (DOD Dictionary of Military Terms) National security information is assigned a classification according to the degree of damage that unauthorized disclosure would cause to national defense or U.S. foreign relations and denotes the degree of protection required. Information is classified only by specially-trained individuals who determine if the material should be classified and at what level. The three prevalent levels are Top Secret, Secret, and Confidential. (See Glossary) A security clearance is required to access and handle classified information and the individual must present a legitimate reason to view the material. All material of permanent historical value is declassified after 25 years unless exempted and subjected to external review, but material can also be declassified before then if it's no longer considered to be sensitive.

Government contractors tend to be especially vigilant with respect to classified information as any violation of classification rules would jeopardize national security as well as a company's capability to win future contracts from the government.

There are nearly two dozen pieces of legislation that are relevant to classified information. But it is U.S. Code, Title 18, Part 1, Chapter 37, Section 798 on Disclosure of Classified Information that makes unauthorized disclosure — or leaking — a crime. *Both the person who discloses classified information and the recipient are considered in violation of this law.*

But whatever frustration they felt about Hersh possessing a classified document, and whatever doubts London may have had about Taguba's conclusions, some things were certain. CACI was among a number of contractors providing services in support of the U.S. military effort in Iraq. Among those contracts was one to provide interrogators to assist the army in the collection of intelligence from Iraqis held in detention at various locations in Iraq, including the Abu Ghraib prison just outside of Baghdad.

A quick check with CACI's personnel department project office confirmed that Steven Stefanowicz was working as an interrogator at Abu Ghraib, and had been at the prison since October 2003. There was no indication that Israel was employed by CACI, a puzzling disconnect with Taguba, and one that the company could immediately explain since he was never an employee of CACI. But without possession of the report, CACI could do little more than respond to what Hersh had told them on the phone. Though the *illegally leaked* Taguba document would soon find its way to the Internet, it wasn't legally available to the public. As far as CACI knew, Hersh was the only unauthorized individual with a copy, and he was demanding CACI say something about Stefanowicz and Israel.

"We had to start communicating, but we didn't have the facts. For that matter, we didn't know if anybody had all the facts. That was one of our biggest challenges," Brown said, adding that, "the army was pretty much blindsided, too. Before long, they were calling us to find out what we knew about the situation."

In fact, one of the most frustrating aspects of the first days of the crisis was the lack of information from its customer, the U.S. Army, whose own investigation had generated the very report that raised the issue at hand.

Brown was not usually involved in the details of CACI's contracts. But others in the organization were on top of managing the interroga-

---

The Taguba report had been classified as SECRET/NO FOREIGN DISSEMINA-
TION, meaning the material therein could cause serious damage to national security if made public and that it included diplomatically sensitive information that no foreigners should see. The leaking of the report to the media was by all definitions and reasonable conclusions a criminal act, but neither the leaker (who has yet to be identified) nor reporters who received the report, presumably to include Seymour Hersh, have been held accountable. Such is the state of affairs in upholding these laws.

tion assignment. These company officials had made earlier inquiries after news reports and public announcements from the army in Iraq alerted them at the beginning of 2004 there might be problems at Abu Ghraib. The army had announced to the press on January 16, 2004 that an investigation had been opened into alleged abuse at an unspecified prison in Iraq. On February 23 it was announced that seventeen U.S. soldiers including a battalion commander and a company commander had been suspended pending outcome of the abuse investigation. And on March 20, 2004 the army held a press conference to announce that charges had been lodged against six soldiers.[31]

Upon inquiry with Major Eugene Daniels, the army Contracting Officer's Representative in Iraq who was overseeing CACI's contract, the company was assured that nothing was amiss. Chuck Mudd, the CACI vice president responsible for this CACI work in Iraq, was in Baghdad at the time of the army's March announcement, and immediately called his army contact just to make sure that no one from CACI was in trouble.

"We were told nothing was amiss. It ain't you," one CACI official recalled that the army had commented. The official reported that, "We hadn't had any complaints and some of our folks had been promoted at the army's request. So we figured we were okay."

"We always heard from the army if they had any questions or issues about the contract," the CACI official added, "so we believed we would hear about any other problems, too. Hersh's call was a stunner." Nonetheless, CACI needed to respond. It also needed to establish the facts as quickly as possible because once Hersh went public, other media were sure to follow.

London also asked his new consultant, Z. Selin Hur, to find out everything that was available to the public about Abu Ghraib prison. But practically no information was found. An online search yielded less than a dozen results, and these were only brief and general references to the prison.

With little information about the (classified) abuse allegations, but pressed for time, CACI's leadership put together a statement of basic facts. The company could not respond either affirmatively or negatively about the allegations against Stefanowicz, though it did confirm that

---

[31] Barbara Starr, "Soldiers charged with abusing Iraqi prisoners," CNN.com, March 20, 2004.

CACI employees at Abu Ghraib had been interviewed by army officials several months before. The interviews did not seem to be unusual at the time. Inquiries at the prison, including questioning of CACI employees, occurred fairly frequently, taking place after every prisoner escape attempt or mortar attack and also over a variety of other incidents. Indeed, being interviewed by army investigators seemed to be a routine part of the job to the CACI team at the prison.

CACI's statement to Hersh also made clear that the company had not received any indication from the army of any improper conduct by its employees. It noted the sacrifices of all the Americans serving in Iraq under difficult conditions and stated that the company continued to support the army's vital mission.

With the response to Hersh completed, CACI awaited publication of the *New Yorker* article — its corporate fingers figuratively crossed that the article wouldn't focus unduly on the company or its employees.[32] Company leaders hoped that after CACI had a brief moment in the spotlight, the glare would fade away.

What they didn't know was that on Wednesday, April 28, 2004, CBS's *60 Minutes II* program was about to scoop Hersh with some photos from Abu Ghraib that would be some of the most startling and disgusting pictures ever shown on American television. Literally overnight, the release of those photos would sear the words "Abu Ghraib" into the world's collective mindset and catapult CACI into the middle of a political and media firestorm of a magnitude that very few companies have ever experienced or survived.

---

[32] Seymour Hersh, "Torture at Abu Ghraib," *New Yorker*, May 10, 2004 (posted online April 30, 2004).

CHAPTER TWO

CACI ON TOP OF THE WORLD

Who are CACI and where did they come from?

> **"Since 1962, Providing Opportunity for
> Our People, Solutions for Our Clients and
> Return on Investment for Our Shareholders"**
> ∼ ABOUT CACI — WWW.CACI.COM

FOR THE CACI TEAM, THE NEWS ABOUT ABU GHRAIB WAS HORREN-
dous, hitting them like a speeding train. The shocking photographs,
along with the allegations that a single CACI employee might be involved, arrived just as the company prepared to celebrate the completion of the largest acquisition in its history, the $415 million purchase of
the Defense and Intelligence Group of American Management Systems
(AMS). CACI was also about to achieve, one year ahead of schedule, a
long quest to record $1 billion in annual revenue. Both personally and
professionally, key company people were celebrating some major
achievements.

Jack London, the company's plainspoken and highly energetic chairman, president, and CEO, was toasting the birth of his third grandchild
on April 27. He had just received a *"Federal 100"* award that acknowledged his technology leadership and the outstanding work of his company

among the government contractors working for the federal government. A highly principled individual, London's longstanding emphasis on business ethics, corporate responsibility, and service excellence had earned him public recognition for which he continues to be sought out as a speaker and role model. The sixty-seven-year-old London had put off retirement in a drive to lead his company to the first tier of defense contractors and, as a former navy reserve captain, to support America's increased defense and security needs. While CACI still did not match with the size of giants like Lockheed Martin, General Dynamics, or Northrop Grumman, the company was at the top its game and had closed four acquisitions during the fiscal year that would end on June 30. The largest of these deals, the AMS acquisition, was set to close officially on May 3. It would make CACI a billion-dollar company and a top tier contractor.

Jody Brown was just beginning to think ahead to preparation of the company's annual report. As if to signal CACI's maturation and its new breadth of services, the annual document would be prepared entirely in-house in 2004. Comfortable in the familiar responsibilities of her communications job, Brown was looking forward to spreading the good news about CACI to the reporters who regularly followed the company's daily business affairs.

Another CACI executive, Senior Vice President Ron Schneider, had recently completed his twenty-fifth year at CACI and was recovering from a gala fiftieth birthday celebration at a favorite restaurant in nearby Annapolis, Maryland. Reflecting on his personal milestones, Schneider felt justifiable pride in working his way from a junior researcher to his current job as a senior officer with responsibility for all competitive proposal development. His life would soon be turned upside down as well, when London asked him to be the company's Abu Ghraib affairs project coordinator.[33]

At Abu Ghraib prison in the outskirts of Baghdad, Steve Stefanowicz was likely feeling the satisfaction that comes with a job promotion. Recently elevated to CACI site manager with the agreement of the army, he believed he was making an important contribution to his country's security. Hired initially as a screener, the former navy intelligence analyst had

---

[33] A full listing of Who's Who at CACI and others in the Abu Ghraib ordeal can be found in Appendix B.

been twice promoted, first to an interrogator position with the army's agreement and more recently in the late spring of 2004 as the company's on-site administrative liaison between the army and CACI personnel at Abu Ghraib. Despite the physical hardship and risks, his decision to join CACI must have appeared to him at the time to be a good choice.

The company itself was growing at an astonishing rate. On April 21 — less than a week before Hersh's first phone call — CACI had reported earnings for the first nine months of its fiscal year. The news was sensational. On increased revenue volume, net income was up 37 percent for the first three quarters of fiscal 2004. During the third quarter alone, net income rose 38 percent and the company signed new contracts worth $395 million.

It's doubtful that CACI's founders could have imagined the heights to which the company would travel under London's leadership. Often referred to as the "grandfather of defense technology firms,"[34] CACI was founded in 1962 by Herb Karr and Harry Markowitz, two former RAND Corporation employees who pooled $1,000 to advertise their new company's seminars on the SIMSCRIPT programming language.[35] Described by A.G. Edwards' analyst Mark Jordan, CACI was a company with "a very long, enviable and consistent history with lots of M&A [mergers & acquisitions] activity."[36] CACI had become by 2004 a billion-dollar company that was acquiring smaller contractors at a rapid pace and diving into new business niches as part of its plan to grow steadily year after year.

In the early years, however, CACI had operated on the proverbial shoestring. Calling themselves the California Analysis Center, Inc., Karr and Markowitz peddled their software expertise to both private and public sector customers. Very slowly, the company got bigger and, in 1967, they opened offices in New York and Washington, D.C. The change in the company's geographic scope triggered a name change to "C-A-C-I" (pronounced "see-aye-see-eye"). Karr and Markowitz retained the

---

[34] Peter Galuszka, "Brains Behind the Brawn," *Chief Executive*, June 1, 2004.

[35] RAND Corporation is a Santa Monica, California "think-tank" with government sponsorship roots with the U.S. Air Force. CACI's SIMSCRIPT is a programming language specialized for developing digital computer simulation models from analytical and mathematical expressions and formulations.

[36] Galuszka, op. cit.

acronym that had already become popular among its customers while dropping the geographically limiting identification with California.

By 1968, CACI had become a public company trading on the over-the-counter market. Its initial public offering brought in $500,000, necessary capital, but a small stake looking back. The following year, CACI's revenue reached one million dollars for the first time. At that point, co-founder Harry Markowitz left the company to return to the academic pursuits that would win him a Nobel Prize for economics in 1990.

With Herb Karr, the founding entrepreneur, remaining as chairman, the company grew more rapidly over the next decade. That decade also marked Jack London's arrival at CACI. After being hired as a program manager in 1972, when there were fewer than fifty people in the company, London would quickly rise up the corporate ladder and place the stamp of his personality on the company. In his tenure, London would order a number of significant changes in corporate strategy, entering new fields of business and pulling CACI up the industry rankings to a spot just behind the industry behemoths.

Although taking command of CACI in an era of celebrity CEOs, London did not pine for public stardom. His gratification derived from personal challenge and achievement, the satisfaction of a job well done, and the success and accomplishments of CACI. His aim wasn't public plaudits but building a company that made a positive contribution to America and the world through quality service to customers, solid career opportunities for employees, and strong returns to shareholders. This commitment was captured in the company motto, "Ever Vigilant," and fulfilled through corporate growth. London also had a private, but patriotic theme to his leadership of CACI, and his branding of "Ever Vigilant" was another reflection of this cultural theme.

Forthright and direct, London's unique personal vernacular is unlike the button-down corporate language favored in many boardrooms. With a raspy voice, he does not mince words. Becoming quite passionate when his core values and integrity are challenged or his company is under hostile fire, London's initial impassioned reaction can catch others off guard. But he quickly regains his intense focus and steely composure as he directs his attention on sound analysis and decision-making.

Known for his strong, diligent, and detailed leadership style, London leaves little doubt about who is in charge. An entrepreneurial and visionary leader, he exudes the assurance and confidence of somebody who knows his trade and is adept at reading market trends in setting and achieving company goals. He is confident of his own instincts, values and ethics, and has a reputation for facing challenges straight on.

London had experienced crisis firsthand as a young naval officer serving as a carrier helicopter pilot during the historic Cuban missile crisis of October 1962 and the tense months following the blockade. He had also tasted a tiny whiff of glory as part of the airborne recovery team that was assigned to fish Colonel John Glenn's space capsule out from the Caribbean Sea after America's first manned orbital space flight in 1962. London is fond of recalling the thrill he felt watching Glenn stride across the flight deck to the cheers from the officers and crew of London's ship, the aircraft carrier USS *Randolph*.[37]

London's navy experience has served him well in his business. In March 2004, *Federal Computer Week*, in describing London among other 2004 "*Federal 100*" award winners, stated, "Jack London knows his way around the military world. With more than twenty years of service under his belt as a navy aviator, London has an in-depth knowledge of just what today's soldier [military] needs from the world of information technology."

Describing the bygone era of his days at sea in the U.S. Navy, London noted: "We didn't have the Internet; we didn't have satellite TV; we didn't have the communications you do now. What you had was a [messages] clipboard carried around the flight deck [ship's decks] by a private in the Marine Corps with a pistol on his side." Forty years later, London noted, the clipboard is gone, replaced by an array of digital communications gear, GPS indicators, and satellite imagery, all linked by sophisticated software. What had been a trickle of combat operations data in 1962 became a torrent by the First Gulf War in 1990. When the U.S. entered Iraq in 2003, the volume would increase to eight to ten times greater still.[38]

---

[37] John Glenn and his space capsule, *Friendship 7*, were recovered by the USS *Noa* on February 20, 1962 after Glenn's space capsule overshot the planned landing zone for London's ship, the aircraft carrier USS *Randolph*. Glenn was later transferred to the *Randolph* by helicopter. London served 12 years in the U.S. Navy Reserve, retiring in 1983 with nearly 24 years total service.

[38] "Profile of J. P. 'Jack' London for the 2004 Federal 100 Winners," *Federal Computer Week*, March 16, 2004.

London's patriotism is evident from his collection of American flag neckties. And his business conversations over the years have often been as much about CACI's service to national security as about dollars and cents.

The September 11 terrorist attacks on the World Trade Centers and the Pentagon had convinced London that CACI's expertise in intelligence and homeland security provided the opportunity to serve America much as he had decades before as a young man wearing navy pilot wings on his chest.

Combining his patriotism with business was possible only because of the company's vast expansion under London's leadership, which had pulled CACI out of a worrisome slump in the early 1980s and turned the company into an engine of growth that also had endeared him to many on Wall Street.

Although reaching the $100 million mark in gross revenue in 1983, the company's underlying financial data was not good. Due in part to weak performance in its European division, the company lost nearly $1 million in fiscal 1984 after earning about $3.7 million the year before. For London, the dip opened the door to the chief executive's suite and also made it possible for him to act boldly upon becoming CEO in 1984. "If [CACI] hadn't been in trouble," he told an interviewer years later, "I wouldn't have had the opportunity to sit in the seat."[39]

In one critical move, London dismissed the company's senior European executive and asked U.S. executive Gregory Bradford to transfer from U.S. operations to take the reins for CACI in London, England. Together, they closed some underperforming units and cut back on real estate leases to build the company's cash supply. London cut the salaries of the company's top executives, even making a 10 percent reduction in his own pay. And he instilled new discipline by calling quarterly meetings where all the top managers had to report on progress — or failures — in their areas of responsibility. Several company airplanes, favorites of Chairman Herb Karr, were put on the block by London after a number of heated debates with the co-founder.

London also reshaped the domestic company to leverage the 1984 change in government rules that opened more contracts to competition.

---

[39] Tania Anderson, "Survival of the Fittest. Jack London is hunting down deals that could turn CACI International into a major player in homeland security," *Washington Business Journal*, January 3, 2003.

The changes took hold, and by 1986, fully 70 percent of CACI's revenue came from competitively bid contracts — a nine-fold increase during the first two years of the new government rules. The company was also riding the wave of new government interest in privatization, driven by the Reagan administration's belief that public services could often be delivered more efficiently by private sector companies that knew how to manage costs in order to earn a profit and stay in business.

Aside from the policy trends, the company credited its success to a business philosophy built around strict compliance with bidding requirements and solid service to its customers. Two decades later when the stain of Abu Ghraib threatened to darken the company's future, London pointed to that philosophy as evidence that CACI had a good track record that gave it the right to be respected and accorded due process under the law, with the presumption of innocent until proven guilty.

"The culture we adhere to at CACI has been stabilizing and steadfast since our company was founded. We value honesty and integrity above all else and demand accountability," London remarked in a 2003 address on business ethics.

In a speech given to a George Mason University audience, London said: ". . . to me, ethics is about leading a well-run operation, where employees obey the law and comply with applicable rules and regulations . . . and at the same time are producing quality products and services and creating value for our shareholders."[40]

In an after-dinner speech to young midshipmen who had taken part in the Naval Academy's Ethics Essay competition in the fall of 2002, London reaffirmed his belief in the Navy's core values of honor, courage, and commitment. Those three words had guided London in the military and in the boardroom. He would return to them again and again throughout 2004 as CACI worked through the issues presented by the mass confusion and inaccurate publicity about the company at Abu Ghraib.

Others also recognized London's commitment to ethical conduct. In 2002, London was honored to learn that the Human Resources Leadership Awards of Greater Washington had created a new Ethics in Business

---

[40] Jack London, "Keynote Address to Century Club of George Mason University," November 5, 2003.

Award in his honor. "I can't think of a greater tribute to CACI's cultural and ethical values," London said at the award's inauguration.

CACI board member Michael Bayer, also a member of the Naval War College Board of Advisors and the National Security Advisory Panel, provided an apt description of London: "His vigilance to the highest ethical business standards has reinforced CACI's reputation for service, responsiveness, customer loyalty, and technical excellence."[41]

By the early 1990s, the marketplace was changing again. The combination of slower growth and technological change suggested that CACI either needed to revamp its business or accept that its rapid growth days were over. London, who added "Chairman of the Board" to his list of titles in April of 1990 upon the death of co-founder Karr, defied demands from some shareholders who believed the best way to cash in was to sell the company.

While agreeing on the need for improving returns, London believed expansion was a smarter strategy than selling out. His response was an acquisition strategy that would bring the company the expertise necessary to change to a more profitable business mix and enable it to move fast when technology or external events signaled the arrival of new opportunity.

"By the mid-1990s, it was clear we weren't going to get to heaven with the kind of work we were doing," London said in 2002 of his decision to shift CACI's focus from professional services and software tools to information technology (IT) solutions and network management. "We were facing a need to redefine the company."[42]

Beginning with its purchase of American Legal Systems (ALS) in 1992, CACI would acquire twenty-nine companies over the next dozen years (there were thirty-eight acquisitions by the end of 2007). The first wave of acquisitions built on the company's existing competencies. The ALS acquisition added to the company's already extensive litigation support work. Other transactions followed, including the acquisition of SofTech Inc.'s federal government business divisions in 1993; the 1995 purchase of Automated Sciences Group, which added IT assets in engineering and scientific services; and the acquisition, in 1996, of IMS Technologies, an information management business. Each acquisition

[41] Tania Anderson, "Survival of the Fittest." op. cit.

[42] Ibid.

added to existing business or filled a gap in CACI's roster of services. By 2002, *Business Week* placed CACI among the top companies in its "Information Technology 100" and *Washington Technology* coincidentally ranked the company eighteenth in the category of federal prime IT contractors.[43]

Seeing the opportunity presented by the transformation of the U.S. military to a lighter, leaner operation that required an increasing amount of outside support, London recognized CACI's potential to grow still more. Since 1970, the number of U.S. active military had been literally cut in half, from about 3 million to 1.4 million in 2002. The army was down from more than 700,000 active duty troops at the end of the Persian Gulf War in 1991 to just about 500,000 when the U.S. entered Iraq twelve years later. With the reduction in uniformed personnel, the Defense Department concluded that it should focus on its core competency of fighting, and other jobs could be contracted to the private sector. The system of contracting was set up to save taxpayer money by using contractors on an "as needed" basis rather than maintaining military salaries year round, year after year to do non-military work. When support services were no longer required, contractor work could be cut back quickly.

With the end of the Cold War, followed by President George H.W. Bush's success with a U.S.-led international coalition to oust Iraq from Kuwait in 1991, the world suddenly seemed a much safer place to Americans. During the Clinton administration, the government began stripping back military assets, reducing manpower, trimming the size of the navy fleet, and even drawing down intelligence capabilities. For London and CACI, that meant potentially more DoD contract opportunities: "As night followed day, these cuts meant military and intelligence organizations were going to turn to outside experts for special services," London recalled.

In particular, he anticipated a growing need for intelligence analyses to meet new challenges in such areas as preventing nuclear proliferation. The demise of the Soviet Union threw thousands of nuclear scientists into the marketplace, at least some of whom were willing to work

---

[43] Stan Crock, "Homeland Security Is CACI's Domain; Specializing in IT work for the intelligence community, this Beltway company has zoomed to a higher profile since September 11 attacks," *BusinessWeek*, November 25, 2002; and Nick Wakeman, "9th Annual Top 100 Federal Prime Contractors," *Washington Technology*, May 6, 2002.

for rogue regimes and stateless political groups who saw nuclear weapons as a way to create risk for the United States and other major military powers.[44]

"The only way to deal with that threat is information technology dominance," said London, "not through bigger ships or tanks or faster airplanes or more missiles. That's a Cold War strategy." The restructuring of the armed forces created the initial business opportunity in national security and intelligence support for government contractors. CACI would soon step in to provide some of the needed services (unexpectedly, the business would grow faster still following the tragedy of September 11).

CACI began moving into intelligence work — its new niche — beginning with its acquisition of QuesTech, Inc. in 1998. In addition to enhancing existing information security capabilities, that acquisition enabled the company to move into signal and information processing and analysis, electronic and information warfare, and command and control systems.

With QuesTech, CACI became a significant player in the intelligence market. The company then acquired XEN Corporation in February 2000 to bring aboard new and expanded intelligence capabilities. With QuesTech and XEN on board, CACI had built a powerful combination in "strategic intelligence," the ability to monitor and analyze global activities, often with distant electronic technologies, including data collected by satellite and signal analysis systems. But CACI lacked "tactical intelligence" capabilities — the up-close, real-time collection and analysis of data at a local level that can make the critical difference in battlefield outcomes. To close that gap, CACI acquired the assets of Premier Technology Group (PTG) in 2003.

According to John Hedrick, a retired army brigadier general whose business unit at CACI absorbed PTG, it was "a great fit, perfect synergy because they brought work [that was new to CACI's portfolio] we didn't do."

---

[44] The Nunn-Lugar program (named after former Senators Sam Nunn and Richard Lugar who originated it in 1991) provided U.S. money to Russia and several former Soviet republics to pay for deactivation of nuclear warheads, tightened security surrounding nuclear facilities, and even employment of some Russian nuclear scientists. These efforts reduced the chance of nuclear materials falling into the hands of terrorist groups, or nations that sanction terrorism. For their efforts, Nunn and Lugar were nominated for the 2000 Nobel Peace Prize.

The addition of PTG gave CACI an entire theater of operations to work for the army. Since 1999, PTG had been providing intelligence support to the army in Europe (USAREUR–G2), and some of its people had been on the ground providing tactical intelligence support (but not interrogation) for U.S. operations in Bosnia and Kosovo.

Since interrogation is one of the commonly accepted methods for obtaining intelligence, CACI's interrogation work in Iraq would emerge out of the acquisition of PTG.

Interrogation, simply defined, is examination by questioning an individual, typically in a formal, official, and systematic manner to obtain specific information. Intelligence gained through interrogation can aid in the interdiction or prosecution of criminal or military operations. Intelligence, on the other hand, as defined by the Department of Defense, is "the product resulting from the collection, processing, integration, analysis, evaluation and interpretation of available information concerning foreign countries or areas [or individuals]; information and knowledge about an adversary (enemy) obtained through observation, investigation, analysis, or understanding."[45] It is logical that interrogation is a method by which intelligence can be gathered. The two terms — intelligence and interrogation — however, are not synonymous. Intelligence covers a much wider scope of activities that has enabled CACI to apply its core skills in information technology to the management and analysis of information about possible adversaries.

By 2004, CACI was considered to be a high-end information technology and communications services firm. Company marketing materials listed "focus on national security" as the first item under "Growth Strategies." In his annual letter to shareholders in November 2004, London described the company focus as "supporting our customers who have key roles in national security, fighting the global war against terrorism, and the reshaping of the way government agencies communicate."

But those words only touched the surface of what London had in mind. To him, intelligence was not just a driver of growth for CACI, but also the key to America's national success and to international security against terrorism. The increasing number of attacks by terrorist groups

---

[45] Department of Defense Dictionary of Military and Associated Terms (http://www.dtic.mil/doctrine/jel/doddict/). See also the Glossary and Terms of Interest.

on civilian targets with low-tech weaponry, using asymmetric warfare strategies, made it clear that security challenges surely included but also went well beyond nuclear proliferation and other weapons of mass destruction.

London noted in a 2002 speech that President Reagan had ended the Cold War by outrunning and out-resourcing the Soviets. But against terrorist groups like al Qaeda or the Taliban, or rogue states like North Korea, the old model doesn't work: "Information systems and information technology are the only viable ways to address these challenges — nuclear proliferation, weapons of mass destruction, and homeland security. We can't protect everything and we can't all wear armor and live in a fortress. Information dominance will drive homeland security and border security and the global war on terrorism. . . . That's why CACI is in this space. This is the critical path of security for the American people at home and around the world."

London also pressed on with his acquisition program to remain competitive and sustain corporate growth. He believed standing still brought stagnation. He took a Darwinian view: adapt or become extinct. Perhaps, even more accurately, he believed the company must *choose* how to adapt or fall behind those who did. If change is a constant, London aimed to direct that change.

After acquiring four companies in 2003, he told the *Washington Post*, "That's not going to satisfy our appetite." Then he added, "The trick in this business is to be opportunistic, to observe, and be a participant in the marketplace."[46]

With each acquisition, CACI acquired new skills, contracts, and additional personnel with security clearances — among its industry's most valuable commodities. That meant new revenue, too, and when the company's fiscal year ended in June 2003, CACI's revenue had grown to $843 million. Perhaps more impressive, revenue from existing operations — excluding each year's new acquisitions — had been growing 12 to 15 percent each year. And, despite warnings from his own people that as CACI became larger, growth rates would inevitably slow, London continued to aim for percentage growth in double digits each year.

---

[46] "CACI Hungers to Reach the Top Tier," *Washington Post*, October 20, 2003.

"People have been telling me for, I guess fifteen years, that growth at these rates is not achievable, and we just continue to do it," he said.[47]

Wall Street applauded the company's performance record, driving share prices up steadily from $5.06 a share at the end of 1994 to $11.51 as 2000 closed. Although the small profit margins of government contractors did not generally appeal to Wall Street investors, this trend changed significantly in early 2001 when the bubble of the overvalued "dot-com" IT companies burst. As stock values in the dot-com's declined in early 2001, the investor trend line in government contractor stocks began to increase. Wall Street started to take a closer look at the sound business values and steady performance of the traditional, established government IT contractors such as CACI. CACI share prices had closed at $48.62 as 2004 got underway (following a two-for-one split in December 2001).

CACI's acquisition drive continued into 2004, capped by the announcement on March 10, 2004 that CACI would spend $415 million to buy the Defense and Intelligence Group of American Management Systems (AMS). With AMS's revenue added to CACI's books, the company pushed past the $1 billion revenue mark, a year in advance of its long-stated goal, and put it on track to double again to the $2 billion mark within another four years.

Analysts hailed the AMS acquisition, calling it "a breakout deal" that was three-to-four times larger than any of CACI's earlier purchases.[48] *InformationWeek* dubbed it "the best deal in recent activity."[49] Equally important, the company's reputation was outstanding and, as news reports noted, even as they honed in on Abu Ghraib, CACI's history was free from scandal.

As CorpWatch wrote on May 7, 2004, "Unlike the other military contractors — aerospace giant Boeing, whose former chief executive Darleen Druyun pled guilty last month to criminal conspiracy charges, or Halliburton, which is suspected of massively overcharging the Defense

---

[47] "At CACI, Concerns About Growth; Some Worry AMS Will Drag Revenue," *Washington Post*, March 15, 2004.

[48] "Local, Canadian Firms to Buy and Split AMS," *Washington Post*, March 11, 2004.

[49] William Schaff, "Taking Stock: Enterprise Software: Let's Make a Deal" *InformationWeek*, March 22, 2004.

Department for gas trucked into Iraq — CACI has generally stayed out of trouble."[50]

CACI's name was respected throughout the contracting community as well. As Brookings Institution Fellow Peter W. Singer noted at the outset of the crisis, CACI did not have any "skeletons" or unusual controversy in its past. "This is the first time it's really been dragged into the public venue," Singer said shortly after the Abu Ghraib scandal was publicized.[51]

"These people are as good as gold," William Golden, a former military intelligence specialist with twenty years of army experience who turned recruiter for intelligence experts, said of CACI. "They could not cut any corners."[52]

With the celebrations about to begin to mark the official closing of the AMS deal, news from Iraq stamped a question mark over CACI's name and future. The effort to find out the truth about Abu Ghraib was about to begin; before long London was to set forth CACI's approach to the crisis. He declared CACI would make sure that the company's position would reinforce its goal: "The Truth Will Out."[53]

---

[50] Pratap Chatterjee and A.C. Thompson, "Private Contractors and Torture at Abu Ghraib," CorpWatch, May 7, 2004. Although the notation about CACI was correct, the reference to Druyun was inaccurate. She was never a Boeing executive. Rather, Druyun was a former Air Force acquisitions executive. In October 2004, she was convicted for negotiating a job with Boeing while she was involved in contracts with the company. Druyun was sentenced to nine months in prison. This is an important published mistake and not at all unusual in today's media. This type of reporting carelessness became more and more apparent to CACI as the Abu Ghraib scandal unfolded.

[51] Peter W. Singer, "Fresh Air," *National Public Radio* May 11, 2004.

[52] Lisa Hoffman, "Prison Scandal Spotlights Role of Civilian Intelligence Operatives," Scripps Howard News Service, May 3, 2004.

[53] "The truth will out" is a line from Act 2, Scene 2 of William Shakespeare's *The Merchant of Venice*.

CHAPTER THREE

CBS SHUFFLES THE DECK

Photos That Shocked the World

"A picture is worth a thousand words."

~ **POPULAR PROVERB**

EVEN AS CACI'S EXECUTIVE TEAM FOCUSED ON RESPONDING TO Seymour Hersh's April 26 call, CBS News was moving forward with a broadcast scheduled for Wednesday, April 28 that would ignite new doubt about America's presence in Iraq and change the dynamics for the war. The incident would also create the biggest crisis in CACI's history.[54]

Hersh possessed a classified report, a damning indictment of military leadership at Abu Ghraib that also reported a breakdown of discipline among at least one company of the 800th Military Police Brigade, a reserve unit that had been put in charge of "high value" detainees in Tier 1-A of Abu Ghraib. The dry formal language of the Taguba report accused the reservists, who were working the prison's night shift, of "forcibly arranging detainees in various sexually explicit positions for photographing." Among other humiliations, the document accused MPs

---

[54] A timeline highlighting the key events in CACI's Abu Ghraib ordeal can be found in Appendix C.

of "forcing detainees to remove their clothes and remain naked for several days at a time," "forcing groups of male detainees to masturbate themselves while being photographed," and "forcing naked male detainees to wear women's underwear." It also listed a range of physical abuse, including punching and kicking prisoners, beating detainees with a broom handle, and pouring cold water on naked detainees.

But CBS had something even more emotionally gripping — photographs of the humiliating behaviors and abuses. It also had a medium and an audience that Hersh could not match. In a classic understatement, CBS would warn its viewers that, the pictures were "difficult to look at." The visuals of laughing GIs cavorting among naked and sometimes bleeding detainees made an impression that could never be equaled by Taguba's printed words alone, nor by Hersh's journalistic overtones.

The images of Abu Ghraib were potent and CBS had reportedly held off on the story for two weeks in deference to a Pentagon request to delay broadcast because of "the danger and tension on the ground in Iraq."[55] But on learning that the *illegally leaked* Taguba report was now circulating and that Seymour Hersh, for one, was about to break his *New Yorker* article, CBS apparently felt free of any obligation to delay its own release. The power of competition and pressure to "break" a story apparently compelled CBS to claim its all-important scoop. "What is clear is that CBS had some qualms about broadcasting the photographs and deferred to the Pentagon when General Richard Myers, chairman of the Joint Chiefs of Staff, asked it to delay showing them. It waited two weeks, finally moving ahead for that most compelling of journalistic reasons — the fear that someone else (the *New Yorker*) would beat it to it," wrote Michael Schudson in the *Financial Times*. "It's not a noble motive. It's the lowest of the journalistic low — competition, ego, perhaps dollars.[56]

The photos were aired by *60 Minutes II* on Wednesday night, April 28, triggering worldwide condemnation of the United States and the Bush administration. Christopher Hanson wrote in the *Columbia Journalism*

[55] "Abuse of Iraqis POWs by GIs Probed, 60 Minutes II has Exclusive Report on Alleged Mistreatment," CBS, April 27, 2004.

[56] Michael Schudson, "For a few dollars more never mind morality, objectivity or contextuality," *Financial Times*, July 31, 2004.

Review, "In short, CBS justified holding the piece on humanitarian grounds and in the same breath justified airing it for reasons of expediency. That position might seem brash, but is it defensible?"[57]

At CACI, the photos elevated the company's anxiety about Hersh's inquiries. At a minimum, Hersh's call had signaled bad publicity and the glare of a national spotlight that CACI's leaders were not used to and had never sought. In their mind, the role of government contractors was in working in the background, not seeking the public spotlight. The CACI team just wanted to go about its business and do a good job for its clients. And this was perhaps even more so because the company largely served the military and intelligence community. CACI's world was one of classified information in which security and confidentiality were specifically required by law.

For much of the Abu Ghraib controversy, the obligations that CACI's leadership felt to respect the laws governing classified documents left the company at a disadvantage — forcing it to react to journalists who possessed highly sensitive documents that, by law, CACI and other such organizations and individuals could not possess.

The CBS broadcast hadn't mentioned CACI or its people, so the company had a small reprieve. But the broadcast *had* referenced civilian interrogators and it presaged how news of CACI's connection would be perceived when some news anchors described the involvement of civilians as "really troubling." Such comments foreshadowed what lay ahead. The Hersh story was about to go public, and whatever chance existed that other journalists might ignore it had vanished with the broadcast of the photos. The first wire service stories moved within minutes of the CBS broadcast, and the Internet was quickly popping with commentary about the pictures and criticism of Bush administration policy.

The photos invoked serious concerns among CACI's leaders. Was it possible that in the haste of a wartime emergency, CACI's hiring process had delivered individuals who had somehow participated in the behavior in the pictures? Of equal concern was what if a CACI employee showed up in one of the photos? How could the company possibly explain that? At the time, of course, nobody — at CACI or anywhere else — knew.

---

[57] Christopher Hanson, "Tortured Logic. CBS held the Abu Ghraib photos on principle, right?" *Columbia Journalism Review*, Issue 4, July/August 2004.

The CACI team recognized, however, that if somehow a CACI employee had done wrong, they would need to deal with it promptly and openly.

"We kept waiting everyday for news services to run more pictures so we could make sure our people weren't in them," explained one CACI executive. The CACI team was concerned about the allegations for sure, but if no employee appeared in the photos, it would take one aspect of the charges off the table.

The Abu Ghraib abuse photographs were powerful, but there were other powerful images showing up at the same time. Images of charred bodies of contractors at Fallujah, Iraq and the images of mass graves of victims of Saddam Hussein's atrocities were also in the media.

Just a month before the Abu Ghraib photos were published, four contractors, working for Blackwater Security Consulting providing security services to U.S. officials and other contractors, were ambushed and murdered in Fallujah, Iraq. The bodies were dismembered, burned, and hung from a bridge while some townspeople danced in celebration, rejoicing at the Americans' death. The event produced its own set of grisly, gut-wrenching photographs. Those images, too, stunned the civilized world, but within days the world moved on. The Abu Ghraib photos, however, created more sensation and, somehow, were more potent — and lingered on in the media.

Other civilians, including contractors, were being taken hostage and even murdered, some by beheadings that were videotaped and distributed by the perpetrators.[58] A growing number of Americans now questioned both the wisdom of the war and the Bush administration's man-

---

[58] Though captivating in their range, the disturbing images from Abu Ghraib, in fact, could not even begin to compare to the brutality of the images of the corpses of the American contractors, charred and mutilated, hanging from bridge girders in Fallujah, Iraq in March of 2004. Nor did they rival the savagery of the videotaped beheading of Nicholas Berg, the American murdered by sadistic Islamic terrorists near Baghdad, nor the later vicious video coverage of the Paul Johnson beheading tragedy later that year. The detainee images also paled in comparison to the methodical and premeditated atrocities committed by Saddam Hussein and his sons in the very same Abu Ghraib prison only a few years earlier. Since the U.S. entered Iraq in 2003, hundreds of Americans and other foreigners have been victims of kidnappings and beheadings. See also Appendices G and K.

agement of it. In that environment, the allegation that contract employees were suspected of abusing prisoners would not only be treated as big news, it also had the potential to trigger inquiries on Capitol Hill, especially among those who had concern about the government's outsourcing of its services and the role of contractors in providing those services. It was an unnerving atmosphere as CACI executives pondered what lay ahead for their people in Iraq, especially those working at Abu Ghraib.

"We didn't know the depth of the trench or how wide it might be," London said months later. "Nobody was telling us anything, so it was hard to assess. But the Abu Ghraib pictures were a total shock. This was clearly a matter of international magnitude and, understandably, our concern was that some of our people might, somehow, be caught up in the middle of it."

The first imperative for London was to get the facts. He summoned his top people, among them Jeff Elefante, CACI's General Counsel; Ken Johnson, a West Point graduate and president of CACI's U.S. Operations; Harry Thornsvard, a senior vice president who had joined CACI just a year earlier when it acquired Premier Technology Group and whose division had hired the CACI interrogators; Thornsvard's immediate boss, Executive Vice President John Hedrick; Jody Brown, CACI's communications officer who had taken the call from Hersh and would now have to develop the plan and deal with the media horde; Chuck Mudd, the vice president and country manager for all CACI interrogator work in Iraq; Mike Gray, who was in charge of managing all of CACI's contracts; and Bill Koegel, the company's outside counsel and widely considered the most indispensable member of London's legal team, who as a partner in the Washington, D.C.-based law firm, Steptoe & Johnson, had helped CACI with many of its legal affairs and other key issues for some thirteen years. Together, they started to assess how to get the job done. Senior Vice President Ron Schneider would be the project coordinator and London, Koegel, and Brown would be the executive steering group, and outside business consultant Dr. Jennifer Burkhart would be London's independent external business advisor.

That same week Burkhart, who advised CACI on mergers and acquisitions (M&A) activities, was attending her nephew's wedding. The best man was his younger brother, Lieutenant Aaron N. Seesan, U.S. Army, who would volunteer to go to Iraq only a few months later. It was a happy, memorable occasion for all the family, but it was the last time many of them would see Lieutenant Seesan.[59]

Burkhart, who was a licensed Ph.D. in psychology, had been tapped several years earlier to assist the company in its M&A search program. She had prior experience in business development with some of the largest certified public accounting and professional consulting firms in the country. Proud of the five companies she had helped CACI acquire to date, with total revenue volume approaching $200 million, she was thinking about her next potential acquisition candidate when news of Abu Ghraib came through. London would soon ask her to shift focus to provide CACI analytical support and recommendations having to do with the psychological and public relations aspects of the unfolding events generated by the Abu Ghraib scandal.

London moved quickly. He tasked some of his key executives and staff with researching the accusations that were being leveled at CACI. At the time, there was no way of knowing how long or how large this story would become. Brown was already inundated with the media: inquiries, reports, and press releases. Other senior leaders were busy staying on top of other areas, like the stock markets and CACI's contracts with the government. But when it became evident that the pace of events related to Abu Ghraib would only intensify and quicken, London decided that the company would have to switch from a reactive position to a proactive strategy — and fast.

First, there had to be a focused, comprehensive, and immediate approach to tackling the crisis. London convened the newly formed CACI Iraq Steering Group (CISG) — a team of all the senior executives and managers whose groups dealt with the company's work in Iraq. The personnel department would have to pull up the files of all CACI staff in Iraq and re-examine their hiring processes. CACI's contracts and audit departments would be tasked with reviewing every detail of the contract documents and the process by which the contracts were obtained and

---

[59] One year later, in May of 2005, 1st Lt. Seesan was tragically killed, the victim of a roadside bomb (IED) in Mosul, Iraq, while leading his platoon on a reconnaissance mission to clear roads of explosives.

administered. The company's finance group would be called upon to assess the revenue from the Iraq contracts, and project the legal and PR costs of representing the company. Also included in the CISG activities was the investor relations (IR) function, which would monitor any market risks to the company and shareholders. Meanwhile attorneys and staff in the legal department would assess whether the company had acted appropriately and would ensure that it continued to do so. Additional members from external legal and public affairs groups would eventually join the team.

All of these activities were directed by London in the (often twice) daily CISG meetings while Schneider, as project coordinator, helped keep the process moving along. Although the CISG had a full but well-organized agenda, not everything would go smoothly. For the first few months particularly, every day brought new challenges, posed new questions and required an adjustment in strategy or some new action. Each member of the CISG possessed particular knowledge of different aspects of CACI's Iraq operations. While decisions about how the company would address certain issues were resolved simply by discussion, others induced heated arguments particularly with respect to how the company would push back against the media onslaught.

This was not the time for consensus building, but decision-making. London would always listen to his senior leadership team, but as the leader of CACI for the past two decades, the final answers would come from him.

The CACI leadership group, which would meet in full session twice a day and once daily on weekends for the next several months, agreed it needed to be briefed on exactly what the roles were of those who were assigned to Abu Ghraib, and what — if anything — the army had said about them. They also had to know, to the greatest extent possible, what had transpired. Had any CACI people participated in abuses like those shown on CBS and described by Taguba? If not directly involved, had any of CACI's people been aware of any misconduct and what, if anything, had they done about it? And what of Taguba's most fundamental accusation — that someone who was employed by CACI had in some way been responsible for the abuses alleged?

Koegel, the outside litigator and legal investigator, was immediately tasked with the job of gathering the information and answering key questions. With a team of Steptoe attorneys that would work exclusively on CACI's internal investigation, he was told to tear down CACI's internal processes piece by piece — finding out who was hired and why. He needed to determine as best he could exactly what CACI employees had or had not done at Abu Ghraib. Taguba had "urged" in his report that Stefanowicz be fired. But before making that decision, London and his colleagues wanted to know for themselves everything they could about Stefanowicz. Without seeing any evidence beyond Taguba's broad accusation, London felt he didn't yet have a basis for firing an employee. Doing so before the facts were available would be wrong, signal premature acceptance of blame or guilt, and be a negative sign to the CACI workforce. Furthermore, the company was receiving positive feedback from the army on CACI employees' performance at Abu Ghraib. He wanted Koegel's help to get some answers fast.

Koegel had served as outside counsel to CACI since 1991. His specialty was litigation and much of his practice involved corporate clients. Koegel's relationship with CACI was mostly in support of the company's Board of Directors in matters of legal defense, litigation, executive agreements, and contract assessments. Over the years, his role had been in many ways that of a legal advisor to London and to senior board member Warren Phillips. Koegel was one of the best litigators in town, and he had a mind that could retain and articulate the most intricate arguments and details.

Koegel was as surprised as anyone when he was called by London to discuss the impact of the breaking Abu Ghraib story. Koegel had known CACI's reputation as a valued government contractor and was stunned, like everyone at CACI, when the news was first heard. In all of his years working with CACI, he had known the company to be nothing less than exemplary among government contractors.

In fact, at this point, the company didn't even know for certain whether anything had really gone wrong at all with its personnel. It had not had any earlier indication at all. It did not know whether it had a substantive problem or just a public relations challenge. It didn't know whether any misconduct by Stefanowicz (or any other company employee) indicated a crack in the administrative process or if someone had simply run amok. And if any individual had gone bad, just how culpable was that person? Had somebody clearly crossed the line by taking part in the activities shown in the photos? Was it a case of guilt by association? Or might they be wholly innocent?

It was Koegel's job to find out.

* * *

Even as it was gathering facts, the CACI team was going to be faced with a host of other issues, including scores of inquiries from the news media. It would have to address the concerns of employees, customers, and investors, while also keeping the business running day-to-day. And it was also likely that additional investigations were going to take place.

Over the next several days, the senior team would seek a way to organize itself for the tasks ahead — while also hoping the crisis might turn out to be short-lived given the suspicion of only a single employee. Ultimately, the work divided itself into three relatively clear spheres: investigations, with Koegel and in-house counsel Elefante in the lead; the broad area of external communications, essentially under Brown's aegis and including not just the media but the investment community as well; and daily business operations, where Ken Johnson and other senior staff would continue the daily operational activities. Over time, the CACI team would encounter unexpected and simultaneous issues that would represent additional crises within the larger initial crisis and which would necessitate additional expertise and expansion of the team.

None of the spheres were mutually exclusive and all of the sphere leaders would have significant internal and, eventually, external support. Brown, for example, would deal primarily with the news media while Dave Dragics, vice president of Investor Relations (IR), would organize most of the IR work. But it was also Brown's job to make sure that the IR and other external messaging was consistent. Brown also would have the task of outreach to employees. And, in the center of it all, very much hands-on, would be Jack London, who provided the strategic direction and focus.

Beyond the organizational structure, the company was going to need a strategic framework to guide the overall effort. As part of that effort, London asked Burkhart to help him assess the unfolding events and shifting public perceptions, and identify the strategies to address them. London credited Burkhart with helping to shape his "Tylenol model" of self-assessment and full and frequent public disclosure in a crisis environment.[60]

Indeed, in considering how to respond to Hersh, CACI had already begun the process of developing an overarching strategic approach beginning with the broad issue of how much to say to the public. There was some sentiment for a minimalist posture — offering only the briefest, factual statements in hopes that the story might burn itself out or pass from CACI and Stefanowicz to larger concerns in a relatively short time. Some argued that it was unwise to comment at all until the company had more information. In their view, the company might simply say that it planned to cooperate with official investigations, but refuse to comment beyond that, lest it jeopardize those inquiries.

Of course, retreat into silence is a common corporate response to trouble — like taking cover during a rainstorm. This approach can have merit if the company is confident that there is no additional information floating around that would provide a new angle or "hook" for a news organization to report on further.

Before the photos became public, there seemed a possibility that the story might not take hold. In fact, allegations of military prison abuse had already been circulating for several months. The Associated Press had written at least two stories in late 2003 about alleged abuse. And the army itself had announced to the press in January that it was beginning an investigation into alleged abuse, and in March that six soldiers faced a court martial for mistreatment of prisoners. But these stories passed with virtually no notice. Some at CACI wondered if Hersh's story might similarly fade away. London conceded: "I was in that camp for a day or two myself."

Absent the photos, it seemed that possible mistreatment of prisoners might not be regarded by the news media as a sensational event. But seeing *is* believing. Writing in the *Columbia Journalism Review*, journalism professor and former Reuters reporter Christopher Hanson concluded: "Taken by the perpetrators themselves, these digital photos

---

[60] In the 1980s Johnson & Johnson faced a crisis when it was found that bottles of Tylenol were tampered with and pills were poisoned, leading to several deaths. The company responded with a forthcoming strategy that acknowledged the crisis and championed its resolution.

transformed a sketchy, abstract page A20 filler story into a page-one story that conveyed horror in unforgettable images."[61]

New York Times' executive editor Bill Keller agreed: "Any honest editor will give you the same answer. It's the pictures; that's what did it."[62]

Even if it were plausible before the photos surfaced, once they became public it seemed imprudent for CACI's planners to assume the story would wither. Given the chaos described by Taguba, the inevitable fog of war, and the likelihood that individuals and critics with policy or political agendas would try to keep the story alive, this particular "rainstorm" seemed very unlikely to pass quickly. If anything, it seemed certain there were more storm clouds on the horizon.

The prevailing view at CACI was that refusal to talk publicly or to limit itself to bland statements that provide little information would forfeit any chance to affect media coverage or influence public perception. On the suggestion of Burkhart and supported by other colleagues, London took the Johnson & Johnson (J&J) Tylenol crisis model of self-investigation and full and frequent public disclosure as an initial reference point and broad framework for the response strategy. Although conceding that he could not recall specific details, he said the impression of J&J as a "stand up" company was fixed in his mind. He recalled that J&J's decision to openly confront and investigate the tragic deaths caused by poisoned Tylenol capsules had enabled the company to quickly regain public confidence.[63]

London also was impressed that J&J's approach, led by then CEO James E. Burke, was rooted in a fundamental corporate commitment to its customers' health and well-being, which J&J put before profit and financial concerns in dealing with its crisis. In London's mind, J&J had prevailed because it resisted the urge to reinvent itself during crisis.

---

[61] Hanson, op. cit.

[62] Sherry Ricchiardi, "Missed Signals," *American Journalism Review*, August/September 2004.

[63] A big advantage in the Johnson & Johnson situation, however, was that Tylenol was already a popular well known product before the company faced its crisis. CACI had a bigger challenge in overcoming the fact it was unknown and its services were not well understood. Further, the media explosion from the Internet, 24/7 cable news, worldwide satellite TV coverage and the ubiquitous blogs made CACI's challenge more complex and incomparably more vast.

Instead, the company clung to a long-established style of operation and corporate philosophy. Robert Wood Johnson, J&J's leader for fifty years, incorporated in the company's credo his belief that business should have responsibilities to society beyond sales and profit.[64] CACI also had a longstanding credo of ethical behavior and a leader in Jack London who believed in contributing to his country including through the company's support work for its government clients.

Johnson & Johnson was applauded in the media for its socially responsible behavior. The *Washington Post*, for one, praised the company for being honest with the public.[65]

London intended for CACI to develop a similar crisis management model. Elements of the Tylenol model would remain evident in the months ahead even as CACI developed its own distinctive mode of operation.

In the end, London's view was the one that mattered. The CEO would consider advice and could alter an initial decision that colleagues disagreed with. But he trusted his instincts and typically stuck with them. And in this instance, London's preference for the Tylenol approach of "telling it like it is" represented a genuine consensus. The group felt firmly that the right way to best serve its country, its government and its military client while also protecting the company's reputation and good name was to find the facts and state them plainly in every available forum.

Looking back, London and his colleagues reassembled the list of principles by which they agreed to operate. Though not written down in any one place, the hours of discussions led to a common view about how the company should conduct itself as events unfolded. Most remarkable in hindsight is the degree to which London and his team clung to these rules of conduct throughout. Also notable is their belief that the principles remain as sound in retrospect, as they had been at the time looking forward. In their view, it also helped tremendously that even before the crisis, the company had a written creed, mission statement, and code of

---

[64] Lawrence G. Foster, "The Johnson & Johnson Credo and the Tylenol Crisis," *New Jersey Bell Journal*, Vol. 6 No. 1, 1983.

[65] Jerry Knight, "Tylenol's Maker Shows How to Respond to Crisis, *Washington Post*, October 11, 1982.

ethics to guide them.[66] The Tylenol case was the added point of reference to further build their approach.

Fully fleshed out, CACI's approach meant that company leaders would do all of the following:

- ☐ Get the facts and get them straight
- ☐ Establish clear priorities early on
- ☐ Trust in CACI's core values, "do the right thing," and tell the truth
- ☐ Look to the company credo and mission statement to help focus on doing the right thing
- ☐ Cooperate fully with all official investigations
- ☐ Publicly and clearly commit to correct problems quickly
- ☐ Make clear that CACI supports the rule of law, including due process and the presumption of innocence; no "kangaroo courts" or "lynch mobs"
- ☐ Emphasize that the company will take firm action upon confirmed evidence of wrongdoing
- ☐ Honor the public record and seek to set it straight whenever it strays
- ☐ Push back against every instance of false or erroneous news reports or other inaccurate public statements
- ☐ Recognize that the media is not an ally and cannot be relied upon to get the story and facts straight
- ☐ Seek public corrections for every error or distortion
- ☐ Tell the company's story over and over again in every available forum — state it clearly and firmly in a straightforward manner — in plain English
- ☐ Communicate directly, fully, and frequently with customers, employees, shareholders, and the public

---

[66] CACI's business codes and value precepts are presented in Appendix D. CACI's credo encapsulates a commitment to quality service and best value for clients, individual opportunity and respect for each other, integrity and excellence in the workplace, and distinction and the competitive edge in its markets. CACI has for many years published policy documents that address the dealings and conduct of its employees and business units. CACI's Code of Ethics and Business Conduct Standards are required to be read and signed annually by every employee. CACI also published a Code if Conduct in Iraq that was similarly required to be read and signed by employees working in Iraq.

☐ Accept that things may get worse before they get better
☐ Resist media intimidation and political "witch hunt" pressures to find a scapegoat
☐ Work to defend CACI's *good name* by doing whatever is proper and appropriate to preserve the company's reputation

In the weeks ahead, when CACI was battered by attacks in the media, reporters' misstatements, unsubstantiated accusations, baseless lawsuits, hate mail, and protest demonstrations at its doorstep, London and the team worked within this newly developed CACI model to respond honestly and fully and forcefully to every audience and in every forum. They would not speak without knowing the facts. But they would when they knew something for certain.

To London's team, the goal wasn't just to ride out the storm. Even more important was a determination to avoid any undeserved and unjustified tarnish on the company's name. It was entirely appropriate to assume no wrongdoing initially since the company had received only positive and no negative feedback from its army client. And the facts of the situation were still uncertain. It would be the facts that would draw the conclusions, not the media's opinions and speculative reports. As a matter of principle *and* business, they believed a good name was critical because a solid reputation can help get contract awards and keep customers but a bad reputation does just the opposite.

"We were going to drown if we didn't push back," London explained later. "Hiding was tantamount to suicide because then the media mostly steers the agenda. And when the media is out of control, it's a monster."

In a groundbreaking strategy that was uniquely geared to the twenty-four-hour media machine, London devised his so-called "targeted media response strategy," which he assigned to Burkhart. This was a multi-page document in letter form sent to virtually every news organization that wrote about CACI in an erroneous, incomplete, false, or misleading manner. London's concept was to lay out all of CACI's factual points in a single place so that the reporters would have the full picture at their fingertips. While drawn from a common, consistent template that was updated over time as more issues surfaced in the media, each response letter would be customized with information specifically tailored to address every issue raised by each individual news story.

And the company's response would go further than answering media queries. Like a military commander, London formalized CACI's effort by assigning it an operational name: *"The Truth Will Out:"* a famous phrase from William Shakespeare's play, *The Merchant of Venice* that signaled both his commitment to finding the facts and his firm conviction that inaccurate information was wrongly casting a shadow over CACI. When the facts were fully assembled, he expected CACI to be cleared, especially considering the company's four decades long clean track record.[67] But if the truth showed otherwise, he also would accept responsibility and fix whatever had gone wrong.

London also tasked Brown to assist him in designing and implementing a comprehensive external and internal communications program. The scope of the program was extraordinary, as it grew to include twenty-seven lengthy external news releases issued at a steady flow throughout the crisis,[68] numerous direct mail campaigns to eventually include members of Congress, dozens of written responses to a variety of individuals, ongoing coordination of outside consultants and a daily report to senior management of all media stories, both print and broadcast, sometimes exceeding one hundred a day, related to Abu Ghraib. "You must have the 'A' team who are fully committed when you are faced with a crisis of this magnitude," Brown explained.

In addition, London directed Brown and her team to build a special section on the company's website to provide information about CACI's work in Iraq. Every press release, every company statement, every communication about Abu Ghraib and CACI was posted for public view. A list of frequently asked questions (FAQs) was developed and maintained on an ongoing basis. Employees were encouraged to tell everyone they could think of — customers, family, friends, and neighbors — to log on

---

[67] The company had a fine track record of relatively trouble-free business operations with the U.S. government for over a forty-plus year period. At any point where an issue or problem had arisen with its government client the company moved promptly to a solution. The company's officers and managers operated by a code of conduct and ethics that had been in place for years (signed and renewed by all employees each year.) The company also had a number of former military personnel who had served honorably (many with distinction) in their active duty careers. And overall, CACI had a remarkably clean and trouble-free record for the work behavior of individual employees.

[68] Select CACI News Releases on the Abu Ghraib scandal are presented in Appendix E.

for information. It was another way London strived to get the facts out and the truth known.

The thousands of communications CACI engaged in were not limited to the media. The company delivered its message to its customers, the investment community, employees and their families, special interest groups, political activists, and, eventually, emerging CACI detractors.

CACI's leadership organized conference calls with shareholders and financial analysts, briefed members of Congress, met with local peace activists, and wrote direct letters to anti-war groups. As best she could, Brown tried to answer every press inquiry — though at times they flooded in at a rate of twenty-five calls an hour. And, in the first few weeks at least, London — like the CEO of J&J's Tylenol crisis — personally took CACI's case to the public — submitting to dozens of interviews with individual reporters. Under London's direction, Brown worked with the PR team to develop the strategy and message points for every single interview.

The path had been set: The CACI team would find out the truth and consistently tell its story to every audience: "The truth will out."

It was all part of what London and his colleagues called "doing the right thing." In every dark moment or every decision point in the months ahead, they would look to the operating principles they had devised and turn for comfort and guidance to the same fundamental statement, first made to London by CACI Board member Larry Welch when he remarked "Jack, just do the right thing."

CHAPTER FOUR

CACI IN THE SPOTLIGHT

The media spins out of control while CACI looks for answers

> **"American journalists were in a**
> **catch up frenzy [over Abu Ghraib]."**
> ∽**AMERICAN JOURNALISM REVIEW, AUGUST 2004**

T HE PHOTOS CREATED A MEDIA FIRESTORM. IN EVERY PART OF THE media world, pictures of U.S. soldiers at Abu Ghraib assaulted the eye. They showed a sad, but limited, alternative reality — there were a number of American soldiers engaging in acts of torment — not pictures of the jubilant liberation Americans had wanted and hoped would be seen.

Arab media aired the images around the clock. A leading Egyptian newspaper was reported to have splashed the word "The Scandal" across the front page above the photos while other Arab media warned that the abuses would rally Islamic fundamentalists.[69] In every part of the world, the photos blazed from TV screens and newspaper pages — evidence of either the baseness of America's war or the betrayal of a just effort to topple Saddam Hussein. In the United States, for those journalists who had not reacted to earlier published reports of prisoner

---

[69] "Arabs Outraged By Photos of U.S. Forces Humiliating Iraqis," *USA Today*, May 2, 2004.

abuse, they were now making up for that lost opportunity in what the *American Journalism Review* called "a catch up frenzy."[70]

Though not named in the first stories, CACI leaders could glimpse the company's immediate future. Once Hersh's report was published, other news organizations would inevitably follow, telling their own audiences about the government contractor whose interrogators were included in the accusations swirling around the Abu Ghraib scandal. Moreover, every one of those reports would now implicitly link CACI to those awful photos — which before long would seem to be the *whole* story of Abu Ghraib.

"Sometimes a particular picture or image takes hold and becomes 'the truth' about some event," explained Don Foley, a public affairs strategist who counseled CACI throughout 2004. "In politics, when somebody thinks of Michael Dukakis, they think about the picture of him in the tank. When you hear 'Abu Ghraib,' you think about those pictures and you assume that anybody accused of misconduct did the same thing we saw in the photos."[71]

As business advisor and psychologist Burkhart pointed out, "Pictures evoke an emotional dimension that words can't capture. And for the media the abuse photos were the 'emotional hook' that kept their audience transfixed and continually engaged in the story they wanted to tell."

"They never lost their shock value, no matter how many times they ran on TV," Foley added. "The words 'Abu Ghraib' became synonymous with a certain kind of 'abuse' and became a taint on anybody associated with the prison in any way."

Of paramount importance to CACI was the fact that neither Taguba's report nor any other publicly available investigation had ever suggested or concluded that any CACI employee was present during the degradation shown in the photos.

Significantly, there was never any information or evidence made available that linked Stefanowicz to Taguba's allegations or the specific abuses

---

[70] Ricchiardi, op. cit.

[71] In September 1988, former presidential candidate Michael Dukakis visited a General Dynamics plant in Michigan to take part in a "photo op" in a military tank. Dukakis appeared awkward and uncomfortable in the military setting, especially wearing a safety helmet that appeared too big for his head. The George H. W. Bush campaign used the Dukakis footage as evidence he would not make a good commander-in-chief and the event remains a prime example of backfired public relations.

at Abu Ghraib. But, before long, on Web sites, in lawsuits, protest demonstrations, and in the mainstream press, CACI was accused of all the extremes, not only of abuse, but also of profiting from *torture* or backing rape and murder as a matter of corporate policy. These more extreme and vile allegations were truly shocking; "preposterous" in London's words, but vile accusations — lies — nonetheless, that he knew had to be dealt with forcefully.

Some might argue that the wilder accusations of torture, rape and murder could be allowed to fall of their own weight. But London was constitutionally opposed to allowing such slurs to stand without challenge. In his mind, lies unanswered have the potential to be misconstrued as truth. He reflected on the opposite views of two famous World War II leaders, Franklin D. Roosevelt who said, "Repetition does not transform a lie into truth" and Joseph Goebbels who said, "A lie repeated often enough becomes the truth."[72] He was determined that the record would show that CACI challenged the untruths, and that the record would include CACI's truthful and factual answers as well.

The linkage of his company with the word "torture" stuck in his craw.[73] To him, and probably to most Americans, torture had especially sinister connotations that went well beyond mistreatment or abuse. Variously defined as "the intentional infliction of severe physical pain," the word torture carries with it the implication of deliberate cruelty and pre-meditated action often for the sole purpose of making the victim suffer great agony.[74] Thus torture implies cruelty for its own sake and, in London's mind, the word's connotations were so evil that to accuse somebody of torture without verifiable proof (solid evidence) was itself a malicious act.

There is a fairly common misconception that interrogation equates to torture or that the two cannot be mutually exclusive. This misconception is not even close to the truth. However, the frantic media and an uninformed public quickly jumped to the conclusion that, not only abuse, but torture had taken place in Abu Ghraib and, in some cases, in the form of

---

[72] Http://www.en.thinkexist.com/quotes/top; Franklin D. Roosevelt, 32nd President of the United States and Dr. Joseph Goebbles, Nazi propaganda architect of Hitler's Third Reich.

[73] The word "torture" first surfaced in media descriptions but was not among the initial Taguba report allegations against Stefanowicz at Abu Ghraib or in findings pertaining to him throughout the subsequent official investigation process.

[74] Merriam-Webster Online Dictionary, http://www.merriam-webster.com.

interrogations. Yet not a single one of the infamous abuse photos depicted an interrogation or showed a CACI interrogator. The notorious
photographs simply did not link detainee abuse (or torture) to the interrogations efforts of CACI employees.

The definition of these terms may be simply semantics to some, but
there is a crucial difference. Interrogation is a process of questioning to
obtain usable and reliable information, in a lawful manner. Torture is a
means whereby extreme suffering is intentionally inflicted. "Abuse" and
"humiliation" were also used to describe what had happened at Abu
Ghraib. And adding further to the confusion, the media and other commentators all too often used these words and concepts inaccurately,
improperly or interchangeably.[75]

While torture is morally wrong, illegal, and arguably ineffective during interrogations, the insinuation made by the media from the Abu
Ghraib scandal was that the Americans and the American military inten-

---

[75] Torture is forbidden by the Geneva Conventions, although the term is neither
directly nor precisely defined. The first Geneva Convention was signed in 1864 to
protect the sick and wounded in wartime, but it wasn't until 1949 that the Third
Convention listed the better-known rights of prisoners of war. Article 3 of the Conventions refers "to violence to life and person, in particular murder of all kinds, mutilation, cruel treatment and torture" and "outrages upon personal dignity, in particular
humiliating and degrading treatment," with addition in Article 17 of both physical and
mental torture or any other form of coercion. The Third and Fourth Conventions
later stated that both civilians and prisoners of war must not be subjected to physical
or mental coercion. In 1993, the United Nations established an Office of the High
Commissioner for Human Rights, whose Convention Against Torture (CAT) has
been the foundation for international law and cooperation on the subject. Article 1 of
the CAT defines torture as "any act by which severe pain or suffering, whether physical or mental, is intentionally inflicted on a person for such purposes as obtaining
from him or a third person information or a confession, punishing him for an act he or
a third person has committed or is suspected of having committed, or intimidating or
coercing him or a third person, or for any reason based on discrimination of any kind,
when such pain or suffering is inflicted by or at the instigation of or with the consent
or acquiescence of a public official or other person acting in an official capacity." Article 11 of the Convention acknowledges the role and rules of interrogation including
the requirement of systematic review and training.

Torture, according to Title 18 of the U.S. Code, is defined as "an act committed by
a person acting under the color of law specifically intended to inflict severe physical
or mental pain or suffering (other than pain or suffering incidental to lawful sanctions) upon another person within his custody or physical control." The U.S. Army

tionally used torture in the interrogation process. There was further erroneous conjecture that contract interrogators were employed to allow the U.S. military to get around existing rules and laws in order to use methods of torture. This, too, as far as CACI was concerned, could not have been farther from the truth. Further, Secretary of Defense Donald Rumsfeld proclaimed during testimony to a Senate hearing on the abuses, "I can't conceive of anyone looking at the pictures and suggesting that anyone could have recommended, condoned, permitted, encouraged, subtly, directly, in any way, that those things take place."[76] While many headlines made accusations of torture, there were, as of December 2007, no charges of "torture" brought against anyone, under the Uniform Code of Military Justice (UCMJ) or any other legal code, alleged to have been part of the detainee abuses at Abu Ghraib.[77]

---

incorporated these definitions into its own policies. In the version of the Army Field Manual in use at the time of the abuses (Army Field Manual. FM 34-52, September 1992), interrogation is defined as "the process of questioning a source to obtain the maximum amount of usable information. The goal of any interrogation is to obtain usable and reliable information, in a lawful manner and in a minimum amount of time, and to satisfy intelligence requirements of any echelon of command." Force is also prohibited "as a means of or aid [in] interrogation" and violations of these prohibitions are criminal acts punishable under military justice. The Manual also requires clearance from a command judge advocate before a questionable method can be used.

[76] "U.S. Senate Armed Services Committee held a hearing on the treatment of Iraqi Prisoners Friday," *Washington Post*, May 7, 2004.

[77] While there is no specific offense of "torture" under the Uniform Code of Military Justice (UCMJ), Subchapter X, Punitive Articles, at Section 877.77 through 934.134, lists all charges that may be brought that carry punitive measures. The two most serious charges brought against the soldiers at Abu Ghraib for the acts depicted in the Abu Ghraib photographs were Section 893.93 "Cruelty and maltreatment" and 928.128 "Assault." Section 893.93 "Cruelty and maltreatment" is defined as "Any person subject to this chapter who is guilty of cruelty toward, or oppression or maltreatment of, any person subject to his orders shall be punished as a court-martial may direct." Section 928.128 "Assault" is "Any person subject to this chapter who attempts or offers with unlawful force or violence to do bodily harm to another person, whether or not the attempt or offer is consummated, is guilty of assault and shall be punished as a court-martial may direct. (b) Any person subject to this chapter who — (1) commits an assault with a dangerous weapon or other means or force likely to produce death or grievous bodily harm; or (2) commits an assault and intentionally inflicts grievous bodily harm with or without a weapon; is guilty of aggravated assault and shall be punished as a court-martial may direct."

London was disgusted by such preposterous theories. The principles and rules remained the same regardless of whether the interrogator was contractor or military. No one was above the law.

Over the months ahead, few things would disgust him more than the casual way in which commentators tossed the words "abuse" and "torture" at his company.[78] Some even maliciously accused CACI of deliberately indulging in torture as a part of the company's business plan.[79] Every repetition of these appalling and vicious allegations just stiffened London's resolve to push back even harder on the falsehoods and move more forcefully to find the truth and confront the false accusations.

On April 30, 2004, ironically Jack London's sixty-seventh birthday, Hersh's piece was posted on *The New Yorker* Web site and provided the world with the first detailed account of Major General Taguba's report. Titled "Torture at Abu Ghraib," the article mentioned CACI only briefly and even that reference was deep inside the article.[80] But the brief mention was damning. Hersh quoted Taguba's suspicion about Stefanowicz and Taguba's suggestion that the civilian "be fired from his army job, reprimanded, and denied his security clearance." Although Stefanowicz had no authority over the MPs, Taguba, in imprecise words, said the CACI employee "allowed and/or instructed" military police in actions "which were neither authorized and in accordance with applicable regulations/policy." It was a strong sweeping statement, without corroborating evidence. And London, the former military officer, felt confident that a civilian contractor like Stefanowicz would never have been permitted to act with that type of authority.

Hersh withheld any comment of his own on CACI. But the placement of the CACI reference — after several pages detailing the abuses — and the timing of the article, which ran just as the public was

---

[78] For example, a August 13, 2004 headline in the *Washington Post* read, "CACI Finds No *Torture* Involvement" while the first line of the article stated that, "no evidence that [CACI] employees were involved in the *abuse* of detainees at Abu Ghraib prison." [italics added]

[79] While fringe media often put out headlines like "Torture for Profit" (Guerilla News Network, September 21, 2004), mainstream voices also made similar accusations. "Companies looking to profit from the torture of human beings don't belong in our portfolio," said California state controller Steve Westly (Leon Worden, "State Controller, Treasurer Questions Investments in CACI," *The Signal*, July 10, 2004).

[80] Hersh, op. cit.

seeing the pictures for the first time, had the lasting effect of connecting Stefanowicz and CACI to the worst of the misdeeds.

Attorneys for the accused MPs also tried to create a link between CACI, the Abu Ghraib scandal, and the infamous photographs. Gary Myers, who represented accused MP Sergeant Ivan "Chip" Frederick, described the contractors as "central to the case" and said their inter-actions with the MPs "creates a laissez-faire attitude that is completely inappropriate."[81]

Guy Womack, the attorney for Charles Graner (who would be convicted of several charges, including assault and obstruction of justice, by a court martial in January of 2005), was even more strident in his accusations against the contractors. Womack appeared several times on national television depicting his client as a soldier who was simply following orders and acting on the direction of interrogators. But months later during the court martial hearings, the blame placed on the interrogators by the accused in the early days of the scandal did not gain the expected attention or hold any significance in the military trials.[82]

This fact alone is probably the single most important element in telling the story about the interrogators at Abu Ghraib. If the defense attorneys could have proven the interrogators (military or civilian contractors) were responsible for the MP's abuses at Abu Ghraib, they would have made every possible effort to do so. But they apparently could not and did not.

Working with Myers' words, both Britain's *Guardian* newspaper and the *Los Angeles Times* reported on April 30, the same day as Hersh's story, that contractors were conducting interrogations at Abu Ghraib.

---

[81] Julian Borger, "U.S. Military in Torture Scandal," *The Guardian*, April 30, 2004.

[82] An uncle of Sgt. Frederick told the press on April 30, 2004 that Frederick had informed him through an email that it was the civilians who attached electrical wires to a prisoner who was forced to stand on a narrow box with his head hooded and body draped with a blanket. An army reserve officer responded to this by saying, "That's nonsense, these soldiers are military policemen, and they all were trained for their special duties. They all were drilled thoroughly in the rules of the Geneva Convention, and they all certainly knew that what they were doing when photographed was flat-out wrong." (John Moreno Gonzales and Arnold Abrams, "Families of accused soldiers blame civilians," Newsday.com, April 30, 2004.) Frederick later pled guilty to participating with another soldier in placing the hooded detainee on a box and attaching wires to his fingers.

Unlike Hersh's article, these articles made the contractors their primary focus, and raised questions about the propriety of contracting out the interrogation function.[83]

In seeking to shift the onus from their clients to CACI and Titan, Myers and Womack had taken advantage of journalists' greatest need — new information that moved the story forward. The result is that journalists get a new story that keeps them in the paper, and the source gets a story more to his or her liking.

In this case, Myers and Womack effectively enlisted the newspapers in a test of their clients' defense. They also tried to redirect attention away from their clients by suggesting that there were bigger fish to fry. In effect, they provided a road map for the next phase of media coverage. Myers was among the first to raise broader questions of public policy and also to suggest that the world should look for culpability elsewhere — to senior U.S. military officers and policymakers in Washington but also to corporate contractors such as CACI.

Although never successfully obscuring his client's complicity in the abuses (Sergeant Frederick ultimately pled guilty to the charges against him), Myers' finger-pointing cast a wider net and provided fresh fodder for the journalists. When Myers identified CACI and Titan, the Taguba report was still only available to a very limited circle. Of the journalists, Hersh appeared to have the only full copy of the document, while Borger at the *Guardian* said he had been provided with "parts" of the document. Myers, therefore, became a critical source for reporters who wanted to write a story that didn't just repeat what CBS and then Hersh had already said.

The new stories also showed the risks of reliance on secondhand sources. Without seeing the document themselves, the *Times* and the *Guardian* incorrectly quoted the Taguba language and wrongly reported that a CACI employee had been fired.[84] It was a prelude to the voluminous errors that would appear in news coverage over the next several

---

[83] "Iraq Prison Staff Seen as Issue; Lawyer for a U.S. Soldier Accused of Abuse Alleges Contractors Are Used to Question Inmates There," *Los Angeles Times*, April 30, 2004; Julian Borger, "U.S. Military in Torture Scandal," op. cit.

[84] Ibid. *The Guardian* erroneously stated "A CACI instructor was terminated . . ." and the *Los Angeles Times* mistake read, "According to the report, a CACI employee was terminated from duty at the prison because of the infractions."

months and which would continue to fuel future false reports. London would note that the story started off all wrong, and over the next few months became even more distorted.

Reluctant to talk while it sorted out facts, the CACI team withheld comment on the *Times* and the *Guardian* stories — a stark contrast to the massive response strategy that it would implement over the months to come. On the theory that a refusal to comment may leave the impression that one has something to hide, most public relations experts would have advised CACI to provide a bland statement. But the media calls often came up against the reporters' deadlines, leaving CACI's leadership with little time to respond. With time short and concerned that they might do long-term damage by providing wrong information, CACI's leaders chose to risk short-term embarrassment by declining to respond to the newspapers' phone calls. Both papers reported that CACI did not provide a comment — and this was the press' way of signaling to readers that the silent corporation may be hiding something.

In contrast, a Titan Corporation spokesperson reportedly told the *Times* that none of its staff was working at Abu Ghraib — an unfortunate inaccuracy that probably did not help the company's long-term credibility.[85]

Ominously, the *Times* also reported that five Democratic senators had already requested a congressional inquiry into the use and activity of military contractors — an indication that CACI's growing task list probably would have to include talking to Capitol Hill if it hoped to successfully defend its good name.

With these few exceptions, the earliest news accounts largely bypassed CACI and focused on the photographs. That bought the company precious time to begin assembling facts. At attorney Koegel's suggestion, London ordered an internal CACI team to reconstruct the hiring process for the interrogators. He told his people to re-examine every resume and to assess again whether every person hired met the qualifications in the army's Statement of Work (SOW) for the contract and project. To ensure independent judgment, London decreed that the review must be led by somebody who had no involvement at all in the hiring decisions. To manage the taskforce, he turned to Ron Schneider

---

[85] "Iraq Prison Staff Seen as Issue," op. cit.

who, in his "day job," was in charge of assembling CACI's new contract proposals and who now would also serve as CACI's Abu Ghraib project coordinator for the SOW and employee qualifications review.

CACI headquarters quickly became a home away from home for many of its key people as long days quickly became the norm. News was breaking daily and CACI's team had to react quickly. During the first months, many of the senior and support staff involved in the CISG stayed even later than usual every night and throughout the weekends. When seeing each other on Saturdays, some would jokingly wish each other a "Happy Friday, part 2." London realized that his people were keeping an extraordinary pace just as he was, and that there had to be some respite if his team was going to face a long haul. An "on-call" schedule of executives and administrative staff was created to allow others on the team time off while keeping leadership on top of everything, including running the company's day-to-day business operations.

It was, Schneider said later, a 24/7 operation. There were nights that some members of the team slept at the Holiday Inn across the street from CACI headquarters instead of heading home. Schneider, the father of a young child, made a personal decision to avoid the hotel. Summoned to the executive suite by London, Schneider said he would take on the assignment, but "not at the expense of my family."

"I intend to see my five-year-old every day," Schneider told his boss.

The résumé-checking exercise quickly expanded to cover almost everything about CACI's work in Iraq. As the number of inquiries grew, both internal and external, the group took on the role of a twenty-four-hour "Shell Answer Man," said one member. Schneider's team waited each day for new inquiries from government agencies or the company's top executives and then set about finding the answers.

Delivering the information where it needed to go sometimes assumed comic overtones. When materials being assembled at corporate headquarters in Arlington, Virginia required the signature of an employee some twenty miles away in Chantilly, the employees arranged a nighttime rendezvous at a convenient meeting point about halfway between each other's homes.

"We'd meet at the Sheetz gas station in Haymarket (Virginia) and sign out the documents in the parking lot," recalls CACI executive Mark Billings. "The next morning I'd take the boxes to Dulles Airport, send them to Fort Huachuca (a government contract office), and head for work."

In scrutinizing the Taguba report, London also ordered his people to find out for certain whether or not John Israel ever worked for CACI, as Taguba had said. CACI's managers couldn't recall Israel as one of their own and had been puzzled when Hersh brought up the name from Taguba's report. But instead of issuing an instant denial CACI wanted to verify all the facts by looking through its full employment roster — more than 9,500 names — and checking its data history and subcontractor records to find out if Israel had *ever* collected a paycheck from CACI, a subsidiary, or any organization even remotely related to CACI. The answer was he had *never* been at CACI or worked for CACI.

London liked to move fast and hit hard with a public statement. But he recognized the importance of getting the facts right before saying anything. In the long run, he was certain it was more important for the company's credibility to have its facts in order every time. As with managing the business, it was vital to focus on the long-term. Job One in this crisis was to protect the company's good name while preserving customer service and shareholder relations. And putting out erroneous information inadvertently would undermine the larger, more important goal.

Part of that goal was staying on top of all the information flying around. The scope and scale of information was enormous. What didn't flood CACI inboxes every day had to be found. CACI had to keep track of what was being said about it and also what members of the team were reporting to each other. London knew the amount of information would grow every day and that it would need to be managed. He looked to Z. Selin Hur, a management consultant who had joined the company only two weeks before the Abu Ghraib story broke. It turned out that she had recent experience in knowledge management. She knew how to organize and maintain what quickly became the company's knowledge repository.

There was mention of CACI throughout the media, in the print press, on TV news and talk shows, in blogs, and on all kinds of Web sites. All items had to be reviewed and responded to, then filed in the repository. There were reports, research papers, and congressional testimony. Internet message boards were monitored to gauge individual investors' attitudes. Hate mail was kept as well as letters of support. Whatever anyone needed, from a specific article to an e-mail sent out by London, it would be easily found in the repository. Internal and external communications were categorized. Agendas and task lists were retained. Even videotapes of CACI mentioned on TV were logged in and tracked. When two lawsuits were subsequently filed against the company, all information was reviewed by a deputy general counsel. The CACI team knew that with the media's preposterous distortions and allegations triggered by the *illegal leak* of Taguba's Abu Ghraib report, they had a considerable challenge in front of them. Perhaps one of the important reasons the Taguba report had such an impact for the media was precisely because it was *illegally leaked*. This somehow made it seem more credible than the formal investigative reports that would be released in the months to come.

"We wanted to get good results, as Schneider explained, but we absolutely had to get it right. From the very moment Jack asked me to do this, he made clear that it was not an exercise to hide anything. We were going to put out the truth — even if it was damning." London's choice of their motto, "The Truth Will Out" was not an accident.

CHAPTER FIVE

MAY 3: THE NEWS GAINS MOMENTUM
A story and a strategy unfold

> **"The company further stated that one of the people
> reported to be an employee [John Israel] . . .
> is not and never has been a CACI employee."**
> ~ CACI PRESS RELEASE, MAY 3, 2004

O N MONDAY, MAY 3, CACI's GREATEST HOPES INTERSECTED WITH
its greatest fears.

That morning, the company proudly announced the completion of
its largest acquisition. In a single stroke, the purchase of the AMS Defense and Intelligence Group had increased the company's workforce
by some 23 percent and added a potential of $275 million in revenue
for the coming year.[86] Literally overnight, the company's projected revenue for the fiscal year that would begin on July 1 rose by 25 percent to
$1.5 billion.

Completion of the transaction also boosted CACI into a higher strata
in the contracting arena. For the first time, CACI had the scale to bid
for larger government contracts worth up to $1 billion. With the former

---

[86] CACI acquired the assets of AMS Defense and Intelligence Group while the remaining assets of AMS were acquired by a Canadian firm.

AMS assets as part of its portfolio, the company could now go head-to-head for selected contracts with competitors such as Lockheed Martin, General Dynamics, and Electronic Data Systems.[87]

The fate of AMS, founded in 1970 and roughly the same size as CACI before the transaction, also was a warning about the hazards of the marketplace. Once one of the premier providers of software services to government, AMS had struggled after some highly publicized disputes over its performance on a number of high-dollar and high profile government contracts.

But the satisfaction of adding the AMS business to CACI's holdings was tempered by the other news in Monday's newspapers. May 3 also was the day that the nation's major media trumpeted CACI's alleged involvement in the abuses at Abu Ghraib.

"Prison Scandal Throws Spotlight on Private Contractors," announced the *Financial Times*, in a story that also postulated that gaps in the law might spare the civilians from prosecution for wrongdoing, even though several more investigations following up on Taguba's report were still being conducted.[88] These further investigations were not yet complete, their conclusions had not been reached, their reports had not been published, and above all, no contractors were facing any charges for any wrongdoings. But over time, this media conjecture would help feed speculation that the Pentagon had deliberately turned to contractors because the civilians could somehow be shielded (according to this theory) from punishment. Such baseless conspiracy theories by the media were yet another obstacle for the company to overcome. It prompted London to believe that the media embraced that long-standing credo: "Never let the truth stand in the way of a good story."

The *New York Times* and the *Baltimore Sun* also reported on CACI's alleged involvement. Both papers repeated the erroneous information from Major General Taguba's report that John Israel as well as Stefanowicz were employed by CACI — misinformation that added to the perception that CACI was deeply involved in prisoner abuse. Taguba had identified four individuals that he suspected had responsibility for the MPs behavior. Two of these were military officers and, according to

---

[87] "At CACI, Concerns About Growth," op. cit.

[88] Joshua Chaffin, "Prison Scandal Throws Spotlight on Private Contractors," *Financial Times*, May 4, 2004.

his misinformation, the other two were from CACI, when in fact, one was *not* an employee of CACI.

The *Washington Post,* CACI's hometown newspaper, had a somewhat different perspective. Notified by an e-mailed statement from Jody Brown, the *Post* was the first news outlet to report that CACI was launching its own internal investigation. But the *Post*, too, incorrectly reported that *two* of CACI's people were involved. Despite the company's e-mail, the *Post's* story also took a swat at CACI, complaining that neither Brown nor London would speak with them. This presaged a contentious relationship between CACI and the *Post* that lay in the months ahead.

The ironic juxtaposition of the news from Iraq and the AMS acquisition was clear to those in the CACI executive suite.

"We had been briefly on top of the world, and now we were facing adversity beyond measure," London recollected.

The first news stories were largely devoid of comment from CACI. In part, this reflected CACI's lack of information. Without access to the *illegally leaked* (SECRET/NO FOREIGN DISSEMINATION) Taguba report and with no new information from its military customer, it was hard for CACI to advance the story. It was a disturbing and dangerous position to occupy.

Taguba's *illegally leaked* report was, unfortunately and erroneously, fast gaining circulation as *the* truth about what happened at Abu Ghraib. Ironically, the media was not challenging the Taguba report, even as its errors were being revealed. Reporters continued to produce erroneous stories on the basis of partial information.[89] Many had seen Taguba's fifty-three-page summary document, but not the thousands of pages of "annexes" that presumably included supporting evidence for Taguba's conclusions. Others simply repeated stories or parts of stories picked up from other media sources. Still, having seen the pictures, the media seemed certain that abuse had taken place and were willing to claim that it was CACI's fault.

In hindsight, reporters should have made clearer that their accounts reflected partial information and that they had no independent way to

---

[89] For example, *The Guardian's* Julian Borger admitted so in his piece, "U.S. Military in Torture Scandal" (April 30, 2004) when he stated that, "A military report into the Abu Ghraib case — *parts of which were made available to the Guardian* — makes it clear that private contractors were supervising interrogations in the prison, which was notorious for torture and executions under Saddam Hussein."

corroborate allegations about the CACI interrogator or other individuals who had not appeared in the photos. They consistently failed to convey that Taguba's report was only one in a series of ongoing investigations that had *not* all been completed at the time of the leak.[90] More importantly, they failed to report that Taguba was assigned to investigate and report on MPs at Abu Ghraib, whereas the investigation aimed specifically at looking into the intelligence and interrogator aspects of the Abu Ghraib incidents was still underway. (This would be known later as the Fay report.)

But whatever the shortcomings of the news reports, CACI was beginning to understand the public relations axiom that you must define yourself or others will do it for you. Most Americans had never heard of CACI until the Taguba report became public. Unless CACI began explaining itself soon, it seemed highly likely that large numbers of Americans were going to take the voluminous media renditions, opinions, and embellishments of the Taguba report and wrongly conclude that CACI employees were to blame for the activities shown in the photographs and at Abu Ghraib.

And, as advisor Burkhart noted, "from a psychological standpoint it is hard to reverse a negative perception, particularly when the perception occurs with the first and only encounter, as was the public's experience with the interrogators and CACI." Being well-known was the most significant difference, she observed, between CACI's plight and that faced by Johnson & Johnson with Tylenol. Johnson & Johnson had a popular product, which was known around the world. CACI was a virtually unknown company, offering not a product but a set of complex services in the finite space of federal contracting that was not widely understood by the American public, much less the world at large.

The volume of media calls to CACI was staggering. At times, messages from the media arrived every other minute. Other than London, Brown was the only person authorized to speak for the company. She simply couldn't dial fast enough to respond to every reporter.

Of increasing concern to CACI leadership, news reports were beginning to include gross errors, some of them potentially harmful to CACI, and these would take root — to be repeated again and again — unless

---

[90] A list of all the investigations in which CACI was involved can be found in Appendix F.

CACI found some way to correct the record.[91] The company began to get a sense of what high-profile celebrities feel like when they see distorted tabloid press portrayals. CACI had to take a far-reaching approach to communicate not only with journalists, but with its employees and the general public. The message had to be consistent, and the facts as CACI knew them had to be repeated again and again to counter the growing tide of errors.

London's solution was to create a hypercrisis PR (Public Relations) response mechanism. Dealing with the media involved a three-pronged approach. First, the CACI team would provide lengthy press releases that covered what was known and that enabled the company to reach many reporters, their own employees, and the public, all at once. The second part of the strategy was to provide targeted media responses to correct reporters' errors with known and verified facts. And the third was to post updated information on the CACI Web site. Though a written document cannot possibly respond to every specific journalistic query, it offers a relatively efficient way to get the company on record. All three parts of London's unique approach for dealing with the press overlapped and supported each other. The press releases would be reinforced with targeted media responses and all of the known information would also be placed on the FAQ section of CACI's Web site.

In its first extensive public communication, London insisted that the company spell out some key points that would remain consistent throughout the ordeal. The company stated as a bedrock principle that it would not tolerate illegal behavior by its employees and that it would take swift action in the event of wrongdoing. But the company also noted that its employees were supporting the military and were also risking their lives to protect America's freedom. With this statement, CACI's messages began taking shape.

---

[91] For example, many media outlets were still calling John Israel a CACI employee. Other errors would cause greater confusion still. A May 9, 2004 *New York Times* article by Douglas Jehl and Eric Schmitt, "In Abuse, a portrayal of ill-prepared, overwhelmed G.I.'s," incorrectly stated that, "In mid-August [2003], a team of civilian interrogators led by Steven Stefanowicz . . . began work at Abu Ghraib . . ." when, in fact, Stefanowicz wasn't even hired until September 2003 and had gone to Iraq in October 2003 as a screener (although promoted later to interrogator) and had not been sent to Iraq as the team leader.

The first CACI press release following the *60 Minutes II* broadcast and *New Yorker* article noted pointedly that the company had yet to receive any information from the army about any misconduct or any actions against any employee because of prisoner abuse. Absent any supporting evidence or an opportunity to examine evidence, the statement strongly implied that it was just too soon to take any disciplinary action — a position London would soon state more explicitly in later press releases and interviews with journalists. It was a view he would never abandon throughout the ensuing months of ongoing investigations.

Although not directly challenging Taguba's accuracy, this first CACI press release implicitly raised the possibility that the Taguba report did not represent the true picture in its entirety. It pointed out that one individual identified by Taguba as a CACI employee "is not and has never been a CACI employee." The CACI release also said it had retained independent outside counsel to lead its own investigation of its employees' behavior — an indication that it would take responsibility to get the facts — for its customers, the public, and its employees. London and CACI management were not prepared to simply accept Taguba's Military Police report as gospel. Indeed, as more information came to light, it became evident to CACI, that on the issues most critical to the company, Taguba's account had errors and presented questionable, inconsistent conclusions.

By initiating their own inquiry, London's team chose a fairly aggressive PR course that many other companies traditionally had shied away from. But London's team, through his determined leadership, was now inventing their own groundbreaking PR crisis management strategy. This crisis and the CACI team's response would fall outside current conventional modes of journalism and crisis management.

As a general rule, companies aim to avoid creating new stories in the midst of a crisis, because even the most sympathetic reports will repeat the allegations one is trying to combat. Typically, a key tactical goal is to avoid any action that provides new "legs" to the story. On the other hand, CACI offered an alternative for reporters. Instead of focusing on alleged abuse, which was still under investigation, CACI's initial press release sought to generate the facts about a responsible company working hard to get answers. The company was apparently heard. After receiving the release, Reuters, for example, replaced a headline reporting

"Iraq Prison Abuse Puts Spotlight on Contractors" with the more objective lead-in that CACI "looks into" the abuse. Gaining some ground and a brief reprieve for the company, the initial news release generated somewhat more positive stories than had been the case prior. Reuters also reported London's declaration that, "I would be prepared to go over there myself to get to the bottom of this."[92]

But the Abu Ghraib story, including CACI's alleged involvement, played to too many agendas to fade away in a hotly contested election year. In the short term, at least, the story was only going to get bigger no matter what CACI did. With the story certain to linger, the CACI decision to engage was most likely a smart choice.

For the moment, at least, there were a few news stories that depicted CACI a bit more favorably — as a company trying to find the truth, but handicapped because nobody in the government was officially disclosing details. Reporters, often suspicious in believing that the government tends to hold back information, could for the moment relate CACI's plight to their own. But it was not enough. It was a bond that wouldn't last long.

---

[92] Sue Fleming, "U.S. Contractor Looks Into Iraq Prison Abuses," Reuters, May 3, 2004.

SECTION TWO

THE MEDIA'S HYSTERICAL RAMPAGE

CHAPTER SIX

THE SECOND-DAY STORY
New details, errors, and security concerns emerge

> **"A lie can travel halfway 'round the world**
> **while the truth is putting on its shoes."**
> ∾ **POPULARLY ATTRIBUTED TO MARK TWAIN**

AFTER THE FIRST NEWS BREAKS, LARGE AND SMALL, NEW INFOR-mation is the life blood that enables journalists to tell what they call "the second-day story." To journalists, good stories are the ones that go for a third and fourth day. The biggest stories last for weeks and possibly months. These stories are said to have "legs." Abu Ghraib's legs were about as long as they come.

Abu Ghraib was an easy story to keep alive. Eager "sources" con-stantly materialized to add their speculations and opinions.

Some sources, including academics and "experts" in consulting busi-nesses look for opportunities to promote themselves by getting their names in the newspaper or appearing on TV. To them, getting visibility in a news story is a form of marketing. Other sources, who "decline to be identified" or "request anonymity," are those who generally have an agenda to advance.

But whatever reservations the reporters might have had about their sources' reliability, Abu Ghraib was a hot topic and the stories were being filed everywhere — on television, in the newspaper, and around the world on the Internet — and CACI was getting pummeled.

One thing that often astounds people and companies who find themselves in a public relations crisis for the first time is the speed with which the media identifies new issues — or changes course. Since every day is a blank slate for journalists, even when covering an ongoing crisis, each day's journalistic challenge is to find something new to say. By definition, "news" is what just happened that wasn't known before, and yesterday's story is "old news." Editors and the public want something fresh. Journalists call it a "hook" or an "angle." For those in the spotlight, it can mean a new challenge almost every day. Having struggled to provide answers to one day's news, the company was forced back to the conference room so the team could work out the right words to address the latest issue.

As Jody Brown remembers, "Every day there was a journalist dropping a bomb on us, calling and saying 'we've got a source who says 'such and such . . .' and we (at CACI) had no way to verify any of it." Her experience on the firing line convinced Brown that "some reporters were almost desperate to get on page one. It seemed more important to them than getting the story right."

The emerging new themes are clear from a look back at the headlines: "Dismay and Surprise that U.S. Army Outsources Interrogation," said the *Financial Times*. "Contractors in Sensitive Roles, Unchecked," trumpeted the *New York Times*. "Hiring of Civilians to Question Prisoners Raises Accountability Issues," offered the *Baltimore Sun*. The *New York Times* and the *Washington Post* made an issue of the fact that the accused contractors were still on the job two months after the Taguba report was filed. Taking on a legal angle ahead of their media colleagues, the *Financial Times* and the *Wall Street Journal* on May 3 and the *Boston Globe* on May 4 raised the possibility that civilian contractors, even in the absence of any formal charges being made, might fall outside the reach of U.S. law. "Legal Loophole Arises in Iraq Abuse Case," the *Journal* said, while the *Globe* reported "Civilians Identified in Abuse May Face No Charges."[93]

---

93 Joshua Chaffin, "Dismay and Surprise that U.S. Army Outsources Interrogation," *Financial Times*, May 7, 2004; Joel Brinkley and James Glanz, "Contractors in Sensitive Roles, Unchecked," *New York Times*, May 7, 2004; Gail Gibson and Scott Shane, "Contractors act as interrogators; Control: The Pentagon's hiring of civilians to

These eye-catching headlines, designed to be inflammatory if not entirely accurate, smeared CACI. But they sold papers.

Some of the reporting showed evident attempts at balance. Other stories were examples of dubious journalism. A highly charged, but thinly sourced report in the *Washington Times* mislabeled CACI as a "security firm" and quoted an unidentified lawyer wrongly speculating that CACI's contract was a "black world" operation run by the Central Intelligence Agency.[94] In fact, CACI had openly advertised for interrogators and the work was openly contracted for under the General Services Administration's schedule through a contract managed by the Department of the Interior at its Ft. Huachuca, Arizona office. The contract and its award process were open and always available from the government, as CACI had said from the beginning. Furthermore, the CIA had absolutely nothing to do with the contract and CACI's work for the army had nothing to do with the CIA. But it seemed that some in the media had no qualms about making baseless and absurd claims otherwise.

London and Brown were also disappointed by the lack of interest among some reporters in understanding the business of government contracting. It seemed logical, especially when questions arose about the contract vehicle the army used to hire civilian interrogators, that a reporter would be eager to learn how contracting worked. Government contracting is an arcane process that most reporters covering Abu Ghraib had never before had a reason to understand. But now that understanding the contract process was relevant, Brown sensed that many of the journalists were embarrassed to admit their lack of knowledge and wouldn't ask questions lest they betray their ignorance.

"They didn't know what a 'contracting officer' was and when we'd try to explain it, too many of the reporters we dealt with weren't interested," Brown recalled with a shake of the head.[95]

---

question prisoners raises accountability issues," *Baltimore Sun,* May 4, 2004; Greg Jaffe, David S. Cloud and Gary Fields Wall, "Legal Loophole Arises in Iraq," *Wall Street Journal*, May 4, 2004; and, Farah Stockman, "Civilians Identified in Abuse May Face No Charges," *Boston Globe*, May 4, 2004.

[94] Sharon Behn, "U.S. Addresses Control of Security Companies," *Washington Times*, May 5, 2004.

[95] The contracting officer is the government's official agent who enters and signs contracts with business organizations, and has considerable authority over the administration of the contract and all of its details, e.g., price, cost, payment, delivery, etc.

The media's hunt for new angles encourages conjecture and can lead to mistakes, which are then repeated. Some errors are matters of nuance or omission, not outright misstatements. Other times, the media says things that are just wrong. Moreover, the corrections never seem to catch up with the mistakes. As Mark Twain is popularly believed to have said, "A lie can travel halfway round the world while the truth is putting on its shoes." Twain's nineteenth century characterization is an understatement in the twenty-first century, when the Internet spreads information around the globe in a matter of seconds. Once posted online (or in print or on video tape), "the news," including the errors, becomes part of the record, to be repeated over and over.

USA Today posted on its Web site (though not in the newspaper) a "chain of command" chart that showed CACI reporting to the CIA. Responding to a demand for correction, after a complaint from CACI leadership, an email from *USA Today* lamely explained: "Our source on this warned us there may be different interpretations. With your nudge, we re-examined the graphic and have changed it."[96]

There was no apology or admission of error from *USA Today*. The outlandish mistake was casually pushed off on an "unnamed source," who had apparently signaled that caution was in order. It was a pattern of conduct that CACI found distressingly unacceptable but would see again and again as the media rushed to put out the news. As London complained to one of the newspaper's reporters, "Nobody called us to even ask. If you don't believe us that's one thing, but not to call. . . ."

Mindful of the potential damage to his company's good name, London lectured the journalist: "Hundreds of thousands of people have seen that organization chart. It's very discouraging. I have to monitor, edit, and correct material put out by journalists who should do it as part of their own jobs!" London would later note, "The media's hysterical rampage and thoughtlessness made our efforts to correct the record more difficult — and even more important."

It was the sort of thing that convinced the beleaguered CACI team that at least some in the media didn't check facts. Many media critics believed ever since the Watergate scandal catapulted *Washington Post* reporters Robert Woodward and Carl Bernstein to media cult hero status,

---

[96] E-mail from Jody Brannon, Executive Producer for News, USAToday.com to Jody Brown at CACI, May 12, 2004.

that finding the "smoking gun" of scandal was the only measure of journalistic success. Woodward and Bernstein, with the clandestine help of a high-level government mole, apparently spent days pinning down facts.[97] But instead of emulating that level of diligence, many of the journalists seemed to confuse speculation by a "source" or an opinion by an "expert" with fact — or worse yet, did not care.

CACI longed for the opportunity to educate journalists about their business and their work in Iraq. They believed the detailed story would demonstrate that the company did its business the right way.

At first when the Abu Ghraib story broke, CACI lacked the facts to answer media questions with complete certainty. Without confirmed facts, the company had to decline some interview requests and was only able to provide limited information. But as CACI representatives tried to reach out to the media when they could say more, the team observed that the approach of many reporters was to try to catch their interviewees off guard or attempt to trap them in an inconsistency rather than listen to what the company had to say.

Some reporters' tactics were sneaky and manipulative. In one instance, a reporter misrepresenting himself contacted the company's human resources department asking for "employment verification" as if he were conducting a credit check. Others tracked down private e-mail addresses of employees in Iraq and sent them various "best wishes" messages and offering sympathy in attempts to solicit a response.

In one incident, Jody Brown was alerted to a *Washington Post* reporter e-mailing an Iraq-based CACI manager after being given "no comment" from Brown. The manager notified Brown. Brown confronted the *Post* reporter, who attempted to proclaim innocence. Several reporters (or people claiming to be) used scare and intimidation tactics that came close to stalking behavior. For example, one reporter found the private cellular phone number of a younger sibling of a CACI employee in Iraq and started harassing her for information. Her

---

[97] Woodward and Bernstein's secretive source was a man identified only as "Deep Throat," who leaked information about the involvement of U.S. President Richard Nixon's administration first in the Watergate break-in and then in subsequent events that came to be known as the Watergate scandal. The source revealed himself in 2005 as Mark Felt, who had been in the government in the position of the Deputy Director of the FBI at the time of the scandal.

mother would later call Brown to report the incidents and ask what she should do.

Encounters between employees and the media placed additional pressure on CACI team members. But they took on the task of assisting the family members of their CACI colleagues who were serving their clients in support of national security.

While a few journalists would earn respect in the weeks ahead, the overwhelming impression from CACI's experience was that the media's collective work was ridden with mistakes, half-truths and sloppiness. The lack of fact-checked work was overwhelming.

The experience also caused London to wonder how the benefits of a free press balanced with the media's largely unchecked ability to influence public opinion. He did not believe in a "media conspiracy" that deliberately sought to shape public policy because the media was too diverse for that. But the repeated errors, and a seeming lack of diligence in pursuing facts, led the public to ill-informed conclusions about CACI (as hate-mail and a later protest demonstration would help prove). London feared for his company's reputation, which he believed lost a bit of its luster every time a journalist failed to draw the distinction between *allegations* about misconduct by a company employee and the *conclusion* that any employee was guilty. He believed that his company suffered unfairly by a media shorthand that seemed to suggest that the alleged act of a single employee, if in fact he had behaved improperly, was also a statement about the values and actions of an entire company of 9,500 employees. These distinctions were not forthcoming from the media.

London also was deeply troubled that there was no evident process: no court, oversight boards, or serious self-regulation to redress the mistakes or impose consequences for repeated errors (intentional or otherwise) in news reports. He would later tell associates that the Society of Professional Journalists divided its Code of Ethics into four categories: "Seek the Truth and Report It," "Act Independently," "Minimize Harm," and "Be Accountable."[98] But he was coming to believe that too many journalists simply forgot or ignored these objectives. Perhaps too, he thought, many did not even know of their existence.

---

[98] Society of Professional Journalists, Code of Ethics (http://www.spj.org/ethics_code.asp).

He worried that errors in news reports were painting a grossly misleading picture of his company that would be almost impossible to erase.

The media's frenzy in covering Abu Ghraib gave CACI another new problem — security. Instead of requesting an interview with the company, some camera crews and reporters decided to make surprise visits to CACI headquarters and local offices demanding interviews with London and other executives. Crews from network news would camp out in the headquarters' lobby until they tired of waiting for the unlikely meeting. At a couple of smaller CACI field offices, reporters were found in the buildings in search of CACI employees who might speak to them. Although London and his team wanted the chance to tell CACI's story as the facts developed, they would not respond to ambushes. When alerted to the unannounced media visits, the CACI team leading the orientation of new employees from AMS sought protection by locking the doors of the conference rooms they were using at a local hotel.

For the first time, the company had to consider whether its employees' safety might be at risk because of the negative news reports about the company and backlash from the public over what they read about CACI. Before Abu Ghraib, CACI was known simply as one of the Washington Beltway consulting firms that served the government. Though respected by those who knew its work, CACI was not well known by the average American or even Washingtonians. Literally overnight, the connection to Abu Ghraib was making CACI's name familiar. But it was the sort of recognition the company dreaded.

CACI was now a topic of heated and often nasty Internet discussions. Vicious electronic hate mail and voice mails to individual CACI employees or to the company's main headquarters and field offices added to CACI's growing concerns. Shockingly explicit e-mails to Jody Brown were full of frightening and abusive language. One e-mail, for example, called her "the MANURE of the human race." Another proclaimed that, "You and your co-workers propagate racism and enjoy humiliation of Muslims." Another email with the subject line "CACI Monsters," asked: "Do you reach orgasm when you torture people, you sick cow." "You are one sick bastard," wrote another commentator to CEO London. The parent of two soldiers serving in Iraq left a voice mail for a CACI executive complaining that, "so-called military intelligence people have destroyed American credibility." The caller warned: "So f*** you and your professional torturers. And, if anything happens to my kids, God d°°° it, you will know me. I guaran- f°°°ing-tee it."

CACI's security concerns were also heightened by the ability of news organizations to obtain unlisted phone numbers and addresses of CACI employees, including some based in Iraq, as well as the company's most senior executives in the United States. CACI reasoned that if journalists could get this information, violent individuals might also. "It's scary," one executive said of the ease with which people could be located despite attempts to keep their phone numbers and addresses private. The anxiety was so widespread that the wife of one senior executive suspended her habit of dropping by the office and refused to let the couple's child visit her father's workplace until CACI began to fade from the news in the fall of 2004. Another senior executive's convalescent wife who was confined to their house was terrified to find reporters congregating and waiting in the driveway, randomly knocking on the door and making frequent, disruptive phone calls to their unlisted phone number.

Also, in some cities, anti-war groups and far left organizations were targeting CACI offices for demonstrations. In one CACI community, a local business occupying a *former* CACI address was being harassed by protestors looking for CACI. The old address was still listed on CACI's Web site and the new occupant, getting a taste of what CACI faced, anxiously implored CACI to update its online information.

As it worked overtime to find out what had happened at Abu Ghraib, CACI also now wondered: what if security was breached by somebody with deadly intent? For instance, in Texas a so-called anti-racism group pronounced a "corporate death sentence" on the company.

General Counsel Jeff Elefante circulated a note advising headquarters' employees that the company had hired additional security people, and asked them to report anything out of the ordinary. Guards were engaged around the clock at headquarters, and additional security personnel were retained at locations around the country.

In a more detailed memo a few days later, the company provided its workers with ten specific steps to ensure security. This included a lockdown of CACI buildings to make sure that all visitors were carefully screened, strict attention to requirements that employees display ID badges when on premises, and a suggestion that employees remove all CACI identification when outside of the office. It was a sobering, but necessary chore — one more challenge of running a business in the glare of a negative and threatening spotlight.

Over the next several weeks, protestors would target CACI offices in California, Colorado, and Texas. They marched beneath banners that denounced CACI as "corporate torturers" and complained that CACI was "privatizing torture," or identified CACI as "Corporate Asshole Creating Injustice." The Texas group that passed a "corporate death sentence" against CACI circulated leaflets accusing the company of "Torture for Profit." The protestors' banner denounced "men who trade in blood." And while a close reading showed the group was aiming to shut down business operations, not inflict bodily injury, the record showed that some of its activities had turned violent. No threat could be ignored.

So much more than simply being another issue to deal with, to London, the demonstrations were a vulgar personal affront. When demonstrators showed up at corporate headquarters, London's reaction was anger and disgust. In his mind, his company was engaged in acts of patriotism — trying to help American troops win a war that had toppled a tyrant. Now, he and his people were being vilified as torturers — accused of human rights abuses that were being construed as a matter of company policy. Surely if the demonstrators had known the relevant facts or CACI's reputation, he believed the reaction would have been different. He believed that if they knew that only one of CACI's 9,500 employees was under question — without any evidence — and that less than 1 percent of the company's revenue came from this work in Iraq, it would show that the company was not attempting to do anything but support the troops and the U.S. government. In addition, CACI was cooperating with all government investigations and was about to initiate its own internal investigation to be conducted by outside legal counsel. But he was powerless to stop the name-calling and it came across as deeply offensive and unjustified.

As a result, the company was forced to issue a warning to all employees that media were showing up unannounced at offices, that they should not engage reporters in any conversation and that they should escort them off the premises and notify CACI administrators of the incident. The company also hired guards to monitor the headquarters lobby and other entrances to ensure reporters didn't get in. The sight of the guards made employees feel both uneasy and reassured. As Schneider recalled, "I remember looking outside my office window and seeing a black Suburban bringing the guards for the next shift. Watching them strap on shoulder holsters was a little disconcerting, though comforting."

Although no incidents ever occurred, there were reports of suspicious activities, like strangers video-taping the headquarters building or holding up gadgets, likened to recording devices or cameras, toward office windows. Fortunately for CACI, nothing came of these incidents and the guards blended into daily office life.

This was CACI's new reality.

CHAPTER SEVEN

WORKING TO CATCH UP

Under attack, CACI rechecks its work

**"For [obvious] security reasons, we do not disclose or
discuss the assignments or locations of our employees."**
~ JACK LONDON, CACI NEWS RELEASE, MAY 3, 2005

RON SCHNEIDER WASN'T HAPPY. PLOWING THROUGH RÉSUMÉS TO reassess the qualifications of the people CACI had hired for the work at Abu Ghraib, he wondered whether the operations team responsible might have messed up his company.

"I was angry at the operations folks. The company's reputation was very important to me," Schneider recalled. "I'd spent half of my life at this company and was concerned they had somehow let us down."

Next to the abuse itself, among the most surprising news in the Abu Ghraib affair was the revelation to the public that contractors were involved in interrogation even though contractors from other companies had already been providing interrogation support for some time in Afghanistan and Guantanamo Bay, Cuba. The contractors' large role in Iraq was public knowledge, but there was a common misconception that civilians were performing work that didn't require interrogator-related expertise — military or otherwise (e.g., interrogation experience from detective, police work, or other federal agencies). Yet handing off non-military work to the private sector was part of a transition that had been occurring over the past twenty years designed to free troops for the military's core war-fighting mission.

As former Director of Naval Intelligence, RADM Thomas A. Brooks (Ret.), stated, "The Abu Ghraib prison scandal cast a spotlight on the use of contractors to perform functions normally associated with military personnel, and all the contracting, control, discipline, and training issues associated therewith. The sometimes-overheated rhetoric of the press created an impression that the use of contractor personnel to perform functions traditionally considered to be the realm of uniformed personnel was something new and extraordinary. It is neither, though the number of intelligence-related functions performed by contractors during combat operations in Iraq and Afghanistan may, indeed, be unprecedented."[99]

There were many opinions on the outsourcing of interrogation. "This is just one more example that we've delegated an awful lot to our contractors," Steven Schooner, a law professor and government contracts expert at George Washington University, told the *Financial Times*.[100] Former CIA agent Robert Baer was blunt and dismissive: "It's insanity . . . these are rank amateurs."[101] (Baer's assumption, though not uncommon at the time, was later rejected by several official inquiries, which concluded that the civilians were not only qualified but, in many instances, were *better* qualified and more experienced than their military counterparts.)[102]

In fact, contractors were edging closer to the fight. Given the growing sophistication of modern weaponry and its dependence on computer expertise, skilled computer and communications specialists from the private sector were often involved in aspects of combat operations. But interrogation was something many did not expect to find on the outsourcing list. The reaction to news that civilians were interrogating

---

[99] Glenn J. Voelz, "Managing the Private Spies, Use of Commercial Augmentation for Intelligence Operations," Discussion Paper No. 14, Joint Military Intelligence College, June 2006.

[100] Chaffin, "Prison Torture Scandal Throws Spotlight on Private Contractors" op. cit.

[101] Julian Borger, "U.S. Military in Torture Scandal," *The Guardian*, April 30, 2004.

[102] Church Report op. cit.

prisoners guaranteed that there would be close scrutiny of CACI. Schneider's job was to find out whether CACI could withstand the examination, by assembling the facts and data and presenting the results — the facts, not the allegations.

In setting out his approach, Schneider, a competent analyst, fell back on what he knew best — how to put together a complex contract proposal and technical document and then have an internal "red team" (an objective and expert third-party review team) thoroughly dissect it to see if it held up under closer inspection.

He put together a team from the staff at CACI's Arlington, Virginia headquarters and combined them with a senior group from operations, the division responsible for much of CACI's intelligence work, but independent from the interrogator services unit. Then he virtually locked them in a conference room for three weeks, where they worked nights and weekends. The task was to examine in detail the credentials of everybody hired by CACI for intelligence work in Iraq, beginning with the interrogators, and determine, once again, whether they met all the requirements stated in the contract. The team was going to take another look at every résumé, verify U.S. government security clearance information, confirm U.S. citizenship, and examine military discharge papers for those who were previously in the armed forces to make sure every employee's information was correct and met all the job requirements. Then the team would match that information against the job qualifications spelled out in the contract and the contract's Statement Of Work (SOW) to verify that the right people had been hired, and ensure nothing had been overlooked when employees entered the company.

At issue were fifty-five people hired by CACI and sent to Iraq — twenty-five as interrogators and thirty as screeners (of which nine were later promoted with the army's agreement to interrogator). The screeners (a differentiated skill category and function from that of an interrogator) were to be assigned tasks for determining a detainee's category, such as "enemy prisoner," "combatant," "criminal," "insurgent," etc. Each candidate's résumé would be rated against the SOW and the Military Occupational Specialty (MOS) requirements of the positions.[103] Because seven individuals were hired as screeners and received field

---

[103] The U.S. Army maintains the MOS codes for its various skill needs. The interrogator MOS in the U.S. Army was coded "97E" (in 2004).

advancements to interrogator, their resumes were evaluated twice —
once for a screener position and a second time as an interrogator.

The results from Schneider's team would be evaluated again by a
company employee with twenty-five years of Military Intelligence (MI)
experience — providing another, highly qualified set of eyes on the
team's work. To ensure consistency, the team scrutinized the application of equivalent civilian experience for interrogators and screeners
who did not have military training in interrogation. The equivalent
civilian experience was specifically permitted by the army's SOW for
CACI's contract. In fact, the use of equivalent experience categories is
quite common in U.S. government services contracts, and was *not* a
new concept at all for CACI's Iraq interrogator services contract.
Equivalent experience could include relevant experience from other
government organizations, such as police departments, or the Federal
Bureau of Investigation, Central Intelligence Agency, Department of
Justice, Bureau of Alcohol, Tobacco, Firearms and Explosives, or the
Drug Enforcement Agency.

The review began with internal tension, as the two CACI groups
each brought different backgrounds and perspectives to the table. The
members of the operations group were relative newcomers to CACI,
having joined the company within the past year when CACI acquired
Premier Technology Group, which was the source of the initial Iraq
work that had hired the interrogators. They felt a natural loyalty to their
colleagues who had done the hiring — but they contributed an understanding of the process that Schneider and the review team did not
have and found helpful. They also brought some reservations about
Schneider, who they thought might not understand the practicalities of
finding qualified interrogators willing to go to a war zone to work. For
their part, Schneider and his colleagues from CACI's business development department brought fresh eyes that were critical, analytical, and
independent.

"We weren't 'tainted' by having hired anybody in the first place,"
Schneider explained. "I was brought in because I was outside the hiring
chain of command."

The long hours drew the team closer to their mutual commitment to
the task. CACI's Mark Billings, a retired army lieutenant colonel, said
some nights he simply skipped his forty-five-minute drive home to stay at

a nearby hotel. He was reporting at 6:30 A.M. and working until 9:00 P.M. or later. There simply wasn't time for home. The work was so intense and the dedication so high that he recalled making a point of announcing days in advance that "on Saturday morning I will be taking time to get a haircut. I am going to the barbershop."

This process of a detailed review and scrutiny by the CACI team was now working in an audit and investigation sense, looking at the data and records that had been used during the recruiting and hiring phase for each employee. Pulling it all together was a case study in thoroughness, persistence, and objectivity.

The occasional gaps in paperwork, Schneider recollected, led to "some very tense face-to-face meetings and phone calls" as he had to deliver the news to the executive suite. Asked if he was ever tempted to shade the facts to avoid London's displeasure, Schneider chuckled in amazement: "The consequences of not telling Jack something are much worse than telling him," Schneider explained. "If he finds out twenty-four or thirty-six hours later, you hear about it."

In the end, the team resolved every issue but one. It turned out that a single employee, a screener, who was hired from another company while working in Iraq was believed to have a security clearance because his previous job had required it. In fact, he did not have the appropriate clearance. Once discovered, the oversight was reported in mid-May 2004 to the U.S. Army's Contracting Officer's Representative, Major Eugene Daniels, who was CACI's army liaison in Baghdad for its intelligence work in Iraq. The information also was sent to the contract office at Fort Huachuca, which was also responsible for contract oversight. The company promptly submitted a request for the needed clearance, but the screener resigned shortly thereafter.

Among the interrogators (including those employees promoted to interrogator from screener) all were determined to be qualified in accordance with the contract's criteria. Twenty-two of the twenty-five interrogators (88 percent) had direct experience or military schooling in interrogation before joining CACI. The others had related military or civilian experience. The bottom line finding was that all the CACI hires were confirmed to be qualified under the contract's SOW criteria and requirements. Among the thirty individuals hired as screeners, Schneider's team found that all met the army's SOW requirements.

The conclusion was good news because London was already describing the company's hiring procedures and practices publicly in conversations with the *New York Times*. He knew for certain that strict company policy and procedures for hiring qualified personnel were in place. In fact, London had personally written a company recruiting manual entitled "How to Hire Heroes," which was initially published by CACI in the mid-1980s.

"The way the process works is that the United States government sets forth their needs and what the requirements are in terms of these skill sets" London told the *Times*. "We put together a project team and roster, if you will, of team staff that we believe meets the terms and requirements and so on that are set forth. I have every confidence that the skills are such that you're dealing with experienced people to meet these interrogator requirements. You're not talking about people that have been picked up at the bus stop."[104]

Subsequent formal U.S. government inquiries reached the same conclusion — that ***every CACI interrogator met the qualifications set out by the army in the CACI contract Statement of Work***.

Confirming that the interrogators were clearly qualified was just one challenge. Over the weeks ahead, CACI would be confronted with a number of new "issues" — some raised by news organizations, others presented by Congress, financial markets, government agencies, "expert" commentators, political activists, and other third parties. All required hard thinking and tough decisions about whether and how to respond.

With safety issues foremost, London's determination to make the company's case to the public was complicated by an equally strong determination to withhold specific information about employees' names and work locations. In addition to providing for the safety of CACI's U.S. employees, London and his team knew the news from Iraq provided dramatic evidence of the need for caution abroad as well. Civilian contractors were being taken hostage and sometimes murdered. Most notably was the group of American contractors that had been mutilated, burned, and hung from a bridge in Fallujah — all of it captured by TV (video) cameras. One CACI interrogator, concerned for his family's

---

[104] Joel Brinkley and James Glanz, op. cit.

safety, resigned after his name showed up on several Web sites, including one belonging to the Arab news agency al Jazeera.

Careful lest he unintentionally discuss confidential or classified information, and concerned about working at cross-purposes with the army, London also was reluctant to discuss details of CACI's contracts. Operating within these constraints, London's first few interviews with reporters were sometimes cryptic exchanges in which the reluctance to share certain types of information undermined his ability to make critical points. In some instances, the discussions may even have left some matters open to interpretation. It seemed, in these situations, the media filled in the gaps with speculation and "theories" or by linking together unrelated facts.

London, forgetting the audience's unfamiliarity with the subject, at times was not clear in distinguishing between the very broad range of intelligence work and the very small subset of interrogation work. In a few instances, the press also seemed to have the impression that CACI had interrogation contracts in locations other than Iraq. From time to time over the next several months, news reports or third-party statements would erroneously report that CACI interrogators were at work in Afghanistan and/or Guantanamo Bay, Cuba. In fact, CACI's only interrogation contract involved Iraq.

Later, the company spent considerable time trying to correct this error. But in the first interviews, London declined to address the matter specifically, explaining it was due to concerns about employee safety or breaking government security. As a result, the media reached its own conclusions and reported and reprinted the story — without verification from CACI.

Compounding the situation was the company's decision not to release the names of its employees. In its May 3 release, CACI noted that, "one of the people reported to be an employee . . . is not and never has been a CACI employee." But since London had made a decision not to discuss employees by name, the release didn't identify whether Stefanowicz or Israel was the individual wrongly linked to CACI. Asked in several interviews on May 5 to say who worked for CACI and who didn't, London refused because "I need to protect the safety of these people."

"I've seen bodies of American contractors hanging from bridges," he told a reporter for National Public Radio. "I take this very seriously." And by implication, he thought the reporter should take it seriously, too.

It was a conscious decision that London insisted months later was the right thing to do to protect his people's privacy. It also drew attention to an important factual error in the Taguba report and demonstrated that the report was not 100 percent correct. But no one in the media was scrutinizing the Taguba report to uncover these inconsistencies and discuss them in public.

The fact that London was not precise in some cases and the failure of the press to dig for facts and see the obvious discrepancies in Taguba's report made it harder to set the record straight in the long run. Thus, the errors continued. A May 7 story by Cox News Service mistakenly described John Israel as a CACI interpreter and implicitly questioned the company's hiring practices with the observation that Israel, actually a Titan employee, "did not even have a security clearance."[105] It was a double error by the reporter, as the military, contrary to the Taguba report, later reported that Israel did in fact possess a valid security clearance.

As journalists reread the Taguba report, most ultimately recognized that John Israel had been identified variously as an employee of Titan and also of CACI (other individuals also were misidentified by the Taguba report). Titan eventually acknowledged that Israel was employed by one of its subcontractors. Most news organizations ultimately got this right but often media corrections occur after the wrong (or false) information has already been spread in a damaging way around the world.

Yet, months later, some would continue to repeat Taguba's initial mistakes. The continuing misstatements demonstrated the difficulty of getting corrections to stick once the media had accepted and widely published the erroneous information. It was also particularly frustrating that the original source of the error in this case the Taguba report, remained available without correction. There was no way for CACI to reach the thousands of journalists who had covered the story around the world or might some day report about Abu Ghraib. The ongoing failure of the media to verify its facts and correct errors, even seemingly small and simple ones, would pose ongoing difficulties for the company.

---

[105] Bob Dart, "Prison Abuse Allegations Put Pentagon's Use of Private Contractors Under Scrutiny," Cox News Service, May 7, 2004.

Some of CACI's critics outside the media seemed almost indifferent to the facts. Long after most news organizations understood who worked for whom, an email to Jody Brown about John Israel challenged CACI for "some further specification of this mysterious figure." A lawsuit that woefully lacked its own due diligence, and that was filed against the company (a month after the news broke) before the official investigations were completed, also persisted in misidentifying Israel. So did anti-war groups, which included the misinformation in the materials they distributed in their efforts to generate protests against CACI.

For CACI, the widespread attention compounded by mounting media errors created a multi-front challenge it would continue to confront in the ensuing years.

CHAPTER EIGHT

BEYOND THE MEDIA

Concerns surface as CACI takes stock

**"I have confidence in the employees here at CACI. . . .
Please continue to do the fine job you've been doing."**
~ JACK LONDON IN NOTE TO ALL CACI EMPLOYEES, MAY 3, 2004

WHILE THE DRAMA OF ABU GHRAIB PLAYED OUT IN THE NEWS media, other groups also were scrambling to learn what had taken place and decide how they should respond.

At the Pentagon, civilian and military leaders were trying to understand the implications of the abuse and where responsibility lay. Harsh, skeptical questions were rolling in from members of Congress and the news media who wanted to know who knew what and when they knew it. The statement of Defense Secretary Donald Rumsfeld and Joint Chiefs of Staff Chairman General Richard Myers that they had not read the Taguba report before it had been *illegally leaked* to the public created some consternation.[106] Many wanted to know why, two months

---

[106] The military investigation process is carefully designed to be objective and unbiased to avoid influencing investigations or prejudicing findings. Problems are investigated at their source and these findings are reported to the next level in the chain of command for review and decision, including potential referral for further investigations. Those at the higher levels in the chain of command refrain from review and

after the report was completed, nobody had informed Titan and CACI that their employees were under suspicion or had asked the companies to do anything about it. In the Pentagon, military and government personnel were trying to fit all the pieces together — even turning to CACI with questions about the contract because some offices in the Pentagon

---

comment on proceedings until the investigation process is fully completed throughout the appropriate levels and chain of command in order to avoid biasing the results by influencing the process. This process is similar to the civil system in which efforts are made to provide an unbiased jury or judge, to avoid undue influence of witnesses and prevent prejudicial proceedings. The media's criticism of those within the higher ranks of the chain of command for not prematurely seeing the *illegally leaked* document demonstrated the media and observers' lack of understanding of this process. They apparently lacked awareness of how even the media's own saturated coverage along with its constant speculation on the matter in the middle of the Abu Ghraib investigation could significantly compromise the ongoing investigative process.

Taguba's report resulted from an Article 15-6 investigation (as did the Fay report). Listed as one of his references, *AR 15-6, Procedures for Investigating Officers and Boards of Officers, 11 May 1988*, contained the guidelines Taguba was required to follow for his investigation into events at Abu Ghraib. According to section 3-18 of the AR 15-6 procedures, a "written report of proceedings should be submitted, in two complete copies, directly to the appointing authority or designee, unless the appointing authority or another directive provides otherwise." Section 3-19 then states that the "appointing authority will notify the investigating officer or president of the board if further action, such as taking further evidence or making additional findings or recommendations, is required.

On page 6 of his report, Taguba states that on January 19, 2004, Lieutenant General Ricardo S. Sanchez "requested that the Commander, U.S. Central Command [CENTCOM], appoint an Investigating Officer (IO) in the grade of Major General (MG) or above to investigate the conduct of operations within the 800th Military Police (MP) Brigade." Taguba elaborated that five days later, (erroneously dated as '24 January 2003' instead of 2004), "the Chief of Staff of U.S. Central Command (CENTCOM), MG R. Steven Whitcomb, on behalf of the CENTCOM Commander, directed that the Commander, Coalition Forces Land Component Command (CFLCC), LTG David D. McKiernan, conduct an investigation into the 800th MP Brigade's detention and internment operations from 1 November 2003 to present." Taguba was appointed on January 31st to conduct the investigation by "appointing authority" LTG McKiernan.

On page 14, Taguba states that, "On 9 March we submitted the AR 15-6 written report with findings and recommendations to the CFLCC Deputy SJA, LTC Mark Johnson, for a legal sufficiency review. The out-brief to the appointing authority,

presumably couldn't readily locate a copy of the agreement under which the interrogators had been hired. Other government workers involved in contract administration, such as the Department of the Interior and the Defense Contract Audit Agency, also began asking CACI for data that would show whether or not the company was fulfilling the terms of its contract commitments.

At issue too were America's reputation and the merits of the war itself. For some, the photos and the Taguba report crystallized their broader concerns about the Bush administration's policy. "This administration has failed the military, the American people, the Iraqi and the international community," said Democratic House member Henry Waxman of California. He said a congressional investigation was necessary "to salvage what is left of our standing in the world."[107] Both House and Senate Committees summoned Defense Department and military leaders to testify, and were asked "to please get to the bottom of what actions the CIA and CACI officials had taken, since their names were not on their uniforms, as they directed our troops."[108]

Also on Capitol Hill, five House members formally petitioned the General Accounting Office (GAO) to investigate contractors working in Iraq.[109] The congressmen's six-page letter asked, among other things, how many contractors were in the country, whom they worked

---

LTG McKiernan, took place on 3 March 2004." Despite other mistakes, Taguba did follow army rules and submit his report to the appointing authority. No official beyond the appointing authority would have been required to read the report unless the appointing authority, LTG McKiernan, directed so. Therefore, it is the norm for Defense Secretary Rumsfeld, Chairman of the Joint Chiefs General Myers, or anyone else up the chain, not to have seen or read Taguba's report at the time it was *illegally leaked*.

[107] "Statement by Rep. Henry Waxman on H.R. 627." May 6, 2004.

[108] Remarks of U.S. Rep. Curt Weldon (D-PA) at Hearing of House Armed Services Committee, May 7, 2004. Notwithstanding this comment, CACI personnel never "directed" U.S. troops or anyone else in the government nor had any authority whatever to do so.

[109] The General Accounting Office, which initiates investigations and studies at the request of Congress and other government agencies, changed its name to the Government Accountability Office on July 7, 2004 during the midst of the events described here. This narrative and this book use the old name for consistency and because referenced GAO reports were generally completed under the old name.

for, what the employees' nationalities were, how the contractors interacted with the military, whom they reported to, and what laws applied in the event of misconduct. U.S. Representative Janice Schakowsky (D-IL) sent a letter to President Bush requesting the suspension of all contracts with civilian firms for security, supervision, and interrogation of prisoners.[110]

On Wall Street, financial analysts were trying to assess the prospects for CACI and Titan — and whether events at the prison exposed either company to significant financial risk. Both companies had experienced a sharp fall in their share value when the Abu Ghraib news first broke (CACI shares fell almost 9 percent in a single day, from $45.28 to $41.45) and analysts wanted to know if the decline was an overreaction that signaled a time to buy, or whether more trouble lay ahead. Titan had just struck a deal to sell out to Lockheed Martin and some on the Street were worried that the transaction might now be in trouble.[111]

CACI employees experienced a range of emotions. Some were angry, some perplexed, and others feared that problems for the company could ultimately threaten their careers. Some CACI employees sent encouraging notes to their bosses. A few mistakenly concluded that the company was, in fact, complicit in abuses at Abu Ghraib: "Management has to make an important and painful decision — to cancel the [interrogation] contract, due to the fact that directly or indirectly employees are expected to act in an illegal and morally repulsive manner," wrote one uninformed employee. Another worker reported that he was looking for another job because "I WILL NOT be associated with the immoral animals that commit these types of war crimes and perversions."

These anxiety-ridden letters did not go unanswered. London insisted on a response to every communication, particularly those that included radical misperceptions about CACI.

---

[110] Roseanne Gerin, "Contractors caught under a microscope, Iraq prison scandal raises questions about outsourcing," *Washington Technology,* May 24, 2004.

[111] In late June of 2004, Lockheed Martin announced that it was calling off the $2.2 billion merger with Titan "because Titan did not satisfy all the closing conditions," citing failure to resolve an investigation of alleged Foreign Corrupt Practices Act (FCPA) violations. (Lockheed Martin Press Release, "Lockheed Martin Terminates Merger Agreement with the Titan Corporation." June 26, 2004).

To the employee who urged the company to cancel the interrogation contract, London wrote a lengthy response. He began by stating, "Our work for government agencies plays a vital role in protecting America's security." He went on to provide not only the relevant facts about CACI and its role in Iraq, but also an extensive history of terrorism and the brutalities of the Saddam Hussein regime. London emphasized in his response that "the truth is vitally important to us, and we look forward to helping in the process of shedding light on the truth as well as dispelling the deeply offensive and false information that has been circulating about CACI's project at the Abu Ghraib prison. As a company that has long placed ethics and integrity in the forefront of our performance, we find the widely published distortions about CACI particularly disturbing. CACI was founded on the principles of integrity, honesty, and a steadfast commitment to providing quality services and best value for our customers. The company was built on and continues to stand firmly on these principles, and we believe they have been, and indeed, remain the formula for the company's continuing success."

Another employee wrote London that despite his great appreciation to the company for providing him with extensive business experience and moral support as a disabled man, he would withdraw his support for CACI. "Sadly I must now count YOU as one of the enemy," he proclaimed. London replied, "CACI is proud of its over forty-two years of commitment to its many thousands of employees for creating a company built on sound values, career opportunity and a livelihood that also has a patriotic component." He again provided the facts about CACI, the history of terrorist attacks on the U.S., and the Saddam Hussein tortures, and concluded with a statement about the value of CACI's work in "protecting Americans' security, improving the performance of domestic programs and enhancing the country's intelligence capabilities at home and abroad. We are proud of that work and will continue to serve our customer, the U.S. government in the tradition of excellence that has made CACI a truly outstanding organization."

While his public statements were important, London believed that it was crucial to directly communicate with his employees. In his mind, employees are the true key to any company. During his time as CEO, London had worked hard to build a company culture of ethical behavior. The company had adopted a mission statement and credo that embodied its values and made plain to employees what was expected of them. Among the core phrases in these statements were "integrity," "excellence," "accountability," and "quality service." At the end of 2004, addressing a company dinner, London remarked that throughout the tough times of the Abu Ghraib affair, "we looked to our valued employees, and our company values."

CACI was fighting on many fronts, not the least of which was to inform and retain its employees. Having been blindsided by an international furor of immense magnitude, the company was at an enormous disadvantage, and its own employees were learning of the situation at the same time as the rest of the world. Furthermore, this information was coming primarily from an unreliable source — a twenty-four-hour-a-day media machine that frequently gave into sensationalism, speculation and spin.

CACI was not alone in this dilemma. The media was churning faster than the U.S. Army, Congress, and the administration could respond. The reality was that the media madness did not allow for diligent investigation, thorough examination or objective review. Speculation, accusation, and premature judgments were outpacing the army's investigation results and verifiable conclusions.

As the crisis continued, London fell back on the fundamental principles of leadership that he had learned as a young midshipman at Annapolis. He had recruited a number of his employees from military retirees and, as their business commander, he had the responsibility to rally them when under fire. He had to demonstrate, by example, that CACI's credos and codes were not just words but real beliefs, and he wanted to remind them of their responsibilities.

It was about this time that he also settled on a symbolic gesture by wearing a specific necktie that would let his people know how he felt. He awoke one morning and selected from his collection of ties his "Navy Jack" — the red and white stripes of the American flag, the blue field of stars, and the words "Don't Tread on Me" printed below a rattlesnake coiled and ready to strike. The tie's Navy Jack flag reminded him of his midshipman days at the U.S. Naval Academy, and signaled his confidence and determination. It was, one colleague said with admiration, "Jack's 'f*** you' tie," a way to say that neither he nor his company would be defamed. London would wear it for the duration —

every day from May through October — as a way to bolster his employees. Recognizing the tie needed to look crisp and the colors sharp, London had an aide buy three more. Like a good military man, London attended to detail, knowing that ample supplies were critical to the success of any campaign. In fact, he still owns and frequently wears those four Navy Jack ties.[112]

But before the symbols would do any good, he had to communicate to his employees directly. No matter how dedicated they were, the news about Abu Ghraib and the accusations that their company was somehow involved were shocks that could shatter confidence. With the media storm likely to last for some time, it was vitally important that CACI employees hear from their leader about what was going on and how the company intended to handle it. Going forward, it seemed clear to CACI's senior managers that whenever possible, employees should learn about new developments — good and bad — from their leaders before they heard about it from the press. With this guiding principle, London directed Brown to develop a comprehensive, long-term, internal communication effort. It was all part of the strategy of openness that London and his team had settled on in their early conversations.

On May 3, the same day CACI sent its first news release to the media, the same day it began the full integration of AMS, and the beginning of the first work week after Hersh's report linked CACI to Abu Ghraib, London sent a statement to CACI's people — all 9,500 — in posts around the world to assure them that the company would find the truth. In anticipation of the concerns that employees would likely have, London had tasked Brown to set up a comprehensive list of frequently

---

[112] In the fall of 2003 on a visit to CACI staff and customers at the Naval facility at Yokusuka, Japan, London had noted the old Navy Jack flying from the stern of the USS. *Kitty Hawk (CV-63)* as he boarded her. She was recently coming out of her yard (repair) period, and was still tied up pier-side being readied for sea. London had always liked the idea of the Navy Jack with its famous "Don't tread on me" slogan and symbolic rattlesnake. At the time, the USS. *Kitty Hawk*, commissioned in 1961, was the oldest ship (42 years old) in the U.S. Navy on active sea duty, boiler-fired and steam-driven. Being non-nuclear, she was accepted for permanent forward deployment status in Japan. In late 2005 the navy announced that the USS. *Kitty Hawk* would soon be retired. London was proud of the work CACI did for the U.S. Navy in Japan.

asked questions (FAQs) on the company's intranet Web site. In his view, not only was this strategy a way to relay up-to-date information to all of CACI's employees, but London wanted the FAQs to become integrated into the overall internal communications program.

In the same way he was limited by lack of knowledge in dealing with the press, London was restricted in what he could say to company personnel. The key messages in his statement were similar to what London said publicly — we do not tolerate abuse, and we are launching our own investigation. But he also tried out a new thought. At this point, it was largely a plea for calm. Later, as the crisis persisted, the same words would become more urgent, signaling a principled stand, and a reminder that in America convincing evidence was necessary before conviction. On May 3, London would assert for the first time: "We must not jump to conclusions."

London also thanked his people for their work and reassured them of his faith in CACI. The worst case, London told himself, was that one or two employees in Iraq might have "gone off the ranch." But that shouldn't reflect on the rest of CACI — he simply wouldn't allow it.

"Regardless of the media allegations . . . I have confidence in the employees here at CACI. I am proud that you conduct CACI business with the utmost care and professionalism. Please continue to do the fine job you've been doing," the statement said.

And he promised to keep them up-to-date. "Jack insisted that our employees be informed in a consistent and timely manner to reassure them that we were doing the right thing and they could trust us," Jody Brown noted.

In addition to the formal communication, London also turned to his established habit of walking the halls of CACI. He had always believed one gets a better feel for what people are thinking through spontaneous hallway conversations than from formal or large-scale events. When people are summoned to a meeting or asked to speak in front of large groups of peers, candor tends to disappear. In those settings, many people fall back on platitudes or silence. London believed that more real and candid information could be exchanged when a few people just talk informally in the hall — even when one of them is the boss. From there, the grapevine can take over as colleagues tell one another about such conversations and the facts get passed along, with answers to questions and assurances about uncertainties.

Next, London knew he must talk to the financial community. For the sake of the shareholders, he needed to do what he could to keep the stock attractive to investors on the basis of sound business fundamentals. The message here was that much more investigation needed to be done before any conclusions could be reached. And the company's leadership had made its pact to do the right thing, no matter the outcome. Once again, in London's mind, it meant standing up straight, saying his piece, taking the questions and showing CACI had nothing to hide. Convinced that the way you present yourself can be as important as what you say, London scheduled a teleconference call for May 5 to address Wall Street analysts. He opened the call to any reporters who wanted to take part as well.

London began the call with a lengthy statement, which was separately released to the news media to maximize the chance that the company's messages would be heard.

He repeated the pledge to take action if the evidence showed misconduct.

"We will be relentless in identifying and punishing any improper behavior," he said, while also defending the company's honor. "If there is illegal behavior on the part of any employee, it is not indicative of the mode of operation of this corporation or the patriotic service of thousands of CACI's honorable, hardworking people diligently pursuing their assignments."

He again noted that the company did not have any direct information from the government, and also that it had not received any requests to stop work or to terminate or suspend any employees. He noted that interrogation was but a small part of the company's portfolio, amounting to "less than one percent of our entire business base." He reported that unfolding events had not had any economic impact and that the company's core was still strong.

London promised that CACI had, and would continue to cooperate with any and all government inquiries and also was conducting its own internal investigation with independent outside counsel. "We are eager to find out as soon as possible what has happened, and we've taken steps to inquire," he reported.

He defended the company's work and the quality of its people and pledged to continue to support the military mission in Iraq.

"The government is shorthanded in some of these critical skill set areas, and relies on qualified contractors to provide a wide variety of competent, professional services related to the global war on terrorism. We have been proud to support those initiatives and requirements. The people we have recruited have been competent and capable," he said.

He pointed out the wide range of CACI's services and, finally, noted that the appalling actions at Abu Ghraib should not cloud the patriotism of those who "are sacrificing so much to defend our country against terror and to support the freedom of Iraq."

During the question-and-answer session that followed, London also drew a distinction between possible misconduct by an individual and misconduct by the company. He observed that companies survive because people understand that solid corporate business practices are separate from instances where individual human beings sometimes step out of line of their own accord.

Initial reaction to the call was gratifying. In a report to investors, Raymond James & Associates credited CACI with "an excellent job." It reiterated its "buy" rating on the stock and said that the decline in share price, which fell about 8 percent after the first reports linking CACI to Abu Ghraib, was "unwarranted."

"We were very impressed with management's conviction, candor, commitment and patriotism," Raymond James said.

Though somewhat less effusive, Morgan Stanley said the decline in shares was a buying opportunity. It said Abu Ghraib would only be a concern if the Defense Department pulled contractors out of the region, but rated that prospect "highly unlikely."

"The government simply does not have the internal manpower or expertise within its ranks to forego outside contracting," Morgan Stanley added in its "quick comment" to investors on May 5.

Among the few dissents from the investment community was one from the Motley Fool, which counseled a more repentant tone.

"Legislators love their witch hunts, and innocent or guilty, it doesn't look to me like CACI is doing nearly enough to ward off a trip to the pyre," Motley Fool's Seth Jayson opined. The "witch hunt" fear also had been raised on the conference call by Tim Quillen, an analyst with Stephens Inc.

Reaching out to Capitol Hill was less natural for London. CACI was just not a company that sought out political connections. Though individual employees and officers contributed some money to political candidates, the amounts were not large. The company did not sponsor a political action committee. It did not spend large sums of money on lobbyists, nor did it employ an aggressive internal team for political outreach.[113] Instead, CACI had focused its energy on playing by the rules, figuring that if it had the right skills and served its clients well, it would be recognized for its capabilities and work ethic and would do just fine.

Watching the congressional hearings, it was obvious that there was very little knowledge on Capitol Hill about CACI, and, in particular, about the support it was providing the military with regard to interrogation services. Burkhart, London's business advisor, reminded him that people could not identify with an entity with which they had no knowledge. She suggested that the company develop an information package about CACI that would be different from the usual marketing materials, something to supplement existing information with a human-interest component that would help people relate to and understand CACI and its employees.

Burkhart also stressed: "It is important to get this information out as soon as possible, before negative perceptions are solidified." It was critical, she believed, to tell the whole story about CACI. Any void in the public's knowledge of the company was going to be filled each day by media commentary, opinion, and speculation, and just as importantly, by Web sites, bloggers, and rumor mills. "It is vital," she said, "to get a full, accurate story about CACI out so those who care enough to inquire, or are aware of the evolving story, will at least have the company's history and position to review."

What resulted was a four-piece package that included the historical human-interest element drafted by Burkhart and incorporated into a corporate technical piece prepared as a mailer by the communications team. Included in each mailer were an introductory letter, one handout about the company's history and services, and another handout about CACI's corporate culture. These documents were placed in large envelopes, that featured CACI's characteristically patriotic imagery, and

---

[113] Before Abu Ghraib CACI had, in only one situation, hired a firm associated with lobbying activity. The Livingston Group was engaged by CACI's Director of Business Development for marketing support in the New Orleans area to assist the company in identifying and developing new business opportunities.

hand delivered to every member of Congress. This package became a useful supplement to CACI's introduction to Congress, which was about to get underway.

Later mailings would include a copy of two August news releases announcing the results of CACI's internal investigation and army contract extension, and a feature card with the CACI logo and a brief message asking the reader to take a few minutes to look at CACI. This package would be distributed not only to members of Congress, but to CACI's customers and business contacts.

While Congress may not have known CACI, the company was not completely unconnected to Congress. Among London's acquaintances in Congress were Representative Tom Davis, a Republican from Fairfax County, Virginia, who chaired the House Government Reform Committee, and Democratic Representative Jim Moran of Alexandria, in whose district CACI's headquarters were located. London had recently traveled with the two men to Amman, Jordan, as part of a delegation of business and political leaders from Northern Virginia. He had enjoyed their company and the casual conversations and experiences they shared while there. London now decided to get in touch with the two men as a first step to introduce CACI on Capitol Hill. Davis and Moran listened to London's position, and in London's view they both seemed receptive to information about the company and the Abu Ghraib situation. He chalked that up as a positive result.

London doubted, however, that conversations with only two congressmen were sufficient by themselves to meet CACI's need for recognition on Capitol Hill.

Because CACI had virtually no profile in Congress, the company had no staunch supporters who might speak up for CACI if it were to come under intense congressional scrutiny. Without political connections CACI seemed vulnerable. London and his senior executives did not have a history of participating in political affairs.

CACI's predicament would seem even more precarious should any lawmaker or group of lawmakers decide to make CACI an example or summon CACI executives for questioning by a committee. If this were to be the case, it would be difficult to find allies to support CACI. It would be especially difficult if that support could be construed as defending prisoner abuse, should the findings show a CACI employee to be involved in some culpable way. In these circumstances, many members of Congress were likely to make the calculation that speaking up for the company was all risk and no gain. If brought into the congressional spotlight, CACI would at that point almost certainly have to stand or fall on its own.

Recognizing this reality, London began to ponder the need for some assistance with congressional relations. He was aware that the political fever on Capitol Hill over Abu Ghraib might bring a request to testify and potentially focus negative publicity on his company even though this was a matter of allegations and "suspicion" about one employee. He wanted to avoid that negative publicity if he could, but he also wanted to get some information on how to introduce the company and interact with this new environment. Before long, consistent with the general strategic decision to use external resources when needed, he would begin a search for the right people to help.

CHAPTER NINE

WHACK-A-MOLE
CACI hits back with the facts

"Truth lives on in the midst of deception."
∾ **JOHANN FRIEDRICH VON SCHILLER**

THE VOLUME OF ERRONEOUS MEDIA REPORTS AND THE HUNDREDS of self-styled commentators cited by various news reports about Abu Ghraib, conjures up the children's game "Whack-A-Mole." In the game, a player uses a padded hammer to hit moles that pop up briefly, disappear, and then re-emerge, but at a faster and faster speed as the game progresses. No matter how many successful hits one scores, some numbers of the moles escape unscathed. For CACI, whacking enough "moles" to keep the record straight presented an enormous challenge. The volume of false information was overwhelming and a new approach was needed.

Just tracking the news reports was a job in itself. Printed out for London and his Iraq team, clips from daily newspapers and magazines about Abu Ghraib totaled two hundred pages or more each day for weeks. On top of that, there were countless hours of broadcast news, Web site reports, and Internet blogs to keep track of and review.

Having digested the daily "book" of news reports, CACI needed to compile the commentary, identify errors or observations that required response or clarification, produce the individual responses, and deliver them. London vowed that every significant factual error required a direct response and immediate correction.

As she battled to direct the response process, Brown believed that consistent and, in some cases, customized messages would be required. Despite the strategic commitment to respond to every error, however, the days simply weren't long enough. But London would not tolerate having any misleading issue go unanswered. There were many times when he drafted language himself for responses to new issues.

This drove home the reality that despite popular reference to "THE Media," no such monolith exists. Brown's days were taken up by responding to hundreds of different reporters for scores of different organizations. Some news organizations seemed to check facts meticulously; most were less careful. Some tried to connect every dot. Some organizations, when quoting a source, provided full context and shared conflicting evidence where it existed. But often, each day's story stood on its own without much reference to what was reported the day before. The words of an "expert" might be given prominence even when at odds with what the same or some other expert said the day before — and that was a problem because most readers or viewers will see only some of the stories.

In a crisis, most corporations calibrate their responses, typically identifying the news agencies that they *must* respond to right away while relegating other media segments to a lower category to be dealt with when time allows. Some companies adopt a policy of near silence except when the issues on the table are so significant that some type of statement is unavoidable. But London believed, as Abraham Lincoln had stated, "To sin by silence when they should protest makes cowards of men."

And despite the most diligent efforts or persistence in making corrections, some errors will pass, unamended, into the permanent record. Like the whack-a-moles, the mistakes will pop up again and again, repeated by journalists, experts, and politicians who find them when "Googling" the Internet or searching a media database such as Nexis. Keeping abreast of this deluge was the greatest media challenge for CACI.

Still, London's goal was to answer *every* mistake and every misstatement about CACI. No media outlet was too small or so extreme that it could be ignored, because every report wound up in the record somewhere. And this was the case more than ever because of the Internet and its vast array of blogs and Web sites.

At London's direction, the CACI team even responded to college newspapers and fringe Web sites, such as the aptly named "Conspiracy Planet." It took serious note of Arabic and leftist media speculation about links between CACI and Israel. The basis of the latter speculation was London's participation in a trade delegation titled "Defense Aerospace Homeland Security Mission of Peace" that had visited Israel and Jordon in January of 2004. Participants also included Senators Evan Bayh (D-IN) and Ben Nelson (D-NE) and Congressmen John Linder (R-GA) and John McHugh (R-NY), former under secretary of the army Joe Reeder and assistant secretary for infrastructure protection at the Department of Homeland Security, Robert Liskouski.

One of the earliest of these reports on May 11, 2004, by Ali Abunimah of Lebanon's *Daily Star*, acknowledged that, "no evidence has emerged directly linking CACI's involvement in the Abu Ghraib atrocities to Israel." But that lack of evidence didn't stop Abunimah from putting his uncorroborated theory into circulation.[114]

As the story developed, so did the conspiracy theory. Abunimah's piece obviously provided no support for this hypothesis other than London's brief presence in Israel. But despite his acknowledgment that he lacked specific proof, Abunimah wove together happenstance and coincidence with speculation and spin to suggest a conspiracy. His work triggered similar reports in fringe media such as dissidentvoice.org, which ran an item called "United Kingdom, United States and Israel: Kings of Pain," and credited Abunimah with "a gold-mine worth of resources."[115] "Kings of Pain" was widely reprinted, showing up in the Russian news agency Pravda and the Palestine Media Center Web site, among others.

---

[114] Ali Abunimah, "Israeli Link Possible in U.S. Torture Techniques," *Daily Star*, May 11, 2004.

[115] John Stanton, "United Kingdom, United States and Israel: Kings of Pain," Dissidentvoice.org, May 13, 2004.

Shortly after it was incorporated into a similar story in *Arab News* called "What Might Sharon Know About CACI?"[116]

This ongoing media frenzy also extended to mainstream media such as the *Washington Post*, the *New York Times*, and the *Baltimore Sun* throughout the summer of 2004. To the CACI team's consternation, the fringe media reports also helped stimulate inquiries from mainstream news agencies, including National Public Radio and *USA Today*.

London was amazed that the story was accorded any credibility. And so it was that he was pressed into service strenuously rejecting the unfounded charge of this bizarre theory in a series of interviews with journalists.

With London's guidance, CACI practiced zero tolerance for errors. Small mistakes would not be allowed to slip by. Each word would be weighed for misleading implications or dubious conclusions that might be as damaging as factual errors.

But errors, large and small, continued. For example, some news articles referred incorrectly to CACI as a security firm and others wrongly lumped its employees into the category of "mercenaries" even though nobody employed by CACI ever carried a gun as a mercenary or paid combatant. Germany's *Der Spiegel* made such a sweeping declaration when it wrote that, "no one feels responsible for the private interrogation specialists who were allowed to do their dirty work in Abu Ghraib. These mercenaries do not fall under military jurisdiction."[117] The truth was CACI simply did not provide personal or industrial security services or para-military mercenary services of any kind. These and numerous other similar inaccuracies and accusations were intolerable to CACI.

In the context of Abu Ghraib and an environment where some terrorists and insurgents in Iraq had used the abuses as excuses for beheadings, the consequences of getting information wrong were potentially dangerous, life-threatening, and far-reaching. At the very least, when repeated often enough, especially in a wartime context like Iraq, such mistakes resulted in a badly distorted picture. To London, whose company was

---

[116] Sarah Whalen, "What Might Sharon Know About CACI," *Arab News*, May 14, 2004.

[117] Rudiger Falksohn, Siegesmund von Ilsemann, Susanne Koelbl, Gerhard Sporl, Volkhard Windfuhr, Bernhard Zand, "Excesses of Sex and Violence," *Der Spiegel*, May 10, 2004.

working in the war effort and had been from the beginning, this trend seemed to resemble propaganda — if the events were recited often enough they became accepted by some as fact.

Journalists sometimes call their work the "first draft of history." But by the time a "fully proofed" and accurate history is written the CACI name might be critically damaged. For Jack London, it was his company on the chopping block. To him, every error or misperception in the press was one more unjustified stain on his company's reputation. His mission, he believed, was to note every mistake and try to fix it.

At the heart of London's media strategy was the creation of a multi-page letter to be sent to nearly every news organizations that talked about CACI in an erroneous, incomplete, false, or misleading manner. London wanted to have a response for every story and every comment that represented CACI inaccurately in any way or failed to provide a complete picture of the situation that CACI was encountering. London had charged this "response" task to outside business advisor Burkhart and consultant Z. Selin Hur. London, Burkhart, and Hur entered CACI's boardroom one Saturday in early May of 2004 to draft the language. Nearly ten hours later, the team had developed a fact file and template for the letters. Drawn from the template and fact file (which were updated frequently), each response letter would be specifically tailored to address every issue raised by each individual news story that had mistakes.

Every day, Burkhart and Hur would pour over the day's press coverage and identify errors, misleading reports, or incomplete information that needed clarification. In what would become their routine for months, Burkhart would be the first to review the press coverage each day. Drawing from the previously approved specific and consistent language from the fact file, she would assemble responses. These would be the media response letters, which she would then send to Hur, who would review them again, making sure each letter contained the most up-to-date information CACI had. Hur would then identify and attach the contact information (including all outlets in which the piece appeared), after which the responses would be sent out by the company's corporate communications team.

As the stories mounted and new aspects, new "experts," and consequently new problems arose, Burkhart worked feverishly to keep up with the pace. "At times," she said, "I felt like a one-person army defending the truth about CACI against thousands of reporters who had far more resources for getting their stories out." She was frustrated and dismayed to find that the same media errors continued to be repeated. And the volume of mistakes would increase when new aspects of the story broke. Reporters who failed to note previous corrections would pick up and repeat the same errors in the new news cycle. Burkhart would then have to repeat previous corrections along with correcting any new errors that emerged with the new waves of breaking news stories.[118]

Hur marveled at how difficult it often was to track down the author of an article. Reporters seemed to rarely provide direct contact information in their pieces or on an outlet's Web site. Even reporters from the mainstream newspapers and media were hesitant to give their contact information when asked. In some cases, there was no author or source, like a newswire, cited for the article in question. She got creative and either tracked down the article's author from multiple posts of the piece or made sure that the editor of the publication received the letter.

Between May and September, Burkhart and Hur sent out more than 350 targeted response letters. It was tedious work that required constant attention and considerable resources. And it was a task that had to be renewed at various times thereafter.[119]

Constructing the response letters took considerable time and effort to research and draft the appropriate language in order to ensure accuracy and consistency. Many of the targeted response letters included statements addressing widespread misperceptions. For example, some media reports misconstrued CACI job listings for interrogators as implying that interrogators were out of the chain of command and operating on their own. The response letter to these reporters would include the statement that "Employees were recruited with the knowledge that

---

[118] See Appendix A Setting the Record Straight for additional corrections.

[119] The heated midterm elections of 2006 which raised the Iraq war and revisited the Abu Ghraib scandal as campaign issues, generated an increase in the volume of erroneous reporting, opinion articles, blogs, and video clips that often repeated the previous false and distorted information about CACI's interrogation work. The one dimensional and politically driven propaganda film *Iraq for Sale*, by Brave New Films was loaded with false statements and malicious innuendo about CACI and London.

'minimal supervision' would be involved and this meant that they must have experience and maturity, that they would be responsible and accountable for their actions and their work performance and dependability. At all times the U.S. government has had and continues to have oversight of CACI's employees reporting for work. CACI personnel have no management, supervisory, or command authority whatsoever over any non-CACI personnel."

Another example was a letter to *Financial Times* correspondent Joshua Chaffin that required a brief paragraph outlining the difference between a "spy" and an "interrogator." So too, student journalists at Berkeley and Stanford were corrected with the information that CACI did not then, nor had it ever provided combat soldiers or mercenaries.

Reaching out with accurate information was a huge challenge. The unique and ubiquitous nature of the Internet enabled rapid dissemination of information, whether fact or fiction that could be fired off all over the globe instantaneously. This was new in crisis management. And it was clearly not the communications world that Tylenol's Johnson and Johnson management team and CEO had faced in the early 1980s.

Since reporters generally cover a story throughout its duration, there would be articles by the same reporters nearly every day. And many articles rehashed the main points of previous pieces. Sending a response letter to those reporters every day would be counterproductive and the CACI team wanted to avoid a "junk mail" effect in which the letters would possibly be dismissed or discarded. So the team developed a timing strategy on when to send out letters to the same reporters or media outlets allowing at least two to three days between letters. In this way, each letter was still relevant to the reporter's recent articles, but also contained the most up-to-date information on the company. At the same time, if there were new developments in the Abu Ghraib story or new items on CACI that included mistakes, Burkhart, Hur, and the PR team would address any and every error immediately.

With the targeted media response letters, CACI would achieve one of its primary goals — the facts about the company would be heard. London knew that a letter from a company so prominently mentioned in the news would, at least, be opened and read. The concept of the targeted response letters was not only to address mistakes in individual news articles, but also to provide those corrections in an informative and non-accusatory way. The tone of the letters was firm but friendly. London insisted that the end of each letter also invite the reader to visit the company Web site (www.caci.com) and CACI's Iraq FAQs (frequently asked questions) section which gave CACI another opportunity to present its story and the facts — and present a wider view than the media was delivering.[120]

This targeted media approach had another distinct advantage — broader coverage. In addition to the wide scope of topics and corrections that could be covered in the email letters and Web site, CACI could also reach a much larger number of journalists and media outlets. Response letters could be sent as often as necessary and without delay. In fact, CACI responded to publications in France, India, Germany, Israel, the United Kingdom and Lebanon at the same time that it communicated with media outlets in Boston, Denver, and Los Angeles. Every letter was also emailed to the reporter, editor, or publisher of a targeted article, providing additional insurance that the CACI message would be received.

The scope and efficiency of such an operation on a corporate level was unprecedented as far as the CACI team knew. The letters were also a useful supplement to the company's standard outreach efforts, such as press releases and teleconferences. And continuous updates from the letters were channeled into the FAQ section of the CACI Iraq Web site. Updates by CACI were prepared on an ongoing basis as new information and errors in stories emerged and the targeted media response letters were the best way to address them.

The letters clearly had an impact. The fact that a number of reporters responded to the letters let the CACI team know that it was being heard. The media was clearly not used to receiving such a direct and comprehensive response to its stories. Some reporters were puzzled; others were miffed when the message hit their hot buttons. The letters began by citing "some aspects of your article for which we would like to provide additional factual information." To the reporters, this implied they had made mistakes but stopped short of confrontational language. But the letter sometimes drew irritated reactions. "I'm confused. What, specifically, are you alleging that I got wrong?" asked an AP reporter in a

---

[120] CACI's Iraq FAQs section remained on the company's Web site as of December 2007.

fairly typical reply. "I cannot determine what you believe was wrong in any of my articles. . . . If there were indeed factual errors in any of my articles, I want to correct them."

London was convinced that if he distributed the truth widely, at least some of it would make its way into circulation. Some reporters might be irritated, but if even a few listened to what CACI had to say, London believed that the price was well worth paying. Moreover, at least one small West Coast newspaper ran a CACI dispatch in its entirety as a letter to the editor. To London, Burkhart, and Hur, that was the sort of victory that made the effort worthwhile.

This comprehensive media response strategy became a systematic and circular process to ensure accuracy, consistency, and repetition of the facts in order to get the truth out — London's overriding objective when it came to the public and the media. Issues and factual answers drafted for the targeted media responses were also added to the FAQs on the company Web site, and answers from the FAQs were fed back into the "fact file" to be used for the targeted media response letters in addressing the daily media. The answers in the FAQs and the fact file were scrutinized rigorously by the CACI team before being printed and disseminated. And information used in the media response letters and the FAQs were also used in CACI press releases. All three prongs of London's unique hypercrisis PR approach in dealing with the media — regular press releases, the FAQ section of the CACI Web site and the targeted media response letters — broadened the forum in which the CACI team got the facts out.

London's hypercrisis PR strategy for CACI was designed and built on the motto: "The Truth Will Out."[121]

---

[121] CACI's Hypercrisis Management Model is presented and discussed in Appendix H.

CHAPTER TEN

THE ROAD TO ABU GHRAIB
The history behind the prison of infamy

> **"But Abu Ghraib has always been a desolate and dreaded place, the most infamous of all jails [under Saddam Hussein] in a country saturated with horrific prisons."**
> ~ *THE TORONTO STAR*, APRIL 13, 2003[122]

O VER SUBSEQUENT WEEKS IN TWO MORE *NEW YORKER* ARTICLES, Seymour Hersh spun a larger story of government misconduct. To him, the story was not about the misbehavior of a few MPs in Iraq, but rather of an administration in Washington that had turned its back on America's long-term commitment to international law. In the trauma of September 11, the Bush administration, according to some, had set new rules for a new type of war. To Hersh and others, the new rules somehow, and in some way, had paved the road to Abu Ghraib.

Leaked memos written by White House Counsel Alberto Gonzalez had reportedly portrayed the Geneva Conventions as "obsolete" in an age of terrorism. He noted that setting the Conventions aside would make it harder for prosecutors to charge Americans for allegations of

---

[122] Rosie Dimanno, "Abu Ghraib Prison: Nowhere in Iraq Was Butchery More Rife." *Toronto Star*, April 13, 2003.

crimes against prisoners — exactly what some said was happening at Abu Ghraib. It could have been expected that some detainees — e.g., suspects — would attempt to criminalize their captors, using America's justice system in any and every possible way to obfuscate and detract from their terrorist complicity. Though the administration had said it would honor the Geneva rules in Iraq, skeptics argued that the earlier suspension of the rules in Afghanistan and for detainees at Guantanamo Bay only sowed confusion among American soldiers, and may have contributed to the abuses at Abu Ghraib (although this theory has never been proved one way or another).

Even as President Bush declared the abuse shameful and spoke on Arab television in direct apology, many critics pointed the finger of blame at the White House and Defense Secretary Donald Rumsfeld and called for Rumsfeld's departure. Others, including supporters of America's intervention in Iraq, worried that the scandal had undermined American credibility and would impede the effort to bring stability to Iraq. George Melloan wrote in the *Wall Street Journal* "Since the Abu Ghraib disclosures, the president's natural enemies in America have been emboldened. . . . The chattering classes on the left, along with a few on the right, are reviving the memory of the 'Vietnam quagmire.'"[123] Charles Krauthammer, in the *Washington Post*, said the calls on Rumsfeld to resign were, for partisans, "a convenient way to get at the president." For those with no partisan agenda, but shocked by the photos, "it is a way to try to do something, anything, to deal with the moral panic that has set in about the whole Iraqi enterprise."[124]

But both sides were vastly oversimplifying. The United States had never planned to use the prison as a military detention center. Indeed, the military planners never anticipated the need to run long-term detention facilities for insurgents or others who might be a security risk. But, as often happens in war, plans are upset by unanticipated contingencies.

History argued against American forces being involved in any way with Abu Ghraib. Built by British contractors in the 1960s, and located

---

[123] George Melloan, "Wishing Won't Make Terrorism Go Away," *Wall Street Journal*, May 18, 2004.

[124] Charles Krauthammer, "The Abu Ghraib Panic," *The Washington Post*, May 14, 2004.

about twenty miles from Baghdad, Abu Ghraib covers 280 acres and has been described as "a square kilometer of hell."[125]

Abu Ghraib had a terrible and brutal history. According to the U.S. State Department, Saddam Hussein's rise to power in 1979 introduced a regime of torture and terror in Iraq that was arguably the most brutal in contemporary history.[126]

Under Hussein, the prison became known as "the death chamber." In February 1998, 400 prisoners at Abu Ghraib were executed summarily and two months later, one hundred detainees from Radwaniyah Prison were buried alive in a pit in Ramadi province. These killings were carried out to "clean out" the prisons. It has been estimated that an additional 3,000 were killed in a similar manner between 1997 and 2002.[127] Under Hussein's orders, the security arm in Iraq routinely and systematically tortured its citizens — beatings, rape, breaking of limbs, and denial of food and water were commonplace in Iraq detention centers. According to official documents, Hussein's rule of terror resulted in the execution of 30,000 Iraqis who disappeared to the anonymity of mass gravesites, as well as the mutilation of countless others who returned to society physically and emotionally scarred, maimed, or handicapped from methodical acts of torture.[128]

---

[125] A profile of Abu Ghraib prison and its history is presented in Appendix G.

[126] American Prisoners of war from all branches of the military captured during the Persian Gulf War of 1991 said they endured torture under Hussein and his intelligence service that included beatings, starvation and mock executions. Adam Piptak, "17 Ex-P.O.W's Set Back Again in Claim Against Iraq," *New York Times*, June 5, 2004.

[127] U.S. Department of State International Information Programs, "Silence Through Torture", *Iraq, A Population Silenced*, February 2003.

[128] Ibid. According to official records from the U.S. Department of State numerous methods of torture were implemented during Saddam's regime, including medical experimentation, beatings, crucifixion, hammering nails into fingers and hands, amputating sex organs and breasts with an electric carving knife, spraying insecticides into a victim's eyes, branding with a hot iron, committing rape while the victim's spouse was forced to watch, pouring boiling water into the victim's rectum, nailing the tongue to a wooden board, extracting teeth with pliers, using bees and scorpions to sting naked children in front of their parents. Hussein's sons, Uday and Qusay, were also responsible for the invention of horrific methods of torture used in Iraq's detention centers, including electric shocks to males' genitals, pulling out finger nails, suspending individuals from rotating ceiling fans, dripping acid on victims' skin, gouging out eyes, and burning victims with a hot iron or blowtorch.

Surrounded by twenty-four guard towers, the complex was divided into five separate walled compounds for different types of prisoners, one section each for foreign prisoners, long sentences, short sentences, capital crimes, and "special" crimes. The special crimes section, primarily for political prisoners, was itself divided into open and closed wings. In recent years the closed wing, named initially because those held there were denied any visitors or outside contact, was reserved for Shiite

---

In 2000, to silence dissenters, Hussein issued a decree authorizing the government to amputate the tongues of any citizens who would dare to criticize the Hussein government.

The daily *Babel* newspaper, owned by Uday Hussein, contained a public admission printed on February 13, 2001 of beheading women who were suspected of prostitution. According to the Iraqi Women's League in Damascus, Syria, "Under the pretext of fighting prostitution, units of 'Fed'iyee Saddam,' the paramilitary organization led by Uday, beheaded in public more than 200 women all over the country, dumping their severed heads at their families doorsteps."

An Iraqi citizen and advocacy director of the International Alliance for Justice described Saddam's torture regime as "a country where people are ethnically cleansed [and] prisoners are tortured in more than 300 prisons in Iraq. Rape is systematic . . . congenital malformation, birth defects, infertility, cancer and various disorders are the results of Saddam's gassing of his own people . . . the killing and torturing of husbands in front of their wives and children. . . . Iraq under Saddam has become a hell and a museum of crimes." Press Conference, National Press Club, Washington, D.C. October 22, 2002.

Hussein's systematic torture machine at Abu Ghraib also included collective punishment of entire families or ethnic groups for acts of one dissident. Women were raped and often videotaped during the rape to blackmail their families. Citizens were publicly beheaded and their families were required to display the heads of the deceased at their homes as a warning to others who might question the politics of the Saddam regime. Dissidents were tortured, killed, or disappeared in order to deter others from speaking out against the government. Iraqis were not allowed to vote to remove the government. Each ballot read "Saddam Hussein: Yes or No" and a "No" vote could be traced from the numbered ballot to the voter who would disappear forever. For more than 20 years Hussein executed perceived opponents, arresting many as political prisoners before executing them.

Hussein's regime also used chemical weapons against its own people. Between 1983–1988 alone, over 30,000 Iraqi's were murdered with mustard gas or nerve agents. It has been estimated that more than 60,000 Iraqi citizens were killed with chemical agents. During his two-year campaign against the Kurds, chemical weapons were used against more than 40 villages.

prisoners. "Abu Ghraib has always been a desolate and dreaded place, the most infamous of all jails in a country saturated with horrific prisons, warehousing in misery an entire sub-population of the incarcerated. The condemned and the damned: murderers, thieves, political prisoners, dissidents, Communists, Baath party opponents, and just about every poor wretch who happened to make a passing, overheard, intemperate remark about the Saddam regime," the *Toronto Star* wrote in April 2003 when the gates were opened upon Saddam's fall from power.[129] Torture was a significant aspect of Saddam Hussein's rule, and to many Iraqis, Abu Ghraib was hell on earth.[130]

Stating that, "Much of the recent controversy surrounding Abu Ghraib has made only vague reference to the prison's nightmarish past," the American Enterprise Institute held an event on June 2004 open to the press called "The Tortures of Saddam's Abu Ghraib and Their Place in the New Iraq." The event included a video obtained from the Pentagon showing the routine torture, beating, dismemberment and decapitations that occurred at Abu Ghraib under Hussein. Despite the saturated coverage of Abu Ghraib at the time of the video's showing, only four to five reporters attended the event. One such reporter, Deborah Orin reported "The video only lasts four minutes or so — gruesome scenes of torture from the days when Saddam Hussein's thugs ruled Abu

---

[129] Rosie Dimanno, "Abu Ghraib Prison: Nowhere in Iraq Was Butchery More Rife," op. cit.

[130] Saddam Hussein Al-Tikriti, age 69, was executed by hanging in Baghdad, Iraq on Saturday December 30, 2006. Convicted of being guilty of war crimes against the Iraqi people by the Iraqi government, Saddam Hussein's execution was conducted not at the Abu Ghraib prison where he carried out torture and murder against his own people, but at the facility in Baghdad that housed his intelligence and security group during his regime (1979–2003). He had been captured by the U.S. Army's 4th Division, 1st Brigade on December 13, 2003 (Operation Red Dawn) in Ad Daur, a small town near Tikrit where Hussein's family and close friends lived. He was pulled from an underground pit (spider hole) on a rural farm site. Hussein was betrayed by Mohamed Omar al-Musset, a cousin of Abid Hamid Mahmud (Hussein's personal security officer), and #4 on the U.S.' Wanted List, after Hussein and his two sons (Mahmud also was the 'Ace of Diamonds' in the "wanted" deck of cards). Mahmud was captured in July 2003 while al-Musset was captured on December 12th in Baghdad and *gave up Hussein's whereabouts after only a few hours of interrogation.* Intelligence teams knew that Mahmud was the only person at the time who knew the day-to-day whereabouts of Hussein.

Ghraib prison. . . . Saddam's henchmen took the videos as newsreels to document their deeds in honor of their leader."[131]

As it turned out, the course of the Iraq war produced an entirely different class and number of detainees than expected, and American forces needed a place to house them. Having initially designated Abu Ghraib as the place where Iraqi police would detain common criminals, the military began to put its prisoners there as well. Located by a main road in an urban area not far from Baghdad, Abu Ghraib presented significant security challenges. It would be subjected to almost daily mortar attacks by insurgent forces, exposing soldiers, contractors and detainees to constant danger and greatly exacerbating the ability of U.S. forces to maintain order and discipline in a facility that was typically overcrowded.

The *Washington Post,* in describing the challenges the U.S. forces faced at the prison, stated that, "the Abu Ghraib prison was particularly hellish. Insurgents were firing mortar shells and rocket-propelled grenades over the walls. The prisoners were prone to riot. There was no PX, no mess hall, no recreation facilities to escape the heat and dust. About 450 MP's were supervising close to 7,000 inmates, many of them crowded into cells, many more kept in tents hastily arranged on dirt fields within the razor-wired walls of the compound. Around the perimeter, GIs kept wary eyes on Iraqi guards of questionable loyalty."[132]

The riots were especially disturbing. "The uprisings rattled even the most seasoned of soldiers. Detainees would cut themselves on the concertina wire . . . and try to smear their blood on MPs. They rushed the wire and threw rocks they had stored up in empty meal containers."[133]

Tensions increased when a mortar attack on the prison in September 2003 killed two soldiers and a prisoner was subsequently found with a 9m pistol believed to have been smuggled in by Iraqi guards. In his report, Major General Taguba noted "The Iraq guards at Abu Ghraib demonstrated questionable work ethics and loyalties and are a potentially dangerous contingent within the [prison]. These guards have furnished the Iraq criminal inmates with contraband, weapons, and infor-

---

[131] Deborah Orin, "Reporting for the Enemy; Media Won't Show Saddam's Evil," *New York Post*, June 16, 2004.

[132] Scott Higham, Josh White and Christian Davenport, "A Prison on the Brink; Usual Checks and Balances Went Missing," *Washington Post*, May 9, 2004.

[133] Ibid.

mation. Additionally, they have facilitated the escape of at least one detainee."[134]

The *Washington Post* noted, "Confusion was high. Morale was low. The checks and balances established to hold soldiers accountable during vagaries of war were virtually nonexistent." Abu Ghraib was also "a dangerous place that smelled of sewage and sweat. Flies infested the camp. Those who have been there describe it as an outdoor cesspool where detainees stockpiled their feces to throw at the MPs."[135]

Isolated without amenities that were available to other troops in Iraq, the prison was painfully short on supplies including prisoner jumpsuits. One soldier reportedly handed out personal items from his own care package from home and issued female underwear from the sparse prison supplies, to male detainees because "The only thing I had was female underwear."[136]

U.S. planners had anticipated the surrender of large, relatively disciplined units of Iraqi troops who would be relatively easy to manage. But instead of surrendering formally en masse, the Iraqi Army essentially disbanded itself.[137] The soldiers simply went home, and blended into everyday Iraqi life. Coalition authorities later announced as much in the stand down of the Iraqi Army.

The disintegration of the Iraqi Army had hastened the end of major combat activities. The set-piece battle for Baghdad and other major cities never occurred. By April 9, 2003, U.S. forces had taken control of Baghdad. On April 14, less than four weeks after the start of the Operation Iraqi Freedom (OIF) campaign, the U.S. military said the Iraqi Army had virtually ceased to exist and that "major combat engagements" were essentially over. It was a stunningly swift victory. But if major organized combat had ended, it soon turned out that the war had not.

---

[134] Taguba Report, op. cit.

[135] Scott Higham, Josh White and Christian Davenport, "A Prison on the Brink; Usual Checks and Balances Went Missing," op. cit.

[136] Jim Loney, "Abu Ghraib was Hell, U.S. Soldier tells Abuse Hearing," Reuters, August 6, 2004. The later Fay investigation's report would note that, "A severe shortage of clothing during the September, October, November 2003 time frame was frequently mentioned as the reason why people were naked."

[137] John Diamond, "Prewar intelligence predicted Iraqi insurgency," *USA Today*, October 24, 2004.

It was shortly thereafter that a suicide car bomber killed four U.S. soldiers. By the summer of 2003, coalition forces were facing a growing insurgency marked by suicide bombings and other urban guerrilla-style tactics. In August of 2003, both the Jordanian embassy and the U.N. mission in Baghdad were victimized by bombings that killed thirty-three people. In Najaf, a car bomb killed 125 civilians, including Shiite leader and Imam Ayatollah Mohammed Baqr al-Hakim. Then, a year later, in December 2004, the U.S. Army was attacked by a suicide bomber who entered an American military base cafeteria in Mosul, Iraq killing twenty-four U.S troops.[138] This was the deadliest attack on U.S. forces since the war began.[139]

As both the insurgency and the number of prisoners held by U.S. forces grew, so did the number of prisons managed by U.S. forces. But instead of disciplined Iraqi Army troops, the U.S. held a mixture of insurgent fighters, including terrorist operatives from outside of Iraq, plus common criminals and Iraqi civilians swept up in the events of war. As in any guerrilla conflict, it was hard to distinguish between combatants and innocents, to know who posed a risk if released and who could provide valuable intelligence. Every type of prisoner wound up at Abu Ghraib, where they were turned over to a widely acknowledged undermanned and under-trained military police brigade and leadership that would later be found incapable of managing this heavy burden.

In the year after the end of major combatant operations, the military detained tens of thousands of Iraqis. All of the detention facilities were filled to capacity or beyond. Abu Ghraib alone, reportedly, would come to hold as many as 7,000 prisoners in the fall of 2003, when the infamous photos were taken. These prisoners and detainees were guarded by a single, under-strength battalion, even though army doctrine calls for one battalion for every 4,000 detainees. At Camp Cropper, outside the Baghdad Airport, the detainee population at times reached 1,000 — five times the facility's

---

[138] In January 2005, a month after the Mosul cafeteria bombing which killed 24 U.S. soldiers, including six from his own unit, 1st Lt. Aaron Seesan, Burkhart's nephew, stood up at Ft. Lewis, Washington and volunteered to go to Iraq to replace a wounded platoon leader. As a combat engineer "sapper," he would take on the dangerous job of conducting explosive sweeps so others could travel more safely.

[139] "Deadliest Attack On U.S. Base, Insurgents Previously Attacked Flimsy American Dining Hall Tents," CBS/Associated Press, December 21, 2004.

intended capacity. There were simply more prisoners than the army had prepared for or had the facilities and military guards to accommodate. The result was detainee riots, escapes, and repeated escape attempts.

Compounding this were apparently differing U.S. policies for the three different forward locations in the war against terrorism. At Guantanamo Bay, for example, where the United States held several hundred al Qaeda and Taliban operatives, it is widely reported that interrogation techniques were used that were not part of published army doctrine.[140] Some, including the military's own investigations, said that the distinctions may have confused the troops and that soldiers at Abu Ghraib may have unwittingly misinterpreted and violated the rules of engagement by using techniques approved for another theater, but not for Iraq.[141] Whatever the case, CACI personnel said that at Abu Ghraib, the rules of engagement were clearly posted on a bulletin board at the Joint Interrogation and Debriefing Center (JIDC).

As military units and individual soldiers moved from one theater to the next, it appeared that at least some of them took knowledge about army doctrine or theater-specific interrogation rules with them. For example, the 519th Military Intelligence Battalion from Fort Bragg, N.C. was posted for detention duty at Bagram, Afghanistan in 2002 and then in the summer of 2003 was moved to Abu Ghraib where one of its captains, Carolyn Wood, posted interrogation rules that were based, in part, on the rules she had developed for Afghanistan.[142]

"These techniques, approaches, and practices became confused at Abu Ghraib and were implemented without the proper authority or safeguards. Soldiers were not trained on non-doctrinal interrogation techniques such as sleep adjustment, isolation and the use of dogs," the army's Fay report would later conclude.[143] In the follow-up investigative report to the Taguba and Fay reports, the March 2005 report by Vice Admiral Albert T. Church, the Navy's Inspector General, would also

---

[140] The army used some civilian interrogators at Guantanamo Bay, but CACI interrogators were never engaged there. Interrogators were only provided by CACI for work in Iraq.

[141] Church Report, op. cit.

[142] Ibid.

[143] Fay Report, op. cit.

express concern about the migration of interrogation techniques. Church would note that policymakers spent significant time on designing procedures for Guantanamo, and should have done the same for the other theaters. "We consider it a missed opportunity that no specific guidance on interrogation techniques was provided to the commanders responsible for Afghanistan and Iraq," Church concluded.[144]

Some in the media and public apparently believed that the abuses could be traced to the tone of internal Bush administration memos that debated interrogation techniques, which were interpreted by critics to suggest that the administration held the Geneva Conventions in low regard. How this related to non-affiliated, non-uniformed "terrorists" and Islamic-jihadists captured in the field under "hostile or combatant" circumstances was apparently not clarified at the time. However, the Geneva Conventions do not, in general, relate to terrorists or non-uniformed combatants.

Others disputed or rejected the supposed link between these internal staff memos and conduct in the field. Heather McDonald, writing in the Manhattan Institute's *City Journal* in early 2005, argued that these memos had no effect on interrogators in the field because individuals in the field were unaware of them. "We had no idea what went on in Washington," Chris Mackey, a former military interrogator in Afghanistan, told McDonald.[145]

McDonald further noted, "The abuse at Abu Ghraib resulted from the Pentagon's failure to plan for any outcome of the Iraq invasion except the rosiest scenario, its failure to respond to the insurgency once it broke out, and its failure to keep military discipline from collapsing in the understaffed Abu Ghraib facility. Interrogation rules were beside the point." McDonald added that an overreaction to the abuses at Abu Ghraib needlessly tied interrogators' hands and prevented them from using legitimate methods and approaches for obtaining valuable intelligence.[146]

Mackey, too, separated the events depicted in the published Abu Ghraib photos from both policy decisions and successful interrogation.

---

[144] Church Report, op. cit.

[145] Heather McDonald, "How to Interrogate Terrorists," *City Journal*, Winter 2005. It should also be noted that "Chris Mackey" is a pseudonym that this former interrogator adopted for personal security reasons.

[146] Ibid.

Indeed, the fact was that the abuse-related photographs showed MPs — not interrogators or interrogations.

Writing in *The Interrogators*, the book he co-authored with *Los Angeles Times* reporter Greg Miller, Mackey said administration rules exempting al Qaeda and Taliban fighters from the Geneva Convention were largely beside the point.

A military-trained interrogator (but not a CACI employee), Mackey acknowledged in his book that he and his colleagues sometimes tested the limit of military interrogation rules and said that "the harsher the methods, the better information we got and the sooner we got it." But Mackey insisted that he and his fellow interrogators always stayed within the limits of the Geneva Conventions and did not use techniques that could be construed as torture. According to Mackey, the real challenge for interrogators in every theater in the war on terror was adapting a military rulebook and techniques that had been crafted for Cold War adversaries (i.e. U.S.S.R., Soviet bloc and communism) with cultures that were relatively familiar to Americans, to a completely new type of enemy (i.e. insurgents, violent religious extremists, radical Muslims) that thought in entirely different ways (viz. cultural and religious) from those in western society. He said that more effective than torture was the exploitation of the prisoners' own cultural biases "and convincing prisoners they were being sold out by somebody they knew." In a conversation with a CNN interviewer, Mackey elaborated: "For example, a Moroccan being sold out by an Algerian. There's tension there. And when we were able to exploit that, we achieved our ends . . . basically exploit their own prejudices that they had against one another."[147]

Mackey dismissed the notion that the abuses of Abu Ghraib reflected the migration of interrogation techniques from Afghanistan to Iraq. In an interview with National Public Radio, he drew a sharp distinction:

"When I was in Afghanistan, we never operated with these additional sets of rules. We were armed with the interrogation approach strategies that we had been taught in [military] school. And

---

[147] Interview on CNN's "American Morning," July 19, 2004 (http://transcripts.cnn.com/TRANSCRIPTS/0407/19/ltm.04.html).

although these certainly did evolve in order to sort of accommodate the cultural issue and a lot of realities that we encountered on
the ground, we never had sort of envisioned the idea that there
were a whole 'nother set of rules."[148]

Clearly there were different views and attitudes regarding interrogation
techniques and intelligence gathering and relevant policies, practices
and authority. Determining facts and finding the truth of it all would
take time. But for CACI the only issue that mattered at the moment was
finding out the truth about the allegations in the *illegally leaked* Taguba
report. While the company was seriously concerned about the harm Abu
Ghraib had caused America and its military, as a contract and business
matter for CACI, it was all coming down to the Taguba report, Abu
Ghraib, and Steven Stefanowicz.

---

[148] Interview on National Public Radio's "Fresh Air," July 20, 2004.

CHAPTER ELEVEN

THE BAYING HOUNDS

Assaulted with tough questions CACI has firm footing in its Statement of Work

> **"No matter where you go, they [the media]
> are barking and baying at you."**
> **~ JACK LONDON ON BEING THE TARGET OF MEDIA
> HYSTERIA, NOVEMBER 2004**

WHATEVER THE ROAD THAT TOOK THE U.S. ARMY TO ABU GHRAIB, CACI had ridden along it. And the continuing controversy fanned a blaze of negative coverage that singed the company. For journalists who wanted a piece of the big story, new angles about CACI were a way in the door. For political activists and "experts" riding the coattails of the Abu Ghraib story, CACI's dilemma was a way to be heard.

Having reported the sparse information laid out by Taguba, the media now wanted to know if CACI employee Steven Stefanowicz would be held accountable — either by CACI or the law — or whether legal loopholes might enable him to avoid any responsibility for the alleged misconduct at Abu Ghraib. The questions also reopened the debate about the appropriate role of contractors in military operations and to what extent those in the army or the government were paying attention.

From CACI's perspective, the questions meant more scrutiny, more anxiety from shareholders, more uncertainty among employees, and more time in the spotlight. There was a precarious balance between addressing these issues and ensuring that they did not affect the company's business operations. The CACI executive team wanted in no way for the Abu Ghraib events to distract their employees from the work CACI was performing for its many customers. In any case, all of this media coverage was from a disparate group of reporters, and there were no fixed rules for CACI to use in its push back to get the facts straight and on the record.

As with personnel in any enterprise, reporters vary greatly in quality and capability. Some meticulously check their facts and make sure they've got the known details right. Others, whether through inexperience or tight deadline pressure, get the facts wrong or report speculation as if it were truth. Even a single instance of bad (inaccurate) reporting read by thousands can inflict immense damage on a reputation. With thousands of reporters writing about Abu Ghraib, the chance for error was immense and the potential business and reputational damage incalculable.

To CACI, it felt like the company was caught in a political whirlpool where different interpretations of events at Abu Ghraib being tossed around were a proxy for debate over the war in Iraq itself. The company's managers were concerned that misinformation repeated about the company could cause irreparable damage.

For the next several months, nearly every story about government contracting and almost every story about Abu Ghraib referred, to some extent, to CACI. And no matter how small, nearly every story about CACI — any business transaction, any contract award, even any personnel action — now included a boilerplate comment about Abu Ghraib. This was hard for the company to accept or understand in light of the fact that only one CACI employee was mentioned in a single paragraph in the Taguba report. And that mention referred to a "suspicion" — not a direct charge — with the recommendation for further investigation of that suspicion.

CACI had brought Stefanowicz back to the USA in May of 2004. However, the company did not have any facts regarding the allegations against him. Moreover, the investigation specifically aimed at the intelligence gathering aspect of Abu Ghraib, in which Stefanowicz was a part, was just getting underway. So no specific conclusions would be coming soon.

Abu Ghraib looked like it would become CACI's scarlet letter. And CACI was becoming the one-word shorthand for journalists, critics, and activists who wanted to point to problems with the military's contracting process. If you wanted to debate the role of contractors with the government or question the government's outsourcing of its services, it was convenient, though fallacious, to simply point to Abu Ghraib and CACI. History would soon show that contracted services at Abu Ghraib were not the cause of the difficulties.

For CACI, the experience was nearly overwhelming. At various times, London likened it to a "tsunami" with a new wave breaking over the company almost every day. Other times, he felt cornered like a fox at a foxhunt. "No matter where you go, they [the media] are barking and baying at you," he recalled. For many weeks, London and Brown played "dialing for reporters." At the close of the day's business, they took the list of media calls and began phoning back in hopes that time on the phone with reporters — sometimes thirty minutes or more per call — would help CACI get its facts into print.

The questions were endless. The accusations stung. CACI prided itself on its ethics and integrity, and its focus on customer service. The company took comfort in its good reputation, built over more than four decades of quality client support. Now, within CACI, the goal was to make the world understand that what happened at Abu Ghraib — even if one employee may have violated rules — certainly did not, and could not define the company. It did not represent who the people of CACI truly were, what they had accomplished, or what they remained capable of accomplishing in the future.

★   ★   ★

Even though the CACI team and company leadership believed their work in Iraq had gone well (had not the army consistently said so?), questions continued to blast out from the media. The questions about CACI's contract and what they were doing at Abu Ghraib were incessant. But CACI knew its contract and its Statement of Work were straightforward, proper and completely aboveboard.

Furthermore, the Statement of Work for the interrogation support services contract between CACI and the army in Iraq, for example, demonstrated the working level capability and commitment that CACI brought to its customers.[149]

The SOW for the interrogator support to the army by CACI at Abu Ghraib, by all current standards, was thought out and thorough. It specifically stipulated that the interrogation support program was designed "to increase the effectiveness of dealing with detainees, persons of interest, and Enemy Prisoners of War (EPWs) that are in the custody of US/Coalition Forces in the CJTF-7, in terms of screening, interrogation, and debriefing of persons of intelligence value."

At the on-site supervisory level, the requirements for the C2X Screening and Interrogation Operations Coordinator were "proven CI/HUMINT experience at tactical and operational levels" and required that the individual "must be a U.S. citizen and possess a Top Secret/SCI security clearance." The SOW also stipulated that the supervisor "Candidate will be required to work twelve hours per day, seven days per week" and that the "Contractor is responsible for providing supervision for all contractor personnel."

The Interrogation Support Cell Manning requirements for other positions stated "All positions will require work to be performed twelve hours per day, six days per week. The work schedule will be staggered, in order to provide one day of rest for employee, while still maintaining support seven-days per week."

The Statement of Work also called for the following:

a. "Database Entry/Intelligence Research Clerk (D/IRC). Six (6) D/IRC's are required at minimum, to support the interrogation operations of the Theater Interrogation Facility. Identified D/IRC'S should be the civilian equivalent to one of the following; 96BE, 350B/E or an individual with a similar skill set, and U.S. Citizens; three with a Secret clearance and three with Top Secret clearance."

b. "Screeners. Six (6) screeners are required at minimum, to support the interrogation operations of the Theater Interrogation Facility. Identi-

---

[149] CACI's Statement of Work for Iraq, presented here in brief part, contained or referenced numerous DoD acronyms, military terminology, government forms and military organizational designators. Some of these terms are provided in the Glossary, others are left undefined.

fied screeners should be the civilian equivalent to one of the following: 97B/E, 35BV5, 95BV5, Strategic Debriefer or an individual with a similar skill set:, and U.S. Citizens with a Secret clearance."

c. "Interrogators. Ten (10) interrogators are required at minimum, to support the interrogation operations of the Theater Interrogation Facility. Identified interrogators should be the civilian equivalent to one of the following: 97E, 351E, Strategic Debriefer or an individual with a similar skill set, and U.S. Citizens. Five positions, at minimum, require a Top Secret clearance; the other five positions can be either at the Secret or Top Secret clearance levels."

As an IT company that contracted for intelligence systems and technology, CACI was qualified to meet the SOW requirement that stipulated IT services and equipment use to carry out its work in Iraq. ADP Equipment requirements "for effective interrogation support operations" to "be purchased by the Contractor" included:

a. "11 Dell Optiplex GX 400 computers . . ."
b. "1 × Computer with a minimum of 2 GHZ processor . . ."
c. "2 × Dell Laptops . . ."
d. ". . . 2 × 2400dpi scanners, 2 printers; 1 × HP laser jet 4100 and 1 × HP Color Laser Jet 4550 . . ."

IT requirements of the contract also included "Work space for the contractor, with access to office supplies, office furniture, computer and systems automation, internet access, and local and long distance telephone access, including DSN, as required to fulfill contract/mission requirements." (Contrary to later misunderstandings, the contract *did*, as shown here, include an IT performance and support component).

Showing confidence in CACI's ability to continue to provide the interrogation work, if necessary, the SOW, as initially prepared, allowed for the extension of service (option years) beyond the initial contract year according to the following section of the SOW:

Period of Performance: 01 AUG 2003 to 31 JUL 2004 (Base Year)
01 AUG 2004 to 31 JUL 2005 (Option Year 1)
01 AUG 2005 to 31 JUL 2006 (Option Year 2)[150]

---

[150] Two option years were originally included in the Statement of Work, but were excluded in the actual contract, which was for a one year period of performance.

The SOW also showed that CACI was willing to take on hazard duty by stating that "the Government shall provide the following services when the Contractor is deployed in support of CJTF-7 Contingency Operations. . . ."

For hazard duty the SOW stated the requirement for: "Organizational clothing and individual equipment (OCIE) and protective clothing/equipment to include protective mask and chemical protective over-garments required in the Theater of operations. . . ."

For support the SOW stated the need for: "The appropriate documentation commensurate with that given to DoD civilians in the Theater of operations: deploying Contractors will be issued a Uniform Services Identification Card, DD Form 1173, and a Geneva Conventions Identity Card, DD Form 489. CJTF-7 will provide the Contractor with a Letter of Authorization (LOA) that allows army Units to issue necessary equipment, tests, shots, and training to the Contractor employee."

For protection the SOW stipulated: "Force protection measures commensurate with that given to DoD civilians in the Theater of operations. This includes training Contractors in self-protection and NBC [nuclear, biological and chemical]." Noting, "Contractors are considered non-combatants and are not authorized to be armed." CACI personnel were not armed and did not carry weapons.

Provision was also made in the SOW for the event of death stipulating, "Remains processing in the event of an employee's death while in the theater of operations. This includes the transportation of remains back to CONUS."

The SOW also demonstrated CACI's recognition that further training would be provided by the army to its interrogators once they were deployed to Iraq: "Appropriate individual readiness training (IRT), area orientations and training/briefings on rules of engagement and general orders applicable to U.S. Armed Forces, DoD Civilians, and U.S. Contractors as issued by the Theater Commander or his/her representative."

Despite the incessant criticism and increasingly damning accusations that were gaining momentum in the media from the single paragraph in the Taguba report, CACI executives knew the company had a fine reputation and a firm footing in the SOW. And the company believed it had fully complied with the plan outlined in the SOW. If any employee had violated the law, failed to follow rules of engagement, or otherwise not complied with the contract SOW, it was certainly not condoned nor authorized by the company. Furthermore, any such behavior was fully against company policy and standards of behavior and the company would take any necessary and appropriate action if employee violations were proven.

Outside CACI, however, people reached other judgments and developed different opinions. They had seen the pictures of the army MPs with the detainees and they had heard CACI's name. "We have now lost confidence in you [CACI] . . . since you have not taken any action," one correspondent emailed the company less than a week after its alleged involvement first became public. People seemed to assume that CACI *must* have done something wrong, regardless of the terms of the SOW and its execution by CACI, or the actions of the company or some of its employees. It became a case of guilt by association, and guilty unless and until proven innocent.

The public, understandably, had no knowledge of CACI's project and nor would they typically have been so informed. In any case, CACI had no requirement or authority under the circumstances at the time to make the SOW available to the public, so the questions persisted. For the time-being CACI would be bombarded, assaulted by tough questions, and confronted by a virtual "piling on."

But in particular, people wanted to know: What was CACI going to do about Stefanowicz? Why hadn't he been fired yet? And why was CACI interrogating prisoners?

Further, there was an important overarching question: What took CACI to Iraq in the first place? For that query London and his team had a ready answer: the U.S. Army needed help, it was in CACI's line of intelligence-gathering business, and the company answered the call.

CHAPTER TWELVE

CACI GOES TO IRAQ
Answering the U.S. Army's call for help

> **"When you run out of soldiers and they don't have an expertise, one way to get that capability is to contract it."**
> ∾ **U.S. ARMY SPOKESMAN MAJOR GARY TALLMAN, MAY 2004**

THAT CACI WAS IN IRAQ SHOULD NOT HAVE BEEN A SURPRISE. THE surprise would have been if CACI were *not* providing services in Iraq.

For the United States military and the growing number of contractors that supported it, the war in Iraq reflected a deliberate decision by U.S. policymakers and presidential administrations over the previous twenty years to change the way America fights its wars. With the end of the Cold War, the United States decided to reduce the size of its permanent military force — a decision that was aimed at saving taxpayers money. From more than three million individuals in 1970, the combined permanent force of all of the U.S. military services had fallen to about 1.4 million when the United States went into Iraq in 2003.

In part, the shift represented advances in technology and weaponry, which reduced the number of troops necessary to achieve military objectives. Changing geopolitical circumstances as well as the overwhelming superiority of U.S. combat forces seemed to reduce the likelihood of extended combat involving massed armies, further encouraging the movement toward a swifter and more effective, but smaller permanent force.

These force reductions also meant that sustaining a military effort would require others to take on critical logistical and other non-war fighting tasks. The answer was the government contract support industry, which took up a range of logistical and operational support activities, including cooking, cleaning, property management, vehicle maintenance, computer network installation and management, information technology and management, intelligence analysis, surveillance system management, and the management and maintenance of sophisticated weaponry and communications systems.

High technology also drove the shift toward contractors, who possess proven computer and technical skills that are not readily available in an all-volunteer force in the numbers required. In addition, the contractors' expertise remains readily available for years at a time, without training reinvestment. For example, the Global Hawk and Predator unmanned drones used in Afghanistan and Iraq are sometimes operated by contractors, and some surveillance systems are now being designed from the outset for operations by contractors.[151] As U.S. Army spokesman Major Gary Tallman put it, "When you run out of soldiers and they don't have an expertise, one way to get that capability is to contract it."[152]

In Iraq, the military did not have the necessary personnel for screening and questioning the increasing number of detainees. They needed to gather and analyze field source intelligence data and information. The large and growing number of detainees made the requirement increasingly more urgent. Since CACI already provided intelligence support in the form of IT solutions and technology services to the U.S. intelligence community, the interrogation requirement coming from Iraq was a logical extension of CACI's tactical intelligence and field services for information collection, data analysis, and decision support. CACI agreed to perform these intelligence and interrogation support contract services because of its long-standing commitment to its U.S. Army clients and

---

[151] Victoria Burnett, et al., "From Building Camps to Gathering Intelligence, Dozens of Tasks Once in the Hands of Soldiers Are Now Carried Out by Contractors," *Financial Times*, August 11, 2003.

[152] David Washburn and Bruce V. Bigelow, "Debate on Military Contractors Heats Up" *San Diego Union Tribune*, May 7, 2004.

the army's urgent need under critical wartime conditions. Indeed, in his March 2005 report on interrogation operations Vice Admiral Church specifically noted that civilian interrogators provided mission continuity that was not available from purely military resources.

In his 2003 book *Corporate Warriors*, the Brookings Institution's Peter W. Singer, a recent doctoral graduate who was a critic of military outsourcing, even observed that these specialist firms "build capabilities and efficiencies that a client [nation] military cannot sustain. The client's own military, in turn, can concentrate on its primary business of [war] fighting." Singer also pointed out that a growing number of firms were providing intelligence and information analysis. Noting that the private Pinkerton detective agency had been the primary source of intelligence for the Union forces in the U.S. Civil War, Singer observed: "Although it sounds somewhat shocking that private firms could undertake such roles, in a sense their growth is a throwback to the past." He surmised that the private intelligence business seemed to be in the initial stage of "a huge boom."[153]

The United States increased military outsourcing during the 1990's under the Clinton administration after the Cold War brought reductions in force size. Since the Persian Gulf War of 1991, contractors have played a vital role in every major U.S. military engagement. The Clinton administration, for example, turned to private firms like Kellogg, Brown & Root (KBR) and DynCorp to handle supplies and provide a variety of other field services in the Balkan conflict, rather than take the unpopular step of calling up military reserve forces.

"Only those functions that must be performed by the [DoD] should be kept by the [DoD]," a Pentagon study said in 2001.[154]

"It's an acceptance of what companies are already thinking in terms of core competencies. Do we need to have privates on KP duty slicing potatoes? Probably not. So I think this trend is just starting," said Ken Krieg, an adviser to U.S. Defense Secretary Donald Rumsfeld.[155]

---

[153] Peter W. Singer, *Corporate Warriors: The Rise of the Privatized Military Industry* (New York: Cornell University Press 2003), 97–99.

[154] U.S. Department of Defense, "2001 Quadrennial Defense Review Report," September 30, 2001.

[155] Nelson D. Schwartz, "The Pentagon's Private Army," *Fortune Magazine*, March 17, 2003.

During the first Gulf War in 1991, the U.S. deployed about one contractor for every fifty active duty personnel. During the conflicts in Bosnia and Herzegovina in the mid 1990s and Kosovo in 1999 that ratio increased to about 1 to 10, roughly the same ratio as at the outset of the Iraq war. By 2004, an estimated 20,000 contractors (not all of which were U.S. contractor workers) were put to work in Iraq.[156] By 2006, there were reportedly 100,000 contractors in Iraq (but most of these were not doing military combat-related work).[157]

In Iraq, and earlier in Afghanistan, the private firms took on new roles. Blackwater USA, a security consulting firm, for example, provided security forces responsible for the protection of other contractors as well as senior government officials. CACI had long provided traditional IT and network services and logistical property management support as well as intelligence analysis to the U.S. military, and was doing so in Iraq. But, for the first time, it was requested to also provide interrogation support. Other private firms were already providing interrogation services at Guantanamo Bay and Afghanistan.

There were risks that came with the government contractor work as with any war situation, and tragedies did occur. A number of contractors were killed or abducted. The most tragic and gruesome occurrence was the death of the four Blackwater employees who were killed and publicly mutilated, burned, and hung from a bridge near Fallujah in Iraq in April of 2004. The publicity surrounding the subsequent abductions and beheadings of Nick Berg and Paul Johnson was bringing the hazards of the contractor work to the forefront of the public's attention. According to the Department of Labor, some 650 contractor deaths had occurred in Iraq between March 1, 2003, and Sept. 30, 2006, and some 150 of these were believed to be American contractors.[158] By May 2007, the number of contractor deaths had risen to 917, at least 146 in the first three months of 2007 alone.[159]

---

[156] Deborah Avant, "Think Again: Mercenaries," *Foreign Policy*, July/August 2004.

[157] "Census Counts 100,000 Contractors in Iraq, Civilian Number; Duties are Issues," *Washington Post*, December 5, 2006.

[158] Bernd Debusmann, "In Iraq, contractor deaths near 650, legal fog thickens," Reuters, October 10, 2006.

[159] John M. Broder and James Risen, "Contractor Deaths in Iraq Soar to Record," New York Times, May 19, 2007.

The increasing contractor presence in Iraq generated significant debate in the United States even before Abu Ghraib because of concerns about the role of contractors in the government. Some argued that the government lacked a clear policy for military contractor relations, which they said contributed to a range of problems across Iraq, not just at Abu Ghraib. As would be logically expected, contracts were awarded from different offices and different agencies, and for different duties, tasks and requirements. At the time the Abu Ghraib abuses became public, nobody (apparently) could say for certain how many contractor workers the U.S. employed in Iraq. A General Accounting Office study in 2003 even chastised the Defense Department for its failure to establish policies for the use of contractors and how they interact with forces in the field.[160]

Deborah Avant, a George Washington University professor who studied the industry, wrote in the *Washington Post* on May 7, 2004: "There are no standard procedures for deploying private security workers under military contractors, which makes it far more difficult to gather information about who they are, what they're doing and for whom."[161]

"You've got thousands of people running around on taxpayer dollars that the Pentagon can't account for in any way," asserted Dan Guttman, a Fellow at Johns Hopkins University who teaches classes on government contracting.[162]

U.S. law asserts jurisdiction over American contractors employed by the Defense Department, but there is debate about its applicability if *non*-American contractors engaged by the Department are found guilty of law violations — and in Iraq thousands of the contractors were not Americans. However, this was not an issue for CACI, whose employees in Iraq providing intelligence-related services were all U.S. citizens with Top Secret, Secret, and Special Compartmental security clearances. But

---

[160] U.S. Government Accountability Office, "Military Operations: Contractors Provide Vital Services to Deployed Forces but Are Not Adequately Addressed in DOD Plans, GAO-03-695," June 24, 2003.

[161] Deborah Avant, "What Are Those Contractors Doing in Iraq?" *Washington Post*, May 7, 2004.

[162] Matt Kelley, "Pentagon Memo Warned in 2002 About Lax Oversight of Army Contractors" Associated Press, May 7, 2004.

the debate on all of these issues elevated substantially after the Taguba report had the effect of raising questions about the role of contractors at Abu Ghraib.

CACI had been a leading competitor in the government contracting industry and, over the last ten years, was part of the growth of government outsourcing. Indeed, its business strategy under London, including the decision to move into intelligence work, reflected the judgment that the needs would grow larger still and that the company would acquire a skilled and sizable workforce to address them. CACI employees, led by London, also felt deeply about their patriotic duty to support the U.S. military, including its effort in Iraq. The Iraq conflict was an opportunity to demonstrate this support, and CACI was ready to do its part. Moreover, CACI was willing to support its army client at the earliest, most undefined and unpredictable stage of the war, when the terrain was unknown and untried.

The first CACI employee engaged in Iraq-related activity had deployed from Germany to Kuwait in February 2003 along with the U.S. Army's V Corps as part of an ongoing arrangement for logistics support to V Corps' G4, which was preparing to participate in the invasion of Iraq. CACI's people (these were PTG, Inc. employees until May 15, 2003) crossed into Iraq with V Corps in March and traveled with it all the way to Baghdad. CACI's first intelligence support personnel, also attached to V Corps, flew to Iraq from Germany in June 2003 after the announced end of the major combat operations phase.

"We've been in this thing (Iraq) for the entire war. We had logistics people who deployed from Germany and went in with V Corps when the attack went on. We've been supporting this since February 2003. We didn't just come in after the troops were on the ground and start getting business," explained Mark Billings, who had been part of the CACI team that poured over interrogator resumes for a second look as part of the company's internal investigation of Abu Ghraib.

Contractor work scope under the V Corps G3/G4 task order that took the Premier Technology Group (PTG) of CACI to Iraq included providing support and assistance for "planning guidance, advice, and technical assistance in the development of operations plans and orders and time-phased force deployment data to support real-world contingencies and exercises." An additional task order supporting the V Corps

G2 called for "security input for the Division's anti-terrorism force and protection effort." Under a separate task order, USAREUR would be supported by an expert anti-terrorism analysis team provided by PTG.

PTG was acquired by CACI in May of 2003 — some two months before there was a confirmed need by the army for interrogation services — but after the PTG employees had gone into Iraq with the V Corps. The intelligence and support contract was initially awarded to PTG in 1998 under the General Services Administration schedule contract for information technology when the GSA Washington, D.C. office issued a limited competition Request for Proposal (RFP) for holders of a GSA IT Schedule to perform Intelligence Support to USAREUR G2. Later that year PTG's IT schedule was submitted to the Fort Huachuca Contracting Office in response to Huachuca's request to establish a Blanket Purchase Agreement (BPA) to streamline the procurement process. PTG was awarded a BPA on January 12, 1999. The BPA became the base document for numerous intelligence delivery orders supporting the U.S. Army in Germany, Italy, Bosnia and Kosovo. The contract was transferred to CACI in 2003 when it acquired PTG's assets. At the time of initial deployment to Kuwait, these employees were still on the PTG payroll and not employed by CACI. By the time two of these employees deployed to Iraq in June 2003, they were employed and being paid by CACI. Over time, the army tapped this contract to cover eleven separate task orders for CACI services in Iraq. Six of the orders involved intelligence work of which two were issued for interrogation services.

Although CACI's interrogation work captured public attention after the Abu Ghraib story broke, interviewing detainees was a smaller part of what the company was doing in Iraq. All told, CACI hired a total of three dozen interrogators between August 2003 to serve at various U.S. Army sites throughout Iraq, when it was first asked to provide this service, and in April 2004, when the Abu Ghraib photos were published. But at no time did the company have more than ten interrogators assigned and working at Abu Ghraib prison.

During that same period, CACI employed roughly 175 other people for a wide range of intelligence, technical, and project support work in Iraq. That number would grow appreciably in the following year. These employees provided intelligence support, background investigations, property management, and logistics record keeping. They supported the installation and management of computer systems and the software and hardware to support property management functions. By early 2004, CACI had about fifty logistics people spread across the country to help the army keep track of its property.

CACI also was providing a range of intelligence support and analysis services. CACI supported the military with more than a dozen "human intelligence support teams" that assembled and interpreted raw data located by the military in small unit operations. It also provided "open source intelligence," compiling public information from Iraqi and regional media into a daily newsletter called the *Mosquito* to help political and military officials understand what was on Iraqis' minds.

Although not accompanying the troops into combat, CACI's people worked twelve-hour days or longer, often seven days a week, to meet the needs of a military at war. They faced all the inherent risks of life in Iraq: mortar attacks, roadblocks, and shootings, including having windows shot out of their vehicles. When one government contract reviewer asked whether CACI qualified for higher, risk-based fees for its services, CACI answered with a photograph of the bombed out work area of one of CACI's logistics support employees. Some U.S.-based government officials who lacked firsthand experience in Iraq did not seem to fully understand or grasp the extent of what contractors were doing or the risks incurred from working in Iraq.

On the other hand, CACI's contract did not authorize employees to carry weapons. Nor did CACI provide armed security services. Most importantly, the company did not engage in any paramilitary or other type of "mercenary" war-fighter combatant work.[163]

After Abu Ghraib, the public disclosure that the army was using civilian interrogators triggered significant debate over outsourcing this work. The argument was fueled by the abuse scandal even though the pictures and charges were pointing directly to military personnel and not contractors. Some commentators argued that interrogation was the type of core military service that should be reserved for uniformed personnel. In this

---

[163] The word mercenary is often misused. According to the 2005 *New Oxford American Dictionary*, mercenary is defined as "a professional *soldier* hired to serve in a *foreign* army" [italics added]. CACI support to the U.S. Army cannot be described as "mercenary" under any circumstances. See also Glossary and Terms of Interest.

view, "tactical" intelligence involving immediate, on-the-ground combat-related activities such as a possible enemy attack, is simply too sensitive to be outsourced to contractors. But this was only one viewpoint and several government contractor companies continue to provide interrogation support services in Iraq, Afghanistan, and Guantanamo Bay.

There was another view. The Church report that would be released in March of 2005 would reveal that, in many cases, contract interrogators brought more experience and maturity to their work than their military counterparts. These comments and findings added weight to the view that there is considerable value from contractor support in this arena.

The commanders in Iraq, at the time CACI was contracted to provide interrogators, were intensely concerned about meeting their immediate needs for information. Given the vast and growing number of Iraqis in custody and the demand for army interrogators in Afghanistan and Guantanamo Bay, the army simply did not have enough trained interrogators to get the job done. Yet there were hundreds of U.S. civilians (citizens) who had interrogation related skills and experience that could be tapped to support the army — if they would indeed apply for the position.

"The sheer number of interrogation units is way down, personnel is way down, and the people they do have, except in reserve units, really haven't been concentrating on that part of the job," Major Thomas Barbeau, who headed an interrogation company in the 325th Military Intelligence Battalion, told *USA Today*.[164]

Indeed, the military had previously turned to contractors to assist with interrogation of prisoners at Guantanamo Bay and believed the system had worked well. As later noted in various government inquiries, the civilian interrogators at Abu Ghraib were in many regards, considered better qualified than their military counterparts. The civilians, for example, tended to be older and have more experience than those in uniform. They combined military experience and training with civilian work in interrogation. And contractors who lacked military interrogation experience often made up for it with considerable experience in related law enforcement work. Just as importantly, the contractors were highly valued because they often served longer tours than the soldiers (who in

---

[164] Kevin McCoy, "U.S. Missed Need for Prison Personnel in War Plans," *USA Today*, June 15, 2004.

2003 were serving six month tours) providing the continuity needed for successful intelligence gathering.[165]

For the CACI team, there was no hesitation when the call came from the army for interrogation support. After Abu Ghraib, some said CACI management had not sufficiently calculated the risks of the engagement aside from the physical dangers, but in August 2003, the assignment did not seem to involve the kind of unusually high-risk work that CACI would be inclined to avoid. To CACI, interrogation also seemed a natural extension of its intelligence support work — in particular, the specialty referred to as "human intelligence."

"Interrogation has gotten a bad connotation, but it's just another form of intelligence," said Billings. "It's just asking questions. It doesn't mean we are abusing people or mistreating them. It's another technique — asking questions — to save American lives."

The questions being asked were easily surmised. Where are the hostile forces? How many are there? Where do they come from? What kind of weapons do they have and how many? Where do they get their weapons? Answers to such questions have obvious immediate tactical value to U.S. military forces. Such information can — and does — save the lives of troops.

But as the Church Report later noted, "Military interrogators are trained to use creative means of deception and to play upon detainees' emotions and fears." Therefore, the report noted, those who are unfamiliar with interrogation might find it "offensive by its very nature."[166] That was especially true after the Abu Ghraib pictures were juxtaposed with discussions and reports about interrogation procedures, leading many, particularly those with little knowledge about such procedures, to conclude there was a direct link. The important goal of all interrogation efforts was essentially ignored — to discover information that is used to save lives and defeat the enemy.

Interrogation, initially, was not a line of business CACI anticipated or sought out. CACI did not have a corps of interrogators on the payroll. The army's request meant CACI would have to identify people with the

---

[165] The Army Inspector General would later report that CACI civilian contractors who had formal military interrogation training averaged 9.5 years of interrogator training experience prior to employment by the company.

[166] Church report, op. cit.

right skills for this new line of business. But when requested by the customer, providing these services seemed to CACI's decision-makers to make eminent sense in meeting an urgently requested need.

After all, CACI's team reasoned, the interrogators would be under army command, in a reasonably secure environment, operating under army rules of engagement in facilities run with military precision. Nothing in American military history or tradition would suggest that prisoner abuse, historically never a practice or a problem, under any circumstance might be a significant concern or that CACI's interrogators would be implicated. As London asked in wonderment months after the Abu Ghraib photos came to light: "Why would I even imagine such a thing?"[167]

In fact, from the company's perspective, in August of 2003 providing interrogators seemed far less risky than other services that might require contractors to travel across exposed terrain or provide logistical support to combat troops in the field. There were instances where fuel tanker convoys driven by contractors had been attacked with fatal results. And if personal safety were the considered criteria, providing interrogator support certainly seemed less risky than providing armed security guards.

Certainly the company was aware of the general risks to its employees in Iraq. In a war zone, nobody's personal safety can be guaranteed. In that regard, CACI had been fortunate. While 50 or more civilian contractors had died in Iraq as the spring of 2004 approached, none of CACI's employees had been killed; none had been taken hostage. And the company was thankful.

The possibility that an employee might be killed, while remote, seemed more likely to CACI than a breakdown in military discipline that would open the door to the abuses that took place in the photos at Abu Ghraib.

"We took great care thinking through how to handle a death. How to get a body out. How to notify the family quickly, so they wouldn't hear about if from the media," explained Harry Thornsvard, the senior vice president who had come to CACI when it acquired PTG.

If Thornsvard had any concern about the interrogator contract, it wasn't possible prisoner abuse, but rather, whether or not he could find enough of the right people to do the job.

---

[167] Liberated citizens and prisoners in WWII reported that when overtaken by the allies, they were relieved in cases where their captors were U.S. forces because of the fair and humane treatment they would receive by the U.S. military.

"There aren't a lot of people with these skill sets," he observed. There were fewer still that wanted to leave their families and live in an enemy prison camp environment thousands of miles away in war-torn Iraq.

Based on the army requirements spelled out in the Statement of Work, exacting standards were set by the Program Management Team for the recruitment effort. The army wanted people who already had the training and experience for the job, primarily the 97E MOS, the army's skill classification and code for interrogators. But other sources for these interrogator skills and experience were also deemed acceptable, such as from organizations like the FBI, CIA, DEA or major police departments. The army wanted people who could be familiarized with local conditions and then, after several successful interrogations side-by-side with an army interrogator, be trusted to assemble an interrogation plan and put it to work. Qualifying and screening recruits for the job would be intense and demanding. Every one of those hired must be a U.S. citizen, already possess an active government security clearance at the Secret or Top Secret level, and have passed the intensive background checks that these clearances entailed. These criteria assured the likelihood of hiring the right people.

As it turned out, given the high level of scrutiny required by CACI's hiring standards, the company was unable initially to find enough people to fill all the authorized interrogation positions. Of some 1,600 applicants, the company hired only three dozen that qualified as interrogators, were U.S. citizens with the required security clearances, *and* were also willing to go to Iraq. Many people just weren't readily available to go to Iraq. Not being able to fill all the requested billets also meant less revenue for CACI. "We left money on the table," Thornsvard said. But the company would only send people who had passed the screening, position criteria and job requirements.

And, for a variety of reasons, some of those hired didn't stay for the duration. Some simply didn't realize the degree of hardship they would have to endure. "There was a lot of hostile action. There were a lot of mosquitoes. No electricity at first, no hot meals, and you had to sleep outdoors," said Chuck Mudd, CACI's Division Vice President for the interrogation services in Iraq.

One interrogator resigned after a single day on the job because conditions were so bad. Another resigned because "he didn't like being mortared at night." Others went home early for family reasons. One new hire quit, ironically, because the company (acting on army security precautions) "wouldn't let him go sightseeing in downtown Baghdad," recalled Mudd.

Moreover, Abu Ghraib was quite obviously a dangerous place to work. None of CACI's employees were armed, and some who were concerned about their personal safety asked the company to send them handcuffs to restrain prisoners during interrogations. The company declined because sending restraints would have implied that the company was doing the MPs' job. Instead, CACI promptly requested that the army pursue the matter of the needed additional prisoner restraints.

The Statement of Work required the army to provide protective gear to contractors. But when the government's supplies at the departure center at Ft. Bliss ran short, the army authorized the company, to buy protective vests with bulletproof inserts themselves. "We didn't know how to do that when the first request came in, but we found a vendor in Pennsylvania who sold us five vests a week," recalls one CACI official.

After the Abu Ghraib scandal became public, recruiting and hiring interrogators to fulfill the army's contract became even more difficult for CACI. In July 2004, one counter-intelligence analyst supplied by a subcontractor, L-3 Communications Corporation, was released by L-3 with the explanation that a corporate decision had been made to cease work in Iraq due to the Abu Ghraib fallout and because L-3 corporate policy did not allow it to do interrogator work. Needing qualified staff, CACI subsequently hired that same analyst on July 30, 2004.[168]

Whatever the difficulties, nobody at CACI headquarters ever considered refusing the Iraq work needed by the army. Because the company was already under contract for intelligence services to units that had deployed to Iraq, it wanted to continue with the work that the army

---

[168] Ironically, exactly one year later L-3 was bidding to do full-scale interrogation work in Iraq, *after* the hostile prison environment had been stabilized and CACI had built up a quality team that clearly met the army's satisfaction in Iraq. This was evidenced by the fact that the army authorized this CACI team to stay in place in Iraq under the new contractor. And by then, the sensational aspects of Abu Ghraib had subsided.

needed to have done. Besides, the company team felt confident it could field the requirements. At a minimum, refusal to support the army could impact the bond of loyalty and commitment between the company and the army. In London's view and that of his team, the customer had to be able to count on CACI for the tough job.

In a company that employed military veterans, men and women who had taken an oath to serve and whose commitment to the oath remained, supporting the U.S. mission in Iraq was also viewed as a matter of duty.

"We are proud of our work in Iraq. This is clearly meaningful," said Thornsvard, a veteran with more than two decades of army service. And Mudd, a retired army colonel who spent a week every month in Iraq to check on CACI's people, said "dedication" was the main reason CACI's people were committed to staying on the job.

"Yes, they're making good money. But they are there because of dedication," Mudd noted. "It's a war zone and you pretty much have to be former military to do these jobs. But our interrogators are saving American lives. I feel pretty good about that. Otherwise I wouldn't be going back to Iraq all the time."

What's more, declining the work would have violated every one of CACI's core values. CACI's credo emphasizes "quality service" to its clients; its mission statement promises "solutions for our clients," its business values emphasize, "putting clients first." As to these values, Jack London believed them and lived them, and he surrounded himself with an executive team that shared them too. At the end of 2004, as he thanked his senior people for shepherding the company through the shadow of Abu Ghraib, London turned back to these foundation documents.[169]

"You have demonstrated a wonderful understanding of our commitment to our clients — we never leave their side," he said of the company's loyalty to the army.

"Of course CACI's Mission Statement and overall culture influenced our actions during this trying period. When we needed guidance we didn't have to look far. We looked to our valued employees, and our company values," London said as he recited the CACI values and the Credo, slowly and with passion.

---

[169] See Appendix D—CACI Corporate Philosophy: The Company's Foundation Documents.

"These are not just words," he assured them. "Because we follow this Credo we have built a great company." And he reminded his people: "We have pledged to 'always do the right thing.' It's this attitude that always sets us apart from others. Other companies may have abandoned their commitments when the going got tough. Not us."

Thus was CACI set upon the path to Iraq.

CHAPTER THIRTEEN

THE ECHO CHAMBER

Speculation: Everything and everyone suddenly under suspicion

**"Early in life I had noticed that no event is
ever correctly reported in a newspaper."**
∽ **GEORGE ORWELL**

NEWS STORIES ABOUT ABU GHRAIB BEGAN TO ROLL OUT IN WAVES
of discernible themes that would appear in numerous media outlets at roughly the same time. As they freely admit, reporters borrow
ideas from one another. That means the same issues bounce against one
another to create an echo chamber that tends to amplify each new
theme. The echoes grow louder as policymakers and commentators enter the discussion — creating more reverberations for another day's
story. For those in the news, like CACI, the cacophony of echoes means
multiple challenges in multiple venues, even as the clamor has already
filled the echo chamber.

Some of the issues that enter the echo chamber are predictable and
can be addressed with simple facts. Others arise without warning.
Unteathered from fact, some issues are barely more than conjecture
cloaked in journalistic form. Ironically, allegations of wrongdoing are
often the most difficult to lay to rest. As hard as it may be to prove that

something happened, it is often harder still to prove that it did *not* happen.

The fact that new investigations were getting underway in May 2004, including one specifically aimed at assessing the intelligence aspects of Abu Ghraib, seemed to have been lost on the media, which continually churned the past news of the Taguba report. The media apparently did not want to relinquish the opportunity to get more mileage out of an already "hot" story or to wait for the facts to emerge from the yet unfinished investigations.

As public discussions unfolded, attention moved to the question of "accountability." As if assuming that Taguba's suspicion of Stefanowicz and Titan employee Israel was tantamount to guilt, people wanted to know who would make sure that the contractors were punished for their alleged actions. This was the case regardless of the fact that no proof had been provided — no evidence, no testimony — nothing but unsubstantiated allegations. Still the questions came like a torrent. What laws would apply? Who would prosecute? And, in one of the more revealing questions, what was taking so long to exact a punishment? This implied a presumption of guilt, without waiting for the evidence to be set forth. The Taguba report continued to be viewed as the absolute truth and final word, unvarnished, unquestioned, and unchallenged. But at CACI, the view remained unchanged: all personnel actions would be based on fact.

Along with the questions also came endless theorizing. Some news stories hypothesized that the decision to employ contractors for interrogation reflected a deliberate attempt by the Bush administration, the military or, perhaps, the CIA to farm out the dirty work to civilians. This cynical theory held that because civilians were not covered by military law, they could escape scrutiny or prosecution if their behavior was deemed illegal.

As the *Financial Times* suggested on May 20, 2004 in a report that did not identify even a single source by name, "Several high ranking military legal officers believed the Pentagon used contractors to interrogate prisoners in Iraq and Afghanistan in a deliberate attempt to obscure aggressive practices from congressional or military oversight." At CACI, the company considered such comments and speculation dangerous and irresponsible.

The *Times* said it learned of the military lawyers' concerns from a "civilian lawyer" who was allegedly relaying complaints he said he had heard months earlier. According to the unidentified civilian lawyer's secondhand account (hearsay), the military lawyers presumably believed there was "a conscious effort to create an atmosphere of ambiguity, of having people involved who couldn't be held to account."[170] London and the CACI team couldn't help but feel that the *Times* was being driven by what seemed to be a rumor mill augmented by biases against the war, whether military or civilian in origin.

Or, as the *Guardian* speculated more precisely on its own accord just a week after the Abu Ghraib news first broke, "This legal grey area may well not be entirely accidental of course. It means private contractors can be used to do dirty work for the military or the CIA with plausible deniability and relative immunity."[171] This prompted London to ask, "How do people conjure up these absolutely absurd ideas?"

Although not directed specifically at CACI, such conjecture carried significant reputational risks for the company. To CACI, these Abu Ghraib stories implied that the alleged involvement of a CACI employee in abuses at the prison was part of a deliberate pattern of questionable conduct by the company. This abhorrent implication was particularly difficult to address. How could CACI or the military *disprove* speculation about what somebody may have intended when CACI was hired?

Yet by the traditional standards of journalism, there was nothing unusual about the *Guardian* or the *Times* stories. Shielding sources' identity enables journalists to collect information that would otherwise not be available and allows "whistle blowers" to reveal alleged misconduct without jeopardizing their jobs while at the same time providing a venue for disgruntled individuals to expose their biases in support of their personal or political agendas without consequence.

While there have always been laws against leaks, the premeditated, illegal disclosure of classified (e.g. Secret, Top Secret) information

---

[170] Joshua Chafin, "Contract Interrogators Hired to Avoid Supervision," *Financial Times*, May 21, 2004.

[171] Julian Borger, "The Danger of Market Forces," *Guardian*, May 6, 2004.

seems to have become common.[172] The Justice Department investigations exposed long-standing tensions. As one op-ed piece explained, "Government and the press are natural antagonists. Government wants to keep secrets, while the press wants to expose them."[173]

Nonetheless, for all of this, there was still no comment, no call to look into the facts surrounding the *illegally leaked* Taguba report, nor any apparent attempt to discover who had broken the law by divulging classified military information by putting the report in the hands of the press.

But all of this speculation was premature since charges had not been brought against any CACI employee and there was no evidence that had been presented — only allegations. In fact, military investigations were still underway, particularly the investigation that was assessing interrogators. Moreover, as London related to the press, "It's been reported to us that we're doing a fine job. That's from our customer (the army), and those are the people who count."[174]

The details of the CACI contract would also soon enter the echo chamber with words that the army's request for interrogators had been processed as a task order on a longstanding contract for information technology services. The contract, issued to PTG in 1998, had been converted to a U.S. government blanket purchase agreement (BPA) with the Interior Department and, in this case managed on behalf of the U.S. Army who received the services. The army paid the Interior Department for contract administration services performed by Interior employees based at the Interior's National Business Center located at Fort Huachuca, Arizona, which also houses the U.S. Army Intelligence Center.[175]

---

[172] The Espionage Act of 1917 stipulates that the *unauthorized* communication (both receipt and disclosure) and publication of information "relating to the national defense" is illegal [italics added].

[173] Peter Scheer, "Press freedom undermined by prosecutions," *San Jose Mercury News*, March 13, 2006.

[174] Mathew Barakat, "Contractor: Army Happy With Interrogators," *Guardian*, May 11, 2004.

[175] The Ft. Huachuca contract was a General Services Administration (GSA) Schedule 70 Contract for Information Technology Services and that was later converted to a blanket purchase agreement (BPA).

Federal government procurement regulations provide for BPAs as "a simplified method of filling anticipated repetitive needs for supplies or services by establishing 'charge accounts' with qualified sources of supply."[176] BPAs are designed to increase efficiency and may enable the contracting agency to receive volume discounts or other price benefits. This contracting procedure was in wide use throughout the U.S. government with many companies before 2003 and Iraq. There was nothing unusual about CACI's contract arrangement.

CACI inherited this GSA schedule contract, and BPA, as part of the assets it acquired (bought) from PTG in May 2003. Issued initially by the contracting office at Fort Huachuca (then an army contracting office), administration of the contract was transferred by the government to the Interior Department as part of the Clinton administration's efforts to streamline government. Also at that time, the contract was extended for five years until January of 2006. The BPA was modified in July 2003 to reflect CACI's acquisition of PTG assets.

News that CACI interrogators had been hired under an information technology contract raised eyebrows among those who did not know the history behind it. In some quarters, it seemed to substantiate the speculation that the army had hoped to hide the outsourcing of interrogation work. That the contract was actually administered by the Interior Department seemed to enhance suspicion among those who were already suspicious. Even London observed much later: "Heck, if I didn't know the legitimate background, that might have even sounded fishy to me." But the suspicions concerned him greatly because they fueled misperceptions and false allegations.

The contracting goal was speed, never secrecy. The agreement to use the existing BPA contract was approved by the army, which had worked with the contract officers at Fort Huachuca and wanted to get resources in place as fast as possible. The urgency was necessary to protect the lives of American soldiers not to support any imaginary secret agenda.

"The army was in a world of hurt. Troops were getting killed because we didn't have enough good intelligence," explained CACI executive John Hedrick, a twenty-eight-year army veteran whose business unit at

---

[176] U.S. Department of the Interior, *Blanket Purchase Agreements Handbooks*, September 2000.

CACI had absorbed PTG. Overwhelmed by thousands more detainees than it was prepared for and struggling to subdue an insurgency that was killing more American GIs than the Iraqi Army, the military was concerned about getting interrogators in the field — quickly.

On receiving final information about the army request for interrogators, CACI executives went directly to the army contract officers in Baghdad and Kuwait and asked the army to initiate a new contract process. But issuing a new contract would, apparently, require a lengthy and workload-intensive competitive bidding procedure. All parties knew that delays were unacceptable. CACI officials recalled later that the army officials in both places had responded with the question to CACI: "Do you have an existing contract vehicle?" CACI noted the BPA already in place at Interior which was currently providing intelligence support to the U.S. Army in Europe and the army said, in effect, "Let's go with it." It was a matter of efficiency and effectiveness, and never an attempt at evasion, nor could it be, as the contract was completely open and public.

The use of pre-existing contracts such as BPAs and large purchasing agreements known as "indefinite delivery-indefinite quantity" (ID-IQ) contract vehicles reportedly became a staple for the army as it worked with contractors to add resources in Iraq at a time of extreme need and urgency.

Over the BPA contract's life, Interior issued eighty different task orders to CACI, including eleven for work in Iraq. Of those, six involved intelligence work or interrogation at a combined worth of about $52 million — a significant amount of money, but still a relatively small amount for a $1.5 billion company like CACI. And this involved groundbreaking work CACI would have to do in a combat zone, during the early days of the war and during the height of the detainee collection activity in 2003. The $52 million effort would pale compared to the $450 million contract for these very same services the army was to later award to another company in July 2005.

After Abu Ghraib, when CACI's PTG contract first came under scrutiny, Interior Department spokesperson Frank Quimby insisted that the contract awards were appropriate because the interrogation work involved the use of information technology, including computer integration, data entry, and data processing.

"The Department of Interior received no indication . . . that anything was amiss with the contractor's performance," Quimby said at a news conference in late May, and he noted that an army representative had said just a week earlier that the military "is satisfied with CACI's personnel and performance."[177] CACI took very careful note of those statements.

But as the glare of scrutiny increased, Interior's defensiveness grew. Having defended both his Department and CACI's performance, Quimby then created new confusion. He announced that "in the interest of prudence," Interior would not allow the army to order any new services under the contract. Then he added that existing contracts would stay in place. The Associated Press misconstrued Quimby's announcement as a "suspension" that would block the hiring of new interrogators. The media's lack of knowledge about the government contracting arena, and their resulting mistakes, would be a continuing problem for CACI. The din of the echo chamber was growing louder.

At CACI, the events caused consternation, as it had not received any notice to stop work. The company hurriedly got clarification from Interior and, within an hour, was issuing its own statement to try and set the record straight. A fast correction was essential to calm investors lest the misleading news report drive share prices down further. "Any modifications, extensions, or additions to CACI's work will be the subject of separate contract actions," CACI's statement explained, "a number of which DOI [Department of Interior] informed the company are currently in process."

A new wave of media reports ensued which carried the same confused language that the Associated Press had put out. As a result of the media and DOI confusion CACI targeted media response letters were quickly launched to clear up the misunderstandings.

To the CACI team, it was one more significant mistake by a hasty media, and growing evidence that its corporate commitment to vigilance was going to be tested mightily. To the people at CACI it was all beginning to seem like a bizarre nightmare.

---

[177] "CACI Contracts Blocked; Current Work Can Continue," *Washington Post*, May 26, 2004.

CACI STANDS ITS GROUND

CHAPTER FOURTEEN

FALLOUT

CACI in the media glare is scrutinized from every direction

> **Sir, they [contractors] were not in any way
> supervising any soldiers, MP or otherwise."**
> ~ **MAJOR GENERAL ANTONIO TAGUBA, MAY 2004**

ALMOST OVERNIGHT, THE NEWS REPORTS ABOUT ABU GHRAIB triggered a defensive mechanism, a "self-interest" reflex in groups and individuals connected to CACI. For some, it may have seemed a matter of survival. Government contract officers, for example, began asking tough questions so they would not find themselves under fire for failing to exercise proper oversight. Agencies that had seemed satisfied with the company's performance before learning of Abu Ghraib suddenly were directing a stream of inquiries the company's way.

The Interior Department, which had approved every army request for CACI's services, (and well before that, all of PTG's contracts), distanced itself from CACI by ordering its own investigation of the contract management process. Barely a week after CACI's name first surfaced in public, contract officers at Fort Huachuca suddenly suggested that CACI may have hired "unqualified individuals" for interrogation — even though every person hired had been approved or agreed to by the army for work in Iraq. "Please identify the individuals involved with this particular task, and documentation of how they meet this requirement," the contract officers requested.

In Iraq, Major Anthony Daniels, the Baghdad-based contracting officer's representative responsible for CACI's work, met with the company's Abu Ghraib employees. Daniels came as a customer and a friend, not an adversary. He needed the CACI team's work to continue. He assured the civilians that their work was respected and appreciated, but he also cautioned that they could expect more scrutiny. Subsequent remarks to the employees by Major General Geoffrey Miller, who had been given responsibility for running the prison in May, were more pointed. Noting "difficulties in the past," Miller made clear he would run a tight ship. By all accounts, the prison environment had been chaotic at best. Miller's job: fix the situation and make Abu Ghraib better for soldiers, contractor civilians, and detainees alike. But for the CACI team, it may have seemed as much threat as promise. If there was any inclination to find scapegoats, who better than employees of the company that already had an accused employee? Some CACI employees believed that the Taguba report had, in effect, set them up to be scapegoats.

In England, CACI suffered its only business loss related to Abu Ghraib. One local government agency, the Gateshead Council, pulled a £90,000 contract because of the prisoner abuse allegations. The contract loss was discouraging because CACI's United Kingdom division was not engaged in Iraq and did not provide services to the military or intelligence agencies. It provided basic computer and technology services to its customer base of commercial business and local government.

Anxiety about additional losses seemed validated a week later with word that Adam Price, a member of Parliament, planned to ask U.K. Health Secretary John Reid to suspend all of the agency's contracts with CACI while investigations went forward. British taxpayers, Price said, would be upset to know that their money was supporting a company accused of "torture of prisoners."[178] At stake for CACI was some $1 million in Health Ministry contracts. To the relief of CACI, a meeting between Price and CACI's U.K. President in London, Greg Bradford,

---

[178] Kirsty Buchanan, "Block British Firm's Iraq Deals, says Plaid MP," *The Western Mail*, May 22, 2004.

defused the threat. Price agreed to hold off on his letter, though he urged CACI to abandon the interrogation business.

Back in the U.S., CACI withdrew from a competitive bid on an army contract for linguist services. "In light of the ongoing investigation of the treatment of prisoners in Iraq, we have regretfully concluded that any CACI submission would be clouded by allegations that a CACI employee has been implicated in the investigation. . . . [W]e do not believe this issue will be satisfactorily resolved by proposal submission and evaluation," CACI President of U.S. Operations Ken Johnson wrote in the withdrawal letter.

Additionally, fifteen minutes around the Washington Beltway from CACI's headquarters, the company was under review by the Calvert Group of mutual funds, which said it might drop CACI from its list of socially responsible firms because of the Abu Ghraib publicity. Calvert's "Social Index Fund," which invested only in companies that met its social responsibility criteria, had added CACI to its list of responsible companies just two years earlier. In a statement Calvert said its research department had recommended dropping CACI for falling short of Calvert's separate "human rights" and "weapons" criteria. As a matter of policy, Calvert did not invest in companies that make weapons. But dropping CACI on these criteria was puzzling because CACI had never dealt in arms and no one had ever been charged with any human rights violations. Yet Calvert's policies, posted on its Web site, stating that it avoided investments in companies with "a pattern or practice of human rights violations," suggested that Calvert, too, was accepting what was becoming a false and distorted characterization of CACI.[179]

Calvert's threat to drop CACI from its list of approved companies as well as the lost contract in the U.K. reflected an increasing tendency to equate an allegation toward an employee with pervasive corporate guilt in the court of public opinion. It highlighted the ability of the media to shape others' behavior. A Calvert investment director, Julie Gorte, admitted as much at the time. Without any direct evidence of the role played by CACI, Titan, or their employees, Gorte told Bloomberg News that the recommendation to drop CACI was based on "what we've all seen in the media in the past 10 days." Referring to the photos, Gorte

---

[179] Calvert Online, "Social Analysis Criteria" (http://www.calvert.com/sri_ib_21.html?) and "Issue Brief, Weapons" (http://www.calvert.com/sri_647.html).

concluded: "It's quite clear there was abuse in Abu Ghraib that wouldn't meet anybody's definition of human rights."[180] Gorte may have been right about Abu Ghraib, but no evidence linked CACI to the abuses.[181]

London's business advisor Burkhart explained the reason for the immediate tendency to pin blame on contractors. "With the intense emotions triggered by the pictures and descriptions of the abuses at Abu Ghraib, people had to direct their anger and negative feelings toward a target. And the most vulnerable target was the least well-known and most poorly understood group — the contractors. This would be the likely reaction, even though the faces and names that were emerging in the scandal were those of military personnel." She added that for many, "it would feel unpatriotic to blame the military or even the government during a war. But contractors — whom most people knew nothing about — are not associated with such emotions." To London, the analysis made sense. And he was watching it all play out in real life.

Another concern Burkhart raised was the impact the photos would have on viewers when shown in reference to CACI and contractors. In fact, the photos would continue to plague CACI. The pictures depicting the detainee abuse were frequently shown together on TV and in the print media with CACI's name, even though *none* of CACI's people were in the abuse pictures and *no* evidence had ever been presented to support the Taguba report's allegations. Concern mounted within CACI that people seeing the photos would immediately think "CACI" or "contractors," adding further to the perception of guilt by association.[182]

---

[180] Edmond Lococo, "Fund May Dump Firms Linked to Iraq Prison Scandal," *Bloomberg News*, May 14, 2004.

[181] CACI and Titan were removed from Calvert's Social Index in June 2004 along with fourteen other companies (eight because of mergers). Jeff Clabaugh, "AES and CACI Struck from Social Index," *Washington Business Journal*, June 14, 2004.

[182] This, indeed, turned out to be the case. By December 2007 and the publishing of this book, the preferred hate-media visualization of Abu Ghraib often wrongly associated with CACI, was the photo of a hooded detainee standing on the wooden box, cloaked in sack cloth, with arms outstretched and electric cords hanging from both arms. However, it was army Staff Sergeant Ivan "Chip" Frederick who had pled guilty to attaching electrical wires to a detainee's arms, forcing him to stand hooded on a box, and for photographing the detainee. CACI people were not shown in any of the notorious abuse photographs, and there has never been any facts or evidence offered anywhere to link any CACI person with them.

This was yet another challenge in managing the negative influence of the media.

CACI was hardly alone in falling victim to the presumption of guilt, but as a relatively unknown company it may have been more vulnerable. Better known companies often benefit from name recognition that gives them a foundation of goodwill to help minimize the sense of "guilt by accusation, association or proximity."

With the accused seemingly convicted in the public mind, pressure may grow for quick sanctions. Lengthy investigations are typically necessary to provide a clear picture of guilt and innocence. In CACI's case, impatience was manifesting itself with complaints about the slow pace of sanctions being leveled against the civilians that Taguba had named in his report on Abu Ghraib.

Yet, the case was already being tried in the media. Just days after the Taguba report became public, a *New York Times* report marveled that the companies had not yet removed any employees from Iraq.[183] Peter W. Singer of the Brookings Institution, in apparently failing to balance his opinions with the rule of law and employee rights, complained to news organizations that not only hadn't the civilians been prosecuted, but "none of them have even been fired yet."[184]

Singer was becoming more visible in public appearances following the *illegal* leak of the Taguba report, voicing his long-standing criticism of government outsourcing and Defense Department contractors. What Singer did not explain was on what basis he thought the companies should act in summarily firing employees. His view did not take into account issues associated with "wrongful termination" (firing) in an unsubstantiated, prejudicial, discriminatory manner. Less than a week after allegations about Stefanowicz and Israel had become public and with only a few sentences that said their employees were under suspicion, it was not clear that the companies had sufficient information to justify disciplinary action, like a prejudiced termination. But people working from second- or third-hand information who could give opinions without

---

[183] Joel Brinkley and James Glanz, "The Struggle for Iraq: Civilian Employees; Contract Workers Implicated in February Army Report on Prison Abuse Remain on the Job," *New York Times*, May 4, 2004.

[184] "Military Contractors Take the Heat," *Daily Dispatch (South Africa)*, May 7, 2004.

consequence to themselves spoke out freely with an air of certainty even as the facts were not yet known.

In any case, CACI was unable to get the necessary information for in-depth decision-making concerning the Taguba report's allegations. Repeated requests to the army for an official copy of the Taguba report had been fruitless. More importantly, CACI did not know what was in the 6,000 pages of the Taguba report "annexes" that presumably fleshed out the vague accusations pertaining to its employee in the fifty-three-page summary that had been posted on the Internet.

Ironically, the first copy of the Taguba report provided to CACI came courtesy of a reporter from National Public Radio (NPR). Apparently trying to be helpful, NPR's Ari Shapiro believed that CACI would have a better opportunity to answer questions if the company could see the document. Shapiro e-mailed the fifty-three-page document to Jody Brown, either not realizing or not concerned that for a government contractor, possessing a classified document without authorization was a breach of security.

Although assuming the gesture was well-intended, Brown's reaction was terse and unappreciative: "Crap!"

"I had to report to security, file a written report, and get my computer cleansed," Brown recalled with a wince.

Watching in horror as her computer was carted away for what she knew would be several hours of file clearing, Brown could only shake her head at the irony. In the midst of her most serious professional crisis, she had just lost one of her most important tools. "It was not helpful," was her understated assessment. She was not alone. Many at CACI thought that the irony of the company's compliance with security regulations in the face of journalists' abuses of the same was just "too much."

The incident also spoke to the cultural gap between the media and CACI. Journalists come to possess secret documents provided to them by a source that is breaking the law. To the journalists, the classified document is another piece of information — perhaps even more valuable because of its illicit nature.

But at CACI, the classification stamp carries the weight of law, respect, and principle. Some at CACI believed the media's disregard for the law and its inaccurate reporting on top of that were at the core of even deeper problems.

As far as London was concerned, leaking of classified materials was both illegal and wrong. He believed documents were classified to protect America's national security. As a young man, he had taken an oath to respect and protect such secrecy of information that could result in dangerous consequences if placed in the hands of America's enemies.[185] His company employed a significant number of former military people who had taken the same lifetime oath upon entering military service. To them, respect for classification stamps was not just a part of doing business, it was a way of life. Ultimately, the CACI team examined the version of the Taguba report that was posted on the Internet, but the fact remained — despite being leaked, it was still a classified report.

With that in mind, London persistently inserted the phrase *"illegally leaked"* whenever a CACI press release or statement discussed the Taguba report. To most journalists and probably a number of Americans, regrettably, the legality of the leak may not have been significant. But to London and his colleagues at CACI, the fact that a document was leaked and that a law had been broken was an *essential* piece of the story. It struck London as wrong for the journalists as well as those who had leaked the documents, to decide which laws to respect and which to break. This was going above the law. That was irresponsible and potentially dangerous, especially to the servicemen and women in Iraq.

Having finally read Taguba's conclusions, CACI still lacked the specifics of what had happened at Abu Ghraib. Details were presumably laid out in the annexes, including the testimony of every person Taguba had interviewed. What had Stefanowicz and other CACI employees told the investigators? What exactly had been said about Stefanowicz? Who had said it, and was there tangible physical evidence to support Taguba's suspicions and allegations? This was vital information for CACI's own investigation and also for London's assessment of what steps management should take.

---

[185] When the secrecy of "need to know" is breached, the loss of life in times of war can be expected. Consider how deadly fallacious reporting can be. *Newsweek* magazine's false portrayal and misrepresentation of Koran abuse at Guantanamo Bay, Cuba, in the late summer of 2005 reportedly resulted in numerous riots and at least seventeen deaths. Despite this destructive outcome including the tragic loss of life, *Newsweek* suffered no material consequences for its inexcusable, incompetent, and damaging reporting.

CACI was under fire for not moving fast enough against Stefanowicz. But to CACI management and its advisers, punishment was premature and unsupportable without a bill of particulars and the evidence to back it up. The CACI team was working hard on its interviews with its people in Iraq. It was reviewing every bit of internal documentation, every email and every letter it possessed. But that process would move faster if London and his advisors knew what evidence Taguba had.

As it worked to put the pieces together, CACI continued to make its case in the media. He felt his way carefully at first, but with each discussion, London became more comfortable. The uncertainty about what happened at Abu Ghraib persuaded him to take extra care with his words. Not knowing the hand he was holding, London was careful. As concerned about avoiding missteps as in making his points, he answered questions, but limited his commentary.

Day by day, as he grew accustomed to the journalists' style and more confident that CACI — as a company — was not culpable concerning the Abu Ghraib scandal, his normal forcefulness returned. He began to see the media interviews less as an exercise in answering questions than in delivering his messages. He began to think of the conversations with reporters as part of CACI's strategic decision to make sure the public record was accurate. The interviews became a chance to advance his agenda of correcting media mistakes and finding the truth — just one more part of building CACI's business and preparation for the company's "comeback" from the negative publicity.

Determined that the journalists should hear and understand certain key points, London would cut off the reporters' interruptions. "I'm going to have my say," he insisted and ticked off his main points:

- ☐ We have not heard anything directly or officially from the army about any misconduct.
- ☐ These are unsubstantiated and unproven allegations, not charges.
- ☐ We do not tolerate illegal conduct, and we will act quickly if evidence shows one of our workers has been guilty of breaking the law.
- ☐ We are cooperating fully with all government investigations.
- ☐ In America, people are innocent until proven guilty; we believe in due process and the rule of law.

□ The army in the field has been pleased with our performance at Abu Ghraib and elsewhere in Iraq.

□ We continue to support the U.S. mission in Iraq, and we are proud to serve.

Whatever the question, London learned to return always to this same set of points — convinced that if he could say it often enough, to enough reporters, eventually it would show up in their news reports. If the media would report the facts and resist speculation and spin, he believed the world would finally understand that CACI acted professionally and responsibly.

London always thanked the journalists for their time — even though he was certainly one whose time was incredibly stretched. He also thanked them for a willingness to listen, though over time he became less convinced that they would accurately relate what he said. At the same time, he would find the occasional need to subtly put them on the defensive and take them to task for their own missteps.

Questioned about his trip to Israel and the wild speculation that CACI's interrogators had been trained in torture by Israel's Mossad agents, London bristled when Tom Squitieri of *USA Today* half-jokingly suggested his visit to Israel was a "recruiting" call.

"I think that's a little over the top," London objected. "I understand you're joking. But that's the kind of stuff that's going around; you've got to understand I take this very seriously. I've got a public corporation with public shareholders, I've got 9,500 hardworking people trying to do a good job for the country," London lectured, as the backpedaling journalist insisted: "It was a joke, I was joking," pleaded Squitieri.[186]

---

[186] Tom Squitieri, a sixteen year veteran of *USA Today*, resigned under pressure in May of 2005 after the paper learned he had lifted quotes from another newspaper (*the Indianapolis Star*, owned by Gannett, the same parent company as *USA Today*) for a front-page story and used several other quotes, without attributing them to other publications, that were later cut during editing. (Howard Kurtz, "USA Today Reporter Resigns, Tom Squitieri Used Other Papers' Quotes," *Washington Post*, May 6, 2005.) Squitieri soon joined Dittus Communications, a Washington, D.C. public relations firm, as a senior media adviser in July of 2005. In an ironic twist, Jody Brown received a letter and package of marketing materials from Squitieri offering their PR services to CACI.

In another characteristic exchange to another reporter who impatiently interrupted his answers, London sternly countered: "I need to explain the story to you so there will be at least one person who knows what's going on."

The company also remained alert for specific issues requiring quick response. One recurring challenge was media reports, beginning in early May, about CACI advertisements for interrogators who could work under "minimal supervision." As CACI explained on its web site: "We use the terms 'under minimal supervision' and 'under moderate supervision' in our job descriptions to communicate that we are looking for highly responsible individuals with a comprehensive understanding of the requirements of the position and the ability to work without continuous and specific instruction in the details of how to perform the job. These phrases are not intended to imply that employees are left unsupervised so they can violate laws or commit wrongful acts."[187]

In a teleconference with financial analysts, Ken Johnson said the supervision language simply indicated that, "they're going to have to operate without day-to-day or minute-to-minute supervision from a CACI manager." He added, "We've been hammered and indicted in the press about that. But it's a fairly simple, unremarkable statement in terms of the levels of seniority and the kind of people that we provide over there."[188]

The phrase's meaning was misinterpreted and distorted by reporters to suggest that CACI's interrogators would have free rein without regard to military direction. It was an angle that different reporters repeated throughout the summer. Each time it came up, London corrected the misinterpretation, and it was consistently addressed in the targeted media response letters sent out by Burkhart and Hur. This information had

---

[187] The term "minimal supervision" is commonly used in job descriptions by companies in the same manner that CACI used the phrase and to convey the same meaning (e.g., no need for constant observation or the need to watch over the employee continually in doing a job). However, in CACI's case, these terms were taken out of context and given a different interpretation by those critics and activists who were putting forth the notion that there was no oversight or supervision of CACI employees. In fact, CACI employees reported to and were supervised by the army chain of command. They received administrative and personnel function supervision from CACI management (e.g., pay and benefits, leave and travel, living accomodations).

[188] CACI teleconference call with Wall Street analysts, May 27, 2004.

also been posted on CACI's Web site on its Iraq FAQs section. But no matter how hard CACI pushed back, it couldn't seem to put the matter to rest.

Pointing to congressional testimony from Secretary of Defense Rumsfeld, and then acting secretary of the army Les Brownlee, and Lieutenant General Lance Smith, London said in a press release distributed by CACI on May 9: "As stated, CACI employees are monitored and are under the supervision of U.S. Army personnel."[189]

The CACI release also quoted the sworn testimony of Brownlee: "And these people [civilian interrogators] had no supervisory capabilities [authority] at all; they work under the supervision of [army] officers in charge or non-commissioned officers in charge of whatever unit they are in."

Those skeptical about the Bush administration and Pentagon leadership may have regarded Brownlee as an unreliable source. But Taguba himself would offer a similar report in his own Senate testimony two days later.

In responding to Senator Daniel Akaka's question during the May 11, 2004 Senate Armed Services Committee Hearing on Iraqi Prisoner Abuse about Taguba's suspicion "that two contractors were either directly or indirectly responsible for the abuses at Abu Ghraib: Were either of these contracted personnel supervising soldiers or in a position to direct soldiers to take specific actions?" General Taguba stated under oath, "Sir, they were not in any way supervising any soldiers, MP or otherwise."[190]

This was an astonishing statement, given the sparse language on page 48 of his 53-page report that was now out in the public domain. To the careful listener, the question immediately becomes: What then does

---

189 CACI Press Release. "CACI Emphasizes Facts Presented During Congressional Testimony on Iraq Prison Investigation and Requirements Related to Company's U.S. Military Contract, No information on improper behavior reported to company by U.S. Government; Company does not tolerate illegal behavior by employees." May 9, 2004. Original testimony from the U.S. Senate Armed Services Committee's Hearing on the treatment of Iraqi Prisoners on May 6, 2004.

190 Testimony of Major General Antonio M. Taguba; Stephen A. Cambone, undersecretary of defense for intelligence; and Lt. General Lance Smith, deputy commander of Central Command, before the Senate Armed Services Committee, May 11, 2004 (http://wid.ap.org/transcripts/040511iraq_senate.html).

Taguba mean in his allegations against Stefanowicz? Did he participate in directing the infamous behavior or not?

Taguba clearly stated in his testimony that the contractors, presumably to include Stefanowicz and Israel, were not supervising military personnel. Therefore, logically they could not have directed any actions.

Taguba's testimony clearly did not appear to confirm his earlier report about Stefanowicz with any degree of conviction.

Nonetheless, the damage had already been done. CACI was squarely in the media glare. As noted by Brian Williams of *NBC News*, "Media attention is often like the spotlight in a prison yard. When it's on you, it's blinding."[191]

---

[191] CNN Interview with Brian Williams, December 4, 2005. (http://transcripts.cnn .com/TRANSCRIPTS/0512/04/rs.01.html).

CHAPTER FIFTEEN

WHAT TO DO ABOUT STEVE?

Behind the name, in front of the world

> **"We will not condemn any employee prematurely on the basis of unproven allegations, rumor, speculation or incomplete investigations. No lynch mobs."**
> ∼ JACK LONDON, OP-ED, AUGUST 19, 2004

O F ALL THE QUESTIONS BEFORE JACK LONDON, NONE WOULD BE more persistent or have a greater short-term influence on public discussion of CACI than what to do about Steve Stefanowicz, the one CACI employee singled out in the Taguba report.

London now believed firmly that press reports overstated what Taguba had concluded about Stefanowicz, and that Taguba's carefully chosen words suggested that the conclusions he reached about Stefanowicz relied more on speculation than evidence. London's belief was supported by advisor Burkhart's analysis of the situation.

But the media shorthand and the public understanding was that Taguba had "found" that Stefanowicz was somehow responsible for what the MPs in the photos had done. This interpretation was also being used as an argument by the defense attorneys in the Abu Ghraib courts-martial proceedings who were attempting to shift blame from their clients. But in the trials, the Taguba mislabeled "finding" was never introduced. In fact, Stefanowicz was not called or deposed in any of the proceedings. Nevertheless, that perception — Taguba's "finding" — created immense public pressure on London in 2004 to make a clean break between Stefanowicz and CACI. Taguba *had* recommended in his report that Stefanowicz be fired.

But, as a CEO of a public company, London had corporate responsibility. He was obligated in his duties to make defensible decisions based on sound judgment and reliable information. He could not yield to pressure and allegations alone. He made it clear: there would be no lynch mobs at CACI. He would continue to reiterate this position in the coming months stating firmly: "We will not condemn any employee prematurely on the basis of unproven allegations, rumor, speculation or incomplete investigations."[192]

London's reluctance to condemn Stefanowicz had consequences. To critics, his stance suggested indifference to the abuses at Abu Ghraib. To London's colleagues at CACI who knew their principled CEO, it was one of his finest hours.

There is little doubt that firing Stefanowicz would have deflected criticism of CACI and likely won it applause for moving quickly to address its employee's alleged complicity. But this action was *not* "the right thing to do."

In fact, to London, the public demand — without seeing the evidence or hearing the man's defense — was extremely unsettling. London firmly believed that in America people are presumed innocent until proven guilty. He wanted to see solid evidence before imposing a *permanent* punishment — potentially damaging a man's career and ruining his reputation. In his mind, the core principles of fairness and law didn't disappear just because Stefanowicz had been publicly accused.

While London had committed to act quickly if the evidence showed any CACI employee had broken the law, he was insistent on firm evidence of misconduct before he acted against Stefanowicz.

The first caution flag for London was the mistakes in the Taguba report. The report had misspelled names and associated employees with

---

[192] Jack London, "Angelides Takes Wrong Tack With CACI Investment," *The Sacramento Bee*, August 19, 2004. See Appendix I for the full text.

the wrong companies. Those mistakes could be ascribed to carelessness and might not affect the fundamental conclusions. But in London's experience, small mistakes often suggested larger errors.

"One thing that jumped out at me real quick was that if the report got these things wrong, what other mistakes might be in there?" London explained. "Maybe all this isn't quite what Taguba says it is." Confusion about peoples' names and companies could also mean confusion about who did what and when?

And London kept in the forefront of his mind what the media and the public ignored: that Taguba's report was only one in a series of investigations. Several other investigations were getting underway, including one aimed specifically at the military intelligence group in Iraq, including the interrogators. London's own military background made him acutely aware of the importance and value of this thorough and unbiased investigative process.

Difficult as it was to bear the negative publicity, London held his ground and waited patiently for the investigative process to complete its course. He was not going to give in to the public pressure, the media hype, or his own discomfort.

London was adamant about finding out what happened at Abu Ghraib. But he was not convinced by the Taguba report with its shortfalls, including the lack of any specific evidence against Stefanowicz. London remained resolute while digging in his heels and waiting for the investigative process to draw factual conclusions. Unfortunately, this would take many more months.

Reconciling the demand for action concerning Stefanowicz with the lack of facts to support such action was one of the most difficult challenges for the CACI leaders. "Don't think it didn't cross my mind," London said later when asked about firing Stefanowicz, "That would have been a slam dunk that made a lot of our issues go away. But we were hearing a lot of inconsistencies."

Furthermore, London did not want to be seen by his worldwide workforce, especially in Iraq, as a manager who would fire people without justifiable reasons and supporting factual evidence. This just wasn't going to happen.

Because of the photographs, many journalists seemed to turn off the skeptical side of their nature and treated Taguba's conclusions as final.

London sensed this was not right. Neither General Taguba nor the journalists drew clear distinctions between the actions captured in the photographs and other alleged misconduct, including misdeeds that allegedly involved contractors — a failure that was unfair and damaging to those cited.

Despite the inconsistencies in his report, it was hard to find any journalist who publicly asked whether Taguba presented a complete and accurate picture. They failed to note that Taguba's investigation focused on the MPs — not the interrogators — and that the investigations of interrogators would be the subject of a separate, upcoming report. Notwithstanding their focus on Abu Ghraib, the media overlooked the errors and the lack of supporting details of the Taguba report and ignored other investigations, showing a real lack of journalistic integrity.

In fact, despite Taguba's suspicions, the army appeared more than satisfied with CACI's civilian interrogators' work. Even as others questioned whether civilians should be conducting interrogations, the army provided positive feedback on CACI's performance and requested more CACI interrogators, not fewer. These signals raised further questions by the CACI team about the basis for Taguba's allegations.

Few news accounts made any note of an earlier report by the army's Provost Marshall General Donald J. Ryder on detentions and corrections in Iraq, a secret army document that Taguba cited at length and disagreed with in some important aspects.[193] The fact that two army reports about the same matter came to different conclusions should have cautioned journalists. Most did not even reference the earlier Ryder report even though Taguba himself had discussed it extensively. It was as if the Ryder report didn't exist or matter to the media.

Further, many news stories were careless in their descriptions of what Taguba said, drawing firm conclusions that went well beyond Taguba's words. For example, Taguba wrote that he "suspected" two military intelligence officers and two contractors of responsibility, but many news stories exaggerated this statement reporting that he had *found* them responsible. Perhaps signaling the lack of definitive evi-

---

[193] "Report on Detentions and Corrections in Iraq," also known as the Ryder report, was written by Donald J. Ryder, the Provost Marshall General of the Army. The report was completed in November of 2003 but was not publicly released until October 15, 2004.

dence, Taguba wrote that Steve Stefanowicz "allowed and/or instructed" MPs to facilitate interrogations in unauthorized ways. The difference between allowing something to happen and instructing somebody to do something is in fact vastly different and quite significant. News reports generally did not take note of this substantial difference, nor did they note Taguba's lack of clarity.

These allegations are particularly disturbing because Stefanowicz, as a government contractor and individual, was not in any position of authority to instruct, allow, disallow, or prevent the MPs' actions.

Later, in Senate testimony, Taguba said that the MPs were "probably influenced" by others — presumably including the contractors. While conceding that the contractors did not supervise the MPs captured in the infamous photos, Taguba said the MPs regarded the contractors as "competent authority."[194] To London and his colleagues, these vague and somewhat contradictory allegations were not the solid evidence they believed necessary to fire Stefanowicz. Taguba's testimony only exacerbated the situation.

Taguba's choice of words, on the other hand, may have reflected his understanding of the forums in which he was operating. His written report was not intended for public consumption. It was drafted for internal use by the military to supplement ongoing investigations, raise further questions for investigation, and help guide its future policy decisions or the bringing of charges.

Under oath in a public forum, Taguba stuck very carefully to what he *knew* to be true. While he seemed to surmise that the MPs had been "probably influenced," he did not elaborate with proof. This all, again, seemed to be speculation or "suspicion" — without concrete evidence.

Still the media did not pursue the Taguba report with anything close to a critical eye. Journalists never considered whether, in writing his report, Taguba's choice of words may have been influenced by the assumption that it would remain a classified internal document. Nor did the media note the indications of ambivalence. Introducing that kind of nuance would have significantly complicated the clean story line.[195]

---

[194] Testimony of Taguba et al., op. cit.

[195] Toward the end of 2004, London even thought about contacting Taguba himself to better understand the basis of the allegations, but decided against it concluding it was not his position to do so.

Worse still, careless paraphrases in some news reports attributed things to Taguba that the report simply did not say. For example, an Associated Press story wrongly stated that the Taguba report said Stefanowicz "ordered soldiers to abuse prisoners."[196] Another example was a lengthy May 9, 2004, article in the *New York Times* that referred to the August 2003 arrival in Iraq of "a team of civilian interrogators led by Steven Stefanowicz."[197] But Stefanowicz did *not* arrive at Abu Ghraib until October and, when he did, he was *not* a team leader. At the time of his arrival, he was not even an interrogator — he was a screener.[198]

Where the media was careless, London could not be. He was accountable for his decisions. London appreciated the value of a free press as one of the foundations of American liberty, but just as government had a system of checks and balances, shouldn't there be some way to hold the media accountable for its mistakes? After all, he reasoned, other professionals (ranging from attorneys and doctors to electricians and hair stylists) are governed by industry codes of conduct or professional or government licensing requirements. They have to demonstrate knowledge in prescribed areas and prove a basic level of competence to enter their fields, and they can lose the right to practice their professions if they make mistakes or violate ethical canons. Licenses could be revoked by their governing bodies for causing harm in the practice of their professions. During trips to the United Kingdom, London had become familiar with the Press Complaints Commission, an independent body which deals with complaints from members of the public about the editorial content of newspapers and magazines. A free and efficient service in the UK, London wondered if such a self-regulatory mechanism would work in the U.S.[199] But it seemed to him that journalists were only governed by their own directives and disparate traditions.

Journalists' words carried enormous weight, and London was convinced that not enough of them truly recognized the responsibility that should rightfully accompany this power. London believed that the

---

[196] Kelley, op. cit.

[197] Jehl and Schmitt, op. cit.

[198] Steve Stefanowicz: Arrived in Baghdad — 10/06/03; Arrived in Abu Ghraib prison and began work as a screener — 10/07/03; Returned to U.S. — 5/16/04.

[199] The Press Complaints Commission is discussed in further detail in the CEO's Post Script.

collective coverage of the Taguba report was, in effect, convicting Stefanowicz before the facts were even examined. At the same time, London wanted it to be clear that he was prepared to act against Stefanowicz if the evidence showed it was the right thing to do. It was a difficult balance to maintain as the media pressure mounted.

London reiterated emphatically that CACI would not condone, tolerate, or in any way endorse improper behavior by its employees, and he would take swift action if the evidence demonstrated Stefanowicz was culpable of wrongdoing. To him, however, the facts were a prerequisite for action.

The information from CACI's people and their military contacts in Iraq painted a more positive picture of Stefanowicz than the Taguba report did. It also suggested that the military itself was not convinced of Taguba's preliminary conclusions about the civilian contractors at Abu Ghraib.

In fact, Taguba himself, in an apparent contradiction to the language of his own report, shifted focus and culpability away from the contractors in his May 11, 2004 testimony to Congress. In response to questioning by Virginia Senator John Warner "How did this happen?" Taguba replied, "Failure in leadership . . . lack of discipline, no training whatsoever and no supervision."[200]

And in response to West Virginia Senator Robert Byrd's question, "who gave the order to soften up these prisoners . . .?" Taguba responded, "Sir, we did not find any policy or a direct order given to these soldiers to conduct what they did. . . . We didn't find any order whatsoever, sir, written or otherwise, that directed them to do what they did."[201]

Yet Stefanowicz remained prominent, and was repeatedly called out as a central figure in the media coverage and in the perception of the public.

Who was Steve Stefanowicz anyway?

The second of four children, Stefanowicz was born in 1970. A high school basketball player in suburban Philadelphia, the six-foot, five-inch Stefanowicz was the tallest member of his high school graduating class. Friends say he was popular in high school, a natural leader who participated in a wide range of activities, including basketball. Later,

---

[200] Testimony of Taguba et al., op. cit.

[201] Ibid.

associates at CACI described him as smart and charismatic, with an engaging presence.

A 1995 graduate of the University of Maryland, Stefanowicz joined the
Navy Reserve in 1998 where he was assigned to the Naval Reserve Joint
Intelligence Center in Jacksonville, Florida. While in Florida, he also sold
recreational vehicles like motorcycles and jet skis in Panama City.

The Reserves would take Stefanowicz to Afghanistan in 2000 for a
short-term assignment. Later that year Stefanowicz moved to Australia
where he worked as a job recruiter for Morgan & Banks and specialized
in filling information technology positions.

As a naval reservist, Stefanowicz had volunteered for active duty after the September 11 terrorist attacks. Returning from Australia after
eighteen months, he was posted to the Middle East. Stefanowicz spent
the better part of a year as an intelligence specialist in Muscat, Oman,
and won a medal for meritorious service. He joined CACI after muster-
ing out of the service in September 2003.

As events unfolded over the publicity about Abu Ghraib and certain
people emerged as key figures, London asked Burkhart to provide
thumbnail psychological profiles, sketches, on certain people in order to
better understand and gauge their behavior and motivations. While they
were done with third-party sources and never intended to be in-depth
or comprehensive analyses, London had come to find Burkhart's profiles
insightful and informative.

In the case of Stefanowicz, the bulk of information that Burkhart re-
searched and evaluated contradicted rather than supported the accusations against him. What Burkhart found was the profile of an individual
who appeared cooperative, compliant, and more likely to follow the
rules than to break or bend them. She ascertained that he was used to
working in structured situations that required taking orders and carrying
out directions and, in fact, had received commendations for his service
orientation.

Burkhart noted quotes from others, most of whom described
Stefanowicz in positive terms — which she considered a telling piece of
information given the public accusations against him. He was described
as a "team player" and "patriotic." Burkhart observed that his former
girlfriend was quoted as saying, "He's American through and through"
and "There's nothing in his behavior that makes me think he was capable

of doing this" (referring to the abuse accusations). She added that after September 11, he left Australia to voluntarily return to active duty. Phoning his reserve commander, Stefanowicz was reported to have said, "Do you want me home? If so, tell me when and I will leave immediately."[202]

Army Chief Warrant Officer John D. Graham, an interrogation operations officer at Abu Ghraib, said of Stefanowicz: "He was arguably one of the best that we had. He was very perceptive in his conversations with detainees. What Major [General] Taguba had said didn't match anything I had observed with Steve — didn't sound like Steve at all." Graham stated that Stefanowicz never interrogated a prisoner alone and he never saw Stefanowicz give orders to soldiers.[203]

One comment from a former employer stood out in particular for its description of Stefanowicz as "the most reliable, straight-up-and-down, good human you could imagine, gentle as a lamb."[204] These were words far and above what an employer would typically use or volunteer in describing an employee, Burkhart noted. These types of statements revealed the way Stefanowicz was viewed by people who knew him.

But it was Stefanowicz's own words, according to Burkhart, that held the most clues about him. In his sworn statement, Stefanowicz referred to "approved interrogation plans" and "interrogation rules of engagement."[205] He repeatedly emphasized the review and approval process and cited "specific and detailed rules required for implementation." He consistently spoke of assignments that needed to be "written out in detail for each day" and "approved through the appropriate chain of command." He referenced "a copy of the detailed, written program that they receive and keep on record in the office," and told of adhering to

---

[202] Susie O'Brien, "My Man Was No Torturer, Accused Was a Patriot, Says Ex" *The Herald Sun (Sydney)*, May 10, 2004.

[203] "Family and Friends Close Ranks Around Civilian Interrogator," *Washington Post*, May 14, 2004.

[204] Joel Brinkley, "9/11 Sent Army Contractor on Path to Abu Ghraib," *New York Times*, May 19, 2004.

[205] Taguba Annex # 90 Testimony of [Mr. Steve Stephanowicz-Redacted] [sic] US civilian contract interrogator, CACI, 205th MI Brigade (http://www.aclu.org/torturefoia/released/a90.pdf).

"approved rules of engagement and proper treatment of the detainee."
Asked under oath if he knew of any type of pictures that showed abuse
of detainees, Stefanowicz succinctly replied, "No." His reference to
rules, approvals, and consideration for the detainees gave Burkhart further reason to doubt the validity of the accusations leveled against Stefanowicz, especially those suggesting a direct, active, or independent
role. Burkhart's analysis was enough to raise questions about Taguba's
conclusions — but far from proof of any kind.

But her independent assessment was backed up by other sources.
London was told by CACI's team that soldiers in Iraq had said that
"Steve went out of his way to ensure the safety and well-being of prisoners." And that "Steve would cover a prisoner he was interrogating with
his own body when a mortar attack would occur during an interrogation." According to this account, Stefanowicz reported at least one person for improper treatment of prisoners and relayed his concerns about
mistreatment of detainees to higher ups. The team also reported that,
"Steve's interrogations were always monitored by military personnel and
that Steve had mentioned to higher-ups in the past that he didn't agree
with how the MPs handled the prisoners."[206]

And when CACI went to its army contacts in Iraq, Stefanowicz got
good reviews despite the Taguba report. "To our amazement, they were
positive and supportive," London said. "There was a gross inconsistency.
You've got Taguba, and then we're told something else by the folks who
are working with Stefanowicz, who seem to be saying 'we're glad to have
this guy on the job.'" These were army personnel with excellent reputations, and whose opinions were highly reliable.

Further backing up the compliments from the field was the job
record, which suggested good work. Stefanowicz had soon progressed
from screener to interrogator with on-the-job training in Iraq. With the
army's approval, he had been promoted to site manager for the CACI employees at Abu Ghraib only a few months after his statement to Taguba,
and just a month before Taguba's report became public in April 2004.

At no time, before or after the Taguba report, did CACI ever receive
a complaint from the army customer about Stefanowicz or any indication that he would not be welcomed back as an interrogator at Abu
Ghraib.

---

[206] Internal CACI e-mail from Scott Northrop, May 16, 2004.

This more favorable view of Stefanowicz was reinforced by a little noticed *New York Times* article mentioning that Stefanowicz had reported a military intelligence interrogator for making a prisoner walk naked down a cellblock in an attempt to humiliate the detainee. Quoting soldiers, the newspaper said Stefanowicz "had not thought stripping detainees was an appropriate interrogation technique."[207] Another reporter in early May related a virtually identical account of the incident and said military intelligence soldiers had described Stefanowicz as "a whistleblower."

Similarly, Army Chief Warrant Officer John D. Graham, who was *not* interviewed by Taguba, told the *Washington Post* that Stefanowicz "voiced some concerns about certain things going on, concerning treatment of the detainees." He added, "We brought those issues to a higher-up and somebody who works with us went over to talk with the [military officials] to see what was going on."[208]

* * *

But the company also needed to hear directly what Stefanowicz had to say. CACI's outside legal counsel personally met with Stefanowicz as he returned to the U.S. from Iraq in May of 2004. And the lawyers, veterans of investigations and litigation, concluded he was "believable."

In the CACI teams's mind, the army's overall silence on Stefanowicz suggested doubts about Taguba's conclusions. If Stefanowicz was a troublemaker, or a ringleader that the Taguba report inferred he was, why was there no outcry from the army in Iraq? It simply didn't add up.

Ironically, too, Taguba's report suggested that Stefanowicz lied in his statement to him, raising the question as to how Taguba came to doubt Stefanowicz in spite of the otherwise glowing reports about the employee. Was there other testimony that shed doubt on Stefanowicz, and on what basis or according to what motive had it been revealed? Were "unnamed sources" telling Taguba things about Stefanowicz that held him culpable?

Later, through his lawyer, Stefanowicz had insisted emphatically that he was innocent and that everything he'd done had been authorized.

---

[207] Kate Zernike and David Rohde, "Forced Nudity of Iraqi Prisoners is Seen as a Pervasive Pattern, Not Isolated Incidents," *The New York Times*, June 8, 2004.

[208] "Family and Friends Close Ranks Around Civilian Interrogator," op. cit.

If none of these positive reports proved Stefanowicz's innocence, the other potentially negative views certainly did not prove his guilt — and that's what London needed before imposing any discipline or letting him go.

"If he *was* innocent, I didn't want an innocent guy to get 'hung,'" London explained later. "Plus, we had other employees in Iraq. What kind of message does it send? I didn't want to create a mind set that if somebody is abruptly *accused*, you just haul off and fire him. What kind of management accountability would that signal?"

The truth was yet to be determined through further investigation — as London said, "The Truth Will Out." But at that time there was no justification for punitive measures. London would not take action based on the court of public opinion.

CHAPTER SIXTEEN

"THE TRUTH WILL OUT"

CACI gets Iraq updates and launches a proactive response

> "At no time, did the [military] leadership even hint
> of any abuse problems with CACI employees."
> ~ CHUCK MUDD, CACI MANAGER FOR IRAQ, JANUARY 2005

E VEN AS HE STOOD UP FOR HIS COMPANY IN PUBLIC, LONDON WAS demanding answers internally. He was determined to know the truth and, like other Americans, among his first questions was: what did people in CACI know and when did they know it? He needed to find out why his people in Iraq hadn't had any advance warning of the events in Taguba's report, so he turned to his CACI division vice president, Chuck Mudd.

A retired army colonel with twenty-six years of service, Mudd had joined the military out of need. The idea was to pay for college with an ROTC (Reserve Officer Training Corps) scholarship, much to the dismay of his father, a World War II vet who detested all things military. The animosity was so great that the elder Mudd boycotted his son's college graduation to avoid seeing him in uniform.

Now, in civilian life, Mudd found himself spending a lot of time in a war zone. As CACI's division vice president for Iraq, he was spending at least a week every month in country. The mission was so dangerous that when leaving for his first trip, he told his girlfriend he was headed for Germany. He had not wanted to frighten her at the time. Hopping mad when she learned where he was, she asked him why he had not told her where he was really going. "You would have worried and you would have been mad," Mudd said.

For London, Mudd responded with full candor, spelling out the details of operations at Abu Ghraib and the physical and operational barriers that separated CACI personnel from the cellblock where, reportedly, the abuse had occurred. He also reported back on his own regular inquiries to the military customer about CACI's performance. In addition, Mudd and CACI's Iraq-based manager Scott Northrop had specifically asked their army customer about mistreatment of detainees in January after the army announced it was looking into possible abuse. "At no time," Mudd reported, "did the [military] leadership even hint of any abuse problems with CACI employees."

Mudd's recounting provided important reassurance to London. It bolstered his growing belief that Taguba's conclusions about CACI's single employee had run ahead of the evidence, and it further strengthened his instinctive decision to resist premature and damaging disciplinary action against Stefanowicz.

First, Mudd reported that the mere fact that Taguba had interviewed CACI personnel was not an indication of any significant problem. Investigations and interviews had become the norm at Abu Ghraib — events of such frequency for civilian and military personnel alike that CACI had established a post-interview reporting process to find out whether any of its employees might be under investigation. But until Taguba's report leaked out, there was never any indication of any concerns about CACI's people.

"Every time there is a problem with the prisoners where a prisoner escapes, a major fight or riot happens, a prisoner is shot, or in the event that a prisoner dies under suspicious circumstances, an investigation is done," Mudd reported. Because bad incidents were not uncommon given the wartime circumstances, the interviews by Taguba were just one of three "high-level" inquiries in the previous four months, Mudd said.

Mudd noted that since July 2003 he had traveled to Iraq regularly. On every occasion when he visited Abu Ghraib, he touched base with prison leadership to find out if CACI's employees were providing satisfactory service — standard practice for CACI management. He also met with the army contracting officer's representative, Major Daniels. Separately, Northrop met regularly with military officials, inside and outside of the prison, for status reports that would also reveal if any CACI employee had done anything that warranted some type of counseling or CACI action. In addition, daily reports from CACI's administrative manager Dan Porvaznik, which tracked all CACI and client-related in-country issues, reflected no unusual behavior or indicated there was any noteworthy problem. The information from Baghdad was regularly reviewed by CACI's executive team, including London, during a weekly Monday meeting to assess the company's overall worldwide business situation.

The regular contacts between CACI's managers and military representatives at the prison and at Central Command, in Baghdad as well as the follow up reports to the company's senior managers in Virginia, affirmed the company's diligence. The company had an internal system in place to monitor performance, ensure fulfillment of contracts and protect its shareholders, and it was applying that system to its work in Iraq. And so, there was a continuing and consistent monitoring process for CACI's people and the company's work although that system did not discover or reveal the confidentiality surrounding Taguba's Article 15-6 investigation work.

Based on what the CACI team could observe, as well as what it heard from its army customer (on the typical contract, customers are always the most likely early warning source for any troubles), CACI's managers understood that their interrogators and screeners were doing their job in accord with the standards established by the army. With the publication of the abuses shown in the photos and the *illegal leak* of Taguba's report, it had become apparent that Abu Ghraib was not functioning, as it should. The absence of an alert from the army about potential problems, however, did not necessarily dismiss concern by the company.

What London really needed to know was whether any CACI employee had any involvement in any abuses. Based on Mudd's reports, London had reason to believe that CACI employees were not involved in or even aware of the appalling conduct shown in the pictures.

The abuses shown in the photographs reportedly took place in the cellblock, or "hard site," where high-value and more difficult prisoners were detained. They reportedly occurred after midnight. CACI employees had occasion to visit the cellblock but only when assigned to do so, and visits were less likely during the nighttime. CACI's Abu Ghraib employees were assigned to twelve-hour shifts, which could cover overnight hours, but they only worked beyond that time (their shift) for short periods when the military specifically required it.

Other than the routine interaction between guards and interrogators, Mudd's report suggested very little contact, though some was inevitable, between CACI's people and the night shift MPs who would later be charged and brought up for courts martial for the abuses. And no evidence (e.g., photograph or sworn eyewitness testimony) has surfaced since to contradict Mudd's findings other than occasional testimony at the various soldiers' courts martial (trials) regarding some alleged contact between CACI employees and the night shift MPs.

Because of security concerns at the time, London could not share the details of Mudd's report in any public forum. In addition to reporting on activities inside the prison walls, Mudd had also described the physical layout of the living quarters, the holding areas for prisoners, and other key locations at Abu Ghraib. Since this information could have provided a road map for an enemy attack, and since its public release could have jeopardized safety at the prison it was not publicly discussed.

While briefing Chuck Mudd's report to selected journalists would almost certainly have generated positive coverage of CACI's efforts to monitor its workers, doing so would have violated the company's larger, serious obligations to its employees, the army, and to the effort in Iraq.

The information was important for CACI's own investigation, and the company shared it with the government to help in official inquiries. But giving it to the media was out of the question. Much as he may have wanted to demonstrate in some way that his company had not acted improperly at Abu Ghraib, public release of sensitive information to the media would have undercut London's insistence on doing things the right way.

Around this time, London discovered that, even with his "Truth Will Out" program, many of his employees were not eager to raise this painful subject with their customers. But throughout the ordeal, London constantly pressed them to do just that.

"Feel free to share the information we've posted on Iraq with them [customers] or anyone else," London told his employees in a May 25, 2004 teleconference. He also invited them to e-mail new questions for the CACI Web site that posted FAQs (frequently asked questions) with factual answers for anyone to view.[209]

The May 25 call was a capstone to the ongoing effort to tell CACI's story. In it, London had summed up for his people the work that had already been undertaken to address the ordeal.

For example, his team had worked over the weekend to put out a unique press release on Mother's Day, May 9. Indicative of its 24/7 crisis management mode, CACI broke the unwritten rule that press releases are issued only during the normal Monday-to-Friday workweek.

The release did not break new ground, but London believed CACI should fully respond to issues raised in Senate testimony two days before. For the first time in writing, the company provided a comprehensive and detailed explanation of its hiring practices and the qualifications of the interrogators it hired. And, in his strongest direct language up to that time, London said he would "not permit hearsay or unsubstantiated rumors and accusations to unfairly condemn any individual."

In a written message to employees, London attached the press release, repeated his determination to avoid premature condemnation of any individual, renewed his promises to find out the truth, and reiterated his pride in the work CACI's people had undertaken.

A few days later, in his regular "Chairman's Notes" commentary and correspondence to employees, London aimed once more to buck up his employees' spirits.

He reminded them of the corporate commitment to vigilance, integrity, and honesty, and reiterated that, "we are fully accountable for what we do." He predicted that the company would emerge stronger for the experience and he counseled loyalty to co-workers.

"I urge you to remember that our co-workers in Iraq have not been charged with any wrongdoing and, as such, remain valued members of

---

[209] CACI's Iraq FAQs were still provided on the company's Web site for public review as of December 2007.

the CACI team and fully deserve our support and loyalty," London said, and added, "In my book, people are innocent until proven guilty."

And in a reminder that other business still continued, London closed with a note about the company's climb into the top twenty list of government contractors for IT services and reported on his recent meeting with the Secretary of the Department of Veteran Affairs and the ongoing success of CACI's VA project teams.

Following his comments to his employees, London also decided it was time to reach outside of his familiar circle to engage additional outside advisors for support with press relations and outreach to Capitol Hill and elsewhere in the government. There was a certain regret in the decision because London wanted to believe his in-house team, which had always performed admirably, could handle any task. But he recognized the overwhelming challenges presented by this crisis, and he knew there were limits to what his people could do. He also realized, that given the unusual circumstances, the company needed additional expertise in areas outside its normal scope of activities. The volume of the press demands alone was putting CACI under an almost impossible strain, especially given the compounding inaccuracies along with the extent of the other responsibilities requiring attention during the crisis.

So London and his team turned to two companies: Prism Public Affairs, for communications and media support, and Clark & Weinstock, a government relations firm that included several former members of Congress. The lead communicator from Prism was Don Foley, who had handled press relations for former Democratic House minority leader Richard Gephardt for more than a dozen years, including a 1988 presidential run, and then later for Northwest Airlines. Foley was supported at Prism by Mike Gelb, a former Reuters reporter who had covered the White House and politics, and Dan Casey, a former research director for the Republican Party. To handle direct outreach to Capitol Hill as well as state-based officials, Clark & Weinstock provided former Democratic member of the House of Representatives Vic Fazio, David Berteau, a military affairs and procurement expert who had worked for four consecutive secretaries of defense, and Sandra Stuart, who had been Assistant Secretary of Defense for Legislative Affairs from 1993 to 1999 prior to joining the firm. If appropriate, Clark & Weinstock also could call on former Republican Representative Vin Weber, a partner in the firm.

London also used the help of an additional specialist and consultant in crisis public relations, Claire Sanders Swift, who had worked within the realm of broadcast media, including CBS's *60 Minutes*. Her focus and role was primarily on testing London's media strategies about the sensitive issue of Stefanowicz and offering scenarios about the appropriateness on when and what to say.

The advisors' cultures were not always a natural fit for CACI. One CACI executive conceded that at first he thought the consultants just got in the way. "I didn't have time for them initially. I just didn't care what they did," he explained. "But in the end it would have been more unsettling not to have them. You simply need the outside view — even if you don't take all of their advice."

"This was a particularly interesting period for us." Brown said later. "Even with the best outside consultants on your team, believe me, you will have conflicting advice. At the end of the day, the person on the top has to make the decisions. In each case, Jack would consistently and intently listen to his advisors and weigh his options. But then he'd call the shots — every time."

It took time for the consultants to grow comfortable, too.

"There's a feeling-out period with every new client," explained Foley. "We're from politics and journalism. We're irreverent and informal, and these were former military guys — a little more traditional."

Foley added, "And then Jack [London] wasn't like any other CEO. He was ready to stand up and fight. A lot of companies, when they're in a crisis, claim they want to be open and 'let the chips fall where they may' but they just want to take cover and let it all pass over — not Jack."

Foley, in particular, became a core advisor to London and Brown. According to Brown, Foley and London developed something of a "mind meld." The oftentimes outspoken London and the soft-spoken Foley, with vastly different communication styles, became an effective "odd couple." Berteau also formed a good working bond with his new client and would accompany London to key offices on Capitol Hill so the CACI CEO could introduce CACI and deliver his messages personally to some of his company's severest critics.

CHAPTER SEVENTEEN

NEW FACES

Critics put in their two cents for their fifteen minutes

"They were professional. Many of them were retired military."
∽ **MAJOR GENERAL GEOFFREY MILLER, COMMENTING ON CIVILIAN INTERROGATORS, MAY 4, 2004**

EACH DAY OF A PUBLIC SCANDAL BRINGS NEW COMPLEXITIES AND new players. Finding these new players and introducing them to the public becomes a way for reporters to give the unfolding story a new dimension. For those, like CACI, at the center of the storm, new elements add to the tumult. Often, the issues raised linger long after the individual who raised them has been forgotten.

On May 7, 2004 the *Guardian* introduced to the existing confusion Torin Nelson, a former Abu Ghraib interrogator, who would validate Taguba's findings of disarray at the prison and also complain that many of his fellow interrogators lacked the experience or know-how to do their jobs.[210] Nelson had been a military interrogator at Guantanamo Bay in 2002 and before that in Bosnia. He returned stateside in February of 2003 to prepare for deployment to Iraq and the invasion in March.

---

[210] Julian Borger, "Cooks and Drivers Were Working as Interrogators. Private Contractor Lifts the Lid on Systematic Failures at Abu Ghraib Jail," *The Guardian*, May 7, 2004.

He left Iraq in July of 2003 and quit the military because, as he said, "higher-ups with less experience were making piss-poor decisions instead of listening to lower-ranking, more experienced people."[211] After Nelson finished his military career he applied for a job, and CACI hired him in late 2003 sending him to Abu Ghraib with the army's agreement.

Nelson worked for CACI at Abu Ghraib prison in Iraq as a senior interrogator for little more than two months from November 25, 2003 until February 5, 2004, when he left the company and returned to the U.S. The word within CACI at the time Nelson left the company was that he had struggled with the difficult conditions at Abu Ghraib. Describing it as one of the worst detention facilities he'd seen Nelson stated, "I was worried about working there from the moment I arrived, actually."[212]

Compared to Abu Ghraib, Guantanamo was a safe environment, where Americans had been firmly in control, and conditions were generally regarded as secure for both detainees and interrogators. In contrast, conditions at Abu Ghraib were dangerous and deficient. Abu Ghraib prison had a perilously high ratio of detainees to military personnel, and was lacking in every basic comfort. Soldiers and civilians stationed there, for example, asked their families to send poison to help them kill a growing rat population. There were also frequent mortar attacks as well as threats to the staff by the prisoners.

"You're comparing apples and oranges between Gitmo (Guantanamo Bay) and Abu Ghraib" Nelson later said.[213]

Citing worries about his personal safety, Nelson resigned in February. If he had concerns about interrogation techniques at that time, he kept them to himself. But with the public and media fixated on the abuse story, Nelson found his way into the spotlight. At CACI, some saw Nelson as a self-promoter seeking his "fifteen minutes of fame.[214] He got it — and his comments would be regularly quoted and construed by the media as evidence in alleging that CACI had not been sufficiently diligent in its hiring practices.

---

[211] Pratap Chatterjee, "An Interrogator Speaks Out," CorpWatch.org, March 7, 2005.

[212] Lisa Myers, "Climate at Abu Ghraib distressed former interrogator," *NBC News*, May 10, 2004.

[213] Leon Worden, "Interrogator: Chaos Reigned at Abu Ghraib" *Signal*, June 20, 2004.

[214] The 15 minutes phrase is a reference to Andy Warhol's prognostication that "In the future, everyone will be famous for 15 minutes."

Nelson's first target was the military, which he accused of running an "abysmal" operation at Abu Ghraib. He also accused the military of over-reliance on contractors, who he said often weren't up to the job.

"I'd say about the contractors that it's kind of hit or miss. They're under so much pressure to fill slots quickly. . . . They penalize contracting companies if they can't fill slots on time and it looks bad on companies' records. If you're in such a hurry to get bodies, you end up with cooks and drivers doing intelligence work," Nelson was quoted in the *Guardian*.[215]

Unfortunately, Nelson was wrong with regard to "filling slots", at least as far as CACI was concerned, but the media did not check out his statements. Specifically and factually, there was no penalty at CACI if the company could not "fill slots on time." Not only could the company have easily proven this to be false, CACI also had proof positive that they hired only staff who met the army's requirements. Yet the *Guardian* never called CACI to verify or comment on Nelson's accusations. Rather, they used Nelson's comments in an article titled "Iraq Conflict: Cooks and Drivers Were Working as Interrogators." This quote, though false in all regards, was repeated extensively in the media in the weeks to follow.

Nelson was next interviewed by NBC's *Nightly News* and the *Today* show on May 10, and a day later he turned up for a twelve-minute interview with Deborah Norville on NBC's affiliate channel MSNBC.

"There were a number of individuals, not just on the CACI side, but on the military side that, I felt, needed more experience if they were actually going to be working as interrogators," Nelson told Lisa Meyers of NBC News in a comment that cast aspersions on the military interrogators as well.[216] Nelson alleged that, "Perhaps a third had no formal training." This remark ignored the fact that all interrogators hired by CACI and sent to Iraq were agreed to by the government as meeting the army's requirements for assignment to Iraq.

Nelson declined to say whether he had seen any abuse, but he surmised to Norville that interrogators seemed to have had influence over the military police and that "if someone wanted to do something like that [abuse], I think the guards really probably would have

---

215 Julian Borger, "Cooks and Drivers Were Working as Interrogators," op. cit.

216 Interview with Torin Nelson, *Nightly News*, NBC, May 10, 2004.

complied."[217] These comments were, of course, speculation and opinions, and amounted to nothing more than that.

Nelson also challenged the CACI hiring process. Although he noted that his qualifications strongly matched the requirements for the interrogator position, he complained that the CACI interview process was too short. On the one hand, Nelson boasted openly about his superior qualifications, but on the other hand, he seemed to complain that CACI had recognized those qualifications too quickly. It seems that he didn't consider that CACI might logically streamline its interview process for well-qualified candidates.

London and his team were incensed by Nelson's allegations. The vast majority of the interrogators CACI had hired possessed military backgrounds, even though that was not a set requirement of the statement of work, and many (twenty-two out of twenty-five) were trained, in fact, as military interrogators. Among those without military interrogator background, most had been involved in police work. Subsequent government investigations would confirm that all of CACI's hires met the requirements specified by the army in the contract, and that all but one (who was already in Iraq when CACI hired him from another contractor) had the necessary levels of security clearances. There were no "cooks and drivers" among those hired by CACI. Indeed, CACI believed that many of its interrogators, because of previous experience in the field, were better qualified than some of the soldiers fresh out of intelligence school — a belief that was shared by some military officers, as noted in the later Schlesinger and Church investigation reports.

Up to that time, the company had reviewed 1,600 applicants but engaged only three dozen, all of whom were approved by the army beforehand, or were accepted for work in Iraq by their assignment records on the job. CACI's rigorous hiring process meant it was not able to fill all of the authorized positions. This meant less revenue to CACI, but sending only qualified personnel to do this critical work was, without question, more important to the company than the money.

After news about the Abu Ghraib scandal broke, the media coverage made it even harder for CACI to fulfill its hiring goals. And the already difficult task of finding qualified people willing to travel to a dangerous

---

[217] Interview with Torin Nelson, *Deborah Norville Tonight*, MSNBC, May 11, 2004.

foreign location was further complicated by the turnover of employees due to the harsh conditions in Iraq. One CACI subcontractor, L-3 Communications, notified CACI that it would no longer participate in supplying interrogators to CACI in Iraq because its corporate headquarters had changed its policy and decided not to do interrogation work.

Despite these challenges, one of the things London and his team had been most proud of was their quick response to the army's early needs, and the fact that CACI had remained committed to the army when the circumstances in Iraq and the conditions at Abu Ghraib were so chaotic. One industry representative told the press that companies like Titan and CACI "provided incredible surge capacity and incredible speed," in supporting the military in Iraq.[218]

Besides interrogators, the army also needed translators to support intelligence collection and Titan Corporation was contracted to fill this need. However, the background of translators in Iraq was much more variable than those of the interrogators. As Titan readily noted, the translators that it was responsible for came from a wide range of civilian backgrounds. Its job was to find Arabic speakers who also were fluent in English, and the translators' civilian vocational experience was not particularly relevant to that assignment. Published reports stated that Titan's hires included divergent backgrounds such as doctors, artists, and grocery baggers. "Just because an applicant may be a doctor or a businessman or some other vocation doesn't mean he or she isn't qualified to speak fluent English and Arabic and support the military," Titan spokesman Wil Williams explained.[219]

Of course, as London noted, the U.S. Army Reserve and National Guard personnel activated for service in Iraq also were of widely divergent professional or vocational backgrounds.

In the end, even Nelson seemed to back off the "cooks and drivers" comment about interrogators, telling Norville that while he exceeded CACI's qualifications, "I'm not sure about anybody else that was — that was hired by the company."[220] And he later clarified that his "cooks and

---

[218] Elaine Grossman, "Possible Interrogation Contractor Influence Cited in Senate Vote," *Inside the Pentagon*, June 24, 2004.

[219] "Line Increasingly Blurred Between Soldiers and Civilian Contractors," *Washington Post*, May 13, 2004.

[220] MSNBC interview, op. cit.

drivers" comment to the *Guardian* did not pertain to CACI.[221] In any case, CACI's interrogators were proven to have had the qualifications set forth and required by the contract.

In addition to his TV appearances, Nelson was quoted in a number of newspapers, including the *Washington Post*. Months later he remained a presence as others recycled his earlier comments.

A year later in a report from an interview with Nelson, CorpWatch said that Nelson left Iraq "when other CACI staff became hostile to him when it became obvious he had told the truth to Taguba." This was all news to CACI, and whatever the "truth" was that Nelson claimed to have told Taguba it was not revealed in the article. CorpWatch also credited Nelson as saying that one co-worker told him "he better watch his back." But the article went on to quote Nelson as also saying, "I told the [CACI] project manager that the country [Iraq] was going to hell in a hand basket and the American military was not doing a damn thing about it."[222] Overall, CACI's Iraq team saw Nelson's media appearances as those of a self-promoter looking for an audience.

To Burkhart, more critical than the "what" of Nelson's statements was the "why." She questioned why someone trained in the confidential work of intelligence gathering, and who had also been interviewed as part of a classified military investigation (which was still not completed nor declassified) would give public opinion on that investigation. She concluded that Nelson was probably able to put all of that aside in favor of the opportunity to talk to the press, which enabled him to publicly promote himself in order to advance his career aspirations.

Contrary to his apparent intentions, Nelson's disparaging remarks about his profession would soon undermine his credibility.

In fact, while Nelson was with CACI at Abu Ghraib in early 2004, he had been one of the first to relate his suspicion to Major General Taguba's investigations that John Israel and Stephen Stefanowicz merited scrutiny as perpetrators of abuse. Nelson never claimed to have ac-

---

[221] On May 14, 2004 the Guardian posted a correction to the May 7, 2004 Borger article stating "In the interview below, we quoted a remark Torin Nelson made about "cooks and truck drivers." Mr. Nelson has asked us to make it clear that he intended the remark to be rhetorical. He did not mean that people from those jobs were actually working at the prison as interrogators. . . ."

[222] Chatterjee, "Interrogator Speaks Out," op. cit.

tually seen any abuse by either man, but he apparently felt free to offer his opinions to the army's Criminal Investigation Division. He had begun "quietly pulling files and actively looking for signs of malfeasance."[223] Nelson's "suspicions" as told to Taguba were nothing more than hearsay — he gave no specific, concrete evidence. According to their interview with Nelson GovExec.com stated "All Nelson did was pass on what little he had heard and had been able to document."

Over the next several months, information would emerge from investigations and testimony to contradict Nelson's statements. Nelson would also be unsuccessful in returning to his interrogation work. In October 2005 he was reportedly hired by another contractor to do- interrogation in Afghanistan but en route to that job he received an email from his manager stating, "I must inform you that you have been terminated by the [army] client." "Do not go to Bagram, Afghanistan." A follow up email to Nelson stated, "The decision was based on your association with high-profile issues surrounding Abu Ghraib . . . CJTF-76 [Combined Joint Task Force–76] the U.S. military authority."[224] Ultimately Nelson went to work for a real estate firm and in 2006 he lost his run for a congressional seat in Utah. He also reportedly traveled to Washington, D.C. in an effort to get congressional support for a committee of professionals, including himself, to critique and overhaul military training, recruitment, and operations management. It seemed at the time that Nelson was unsuccessful here as well.

Nearly a year later, London bristled when asked about Nelson. "His remarks were harmful and reckless. He took advantage of this terrible situation at Abu Ghraib to aggrandize himself and hurt everybody else — the military, his former colleagues, and a company that had treated him well and helped him in his career," London said.

Nelson would later confirm one important aspect of CACI's work at Abu Ghraib: that CACI interrogators reported to the military supervisors. In a statement taken under oath, in Salt Lake City on September 9, 2005, Nelson confirmed that CACI's Dan Porvaznik was the supervisor at Abu Ghraib, handling mainly administrative affairs as site manager.

---

223 Jason Vest, "Haunted by Abu Ghraib — Having helped reveal abuses at the notorious prison, former interrogator Torin Nelson opens up about why it happened and how it has wrecked his career," GovExec.com, October 3, 2005.

224 Ibid.

During that same September 9 meeting, Nelson also stated under oath that "CACI interrogators at Abu Ghraib reported, through our chain of command, to the military personnel who were running the JIDC [Joint Interrogation and Debriefing Center] at Abu Ghraib; we would report to them, as far as operational matters go."[225]

Despite his eventual final equivocation, Nelson's allegations created difficulties for CACI. The company found itself confronted by a classic "he said-she said" situation in which the instincts of both the media and the public are to believe the individual in any tussle between a company and disgruntled employee. Nelson also would not communicate with CACI's counsel.

The challenge was compounded by the fact that CACI was relatively unknown. The company had no public marks against it, but it also lacked a public reservoir of goodwill or popularity. Companies like CACI are often stunned to find that presumptions shift quickly against them when they suddenly are *accused* of wrongdoing.

The media also failed to note that Nelson's assessment of the civilian interrogators' worth and performance evaluation conflicted with that of the military. Major General Geoffrey Miller, who had run the detention camp at Guantanamo Bay and who was assigned in early May of 2004 to clean up Abu Ghraib, said his experience showed that civilian interrogators could do the job quite well.

"They were professional. Many of them [contract interrogators] were retired military," Miller told a press briefing.[226]

And Defense Undersecretary Stephen Cambone, in his May 11, 2004 testimony, told the Senate Armed Services Committee that many of the civilians "are quite capable and are, in terms of the interrogators' art, better able to conduct those interrogations than the younger [military] individuals who are new to that activity."[227]

This testimony would eventually be supported by the findings of the Schlesinger report in August of 2004, which stated that, "The Naval

---

[225] "Sworn Statement of Torin Nelson." Formal interview by Burke Pyle, LLC, filed in the United States District Court, for the District of Columbia. September 9, 2005.

[226] U.S. Department of Defense. "Detainee Operations Briefing by Major General Geoffrey Miller." May 4, 2004 (http://www.defenselink.mil/transcripts/2004/tr20040504-1424.html).

[227] Testimony of Taguba et al., op. cit.

Inspector General . . . found some of the older contractors had backgrounds as military interrogators and were generally more effective than some of the junior enlisted military personnel."[228]

The Church report (from the follow-up investigation to Taguba's) which was released in March of 2005 concluded that, "Contractors made a significant contribution to U.S. intelligence efforts." The report further stated that, "on average, contractors were more experienced than military interrogators and that this advantage enhanced their credibility with detainees and promoted successful interrogations." Apparently, there was no link that existed between the *approved* interrogation techniques and detainee abuse.

Nelson was not the only self-styled commentator on CACI and Abu Ghraib. The spotlight also shone on Peter W. Singer, who had found a spot on many journalists' contact lists and had weighed in on the issue early. On paper, Singer must have fit with the media's "expert" profile. Presumably he had all of the necessary paper credentials — a doctorate from Harvard; affiliation with the Brookings Institution, a Washington, D.C. think tank; published works, including a book on military contractors; an ability to talk in the short "sound bites"; and a particular viewpoint. In this regard, Singer had become a publicly recognized commentator and advocate of certain military policy views.

While London did not have any specific concern about Nelson's comments to the media because his views were seen as strictly self-serving, Singer's views came from a different direction.

Despite a label of "expert", it was becoming clear that Singer was an opportunist looking to capitalize on CACI's problems. And his commentary fully encapsulated the criticism and disparagement that the company was facing. Publicly refuting Singer's accusations and exaggerations would simultaneously refute many of CACI's misinformed and mistaken challengers.

Singer had a quite outspoken belief that the U.S. government was wrong to outsource certain military support work and he was entitled to that opinion. CACI had not, and did not, intend to enter that controversy. But to London expressing these views did not require nor justify a focus on CACI where it was not accurate or appropriate to do so, and most especially where the facts did not fit.

---

[228] Schlesinger, op. cit.

Abu Ghraib gave Singer a platform to talk about his, apparently, long-standing criticism of government outsourcing and his opinion that government lacked a clear policy for military contractor relations. The possibility that contractors had been accused in the abuses at Abu Ghraib, however, provided a tailor-made opportunity for Singer to air his views and promote himself and his recent book about military contractors. To Singer it may not have mattered which companies were involved in making his point about the government's outsourcing (contracting out) of certain presumed military-like functions, but his repeated singling out of CACI came across as unwarranted. CACI had had a good reputation for more than forty years, which Singer had freely acknowledged, but that now seemed of no consequence in promoting his views.

From virtually the first day after the abuse photos became public, Singer showed up in news reports. Some of what he said was accurate, telling the *Boston Globe* on May 4 that private companies' ability to punish workers was essentially limited to termination. "No company can properly punish a felony offense. . . . All you do is you lose a paycheck," he noted.[229] For serious crimes, government legal action was essential. But business people already knew this obvious fact. To those at CACI, his comment prompted the question: Did Singer, or the public in general, somehow believe that companies could "punish" their employees? And what was meant by the term "properly"?

More questionable was Singer's apparently foregone conclusion, beginning in the first days after the scandal broke, that contractors were being let off easy. "You have to show that when crimes happen, we punish them to the full extent of the law," Singer told the *Los Angeles Times* on May 4. "So far that doesn't appear to be the case. We've let the contractors fall through a gap in the law."[230] Such premature and unfounded remarks at the outset of the news about Abu Ghraib, before investigations had been completed, were totally inappropriate. The commentary was unjustifiably damaging to both CACI and the contracting industry because Singer did not reference or emphasize the rule of law, due process, the concept of innocent until proven guilty, or that other important government investigations were still underway.

---

[229] Stockman, op. cit.

[230] T. Christian Miller, "Contractors Fall Through Legal Crack," *Los Angeles Times*, May 4, 2004.

Singer aggressively stated his concern about "a free pass" in a nine-hundred-word opinion column that ran in several major newspapers around the country in the first week of May.[231] He also pushed his theories in an international forum. On May 11, 2004, the *Pakistan Daily Times* ran an op-ed by Singer called "Outsourcing Interrogation: the Legal Vacuum."

While there were some questions about how the laws would apply under appropriate situations, Singer's speculation just days after civil authorities first learned of the apparent abuses created the misperception that "the fix was in," although this was never the case. It was certainly possible that history could prove him correct, but it was also possible that the results would show the civilians had not broken the law. Either way, prosecutions, if warranted, should take place after the evidence was gathered, assessed, and indictments filed. But this did not cause Singer to hesitate in promoting his own angle.

In an interview with the *Financial Times*, Singer seemed to suggest that the fact of hiring contractors for interrogation was by itself nefarious. "That's the whole rationale for using these firms," Singer said. "A lot of people focus on the financial cost [benefit], but it's really the political cost [benefit]. It allows you to shift roles that might be controversial to . . . private companies."[232]

Yet a week earlier, Singer had told a radio interviewer just the opposite. "My sense is that it's not a case of trying to pull in private contractors to do the *dirty work*. . . . A lot of reports have stated that in the media, but I don't think that's the case [italics added]. My sense is it's more about a lazy bureaucracy," Singer said in a lengthy interview on National Public Radio.[233]

The self-contradiction continued in the *Guardian* when he stated that, "private military contractors in Iraq are operating in a black hole as

---

[231] Singer's column was published with varying headlines applied by newspapers in *The Record* as "Private contractors and the abuse of Iraqi prisoners" (Bergen County, New Jersey) on May 4, 2004; as "Beyond the law" in *The Guardian* on May 3, 2004; and as "Above law, above decency" in the *Pittsburgh Tribune-Review* on May 9, 2004.

[232] Joshua Chaffin, "U.S. Turns to Private Sector for Spies," *Financial Times*, May 17, 2004.

[233] Singer "Fresh Air" interview op. cit.

they do not fall within the military chain of command." He then turned around and told Minnesota Public Radio that, "at a broader level, though for me, it's not so much this conspiracy theory of trying to avoid culpability, it's actually just bureaucratic laziness, the fact that the Pentagon is often faced with a problem . . . is handling that problem over to private contractors to take care of. And in some cases it works great, and in other cases you get these abuses and failures of jobs and mess-ups, etc."[234] Notably, in these very statements, Singer perpetuated the idea of private contractors doing "dirty work" — just by making these references on national radio.

These loose assertions and contradictory statements were even more evidence of a general lack of accountability in the media and among the self-proclaimed "experts" who could stand on the public soapbox with impunity and say one thing today and something different tomorrow without consequence to themselves.

Potentially damaging to the company was Singer's apparent assumption that the civilian interrogators at Abu Ghraib were, in fact, guilty of serious crimes. London was adamant that his people were entitled to due process. And he intended to call to task anybody — who intentionally, or without justification, maligned CACI or its employees.

While the photos seemed to show misconduct by the MPs, the only implications about the civilian contractors were the few lines in Taguba's fifty-three-page summary report. With Taguba's annexes still secret and other investigations not yet complete, London considered it presumptuous for anyone on the outside to render a judgment about CACI's employees at Abu Ghraib. Taguba's report had simply said that Stefanowicz was only one of four people that he "suspected" of being "either directly or indirectly responsible for the abuses," and no other fact, evidence or comment was provided.

Indeed, a week after Singer's first complaints, Taguba had cast doubt on his own allegations regarding the abuses when he shared with the Senate Armed Services Committee, under oath, his belief that the MPs "did it on their own volition" and "they were probably influenced by others, but not necessarily directed specifically by others."[235]

---

[234] "Interview with Peter Singer." Marketplace — Minnesota Public Radio. June 17, 2004.

[235] Testimony of Taguba et al., op. cit.

But Singer apparently failed to do his research. He commented in Pakistan's *Daily Times* that, "The interrogators . . . are found to have crossed several red-lines of acceptable legal and humane behavior."[236] With regard to CACI's people, there simply were *no proven findings out on any of these allegations.*

These statements by Singer would soon be followed in the months to come by other similar remarks and insinuations in the media, including CNN and Minnesota Public Radio. A June 2004 article in *Inside the Pentagon,* stated that Singer believed that "industry influence played a role in defeating proposed Senate legislation last week that would have *banned contractors from conducting or translating detainee interrogations* at U.S. military installations" [italics added].[237] In fact, London and his team were not even aware that such legislation was being considered. CACI had never engaged in any such legislative lobbying efforts on Capitol Hill and individual employee contributions to various political campaigns (Democrat and Republican) had only added up to less than $20,000 over the previous eighteen months. All of the contributions had been made, throughout the 9,500-person company, privately, by various people in relatively small amounts and at different times.

Despite the free reign the media gave Singer in expressing his opinions, there were those who had publicly expressed certain skepticisms about Singer's views as developed in his book, *Corporate Warriors*, even while recognizing some of its contributions.

Richard Lacquement, Lieutenant Colonel, U.S. Army, writing at the U.S. Naval War College in 2004 noted that while Singer's book was a must-read for military professors and national security experts and that he (Singer) had developed an especially worthwhile framework for examination, many of his suggestions were provocative.

Lacquement further suggested in his review that some of Singer's analysis and conclusions were arguably unsound. "The book [*Corporate Warriors*] contains some significant flaws, but they generally stem from the groundbreaking effort to comprehend the significance of these

---

[236] Peter W. Singer, "Outsourcing Interrogation: the Legal Vacuum," *Pakistan Daily Times*, May 5, 2004.

[237] Elaine M. Grossman, "Possible Interrogation Contractor Influence Cited In Senate Vote," op. cit. Interrogations certainly applied to CACI's work, however, the company had nothing whatsoever to do with the proposed legislation.

firms. There are also many loose assertions, insinuations, and innuendos that are unlikely to withstand closer scrutiny. . . ."[238]

Lacquement used Singer's segment entitled "Implications" as an example of these flaws:

> The words "possible," "might," and "can" show up with inordinate frequency and are indicative of a looser, more speculative analysis. Here, Singer has a hard time maintaining the distinction between the [various categories of] firms [that] he had carefully created earlier. The effect is often to *tar all provider firms* [italics added] that bear the most resemblance to mercenaries or traditional military combat organizations. Singer darkly intones about the pitfalls and potential problems that can arise from the use of private military corporations. In this section, he tends to lump together all flavors of private military corporations, *suggesting guilt by association* [italics added] with a small number of admittedly distasteful companies. This tendency to associate loosely all firms with the sins of the most egregious ones (almost always provider firms) seems even less fair given the fact that elsewhere Singer notes that such firms constitute a small fraction of the overall private military firm population. Many of his accusations do not apply well to support firms.[239]

Lacquement's comments about Singer fit precisely with London's observations, especially with Singer's apparent tendency to lump contractors together and project onto them the "guilt by association" label. This is what Singer did to CACI in using the negative publicity of the Abu Ghraib tragedy to disparage the company.

In their quest for publicity, both Nelson and Singer seemed impervious to the unjustified damage their inaccurate representations would inflict upon CACI — as a company and as a people — and to CACI's customers and shareholders. They did not seem to realize that their unsubstantiated public and widely disseminated commentary also had

---

[238] Richard Lacquement, Book Review of Peter Singer's *Corporate Warriors*, *Naval War College*, Autumn 2004.

[239] Ibid.

the potential, through the media's amplifications and distortions, to undermine and endanger American military and contractor civilians in the field.

Some might even argue that sharply drawn opinions along with media misinformation — tragically and unjustifiably — could add further to the unfortunate misperceptions being created around the world about America itself.

CHAPTER EIGHTEEN

AUDITS GALORE
Investigations, inquiries, and more

**"I have attached a list of questions that we are interested
in so as to gain a better understanding of the GSA
contract that was [discussed] in the *Washington Post*."**
**~ E-MAIL TO CACI FROM DEFENSE CONTRACT
AUDIT AGENCY, MAY 19, 2004**

A s CACI'S PEOPLE TRIED TO ADJUST TO THE NEGATIVE PUBLICITY,
the company was moving forward with its own fact-finding and
data-gathering in response to a growing number of information requests
from government agencies and some independent groups. The latter included Amnesty International USA, which in mid-May wrote CACI for
information about the company's human rights policies and asked the
company to draft such a policy if one did not exist.

CACI responded immediately with a letter from London outlining
its commitment to find the truth and take action if its employees acted
improperly. It also provided a series of attachments, including the company's long-standing ethics policies, credo, and operational philosophy.
Upon reviewing CACI's materials, Amnesty wrote again in June 2004

and January 2005, reiterating its requests for CACI to draft a specific human rights policy closer to theirs. It thanked CACI for responding quickly and thoughtfully, but in a disingenuous move it also posted accusatory articles on its Web site and prompted readers to write condemnations to and about CACI. In the end, the company and the activist group could not agree. London and his team closed off the correspondence in February of 2005 by informing Amnesty that the company believed its policies were fully suitable and responsible and that it was both disappointed and surprised that Amnesty remained dissatisfied.

"We respect your efforts to improve human rights around the world; however, we will not allow any outside organization to try to impose their agenda, especially when we have demonstrated that our policies and procedures are comprehensive and responsible in trying to ensure that all rights and the truth are upheld and protected," London wrote in 2005.

In the midst of the media firestorm, London was trying to keep CACI's business moving forward. On the agenda were an upcoming earnings report and a session with Wall Street analysts, who needed to know about the company's financial numbers, and also whether Abu Ghraib was a threat to CACI's share price or profits.

CACI leadership also learned that the Defense Contract Audit Agency (DCAA) had contacted CACI officials in Iraq on May 19 and requested a range of information about the company's Iraq contracts, the statements of work, staffing, job titles, and billing processes. CACI's managers in Baghdad directed DCAA representatives to corporate headquarters for this information, the company's standard policy for all field audits. The CACI field managers were told that lack of cooperation could result in the issuance of a "denial of access" report. Ironically, news of the unannounced Baghdad request came just as DCAA representatives were also arriving at CACI headquarters in Arlington, Virginia, for a scheduled meeting to raise the same questions.

The DCAA was established by a directive of the Department of Defense (DoD) for the purpose of performing all contracts auditing for DoD, as well as providing accounting and financial advisory services in connection with the negotiation, administration, and settlement of contracts and subcontracts for all DoD procurement and contract administration activities. DCAA also provided contract audit services to other non-DoD agencies as specified in cross-servicing agreements established with these agencies. Basically, its role was to ensure that the government was getting value for its money.

CACI was very familiar with DCAA and its oversight responsibilities. Based on "whether the audit workload at the contractor is of a continuing nature and is sufficient in significance, complexity, and volume," DCAA would place its staff on site at the contractors' offices.[240] In view of the scope and volume of CACI's DoD work, DCAA maintained one supervisor and five auditors on site at CACI corporate headquarters. On May 19, the audit supervisor and three of these auditors were (primarily) assigned to DCAA's audit of CACI's Iraq (GSA-related) contract while the audit was in process. Additionally, the Branch Manager, Regional Audit Manager and a Compensation Technical Specialist would periodically be located at CACI to facilitate the audit.

But it was not the usual, regular DCAA review. A May 17, 2004 article in the *Washington Post* had described CACI's contract with the U.S. Army, administered by the Department of the Interior, as worth up to $500 million.[241] This was for all of the possible work to be placed on the contract, a ceiling amount, not the value of CACI's work in Iraq, which was far less. In the article, Interior spokesman Frank Quimby spoke in detail about the Iraq-related task orders in the contract, including a $19.9 million order under which CACI would provide interrogation support services. This prompted an inquiry from an onsite DCAA auditor on May 17, 2004 to "brief the contract." The initial request was followed by a request from the Branch Manager two days later on May 19. That e-mail stated, "I have attached a list of questions that we are interested in so as to gain a better understanding of the GSA contract that was in the *Washington Post*."

The DCAA e-mail continued, "I would also like to brief the basic contract and task/delivery orders for the Iraqi work. This is the typical brief including type of contract/orders, services provided, audit rights/ clauses, FAR/CAS clauses,[242] special provisions, billing instructions/

---

[240] Defense Contract Audit Agency. *DCAA Contract Audit Manual*, Vol. 1 of 2, Chapters 1–8, 200.1 (Washington, DC: U.S. Government Printing Office, January 2005).

[241] "CACI Contract: From Supplies to Interrogation," *Washington Post*, May 17, 2004.

[242] FAR: Federal Acquisition Regulation, CAS: Cost Accounting Standards.

provisions, task orders and ordering language to purchase the services in Iraq. . . . It would also be helpful if you could show us a recent billing for interrogation work in Iraq." The attached questions, which focused on the role of PTG, also suggested that the scope of the inquiry might look back several years.

The fact that DCAA was crediting the *Washington Post* as the source, or at least the motivation for its investigation, puzzled those at CACI. CACI's concern heightened with DCAA's expectation that the extensive and detailed information requested was to be gathered and presented within six hours and thirty-five minutes of DCAA's issuance of the request. This was quite unusual, in fact probably unheard of in the company's experience, and on such short notice. But CACI knew it was important and would get the job done for DCAA.

CACI Compliance and Contracts staffs were also puzzled by the DCAA request regarding CACI's GSA contract. DCAA did perform contract audit services for other agencies, but to CACI's knowledge GSA was not one of them. In fact, it was believed that DCAA had made an effort in the past to exclude GSA activity from its reports because (it was the company's understanding) a cross-servicing agreement was not in place with GSA. GSA also had its own auditors. Despite the somewhat unusual request, CACI wanted to respond, to continue to offer information that would provide reassurances to those who had their own set of concerns. The Abu Ghraib scandal had broken less than three weeks before and CACI was clearly being scrutinized from every possible angle — DCAA included. Within days of the *Post* article, DCAA had begun submitting requests for information about the contract.

CACI's leadership was fully aware that most everyone with some connection to Abu Ghraib now had a heightened sensitivity toward their own roles and were adopting protective measures. Government agencies were concerned now about their own responsibilities and reputations, and were particularly concerned about what the media might report about them and Abu Ghraib-related events. It was time to recheck their work and previous actions.

For years, CACI had been working with DCAA as its contract business with DoD had grown. The company's people were well aware of the DCAA's competence and capability. And London had thought to himself at the time that, though it would be a virtual mountain of work for his people in responding, having DCAA do its audit on CACI's Iraq projects off the GSA Schedule (and the Ft. Huachuca, DOI BPA) for the U.S. Army would ultimately be very beneficial.

London believed CACI's contracting system, financial integrity, and business ethics would come through in the end. A thorough look by DoD's best at the DCAA in reviewing CACI's task orders at Ft. Huachuca on the DOI's BPA would greatly assist in getting others informed about the company's integrity in the contracting process and the facts made known for all to see and understand. While there was much work yet to be done at the moment, London and the CACI leadership team would eventually be glad to have the results. The government would have its detailed review by its experts and, the CACI team felt confident, would find very little, if anything, at issue.

At CACI, it soon became clear that the media (the *Washington Post* in particular) had a heavy influence in dictating the pace of activities in the unfolding Abu Ghraib affair. It had become clear that the publication and dissemination of information could formulate negative opinion — undue influence — even while lacking the facts or, worse yet, misconstruing and exaggerating them. To London this was not good for CACI, the U.S. Army, or the American people. It seemed that "undue influence" was being exercised inappropriately by the media.

CACI's Government Compliance team led the response to DCAA. With twenty-nine years of contracting experience between the team's two managers, London and his CISG team knew this inquiry would be well addressed. When the appointed time came, senior company finance executives, General Counsel Elefante, and Senior Vice President Thornsvard, whose division had hired the interrogators, joined the company's compliance team at the meeting with DCAA. DCAA brought some of its senior people as well, including the Mid-Atlantic region audit manager.

Although DCAA had already submitted its first questions to CACI, they asked the company what was really of concern to the audit agency. How did DCAA not know about the Iraq interrogators contract? To this, the CACI team readily responded by pointing out that DCAA had only previously asked CACI if it was doing "reconstruction" work in Iraq. The particular e-mail on the topic from DCAA had said, "The first question is whether the contracts involve *reconstruction* [italics added] in

Iraq. If not, we need go no further." The company's response had been simple. "From our contracts department — No reconstruction work." As evidence, CACI produced the e-mail with the exchange. It turned out that CACI correctly answered DCAA's question, but it seemed in hindsight that DCAA may not have been asking the questions needed to get the information it now wanted. Moreover, information had been previously sent to DCAA on the GSA (DOI/BPA) contract. The company, all along, had been open and responsive in every way.

But DCAA now wanted to know more. The audit agency seemed to indicate that it wanted information about the interrogation services contract with the army and it did not want to be left unaware if something adverse arose. Understandably, CACI initially was curious about DCAA's unusual request. Through what oversight authority would DCAA review CACI's GSA contracts? In response, DCAA stated that it had enough authority under certain FAR clauses included in the GSA contract vehicle to allow them access to all requested information.

Feeling the intense scrutiny the company was getting from all directions, the CACI team felt that it had to be questioning everything being demanded of it. At first, the company wasn't fully convinced of the extent of DCAA's authority, as DCAA would technically only be entitled to examine and audit certain records.[243] But understanding DCAA's position in these unusual circumstances, CACI readily complied with this new environment of heightened scrutiny.

As it turned out, there would be a careful and detailed review by CACI and DCAA. And this was in keeping with what London had wanted the process and outcome to be.

But London also fully understood the unusual circumstances, and had established earlier a policy of full disclosure with regard to the Abu Ghraib crisis. The company's compliance staff would respond to DCAA's requests. The increasing scrutiny had put everyone in a reactive position. Yet the current workload in responding to all the inquiries was daunting. But CACI had nothing to hide. The company's relationship with DCAA had always been a good one, professional and respectful.

---

[243] These include records and other evidence sufficient to reflect properly all costs proposed, negotiated, claimed to have been incurred, or anticipated to be incurred or indirectly incurred in performance of the contract.

Before handing over anything to DCAA, the CACI staff did request some clarification. CACI asked the agency three questions. What was the purpose of the inquiry? What information did it need? And how would DCAA use the information? CACI needed to know what DCAA's intentions were to understand how to best meet the agency's objectives. The company also did not want this special circumstance to set an unusual precedent for future audits. Proper protocol needed to be established and followed for all of this.

Typically, whenever DCAA had a question about CACI's work, the onsite auditors would informally inquire of CACI's compliance staff by phone or in an e-mail. And CACI would provide the answers in a similar fashion. But like all the other events triggered by the Abu Ghraib scandal, this inquiry would be different. With all at stake from the various investigations and media scrutiny, this time the process would be more formal. As part of this formality, the CACI team informed DCAA that all requests would need to be in writing. The team also determined that before the company sent anything back to DCAA, it would have its legal department review the responses and document every aspect of the inquiry. The CACI compliance staff made sure that these responses would be thorough and the company's accountability would not be called into question.

By the end of May 2004, DCAA had submitted twenty-eight requests for information. These requests covered the usual topics such as a copy of the contract, specific task orders, the contracting officer representative, and subcontractors. Over the next several months, DCAA's review continued. Initially DCAA seemed to believe that their project would go quickly. The audit agency's branch manager whom CACI reported to for all DCAA matters, would take up a temporary office at CACI headquarters. The DCAA also used the services of five more auditors in the Washington area in addition to auditors in Iraq as part of the review. The DCAA's regional audit manager even set up shop for one week at CACI.

What the DCAA thought would take only several days ended up taking several months. But they also seemed to believe that CACI was slow in providing information because of the company's diligence and caution. Given the seriousness of the situation, however, the company was not inclined to provide information until it was reviewed internally and it could confirm every fact provided. That type of attention would take some extra time but was more than justified given the gravity of the circumstances for all parties.

To the CACI compliance staff, the DCAA requests also seemed to get more detailed and specific than would normally have been the case. By the end of October of 2004, DCAA would make eighty-seven requests for information from CACI. CACI's team replied to every request.

When asked about a few inconsistencies in timecard reporting from Iraq, CACI showed how the lack of a reliable communications infrastructure in the remote Iraq war zone sometimes prevented employees from filing their reports on time. CACI said that the company was working on processes to address the issue. Since this was a "first-time event" for CACI, the company also showed that it was quick to take corrective action.

The company also thought it unusual that DCAA would review whether or not the GSA schedule was properly utilized by CACI. While the statement of work (SOW) requirement and the GSA schedule were not always congruent, this divergence was not at all uncommon in government contracting practices, was widely known about throughout the industry, and was fully known to the government (including the GSA). Nonetheless, CACI, still following its practice of full disclosure, presented its case to DCAA. CACI would demonstrate the path of logic between the SOW and GSA schedule. It would also demonstrate that the customer, the U.S. Army, had agreed to the use of the contract vehicle and was aware of the differences.[244]

CACI also showed how it painstakingly qualified the SOW to track to the GSA schedule when the contract was initially chosen. The CACI team believed it did an excellent job of showing how interrogation support services were brought into the contract by the customer. For instance, GSA itself had historically issued similar intelligence task orders reportedly five years before with PTG in 1998. The same GSA IT schedule contract, it would later become known, was also being used by Lockheed Martin with the army for contractors at Guantanamo Bay, Cuba.[245]

---

[244] The Army Judge Advocate in Baghdad had signed off on the Purchase Request (PR) and use of the BPA at Ft. Huachuca. Officials at Ft. Huachuca's DOI National Business Center had also signed off on its use for the contract with the army.

[245] "Interior Dept. Inquiry Faults Procurement," *Washington Post*, July 14, 2004.

As CACI provided answers to DCAA's questions, the agency had to review the information and determine its conclusions. Was there anything the company was supposed to do but didn't? Did DCAA accept CACI's responses and explanations to its inquiries? As the months progressed, the CACI director of internal audit and compliance later recalled about the DCAA project, as it became understood, "Everyone just stopped talking about it."[246]

Since it was unrelated to alleged detainee abuses, the DCAA audit and review never attracted much interest in the media, but it was triggered by the Abu Ghraib scandal, or more specifically by media coverage of Abu Ghraib. And it was one more major task to the already heavy workload for CACI to address, one more task that directed employees away from their normal work to answer detailed, rigorous questions about contract performance, delivery and pay grades — questions that the government now asked because in CACI's view, Abu Ghraib had raised the perceived headline risks.

No longer focused only on detainee and prisoner abuse, the government's organizations were now examining contract administration issues as well. The echo chamber in late May of 2004 was beginning to drive the story in new directions. The initial interest in contract audit issues in May was an ominous foreshadowing of a looming threat that would, by June, put the company's entire business at risk.

---

[246] It would be December 14, 2004 by the time DCAA issued its draft reports with findings. DCAA's final report was forwarded to CACI at the end of July 2005. There were no surprises and no serious discrepancies or irregularities, but CACI's project management team was dismayed that among the questioned costs was that of body armor for its employees stipulated in the SOW, which CACI nevertheless had purchased. These were, essentially, a safety requirement under the contract for those deploying to Iraq, and the government had been unable to provide them at the time of deployment. CACI managers, however, made sure the body armor was available.

CHAPTER NINETEEN

WALL STREET
Keeping the markets informed

> "Headlines [are] twice the size of the events."
> ~ JOHN GALSWORTHY

TALKING TO THE PRESS TOOK THE MOST TIME AND PROVIDED THE greatest distraction for London. But talking to Wall Street was even more important because if the stock price held up, it could help maintain employee morale and, just as importantly, investor confidence. It would also support the company's strategy of growth through acquisition. In concluding an acquisition, if payment is to be made in shares instead of cash, then persuading a seller to take shares is more difficult when the stock performance has been weak. Though all CACI acquisitions to date had been for cash, stock might, conceivably, be considered for use in the future — or in the outright raising of capital through public stock offerings. A higher performing stock price, therefore, was not just about morale; it was also importantly about shareholder value and keeping the company moving forward.

To Dave Dragics, CACI's Vice President for Investor Relations, the questions about Iraq had certainly intensified his job, but hadn't really changed its essentials.

"In investor relations, you have two responsibilities — maintain management's credibility with the Street and help lower the cost of capital," Dragics explained. "After Abu Ghraib, the challenge was to maintain credibility. That was the whole mission."

A relative newcomer to CACI's senior team, Dragics had joined the company in August 1998 from Microdyne Corporation, where he had been director of investor relations. His résumé showed more than two decades in several positions: investor relations, finance, marketing, and business operations, including ten years working in mergers and acquisitions. He also brought extensive military experience, a valuable asset in CACI's world. A Vietnam veteran, Dragics was called back to active duty to direct the Defense Intelligence Agency's Desert Storm Task Force during the 1991 Persian Gulf War. All told, he had served twenty-six years in active and reserve duty in military intelligence before retiring as a colonel in the U.S. Army Reserve.

CACI's share price had fallen more than 8 percent (from $45.50 to $41.45) in the first days of trading after its name surfaced in connection with the Taguba report. Two weeks later the stock was off more than 10 percent, falling to $40.65. Though painful, the decline was not as severe as might have been anticipated. Many years before, by contrast, CACI shares had fallen more than 20 percent in one day because of some analysts' confusion over a company report on earnings.[247]

Those familiar with CACI knew it was a solid business. The company had a good reputation on Wall Street. In recent years, it had communicated effectively, matched or exceeded its forecasts, and delivered on its promises. The result was a foundation of goodwill that cushioned the stock against a more precipitous decline after Hersh's *New Yorker* article was published. In a testament to Wall Street's regard for both CACI's management and the company's financial strength, the stock had stabilized as the Memorial Day holiday approached and was starting to inch upward again.

---

[247] Despite explaining on a quarterly conference call in April of 2002 that the company had issued more shares, analysts' confusion led them to wrongly believe CACI's earnings performance had faltered that quarter, leading to a 20% drop in share price and over 9 million shares in trading volume in one day.

On May 26, following the market's close for the day, the company released its first projections for fiscal 2005, which would begin in July (CACI's fiscal year runs July 1–June 30). With a boost in revenue from the AMS acquisition, the company projected net income to rise as much as 30 percent in the first quarter and estimated total revenue of $1.5 billion for the full fiscal year. The share price stood at $42.42, up a bit from the post-Abu Ghraib low, and the company had scheduled a teleconference briefing for analysts the following morning at 8:30 A.M. just before the market opened.

London and Dragics considered the call a potentially pivotal opportunity to reassure analysts that the company was doing the right thing about Iraq, and that the uncertainties about Abu Ghraib had not had any significant impact on the company's business prospects.

"We had credibility before this happened," Dragics recalled. He was confident that the company could maintain its reputation on Wall Street with the same strategy it was using with the news media — straight talk and a willingness to answer every question. In his mind, as in London's, the formula was simple: step into the arena, stand up to the questions, and show that you have nothing to hide. To them, the duck-and-cover strategy seemed to signal that there was something to hide.

That was why in the crisis's first week in May, the company had held a brief, special conference with analysts. It was also why the company felt it must keep the analysts informed with another conversation. Dragics had been working the phones, talking to analysts and trying to tell them what he knew. But getting the message straight from the veteran CEO in an open forum would add a measure of reassurance that Dragics alone couldn't provide.

Three weeks had elapsed, and a lot of news stories and speculation had been published and broadcast since the first conversation and brief to Wall Street about Abu Ghraib. That first brief had taken place in the first week in May. During that time, the photos were replayed again and again on television and published repeatedly in the print media. And CACI's name was continuously featured in news reports about Abu Ghraib.

In a vacuum of information about a company, nervous investors tend to sell, driving stock prices down. Wall Street wanted to know, from the top, from the CEO, more about what was going on with CACI.

"We had to keep the communication going. Everyone wanted information at the same time, and they wanted the same information," Dragics explained.

Investor conference calls are carefully choreographed. For CACI, Dragics would act as the unofficial master of ceremonies, introducing London for opening remarks. London would then turn to CACI's CFO for details on the financial numbers and then to Ken Johnson, the President of CACI's U.S. Operations, to talk about operations. London would discuss the integration of the AMS division into CACI and, finally, talk about Iraq.

CACI's investor relations and business communications teams drafted the remarks more than a week ahead of time, and these key themes were pre-tested in internal calls from London to CACI employees in the U.S. and the U.K. just a few days before the conversation with investors. In effect, the internal conference calls on May 21 and May 25 both served to inform employees and provide a dress rehearsal for Wall Street.

The internal sessions revealed some of London's frustrations with the media. He noted that the press was in "stampede mode" and conceded that he understood their temptation to jump to conclusions. He noted that the problem was with media speculation. He said, "The media are experienced at making speculation and rumor sound like solid, proven fact, when they clearly are not."

"We're not used to this kind of media coverage and abuse, and we feel we don't deserve it," he added, giving the loyal CACI audience a glimpse at his innermost feelings. The internal sessions provided a valuable safety valve, enabling London to get things off his chest in a way that would, perhaps, not serve his purposes in discussions with Wall Street. The Street was more interested in financial measures and facts about Iraq than whether journalists were being fair. But he knew his people wanted to know their leadership was on top of the Abu Ghraib situation.

The internal teleconference also included important points that would be repeated to the investor community. To both audiences, London would emphasize his commitment to learning the facts and taking swift action if the evidence confirmed wrongdoing by any CACI employees. He also introduced a personal perspective on events in Iraq.

While stressing his horror at the photos of Abu Ghraib, he also pointed to the brutal attacks on American contractors. CACI's people had so far avoided physical harm, but London felt a deep connection with the civilians who had been kidnapped or killed.

"The crimes being committed against civilian contractors . . . are as atrocious as the terrible wrongdoing against the prisoners at Abu Ghraib," he would say to each audience. In truth, he recognized, like so many Americans, that the terrorist, jihadist atrocities (most notably the kidnappings and beheadings) were vastly grizzlier and more grotesque than the photographed abuses at Abu Ghraib. At the same time, he maintained emphatically that the transgressions at Abu Ghraib were totally inexcusable.

The earnings numbers were good, the scripts had been polished, and Dragics was confident that Wall Street would like what it was about to hear.

And then, London's fax machine rewrote the equation.

SECTION FOUR

CACI'S BUSINESS AND REPUTATION AT STAKE

CHAPTER TWENTY

A COMPANY AT RISK

Under political pressure, the government puts CACI under a microscope

> "I am giving CACI 10 days . . . to provide me with
> information and argument that CACI should
> remain eligible for future government contracts."
> ~ GSA SUSPENSION AND DEBARMENT OFFICIAL, MAY 26, 2004

SHORTLY AFTER 10:00 A.M. ON MAY 26, AS JACK LONDON PREPARED for his first public teleconference with Wall Street investment analysts since the Abu Ghraib story broke, the future changed. As Lillian Brannon, the CEO's executive assistant, waited for the fax transmission to complete, she couldn't know that CACI's world was about to turn upside down.

On hearing the familiar disconnect tones of a completed fax transmission, Brannon pulled three pages off the machine, scanned the cover note, and walked into London's office with the missive. "I have something here you ought to look at," Brannon said as she handed over the fax. The blandly worded subject line: "Contract issues with CACI International, Inc," didn't indicate the dynamite it contained. Signed by the General Services Administration (GSA) official responsible for suspensions and debarments from government contracts, the letter informed London of GSA's belief that the agency's contract schedule had been "misused" to retain CACI's services in Iraq. He said the misuse had occurred "with the knowledge and consent of CACI," and he wanted to know why the GSA shouldn't bar CACI from any new government work. Given that more than 90 percent of CACI's' revenue came from the federal government; the fax threatened the viability of the company. The letter was like having a man standing on a patient's oxygen hose and asking for a reason to pick up his foot.

"I couldn't believe it when I read it. It about took my breath away, it was so unbelievable," London recalled.

Though couched in administrative language, the implications of the GSA letter were clear. Unless CACI came up with satisfactory answers on the circumstances surrounding the contract, GSA had the authority to suspend or debar CACI from bidding on all government contracts. Federal contract regulations say only "responsible" companies with a record of "integrity and business ethics" should be awarded government business, a very broad prescription that meant GSA had great latitude in considering what to do about CACI. CACI had an exemplary record of good corporate conduct and had been on the GSA schedule IT contract for many, many years, but there seemed little doubt that GSA could pursue a debarment action.

Debarment is relatively rare and the length of the punishment and the terms can vary at the government's discretion. London found it hard to imagine that even if the company had done something wrong, the government would use its ultimate punishment for a first-time offender that could demonstrate four decades of reputable service and integrity. But if he was wrong, the penalty could be severe — as long as eighteen months for a suspension or three years for a debarment.

However unlikely debarment might seem, CACI had to assume it was possible. Less than a year earlier, in July 2003, the U.S. Air Force had suspended three divisions of Boeing from eligibility for new contracts because of improprieties in the competitive bidding process on a new contract. The telephone company MCI was barred from pursuing new government business for several months that same year in connection with accounting fraud at its predecessor company, WorldCom. Though special waivers had mitigated the debarment's impact, the distraction alone had created a difficult hurdle as MCI struggled to bounce back from the scandals that had engulfed WorldCom. In 2002, Enron and its auditor, Arthur Andersen, were debarred because of allegations of fraud at Enron. Arthur Anderson did not survive these issues and went out of business (although the firm was later exonerated when the U.S. Supreme Court overturned its conviction in May 2005).

As he worked through his shock, London composed a mental checklist of what needed to be done. He summoned general counsel Jeff Elefante and got outside counsel Bill Koegel on the phone. He needed their expert eyes on the GSA's letter for any nuances he might have missed. London called his communications chief Jody Brown to figure out what to do about possible press inquiries and also how to inform employees. He turned to his investor relations manager, Dave Dragics, to begin rethinking the pending call with Wall Street analysts.

The brainstorming with Elefante produced a recommendation that CACI engage Craig King, an attorney who specialized in government contracts at the law firm Arent Fox and had years of experience in working with GSA. Among the first tasks for King was to consider whether the letter included any signals that might be a tip-off to GSA's inclinations. For example, was it significant that GSA's letter was somewhat different in format than those it traditionally sent to troubled companies? Historically, GSA had simply informed companies that they had been placed on a list of contractors barred from bidding and challenged the companies to tell why they should be removed from the list. In effect, companies were found guilty and then given the opportunity to have their contract eligibility restored by demonstrating innocence or correcting problems. In this instance, GSA was reversing the order of events. The GSA official said he believed there was contract misuse, but he did not immediately place CACI on a restricted list. Instead, he offered the company the opportunity to make its best defense *before* he made a final judgment and to "show cause" why it should not be debarred. (In fact, the letter signaled a permanent new approach to the debarment process in general. Three weeks after the letter to CACI, GSA published for public comment a new rule proposing to adopt as standard practice the "show-cause" approach it had first introduced by sending its letter to CACI).

Brown and Dragics immediately set to work on a possible press release announcing the GSA inquiry. They also had to take a second look at a pending release on the company's earnings projections, as well as the scripted remarks for the analyst teleconference scheduled for the next day to see if any changes were required.

London needed to advise his board of directors. Collectively, the team had to decide whether CACI, as a publicly traded company had an obligation to disclose the GSA letter as a "material event" that could affect its stock price. Under federal security laws, publicly traded companies must disclose material events that could affect the business's finances or future prospects. Such disclosure is intended to give investors the necessary information for informed decision-making and to eliminate any "insider" advantage to corporate officers. Concerned about apparent increases in illegal insider trading, the Securities and Exchange Commission (SEC), in 2000 had greatly expanded disclosure requirements with adoption of Regulation FD ("Fair Disclosure"). Among other things, Regulation FD eliminated a long-standing practice of holding private briefings where Wall Street analysts and select investors, especially those with large holdings, might be given material information that was not available to the public. As a result, virtually every presentation now made by public companies is announced in advance and opened to the general public.

Regulators, auditors, and some individual industry groups have worked hard to establish clear definitions of a "material event," but the determination always comes down to judgment. In the case of CACI, losing the ability to bid on government contracts would certainly be material. Denying access to its single most important customer organization for any significant period could well destroy the business. Though disturbed, London and his colleagues believed that debarment or suspension was unlikely. Still, the slightest chance of such action made the matter hypercritical.

In their minds, CACI had acted properly. All contracting had been done openly in good faith; all parties were fully aware of how the contract was prepared and awarded. If the interrogation contract and other Iraq contract administration had been handled improperly, as the GSA letter was inquiring, CACI believed it was largely the government's responsibility, not the company's. The army had agreed to use the Interior Department contract because it needed help as quickly as possible. The Interior Department at Fort Huachuca had signed off on the arrangement. The army was fully aware of the SOW and all the contract and pricing details, as was the Interior Department. And because interrogators would use information technology to store information, analyze their findings, and cross-reference with other data sources, the Interior Department's contract officer had decided the work was appropriately covered by an IT contract.[248] It was one thing if the government now felt this type of arrangement was no longer appropriate. But to retroactively reverse itself was another story.

CACI was responding to, and providing a required service initiated and defined by the customer according to the customer's terms. The project was urgently needed, and was delivered under hostile, wartime, combat zone conditions. Moreover, CACI had a solid record of good business practices. There had never been any suggestion that CACI was anything other than the sort of "responsible" company that the government was required to hire and wanted to hire. Certainly, other companies made some significant mistakes yet were not debarred. Over the past several decades, a number of large contractors, including several defense contractors, had been taken to court and found guilty of a wide range of lawbreaking without being debarred. And other companies had, in some cases, been fined millions of dollars. It hardly seemed possible that if CACI were found somehow to be a first-time offender, the company could be restricted from government contracts for what, at most, was a procedural and administrative mistake on a relatively small dollar contract — about $19.9 million — compared to much higher dollar contracts with the companies previously cited.

"I never felt they would actually debar us once the facts were fully known. We were not that far off the ranch," London said later. "And I believe that even inside GSA they knew that." Still, he considered the matter quite important and he intended to get things straightened out quickly. He was acutely aware of the heightened sensitivity and defensiveness of anyone somehow associated with Abu Ghraib events.

In early 2004, several government reports, including at least two that were available *before* the Abu Ghraib scandal broke, suggested something was amiss with government contracting — and not only for work in

---

[248] The interrogation support contract included detailed IT requirements for each position.

Iraq. These reports showed a large and growing number of out-of-scope GSA contracts.

But contracts in Iraq had also been questioned. In particular, two months earlier, in March 2004, the Department of Defense's Inspector General (DoD IG) issued a thirty-six-page review of GSA contracts awarded for the Coalition Provisional Authority in Iraq. The study, which examined 24 contracts worth $122.5 million, was itself the result of an earlier inquiry by the Defense Contract Audit Agency (DCAA). DCAA, in May of 2003, said it found irregularities in both the award and administration of contracts to various companies and recommended an in-depth study by the DoD IG. A year later, the IG concluded that "contract rules were either circumvented or liberally interpreted" in several situations. Eighteen of the contracts studied were awarded through the GSA schedule and in ten of these, the IG said the schedule was "misused." The report listed a number of violations, finding that government contract officers did not establish firm contract controls, inappropriately awarded personal service contracts, permitted out-of-scope activity, and failed to support price reasonableness determinations.[249]

CACI was *not* among the companies cited in the March DoD IG report for contract misuse.

However, *none* of the companies named in the report had been placed under investigation by GSA's suspensions and debarment office either, according to an agency spokeswoman at the time CACI received GSA's letter in May of 2004.[250]

Separately, audits by GSA's Inspector General addressing the Federal Technology Service regional centers showed misuse of IT contracts involving numerous government contractor companies. An audit of three regional client support centers, completed in January of 2004, identified "numerous improper task order and contract awards. . . . Inappropriate contracting practices included improper sole source awards, misuse of small business contracts, allowing work outside the contract's scope, improper order modifications, frequent inappropriate use of time and ma-

---

[249] Department of Defense, Office of the Inspector General, "Contracts Awarded for the Coalition Provisional Authority by the Defense Contracting Command-Washington," March 18, 2004 (http://www.dodig.osd.mil/Audit/reports/FY04/04057 sum.htm).

[250] "Contractors sometimes stretch their deals," *Washington Post*, May 31, 2004.

terials task orders, and not enforcing contract provisions."[251] Until Abu Ghraib, the apparent deficiencies drew scant attention.

Then on June 15, just a few weeks after GSA's letter to CACI, the government's General Accounting Office reported that a review of eleven task orders issued under existing contracts to a number of other companies for work in Iraq showed that seven were out of scope and two others might be. The nine questionable task orders to these other companies were worth nearly $715 million.[252]

There were other companies that had been the focus of government concerns in the area of contracting as well, and two of these had also been involved in contracts with the army for interrogation support at Guantanamo Bay, Cuba and translator work at Abu Ghraib in Iraq.

Titan Corporation, also named in the Taguba report, was battling other challenges to its reputation. At the time of the Taguba report, Titan was under scrutiny by the Department of Justice and the Securities and Exchange Commission because of allegations that some of its overseas consultants earlier, prior to its work in Iraq, had violated U.S. law by paying bribes to foreign interests in the pursuit of contracts.[253]

Lockheed Martin Corporation, which had been in discussions to acquire Titan at the time, had been listed in earlier reports by the Project on Government Oversight as having paid the second highest amount in fines to the federal government for penalties and settlement of misconduct allegations, including out of scope work, between 1990 and 2002.[254]

---

[251] U.S. General Services Administration. "Audit of Federal Technology Service's Client Support Centers," Report Number A020144/T/5/Z04002, January 8, 2004.

[252] U.S. Government Accountability Office. "Rebuilding Iraq: Fiscal Years 2003 Contract Award Procedures and Management Challenges," U.S. General Accounting Office, June 2004(http://www.gao.gov/new.items/d04605.pdf).

[253] "Titan Admits Bribery In Africa, Contractor Will Pay $28.5 Million to Settle Criminal, SEC Cases," *Washington Post*, March 2, 2005. The bribery issue was not resolved until February of 2005 when Titan pled guilty to three criminal counts under the Foreign Corrupt Practices Act and agreed to pay $28.5 million in fines and settlement fees.

[254] In June 2004, Lockheed dropped negotiations to acquire Titan citing its refusal to extend for a third time, at Titan's request, Lockheed's deadline for Titan to resolve its litigation under both DOJ and SEC investigations. Elliot Spagot, "Lockheed effectively scuttles merger with Titan," SanLouisObispo.com, June 24, 2004.

However, the Defense Department Inspector General's report on contracting procedures in Iraq, released in March 2004 citing companies where "contracting rules were either circumvented or liberally interpreted," did *not* include a single mention of CACI.[255]

GSA had now chosen, nonetheless, to focus on CACI. The inescapable conclusion was that publicity over Abu Ghraib and the intense media questions about the propriety of the contract with the company in the spotlight had led GSA to CACI, since the company had a clean track record and was *not* on any lists among companies of recent previous concern. In addition, some CACI officials had heard a rumor on the street that GSA had been under pressure from Capitol Hill. According to the rumor, a senior attorney to a Senate committee with oversight of GSA had told the agency's administrator that he wanted to see action regarding CACI's interrogation contract. In any case, the CACI team chose to disregard the rumor. Two days later, CACI received the GSA letter.

But rumors aside, London needed to make the first critical decision — would CACI publicly disclose the GSA investigation? Or, on the theory that debarment was in the end unlikely, would London decide the company could sit on the news — unless and until debarment seemed imminent?

Some on the CACI board of directors posed theoretical arguments against disclosure. London explained in recounting the discussion, "We're a billion-dollar-company with more than 9,500 employees." "There are many important government projects being performed everyday. Are you going to stop the whole show over a small piece of business?" "You're certainly not talking about egregious contract behavior either." "And remember, you had the full knowledge of contract administration and execution by the United States Army and the Department of the Interior." London added, "It's not like someone went behind the barn and secretly cooked something up."

Still, in the end, London and the board all agreed that CACI should go public. It took two separate board meetings, conducted by phone on May 26 and with the last running toward midnight, to get everyone fully informed and the matter aired for all, to gain the board's concurrence. As the board processed the information and deliberated their actions, CACI went ahead with its scheduled release on projected earn-

---

[255] Department of Defense, Office of the Inspector General, op. cit.

ings for fiscal 2005. The upbeat report forecast total revenue of $1.5 billion for the coming year and said net income could grow as much as 30 percent (part of which reflected the recent addition of contracts acquired from AMS).

The ink was barely dry on the financial release when London told Brown to put out an announcement about the GSA letter the first thing the next morning — about the same time he would talk to Wall Street.

"The GSA has requested that CACI provide information to aid in its determination whether CACI should remain eligible for future government contracts," CACI would report bluntly in its release.[256]

Whatever the real likelihood of debarment, the news was stunning. A $1.5-billion-business might now be at risk over an interrogation contract worth just under $20 million. On Wall Street it was like a neon sign flashing "sell, sell, sell." The stock tumbled fast, dropping 12 percent on the day the news hit, a loss of nearly $5 to $37.48. The total decline for the stock was now 17 percent since the first news reports connected CACI to Abu Ghraib. And this was just the beginning of problems precipitated by the domino effect that would be triggered by the fax letter from GSA.

Other companies might have acted differently (as a Lockheed Martin-acquired company did with its interrogation contract at Guantanamo Bay, also awarded through the Department of the Interior, when it apparently decided not to publicly disclose the news that it, too, was getting questions from GSA).[257] A larger company with significant amounts of non-government business, for example, might argue it could weather the storm of debarment. Or it might take the position that its

---

256 CACI Press Release, "CACI to Provide Information to GSA Regarding Department of Interior Contract Work Performed for U.S. Army in Iraq," May 26, 2004.

257 David Phinney, "Firm's Work at Guantanamo Prison Under Review," *Federal Times*, July 19, 2004. Neil King, Jr. and Christopher Cooper, "Army Hired Cuba Interrogators Via Same Disputed System in Iraq." *Wall Street Journal*, July 15, 2004. In October 2002, Affiliated Computer Services (ACS) got a $13.3 million technology contract through the Department of the Interior that was used to hire 30 analysts and 15–20 interrogators to work at Guantanamo Bay, Cuba. The contract was terminated in November 2003 after an internal GSA investigation found the contract was not being used appropriately. In January 2004 the Interior Department initiated management of a similar interrogation contract using an existing engineering services contract Lockheed had with Interior. But in May 2004, GSA initiated another investigation into the interrogator contract to assess the issues of

work was too critical to national defense for the government to shut it down. Even if a major defense contractor was placed on a restricted list, the government had ample opportunities in the law to waive the restrictions for national security reasons (and there was much precedent for waivers, especially during war). But for London, given his style and philosophy of openness and being straightforward, there never was any serious doubt in his mind about disclosure.

However improbable the chance of debarment, he couldn't guarantee it wouldn't happen. Shareholders had a right to know. Those who were willing to run the risk and keep the stock could do so — some shareholders would obviously consider it an opportunity to buy more; there is a buyer for every share sold. But mindful of recent financial scandals in which executives hid bad news, London was determined to do right by the people who had invested their money in his leadership and his company. They should have the opportunity, *now*, to get out if the risks seemed too great. He didn't want to look back years later and find out that he had rolled the dice with other people's money, and in the event he got it wrong, people who had trusted him would have lost large sums.

He had repeatedly pledged — to his shareholders and his employees — to keep them informed as events warranted. He had declared "The Truth Will Out" as the operational name for CACI's fact-finding and informational campaign. Now was the time to prove it. He knew that going public would ignite another round of bad press reports and probably drive share prices down. But his conscience and his judgment told him a press release was the right thing to do.

Pragmatically, too, he knew disclosure was the right course. In defending the company's name against the allegations and rumors swirling around Abu Ghraib, CACI's strongest card was credibility. If word of the GSA inquiry leaked out from a source other than CACI, it could impact this credibility — with journalists, with Wall Street, and

---

scope and the role an employee played in drafting the contract. An administration procurement official said GSA put CACI and the Lockheed subsidiary under review at about the same time. Lockheed Martin commented on the GSA's inquiry to the press in July 2004 stating, "We have answered the inquiry and it is our belief it will not result in debarment or suspension." Lockheed apparently did not issue a press release or make any formally reported statements on the matter.

with its government customers. The company had built a reputation on decades of integrity and couldn't afford to lose that reputation. But there were real risks. There were scores of willing contractors eager to try to get CACI's contracts if the company did something to crack open the door. And London was *not* going to let that happen either.

London was in this fight to defend the company's good name and reputation. Whatever the short-term pain — in more press reports or lower share prices — the company would just have to ride it out.

The decision was, in part, about personal honor. But it was about being a good and trusted company, too.

"We are in a relationship business," London explained. "We operate on reputation. I concerned myself with that because a government contractor has to be forthright and straightforward."

Or, as CACI investment relations chief David Dragics observed, it's always better to deliver bad news yourself.

"It was a lot more important to keep our credibility than our market capitalization," Dragics explained. "If somebody else disclosed it, we would really take a licking [from Wall Street]. And that is not in the best interest of the shareholders. The market will take it out on you and it will punish you."

On the other hand, having a reputation for being forthcoming often pays off. One of the infrequent media bright spots came out in a call on June 21, 2004 to *The Money Gang* on CNNfn. In the response to a caller asking if he should hang onto or "dump" his shares in CACI, Steve Leeb of Leeb Capital Management got straight to the point: "I think CACI has got a bum rap here. . . . No one has charged this employee [Stefanowicz] with doing anything wrong up to this point. Yet the stock, because there was somebody there, has gotten a tremendous amount of bad publicity." Leeb continued, "People have said, well, they're going to lose all their government contracts. Forget it. That's not going to happen."

He also noted about the company's leadership that, "Their chairman, a man named Jack London, is as straight as can be."

Leeb's recommendation was clear. "I would not get too caught up in the headlines involving this company. And I would definitely hold on to it."

CACI's decision would be the right one. But first, London would go out to brief the Wall Street analysts and get the first taste of public reaction to the news about GSA.

CHAPTER TWENTY-ONE

THE PRESS IN CACI'S CORNER FOR ONCE

A positive response to CACI's candor

> "I don't think CACI has done anything to merit
> debarment, but the debarment and suspension
> systems are often used for the wrong reasons"
> ∿ DANIELLE BRIAN, EXECUTIVE DIRECTOR, PROJECT
> ON GOVERNMENT OVERSIGHT JUNE 7, 2004

THE REALITY OF THE GSA INQUIRY WEIGHED HEAVILY. IT ALSO added a significant amount of work onto an incredible workload already brought on by Abu Ghraib. The agency had provided CACI with ten days to respond, which was little time to build the sort of case the lawyers would want to make. Already, employees were quickly pulling records of every contract and every task order and all the individuals that worked on each project. But the company also wanted enough time to be thorough. For both the investor relations and business communications teams, going public with the GSA inquiry meant a new wave of investor analyst calls and press calls, as well as media coverage, ending their short-lived respite. For London and CACI's President of U.S. Operations Ken Johnson and other senior executives, though, the first order of business was the scheduled talk with the Wall Street analysts to try to allay concerns about GSA.

The GSA inquiry significantly changed the dynamics of the call with the analysts. When initially scheduled, the call was viewed by CACI as an opportunity to refocus on the good news such as the internal integration of the AMS division. While it was understood that the Iraq issues had not and would not go away for some time, the share price had steadied in recent weeks, and there was hope that the markets would learn to live with that uncertainty until the issues were resolved and investigations completed. The GSA letter had changed all that. Literally overnight, the conference call had become another exercise in damage control.

Still, the script for the call was fundamentally unchanged from what had been planned prior to the GSA letter. CACI's CFO provided a financial overview, including an upbeat report on the integration of the AMS group into the CACI operation as exemplified by the completed transfer of all of the former AMS employees to CACI's electronic time-card and e-mail systems. Johnson reported on business development efforts, including a new $88 million Navy contract finalized the day before, and noted that even amidst the Iraq turmoil, CACI had proposals pending for almost $750 million in new contracts. The heavy lifting, on the Iraq topic, was left to London.

Even as he discussed Iraq, London signaled that the business of the company also continued. Expanding on the AMS integration, for example, London reported that every former AMS employee had been matched up with a CACI employee who had volunteered to act as a "sponsor." This sponsor would teach the new colleague about the company, its processes, and procedures. He declared himself "very excited" with the integration progress to date.

Turning to Iraq, London listed five primary investigations of Abu Ghraib, including the new inquiry from GSA, and reported, "We continue to actively support every investigation and inquiry that has come our way from federal agencies." He reminded the analysts of CACI's internal investigation and again pledged to act if wrongdoing was confirmed. In response to questions, he expressed the belief that GSA would accept CACI's commitment to remedy any potential mistakes and would conclude that neither suspension nor debarment was warranted.

Consistent with his determination to tell the CACI story at every opportunity, London invited the analysts to visit the CACI Web site and read the FAQs about Iraq. Summing it up, London pointed to the old adage: "The proof is in the pudding."

London said, "Our [U.S. Army] customer is quite satisfied with the professional work being done by our personnel notwithstanding the Taguba report. . . . Our growth, I think, supports the fact that we've done good work and provide good work. We're proud of the people. We're proud of the company. We're proud of our relationships with our customers."

For the most part, the analysts gave the company high marks for the briefing. A "Feedback Report" prepared for CACI by the investment relations firm of Christensen & Associates found that the analysts continued to view CACI as "fundamentally strong" and were impressed by the company's willingness to talk openly in the midst of a crisis. There was natural concern over the GSA investigation as well as the broader issues related to Iraq, and some participants responding to London's passionate delivery complained about his tendency to "sermonize." But only a few analysts were inclined to dump the stock, and some suggested the recent dip had created a good opportunity to buy. Even one analyst who had sold the stock credited the company for candor.

"They were very honest and upfront about the issues and I don't believe they made any promises they can't keep. They very straightforwardly presented this situation, one that is very difficult, and they point out it could get more difficult," this recent seller told Christensen.

At the same time, a number of analysts wondered about the *business* logic of providing interrogation services and suggested the company exit that line of work. Noting that the interrogation work was less than 1 percent of CACI revenue and considering the damage it had caused, one analyst suggested dryly, "I can't believe the forward strategy for that business is good."

Those with an opinion said debarment appeared a long shot. "That's way too far-fetched," said one. But there was little sentiment to buy the stock either. Whether it made rational sense or not, there was fear that CACI could fall prey to political agendas.

Echoing the thinking that prevailed in CACI's executive suite, a buy-side analyst speculated: "For a rational person, it doesn't sound like the company is going to be cut off from the GSA, but you never know. It is their [CACI's] life blood."

And, in words that would show up in a range of news stories, there was a belief that CACI was just the unlucky target of opportunity at a time GSA was apparently looking to make an example.

"We all know that a lot of work is just jammed into contracts. It's easier to just jam it into an existing contract as opposed to getting a whole new RFP set up, the way the government works," said one. "I'm afraid that CACI could be made a scapegoat."

One participant offered a quick fix solution. "Providing a couple of wrongdoers for people to cast blame on would at least provide a little sense of accomplishment for some," one Wall Streeter suggested. He was probably right from a short-term PR perspective. But CACI felt the idea was a knee-jerk reaction that was totally unpalatable since it did not have any evidence about its employees' conduct to justify that kind of action.

Under the circumstances, news media coverage was about as good as CACI could have hoped. The headlines, of course, were bad news — yet another investigation. Journalists, who had been invited to listen in on the analyst call, generally noted the growing roll call of investigations in their reports, which added to the image of a company truly under siege. Unlike the inquiries about possible prisoner abuse, which focused on a small number of individuals, the GSA query seemed to raise the possibility of corporate misconduct and serious company-wide punishment.

Most news reports were skeptical about the merits of GSA's concerns. There was a bit of irony to the media reaction. The first suggestions of something amiss with the contract procedure had come from the media, which had figuratively raised its collective eyebrows upon learning that the interrogators had been hired under an Interior Department contract.

But having set the fire, the journalists now seemed dismayed that somebody was actually taking their reporting seriously enough to act. Now that they saw a response to their coverage, they shifted position. In the early reports about Abu Ghraib, the media had quoted "experts" to cast doubt on CACI; now it turned to other experts to criticize GSA's actions. It was all a bit puzzling.

Among CACI's surprise sympathizers was Danielle Brian, executive director of the Project on Government Oversight (POGO), which two years earlier had produced a lengthy report critical of the government's *failure* to use its suspension and debarment power. Brian's group had compiled page after page of contractor misconduct it said warranted debarment. Since 1990, it said, the top forty-three government contractors had paid $3.4 billion in fines/penalties, restitution and settlements. Four of the top ten companies on the list had at least two criminal convictions.[258] Only one of the forty-three had ever been debarred or suspended, and that penalty was lifted within a week. POGO's theory was that larger contractors had an unfair advantage over smaller firms in navigating through the suspension and debarment system. CACI was growing, but it was still relatively small when stacked up against the Fortune 500-sized contractors that Brian and others said seemed beyond sanction. But Brian, noting CACI's favorable track record, said the attention on the company was politically driven because of the Abu Ghraib headlines.[259]

According to POGO's Federal Contractor Misconduct Database of publicly available information, which ranks companies based on the amounts they have paid in fines, penalties, and settlements of misconduct allegations, General Electric topped the list with $990 million, more than double the second-place aerospace giant Lockheed Martin's $426 million. CACI was not to be found in any of POGO's rankings.[260]

Brian's opinion of CACI's plight with GSA was summed up in her statement to *Federal Computer Week*, where she stated that, "government has a history of cracking down harder on the smaller companies." She also stated that other contractors had far worse records and should be the focus of GSA's attention. Brian's comments about CACI were not particularly encouraging in London's view, even though he could agree at this point with her comment about the government's history of cracking down harder on smaller companies. He also believed CACI's record was excellent and that it, indeed, was "far better" than most other contractors.

But Brian's observation that CACI had a favorable track record yet seemed to have fallen prey to political agendas, suggested that CACI was being viewed more as a scapegoat than a miscreant. "I don't think

---

[258] Project on Government Oversight "Federal Contractor Misconduct: Failures of the Suspension and Debarment System," May 10, 2002.

[259] Michael Hardy, "CACI Faces Potential Debarment," *Federal Computer Week*, May 28, 2004.

[260] Hardy, op. cit.

CACI has done anything to merit debarment, but the debarment and suspension systems are often used for the wrong reasons, she said."[261]

According to GSA spokeswoman Alice Johnson, companies are required to notify contracting officials when they are asked by their government client to perform out-of-scope work.[262] That viewpoint seemed to CACI and other contractors a bizarre Catch-22. And Brian told *Federal Computer Week* that she too found it difficult to fault the contractors in this case stating that the responsibility should rest with the contracting agency.[263] The Interior Department already had acknowledged publicly, at that point, that its contracting officer had reviewed the army's interrogator request and concluded that the IT contract covered it. Now, GSA wanted to fault the company for accepting the work.

Certainly the critical wartime need made the request more pressing than the typical, routine contract request. CACI had conducted firm negotiations with the government in the past. There were times when it felt it had needed to do so, but under these specific circumstances, it hardly seemed logical or professional, or even plausible to the CACI team to do anything else in this case, but promptly accept the job and start work immediately. And that's exactly what they did.

The CACI team had logically assumed that the government knew its own contract approval processes. Why should it argue when the government said it had an urgent, critical need and gave its administrative stamp of approval to proceed? CACI had no reason to start second-guessing those in the army or the Interior Department at this point during the heated war in Iraq. Government decisions about contracting are made all the time based upon considerations and decisions not discussed or shared with the contractor.

"At no point during these delivery orders did the army indicate there was a problem. They still haven't," Interior Department spokesperson Frank Quimby, stated to the press in June of 2004.[264]

---

[261] Matthew French, "CACI Caught in Iraqi Prison Scandal," *Federal Computer Week*, June 7, 2004.

[262] "CACI Faces New Probe of Contract," *Washington Post*, May 28, 2004.

[263] "Matthew French, "CACI Caught in Iraq Prison Scandal," op. cit.

[264] Leon Worden, "Interior: Army Never Reported Abuse, Agency responsible for dealing with intelligence firm hasn't taken action because no problems were ever reported, official says," *Signal*, June 9, 2004.

Even as the army IG was conducting a review of the Interior's contracting procedures, the *Signal* was reporting positive news about CACI from both Interior and the army stating "The federal government didn't crack down on an intelligence firm [CACI] that provided civilian interrogators to Abu Ghraib prison last fall because the army never reported any kind of problem, an official [Quimby] said Tuesday." Quimby indicated that if the army had any problems with CACI's personnel or services it is supposed to tell Interior Department officials who would then deal with the company. Quimby also explained that all three parties to the contract, CACI, the army and the Interior Department have certain legal responsibilities. "CACI's responsibility is to provide the services at a (negotiated) price," Quimby said. "The Interior Department is responsible for administering the contract" including functions such as issuing checks to the contractor. The army is to provide the specifications, (determine) pay, and supervise the contract work and contract firms," he added.[265]

Several aspects of CACI's contract matter were of significance. First, the Abu Ghraib prison detainee scandal could not be blamed, in any way upon the method of contracting. This was simply not the case. Second, the contract could have been implemented in a different fashion, *but* the approach used at the time was apparently considered by the government as both appropriate and faster in light of the urgent, wartime needs in the combat zone. Above all, the contracting method and details for CACI's interrogator support services contract for the army in Iraq were approved by proper government authorities (civilian and military) both in Iraq and the U.S. And these were the facts, not conjecture or opinion.

London remained firm. "We have not knowingly done anything wrong on this. . . . We've never had any issue along these lines before," he told the analysts. "We have an impeccable record of integrity and ethics."

Outside of GSA, most commentators seemed sympathetic to CACI's predicament. The consensus view was that when the contracting system is misused to fund out-of-scope work, the responsibility lies with government procurement, not the contractor. The government's contracting process and authority are the exclusive domains of the government. It seemed to many that any other viewpoint was simply trying to "pass the buck."

"If the government comes to you and says they have more work out there for you to do, why would you turn it down? Somebody else will be

---

[265] Ibid.

right there to do it for them, and they will reap the benefits," POGO director Brian said.[266]

In an interview with the *Washington Post*, Johns Hopkins University Fellow Daniel J. Guttman said hiring interrogators under an IT contract was like buying a chair when your contract authorized you to buy apples and oranges. But, the *Post* noted, such restrictions are commonly ignored "and, until now, such violations got little attention."[267]

Claude P. Goddard, a Virginia-based government contracts attorney with Wickwire Gavin PC, weighed in and echoed these sentiments, stating that, "contractors usually don't turn down government requests for their services, even if those requests are for work that falls slightly outside an agreement." He pointed out that, "Until CACI's case, there had never been a negative reaction to such practices."[268]

Terry L. Albertson, a government contracts lawyer in a Washington, D.C. law firm volunteered words similar to Brian's: "This is an issue that comes up all the time and it frankly makes government contractors uncomfortable. If your customer comes to you and says they want to buy something, you're not going to say you won't sell it to them," Albertson said.[269]

In a follow-up *Washington Post* story three days later, Jacob Pankowski, a government contract attorney with Nixon Peabody, reaffirmed the practice, pointing out that agencies often use an existing contract to order goods and services because it streamlined a process that would otherwise take months or even years. Pankowski added, "I don't know of any cases where a contractor has rejected an order on the basis that it is not within the scope of their government-wide order — nor would one expect them to." Pankowski pointed out the irony: "The gist of this threatened action [against CACI] is to require government contractors to become the policemen of government contracting officials' conduct."[270]

The industry reaction seemed to echo the question about the appropriateness of this convoluted perspective.

---

[266] French, op. cit.

[267] "CACI Faces New Probe of Contract," op. cit.

[268] "Contractors Sometimes Stretch Their Deals," op. cit.

[269] "CACI Faces New Probe of Contract," op. cit.

[270] "Contractors Sometimes Stretch Their Deals," op. cit.

Indeed, given the urgent need for help in Iraq, Comptroller General David Walker testified at a June 2004 House Government Reform Committee hearing that it would have been likely that the out-of-scope work would have been approved for some contracts under a contracting law exemption for such critical situations.[271]

The CACI team regretted all of this industry commentary. While in a way it gave comfort and support to the company, it also gave an impression that the government didn't pay enough attention to scope issues and neither did its contractors. And that didn't reflect CACI's view or long-term experience at all. Though they could not speak for others, the CACI team believed all along that their sense of integrity and their culture of going by the rules would curb any potential out-of-bounds issues at their firm.

At CACI, the experts' comments did have the effect of easing the sting of the recent onslaught. But no matter how sympathetic, Wall Street still crunched numbers. By the end of the week, Wachovia Securities, for one, had downgraded CACI's stock. On June 1, the credit rating agency Standard & Poor's (S&P) said it had adjusted CACI's outlook from "stable" to "negative," a more worrisome change than Wachovia's because it could presage a rating change that would raise the cost of debt if CACI needed to borrow money from the capital markets. Indicative of this potential significance, the S&P action caused at least one company to pay special attention in its business dealings with CACI. "Business Units should be aware of these negative financial developments with CACI and structure new contracts, or monitor existing contracts with this knowledge in mind," said an e-mail circulated within SAIC, a company with which CACI had partnered on projects as both a prime contractor and subcontractor. With the subject line "CACI Credit Alert," the e-mail (passed along to CACI by a friendly SAIC employee) also warned of "possible future payment issues from CACI . . . as well as operational subcontractor risk."[272]

---

[271] Gail Repsher Emery, "Numerous Iraq Task Orders Fall Outside the Scope of Their Contracts," *Washington Technology Report*, June 16, 2004.

[272] An e-mail reportedly circulated within SAIC, June 10, 2004. Ironically, SAIC had apparently avoided the ax itself, having been one of the companies cited in the March 2004 DoD IG report on contracting procedures in Iraq for having had "either circumvented or liberally interpreted" contracting rules. A GAO review also found that SAIC had seven out of 11 task orders, two of which were worth more than $107 million, either wholly or partly out of scope. Ibid.

S&P maintained its BB rating for corporate credit. But it warned that ongoing investigations, including possible debarment by GSA, dictated caution. "Although CACI's revenue from Iraq are a small part of its total business, and bans from government business typically occur only in cases of extreme impropriety, a decision by the General Services Administration to ban CACI from future government contracts would impair the company's business profile and likely result in a downgrade," S&P said in a statement.[273]

Although a total contract ban seemed unlikely, the potential damage would be significant and the uncertainty created problems of its own. The fact was that CACI had its work cut out to persuade GSA of its point of view. It needed to focus intently on that task without distraction. But there was plenty of "distraction" in store, beginning with some of its neighbors in Arlington, who were organizing a protest to denounce the company that they had dubbed "the torturer" in their midst.

---

[273] "S&P Revises CACI Intl Outlook to Negative from Stable," Standard & Poor's Press Release from Dow Jones Newswire, June 1, 2004.

CHAPTER TWENTY-TWO

A NEW PHASE IN CACI'S TRAVAILS

The company pushes back and stands firmly on its principles

> **"Ignis aurum probat, miseria fortes viros**
> **(Fire is the test of gold; adversity, of strong men)."**
>
> ∼ SENECA

A LTHOUGH IT WASN'T CLEAR AT THE TIME, GSA'S INQUIRY INITIATED a new phase in CACI's travails. Prior to the GSA letter, the company was largely battling in the court of public opinion. It was caught in a crossfire of speculation about what happened at Abu Ghraib, including outlandish conspiracy theories of possible CACI links to the CIA or to Israeli intelligence agents.

The inability of CACI — or any company caught in a media frenzy for that matter — to persuade news organizations to provide the company's perspective can be an exercise in frustration. Why is it, London wondered, that after answering a reporter's questions for thirty or forty minutes at a time only a bare sentence or two of what he said found its way into the newspaper? And why, he asked, did the paragraph following his words tend to challenge rather than support what he said? To London, it seemed the reporters' stories were already complete by the time he got their calls and CACI's responses were only sought to give their stories the appearance of balance.

Though the amount of ink directed at CACI would diminish somewhat over the next several weeks, there was not a single day from April 30 until September 11, 2004, that did not have CACI or Stefanowicz cited somewhere in the media, including the Internet. Brown still fielded numerous press calls every day, though the volume levels were down. And the targeted media response letters from Burkhart and Hur continued to go out as articles and commentators in the media continued to paint a distorted picture of CACI.

The media onslaught had set the stage for a second, more dangerous phase, characterized by a growing number of tangible business threats from official inquiries and legal processes aimed directly at the company's financial well-being and management. A bad news report *is* painful. Get enough of them, and the cumulative damage to your reputation may make customers and potential business partners shy away. By making a company appear vulnerable, the flood of negative news stories might even stimulate legal actions or other threatening actions against the company.

Beginning with GSA, CACI encountered a series of direct threats, experiencing the domino effect it was trying so hard to avoid. GSA had the power to put CACI out of business almost overnight. Events yet to come, such as civil lawsuits filed against CACI by advocacy groups and private attorneys, whether motivated by political beliefs or personal financial agenda, also threatened direct economic harm — as did letters of inquiry from the California state pension funds, which attempted to advance the notion that CACI's management had gone astray.

Hanging over it all were a number of government inquiries and the possibility that the Justice Department might bring suits of its own against a CACI employee. But as London called his team together over Memorial Day weekend to plan for the coming battles, he also found himself bedeviled by a group of local political activists who planned a protest at CACI's front door. Though the demonstration would be small in number, few things caused as much consternation. To London, the protests seemed a mean-spirited intrusion on his employees and a gratuitous assault on his company's integrity.

While London understood and fully respected the right of free expression, he just couldn't abide the demonstrators' organizational leaflets, which smeared CACI as "your friendly neighborhood torturers for hire." The notion that CACI would tell an employee to torture another human being was so repugnant to London, that he could barely contain his anger. "A bold-faced lie," London called the accusations, in one of his milder comments. Many at CACI felt the protestors, angered by the reports of abuse, were mistakenly wrapping CACI up into an anti-Iraq war stance without having genuinely looked at the company or its case. Surely, some thought, they were just reacting to the negative media coverage.

Sponsored by a group labeling itself "Arlingtonians for Peace," the protest was set for June 2 — a Wednesday, and one week to the day after the GSA letter. The initial broadcast of the Abu Ghraib photos by CBS had also occurred on a Wednesday. Noticing the coincidence, Brown and attorney Koegel shared the private joke that Wednesday had become the "incoming" day of dread.

The GSA letter and the demonstration had also coincided with CACI's hiring of Prism Public Affairs. The Prism team members, with the detachment of their outside vantage point, doubted that the demonstrations would amount to very much or that the news media would much care. A few dozen demonstrators (that's what the police anticipated) would likely be ignored by all but the local press. And, even for local media, a few chanting marchers would soon be forgotten — unless a misstep by CACI created a bigger story. Their job, the Prism group believed, was to help keep the lid on. No matter how nasty the rhetoric from the street or how annoying the chants, Prism believed CACI had to look the other way, ignore the demonstrators and focus its energy on the substantive challenges in its path.

Quickly, the Prism people fell into a productive partnership with Brown, their daily point of contact. They constructed a "standby statement" with Brown that she could use if necessary to respond to inquiries from reporters. But CACI would not issue a press release or take any other action that would draw attention to an event that the press might largely ignore. The statement was low-key and calm: "Freedom of speech is at the very heart of our democracy and we respect the right of the demonstrators to express their views — even though they are wrong about the facts and about CACI," read the opening line. It was imperative to take the high road; anger or countercharges would not serve

CACI's goals. After the opening nod to the demonstrators, the language was drawn from CACI's official position. The words were like those London, Brown, and Burkhart had been using for weeks — a pledge to respond to proven wrongdoing, but not to act prematurely. And, in closing, there was an expression of the fierce pride in his company that was London's hallmark. Whether the audience was friendly or not, London wanted them to know: "We are proud of the work we do and of our high ethical standards and our long history of compliance with government contracting rules." He also wanted them to know he was proud of his company's work for the Department of Defense and the U.S. Army in Iraq, including the company's willingness to provide interrogator support work at Abu Ghraib.

In ten short lines, the statement acknowledged the demonstrators and summed up the company's position on where matters stood. The idea, a basic principle of communications, is that every event is an opportunity to deliver your message. Better still, in this instance, the statement might never be issued. That would be the best outcome because its issuance would happen only if there was media interest in the demonstration.

To minimize the risks of confrontation, employees were counseled to go about their business with heads up, but to avoid engaging with or debating the demonstrators. They were told to avoid any interaction that might get out of control or create a picture that might stimulate a news story. They were also assured that the demonstration was expected to be peaceful. The demonstrators had been in touch with local police and the FBI and said they had no plans for confrontation. They said they just wanted to make their point and go home. They even called Brown at CACI to assure her politely that they weren't "crazies."

"This was something this company had never experienced. They did not know how large the demonstration would be or whether it might become violent," recalled PR consultant Foley. "All they knew was the media had been notified and there was always the potential that something could happen that would create news."

Foley noted that the demonstration, and others like it, was also disconcerting because they were only nominally about CACI.

"CACI became a proxy for folks who wanted to protest the war," he added. "They became a convenient target for anti-war frustration."

Nonetheless, it was alarming and upsetting to CACI employees to have a group of misguided people milling around in front of the building.

Whatever ire he felt toward the protestors, and however irritated he was by the word "torturers" applied to his company, London concurred with the low-key approach. Indeed, Prism would learn to recognize a pattern that London's long-term colleagues already knew: the CEO would often start with an initial, more passionate, emotional reaction, and then would settle down to objective, intellectual reflection on the issues and consider the advice of those around him. He was like a general who marshaled his forces for a grand assault while also preparing alternative plans. When the reconnaissance reports came back he would assess the risks and benefits and decide how much force to unleash, and in which direction. Carefully sizing up the adversary, opponent or competitor was part of London's standard decision calculus.

* * *

While Prism and Brown planned for demonstrators, the lawyers plotted strategy for GSA. The first challenge for the attorneys was to gather the facts. Then, with facts in hand, they would have to decide the best way to present them.

As a first step, though, the lawyers wanted more time. Drawing on his familiarity with GSA, outside counsel Craig King believed a request for a limited amount of additional time would be granted. It was his first bit of counsel and it turned out to be correct. GSA agreed to give CACI roughly an extra week extension until June 11 to prepare its case. In the end, the meeting would take place on Monday, June 14. June 11th, it turned out, would be taken up by a state funeral for former president Ronald Reagan, who would pass away in early June.

Winning an extension was the easy part. Attorneys are accustomed to months, if not years, to assemble their cases for a courtroom trial. That longer time frame is partly due to processes that are unique to litigation, such as discovery, which allows the parties to request documentation from the other side and also to depose the adversary's witnesses. Each step of the way can involve courtroom arguments and rulings about the scope of the discovery and what documents must be turned over. The session with GSA was more akin to a negotiation. But even for that type of encounter, two weeks was not a lot of time.

CACI would have to be prepared to answer any questions about the contract vehicle, services performed, and even the customer. From the original award in 1998 to Premier Technology to the present, the full history of the contract had to be investigated and documented, including every person, process, task, and change. The lawyers would have to find the answers.[274]

Beyond the questions about the contract, the lawyers also needed to know what the federal rules said. What was the history of debarment and was there precedent — up or down — to match the circumstances surrounding CACI? Pulling all of that together would be a monumental job, not just for the lawyers, but for CACI as well. The company was going to have to assemble a team to comb through every record, assemble the data in one place, and answer every question.

One of the first tasks was a review of the interrogation contract for an objective assessment of whether there was, in fact, a legitimate issue about scope.

CACI general counsel Elefante would oversee the process, and Senior Vice President Terry Raney and his in-house team of contract administrators would carry out the task. Raney, a former U.S. Air Force colonel and military acquisition officer, had joined CACI in 2001 when it acquired Digital Systems International Corp., a neighboring company with its headquarters literally across the street from CACI.

Within a day of receiving the GSA letter, Raney was hard at work holed up in a conference room with eight colleagues, all of whom served

---

[274] The CACI legal team would have to search for answers to an array of penetrating questions and attempt to find answers, if it was possible to do so. The list was long and broad in scope: How did the very first contract in 1998 to Premier Technology come about? How did the work in Iraq come about, who had suggested this contract vehicle — the army or CACI, and had there been any thought of using a different contract vehicle? How and why was the first contract converted to a blanket purchase agreement (BPA)? What were the services performed, who directed the engagement, and what did the army think about the work? Who in the government had managed the process, why and when had administration been transferred from the army to DOI, and had the contractor had any say in the process? Who had written up the work orders and assigned titles and pay rates to each assignment, and did the interrogation work match up with the contract or, as some claimed, was it out of scope? What other task orders had been issued as part of the BPA, how much money had the government spent, and had there been any complaints before now?

previously as military or government contract officers, and each with at least two decades of contracting experience.

With oversight by CACI's legal department, the group broke into four two-man teams, divided up every one of the company's GSA contracts, and began to look for practices and patterns. The goal wasn't just to examine the interrogation contract or the work assignments for Iraq, but to take a broader look — for comparison purposes, and to see if there might be a systemic problem within the company. Then, over three days, they read every contract, examined every BPA, looked at the GSA schedule, and searched for possible mismatches. Raney's group understood the logical progression of the contract from pure IT to intelligence to interrogation. They confirmed that the government had approved the work at every step along the way, which arguably created prima facie, the GSA established precedent to support hiring interrogators under the existing contract vehicle.

Fee-for-service contract agencies that earn money for every contract issued under their schedules, such as the Department of the Interior's National Business Center and GSA, were becoming increasingly "flexible" about what they would buy with a given contract. (Until it changed its fee schedule in June 2004, GSA was earning commissions of up to 5 percent for its procurement assistance services).[275] Further, the Interior Department's Inspector General (DOI/IG) said in a July 2004 review of GSA schedule IT contracting that these types of contracts were an important contributor to the problem of out-of-scope work.

Under the heading "Contributing Factors," the DOI/IG stated: "The inherent conflict in a fee-for-service operation, [is that] where procurement personnel in their eagerness to enhance organization revenues have found shortcuts to Federal procurement procedures and procured services for clients whose own agencies might not do so."[276]

---

[275] Later that summer, following a presentation by a GSA official to the government contracting industry on this new program, the GSA official told a CACI representative that particular emphasis was now being placed on contracting officers to "do their job."

[276] Department of the Interior, Inspector General, "Review of 12 Procurements Placed Under General Services Administration Federal Supply Schedules 70 and 871 by the National Business Center," July 16, 2004 (http://www.oig.doi.gov/upload/CACI %20LETTER3.pdf).

In other words, the contracting process, administered by the Interior Department on behalf of the Defense Department and the U.S. Army using the GSA schedule IT contract and resulting DOI BPA at Ft. Huachuca's National Business Center, was a way of business that GSA had clearly been accepting for a number of years. And in CACI's case, this was further borne out by the contracting arrangement GSA had already established with Premier Technology Group, Inc. (PTG) as far back as 1998, some five years *before* CACI acquired PTG in May 2003 (and as a result acquired the existing contractual arrangement and relationship between GSA and PTG).

Ironically, the team of CACI contract experts said the use of out-of-scope-contracts wasn't necessary. They had simply become a shortcut for those who didn't know the by-the-book way to achieve the same result. A new contract could have been written under emergency conditions, as one example. Also, a contractor often had a large range of contract vehicles that could appropriately be used for many types of acquisitions that a government agency might request. And even when a contract vehicle didn't exist, the government had mechanisms to get what it needed — it typically just took more time.

For example, interrogation services could be acquired on an expedited basis under special government rules for national security or for "urgent and compelling" needs. In the case of Iraq, however, the army contracting representatives on the ground faced many demands and were under extreme pressure to "get it yesterday." They wanted the least cumbersome way possible to get the contract in place and get the interrogator support they critically needed as soon as possible.

With the insurgency escalating and Saddam Hussein and his two sons still at large, the urgent need for interrogators was clear. There were also growing numbers of Americans — soldiers and civilians — being killed by Islamic jihadist terrorists. These were the greatest factors and probably the most compelling reasons that the contracting process that was already in place and available was immediately used in August 2003.

Moreover, there was still a concern that the expedited procedures might delay the arrival of civilian interrogators. While that would be a minimal delay in peacetime, in a war zone, delays for such services were simply unacceptable. The contracting officers must have reasoned that they should do what was necessary to fight the war. *Not* doing so might be seen as causing unnecessary bureaucratic delay or be deemed irresponsible or even deadly for U.S. forces. The people of CACI, too, wanted to help the U.S. troops and the American government win the war. Saying "no" to the army's preferred contract vehicle at that time, under those circumstances, would seem to be the wrong thing to do, and when DOI signed its approval that seemed to settle the matter.

It was clear that the demands of war had taken first priority. There was no doubt that the army could find other ways to hire interrogators through private sector firms, but it would have been a slower process. With pressure for intelligence growing and more soldiers dying every day from insurgent attacks, the army procurement people decided that speed was obviously their higher priority. A new Request for Proposal (RFP) with competitive bidding was nice in theory and could be issued at a later time, but in the immediate emergency, the procurement team apparently, and understandably, took the most direct, efficient, and effective course they could find.

Working with Raney's findings, the lawyers pulled together the information and argument that they believed dismissed the notion that CACI was complicit in the misuse of the contract, and disproved any justification for debarment by GSA. There would be internal debate about the response volume's tone and how directly they should respond to GSA, but the first job was to gather facts and assemble them in the most proper, yet compelling way possible. Elefante with his legal staff and the contracts division pulled all the documents together so the presentation package could be reviewed.

If the contracts were out of scope, the next likely question was, who was responsible? Attorneys King and Koegel would tell GSA that it was the government's job, not the contractors, to monitor contract scope. Based on a conversation Raney had with one senior GSA official in mid-May, even at GSA there was reportedly a sense that the responsibility lay ultimately with the government. The question on many people's mind was, how could it be otherwise?

Raney noted that a government contracting official had phoned CACI when the first news reports said CACI's interrogators had been hired under an IT contract. When told that the news accounts appeared to be accurate, the official remarked: "That's not right. But I guess it's not *your* issue."

Piece by piece, Elefante, King, and Koegel assembled the case. Although GSA was the chief juror in this case, it was also the complainant, so the lawyers for CACI built their argument as if presenting to a jury of its peers. First, they would establish who CACI was — a good corporate citizen with four decades of favorable and responsible government contracting service. They would then let the company's history tell the story. In effect, they would make the company a character witness for itself. A step at a time, they would show the jury the evidence of CACI's commitment to ethics — not a late-life corporate conversion, but a commitment that dated to the company's earliest days, which had continued throughout and into the present.

The lawyers provided CACI's Code of Ethics and Business Conduct Standards, the foundation document that must be signed by every employee and consultant their first day at CACI. To reinforce the commitment, employees must recertify that they understand their ethical and business conduct obligations every year.

In addition to eight pages of specific rules of responsibility and conduct, the code also included CACI's Operational Philosophy, Credo, and Ten Business Values. Running throughout is the theme of accountability. And in the first paragraph of London's cover note, where it couldn't be missed, CACI's leader spelled out his sentiments: "Our long-standing philosophy has been, and always will be, to sustain the highest possible business ethics." A few lines later, London said it again: "Our goal and policy remains one of high ethics." And in closing, he spoke of high standards and ethics that every employee could be proud of. "Let's keep it this way through continued vigilance and pride in our reputation," the CEO concluded in his first words to every new colleague.

Since the early 1980s, London had been both the practical visionary, strategist, and original writer of all of CACI's philosophy, ethics, and values documents, which he proudly called CACI's "culture."

The packet for GSA also would include details on the company's compliance program and the two internal hotlines for reporting possible lapses in ethics, breaches of company rules, violations of law, or concerns about accounting, internal control, and audit matters. GSA also would be provided a July 2002 memo from London to all CACI managers with the single subject word: "ethics," in boldface and italics to emphasize its importance. Noting the various corporate scandals of the preceding year, London reminded his people of their responsibility to do things in the right and ethical way. "Our corporate culture radiates from an uncompromising tenet — honest business ethics. Our credo expresses the values that we live by and with which we conduct our business: honesty and integrity in all we do, mutual respect for each other, and quality service and best value for our customers."

The lawyers' point was plain. In considering the issues, GSA must understand the principles that defined CACI and its leadership. Responsible behavior and respect for the rules and the law were part of the corporate DNA. Any errors on this contract — and the lawyers did not concede this point — was unintentional and would be corrected. "From the outset," the lawyers noted in a presentation outline, "CACI made it clear that it would accept responsibility for and correct any potential mistakes, and be open and forthright in addressing issues." History and intent should matter when passing judgment, King and Koegel would insist.

Having laid bare the company's philosophy, the lawyers next would show the company's commitment to "transparency," the current buzzword for openness about business strategy, challenges and finances. They would detail the company's efforts to communicate, to respond to public queries about Abu Ghraib and CACI's contract work there in every forum, and to tell its shareholders and its employees everything that it knew. Among the exhibits was the transcript of the recent analyst call and a three-page talking point document, prepared by the Prism and CACI communications team. The document laid out for company managers what information the company had to say to customers, employees, and anyone else that they talked to about the company's history, its work in Iraq, its cooperation with all official investigations, and the matters before GSA.

The talking points also deliberately included two thoughtful and cautionary messages to GSA: that the Interior Department had publicly acknowledged that its contract officer had determined the interrogation contract was within scope and that "independent commentators have raised questions about the appropriateness of GSA's use of a suspension and debarment proceeding to address a matter of government procurement policy such as this." The lawyers would say that directly as well, but it didn't hurt to put it in writing. The lawyers wanted to clearly convey to the GSA that on this issue, CACI was not alone.

Having completed the "character" portion of their presentation, according to their plan, the lawyers would show how CACI had already been damaged by GSA's inquiry. It was not just CACI that needed to be held accountable, but the government contracting processes, as such, also had some matters that needed adjustment:

☐ Foremost, it was the GSA itself that, since 1998, had contracted with Premier Technology Group, Inc. (PTG) in the existing arrangement under the IT contract and specifically for intelligence support-related services for the U.S. Army in Europe (USAREUR-G2). CACI also had not entered the picture until May 2003 when it acquired PTG, some five years *after* the GSA's 1998 relationship with PTG had begun.

☐ Numerous government reports had shown that alleged scope violations were endemic across the government contracting process and many, many other companies had been mentioned, both previously and recently, as having more flagrant violations, whereas CACI had not. None of these other companies had turned up in the news, either, as receiving the same GSA scrutiny as CACI. It seemed clear that the reason it was CACI was because of Abu Ghraib and Abu Ghraib alone.

☐ Others (according to CACI's knowledge) with similar issues were being treated less formally or not at all. Especially given its good record, CACI deserved at least equal and fair consideration.

☐ Because of changes in government contracting procedures in the 1990s, out-of-scope work was not unusual across the industry and numerous, widely published and available, government investigations and reports had shown this to be the case.

☐ The policy issue — responsibility for the scope of a delivery order — fell well short of the debarment/suspension standard and should have been addressed in a less threatening context.

☐ CACI had an absolutely impeccable contracting record. CACI would *not* be in the dock now, the lawyers concluded, except for the unsubstantiated allegations of detainee abuse at Abu Ghraib, which were distinctly separate and apart from contract administration.

- It was unseemly for the government to shift the responsibility to contractors for possible failures by the government to manage the government's own contracting processes.
- CACI had been singled out unfairly in a way that compelled the company to publicly announce the inquiry. The government's letter to CACI had prompted the company to disclose the matter at a substantial cost to its business and reputation.
- News of the inquiry sent CACI's share price down 12 percent, hurting investors, costing the company more than $155 million in market capitalization, and triggering a debt rating statement.

It would be a powerful presentation, though perhaps a bit risky, to brief it so boldly and point so directly to the agency deciding CACI's fate. CACI did not want to be the example for all to point to when discussions of contract "scope" were brought up now or in the future. It would be a grave disservice to pin that burden on CACI, a company with a good reputation, when there were reportedly numerous examples of companies with records of serious transgressions. Those at CACI believed that setting CACI up as the "scapegoat" in these broad-based industry matters was simply inappropriate.

From the opening position statement, the lawyers would lay out the substantive case, demonstrating that not only had CACI made good-faith efforts to comply with every rule, but that it *had* complied at every step. And they would remind GSA that the army and DOI had agreed to the use of the IT contract under the existing BPA for interrogator support services. CACI (or more specifically its Premier Technology division) had suggested drawing up specific new contracts, but that approach had been bypassed by the army because a new contract would take a lot of additional time that it couldn't afford. In business, time is money; in war, time often means human lives.

Again, King and Koegel would map it out step by step, beginning with award of the initial 1998 contract to the PTG team that CACI acquired in 2003. They would walk through the contract history, including the conversion of that initial contract, awarded under GSA's IT schedule, to a blanket purchase agreement administered by army contract officers at Fort Huachuca. They would note the transfer as an extension of Clinton Administration reforms, from army administration to the DOI's National Business Center. Significantly, they would point out that four years before the interrogation contract, the BPA had been approved as the vehicle for providing intelligence analysts to the U.S. Army in Europe and that the GSA-approved statement of work for that assignment included a range of human intelligence support work.

Long before Abu Ghraib, the government had approved this contract for providing substantive intelligence analysis that went beyond regular, commercial IT. To document the history, the lawyers would provide contracts and task orders. They would share the PTG work proposal, which laid out every element of the service they would provide. The lawyers also would show the invoices and information about the individuals employed for the intelligence work. The history showed a steady expansion of intelligence work for which interrogation could be seen as the next logical evolution.

The army's Judge Advocate General Corps in Iraq reviewed the interrogation contract and wrote back to the army office requesting the contract on November 10, 2003 that, "There is no legal objection to the proposed [contract] acquisitions." That internal army memo, too, the lawyers would share with GSA. As additional backup, the lawyers also would append a June 1, 2004 article from *Federal Contracts Report*, which reported that Interior's contract officer had ruled that the BPA could be used for the interrogation work requested by the army. The news article also quoted Danielle Brian, the POGO executive and frequent critic of contractors, who said GSA's examination of CACI was a case of "political opportunism" because CACI "happens to be the news of the day."[277]

If there was a problem with contract scope, the lawyers' history of documentation showed it had been going on for years at PTG with the government's knowledge and approval — and long before CACI entered the picture. This demonstrated the government's de facto acceptance of the arrangement. Why then was CACI now so harshly

---

[277] Abby Bowles, "CACI Under Investigation by GSA, DOD, Interior for Role in Iraqi Prisoner Abuse," *Federal Contract Report*, June 1, 2004.

being called to task? And why was CACI the only one called out when numerous other contractors were in identical situations? It was known that some had a much longer history on the issue, with multiple occurrences, too.

Finally, the lawyers would provide the detailed accounting of the interrogation task order itself and show why all involved — the army, the contract officer at Interior, and CACI's PTG division — were confident that they had been complying with contracting rules and precedents. The lawyers also would answer questions about labor categories — "interrogator" and "screener" positions — against the GSA schedule and what role CACI had carried out in providing technical support to drafts of the contract's statement of work. Finally, they intended to show — in the government's *own* rulebooks — that the government, not the contractors, was responsible for determining and excluding out-of-scope work.

The lawyers would simply disagree with GSA's recent claims that contractors had the sole responsibility to decline out-of-scope work orders. Their position was backed by virtually every commentator who had voiced a public opinion. More importantly, there was no support for GSA's claims in any government regulation they could find. Nor were the attorneys aware of any precedent for any adverse consequence for a contractor heretofore accepting out-of-scope work.

Moreover, King and Koegel would note, a contractor's refusal to accept a delivery order under an existing contract could itself expose the contractor to other penalties, including debarment, for defaulting on its contract obligations. The contractor could be caught in a "damned if you do, damned if you don't" predicament. Under this new GSA paradigm, no matter what decision the contractor made, it could always be found "wrong" after the fact.

As an additional measure, the CACI evidence package also noted other directives from the Defense Department — the authority over the army — and also directives from the Air Force asking the contracting community to be "agile and flexible" in using contract vehicles to assist wartime efforts.

"We are telling our people that they are empowered to innovate, be creative, take reasonable and responsible risks and, most importantly, that there is no single right way to do things in the contracting world," said the then deputy assistant secretary for Air Force Contracting, Brigadier General Darryl Scott in 2002.[278]

Certainly, CACI would comply with any new rules if the government decided that *going forward* contractors shared an obligation to police out-of-scope work. Indeed, it noted that CACI was already establishing new internal controls for GSA schedule contracting. Employees would be expected to recognize that government agencies might request out-of-scope work and that contracting officer approval might not be the last word. Should concerns arise, they must be forwarded up the corporate decision ladder for review. In fact, the lawyers would tell GSA, the new procedures had already resulted in revision of a Coast Guard procurement, which was modified after CACI raised questions about the scope of the work.

The lawyers felt good about their work, but there was still the chance that GSA wouldn't be receptive or moved by CACI's presentation. And public commentary from the government side fed CACI's anxiety as GSA and other government officials, critical of the existing practices in the industry pointed to CACI and the interrogation contract as an example of a system gone awry — and all because of Abu Ghraib.

The spotlight created by Abu Ghraib, combined with a series of reports showing that government contract officers had been signing out-of-scope contracts with regularity for years, had created new pressures on GSA to clean up its contracting procedures. David M. Nadler, a well-regarded government procurement attorney at the Washington, D.C. law firm Dickstein, Shapiro Morin & Oshinsky, observed that contract "abuses have become common and more brazen, including the use of IT contracts to provide family counseling services and to construct an office building, all with minimal or no competition."[279]

With the light shining on GSA, the agency had launched its high profile "Get It Right" initiative to make clear to government contract officers and the private sector suppliers that they needed to pay more attention to the rules. But many observers believed that rather than taking

---

[277] "Air Force Streamlines Acquisition Process," *Air Force Link*, August 14, 2002.

[279] David M. Nadler, "The Pendulum Swings Back," *Federal Computer Week*, August 16, 2004. Compared to the reported accusations in Nadler's article, it would appear that CACI's contract order was neither in the same category nor close to it.

responsibility for past mistakes, GSA had found CACI a convenient platform to shift the focus.

According to *Federal Times*, at a June 8 conference for contractors, the Pentagon's procurement director Deidre Lee made reference to CACI in discussing new contracting rules.[280] Similarly, there was a remark referencing CACI at the same conference attributed to David Drabkin, GSA's chief acquisition official, who joined with DoD in vowing tougher rules.

And all the while, London continued to believe there was something unsettling about all of this. These comments, although unofficial, seemed too focused on CACI. For CACI employees in the audience at the conference, the remarks were hurtful and disappointing. It was hard, indeed, for London to fathom it all, when the intention and purpose of the contract was to help save American soldiers' lives.

Nonetheless, with the spirit of a good leader, he would work to set it right — "Get It Right" — for all concerned, including CACI and the GSA.

---

[280] David Phinney, "DoD Tightening Contracting Rules After Iraq Prison Scandals," *Federal Times*, June 8, 2004.

CHAPTER TWENTY-THREE

OUT OF LEFT FIELD:
A CONSPIRACY THEORY
Protests and lawsuits; political activists find a soapbox

"The assassin and the slanderer differ only in the weapon they
use; with the one it is the dagger, with the other the tongue.
The latter is worse than the former, for the first only kills
the body, while the other murders the reputation."
∽ TYRON EDWARDS

A S PROMISED, THE PROTESTORS' MARCH TO CACI'S DOOR HAD
been nonviolent. There was no damage to the property, no attempts to provoke. In fact, one of the organizers sent an e-mail to Jody
Brown the day of the march to assure CACI, "We are a mature, civil
group and our numbers should be relatively small. I just wanted to give
you the heads-up." Unfortunately, the demonstration would turn out to
be quite different from this self-serving message.

The CACI team immediately set about to prepare for the invasion of
protestors. Building facility security and the independent security company CACI had hired were put on alert. The communications team prepared statements for the media. Internal communications were released

to CACI's headquarters employees preparing them for the visual and verbal assault. Despite the protesters' "heads up" e-mail, the result was a mean-spirited, and even hate-filled, demonstration.

London would later recall the day bitterly. He would tell of his daughter, who was unaware of the protests, pushing his tiny grand-daughter's stroller across the intersection from the company headquarters entrance, hearing the protestors chanting "CACI torturers and killers." She was shocked as she moved on briskly to meet her husband (a naval reserve officer) at the nearby Metro station.[281] She later told her father about her disconcerting experience in seeing the graphic placards and angry slogans. She did not understand the protesters' animosity but sensed the danger the protesters could bring.

Although some at CACI saw the demonstration as an inconvenience that could have been far worse, London couldn't help but feel resentment. He found the choice of the "torturers for hire" tagline to be exceptionally spiteful and deceitful. The fact that any group would so harshly protest against CACI without knowing the facts of the case was deeply disturbing. Months later, he still looked back on the whole event with dismay and disgust.

* * *

Having survived the Wednesday of protests, Brown and Koegel wondered what the next Wednesday "incoming" surprise would be. On Wednesday, June 9, they had their answer. The activist Center for Constitutional Rights (CCR) had filed a lawsuit that shockingly accused CACI of a deliberate corporate policy of torture, rape, and even murder at Abu Ghraib.

The suit alleged that CACI and Titan had conspired with some government officials "to direct and conduct a scheme to torture, rape, and in some instances, summarily execute plaintiffs." Their shocking statements left London wondering what kind of people conjure up such outlandish views. Astonishing in its heinous allegations, the suit provided no supporting facts.

Founded in 1966, the CCR group claims it is "dedicated to protecting and advancing the rights guaranteed by the U.S. Constitution and

---

[281] In fall 2006, London's son-in-law would receive orders to report for active duty within the army and deploy to Afghanistan for a one year tour of duty.

the Universal Declaration of Human Rights." An organization that had earned its notice forty years ago during the 1960s by using the courts to help American minorities fulfill their civil rights, CCR had, from all indications, significantly digressed. From a focus on civil liberties at home, it moved into the international arena to bring lawsuits focused on what it now considered matters of social and economic injustice. In recent years, CCR was increasingly being viewed by some as having a far left-wing and distinctly anti-American foreign policy agenda.[282] By 2002, CCR's leaders were broadly attacking U.S. foreign policy. In March of that year, CCR President Michael Ratner declared that the United States "must make fundamental changes in its foreign policies . . . particularly its unqualified support for Israel, and its embargo of Iraq, its bombing of Afghanistan, and its actions in Saudi Arabia."[283]

CCR condemned the Iraq war as "an illegal, hypocritical, politically expedient and dangerous misadventure." In its 2002 pamphlet *No War*, CCR said: "We suspect that Bush's war against Iraq is really about oil and a frightening plan for world domination."[284] But by conjuring up corporate torture conspiracies, the CACI-Abu Ghraib case took CCR in an even more extreme direction.

CCR had its critics. One of them, conservative columnist John Perazzo, condemned the group's activities and agenda in a July 2002 article called "CCR: Fifth Column Law Factory." Perazzo faulted CCR for attacking the Bush administration about the war, but also for their strident views on immigration, foreign policy, and anti-terrorism strategies, as well as intelligence gathering. He noted that CCR blamed anti-American terrorism on the U.S.'s own policies. Perazzo added, "CCR even finds fault with newly implemented procedures by which the FBI, CIA, and INS can share vital information with one another in order to derail terrorist plots." Perazzo further noted, "The Center is in fact a Fifth Column law factory, part of the same political

---

[282] John Perazzo, "CCR: Fifth Column Law Factory," FrontPageMagazine.com, July 31, 2002.

[283] "Making Us Less Free: War on Terrorism or War on Liberty?" speech to NYC National Lawyers Guild Meeting by Michael Ratner, President, Center for Constitutional Rights, May 2002.

[284] Center for Constitutional Rights. "It's Time to Stand Up and Break the Silence About Bush's War Against Iraq," 2002.

Left that has spent decades portraying America as a racist, corrupt, arrogant violator of human rights both at home and abroad." Perazzo concluded, "It is difficult to identify any American action of which CCR publicly approves."[285]

To London, CCR seemed more of a politically motivated and extremist organization than one with any balanced and lofty goals. In his mind, it was one thing to debate social or economic policies at home, but something quite different, especially in time of war, to pursue initiatives that would knowingly and intentionally undermine the U.S. military — the troops in the field — and American diplomatic missions abroad.

London's disgust for what CCR apparently represented, was heightened by CCR's collaboration in a satirical anti-war book, *You Back the Attack, We'll Bomb Who We Want*, in which illustrator Micah Ian Wright reconfigured patriotic posters from World War II into attacks on the Bush administration, the war in Iraq, and domestic policies that Wright claimed threatened Americans' liberties.[286] To London, Wright's book was unsavory and CCR's page-by-page supporting commentary now negated any possible CCR credibility.

It also became apparent that Wright himself lacked credibility. Wright lied in portraying his background, claiming that he was a former army ranger who turned against war after (supposedly) witnessing errant U.S. bombs kill civilians during the 1989 invasion of Panama. Only later, after he was published, did he admit to having *never* served in the military.[287] Ironically, in August 2005, nearly a year after Wright's lies were publicly exposed a search of the CCR Web site revealed that the

---

[285] John Perazzo, "CCR: Fifth Column Law Factory," op. cit.

[286] Curiously, London had found the booklet in a bookstore on Piccadilly Street in London, England while there on business late summer 2004.

[287] The *Washington Post* reported in May of 2004: "Wright, it turns out, is a liar. He never served in the military — and confessed that last week to his publisher." But the *Post* had also been wrong about him. A year earlier, in reviewing Wright's book, the *Post* had cited his military background to distinguish him from what it called "run-of-the mill leftists" (Richard Leiby, "Rangers Lead the Way in Exposing Author as a Fraud," *Washington Post*, May 2, 2004; and, also by Leiby, "The Gadflier," *Washington Post*, July 6, 2003.) Wright's fabricated military background persists on Web sites despite his admitted deception and lies, and is readily found (2006) in excerpted book reviews quoted on such prominent commercial sites as Amazon.com and Barnes & Noble.com.

CCR organization continued to falsely describe him as "U.S. Airborne Ranger-turned-dissident."[288]

Although not a law firm, CCR's activist opinions expressed by their counsel were a vast departure from the historical positions of most law firms, which was to steer clear of public commentary. But CCR's view of the legal profession and the court system seemed to suggest that these were simply the organization's vehicles, and they would use them for the self-promotion of their political activist agendas.

In June 2004, CCR turned its rhetoric on CACI and Titan. In its early years, CCR had a string of legal successes, but the brief against CACI was notable for numerous factual errors, unsubstantiated hyperbole, and insinuations. While others had suggested the companies may have been negligent, CCR tried to characterize the alleged abuses as a deliberate, premeditated corporate business strategy.

"In order to meet quotas and crank out information, they simply violated human rights," a Philadelphia lawyer working with CCR, told reporters.[289] It was a catchy TV sound bite designed to make news, but the lawyer had no evidence to support the claim.

The lawyer's accusation was representative of CCR's press conference announcing the lawsuit. CCR offered dramatic testimony from former prisoners, but no connections to the two companies. In response to reporters' questions, CCR conceded that it could not identify any specific individuals who engaged in alleged illegal acts; nor could it say whether the alleged acts were committed by military or civilian personnel.

At best, the legal complaint filed by CCR's counsel suggested their haste to attract headlines and provide legal standing for a discovery that *might* somehow produce evidence. A review of the complaint showed a pattern of errors and unsubstantiated speculation. Furthermore, it did not verify, but repeated, the errors in the Taguba report. For example, the CCR complaint, as it was originally filed:

☐ Falsely asserted that there was a conspiracy among CACI and Titan and U.S. government officials. However, CACI's relationship with the government was no different than that of other private and

---

[288] Center for Constitutional Rights. CCR Collaborates on New Book "You Back The Attack!" May 12, 2003.

[289] Joshua Chaffin, "Contractors Face Class Action Suit," *Financial Times*, June 10, 2004.

public companies, and had never had any conspiratorial aspects with either Titan, or the government for that matter.

☐ Falsely claimed that CACI, Titan, and an unnamed third party formed an enterprise known as "Team Titan" to provide interrogation services in Guantanamo and Iraq. However, CACI had never been part of an entity known as "Team Titan" or any similar enterprise name. According to CACI officials, the company had never even heard of the name "Team Titan" until the lawsuit was filed.

☐ Wrongly claimed that CACI provided interrogation services at Guantanamo Bay. CACI never provided interrogators anywhere outside of Iraq.

☐ Falsely claimed that CACI engaged in a deliberate business strategy to acquire an interrogation capacity and then to increase the U.S. demand for those services. CACI, in fact, did not employ any interrogators, nor had it offered interrogation services to any potential customer until August 2003 when it responded to the requirement of the U.S. Army to provide interrogators for service in Iraq. At that time, CACI identified, interviewed, and hired about three dozen interrogators out of approximately 1,600 applicants. CACI did not have any idle interrogation capacity, and because of the difficulty in identifying qualified and willing interrogators, it did not use the full government funding that was contractually available for the work.

☐ Wrongly asserted that CACI relied on interrogation for revenue growth. However, the interrogation contract provided less than 1 percent of CACI's revenue.

☐ Falsely accused CACI of being "indifferent" to the quality of the interrogation activities. In fact, CACI conducted an exhaustive search to identify experienced individuals who could meet the requirements of the army's contractual statement of work. Fewer than 3 percent of the applicants were selected by CACI for review by the military and just 2 percent were hired for service in Iraq. A report by the Defense Department's Inspector General, released one month after the CCR suit was filed, confirmed that all of those hired by CACI met the requirements of the contract's statement of work. Subsequent military reports indicated that in many instances CACI's interrogators had more experience and performed better than the military's own interrogators.

☐ Wrongly alleged that CACI interrogators were operating to meet information "quotas" imposed by the United States government. CACI was never provided with quotas or targets. As of winter 2006, none of the several publicly disclosed investigations had produced any evidence of quotas.

☐ Falsely claimed that CACI deliberately sought to recruit interrogators who would willingly participate in illegal acts. An absolute falsehood, there is no evidence to support any aspect of this.

☐ Wrongly said that John Israel was an employee of CACI. Mr. Israel was employed by a subcontractor to Titan. He was never employed by CACI. This mistake in the *illegally leaked* Taguba report had been reported and publicly corrected by both CACI and Titan.

Despite CCR's attempts to sensationalize, including a headline on its Web site that read: "CCR Files Lawsuit Against Private Contractors for Torture Conspiracy — Charges U.S. Companies Conspired with Officials to Torture Detainees in Iraq," most news articles about the lawsuit focused on CCR's lack of evidence, and some speculated that the lawsuit had limited chance of success.

"The suit is short of details about the crimes that the companies and their employees are accused of committing," the *Wall Street Journal* observed. The newspaper also said that lawyers familiar with suits like this believed there was a good chance the case would be dismissed outright.[290] The *Financial Times* reported: "The complaint offered no specific details to prove the conspiracy allegation. It also failed to identify the U.S. government officials said to have taken part in the conspiracy."[291]

The motivation of the suit seemed to be revealed in a piece by the *Legal Times* that stated, "The plaintiffs are seeking unspecified monetary damages and want the defendants barred from all future government contracts. But, [CCR's Assistant Legal Director Barbara] Olshansky says, the message sent by the lawsuit may be more important than the money to the abused." Olshansky's statement that emphasized

---

[290] Mary Kissel, Christopher Cooper, and Jonathan Karp, "Two Contractors Accused of Role in Iraq Jail Abuse," *The Wall Street Journal*, June 10, 2004.

[291] Chaffin, "Contractors Face Class Action Suit," op. cit.

money and publicity, suggested that the plaintiffs were only incidental to the lawsuit, aimed primarily at giving CCR notoriety and making money for the attorneys.

CCR attempted to lay the blame for the Abu Ghraib abuses at the feet of the defendants, stating the companies "diminished America's stature and reputation around the world." This further damaged the lawsuit's — and CCR's — credibility.

Titan described the suit as "frivolous" and CACI labeled it a "recitation of false statements and intentional distortions." Given "the apparent lack of any pre-filing investigation of the facts," CACI said it might seek court sanctions against the attorneys filing the suit.

Reporters attending the CCR news conference seemed skeptical of CCR's case, repeatedly asking for proof of the accusations. But the CCR attorneys only cited the Taguba report, which had made no reference to corporate strategies or responsibility.

Despite the reporters' apparent doubts, the lawsuit received prominent play from news organizations, both print and broadcast. Many of the broadcast reports included photos from Abu Ghraib and the CACI logo — tightening the connection between the two in the audience's mind.

The coverage showed the ability of a determined self-interest group, at least upon occasion, to generate headlines. The lawsuit included explosive charges about an ongoing news story. It was filed by a known organization that could point to a number of courtroom successes in unpopular causes. Ironically, a more reasoned lawsuit might have attracted less attention.

While CCR's complaint was shoddy, it benefited from the residual credibility of the group's earlier courtroom successes. That credibility got a boost a few weeks later when the U.S. Supreme Court agreed with CCR's defense of detainees at Guantanamo Bay, Cuba — that the detainees had the right to challenge their detention in court. "Scrappy left-leaning public interest group," was how the *New York Times* described CCR on that occasion.[292]

At CACI, the suit was hard to stomach. Many legal experts, including CACI's attorneys, were convinced that the suit was less about CACI and Titan than an attempt to advance CCR's broader attack on U.S. policy.

---

[292] Adam Liptak and Michael Janofsky, "Scrappy Group of Lawyers Shows Way for Big Firms," *New York Times*, June 30, 2004.

CACI's lawyers strongly believed CCR's suit had little chance in court. Historically, the issue of war reparations — what the suit was essentially about — has been treated as a political matter to be resolved between governments. Further, the U.S. government, as sovereign, is essentially immune to litigation in this aspect.

CCR's larger interest, Elefante and his colleagues believed, was the opportunity to use the discovery process created by the lawsuit to find evidence about *government* policy, not the contractors. The lawsuit was simply the means to an end in CCR's fight over Iraq and treatment of detainees in the broader war on terror.

In an interview on public television, in which he never once mentioned CACI or Titan, CCR executive director Ron Daniels came close to admitting that he was less concerned about defending detainees' civil rights than in extracting more information from the government. Daniels noted, "One of the reasons why a lawsuit like this is extraordinarily important is 'cause it does give us the right to get discovery. It does give us a right to investigate and examine exactly what was going on. This is in fact an inquiry . . . to some degree on the part of the public. This is the way for average ordinary citizens to conduct their own investigation, for us to get an even deeper view of what was going on."[293] CACI and Titan were apparently convenient vehicles for their attempt to achieve this broader agenda.

To London, there was a lot wrong with all of this, including Daniels' statement. Daniels seemingly implied that anyone could be sued just so the plaintiffs could do "research." Daniels also made it sound like this was all done on the country's behalf. Yet, it appeared from London's perspective that Daniels thought the 9,500 CACI employees at risk of personal and professional loss by his false statement were expendable.

This "fishing expedition" approach was most evident in a statement by one of the attorneys for the plaintiff, Shereef Akeel. Referring to the individuals who might be accused, he said, "One of the common denominators they (the accusers) narrated to me was that the personnel [at Abu Ghraib] were either dressed in military or civilian clothing."[294] This

---

293 Interview with Ron Daniels, executive director of the Center for Constitutional Rights, *NOW with Bill Moyers*, June 11, 2004.

294 Marie Beaudette, "Seeking Payback; Money for Abused Iraqis Won't Come Easily nor Without Some Creative Legal Argument," *Legal Times*, June 28, 2004.

silly assertion left the lawsuit open to accuse virtually anyone working at the prison at the time.

Whatever CCR's motives, CACI and Titan would likely pay a price — in bad press, damage to their reputations, and the uncertainty and expense of litigation that could run for years and cost hundreds of thousands of dollars in legal fees. While CCR had prided itself on defending civil rights and protecting the innocent, it was indifferent, even callous, about the injury it would inflict on the company's employees by using corporate defendants as vehicles to advance its agenda. But given the extensive errors in the complaint and the hints that government was the real target, the lawsuit reflected a questionable "ends justifies the means" judgment by CCR — at odds with its stated commitment to law "as a positive force" and its purported role of defending the U.S. Constitution as well as human civil rights.

In any case — regardless of CCR's allegations and distorted conspiracy theories — London and CACI's leadership team were committed to determining the facts and the truth, and sustaining the rule of law, due process, and the concept of those accused being innocent until *proven* guilty.

CHAPTER TWENTY-FOUR

THE CALIFORNIA SURPRISE
State officials and pension funds play politics

> "Methinks thou doth protest too much."
> ∼ COMMON VARIATION OF WILLIAM SHAKESPEARE'S
> "THE LADY DOTH PROTEST TOO MUCH, METHINKS."
> (*HAMLET*, ACT III, SCENE II.)

CACI GOT ANOTHER UNWELCOME SURPRISE DURING THE SECOND week of June — and as often happened, the company heard about it first from the news media.

In April, CACI learned of the abuses at Abu Ghraib in a phone call from journalist Seymour Hersh of the *New Yorker* magazine. On June 10, it was alerted by a *Washington Post* reporter that California's state pension funds, which held almost 285,000 shares of CACI stock (about $11 million in value at the time, though only 1 percent of CACI's total outstanding shares), were about to demand answers from CACI about Abu Ghraib. Based on quotes the *Post* had collected, it appeared that some of the funds' leaders had concluded, in its own court of public opinion that CACI had behaved improperly. London was skeptical of the Californians' motives from the start. Notably *no one* from the funds had contacted the company before going to the media. The funds' strategy of airing its accusations and grievances in the press foreshadowed its future approach with CACI.

"It's not only bad practice from a social perspective, but it's bad practice from a company perspective," Sean Harrigan, president of the California Public Employees' Retirement System (CalPERS) told the *Washington Post* in explaining his fund's interest in talking to CACI about Abu Ghraib.[295] California State Treasurer Phil Angelides, a board member of the state's pension funds, whose letters to CalPERS and the somewhat smaller California State Teachers' Retirement System (CalSTRS) had sparked the action, also voiced a negative judgment about the company, again without any attempt to contact the company directly.

"I'm deeply concerned about the nature of the corporate conduct here . . . I have been troubled about what seems a denial of reality or a denial of responsibility for what happened at Abu Ghraib," Angelides said in expressing his foregone conclusions about CACI in a *Washington Post* article that ran on Friday, June 11.

"What the management of this company owes [shareholders] is a full explanation of exactly what has occurred, exactly who was responsible and a full accounting of what will be done to reform its practices," Angelides added.[296] Having already condemned the company he was about to launch a publicity stunt supported by others who had apparently come to the same conclusion.

London found Angelides' reference to "denial of reality" ironic when he noted the absence of representatives of the California funds from the CACI investor conference calls and the lack of prior communications on the part of funds, even with all of CACI's outreach. London concluded that it was Angelides' and the California funds' fault, and not CACI's, for being uninformed. The implication from Angelides' demand — that CACI "reform its practices" — clearly sent the message that Angelides had already judged CACI. It was also a clear indication that this was part of Angelides' "posturing" for his further aspirations in California politics.

---

[295] "Pension Funds Press CACI on Iraq Prison Role," *Washington Post*, June 11, 2004.
[296] Ibid.

Deep in preparations for the critical presentation to GSA within three days on June 14, London resented the tone and the timing of the queries from the West Coast. Although weighed down by the various government inquiries, London understood their inevitability. Indeed, given his own distress at the photos at Abu Ghraib, his belief in military professionalism, and the implications for his company, he *wanted* the government to find out what had gone wrong at the prison. But the accusations from CalPERS were something entirely different, which he hadn't anticipated, and which he considered unprofessional and inappropriate.

He knew there was never a question about corporate responsibility and integrity. Even if "one person [at Abu Ghraib] had gone off track," London noted, "that did not indicate *corporate* misconduct." Not only were Harrigan and Angelides suggesting a lapse by CACI, they had clearly decided to publicize their accusations and demand reparations, before they had even called the company for information. It reminded London of the logic from *Alice in Wonderland* as the Queen insisted: "Sentence first — verdict later."

Angelides' pronouncement that CACI owed shareholders an explanation flew in the face of reality, considering the fact that London had spent the previous six weeks on outreach and publicly answering every query. He had spent hours on the phone with reporters, participated in and Web-cast two public teleconferences with investors, told his employees to reach out to discuss Abu Ghraib with customers, issued regular press releases (CACI would issue eighteen written statements on Iraq-related matters between May and the end of August 2004), and established a special section to answer questions on CACI's Web site. In fact, that Web site was a two-way vehicle that included a form for new questions, which were posted and answered as they came in. Moreover, every press release was on CACI's Web site and the conference calls were available for anybody who wanted to listen to them. In addition to all of these efforts, a board-endorsed, independent counsel investigation was well underway.

Continuous communication that responded to every question had been among CACI's core strategies from the first day of the crisis. Certainly Angelides and CalPERS could take advantage of that outreach, not to mention that they could have contacted CACI and asked their questions directly, without creating a public spectacle.

It was apparent to London that if the funds were genuinely concerned about their investment, they would have asked questions before making public accusations. Instead, they first went to the *Washington Post* with the Angelides' letter and offered an exclusive story. The choice of the *Post*, the news organization that had repeatedly portrayed CACI in a negative light, instead of a California newspaper that would be read by the retirees that the pension funds represented, also was telling.

Taking the story to Washington guaranteed it would be seen by Congress, the White House, the army, GSA, the international press corps, and CACI's employees. A story that was published in Washington would almost certainly be noticed just up the Amtrak line on Wall Street and in the New York financial community.

Angelides, who as state treasurer held an automatic seat on both California pension fund boards, was widely expected to seek the Democratic nomination for California Governor in 2006 (he, in fact, announced his candidacy for that office on March 15, 2005). What better way, CACI supporters reasoned, for Angelides to appeal to a segment of voters by defining himself as standing up against the "torture" coming out of the war in Iraq? Plus, a national media outlet could help Angelides raise campaign funds from across the country. To make clear to everyone who to credit for the pension funds' inquiry into CACI, Angelides' office issued a press release on June 14 that said the funds — "at the urging of California State Treasurer Phil Angelides" — would send CACI a letter asking company officials to come to California to answer questions.

Still, London wondered why they would selectively discriminate against CACI, with accusations and demands, if the basis of the concern was genuinely corporate accountability. London believed it spoke volumes that Angelides and the funds directed their fire against a company based in Arlington, Virginia, some 3,000 miles away from the voters of California, but said nothing about Titan, the California company whose employees also had been accused by Taguba. Nor did the funds seem concerned about Lockheed Martin, which had a large presence (and many voters) in California and was supplying interrogators at Guan-

tanamo Bay, and which was under GSA investigation for the same contracting process used for the interrogators in Iraq.[297]

"I was just furious," London recalled. "My first reaction was to throw
the letter in the trash." London was incensed that anyone in public office and position of authority would show such disregard for the rule of
law and accuse and condemn CACI employees of wrongdoing without
the right of due process.

Every outside consultant — at Prism, the government affairs counselors at Clark & Weinstock, the investment relations advisers at Christensen — as well as most of his senior CACI colleagues, told London
that dismissing Angelides was the wrong approach. The only dissenting
voice was that of business advisor Burkhart, who warned that giving attention to Angelides' tactics would only embolden him in his demands
for a public forum where he could get publicity at CACI's expense. Ultimately, London's initial assessment to reject and oppose the California
attack would prove to have been the correct strategy.

The counselors who favored appeasing Angelides set out to convince
London that, in this instance, conciliation was the best policy. With
some $170 billion in assets, CalPERS was the world's largest pension
fund and controlled more money than many small countries. It had a
track record for social activism, had won wide praise for leading efforts
to protect investors through stronger corporate governance, and had
faced down and won fights with other strong companies and CEOs. But
London recognized the distinction between CACI's situation and

---

[297] From the funds 2004 portfolio holdings reports: CalSTRS held 75,780 shares of
CACI, 209,132 shares of Titan, and 1,500,871 shares of Lockheed Martin as of June
30, 2004. Also as of June 30, 2004, CalPERS held 2,158,267 shares in Lockheed
Martin, 479,839 shares of Titan and 209,100 shares in CACI. The GSA reportedly
also presented Lockheed Martin with a show cause notice in June 2004 for their
Guantanamo Bay interrogation support contract. A Lockheed spokesman said, "Our
belief is that it will not result in debarment or suspension action" but declined to say
why that was the case. Shane Harris, "GSA queries Lockheed Martin on interrogation contracts," *Government Executive*, July 29, 2004. The Lockheed contract was
being rewritten for the third time having been determined twice to have been
improperly awarded. "Lockheed's Interior Contract Gets Rewrite; Guantanamo
Interrogation Work Was Improperly Awarded Twice," *Washington Post*, July 16,
2004.

CalPERS' previous examples. And Angelides' heavy-handed approach did not impress London because the CEO had a clear knowledge of CACI's long history of integrity and business ethics.

A year earlier, CalPERS had pressured GlaxoSmithKline, the pharmaceutical giant, to cut in half the price it charged African countries for its biggest selling AIDS medication. The organization's demand for the resignation of New York Stock Exchange Chairman Dick Grasso in 2003 was considered by many the pivotal moment in Grasso's forced departure in a dispute over compensation. CalPERS' public dissatisfaction about the financial performance of the Walt Disney Company helped push that company's board to strip Michael Eisner of his position as chairman. Companies that had refused CalPERS' requests for meetings had often been added to its annual "Focus List" of firms that the fund believed needed change. Ironically, some companies' share prices rallied after announcements that with CalPERS weighing in, changes would occur.[298]

"You cannot name another investor in America who has done as much for shareholder rights," Nell Minow, editor of the Corporate Library and a prominent advocate of corporate governance reforms, had stated a year earlier in 2003.[299]

On the flip side, the fund's power was sometimes illustrated by an opposite action. In spring 2004, CalPERS' decision *not* to divest a $65 million investment in the Philippines was announced on radio by Philippine President Gloria Macapagal Arroyo and helped push the nation's stock market to a twelve-week high.[300]

But there were obvious missteps by CalPERS as well, most notably a decision to vote its shares against any corporate director who allowed a company's public audit firm to also provide non-audit services to the company. CalPERS took the position that allowing auditors to perform non-audit services creates an inherent conflict of interest that threatened auditors' ability to independently review corporate books. This put CalPERS in opposition to 90 percent of America's corporate board members, including Warren Buffett, who had endeared himself to

---

[298] Chris Gaither, "Investing with an Agenda," *Boston Globe*, April 20, 2003.

[299] Ibid.

[300] Kate Berry, "The CalPERS Machine," *Los Angeles Business Journal*, May 10, 2004.

investors by rattling corporate cages and helping improve financial performance at virtually every company he'd been involved with.

Former Walt Disney Co. director Stanley Gold, known for his corporate governance support, even chimed in on the CalPERS/Buffett issue, "I have a lot of respect for CalPERS, but on this one it's nonsense . . . nonsense. . . ."[301] Neil Weinberg of *Forbes* magazine also weighed in on the California funds' Buffet "opposition" decision, as well as others the funds wanted out of director positions at 2,700 public companies — including Steve Jobs. Weinberg stated, "If the pension fund itself were held to the same standards it demands of corporate America, the board of CalPERS might have to fire itself."[302] And California Controller Steven Westly, a pension fund board member like Angelides, conceded the fund "went a step too far" in its opposition to Buffett. "We are trying to do the right thing, but we are going about it the wrong way," admitted Westly.[303]

For an organization that pushed so hard on others' corporate governance, CalPERS seemed to some to have an odd concept of its own reporting responsibilities. For example, CalPERS had *resisted disclosure* of its private equity funds performance and the management fees it paid investment funds, until pressured to do so when news organizations filed suit demanding the data.

CalPERS was also criticized for hewing too closely to a pro-union agenda. CalPERS president Harrigan was simultaneously vice-president of the United Food and Commercial Workers Union which many considered a conflict of interest. Harrigan was accused of letting his union allegiance take precedence over his fiduciary obligation to retirees when CalPERS threw its weight behind the union during a bitter strike against the Safeway supermarket chain in late 2003. By 2004, CalPERS' board was lopsided, composed almost entirely of registered Democrats or union members, which many observers believed had led the group too far to the political left.

The fund had become a favorite and frequent target of California Republicans and of business interests nationally. It also was beginning to take

---

[301] Kate Berry, "Battle for better corporate governance earns cheers for fund," *Los Angeles Business Journal*, May 10, 2004.

[302] Neil Weinburg, "Sanctimonious in Sacramento," Forbes.com, May 10, 2004.

[303] Deborah Brewster and Simon London, "CalPERS Chief Relaxes in the Eye of the Storm," *Financial Times*, June 2, 2004.

fire from investor advocates without partisan interests. At a board meeting in July 2004, the fund got an earful from its former general counsel, Richard Koppes, and former Securities and Exchange Commission (SEC) Chairman Arthur Levitt, who had been appointed by President Clinton.

"We told them they had too much going on. We said they need to be more tactical and less political," said Koppes, the fund's general counsel from 1986–1996.[304] Levitt, who won praise in Washington for standing up to big corporations, warned the fund's board to "avoid wherever possible going off on political tangents which do not directly impact investment performance."[305]

For many on the advisory team at CACI, it was not the small stake that CalPERS held in CACI that was of concern, but rather the sphere of influence the organization seemed to potentially have. The fund's occasional success in ousting executives showed it had clout with shareholders. An increase in companies' stock prices after positive commentary from the fund demonstrated that the markets listened, too. CalPERS' recognition as a champion for the advancement of corporate governance and other activist causes established the fund as an activist in politics. Three of its thirteen members were appointed (two by the governor, one by members of the legislature) and three are *ex officio*, including California State Treasurer Phil Angelides and Controller Steve Westly — both of whom had stated intentions to run for governor in 2006.

But balancing CalPERS' strength against its recent missteps, as well as suspicions that political motivations could be involved, the consensus among London's advisors was to put aside the justifiable irritation and do everything reasonable to respond in the spirit of cooperation to the requests for information. As an admirer of Winston Churchill, however, London likened the situation to Churchill's famous quotation on appeasement: "Each one hopes that if he feeds the crocodile enough, the crocodile will eat him last."[306]

---

[304] Christopher Palmeri, "UpFront: Taking a Firm Swipe at CalPERS," *Business Week*, August 16, 2004.

[305] Jonathan Weil and Joann S. Lublin, "Gadfly Activism at CalPERS Leads to Possible Ouster of President," *Wall Street Journal*, December 1, 2004.

[306] Gretchen Rubin, *Forty Ways to Look at Winston Churchill*, (New York: Random House Trade Paperback, 2003). In 1938, British Prime Minister Neville Chamberlain believed he could avoid a European war with Germany and Italy by agreeing to

In the advisors' mind, CACI had critical issues pending before GSA. It faced a variety of government investigations, while also continuing its response to the media's confusions about CACI. CACI hadn't chosen these issues, but it couldn't avoid them, either.

With CalPERS, and the less political CalSTRS, CACI had a choice. London and his advisors could turn the inquiries into another contest by refusing to answer questions or attend a meeting. But that, they reasoned, would guarantee more publicity from Angelides and Harrigan and more distorted press for CACI. With all the real troubles CACI faced, it didn't make sense to create one that the advisors felt could possibly be avoided.

Still, Burkhart disagreed. She argued that because CACI had more critical issues, it did not need to be sidetracked by a political campaign. "Answer their questions but don't walk into their trap," she advised London. Citing the lack of previous involvement by the funds in CACI's communications, she predicted that the "summoned meeting" was a pretense to lure CACI onto their turf to attack the company and gain more publicity.

The advisors rationalized that stonewalling the pension funds would knock CACI off the high ground. They needed to answer every question, in every forum. Moreover, the advisers argued, Angelides and Harrigan could not by themselves direct the fund's investment policies. They would need additional votes. By sitting down with them and responding to questions, CACI would have an opportunity to inform the open-minded board members and staff, particularly at CalSTRS. While CalSTRS' silence might merely have been a matter of style, there also was a chance it lacked the same enthusiasm as CalPERS for condemning CACI. It seemed reasonable to find out if the two funds were of the

---

some of Hitler's and Mussolini's demands. Chamberlain, Hitler, Mussolini, and Edouard Daladier of France signed the Munich Agreement that year, transferring the Sudetenland (a region in Czechoslovakia that contained a large German-speaking population) to Germany. Czechoslovakia protested but Chamberlain proclaimed that Britain would not go to war over this. The arrangement was popular with most people in Britain because it appeared to have prevented a war with Nazi Germany. However, many critics, including Winston Churchill, pointed out that not only had the British government behaved dishonorably, but it had also lost the support of the Czech army, one of the best in Europe. Hitler broke the agreement by annexing Czechoslovakia six months later and invading Poland in 1939.

same mind. And if CACI couldn't change minds by providing the facts, sitting down with the two funds might at least prevent any further uninformed allegations against the company.

As the advisory team wrestled with how to convince London to keep the door open to a meeting, CACI's Dave Dragics, vice president for investor relations, was authorized by London to open communications with the funds. London wanted to find out if Angelides' views represented a consensus, or whether he was essentially leading a one-man effort.

CHAPTER TWENTY-FIVE

A TIME TO DECIDE
Getting ready for the General Services Administration

**"I do not believe in confessing to things we didn't do. . . . What
I wanted to do was the right thing, the honest, truthful thing."**
$\sim$ JACK LONDON

CALPERS HAD DIVERTED LONDON'S ATTENTION, BUT THE REAL
concern was just a few days ahead at GSA, and he needed to settle
a matter of tone. There were two possible approaches. He could be relatively straightforward and firm, his instinctive style, especially as he believed the merits were on his side. Or he could lean toward conciliation.
Whatever the merits of the case, GSA had the sole power to decide.

Internally, some pushed for a more pragmatic approach. The goal
was to get through the process with little, if any, impact on CACI's business. It wasn't about "winning" or proving GSA wrong. Those who
pushed the pragmatic approach thought it was a matter of realism.
From this perspective, the thing that counted most was avoiding debarment or suspension.

While believing that precedent was on CACI's side, the pragmatist
advocates also recognized that GSA had wide discretion. CACI could

challenge a debarment in court, but that would be a long and expensive process. Even if a court stayed a debarment, business could dry up. What other contractor would want CACI for a partner and what customer would choose it over a competitor while its future hung in the balance in a courtroom? Even now, just the specter of Abu Ghraib had convinced some other contractors to decline partnering opportunities until CACI's future was clear. Winning a protracted legal challenge might prove a Pyrrhic victory by a weakened company.

The best strategy, in this view, was muted protest. CACI did not need to concede guilt on the contracting matter. In fact, it needed to stand up for its legal rights. But tone was important. If decision-makers believe that you are challenging them, they may stiffen their resolve just to prove a point. That possibility argued for making the case, but without harsh rhetoric or accusation.

The other view, represented by Koegel, feared that too much conciliation could be construed as weakness or lack of confidence in your case. A bit pugnacious by nature, Koegel subscribed to the theory that you fight for what is right.

Koegel believed that GSA was wrong on the law and that CACI's best approach was to stand firm. While he did not relish lengthy litigation, he calculated that GSA also would want to avoid a high-profile court contest and even the hint of litigation might encourage the agency to listen seriously to what CACI had to say. Going to court would surely draw attention to what many believed were GSA contracting inconsistencies over the years. In matters involving CACI's disputed contract, the company could point to several years of GSA flexibility in allowing the original PTG contract to be used (*prior* to CACI's acquisition of PTG in May 2003) for intelligence support services. That was precedent that would be powerful in a court of law. And it was buttressed by a variety of recent government reports that showed a clear pattern, with many contractors, of out-of-scope work under GSA and other government contract vehicles.

Legal briefs might point out in court the revenue that these contracts earned for GSA, which for years had taken a percentage of every one of its schedule contracts. Indeed, the Department of the Interior's Inspector General, in a report that would become public in July, referred to "the inherent conflict in a fee-for-service operation . . ." The IG Report also said that, "procurement personnel in their eagerness to enhance organization revenue have found shortcuts to Federal procurement procedures."[307] DOI also benefited from fee-for-service revenue.

These facts would make it hard to lay responsibility on the issue of scope on CACI alone. Koegel believed in letting GSA know directly that CACI would fight in court if it had to do so. In this view, CACI had nothing to concede. It had followed procedure to deliver resources that the army badly needed in time of war. The government's contracting officers had concluded that the interrogation work was within the scope of the contract or, at least, had otherwise approved and authorized the contract. There was no reason to offer some insincere apology from a company that had faithfully followed the rules by initially offering to sign a new contract vehicle, but then used the process agreed to by the government (a common practice in the entire industry at the time).

It all came down to the fact that London and all of CACI's advisors and lawyers knew the company had acted in good faith in accepting the contract orders for the interrogator work in Iraq.

Koegel wasn't interested in pleading for forgiveness if it meant CACI had to confess to wrongdoing that hadn't taken place. CACI was rightly proud of its ethical standards and reputation, and he would not counsel the company to unjustifiably accept any tarnish on its good name.

While a plea bargain deal would likely remove the debarment threat, it also would be part of the permanent record that could be used against CACI in the future. Koegel also worried that such an admission could hurt CACI's business — perhaps as a tiebreaker in a future contract competition in which the contracting agency would pick the contractor with the otherwise "cleanest record."

In the end, and to no surprise to those who knew and respected Jack London, CACI would not offer disingenuous contrition. The company had *not* knowingly done anything wrong. If GSA could identify mistakes, CACI would fix every one of them. If GSA changed its policies so that in the future contractors must report potentially out-of-scope work or even decline it, CACI would follow those rules to the letter. In fact, on its own

---

[307] "Review of 12 Procurements Placed Under General Services Administration Federal Supply Schedules 70 and 871 by the National Business Center (Assignment No. W-EV-OSS-0075-2004)," op. cit.

initiative the company was putting in place new procedures for assessing the scope issue and alerting senior management. The company believed that these self-initiated measures would also be viewed favorably in the light of recent GSA reform.

But that was a different matter than accepting blame retroactively for failing to follow rules that didn't exist at the time and were now being second-guessed, after the fact.

"Some said let's do a *mea culpa* and prostrate ourselves before the powers that be. But that doesn't fit my personality and that wouldn't be right anyway," London said of his decision to take a straightforward approach to GSA. "I do not believe in confessing to things we didn't do."

He and the CACI leadership had worked too hard for decades to establish the company as a solid business, based upon integrity and ethical behavior, to take a disingenuous "easy way out."

"What I wanted to do was the right thing, the honest, truthful thing. What I did *not* want to do was give any indication that CACI had reacted in a way that might otherwise, mistakenly, make us also seem falsely, knowingly, culpable for any wrongdoing concerning our Abu Ghraib contract," London said.

Similarly he did not want to tarnish, in any way, the reputation of the people who worked for him. London honestly believed that, in a very real way, and up to a point, he held other people's honorable reputations in his hands.

"I represent a whole lot of people, employees, customers, and shareholders," he explained.

It was no surprise: London was determined to be factual about CACI. Pleading a conciliatory "guilty" when the company believed that it had neither consciously nor willfully done anything wrong was not truthful — the company had acted in good faith from the start.

As London, Koegel, King, Ken Johnson, and Jeff Elefante got in their cars on June 14 to head to their meeting with GSA, London was confident their approach was the proper one. In doing the right thing, he believed, they would be doing their best to get the "Truth Out."

CHAPTER TWENTY-SIX

THE DESTINY MEETING AT GSA
Making CACI's case

"Courage is rightly esteemed the first of human qualities
. . . because it is the quality that guarantees all others."
~ WINSTON CHURCHILL

A FTER A WEEK OF MOURNING FOR FORMER PRESIDENT RONALD
Reagan, Washington went back to business on Monday, June 14.
Among that business was CACI's meeting at GSA.

In fact the meeting with GSA would be like hundreds of other meetings held in hundreds of other unremarkable conference rooms every
business day all across Washington. The difference was that the result of
this meeting had the potential to reverberate across the government
contracting world, in both government and industry.

Arranged around a horseshoe table were the men from CACI —
lawyers King and Koegel with London, Johnson, and Elefante all seated
on one side of the table. GSA's team sat on the other side, and the GSA
official took his place at the head. It was a spacious room designed to
allow some distance between the parties. The event and the room were
all about business.

For King, who would make the case for CACI, it was a familiar scene. A former navy general counsel and one of Washington's most experienced government contract attorneys, King had participated in many meetings on behalf of contractors. Debarment and suspension meetings were his milieu, though his current client's situation and style were a bit different than most.

The typical company, facing possible sanctions by GSA or another contracting agency, apologized for anything that might have been wrong. Respectful companies, according to King, tended to get better treatment. They ate humble pie, demonstrated genuine remorse, and were allowed to get back to business.

But London had given him a trickier assignment. "We were careful to mind our Ps and Qs," Elefante said later. "'Yes, sir, no, sir' was the order of the day." But London had the evidence to show that CACI had, in good faith, followed the government's operational rules in effect at the time, and he would make certain the company complied with any new rules that might be imposed in the future regarding out-of-scope work. He also stood firm in his belief that his company should *not* be held accountable after the fact, if somebody now decided the old rules and operating process were flawed. There would be proper respect, courtesy, and civility, but there would not be any forced contrition.

Of paramount importance was the fact that there were lists of companies that had pending issues or questions regarding their contract histories, and CACI was *not* on any of those lists. Plain and simple: CACI was at GSA because of the Abu Ghraib publicity, *not* because CACI faced an out-of-scope issue larger than any other company's. In fact, given earlier government reports on the issue, many other companies would likely have had more serious problems in front of GSA's suspension and debarment officials.

King walked firmly through CACI's presentation. He ticked off a lengthy list of reasons why CACI differed with GSA. He was civil, respectful, and non-confrontational in tone. He delivered a straightforward and firm presentation. The GSA official and his team also responded in a professional and lawyerly fashion, listening, then asking questions — no raised voices, no dramatics, just advocates and judges doing their jobs. It was a wholly professional discussion.

At one level, the issue on the table was the scope of the contract, and whether it was proper for CACI to provide interrogators under a contract for information technology. But King never asserted that the contract was in scope, rather the internal review had concluded that use of the GSA Schedule IT contract was not that unreasonable under the given, urgent war zone circumstances, the widespread current industry practice, and the precedent clearly set with PTG by GSA years earlier. Across the breath of CACI's many GSA contracts, out-of-scope issues were negligible, virtually non-existent. But the interrogation contracts were an exception as a result of the urgent wartime request set forth by the army and supported by the Interior Department at Ft. Huachuca.

Instead of defending the contract, King defended CACI's conduct and pointed out that the government was the responsible party for approving any out-of-scope work. A review of the contract's history, dating back to the original task order issued to PTG in 1998, showed that it had routinely been used for intelligence services with the knowledge and approval of the appropriate (and authorized) government contract officers. (PTG was acquired by CACI in May 2003 before the interrogation services contract orders were contemplated or issued in August 2003.)

And interrogation was yet another procedure for gathering field-level intelligence. Based on five years of history, King argued, CACI had no reason to think there was anything amiss when asked by the army to use the BPA contract in this fashion, particularly in a wartime combat zone, under emergency conditions, when the U.S. Army was urgently requesting support. A broader look at government-contractor relations, as illustrated by the government's own reports, showed that the practice of stretching of contract scope was in fact the rule, *not* the exception.

"We were following the long-established pattern of conduct throughout the industry," recalled Elefante. "We couldn't argue that it was in scope, but instead that we weren't crazy or crooked for having provided the [urgently required] service."

Moreover, King argued, it was the *government's* responsibility to make sure contracts were in scope. After all, the government set the rules; the government ordered the services; the government signed and administered the contracts. King had read the contracting rulebook; he had looked at the case law and administrative precedent. Nowhere, he told the GSA team, could he find any language or rule or precedent that said that contractors had a responsibility to make judgments about scope or to report possible violations.

He cited Federal Acquisition Regulations that said contract task orders were the responsibility of "ordering offices." He noted recent reports by the Defense Department Inspector General and GSA itself that "contracting officials must ensure that the appropriate Federal Supply Schedule is used."[308] He pointed to the General Accounting Office's conclusion that remedies for out-of-scope work had traditionally been directed at the ordering agency. The rules at the time of the Iraq interrogation contract were clear that policing out-of-scope work was the government's job, *not* the contractor's. But there was more to it.

In fact, he added, contractors faced a potential Catch-22 because the refusal to honor a delivery order due to scope concerns could expose the contractor to discipline — including debarment — for contract default.

What's more, even if the GSA were to insist that CACI was responsible for the failure to be "in scope" in this instance, King stressed, the company's conduct did not merit debarment or suspension. Those penalties were the most severe available and should be reserved for the most egregious, fraudulent behavior — not for a company with a long track record of good performance — that believed it was supporting the U.S. Army in time of real need.

At this point in the conversation, King also politely sketched out that CACI was prepared to take its case to court, calmly explaining the position that retroactive application of a new regulatory obligation would *not* survive legal challenge — an ex post facto approach wouldn't fly.

His argument completed, King collected his materials and put them in his case. The two sides shook hands amicably and the CACI team exited to await the GSA's decision.

---

[308] "Contracts Awarded for the Coalition Provisional Authority," op. cit.

CHAPTER TWENTY-SEVEN

STEFANOWICZ REAPPEARS
Speaking out in self-defense

> "A June 12 article on interrogation tactics . . .
> quoted inaccurately from a statement given to
> army investigators by Steven A. Stefanowicz."
>
> ∼ CORRECTION PUBLISHED BY THE
> WASHINGTON POST, JUNE 15, 2004

ON JUNE 14, STEVEN STEFANOWICZ'S ATTORNEY, HENRY HOCKEIMER, put his client back in the news by releasing a copy of the statement Stefanowicz had given to Major General Taguba in January 2004. Ordinarily, it would have been counterintuitive to push a man to whom the media had been unkind back into the spotlight. In this instance, though, it was a necessity forced on Hockeimer and Stefanowicz because of egregious remarks and misquotations by the *Washington Post*. Hockeimer needed to make sure that the rest of the media had the facts for fear that other media would borrow or quote from the initial *Post* account and magnify the mistakes. For CACI, it was one more unwelcome opportunity to see its name linked to Abu Ghraib.

In one lengthy *Washington Post* article about the interrogation methods used at Abu Ghraib, reporters R. Jeffrey Smith and Josh White wrote that Lt. Gen. Ricardo S. Sanchez, the top U.S. military officer in Iraq, "borrowed heavily from a list of high-pressure interrogation tactics" used previously at Guantanamo Bay. Citing documents they said had not previously been disclosed, Smith and White wrote that Sanchez "gave officers at Abu Ghraib wide latitude in handling detainees."[309]

The reporters claimed that intelligence officers arranged for military police to impose severe treatment, writing that the intelligence personnel "often failed to specify how to do so, leaving wide latitude for potentially abusive behavior." To support this assertion, Smith and White quoted from Stefanowicz's January 22, 2004 statement to Taguba. But they *omitted* critical words, including Stefanowicz's declaration that everything was in accord with the rules of engagement as laid down by his military superiors. The two journalists replaced the words in his statement with ellipses to indicate that they had omitted some of what Stefanowicz said.[310] In this case, however, the omissions *changed* the essence of the Stefanowicz statement.

Specifically, the reporters quoted Stefanowicz as saying "the MPs are allowed to do what is necessary to keep the detainee awake in the allotted period of time. . . ." But Smith and White omitted Stefanowicz's vital caveat, *"as long as it adheres to the approved rules of engagement and proper treatment of the detainee,"* which showed Stefanowicz's sworn assertion — three months before the abuses became public — that rules mattered and that there were things he was, and was not, allowed to do.

The journalists also quoted Stefanowicz's request that the MPs apply "special treatment" to a detainee, but again, Smith and White omitted Stefanowicz's detailed description of the ominous-sounding "special treatment," which Stefanowicz explained meant *"showering of the detainee (not excessively) daily if necessary, having the detainee brush his teeth and the maintaining of short hair and no facial hair."* "This current detainee," Stefanowicz had explained to Taguba, "does not like to conform to proper grooming."[311]

---

[309] R. Jeffrey Smith and Josh White, "General Granted Latitude at Prison," *Washington Post*, June 12, 2004.

[310] Some news organizations bar the use of ellipses. Others allow their use to shorten a lengthy quote or to remove jargon that may make a statement hard to understand.

[311] Sworn statement by Steven Anthony Stefanowicz, January 22, 2004 as released by Atty. Henry Hockeimer, June 14, 2004.

In a statement released two days later, Hockeimer chastised the media for "innuendo, misstatements and distortion" that "unfairly depicted Stefanowicz." In defending his client, he specifically slammed the *Post* for its deficient and damaging reporting.

"We understand that most reputable news organizations prohibit the use of ellipses because of the risk of misleading the reader. The *Post's* use of ellipses in this quote of Mr. Stefanowicz demonstrates that the risk is real, and can be truly prejudicial to the person making the statement," Hockeimer said.[312]

"When the omitted portions of the quote are restored and the statement is read as a whole, it is clear that Mr. Stefanowicz, far from contributing to the abuse at Abu Ghraib, worked strictly within the confines of the rules of engagement and undertook to prevent any improper treatment," the attorney added.

Hockeimer asserted that his client "did nothing wrong and, in fact, reported several incidents of wrongdoing to the appropriate channels." He added: "This very statement from which the fragmented quotation is taken contains the reporting of one such incident."

While not clarifying the nature of the inaccuracy or conceding the misuse of ellipses, the *Post* reprinted the full quotation in a box labeled "correction." The *Post* conceded that: "a June 12 article on interrogation tactics [authored by Jeffrey Smith and Josh White] . . . quoted inaccurately from a statement given to army investigators by Steven A. Stefanowicz." It is unlikely, however, that nearly as many readers saw the correction as saw the initial error.

---

[312] The *Post* would be questioned again about it use of quotes in August of 2007 when the paper was called on printing two different versions of the same quote in two separate sports articles. Two consecutive Sunday Ombudsman columns addressed the issue. The first column stated, "The *Post's* policy couldn't be clearer: 'When we put a source's words inside quotation marks, those exact words should have been uttered in precisely that form.'" (Deborah Howell, "Quote, Unquote," *Washington Post*, August 12, 2007.)

Yet the second column started as such: "What reporters put between quotation marks isn't simply a quotation. It's a choice about what they believe the person said — or should have said. Post staff members disagree among themselves and some of them with Post policy — as do readers. Gray areas abound." The *Post's* credibility came in further question when the same column stated that, "Some reporters told me they follow their instincts rather than Post policy.") Deborah Howell, "A Dilemma Within Quotation Marks," *Washington Post*, August 19, 2007.)

The fact is that a mistake in a news story can never truly be reversed. Relatively few readers even see the "corrections" box, which typically resides in some unnoticed section of the newspaper. Moreover, the impressions readers take away from the initial erroneous story are hard to remove from the memory. In this case, a very serious mistake had been made, one that could permanently harm a man's reputation.

Hockeimer's release itself triggered a number of other news articles, most notably an article from the Associated Press that was distributed nationwide, an article in the *Wall Street Journal* (as part of a larger story), and a story in the *Baltimore Sun*. Stefanowicz's local newspapers in suburban Philadelphia also reacted to the Hockeimer release.

Having been put on notice by Hockeimer, and, no doubt pleased to have a copy of Stefanowicz's January statement, the newspapers were careful to quote Stefanowicz's exact words. Interestingly, the *Wall Street Journal*, like the *Post*, compared the tactics used at Guantanamo with those used at Abu Ghraib. But whereas the *Post* concluded that Abu Ghraib "borrowed heavily" from what had previously been done at Guantanamo, the *Journal* emphasized that the techniques at Abu Ghraib were implemented "after they were discarded as too harsh" for use at Guantanamo.[313]

Several of the follow-up stories noted an incident in which Stefanowicz said he "heard" a possible instance of abuse when, following an interrogation, MPs escorted a prisoner back to the cell. He said he questioned the MPs and they were unhappy about his questioning. Hockeimer's statement that his client had reported "several instances of wrongdoing" got little coverage — even though a fairly lengthy *New York Times* story just a few days before, on June 8, had said that Stefanowicz had reported a military intelligence interrogator for making a detainee walk naked down a cellblock.[314]

To London, it defied logic that the initial accusations against Stefanowicz merited page one coverage, but information that suggested the man accused of wrongdoing acted properly was virtually ignored. London believed this was ample proof that some in the media failed to

---

313 Smith and White op. cit.; Christopher Cooper and Greg Jaffe, "Iraq Prison Rules Seen as Too Harsh for Guantanamo," *Wall Street Journal*, June 15, 2005.

314 Zernike and Rohde, "Forced Nudity of Iraqi Prisoners Seen as a Pervasive Pattern, Not Isolated Incidents," op. cit.

even attempt to provide a balanced story. This lack by the media weighed heavily on London. One explanation was that the media was losing interest in Stefanowicz. He was "old news." The other explanation was that the story didn't have the salaciousness it did before. Either way, the lack of coverage was not reassuring for those, such as CACI, who were interested in finding the whole truth about Abu Ghraib.

Whatever the reason, a review of the coverage of Abu Ghraib showed that by June, media interest in CACI and Stefanowicz was beginning to ease somewhat — but was far from over. While new developments such as the GSA inquiry, the CCR lawsuit, or the release of Stefanowicz's sworn statement still stimulated "spot" news stories, follow-up stories — so-called enterprise journalism where reporters dig deeper to expand the previous day's story — about CACI and its employees were now less common.

However, as is often the case, hometown papers stayed with the story longer. Unfortunately for CACI, its hometown paper, the *Washington Post*, was among the country's most widely read and most political. And unfortunately for Stefanowicz, the declining interest meant that any positive information about his conduct reached a much smaller audience than the original coverage of the *illegally leaked* Taguba report.

As June unwound, CACI continued to face significant challenges to its business and its reputation. The outcome of GSA's inquiry still hung in the balance. The California pension funds were demanding attention and a range of official investigations remained outstanding. But packages of newspaper clips gathered and analyzed by Prism each day began to show a decline in reports that mentioned CACI or Stefanowicz. In early May, scores of stories had referenced CACI every day — and these reports might total 200 pages. By late May, CACI continued to show up in stories virtually every day, but in fewer publications. But by mid-June, the news coverage began to diminish further although CACI never escaped the media. From that point on, when stories, blogs, or political activists mentioned Abu Ghraib, references to CACI or Stefanowicz would most likely be included. And *months* later the Abu Ghraib abuse pictures in which *no* CACI employees ever appeared still found their way into defamatory stories about the company.

Though the media continued for months to write extensively about courtroom proceedings involving some of the MPs from Abu Ghraib — events that might have had implications for CACI — the company was not mentioned. Even the CalPERS controversy received only limited attention after the initial report by the *Post*.

But the overall issue of prisoner abuse still remained a daily topic in the media. Some in the media, in fact, used the Abu Ghraib incident as a constant headline grabber. The *New York Times*, for instance, reportedly carried the Abu Ghraib story on its front page thirty-two consecutive days between May and June 2004.[315] It was also reported to have run front page stories on Abu Ghraib close to fifty times by September 2005.[316]

However, the focus in the general media had largely shifted from Abu Ghraib to the broader questions about U.S. policy toward prisoners and the Geneva Conventions. In the politics of a presidential election year, partisans on both sides tried to frame the debate in ways that might help their party at the polls. On June 8, for example, (the same day as the *New York Times* story on page A-14 stating that Stefanowicz had reported prison abuse), the front page of the *New York Times* said of a Pentagon memo that "Lawyers Decided Bans on Torture Didn't Bind Bush."[317] The subject of various memos dominated Abu Ghraib coverage for days as reporters and administration critics looked for links to the White House. "The Reach of War: The Memorandums," the *Times* wrote the next day, and the *Washington Post* weighed in with reports on more secret documents, declaring "Ashcroft Refuses to Release '02 Memo."[318] And, when they *did* write about contractor issues that month, reporters often turned back to the company whose conduct might have major political implications, namely Halliburton, where Vice President Cheney had earlier been the CEO.

Still, the CACI team continued to push out its messages through statements drafted by Brown in response to specific media inquiries,

---

315 Penenberg, Adam. "Searching for *The New York Times*." Wired News July 14, 2004 (http://www.wired.com/news/culture/0,1284,64110,00.html).

316 Bill O'Reilly, "Is the Abu Ghraib Ruling Dangerous?", *The O'Reilly Factor*, FOX News, September 29, 2005. A search of Abu Ghraib stories in the *New York Times* in January 2007 revealed a total of 74 articles.

317 Neil A. Lewis, and Eric Schmitt, "Lawyers Decide Bans on Torture Didn't Ban Bush," *New York Times*, June 8, 2004.

318 Neil A. Lewis, "The Reach of War: The Memorandums; Documents Build a Case for Working Outside the Laws on Interrogating Prisoners," *New York Times*, June 9, 2004; "Ashcroft Refuses to Release '02 Memo; Document Details Suffering Allowed in Interrogations," *Washington Post*, June 9, 2004.

and the targeted media response letters by Burkhart and Hur, which continued to be updated and customized in response to news stories that raised concerns for the company. And the FAQs continued to be updated on the CACI Web site.

London was also mindful of keeping employees up to date and reassured that the company was handling the situation with honesty and integrity. To this end, internal communications also continued at a steady pace.

When errors or misstatements occurred, the CACI team continued to point them out and, in some cases, obtained printed corrections. In a number of instances, the company took the additional step of elevating its message by sending a letter from its outside legal counsel. At the same time, CACI continued to issue news releases reiterating its key messages — such as a three-page release on Sunday, June 13, that repeated its core positions on Abu Ghraib, and provided reporters information about the CCR lawsuit and the inquiries from the California pension funds.[319]

Not all of the news and commentary was negative. Occasionally some positive and encouraging messages came through. "We don't want to see the private sector become a political football," said Doug Brooks, president of the International Peace Operations Association, a nonprofit consortium of business and organizations that provide humanitarian peacekeeping and reconstruction services worldwide. "The private sector has worked with the military since before 1776 and will continue to. . . . The better they work together, the more effective the operation."[320]

However, significant news spikes for CACI lay ahead. A GSA decision and release of the pending military investigations were certain to shine the spotlight on CACI again. But in terms of volume, the trends showed that the CACI story was slipping in the media's priorities. Yet that could — and would — change very quickly.

---

[319] CACI Press Release, "CACI Continues to Inform Investment Community and Public at Large About CACI's Business In Iraq, The Company Seeks to Correct Inaccurate Reports," June 13, 2004.

[320] Elaine M. Grossman, "Possible Interrogation Contractor Influence Cited in Senate Vote," op. cit.

CHAPTER TWENTY-EIGHT

TALKING TO THE CALIFORNIA FUNDS
CACI considers its options

"Hypocrisy is the homage that vice pays to virtue."
∼ FRANCOIS DE LA ROCHEFOUCAULD

THE CACI TEAM WORKED TO CONVINCE LONDON THAT THE California pension funds' accusations needed a response and that direct talk was the best approach. As the company's investment relations director, Dragics would be the advance person. He was asked to take the lead — finding the right people at the funds to talk to, gauging reactions, and attempting to prevent any public battles between CACI and the funds' leaders. California State Treasurer Phil Angelides and then-President of CalPERS Sean Harrigan had already taken a couple of swats at CACI, and London resisted the instinct to respond.

Regardless, as he had done from the start of the crisis, London wanted to defend CACI's good name and press the accusers to learn the truth.

Former Pentagon official Dave Berteau and former Congressman Vic Fazio, the government relations counsel from Clark & Weinstock, knew both Angelides and Harrigan from Democratic Party politics. PR consultant Foley, a Democratic Party activist who kept his hand in party politics even after his entry into the private sector, also was familiar with Angelides. They told their client that Angelides and Harrigan had taken on much larger foes than CACI.

Business advisor Burkhart also offered relevant insight on Angelides. She pointed out that Angelides' approach was aimed primarily at attracting attention in trying to prove his political might. That the Californian tended to stage his confrontations with CACI, complete with press coverage, and that he held a persistently accusatory posture led Burkhart to conclude that Angelides was merely using CACI's situation in order to stake out his political positions. As evidence, she cited Angelides' tactic of contacting the *Washington Post* before contacting CACI. His subsequent public "summons" of CACI to California to answer questions before the media had assured her that it was publicity he sought. This, she noted, was a politically motivated power play designed to embarrass CACI and bolster Angelides' own image. She encouraged CACI to stay on the high road and not get pulled into the quagmire of Angelides' political campaign.

Thus, it was not surprising when Brown received an unusual — but revealing — phone call from a reporter at the *San Francisco Chronicle* who wondered if CACI had a response to Angelides' latest statements. Talking with Brown, the reporter referred to Angelides as a "media hound" and stated doubt that the paper would even cover Angelides' most recent pronouncements.

CACI carefully considered its response to Angelides and the California funds. Any fire from London would be returned in kind across the continent, with rhetoric that newspapers would love. For CACI, given its recent experience, more media coverage would probably have an unwelcome outcome.

"Public discussion with a politician is the last thing we wanted," said Dragics rather ironically, since this was where events appeared to be going. But there would be limitations, as Dragics had said. "The first thing we decided was that we did not want this at Jack's level. It's a lot easier to escalate later than to de-escalate. We wanted maneuvering room."

A draft letter from London to Angelides was put on hold while Dragics penned his own response — not to Angelides, but to the officers of the funds. "They were the shareholders," Dragics explains, so that's to whom CACI would respond — Harrigan, but also to CalPERS' CEO

Fred Buenrostro, CalSTRS CEO Jack Ehnes, CalPERS Investment Committee Chair Rob Feckner, and the two funds' chief investment officers, Mark Anson of CalPERS and Chris Ailman of CalSTRS.

Dragics started the letter by noting CACI's disappointment that no one from California had contacted the company with their concerns before talking to the press. He also indicated a willingness to respond to the funds' questions and, if necessary, to meet in person if a convenient time could be arranged. Plus, the CACI letter was signed by Dragics, not London, a signal to the funds' that the company intended to treat their inquiry as a legitimate shareholders' request.

Depending on sentiment at the California funds, this letter could be regarded in two very different ways. It might be seen as a welcome gesture of cooperation. Alternatively, the letter could be taken as a snub because the funds' concerns were not addressed personally by the company's most senior executives. The way the funds responded could reveal to London and his advisors how big a challenge they had on their hands. Dragics' letter, in effect, was partly a way to open the door to a legitimate dialogue and fact-finding venture. CACI needed to know whether CalPERS and CalSTRS truly had major concerns about the company, or whether they were going through the motions in an obligatory follow-up to a political agenda.

On the afternoon of Sunday June 13, just two days after the *Washington Post's* report, Dragics sent the letter — by fax, e-mail, and Federal Express. He had worked fast, not only because of the inherent urgency of the matter, but also to satisfy his CEO's demand for action. Dragics had to move quickly if he was going to persuade London to defer a tougher, and possibly more public, response of his own.

The first returns came in quickly. Though it was a Sunday night, Dragics was still in his office at 6:30 P.M. when his phone rang. The caller ID window showed a 916 area code — Sacramento. On the other end of the line was Jack Ehnes, the CalSTRS CEO. The two commiserated about working on Sunday and then Ehnes said something that Dragics was delighted to hear: "You know," Ehnes said, "We [CalSTRS] didn't write the letter, Angelides did."

Dragics responded in kind. CACI's letter went to Ehnes, Dragics explained, because the fund, not Angelides, was the shareholder. Ehnes indicated that he understood, and said he was handing the matter to one of CalSTRS' staff people, Janice Hester-Amey, who was responsible for corporate governance issues. He promised that Hester-Amey would be in touch.

At one level, Ehnes' words could be viewed as a bureaucratic response — a suggestion that CACI had sent its letter to the wrong place. But Dragics doubted Ehnes was calling on Sunday just to deliver an address correction. In his mind, the real meaning of Ehnes' words was that, left to its own devices, CalSTRS would not be trying to call CACI on the carpet. Though brief, Dragics believed the phone call was a good sign. On the other hand, Ehnes most likely had called on Sunday evening, not expecting anyone to answer and believing he could just leave a message.

While vigorous in pursuing corporate governance issues and proud of its own record of activism on that issue, CalSTRS typically acted with less flamboyance and less notoriety than its larger sister fund, CalPERS. Earlier in 2004, CalSTRS Chairman Gary Lynes, a public school teacher, had frankly discussed the two funds' differing approaches.

"I would say right now their [CalPERS] corporate governance strategy is a little bit more high profile than ours, and my preference is we keep it that way," Lynes told the *Los Angeles Business Journal* in May.[321]

Given the notoriety of the Abu Ghraib scandal, as well as Angelides' interest in amplifying it, there was little doubt that CalSTRS would seek answers from CACI. But Dragics was banking on differences in the two funds' leadership to give CACI some room for maneuver. Based on the discussion with Ehnes, it seemed that CalSTRS had limited enthusiasm for adverse action against CACI. The fund would listen with an open mind, it was thought within CACI, and if CalSTRS declined to act, the belief was that its restraint would temper CalPERS as well.

While Dragics pursued his assignment, London decided to push back in public. Though persuaded against a direct response to Angelides, London wanted CACI's position on the public record, especially to counter the *Post's* Angelides article. The result was a substantial CACI press release — four pages that recapped the company's position on a range of Abu Ghraib issues in order to keep the record straight.

---

[321] Laurence Darmiento, "Content Below the Radar, No. 3 CalSTRS Exerts its Influence," *Los Angeles Business Journal,* May 10, 2004.

CACI's June 13, 2004, press release provided background on the company's history and reiterated its pride in supporting the troops. The company offered responses to almost every major question that had been raised in recent weeks. It explained the evolution of its intelligence business, including its agreement to provide interrogators for service in Iraq, and it noted its continuing cooperation with every government inquiry.

Then, at the bottom of page three was London's response to Angelides. In countering Angelides' publicized complaint that CACI hadn't answered questions from the funds, the release noted CACI's various public briefings on Iraq, the release of numerous statements, and the posting of information on CACI's Web site. It noted that neither Angelides nor the funds had participated in any of the investor conference calls made available to any and all shareholders. Nor had the California group contacted CACI directly for information. Purposefully, to preserve some negotiating space, the release did not include a commitment to respond to the funds' questions.

Contrary to Angelides' accusation that information was somehow not provided or available regarding CACI, the company felt it could not make a move without generating a news story. With all the press swirling around Abu Ghraib, CACI took the opposite position of most companies and PR advisors, deciding in favor of releasing information rather than remaining silent. CACI had been extremely forthcoming and had distributed vast amounts of updated information through several channels to keep the public informed and the media coverage accurate. Furthermore, with several investigations now underway, including CACI's own internal investigation, it was highly unlikely that any information would be left out, or missed by anyone.

The next day, while London was in the critical meeting with GSA, Dragics phoned CalPERS investment director Mark Anson to gauge the sentiment at the fund. As with Ehnes, Dragics explained that CACI was communicating to its shareholders, not to Angelides. When Anson asked if CACI would send a management team to meet with CalPERS, Dragics quickly replied in the affirmative. "Absolutely," Dragics told Anson, "We have nothing to hide."

Anson thanked Dragics and said he would tell his board that CACI was being "forthright." Unfortunately the discussions between CACI and CalPERS would get more difficult after that.

The next day, Anson penned a formal request to Dragics for CACI to meet with the CalPERS investment committee on August 16 at a regularly scheduled meeting. Anson said the board wanted answers to the questions in Angelides' letter and also wanted Dragics or other senior executives to appear in California to answer questions in person.

"I assure you that the CalPERS Board of Administration considers these allegations to be a most serious matter and expects that CACI International will respond in a forthright manner to the questions posed by Treasurer Angelides," Anson's letter stated. The letter from Anson took advantage of Dragics' offer but also was aimed at putting him in a vice.

Dragics believed CACI was now obliged to meet with the two funds, and he pressed London for authority to set up a meeting. While withholding a firm commitment, London told Dragics to keep talking to the people in California. Familiar with the "bait and switch" routine, London could see the writing on the wall in California.

The next conversations — between Dragics and Anson — grew more contentious. Dragics said the August 16 date proposed by CalPERS, which had a regular investment committee meeting set for that day, was difficult for CACI. The company's board was set to meet on the seventeenth and its earnings were due out on the eighteenth — all-hands-on-deck events. The proximity of the earnings release also created the potential of conflicts with the Securities and Exchange Commission's Fair Disclosure rules. Public discussion of a company's business right before earnings raised, at least, a theoretical risk of selective disclosure of information to some shareholders — in this case the California funds. As Dragics noted in a subsequent e-mail to Anson: "It is our practice — and the investment community and our shareholders respect this practice with not only CACI but other public companies as well — to refrain from commenting on analysts' and shareholders' inquiries or to make public comments so close to such a significant corporate event."

Because a meeting would involve the expense of a special trip to California, Dragics noted that CACI officials would be in California sooner on August 3 to participate in an investor conference, and he inquired if CalPERS would meet with them at that time. When Anson declined, Dragics asked if CACI might answer questions in a video conference on August 16. That way, the CACI team could stay close to home for their board meeting and earnings news release activities, and CalPERS could get its questions answered on the day its members were already planning to meet.

The response back to Dragics was revealing. Again, Anson refused. "The board won't like that," he advised. The CalPERS leader, whether directed by Angelides or not, was working hard to get a face-to-face meeting on the Californians' terms — and no doubt with the media in attendance.

It was becoming increasingly evident that CalPERS was less interested in a cooperative meeting that would promote the free flow and exchange of information, and more interested in demonstrating that the fund, not CACI, would decide where and when to meet. The message was now coming across that it would order CACI to appear, not ask or negotiate with CACI.

CalPERS' insistence on scheduling the meeting on August 16 put Dragics in a tough spot with London, who wasn't convinced the meeting was warranted. London didn't like being dictated to, and didn't care for the idea of spending extra money to send people across the country to meet with a group that appeared to have passed judgment and issued its condemnation already. He sensed that the company was being baited under the guise of shareholder dialogue, and the switch to the political, media-driven agenda would come when CACI arrived.

Dragics wondered if he could resolve the matter by negotiating a different date with CalSTRS, which, in his initial contacts with its representatives, appeared to be less dogmatic than its bigger sister fund. He planted the seed in a phone conversation with Janice Hester-Amey, the CalSTRS staffer with responsibility for corporate governance who agreed to consider the early August date and get back in touch.

But before he could finalize the deal, the dialogue was nearly derailed, yet again, by public accusations from California State Controller Steven Westly who, along with Angelides, had a seat on both pension fund boards. CACI was once again forced to take up its own self-defense.

Like Angelides, Westly was considered a possible contender for the Democratic gubernatorial nomination in 2006. But he had broken from his board colleagues in conceding that CalPERS had overreached in its vote against Warren Buffett as a corporate director. Quiet during the first round between Angelides and CACI, Westly suddenly staked out his own position with a July 6 press release that said CalSTRS should not invest in companies "engaged in torture." In his news release, Westly saw fit to publicly cite and implicate CACI.

Westly's release said the fund should amend its statement of investment responsibility to specifically restrict investments in companies that sell "technologies or services designed for use in the torture of human beings or the treatment of people which does not meet the minimum standards of the Geneva Convention." The release went on to state that Westly would discuss his proposal at an upcoming meeting of the board's subcommittee on corporate governance, and that the subcommittee was set to "discuss a proposal to question executives from CACI International regarding its role in the Iraq prisoner abuse scandal."[322]

Oddly, the release did not suggest a similar policy for CalPERS. The omission apparently reflected the upcoming CalSTRS subcommittee meeting, which was scheduled for that week. The conventional thinking was that if CalSTRS adopted the language, CalPERS would undoubtedly follow suit at the next opportunity.

At first glance, Westly's proposal seemed unassailable, though it was hard to know what companies would be barred by his proposed standard. Corporations with public stature and accountability do not sell technologies or services explicitly "designed" for torture. But with CACI specifically cited in Westly's news release, any reader would quickly draw his intended connection.

"This is not about putting one company under a microscope," Westly insisted. Rather, he wanted "every company to respect human rights, whether it's operating in Iraq or Indiana."[323]

But in the context of Abu Ghraib, and Westly's observation in the press release that the upcoming meeting would include a discussion about CACI's alleged "role in the Iraq prisoner abuse scandal," London and his team concluded that Westly's proposal was aimed squarely at CACI. The CACI team was particularly incensed that of the two companies whose employees were named in the *illegally leaked* Taguba report, Westly only cited CACI. The other company, Titan, was Westly's Cali-

322 California State Controller's Office Press Release, "Westly Seeks Anti-Torture Investment Policy," Press Release, July 6, 2004.

323 Ibid.

fornia constituent. To CACI, the failure to mention Titan belied Westly's assertion that he was not singling out any particular company.

London acted swiftly as CACI fired back with its own press release, rejecting Westly's "vile allegations" and accusing him of "political grandstanding" by rushing to judgment before the evidence was in." And to make sure it got its point across, CACI faxed its release to every California State official and every member of the state legislature.

Westly responded with a private letter to London.

"Nowhere in my press release, proposed policy, or statements at the CalSTRS board meeting did I accuse CACI of wrongdoing or participating in torture," Westly again insisted. "I intentionally proposed a broad policy that does not focus on any one company. In fact, I believe the Board should focus more of its time on growing teachers' retirement funds, not on allegations and relatively small investments in any one company." Yet, at the same time, CalSTRS CEO Ehnes, in an e-mail to Dragics, reacted by haughtily suggesting that CACI needed to calm down.

"I do not see any semblance of 'vile allegations' in the controller's release and would suggest that you might take a second and more level headed look at the release," Ehnes wrote. But to London and other CACI insiders, Ehnes had missed or purposefully ignored the point. CACI was responding to a communication that Westly had initiated. And in CACI's view, perhaps the Californians should have calmed down and taken a levelheaded look at their own accusations and communications. To CACI, the California funds' organizational behavior seemed incoherent and, now, fragmented.

In the meantime, Dragics believed he had been near agreement with CalSTRS on a meeting date. If he could close the deal, he could then go back to CalPERS with a blunt message to "join us at CalSTRS or forget about it."

Nonetheless, Dragics felt a need to respond to Ehnes and let the chips fall where they may. He noted that Westly's release, in language very similar to the lawsuit against CACI and Titan by the Center for Constitutional Rights, talked about companies that "profit from the torture of human beings." He observed that both CACI and Titan were targeted in the suit and that CalSTRS held stock in both companies, but "most notably, that CACI was the *only* company cited in Mr. Westly's release."

"We believe we had a duty to respond as we did in order to protect the interests of other shareholders, employees and customers of CACI. We do not want the word 'torture' associated with CACI, and we will not accept any insinuation that we 'profit from the torture of human beings,'" wrote Dragics. London, in reviewing Dragics' letter, fully supported the response.

SECTION FIVE

TURNING THE TIDE

CHAPTER TWENTY-NINE

GOOD NEWS . . . FOR A CHANGE
GSA responds while California waits

**"In no way will mere allegations affect the working relationship
we have with CACI. This situation . . . does not create any
doubt in our minds as to CACI's veracity and honor."**
~ Letter to CACI Senior Vice President Ron Schneider
from a U.S. military officer, July 2004

I T WAS WEDNESDAY AGAIN, THE DAY BILL KOEGEL AND JODY BROWN
had come to expect incoming bombshells. But this Wednesday, July 7,
would be different. There would be more big news, but this time the
news would be good.

As the day opened, however, the focus at CACI was California and responding to Westly's anti-torture policy press release of the day before.
The morning's conference call on the latest media developments, a daily
8:00 A.M. session with London, Brown, Foley, and Schneider, assessed the
damage to CACI from Westly's release. The verdict was mixed. Only
Reuters, the international wire service, had published a report on the
Westly release. But Reuters' stories traveled round the globe to almost
every significant newsroom in the world. Plus, the story's eleven brief

paragraphs cited CACI six times. While Westly insisted he was not targeting CACI, the Reuters' report showed that with the Westly release written
the way it was, the media would zero in on making a CACI connection.

Working with Prism, Brown began developing an op-ed, in conjunction with London, in which the CEO would respond to Westly and criticize the California pension funds and State Treasurer Phil Angelides for
rushing to judgment before they had gathered the facts. London wanted
to act quickly to make CACI's position public before the upcoming
meeting, which would surely be used as a showcase for Angelides.

But within the hour, the day changed. At 9:00 A.M. London's fax connected with a fax machine across the Potomac River at GSA. A three-
page letter from the GSA was on its way. It began with a brief history of
events and then recounted the June 14 meeting. The GSA official noted
that CACI had called the GSA inquiries a "disservice" to the company
and had asserted it was "unseemly for the government to shift blame to
contractors."[324]

GSA seemed to object to CACI's views that, under the law and at the
time the first interrogator services contracts were issued, responsibility
for scope issues resided exclusively with the government. He asked
CACI for additional information on three specific areas.

First, the GSA requested more information about the apparent
involvement of a CACI employee in assisting in the preparation of the
statement of work (SOW) for the interrogation contracts. Second, he
asked for information about all pending investigations "to avoid any misunderstandings," and third, he asked about CACI's experience with
three hotlines the company had established for employees who wished
to express concerns about possible ethics violations. He wanted CACI's
responses within two weeks.[325]

But in the letter's final words, the GSA official indicated that he
would not take any action against CACI.

---

[324] Letter from the GSA Suspension and Debarment Official to CACI CEO J.P. London, July 7, 2004.

[325] Ibid. CACI responded on July 26th to the GSA's questions. The company pointed
out that Federal Acquisition Regulation 9.505-2(b) allowed for a contractor to assist
in preparing the SOW when it is for a sole source award, as it was in CACI's case.
The regulation reads, "If a contractor prepares, or assists in preparing, a work statement to be used in competitively acquiring a system or services — or provides material leading directly, predictably, and without delay to such a work statement — that

"I do not feel that, at this time, it is necessary for me to take any formal action to protect the interests of the Federal government," the letter stated.[326]

Publicly, the GSA investigation and conclusion gave CACI the opportunity to announce the positive outcome, and to reaffirm with an official report that CACI was a "responsible" company.[327] This would reinforce the company's position about its reputation for integrity and ethical behavior.

Within hours of receiving its reprieve, CACI announced GSA's decision with a press release sent nationally over PR Newswire.[328] On Wall Street, the news sent the company's stock up more than $2 to $41.40, a gain of 5.2 percent and its highest point since GSA initiated its inquiry six weeks earlier. Ironically, this added almost $600,000 to the CalPERS and CalSTRS investment portfolios.

In hindsight, some CACI advisors reflected on CACI's decision to publicly announce that GSA was considering debarment. CACI had promptly released news of the letter primarily because it felt it had a legal obligation to disclose material information. It also feared a leak would damage its credibility. It turned out, however, that release of the letter may have also provided an important, if unanticipated, benefit.

The wide-based response to the debarment threat from both the media and third-party commentators ran strongly and consistently against GSA. These reactions showed a general consensus that would criticize

---

contractor may not supply the system, major components of the system, or the services unless — (i) It is the sole source; (ii) It has participated in the development and design work; or (iii) More than one contractor has been involved in preparing the work statement." Nonetheless, recognizing the potential for a conflict of interest, CACI going forward would also develop a policy to identify, report, and avoid such situations. CACI then informed the GSA of the other investigations. Finally, the company explained that there were actually two employee hotlines: one for possible ethics and policy violations and another for accounting matters as required by the Sarbanes-Oxley Act.

[326] Ibid.

[327] The term "responsible," as used here, is from the government contracting lexicon and establishes a company's *bona fides* for contracting with the U.S. government.

[328] CACI Press Release, "GSA Determines That No Suspension or Debarment of CACI Is Necessary." July 7, 2004.

the agency for any adverse action against CACI on this "one-time" and "lesser" mistake.

The media had flogged CACI over Abu Ghraib and the notion that an IT contract could logically be extended to interrogation services. But by late May, most news stories were treating the contract as business as usual, not a nefarious act by CACI or its government customers. Earlier media speculation that CACI or the army was hiding behind the Interior Department so civilians could ostensibly do "dirty work" had been largely discredited in the mainstream media. In this context, a debarment decision by GSA would almost certainly have been regarded as an extreme overreaction by the agency. London believed that the company's straightforward approach, strong stance, and vigorous rejection of the unfounded and false accusations had helped its position all along, including at GSA.

Though evident only in hindsight, GSA's report allowing CACI to continue with its business was the turning point of CACI's Abu Ghraib crisis. Barring some new off-the-wall revelation about contracting misconduct, there was little likelihood the agency would reverse course and take adverse action at a later date. Other investigations were still under way, but GSA's letter dispensed with the most serious financial threat to the company. It was the first of the overhanging questions to be resolved and, from that day on, CACI could point out that it had been cleared by GSA and publicly deemed to be a responsible company. With the GSA's decision, CACI's solid record of contract compliance remained intact and was now public. Some of the tarnish on its good name was beginning to come off.

For a change, the headlines were sweet. "Government Clears CACI for Contracts," announced the *Washington Post*, and *Washington Technology Report* proclaimed: "CACI Leaps GSA Debarment Hurdle."[329]

This enabled London to move his team to the "CACI comeback" phase of his hypercrisis PR model. The news from GSA provided a timely boost for launching one aspect of this comeback plan — customer outreach — organized by Schneider, who had become a "Mr. Reliable" for London as the crisis unfolded. Known for his attention to detail and relentless drive to accomplish the task assigned, Schneider had

---

[329] "Government Clears CACI for Contracts, GSA Decides Not to Bar Firm Over Work for Army in Iraq," *Washington Post*, July 8, 2004; Roseanne Gerin, "CACI leaps GSA debarment hurdle," *Washington Technology*, July 8, 2004.

previously been asked to oversee the company's internal re-examination of the interrogators and screeners hired for work in Iraq. Increasingly, as the need arose for operational oversight of a new, ad hoc task, London turned to Schneider. Subsequently, London asked Schneider to make sure that senior people in the military and civilian agencies that did business with CACI received a firsthand briefing about the company's work in Iraq and how it was addressing the concerns about Abu Ghraib.

This was all part of the CACI comeback process proposed in the first days of the crisis by Burkhart who recommended that London adopt not only an immediate crisis management approach for dealing with the Abu Ghraib scandal, but a broader long term strategy that would help maintain CACI's positive image. This resulted in a more expansive strategy envisioned and designed by London to reaffirm CACI's good name and reputation. This strategy would continue to be an important ongoing effort for the company.

With London's program plan briefed, Brown and the communications team went to work with a determination to see the company's image revitalized and any tarnish wiped away. In the meantime, Schneider's briefings would provide key audiences with all the information the company had to reassure them that CACI was also probing for answers and would reveal any information as it was uncovered.

In consultation with business division leaders and his business development team, Schneider pulled together a list of about a hundred key officials — generals and admirals in the military as well as senior executive service members on the civilian side — and matched them up with a CACI executive who knew them. During June and July, the respective CACI executives were assigned to make contact — in person, by phone, or through e-mail — provide a briefing, and follow up with the information package prepared by the CACI PR and advisor team. They would then report back to Schneider.

Schneider estimated that CACI succeeded in reaching 75 percent or more of those officials on his list, and that most responded favorably. As an example of the positive reception his team received, Schneider shared a letter written to CACI from one military officer it contacted:

"All too often today, we find ourselves on the defensive and responding to falsehoods and exaggerated stories by the media. As such, I know that you sympathize with what the DoD and its members endure every single day. As you always give us the benefit of the doubt, so do we give you the benefit of our support. In no way will mere allegations affect the working relationship we have with CACI. This situation, in its current state, does not create any doubt in our minds as to CACI's veracity and honor."[330]

But amid the good news, the CalPERS-CalSTRS issue remained troubling. CACI's press release response to Westly had generated news coverage. Indeed, there was more press about CACI's counter than about Westly's initial notice. CACI's press release had given the story new legs. But this time the legs were moving in CACI's direction.

Some public relations specialists later criticized the company for making a bigger fire from a little one. Typically, a company wishing to stay out of the news would not circulate a press release that could draw attention to a story that might otherwise be ignored. Rather, it would prepare a statement for use only in response to phone calls from journalists who were already working on a story. And, more than likely — in an effort to make the story less interesting to the media — that statement would reiterate the company's standard defense.

But CACI did the opposite. In the post-Abu Ghraib media climate, the company found the proactive approach preferable. Putting any op-ed-type response to the funds on hold for the time being, the decision was made to issue an immediate news release countering Westly's release. Through a direct response, CACI was thus able to *draw attention to its side of the story*, correcting incorrect statements and confronting the media's distortions. The company stuck with its crisis model of full and frequent disclosure, and its "pushback" strategy against inaccurate, false, and misleading information.[331] London did not believe in delaying confrontation, if confrontation was inevitable. "Better to have a horrible ending, than to have horrors without end," he liked to say of his penchant for forcing matters to closure.

---

[330] Letter to CACI Senior Vice President Ron Schneider from a U.S. military officer, July 2004.

[331] See Appendix H: The CACI Hypercrisis Management Model.

There's no way to know whether London's strong tactics with Westly deterred others, but there's an axiom of politics which politicians like to follow: "it's a lot smarter to look for targets that don't punch back."

Westly sent word through David Berteau and Vic Fazio of Clark & Weinstock that he wanted a truce. Following some communications between the two coasts, a phone call between London and Westly was arranged for later that week. After a bit of discussion over their respective positions, Westly offered an apology for any harm done to CACI, and London respectfully accepted. The two men agreed to pull their press releases from their respective Web sites. While they couldn't undo their previous exchange, pulling the releases was a gesture that signified that the truce had been signed.

Westly insisted that his intent was benign. He reasoned that the anti-torture policy was a way to defuse the issue so that it wasn't just a contest between the pension funds and CACI. He asserted his belief the pension funds had a legitimate interest in corporate governance, but shouldn't be trying to sort out what happened at Abu Ghraib. Indeed, his letter to London indicated a belief that Angelides' complaints about CACI were twisting the funds' priorities.

But Westly's stated good intentions were undone by his singling out CACI in his press release, perhaps with little thought to how it might appear to a company under siege on the other side of the continent. It would have been a simple matter for Westly to say he would make his proposal on torture at CalSTRS' next meeting — without referencing CACI's place on the agenda. Linking the two created an association that alerted reporters. If nothing else, the blowup dramatically illustrated how perceptions can vary greatly depending on where one sits.

While London and Westly parried, Dragics was engaging in more phone diplomacy — trying to tie down a meeting date that did not cause a conflict of interest for CACI with the SEC guidelines, was fair to CACI's board commitment, and addressed shareholder concerns. Despite the disagreeable exchanges over the Westly matter, CalSTRS staff remained flexible. On July 9, after phone conversations with Hester-Amey and Eileen Okada, another CalSTRS staffer, a CalSTRS-CACI meeting was confirmed for 2:00 P.M. on August 2 in Sacramento. Okada indicated that CACI would receive a letter with a list of questions taken from the Angelides' letter as well as some of CalSTRS' own. Dragics, in turn, promised a written response to the questions in advance of the August 2 meeting.

With that resolved, Dragics could turn the tables on CalPERS and invite the fund to join the meeting. London was not going to agree to two meetings, and CACI's objections to the August 16 date were well-founded. If CalPERS said "no," Dragics was content to send them written responses only, even though CalPERS could choose to stir up more trouble. He continued to believe that meeting with them in person was preferable, in order to open the door for genuine discussions, despite CalPERS' posturing. And in concert with outside consultants Foley and Berteau, and investor relations advisor Howard Christensen, Dragics was also determined to provide the most comprehensive response possible to the funds, and ensure that CACI addressed every issue.

"Our strategy was to marginalize it. Make this a non-event. Make our response so robust, so thorough that there was not much they could say [in complaint]," Dragics explained.

The immediate goal wasn't to change minds, but to make clear that CACI was confident enough to answer every question. CACI also believed its position was bolstered by the positive response from the GSA inquiry.

"We were going to respond because we responded to every other shareholder who called, and that maintains [CACI's] credibility," Dragics said. But, as London had believed all along, more problems were on their way. It became clear in hindsight that the California funds wanted a public forum to admonish CACI, and the publicity to advance their political agendas.

Invited to join the CalSTRS meeting on August 2, CalPERS at first declined. By e-mail, Mark Anson of CalPERS asked whether CACI would sit down with his fund separately in September.

Why, London and his advisors questioned, would CalPERS need to have an investors meeting with CACI separate from CalSTRS? What was driving this insistence? Why were the fund's officers being so unyielding if they simply wanted to open a dialogue to address their questions? London and his people already knew the answers to these questions, but, above all, they would not do anything that might even be perceived as inappropriate in light of the SEC's Fair Disclosure regulation. Additionally, they would not incur additional corporate expenses for a separate meeting in September.

Having made CACI's deal for the meeting with CalSTRS, Dragics now chose silence as the response to Anson's September offer from CalPERS.

"We never answered that e-mail," recalled Dragics later.

CHAPTER THIRTY

CAPITOL HILL
Presenting the face and name of CACI

"CACI has been in the defense business since [1962]. Their chairman, a man named Jack London, is as straight as can be."
~ STEVE LEEB, LEEB CAPITAL MANAGEMENT ON
THE MONEY GANG, CNNFN, JUNE 22, 2004

Despite all the debates about policy and the frequent partisan discord, at their core, congressional decisions often hinge on human interaction. Understanding crosses party lines and can lead to collaboration and cooperation beneficial to everyone. But CACI did not have experience or a history on Capitol Hill.

So London shouldered the new task of familiarizing himself and his company to those on Capitol Hill. In both the House and the Senate, there was a growing debate about the role of government contractors and the government's outsourcing of many of its services requirements to government contractors. There was also a belief among some members that the contracting process might be growing beyond the government's capacity to provide adequate oversight. For instance, a number of lawmakers were surprised to learn that interrogations had been outsourced to the private sector, let alone that civilians were also allegedly being implicated in the abuse. Unbeknownst to those at CACI, Senator Christopher Dodd, a senior Democrat from Connecticut, was proposing legislation that would bar contractors from interrogation work. He even cited CACI in his presentations. High-profile hearings seemed possible as summer began, and CACI did not need, on top of its already heavy workload, the prospect of being called before a congressional committee. The CACI team had its hands full addressing all the other inquiries and investigations as well as conducting its day-to-day business operations. Besides, as far as CACI was concerned, the outsourcing issue was a government procurement and policy decision and the company would not participate in that debate.

CACI had generally monitored what happened on Capitol Hill but always as an observer, not a participant. Fully content to function in accord with government policies, the company had never invested any time or money in trying to influence Congress on any policy issue. But its new circumstances mandated a new approach. With the assistance of Dave Berteau, Vic Fazio, and another Clark & Weinstock representative, former congressman Vin Weber, London readied himself for the next phase of his efforts to defend the company's good name by representing his company to Capitol Hill.

In fact, he had already made one foray in mid-May. London had arranged meetings with the two local members of Congress, Republican Tom Davis and Democrat Jim Moran, both of northern Virginia. These meetings, and one with Senator John Warner's Armed Services Committee Chief of Staff, were facilitated by CACI's new association with John Campbell (who had consulted with the AMS organization that CACI had just acquired on May 1, 2004). New to London and CACI, Campbell was known on Capitol Hill and had represented a number of firms there.

London had known Moran for years as he was the representative in whose district CACI's headquarters were located. On several occasions they had had the opportunity to share views concerning issues such as government contracting and defense matters.

Davis, whom London had also known for years, chaired the House Government Reform Committee, which was already examining the work of contractors in Iraq. The committee focused on alleged overcharges and poor performance, including a range of allegations involving Halliburton and its Kellogg, Brown & Root subsidiary. Some committee members reportedly wanted to expand the inquiries to include other companies that had worked on contracts in Iraq. The CACI team was glad to find out that they would not be on the agenda for a mid-June hearing. The workload on the CACI team already had them in overload and another major briefing and presentation effort would have been over the top.

With that context, Berteau went to work developing a CACI outreach strategy in which London would take the lead. The goal was to inform key legislators and their staff about the company, and also about the current role of contractors in supporting the government, including the military services and intelligence communities.

Berteau began by canvassing his contacts on the Hill, which confirmed that CACI was virtually unknown to both the lawmakers and their staff: "CACI didn't have a history on the Hill. Now, the first time they hear about you is in the heart of this [Abu Ghraib] story," recalled Berteau. "We had to redefine the image of the company in the minds of all these people."

The first task was to define the message — figure out exactly how to reintroduce the company to people who knew nothing about it other than its association to the Abu Ghraib story, and to explain what the company had and had *not* done in Iraq. In a sense, crafting the message was the easy part because CACI had been telling its story to reporters and investors on a daily basis for weeks. But on Capitol Hill, everything they had heard about CACI had been filtered through the news media. By the time CACI was ready to reach out beyond the local legislators, many on the Hill had unfortunately already assumed the worst about the company. CACI now had to change minds — or at least provide the counter-balance to misinformed preconceptions.

A significant number of Hill staff, especially Democrats already skeptical of administration policy, presumed that CACI was guilty of wrongdoing. They had come to believe the war was a mistake and that the administration had duped Congress into supporting it. When they learned that the CACI interrogators had been hired under an Interior Department contract, it was an easy leap for these skeptics to assume a hidden agenda. Berteau, who spent more than fifteen years at the Defense Department in both Republican and Democratic administrations, laughed at the so-called conspiracy theory because "it assumes the government you can't see works much more effectively than what you can see, and that rarely happens." But to many in the public and the media at the time, the conspiracy theories apparently seemed plausible and intriguing.

For some of the Democratic legislators there was reportedly a great interest in using the issue of contractors and interrogation as a way to challenge the administration on the larger issues surrounding the war. The president was up for re-election in what looked like a close contest that was getting more and more heated. Perhaps, some Democrats thought, Abu Ghraib could help their party retake the White House. Many House Republicans apparently also saw the issue in partisan terms, reportedly backing off from some initial investigative forays and deciding that the official inquiries by the army and other executive agencies were fully sufficient. In the Senate, however, hearings were moving forward under the direction of Senator Warner, the Republican chairman of the Senate Armed Services Committee, who had the support of committee members from both sides of the political aisle. That was the environment that confronted London as he prepared to take his message to Capitol Hill.

Identifying the people to talk to was the next critical step. London didn't need to talk to every member of Congress. Instead, Berteau needed to identify the individuals and the committees with the greatest ability to affect CACI's future.

In the first circle of contacts were those who were or should be familiar with CACI — congressmen like Moran and Davis, who represented CACI employees living in Virginia. It also meant Virginia senator Warner, whom London had met on several occasions, and Virginia senator George Allen, whom London had met just once before in a meeting between the senators and a group of industry executives soon after the terrorist attacks of September 11, 2001.[332] It also meant other individuals like Republican representative Eric Cantor from Richmond, VA, where a few hundred CACI employees lived. Another Republican con-

---

[332] CACI project management personnel also had supported the Pentagon's repair and reconstruction efforts following the 9-11 attack.

gressman, David Hobson of Dayton, Ohio, represented CACI employees in his district in that state.

The next circle included the committees with jurisdiction over the Department of Defense or that were already taking an active interest in contractors or Abu Ghraib. That included Warner's Armed Services panel in the Senate as well as the Senate Government Affairs Committee; Davis's Government Reform Committee in the House; and the House Armed Services Committee chaired by California Republican Duncan Hunter. The ranking Democrat on the Armed Services Committee, Ike Skelton of Missouri, who was critical of the way the Pentagon was managing contractors, was also a key person to meet.

London wouldn't necessarily talk to the representatives and senators who sat on those committees, but he certainly needed to visit with the key staff people who did the day-to-day work, such as organizing hearings, drafting legislation, and briefing the legislators on the issues.

On June 30, Berteau, with his associate Sandra Stuart, who had been assistant secretary of defense for legislative affairs in the Clinton administration, accompanied London to meet those who represented the likely critics — key staffers for Senator Dodd and Representative Waxman. By plan, London would do the talking for CACI. "The strategy," said Berteau, "was to let Jack be Jack."

Berteau's thinking was straightforward. First of all, congressional staffers weren't used to personal visits from corporate CEOs. They heard from lobbyists all the time and were used to smooth presentations from the professional hired guns. CEOs typically wanted to talk only to members of Congress; many were known to bypass the staff. Berteau believed the staffers would appreciate sitting down face to face with the CEO. Perhaps more to the point, London's personal presence alone sent a powerful message about his own belief in his company and its integrity.

London, true to form, was nothing but genuine. A straight talker, his passion for his company and his country shone through his plainly chosen words.

Intelligent and enthusiastic with an energy level that belies his years (he was sixty-seven in 2004), London bears none of the artificial glitz sometimes associated with twenty-first century CEOs. He can be tough, never backing down from a fight, and he can quickly get people's attention or instill fear when necessary. But upon first impression and during normal conversations London is viewed by most as a down-to-earth, friendly and courteous, regular kind of guy. He stands less than six feet tall, with a quiet raspy voice that masks his steel-hard core. Sit down with London for the first time and you are more likely to think of an affable family friend than the hard-charging CEO of a billion-dollar-company with, as of 2004, some 9,500 employees.

London said of the impression he left behind: "I'm not a kid. I have been around and people soon know it. My style is not threatening and I am sincere. They see and hear me, and they just don't believe I'm designing a system to do torture."

Confident as he was in London's ability to tell the CACI story, Berteau conceded to some nervousness in putting the CEO before some of the congressional staffers. London was traditional and generally conservative in his political views about national security and proudly patriotic in an old-fashioned "salute the flag" kind of way that some, Berteau felt, may find uncomfortable. London believed in and respected political debate (his mother and father had both been active life-long FDR Democrats[333]), but once American troops were in the field, he believed that any public debate that encouraged or emboldened the enemy or undermined or disadvantaged the soldier in the field should stop until the fight was won. London would oppose any action that might compromise the military or place any American troops in harm's way in front of the enemy stemming from any political disagreements at home (Dedicated to supporting the U.S. military, London had a long list of family members and ancestors on both parents' sides that had served in the U.S. military going back to the American Revolution). There were advisors who thought that his beliefs might, mistakenly, put him at odds with the some on Capitol Hill, who, though also seeing

---

[333] London's parents, now deceased, had always voted Democratic. His mother had been a staunch Democratic Party worker in Oklahoma for John F. Kennedy in 1960, and London was a Democrat who voted for JFK in his first presidential election in 1960. After JFK's inauguration, through her party connections to the White House, his mother asked the President to autograph a copy of his book *Profiles in Courage* for her son, Lt$_{jg}$ J.P. London, U.S. Navy. London still has the autographed Kennedy book, with the correspondence to and from the White House in early 1961. It is one of his most cherished possessions.

themselves as patriots, either opposed the war or believed the President was not succeeding in its management.

London's loyalty and commitment to the soldiers — all American military personnel — during wartime stemmed from values and principles he learned at the U.S. Naval Academy in the 1950s. London believed the troops deserved total support, unwavering loyalty, and the very best the nation could possibly do to see to their physical safety and to their victory in combat.

Prior to their meeting, Berteau wondered aloud to one of London's colleagues whether the CEO might doff his "Navy Jack" American flag tie with the famous old words "Don't Tread on Me" (and its coiled rattlesnake) for the meetings. Berteau was concerned that some on the Hill might think that with his tie, "he was somehow flaunting it in their face to make them seem unpatriotic for questioning what was going on at Abu Ghraib." Berteau knew that London wore the tie every day as a statement to his people, but the Hill staff might think he wore it to challenge them in some way.

"It would be very easy for people to assume that [the tie was meant for them]," Berteau added. "We had enough hard work to do on the Hill. I didn't want to add anything to it."

Not that Berteau ever got to raise the matter with London, who, tipped off about Berteau's concern, preemptively snapped back at his adviser: "I'll wear whatever damn tie I want."

In the end, the tie hadn't mattered. London's genuine fervor seemed to overtake the staffers' skepticism.

London didn't just talk about Iraq. In some ways that was the least important part of his presentation. Instead, he talked about who he was and how he built a company that had a few dozen employees when he had arrived in 1972 and by 2004 had become a $1.5 billion corporation with 9,500 people. He gave them a brief outline of his life. He told them about himself as a youngster growing up in Oklahoma, who fulfilled a dream to join the Brigade of Midshipmen at the U.S. Naval Academy. He recalled his service as a young naval officer chasing Soviet submarines across the Atlantic, serving in the Caribbean during the 1962 Cuban missile crisis, and flying a helicopter as a navy aviator and being part of the naval recovery team for John Glenn and his *Friendship 7* space capsule in February 1962. He told them of leaving the navy after twelve years active duty to join a small defense engineering contractor in 1971 before going to work at CACI a year later. He pointed out that he spent another twelve years in the naval reserve, which he believed made a positive impression on his audience of his continuing military commitment at a time when present-day reservists were being shot at in Iraq. London left no doubt that he was proud of his twenty-four years in the uniform and his commission as a U.S. naval officer, and he was proud to have earned the eagles of a navy captain, and the wings of a naval aviator.

London then went on to discuss his pride in his company. Co-founded more than four decades ago by two struggling entrepreneurs including one who would later become a Nobel Prize-winning economist, CACI was steeped in a tradition of ethical conduct and quality service to its customers. Before Abu Ghraib, he pointed out, CACI had a positive image and good reputation. London then told them how CACI evolved into providing interrogators in Iraq — as an unanticipated but logical outgrowth — of a gradual, but planned, diversification of the company into intelligence work. CACI honored the army's request for interrogators not because there were big dollars — less than one percent of company revenue — but because of his belief that you do what you can to help your military customer in supporting your country. And this is especially the case when your country is at war and the requirement is to support an emergency situation in a combat zone.

His impassioned account culminated with concluding remarks in which he assured them that CACI was cooperating fully with every government investigation as well as working hard on its own to find out the truth. Berteau recognized and acknowledged that it was a sincere and compelling presentation.

"He made a very convincing case and defused a number of ideas present in the minds of the staff that needed to be clarified — especially the award of the contract," Berteau said. "Jack could tell that story in a way that made clear [the contract with Interior] was not a subterfuge."

There would be more meetings on Capitol Hill for London over the next several months. He would attend a second session with both Congressmen Moran and Davis in mid-July, and go to meetings with Senator George Allen and Representatives Cantor and Hobson from the original list of officials identified to contact. He would also spend time with Representative Jerry Lewis, a California Republican deeply involved in Defense appropriations, and speak with staff from the Senate Select Committee on Intelligence in September.

London also had an unplanned meeting with Congressman Henry Waxman, and he recalled it later with a smile. While walking with Davis to the underground tram that shuttles members of Congress from their offices to the Capitol building, Davis spotted Waxman and invited the Californian to join him and London on the tram. A little mischievously, Davis introduced London as the guy Waxman was after for Abu Ghraib. Davis added that he'd known London for fifteen years and that the company just does its job, which is why Waxman had never heard of them before. London recalled that he thought that Waxman may have hesitated at first, but seemed to be relaxed by the time their short visit and train ride had ended. London speculated that the chance meeting may have been helpful because, he believed, "it hopefully took a little mystery out of CACI and who I am."

Berteau and his colleagues at Clark & Weinstock would meet and talk with other key staffers without London throughout the rest of the year. They also stayed in touch with those London had met. With every new development, every release of a new investigation, Berteau would work the phones. He was interested in finding out where things might be headed. What Berteau found was a steady decline in interest as it became clear that CACI's association with the Abu Ghraib scandal wasn't as originally reported in the worldwide media, and the *Washington Post*, in particular.

"It became apparent to members [of Congress] that each time the next investigation came out, there was less about CACI than in the previous one," Berteau summarized.

Dodd's bid to block civilian interrogators as a matter of law was voted down on June 16 even before London went to the Hill and interest in pursuing it seemed to diminish as the summer wore on and no effort was made to revive it. Waxman's pursuit of the issues seemed to diminish too as he concentrated his attention on the administration and the larger issue of Defense Department and White House policies that he apparently believed had encouraged the mistreatment of prisoners.

Berteau believed London's talks to introduce and define CACI to the Congressional staffs were at least part of the reason CACI slipped off their radar screen. In Berteau's mind, London had defused the staff's worst suspicions about the company and its work for Iraq. As Berteau explained: "The power of having Jack and letting him talk was that you could see he wasn't trying to hide anything or walk away from responsibility. It was his people, his company, and he was standing up for them."

They could also see London was genuinely serious about helping the U.S. Army and the American soldier. They understood that it wasn't the revenue or profit from CACI's work that motivated him; what mattered was the company's commitment to its customers and its service to the country.

CHAPTER THIRTY-ONE

EMPLOYEES, THE MEDIA, AND THE MILITARY
Reinforcing the troops and reasserting the facts

"There's a lot of bum dope flying around out there."
～ JACK LONDON TO CACI MANAGERS JUNE 8, 2004

BACK AT HIS SIXTEENTH FLOOR OFFICE OVERLOOKING THE BALLSTON area of Arlington, London continued to tend to the business of daily management. Internal communication, always a priority, now took on greater importance as he encouraged his people to focus on the business, despite the questions about Abu Ghraib. He worked diligently with Brown's communications team to provide regular updates to employees. The right timing and frequency was crucial.

"We strived very hard to let employees know in advance about important events or information before they heard it from somewhere else," Brown recalled. "We also maintained the FAQ site on our intranet, posting questions from employees and the company's response. It was quite a campaign and we got good feedback from the employees." Every message to employees strove for the proper balance between the two imperatives of customer service and crisis management. London again urged his people to talk to their customers and let them know the company's view of events at Abu Ghraib, as he had done continuously since the company's situation became clear.

In his monthly "Chairman's Notes" for June, London acknowledged the distraction. He warned employees that media stories about Abu Ghraib "will run for a while yet," but also asked them to "stay focused on our clients." London maintained, "Our reputation is best upheld by continuing to deliver QCS/BV — Quality Client Service and Best Value," (CACI's business motto for over twenty years — one that London had coined for the company).

He noted the successful launch of the new Defense and Intelligence Group that now included the former AMS employees who had joined CACI at the start of May and who were acclimating well. "All integration activities are well underway and on schedule," London reported.

In keeping the company focused on positive developments while dealing with the crisis, London reminded his workers to remember "how successful we are as a business." He proudly reported CACI's strong earnings, including the recent forecast that revenue was expected to reach a record $1.5 billion in the upcoming fiscal year. The forward-thinking CEO also announced a new benefit program that included an additional vacation day benefit for employees beginning July 1 of that year.

In addition, over the next several weeks, London would host conference calls with CACI managers, the company's employees, and its lenders. The talk to company managers was primarily a lesson in how to communicate about Abu Ghraib to their employees, customers, and business partners. He promised a set of message documents to guide the managers in answering questions, and he encouraged them to seek out opportunities to spread the truth about what was going on. He acknowledged that what they said might be received with skepticism because of confusion created by "incorrect information, misleading statements and flat out misrepresentations being circulated by the media." "There is a lot of 'bum dope' flying around out there," London lamented.

Throughout the call there were two recurring themes. Again and again, London and Ken Johnson assured their colleagues that CACI was cooperating with every government inquiry, but also that they would not punish any employee until the evidence made clear that discipline was the right thing to do. The company would not rush to judgment because "that's not right and no one would want to be treated that way," London declared, invoking a deeply felt belief that he had written in his own hand onto the script prepared for him by the internal team.

Johnson pointed out that despite the controversy surrounding Abu Ghraib, the army remained happy with the company's work in Iraq. Johnson said that Baghdad was telling the company that its people were "doing great work and provide huge contributions on a daily basis to intelligence support for combat operations here in Iraq."

Ten days later, London and Johnson delivered the same messages in a teleconference with every CACI employee, though in the interim more challenges had landed at the company's door. In the brief interval between the calls, CCR had filed its lawsuit, the California pension funds had demanded answers through the press, and the CACI team had presented its case to GSA. But before turning to those issues, London began with a pep talk. He thanked his people for their unwavering focus on their work, and he cheered them with news that over the past year, the company had finally achieved its long-term goal of $1 billion in annual revenue (a number that would climb 50 percent further in the year ahead with the integration of the AMS Defense and Intelligence Group).

"This is just monumental! It's clear confirmation that your company has reached 'tier one' level — that CACI is among the largest and most formidable players in the industry," London proclaimed. "And your contributions play a direct role in our continuing and outstanding success."

But then one by one, the two men addressed the outstanding issues related to Iraq. As the company had done in its public comments, they lambasted the CCR lawsuit for statements that "are just plain wrong." They noted that neither CalPERS nor CalSTRS had contacted the company with a single question or joined a single public briefing before taking their complaints to the press.

In between the two internal calls, London and several company executives had laid out the CACI story in a public call to the lenders who were helping finance CACI's various acquisitions, including the recent AMS transaction. In that discussion, London explained how CACI became involved in Iraq, detailed the hiring process for interrogators, and reassured them that the controversy would not likely affect earnings.

While London delivered his public reports, Brown continued to work behind the scenes. At this stage she was working with the team to address media, employee, and messaging or outreach to customers and

Capitol Hill (besides doing her "day job"). Meanwhile, Burkhart and Hur continued the successful targeted media response effort. And Burkhart's human interest piece on CACI was being integrated into the CACI messaging including the information package to Congress.

Among the most worrisome media inquiries during this time was one from Edward Pound, an investigative journalist with *U.S. News & World Report*. Pound said that he had obtained copies of the *secret* annexes to General Taguba's illegally leaked report and was preparing a lengthy article based on those documents. For Brown, it was a flashback to the first days of the Abu Ghraib crisis when first Seymour Hersh and then other reporters called her with questions about a document she hadn't seen — and legally could not see. Now Pound apparently had thousands of pages about Abu Ghraib, and she had no way of knowing what they said — except for whatever Pound chose to share. Frustrated by the uneven playing field and the illegal leaks, Brown was even more perturbed by the question he was asking. Pound said there were rumors that while under contract to CACI, Steven Stefanowicz was, in fact, working as a covert agent for the Defense Intelligence Agency (DIA). In Pound's words, "CACI was providing the cover." And he wanted to know if this was true.

It was a distressing accusation that took Brown back to the worst of the unsubstantiated speculation of the scandal's first week. It dredged up again the false suggestions that CACI was serving as a front for the Central Intelligence Agency or other government offices that were now being widely accused of hiding illegal or unauthorized activity. Brown thought that all of that had been firmly laid to rest, that reporters now recognized it was untrue. Now the charges were back again from a widely read journalist with secret (*illegally leaked*) government information and a high-profile news magazine ready to publish his report.

So back she went to the sixteenth floor at CACI headquarters to notify London of Pound's inquiry. "Preposterous," London exploded when he heard the story. He, too, thought this matter had been resolved. It was simply not true and he wanted to get on the phone and deliver his response directly to Pound himself. Which is precisely what he did, telling Pound exactly that: the speculation was preposterous.

Pound snapped back — how could London be so sure? Abu Ghraib had been a chaotic environment; every day something strange seemed to happen. He assured London that Taguba's secret annexes revealed a lot of ugliness, which he was going to put in his magazine. How could London know with certainty what had or had not been going on? But London forcefully rejected Pound's assertions and thought Pound was trying to get him to somehow reveal an inappropriate or illegal connection. And, of course, there wasn't any.

It was a heated exchange. London's one-word dismissal apparently touched a nerve with the journalist. In any case, Pound did not cite the alleged DIA connection in his report, "Hell on Earth," in the July 19 issue of *U.S. News & World Report.* Pound had posed a loaded question to London and the men had shouted back and forth. But when Pound sat down to write about Taguba's *illegally leaked* secret documentation, there was no evidence presented to support the rumor. London's obvious conviction, despite the argument it ignited, also may have caused Pound to dismiss the notion.

Pound's article turned out to be much different than most of the reporting that preceded it, focusing more on the wretched conditions at Abu Ghraib that created a common misery for soldiers, contractors, and detainees alike, and less on the abuse of prisoners.

Pound reported a prison "spiraling out of control." Abu Ghraib was "a chaotic and dangerous environment" characterized by "riots, prisoner escapes, shootings, corrupt Iraqi guards, unsanitary conditions, rampant sexual behavior, bug-infested food, prisoner beatings and humiliations, and almost-daily mortar shellings."[334] London thought the article was well written, thoroughly documented, and a valuable record of what Abu Ghraib had been like at the time.

There was barely a word in Pound's article about CACI and Stefanowicz. It turned out, based on Pound's published article, that the annexes had nothing new to say about Stefanowicz. Though Stefanowicz was one of the four people who Taguba surmised might bear some responsibility, the annexes apparently did not include any definitive (or factual) evidence to substantiate the suspicion.

If Pound's inquiry to CACI was worrisome, other media issues were exasperating. They convinced London that no subject about Abu Ghraib was too remote, obscure or far-fetched to somehow link back to CACI,

---

[334] Edward T. Pound and Kit R. Roane, "Hell on Earth," *U.S. News & World Report,* July 19, 2004.

leading him to conclude that many of the press followed the popular adage, "Don't let the facts get in the way of a good story." A report by *Inside the Pentagon*, a trade publication that covered the bureaucratic side of the Pentagon, falsely, perhaps intentionally, depicted CACI as a major political donor and suggested that the company had somehow used its lobbying muscle to derail Senator Dodd's attempt to bar government use of contract employees for interrogations.[335] The fact of the matter was that CACI did not make political campaign donations as a company and did not engage in major Hill lobbying efforts.

The Dodd measure had been rejected in mid-June on an almost straight party line vote. With Republicans almost uniformly voting "no," *Inside the Pentagon* speculated that CACI and Titan's campaign donations to Republican lawmakers must have tipped the outcome.[336] It was a far-fetched conclusion that ignored far more likely explanations — the most obvious being that lawmakers recognized the necessity of contract interrogators to support the military's efforts. Senator Warner argued that the measure "cripples America's intelligence system in the middle of a war in Afghanistan, in Iraq, and our operations in Guantanamo Bay," adding, "There is no way in the world the military . . . can hire and train in this short period of time all the replacements that would be required if the senator's amendment became law."

The article specifically noted that Peter W. Singer was among those expressing the belief that "industry influence played a role." John Isaacs, president of the Council for a Livable World, however, disagreed with depicting corporate influence as a factor in voting down the bill. He attributed it instead to several Democratic add-ons to the failed authorization bill.

At the same time, *Inside the Pentagon's* thesis was equally insulting to Democrats and Republicans. If, as the newsletter suggested, Republicans voted "no" to Dodd because of political donors' money, then by the same logic, the Democrats must have all voted "yes" because they hadn't gotten money. The article did note that some in the defense industry felt the role of contractors in the Abu Ghraib scandal was "getting blown out of proportion" quoting one industry representative who observed that when Baghdad fell to the U.S.-led forces in April 2003, gov-

---

[335] Elaine M. Grossman, "Possible Interrogation Contractor Influence Cited In Senate Vote," op. cit.

[336] Ibid.

ernment contractors like Titan and CACI "provided incredible surge capacity at incredible speed."

Upon hearing about the story, London remarked at the time of the *Inside the Pentagon* article that he was completely unaware that the Dodd measure had even been brought up for a vote in Congress. But he hoped that Senator Dodd and others in Congress did not somehow believe the negative and misleading stories circulating about CACI. The company had become aware that Dodd had briefed Congress about CACI's recruiting requirements posted on the company's Web site, but the CACI team did not know if Congress had an accurate understanding of the company overall and of CACI's methods and practice for recruiting.

The amount of money cited in the article was also quite meager in an era when a single big-state Senate campaign can cost many millions of dollars. According to the *Inside the Pentagon* newsletter, CACI employees had collectively provided roughly $13,000 to Republican candidates and $5,158 to Democrats in the past eighteen months. Over the past five years, the newsletter falsely said, CACI had donated nearly $45,000 combined to the two parties, or about $9,000 a year. The fact was that CACI had never made political contributions with company money. It had been only individual employees that had made personal donations on their own. By way of reference, the same article reported that Titan and its employees had donated more than $245,000 to Republicans in the previous eighteen months, and more than $268,000 in the four years before that. These weren't massive amounts by modern political standards either — but they were, in the aggregate, more than twelve times what individual employees of CACI had provided.

Even worse, *Inside the Pentagon* wrongly stated, "The donations included funds from CACI's and Titan's respective political action committees, as well as executives and employees of the companies." CACI had *never had* a political action committee.[337] The contributions were actually made by individual CACI employees as private citizens.

Through Koegel, CACI also chastised *Harper's* magazine for wrongly reporting — nearly two months after the record had been set straight — that John Israel was a CACI employee.[338] It was hard to believe that

---

[337] Ibid.

[338] "Company Mann," *Harper's Magazine*, July 1, 2004.

such an ostensibly "prestigious" publication could lag so far behind the facts — but it did. Curiously, the magazine's July 1 report also wrongly stated that CACI had produced the film *The Battle for Avery Mann* for the U.S. Office of Government Ethics.

Proving that no publication was too unimportant and no error too small for CACI to address, Koegel also corrected the socialist paper *Workers World* for writing that CACI's "involvement" in torture "had been exposed."[339] And Brown notified David Phinney of *Federal Times* that his publication needed to run an official correction for its mistaken statement on June 21 that the Defense Contract Audit Agency (DCAA) was investigating CACI for improper billing.[340] In fact, the agency was seeking to determine if the GSA schedule contract had been properly applied, not whether there was any impropriety in CACI's billing.

CACI also issued one of its periodic compilations of its position on key issues with a press release headlined "CACI Corrects Public Information about its Services Contract for U.S. Army Interrogation Support in Iraq."[341]

Unusual by typical PR standards, the release was not designed to generate a news story and did not provide any new information. But it was important, given the continued erroneous reporting, for keeping the facts correct in the public domain. Still, it triggered short items on the Dow Jones and Associated Press newswires. For journalists, the news release would serve as a handy compendium of CACI's position on important issues and the facts as established up to that point in time.

The press release noted that there were no CACI employees in any of the Abu Ghraib abuse photos, that the company never had more than ten interrogators at Abu Ghraib at any one time, and that it had not provided interrogation services at Guantanamo Bay, Afghanistan, or anywhere else. The statement that CACI's interrogation services were confined to Iraq in small numbers was an important clarification on a matter

---

[339] Susanne Kelly, "Richmond march wants troops home," *Worker's World*, July 15, 2004.

[340] David Phinney, "Firm's Work at Guantanamo Prison Under Review," op. cit.

[341] CACI Press Release, "CACI Corrects Public Information about its Services Contract for U.S. Army Interrogation Support in Iraq," July 20, 2004.

that had created confusion at various times. Burkhart had noted in her daily review of the media that the press coverage of CACI's interrogators was showing an exaggerated focus in both the numbers and scope of their work. Some news articles, as well as the CCR lawsuit, had falsely stated that CACI also provided interrogators in Afghanistan and Guantanamo Bay. This prompted her to suggest that the facts around this subject needed to be disseminated to the press. The CACI news release addressed these issues and also recounted the history of the interrogation contract, noting its original award to PTG in 1998 and the use of the contract for intelligence work for the U.S. Army in Germany beginning a year later in 1999 — *four years* before CACI acquired PTG.

Beyond the day-to-day media fencing, Brown also was preparing a presentation to the *Wall Street Journal* editorial board. Guardedly confident that the worst of the accusations against CACI had been leveled, Brown believed it was time to begin one-on-one conversations with selected media outlets to tell the more complete story about CACI and begin repairing the damage to its good name.

Perhaps more importantly, much as CACI had done on Capitol Hill, the meeting with the *Journal* was a chance to let would-be critics see the real men and women of CACI, especially its CEO. The company's leader, in his direct and unaffected style, left a positive impression on most of those he met as an individual with a strong personal commitment to supporting his country — and always doing the right thing.

On July 20, London and Brown sat down with five of the *Journal's* board members. They would detail CACI's long history of ethical conduct, talk about Iraq and Abu Ghraib, and discuss the California pension funds. It was an outstanding opportunity to meet with the most important decision-makers of a major media organization and provide them with the background and facts from CACI's point of view, all in a non-adversarial environment.

The *Journal* was a regular critic of the California funds, and the board members listened to CACI's side of the story. At this stage, however, there did not seem to be any new story of editorial impact for the *Journal* to publish. Looking back, Brown was not sure of the meeting's benefit, but it had been a chance to present the CACI story face to face with media leaders. And it was an important meeting for CACI, to keep reporters abreast of the story and take a proactive approach, rather than the reactive approach the company had been forced to take over the past months. Furthermore, it continued London's drive to keep the company going forward, to maintain the offensive. He wanted to move CACI's crisis response model further towards the comeback phase of reinforcing the company's fine reputation and image.

To this end, Brown and Prism returned to work on the op-ed piece they planned to have published before the meeting with the California pension funds and State Treasurer Phil Angelides. The column would focus on CACI's role in supporting vital intelligence services in Iraq, and would criticize Angelides for riding roughshod over the basic presumption of innocence to which all Americans were entitled. Though London had allowed Dragics to negotiate a meeting with the funds, the way the situation was unfolding was giving him a glimpse of what was to come, and London wanted the opportunity to state his company's case on his own terms — not in response to Angelides' demands or some reporter's call.

Getting space on an op-ed page is not easy. Prominent newspapers receive a hundred or more submissions a day but may have room for only one or two. Still, Prism advised London that he might be able to use the news from California to submit an article to one of that state's newspapers. He would be writing about a major news story — Abu Ghraib — but with the local angle of the state's pension funds and prominent California politicians. The prospective newspaper, at Prism's recommendation, was the *Sacramento Bee*, based in the state's capital city.

By the second week of July London had finished the article and it was submitted to the *Bee*. A week later, Brown got the good news call from Sacramento that the *Bee* would run the piece, though they needed to verify a few of the statements in London's article.

But the good news was no longer quite so timely. London and Westly had just arrived at their unexpected truce, and criticizing him now would be inappropriate. After huddling briefly to review options, the course of action was clear. Brown had to call the newspaper and pull the piece. As badly as the PR team had wanted the platform to tell the company story before the California meeting, it would have been inappropriate to do so in this op-ed. On July 21, Brown told the editor that CACI wanted to withdraw the op-ed and the editor unhappily killed the column. But as it turned out, there would be another time for the *Sacramento Bee*.

CHAPTER THIRTY-TWO

THE INVESTIGATION ROLL CALL BEGINS
Initial conclusions and findings support CACI

> **"Right is its own defense."**
>
> ∼ **BERTOLT BRECHT**

FROM CALIFORNIA, CACI'S ATTENTION MOVED QUICKLY TO CAPITOL Hill, where the army was beginning to provide more information about Abu Ghraib with the July 22 release of a report by the Department of the Army Inspector General (IG), Lt. Gen. Paul T. Mikolashek.[342] It was the first of three official investigations to be released over the next six weeks. The reports all delivered new information and new conclusions, but each still left questions unanswered.

The reports had different mandates and goals. Mikolashek was ordered to assess the army's detainee operations (procedures, doctrine, and policies), but he was not asked to investigate specific crimes or assign culpability for the abuse of prisoners. A second army report, by Generals Kern, Jones, and Fay (the Fay report) focused on military intelligence and the abuses at Abu Ghraib, but also included discussion of army doctrine. A third report was by an independent panel chaired by former secretary of defense James Schlesinger, who was asked by

---

[342] Lieutenant General Paul T. Mikolashek, *Department of the Army, Inspector General, Detainee Operations Inspection*. July 21, 2004.

Secretary of Defense Donald Rumsfeld to review the Defense Department's detention policies to determine what caused the detainee abuse and how to prevent it from happening again.

Though the reports offered vast amounts of new information and included a significant amount of self-criticism by the military, they were not universally accepted. Some, who believed ultimate responsibility for the abuses *must* lie higher up the command chain, dismissed the reports as whitewashes because they failed to identify high-ranking culprits. To others, the reports seemed contradictory, especially regarding the relative responsibility of senior officials for the abuses at Abu Ghraib. Still, there seemed to be common threads emerging from the reports that contributed significantly to public knowledge about the challenges of dealing with the large number of detainees under U.S. control.

The army IG report, which examined detainee operations in both Afghanistan and Iraq, noted that:

- ☐ Abu Ghraib was seriously mismanaged. The army had provided too few troops, with inadequate leadership, and asked them to do a job for which they had not been trained
- ☐ The rules of engagement, particularly pertaining to the interrogation of detainees, were unclear. They changed in several instances, though the changes were neither clearly enunciated nor well understood
- ☐ At a tactical level, there was confusion over the relationship between military intelligence and the military police, questions about who reported to whom, and what role MPs should play in preparing detainees for interrogation
- ☐ Conditions on the ground were vastly different than anticipated in pre-war planning, and U.S. forces wound up with a much larger and more diverse number of detainees (including hostile detainees) than anticipated
- ☐ Because of the unexpected number of detainees, civilian interrogators were hastily inserted into the chaos to make up for a shortage of available military interrogators

Overall, Mikolashek's report painted a bleak picture of conditions at Abu Ghraib and detainee operations across Iraq. It compared doctrine with performance at each stage of what it called capture, care, and custody of detainees, and found significant deviations between what was supposed to happen and what did happen. Detainees were held longer than usual at each stage of the detention process. The number of detainees so vastly outstripped the number of trained interrogators that valued intelligence was lost because of delays in interrogation. At one time, some detainees at Abu Ghraib were in custody for as long as ninety days before their first interrogation.

Mikolashek said that as of June 2004, more than 50,000 detainees had been captured or processed in Iraq and Afghanistan, and that "shortfalls in numbers of interrogators and interpreters, and the distribution of these assets within the battle space, hampered human intelligence (HUMINT) collection efforts. Valuable intelligence — timely, complete, clear and accurate — may have been lost as a result. Interrogators were not available in sufficient numbers to efficiently conduct screening and interrogations of the large numbers of detainees at collecting points (CPs) and internment/resettlement (I/R) facilities."

The army IG noted that the shortages were offset by the *use of civilian interrogators*, which he concluded, *"provide a valuable service"* [italics added]. On the issue of most direct significance for CACI, the report concluded that the civilian interrogators *all* met the qualification criteria of the army's contract SOW. But it noted that eleven of the thirty-one civilian interrogators did not have formal training in *military* interrogation (though this was *not* required by the contract; other civilian police, detective, or other U.S. government-related experience could be accepted), which it said had the potential to place them at high risk of violating army policies and doctrine (although it also conceded that policy in the theater was unclear, which would seem to be a more consequential finding). It recommended an amendment to CACI's SOW to require, *going forward*, that the civilians either have prior military training in policy and doctrine or that they receive such training before deployment (rather than on-site), adding that the military must ensure that the civilians are trained in military technique and policies.

At the same time, the report indicated that training concerns were not restricted to the civilians. Because of shortages, the army IG reported "tactical intelligence officers were conducting interrogations of detainees without thorough training" and said that, in general, tactical intelligence officers simply lacked the necessary training for effective human intelligence work.

The report also said it learned of two specific incidents in which the civilians allegedly violated military doctrine, but that in one of the instances military interrogators at the location were using the same questionable technique.[343] The alleged policy breaches, however, did *not* appear analogous to the conduct seen in the infamous abuse photos. According to the army IG, one involved pouring water over detainees' heads. The other alleged incident was not described. No further details from the army IG have emerged at the time of this writing.

Of Abu Ghraib, the report said the facility was being used for the wrong purpose. Initially selected by coalition administrator Paul Bremer to house Iraqi criminals under the control of Iraqi police, the prison's mission was expanded to include detention of the U.S. military's enemy prisoners. It was a bad choice, the report observed, because it was too close to a populated urban area and was under frequent hostile fire from mortars and rockets.

Abu Ghraib prison was enormous. It consisted of several separate facilities — the hard site where the infamous MP photos were taken, Camp Vigilant, and Camp Ganci. Except for Tier 1, the hard site prison was under control of Iraqi prison guards. Camps Vigilant and Ganci, both tent encampments, were under U.S. control.

Abu Ghraib was seriously and dangerously overcrowded. Camp Ganci, for example, had eight compounds with a capacity of 500 per compound, but at the time of the army IG inspection, each compound held between 600 and 700 detainees. Guard towers were poorly situated, with numerous blind spots and poor fields of fire. Communication was difficult because of a shortage of radios, at times forcing guards on the ground to converse with their counterparts in the towers by shouting back and forth. Some soldiers tried to improve the situation by buying commercial radios, but that created a security problem because the commercial radios could easily be monitored by outside forces operating on the same frequency. Plus, the commercial radios could not communicate with the military radios that were available at the prison.

---

[343] The question quickly arises that if both military and contractor personnel were using the same "questionable" techniques, what significant "high risk" was at issue because of the "lack of military training" among the fewer contractor interrogators that did not have the training?

In assessing interrogation operations, the army IG noted the fundamental challenge was that army doctrine was written for "a linear battlefield with an identifiable combat zone and rear area, and with the presumption that detainees at the point of capture will normally be enemy prisoners of war" who could be quickly evacuated to secure rear areas. Instead, in both Afghanistan and Iraq, the army was confronted with "non-linear battle spaces and large numbers of detainees whose status is *not* readily identifiable as combatants, criminals, or innocents." The report added that, "doctrine does not address how to effectively screen and interrogate large numbers of captured persons of undetermined status." It also concluded that military intelligence (MI) units simply did not have enough screeners or interrogators. The result was "a backlog of interrogations and the potential loss of intelligence." At every stage of the detention process, the report seemed to say, units were forced to improvise. The army IG, it appears, provided ample, specific justification for the reasons the U.S. Army in Baghdad had moved so urgently to contract with CACI for interrogator support.[344]

Like Taguba, the army IG found confusion over the relationship between the MI's and MPs, particularly the MPs' role, if any, in interrogation. The report noted a seeming contradiction between MP doctrine "that states that MPs maintain a passive role," and the U.S. Army's Field Manual 34-52, which implies more active participation. At Guantanamo Bay, the MPs worked closely with MI as a matter of deliberate procedure, and Major General Miller, who set up the Guantanamo routine, recommended a similar approach for Iraq.[345] In his report, however, Major General Taguba had argued that such collaboration violated army doctrine.[346]

The army IG report concluded that the army's training of tactical intelligence officers was not sufficient for the collection of human intelligence and, most concerning, that policies in the Iraqi theater "were not clear and contained ambiguities."

The report further noted that the military command had issued a series of evolving policy statements as leaders struggled to find policies that were both legal and effective in the unanticipated environment that

---

[344] Mikolashek Report, op. cit.

[345] Ibid.

[346] Taguba Report, op. cit.

evolved in Iraq. The report concluded that uncertainty over the rules "left considerable room for misapplication."

"In a high-stress, high-pressure combat environment, soldiers and subordinate leaders require clear, unambiguous guidance well within established parameters that they did not have in the policies we reviewed," the army IG found, stating that, "implementation, training and oversight of these policies was inconsistent."[347] Still, and quite importantly, the army IG report also said it was *not* able to link any instance of abuse to the policy problems.

On the critical issue of prisoner abuse, the report catalogued ongoing investigations and their status without undertaking its own independent assessment. It reviewed 125 incidents of alleged abuse, including those at Abu Ghraib (it counted the reports from Abu Ghraib as a single incident). The report said thirty-one of those abuse claims lacked merit. Of the remaining ninety-four, it said abuse had been confirmed in forty-nine and that there was potential abuse in the remaining forty-five. Not surprisingly, the report also noted that nearly half of the ninety-four incidents occurred at point of capture, where soldiers tend to be the most stressed, the most threatened, and the least in control of their environment.

The army IG report concluded: "We were unable to identify system failures that resulted in incidents of abuse. These incidents of abuse resulted from the failure of individuals to follow known standards of discipline and Army Values."[348] Of the incidents at Abu Ghraib and other internment and resettlement facilities, the army IG again pointed the finger at individual failure that may have been "compounded by a leadership failure."[349]

Despite all of the problems identified by his team, including doctrine that did not fit the realities on the ground, Lt. Gen. Mikolashek concluded that, "The army's leaders and soldiers are effectively conducting detainee operations and providing for the care and security of detainees in an intense operational environment."[350]

---

[347] Mikolashek Report, op. cit.

[348] Ibid.

[349] Ibid.

[350] Ibid.

London and his team appreciated learning that the army IG had determined that *every one of those hired by CACI met the contracted requirements*. In a short press release, CACI declared itself "pleased" by the IG's conclusion that the company had complied with and met the army's contract requirements.[351] Even then, the company's use of the word "pleased" apparently incensed some reviewers, and CACI heard about it from several sources.

Though the company's own review had arrived at the same conclusion, an official declaration from the army was a far more powerful response to detractors. From now on, CACI would be able to point to the army IG's statements should anybody challenge the company's hiring practices, or if Angelides or other critics suggested that the company had been careless in qualifying those it hired.

Critics and media skeptics apparently did not want to hear the truth as the Army IG documented it.[352] The critics ironically had been willing to take the *illegally leaked* Taguba report as true on its face without any questions. But they used the army IG report to claim a "whitewash" by the army.[353]

Perhaps as significant was the media's relative lack of follow-up interest in what the report said about CACI. To CACI, every new bit of information was vitally important because of the implications for its business and reputation. With the notable exception of their publication in trade journals, the army IG's conclusions about CACI were buried deep inside longer reports on the IG's findings. For the mainstream media

---

[351] CACI Press Release, "Army Inspector General Report Determines CACI Interrogators Met Army Statement of Work Criteria," July 22, 2004.

[352] The media had much to say in its criticisms of the Army IG's findings. The Army IG report apparently did not conclude what the press thought it should conclude. Some of these news stories were: Mark Mazzetti, "Army Calls Abuses of Detainees 'Aberrations,'" *Los Angeles Times*, July 23, 2004; Eric Schmitt, "Army Report Says Flaws in Detention Did Not Cause the Abuses at Abu Ghraib," *New York Times*, July 23, 2004; Josh White and Scott Higham, "Army Calls Abuses 'Aberrations,'" *Washington Post*, July 23, 2004; Farah Stockman, "Army Finds 49 Abuse Cases," *Boston Globe*, July 23, 2004; "Army Inspector General Reports 94 Cases of Prisoner Abuse," Associated Press, July 22, 2004; Jeff Bliss and Tony Capaccio, "U.S. Army Says No Systemic Failure in Iraq Prisons," Bloomberg News Service, July 22, 2004.

[353] "Abu Ghraib, Whitewashed." *New York Times*, July 24, 2004 and "An Army Whitewash," *Washington Post*, July 25, 2004.

and, indeed, for most news organizations, CACI at Abu Ghraib had become a very small part of a very large story. Even the *Washington Post* was reducing the amount of ink it devoted to CACI. But the residual effect of the media coverage compounded by the previously inaccurate and sensationalized reports was leaving a negative impression of the company rather than clearing its name. Salacious news hurt CACI's image, but the lack of it did not necessarily help either. It was a Catch-22 situation.

Like every company accused of misconduct, CACI needed some type of public absolution — or, at least, some kind of finality, some declaration that the story was over and closed on a positive note. But too often, media interest fades away without correcting the initial false reports or tying up the loose ends. The media simply drops the subject and moves on to the next headline. Accused companies and individuals are left to pick up the pieces as best as they can.

Unlike the Tylenol case, it did not appear that CACI would receive praise for its public relations approach in handling its crisis, even though London felt that the company's unique, multi-faceted, proactive approach had done a lot to both correct and balance the media's stories.[354] CACI also coped with the twenty-four-hour worldwide media machine, including cable TV news and the Internet that was not present when companies in the past, like Johnson & Johnson, had to deal with similar crises.

Indicative of the declining interest in the CACI story, none of the *New York Times*, the *Los Angeles Times*, or the *Washington Post* accounts of the army IG's report mentioned the company by name. The *Post's* story did include a single, indirect reference to CACI, noting the IG's observation that many of the "civilian interrogators" lacked military training.[355] This, again, failed to make clear that CACI had met all the SOW requirements for personnel and staffing requirements.

The Associated Press ran a brief, separate report on CACI's statement at 8:00 P.M. that evening and also made a brief reference to CACI near the bottom of its report on the army IG's findings.[356] In one of the more curious references to CACI, the *Boston Globe's* report on the army IG's study noted the Interior Department's finding that CACI's and Lockheed's interrogation contracts were out of scope, but did *not*

---

[354] The CACI Hypercrisis Management Model is presented in Appendix H.

[355] "An Army Whitewash," *Washington Post*, op. cit.

[356] "Army Inspector General Reports 94 Cases of Prisoner Abuse," op. cit.

note the army IG's discussion about the training and qualifications of CACI's interrogators.[357] Only *Washington Technology* paid significant attention to the army's commentary about CACI's interrogators.[358]

But if the media didn't much care about CACI, it had a lot to say about the army IG's report, and most of the commentary was negative. As a group, the media and their news stories simply refused to accept the IG's conclusion that responsibility for the activities captured in the photographs from Abu Ghraib was confined to a relatively small number of individual soldiers mostly of lower rank. In addition, the doubting critics found it hard to square the long list of shortcomings identified by the report — lack of training, lack of doctrine, lack of clear direction, as well as the chaos and the absence of necessary resources at Abu Ghraib — with the conclusion that the army was getting the job done.

One of the newspapers made its views quite clear. "The authors of this 300-page whitewash say they found no 'systemic' problems — even though there were 94 documented cases of prisoner abuse, including some 40 deaths, 20 of them homicides; even though only four prisons of the 16 visited had copies of the Geneva Conventions; even though Abu Ghraib was a cesspool with one shower for every 50 inmates; even though the military police were improperly involved in interrogations; even though young people plucked from civilian life were sent to guard prisoners — 50,000 of them in all — with no training," said the *New York Times* in a July 24 editorial labeled "Abu Ghraib, Whitewashed."[359]

A day later, in a similar editorial called "An Army Whitewash," the *Washington Post* noted that the army IG's report contradicted the Red Cross, Taguba, and testimony to Congress. The *Post* seemed to struggle with how to put the army IG's findings in context. The army IG charter was to conduct an investigation and provide a report about the specific areas of doctrine, policy, and procedure as used at Abu Ghraib — *not* to report about particular crimes or individual culpability. "Oddly, it doesn't even square with some of the findings buried in the inspector general's own report, which confirm that commanders in Iraq and Afghanistan ordered 'high-risk' interrogation procedures to be used on prisoners

---

[357] Stockman, "Army Finds 49 Abuse Cases," op. cit.

[358] Roseanne Gerin, "Report: CACI interrogators lacked training, but met contract," *Washington Technology*, July 26, 2004.

[359] "Abu Ghraib, Whitewashed," op. cit.

without adequate safeguards, training or regard for the Geneva Conventions," the editorial said.[360]

Despite the media's apparent ready acceptance of the Taguba report in its entirety, the "whitewash" label would continue to plague subsequent investigation reports.

Criticism also came from some members of Congress who were apparently frustrated and disappointed in the scope and findings of the IG report. Lamenting the army IG's failure to investigate the existence of so-called "ghost detainees," who allegedly were secretly moved through the detention system by the CIA and other non-military agencies, and the use of unmuzzled dogs in interrogations, Arizona Republican Senator John McCain asked rhetorically: "If you didn't look at the gross and egregious violations, what else didn't you investigate?"[361]

Acting army secretary Les Brownlee countered that the critics mischaracterized Mikolashek's assignment. The role of an inspector general, simply put, is not one of criminal investigation; that function is under the broad domain of the army Criminal Investigation Division.[362] It is unlikely that the army IG would have attempted criminal investigative work. Mikolashek hadn't looked at the questions raised by McCain because that wasn't his assignment or his position. Those questions would be covered in the Fay report due out in late August.

Some of the criticisms of the report could have been brought about by the intense anticipation of more climactic findings. From the media's viewpoint, and likely that of many others, the army IG's investigation report simply did not point the finger of guilt at the people whom they thought it should have — senior military leaders and executives of the administration.

Coming from another direction and more senior position, army chief of staff General Peter J. Schoomaker was among those who warned that overreaction to the abuses could undermine the army's ability to lawfully obtain intelligence that could save lives and shorten the conflict. In the aftermath of Abu Ghraib, there seemed to be at least some tendency to

---

[360] "An Army Whitewash," op. cit.

[361] White and Higham, op. cit.

[362] Criminal investigations in the military fall under the jurisdiction of the Army's Criminal Investigation Division and are conducted under the Uniform Code of Military Justice. The Army's Inspector General is not routinely part of this process.

condemn all interrogation as bad and to forget the legitimate role of interrogation in warfare. General Schoomaker worried that without reasonable balance on the matter, the army would be left with interrogators who were reluctant to act. Many were now coming to believe that the media was actually threatening success on the battlefield.

Similarly, in his book *The Interrogators*, Chris Mackey, a former army interrogator in Afghanistan, observed that U.S. interrogators operated at a *disadvantage* even before Abu Ghraib because al Qaeda detainees were well aware of the limits of authorized interrogation techniques. Further restrictions would make the challenge even greater, he believed.[363]

More directly to the issue, in March 2005, in a subsequent investigative report released on interrogation practices, Vice Admiral Albert Church pointed out: "Military interrogators are trained to use creative means of deception and to play upon detainees' emotions and fears. . . . Thus, people unfamiliar with military interrogations might view a perfectly legitimate interrogation of an EPW (Enemy Prisoner of War), in full compliance with the Geneva Conventions, as offensive by its very nature."[364]

A review of news coverage at the time revealed differing views on interrogation practices. One of the points most often made was that an exaggerated emphasis on detainee abuses might also interfere with, or even prohibit, legitimate interrogations of EPWs, terrorists, and other dangerous or hostile detainees, which would result in more American and coalition casualties. This was essentially the view presented by General Schoomaker. But this view attracted only modest interest from most news organizations. Some might speculate that the media was not sensitive to the fact that its public criticisms and claims of "whitewash" could embolden the enemy in the field.[365]

Of great significance during the MP proceedings was the testimony of over two dozen witnesses, including Specialist Darby who was responsible for turning the abuse photos of Abu Ghraib over to the CID.

---

[363] Mackey and Miller, op. cit.

[364] Church Report, op. cit.

[365] The media's understanding of this potential linkage between its own frequently hypercritical, anti-war, anti-military orientation and a corresponding heightened determination of the enemy — encouraged by the media itself — seemed to be completely lacking. Some might call this the "Uncle Ho effect": the result that North

The *New York Times* noted, "In the three months since the photographs of detainees . . . triggered the Abu Ghraib prison scandal, the soldiers charged with mistreatment have defended themselves by saying they were simply following orders. But as of the end of testimony here on Friday . . . there have been no witnesses and no evidence to back up that central assertion. Yet no one has said there were direct orders to carry out the treatment seen in photos, or even that the military police soldiers were encouraged to "keep it up" as a way of encouraging better interrogations."[366] Darby stated that there was confusion over whether military police or intelligence officers ran the section of Abu Ghraib where the photos were taken but denied claims that MP's were told by intelligence operatives to "soften up" prisoners for interrogation.[367]

Of interest to CACI in the middle of the media blitz and ongoing investigations in July of 2004 was a lone note posted to Yahoo's message board on CACI. Written by someone calling himself "downranger" in Baghdad, the post read: "I'm here at Abu [Ghraib]. I can tell you CACI bends over backwards to insure detainees are properly treated. CACI is a BY The Book Company."[368]

Although this was something the company knew and believed in, it did not seem to be able to get its message across to the media. It was encouraging and reassuring to see that someone unknown to the company, on site in Iraq, who also shared this view, cared enough to try to make it known publicly.

Vietnamese leader Ho Chi Minh was able to achieve in the American-Vietnam War. Widely recognized now, the American media's disparaging coverage of the Vietnam War during the late 1960s helped undermine military efforts in the war zone and eradicated support for the troops at home. Not surprisingly, the fact that Osama bin Laden and al Qaeda, who became well versed in both western culture and the media's influence, particularly on the Vietnam War, were attempting to copy and replicate these propaganda tactics and results, did not garner much attention from the media.

[366] Kate Zernike, "At Abuse Hearing, No Testimony that G.I.'s Acted on Orders," *New York Times*, August 6, 2004.

[367] Allen G. Breed, "Soldier over abuse photos says he agonized before reporting abuse," Associated Press, August 7, 2004.

[368] The finance section of web portal and search engine Yahoo has a message board for nearly every company that is publicly traded. Here, users can post their opinions about a company.

CHAPTER THIRTY-THREE

LAWSUIT REDUX
Opportunists line up

> "The lawsuit is . . . ambulance chasing and piling on activity in a blatant attempt to extort financial gain."
> ~ CACI PRESS RELEASE ON LAWSUIT BY IRAQI TORTURE VICTIMS GROUP, JULY 27, 2004

A S AUGUST APPROACHED, THE ABU GHRAIB SCANDAL WAS NOW IN the fourth month of the crisis. For CACI and its senior leaders, much of the work now was coping with the lingering stain to the company's good name and collateral damage brought on by the media. But the media wasn't the only issue that CACI had to deal with at this stage — there were other challenges on the horizon.

The meeting with CalSTRS and CalPERS was fast approaching, scheduled to take place just ten days after the release of the army IG report. The California funds' meeting would be a challenge even though CACI had been consistently open and forthcoming, putting out all the information as it became available. The plan was to present the pension fund with a display of so much clear and comprehensive information that there could be no reasonable suggestion the company was holding anything back. And the army IG report, no matter how maligned by the press, provided considerable details to support CACI's position. CACI's team would point out the report's observation that the interrogators hired by the company had met *every* requirement in the contract. In fact, CACI had gone far beyond the basic job requirements of the contract by hiring as many interrogators with military training and experience as it could. The company maintained a rigorous approach in its hiring policy, and the qualifications of its interrogator staff were, in fact, extensive. CACI had done the job it was asked to do, the IG report said in its unchallenged conclusion. Nothing in the IG report supported any assertions that CACI had failed to meet its contract obligations or had taken its assignment lightly.

There was also increasing reason to believe that the Taguba report had accused Stefanowicz of wrongdoing without factual support and was based mostly on hearsay. Indeed, as the annexes and information underlying the report trickled out, evidence showing misconduct by Stefanowicz was conspicuously absent. London, Koegel and the CACI team seemed to be the only ones to take notice of this lack of supporting evidence. After accepting the *illegally leaked* Taguba report's suspicions and allegations about Stefanowicz as gospel, the media seemed not to notice that the dramatic accusations lacked factual support. The view of CACI's team would, however, soon be put to the test when the results of two other significant investigations were announced.

Two reports were scheduled for release before the end of August — an assessment of detainee operations by former secretary of defense James Schlesinger (the Schlesinger report) in conjunction with an independent panel of former government officials, and an army inquiry by senior officers tasked with investigating military intelligence operations at Abu Ghraib (the Fay report). London and his CACI colleagues were eagerly awaiting these new reports to find out if these investigations corroborated the Taguba report or whether they would support the growing view that Stefanowicz was wrongly implicated.

Although the details of the company's own investigative findings would be crucial, the operative question was fast becoming when and how to make its findings public. It was this question that London had also asked media consultant Claire Sanders Swift and business advisor Burkhart to ponder. Their final analysis, reached independently, was "the sooner, the better."

The fatigue of crisis and the concern about events ahead may well explain the company's reaction on July 27, a Tuesday, when the morning calm was interrupted by news of yet another lawsuit against the company because of Abu Ghraib.

Evidently tipped off in advance, FOX Morning News ran a brief item about the lawsuit to be filed later that day and aired their report by again showing the photos of the abuses committed by the MPs. This linkage of CACI's name to the photos, which did not depict CACI employees, along with this new lawsuit, once again strengthened the perceived *but false* connections between CACI and the images of Abu Ghraib. FOX News would repeat the story twice more that day, doing so without talking to anyone at CACI, a gross injustice in the CACI team's view.

Later that morning, PR Newswire, which distributes press releases to newsrooms nationwide, made the formal announcement that a group of lawyers led by the small Atlanta, Georgia, law firm of Edmond & Jones was suing CACI and Titan on behalf of five Iraqis who claimed they had been abused at Abu Ghraib.[369] Edmond & Jones' founding partner Roderick Edmond was a former physician who practiced medicine full-time for several years before turning to law. Edmond drew on both of his degrees to concentrate on medical malpractice suits. On its Web site, the firm also claimed its expertise in nursing home negligence, product liability, police brutality, and civil rights violations.[370]

Also in the legal consortium was a lawyer from the Atlanta office of Cochran, Cherry, Givens, Smith and Sistrunk, a firm founded by the late O.J. Simpson defender Johnnie Cochran; a small South Carolina firm that had a relationship with Edmonds; and an attorney from Washington, D.C. Also involved was Australian attorney, Michael A. Hourigan, who had presumably interviewed the alleged victims. Hourigan, the only one of the attorneys who had met the Iraqi plaintiffs, had brought the former prisoners to the attention of Edmond, whom he knew from previous legal work.

The lawsuit did not name any individual defendants but made accusations against CACI and Titan, including an alleged conspiracy.

---

[369] Edmond & Jones Press Release, "Iraqis Civilians File Claim Against Private U.S. Firms Murder, Torture and Abuses," July 27, 2004.

[370] As written on the firm's Web site in 2005. www.edmondfirm.com.

Furthermore, without naming a dollar amount, the suit claimed compensatory and punitive damages for the "Iraqi Torture Victims Group" under the U.S. Alien Tort Claims Act. Like the CCR lawsuit, the Atlanta lawyers alleged conspiracy under federal racketeering statutes, which would entitle the defendants to triple damages and attorney's fees.

But the new suit lacked CCR's inflammatory rhetoric, and the attorneys seemed to also lack CCR's media focus. Where CCR made charges of dark conspiracies and also charged that the companies' senior officers had a deliberate strategy to torture detainees and generate new interrogation business in a plot with the government, the new brief was a fairly bland recitation of what they apparently hoped was the relevant law. CCR had brought alleged victims to a staged press conference; the new suit merely provided a list of alleged abuses.

Much like the earlier suit by CCR, the new suit lacked evidence connecting the defendants to abuses. Two of the detainees presumably had identified Titan translator Adel Nakhla as participating in their abuse. One also was said to have identified "Steven" (the name of more than one American at the site), perhaps a reference to Stefanowicz, but that was unclear. None made specific allegations against John Israel. Apparently the lawyers, like those representing CCR, had simply named the two contractors cited in the Taguba report, CACI and Titan, but with no significant detail provided. The complaint misidentified the employers of Stefanowicz and Nakhla, linking Stefanowicz to Titan and Nakhla to CACI when, in fact, the affiliations were exactly the opposite. The lack of research and the dearth of evidence also limited the prospects for media interest, even though FOX's coverage did considerable damage with its misrepresentation of the photographs linked to CACI's name.

From the media standpoint, the new suit wasn't very well timed. The Abu Ghraib story was now three months old and allegations of abuse at the prison were, in media jargon, "yesterday's news." The Iraqi Torture Victims Group suit was the *second* private lawsuit, which alone diminished its news value. It was also narrower. The new suit charged the private companies, not the government, which was now less interesting to the media than it had been when CCR filed its suit more than six weeks earlier. The media was, by now, much more interested in what the government did or had done. But the government wasn't named in this suit because, according to attorney Craig Jones, "the military seems to be doing a good job of policing their own. They are bringing soldiers to justice."[371] It was obvious to CACI that the real underlying reason was that more "settlement" money might be available by suing corporations.

The CACI team directed the spotlight on the suit with a press release that denounced the attorneys for "ambulance chasing . . . in a blatant attempt to extort financial gain."[372] Jones reportedly responded by telling at least one reporter that the suit was motivated by an interest in human rights, but "we also are interested in a payoff, too. We feel like we are going to get referrals and we may end up with a larger number of cases."[373] CACI also called the suit itself a "malicious and farcical recitation of false statements and intentional distortions." CACI's strategy, which had served it well, was to forcefully and publicly reject the gross distortions and fallacious allegations about the company stemming from Abu Ghraib. This lawsuit was yet another example of the "piling on" phenomenon.

Within hours of the CACI press release, the Associated Press and Dow Jones newswires posted reports of CACI's counterattack — even though neither news agency had filed reports on the lawsuit itself.[374] The news agency's reactions strongly suggest that if not for CACI's own statements, the lawsuit would have generated no additional news that day beyond the FOX News reports. But when under attack, protecting and defending the company's good name was what CACI's media campaign was all about. Some advised London to prepare a simpler holding statement, so as not to draw any more unnecessary attention. But CACI's goal was *not* to minimize news but to declare that it would reject all egregious accusations about the company's good name. London chose to stay consistent with the company's strategy and give the press real-time information in developing their stories.

---

[371] R. Robin McDonald, "New Suit Over Abu Ghraib Abuse Claims Filed," *The Legal Intelligencer*, July 29, 2004.

[372] CACI Press Release, "CACI rejects lawsuit as slanderous and ludicrous, Frivolous suit based on false statements without merit," July 27, 2004.

[373] McDonald, op. cit.

[374] "CACI rejects lawsuit as frivolous," Associated Press, July 27, 2004; "CACI Denies Allegations Made in Abu Ghraib Abuse Case," Dow Jones News Service, July 27, 2004.

Even with CACI's statement, major news media largely ignored the lawsuit. Other than the AP and Dow Jones report, among other print outlets only the *Washington Business Journal* and the *San Diego Union-Tribune* — hometown media for the defendant companies — ran reports.[375] Even then, the *Union-Tribune* took two days to write about it, and the *Washington Post* ignored it altogether. The *Fulton County Daily Report*, a legal publication that covered courtroom and law firm activity in Georgia, wrote a lengthy story that focused mainly on the local law firms and partners involved. A sister legal publication in Pennsylvania, the *Legal Intelligencer*, reprinted that article — perhaps sensing interest among its readers because a lead attorney in the CCR suit was based in Philadelphia.[376]

Other than FOX News and one very brief item on an early morning CNN show the next day, television also largely ignored the new suit. The CCR suit, by comparison, had generated at least a dozen national news items, many of which reran the photos that ignited the scandal in late April. Perhaps the media was tiring of the contractor story which appeared to be leading nowhere, but there was continued association in the minds of many between CACI and the Abu Ghraib photos. London and his team hoped that their efforts to inform the public, coupled with the results of the official investigations, were finally showing the truth and dispelling the myths created by the media through the photographs' repeated connection to the company.

There was also a significant, long-term benefit to CACI's frequent press release approach. By filing a press release, the company assured that its response had a place in almost every permanent media database. This was a key goal. Months, or even years later, a journalist or historian seeking news about the lawsuit also would find CACI's response. Whatever the short-term damage of possibly provoking additional news coverage at the time, CACI's decision to respond to every

---

375 Jeff Clabaugh, "CACI calls new lawsuit farcical," *Washington Business Journal*, July 27, 2004; *David* Washburn, "San Diego-based Titan hit with lawsuit over Iraqi prisoner abuse," *San Diego Union-Tribune*, July 28, 2004.

376 R. Robin McDonald, "Contractors Face New Suit Over Abu Ghraib Abuse Claims," *Fulton County Daily Report*, July 28, 2004; "New Suit Over Abu Ghraib Abuse Claims Filed," op. cit.

egregious and unwarranted attack improved the odds that its voice would be heard in any future media accounts of the lawsuit. Making sure the record included CACI's views on every element of the Abu Ghraib story was consistent with the company's long-term strategy of ensuring that the "Truth Will Out."

On the heels of the lawsuit was a matter even more alarming to CACI. An e-mail had been forwarded to CACI that was being circulated within high levels of the army debating the potential merits of replacing CACI interrogator support work in Iraq. Even while the e-mail framed "breaking off" with CACI as a "political" necessity, the reports the CACI team was getting from the field in Iraq were that the company's employees were doing a great job and their services were important, needed, and valued. At the same time, the army and the Department of Defense were still receiving a lot of media scrutiny and political criticism over the topics of Abu Ghraib, civilian contractor interrogators, and the approval of certain interrogation methods and techniques by officials in the U.S. Army and the administration. The company had no way to know what the internal army views might be, but continued its best efforts in good faith to perform its contract assignments under the difficult circumstances on the ground in Iraq.

The debate and criticism about interrogation would continue to be an issue from the Abu Ghraib scandal that spilled over to Guantanamo Bay and Afghanistan concerning the approval of various interrogation methods and techniques, including the use of guard dogs as part of the procedure. Much of the later political and media discussion would center on Major General Geoffrey Miller — and speculation about whether or not he brought certain interrogation techniques from Guantanamo Bay to Iraq and Abu Ghraib in the fall of 2003.

CHAPTER THIRTY-FOUR

A MONDAY IN SACRAMENTO
CACI's showdown out West

"Fraud and falsehood only dread examination. Truth invites it."
～ THOMAS COOPER

A S THEY BOARDED THE PLANE TO CALIFORNIA ON AUGUST 2, THE
CACI team, Dave Dragics, Ken Johnson, and outside counsel Bill
Koegel, had reason to feel good.

The meeting with the pension funds had been worked out on their
schedules and was taking place at the offices of the presumed less confrontational of the two funds. Further bolstering their position was the
army IG report which provided a strong rebuttal to any suggestion that
CACI had been remiss in its hiring practices. The quick completion of
CACI's GSA review resulted, for all practical means and purposes, in
CACI being publicly declared a responsible company.

Moreover, recent new CACI contract awards — a $75 million con-
tract with the Naval Sea Systems Command and a blanket purchase
agreement that could mean up to $45 million in business from the
Transportation Security Administration — might counter assertions that
management failures existed or that CACI's leaders were jeopardizing
shareholders' interests.

The company's share price, though still down for the year, was up nearly 11 percent from the post-Abu Ghraib low point on May 28. At $41.11 on July 30, the last trading day before the meeting with the funds, the stock was up almost $2 from the date of the letter from California state treasurer Phil Angelides to the pension funds, which triggered the events that led to the upcoming meeting. The price gain since Angelides' complaint had added over $550,000 to the two funds' combined portfolio.

The meeting awaiting them, however, would prove to be a political spectacle to showcase Angelides. As part of that objective, there would certainly be no one from San Diego-based Titan (also accused of Abu Ghraib improprieties as well as corporate misconduct) called to meet in Sacramento, since the California-based company apparently represented a constituency base for the politically focused Angelides.[377]

The team's arrival in Sacramento was preceded by a fifty-page package of information delivered by e-mail and Federal Express to the funds' senior officers and investment staffs on July 28. The package included a twelve-page letter responding to specific questions that the funds had forwarded from the original Angelides letter, as well as supporting documentation that laid out in yet another forum CACI's perspective and position on the issues. It was a comprehensive set of responses that had taken several days to compile. Among the key points in CACI's responses:

☐ Relating to management control of CACI employees at Abu Ghraib, CACI noted that employees reported to a military chain of command that was "responsible for monitoring and supervising CACI employees in the conduct of interrogation operations." In fact, testimony given in courts-martial and depositions in other proceedings had all stated that CACI interrogators were embedded

---

[377] Titan pleaded guilty in the U.S. District Court for Southern California that it bribed foreign officials for business favors and agreed to pay $28.5 million in both criminal and civil fines to the federal government. This plea agreement also included $15.5 million to settle a lawsuit by the SEC. The government had begun investigating Titan during Lockheed Martin's attempted acquisition of the company in 2003 for $2.2 billion. Lockheed called off the deal in June 2004 and L-3 acquired Titan for $2.65 billion in 2005. Roseanne Gerin, "Titan Pleads Guilty to Bribery Charges," *Washington Technology*, March 2, 2005.

into the military chain of command and CACI's supervision was administrative[378]

☐ Based on military interviews with civilians and military personnel at Abu Ghraib in response to incidents at the prison, there was no reason to suspect that the January interviews by Major General Taguba had any relationship to CACI. "Given the conditions at Abu Ghraib prison, in accordance with that standard practice [of investigating all significant events], there were multiple investigations going on during the month of January 2004," CACI reported

☐ Training in local rules of engagement and the Geneva Conventions was, *by contract*, the responsibility of the army, *not* CACI, and the army IG reported that all interrogators hired by CACI met the required army contract statement of work

☐ CACI did not have any reason or precedent to question the manner in which the government went about awarding the interrogation contract, given the history of work awarded to PTG over the previous five years as well as the Interior Department's approval, as the contracting agency, of the interrogation task order. "The orders for work in Iraq were part of a long series of orders for supporting military intelligence operations that had been awarded to Premier Technology Group, Inc, dating from 1998," CACI told the funds

☐ CACI had not made any special or exceptional disclosure of the interrogation work out of respect for security regulations that limit disclosure, the small dollar value of the contract, and its past work with the army. "Because of our long, highly favorable experience in supporting the U.S. military, we did not anticipate that there would be unusual risk associated with providing interrogators such that we would have disclosed this work despite its immaterial size." It is doubtful that anyone — military or civilian — would have anticipated in August 2003 what would later take place at Abu Ghraib. CACI had also openly advertised for interrogators on its Web site and in various trade media

---

[378] CACI's Reply Memorandum in Support of the CACI Motion for Summary Judgment in the *Saleh v. Titan* case highlight statements made under oath by Col. Thomas Pappas, the Army's COR for the CACI contract, the Officer in Charge of the Interrogation Control Element, as well as two CACI managers that support this.

In Sacramento, the three met up with government relations counselor Dave Berteau and made their way to CalSTRS offices on the east side of Sacramento. The office location, removed from the capital building and the town's political center, was appropriate to the low-key fund. The location, they believed, may have lowered the tension and trimmed media attendance somewhat compared to what would likely have happened if the meeting had taken place at the CalPERS office, located in the middle of the government center.

However, their arrival had been preceded by several camera crews and reporters already alerted from news outlets such as Reuters, Bloomberg, National Public Radio, and the *San Francisco Chronicle*. It was no surprise to London when he later got word of this. He had warned the team in advance and coached them ahead of time that they would be walking into a media circus. Earlier in pre-meeting discussions, CACI had hoped for a private meeting outside the media glare. It was a pleasant thought while it lasted. California had a history of government in sunshine, and it was hard to imagine that CalSTRS could have closed the meeting to the press given Angelides' publicity seeking tendencies. Even if CalSTRS staff favored a private meeting, Angelides would have opposed it because that would have deprived him of the political publicity he had worked so hard to achieve, as London's business advisor Burkhart had forewarned.

CACI had insisted, however, that reporters could not ask questions during the meeting. The company had come to meet with its shareholders, who should be given priority to ask the questions. The CACI team expected reporters would seek them out after the fact, but that would allow them the choice of answering or declining to respond at a time that did not take their attention from the shareholders. CalSTRS, too, likely preferred the arrangement, if only to keep the meeting manageable. The pension fund readily acceded to that ground rule from CACI.

The meeting place was inauspicious: a large table in the middle of the crowded room with seats for about fifteen participants. Representing CalSTRS were CEO Ehnes, Chief Investment Officer Chris Ailman, and Janice Hester-Amey and Eileen Okada from the corporate governance staff. Mark Anson, CalPERS' top investment officer, was the only representative from his fund to make the trip across town. California

State Controller Steven Westly, pleading a schedule conflict, did not participate, but sent a senior aide who participated actively.

In the grandstanding style that London expected of him, Angelides arrived several minutes late, apparently staging an entrance to draw attention (as if to say to the media present "I'm ready for my close-up"[379]). He was accompanied by his top deputy, his press officer, and several other aides — his "entourage." It was a calculated entrance that signaled the meeting's dual purpose for him. "A real meeting and also a meeting for show," Berteau chuckled at the memory.

Ailman opened the meeting with introductions and then invited Johnson to talk about CACI. Johnson told the full CACI story as he would to any room of investors. It was an educational presentation, laying out the company's history, business concepts, and commitment to ethics. He talked about the growth plan, including acquisitions, and noted the company's strong financial performance and return on investments. Johnson was deliberate in taking his time before turning to Iraq; if he was going to present to shareholders, he was going to give them the full picture they deserved. He knew the funds wanted to talk about Iraq, but they had claimed the reason was the value of their investment — and Iraq was just one small part of the investment story, less than 1 percent in fact. At one point, in a quite revealing comment, the impatient Angelides urged Johnson to "get to the issues." But Johnson persisted in his obligations to the shareholders by covering the big picture first including the other 99 plus percent of the company's business.

When the question period finally arrived, the staff began with typical investor questions about returns, revenue, and lines of business. Soon, led by Angelides, Hester-Amey, and Westly's aide, the questions turned to Iraq. The anticipated showdown had begun. Over and over again, Angelides returned to his chosen and well-rehearsed theme: interrogation was a "high-risk" service. This was the one and only sticking point the politician could claim. As weak as it was, given the very small percentage of CACI's business base that interrogator services represented, it was still a point Angelides came back to repeatedly. Apparently a pre-planned PR statement, it also had a sound bite factor that would play

---

[379] A popular line from the 1950 movie *Sunset Boulevard* starring Gloria Swanson.

well in the media. Among Angelides' claims was that CACI had simply acted like an employment agency, merely providing bodies without training. He had apparently missed or ignored the army IG report, included in the company's presentation to the funds, that showed CACI's recruiting performance had met or exceeded the contract requirements. Angelides repeatedly asked if this "high-risk" service was "the right place" for an IT company. He demanded to know whether CACI put any limits around the services it would perform as if he had personal prerogative in determining CACI's business portfolio.

It was strikingly apparent that CACI was in the spotlight due to negative media coverage, and *not* for the company's interrogator services work. Now, ironically, the company was being called upon the carpet to respond to these same exaggerated accusations created by the very media machine that had hyped such a slanted version of the story in the first place. In a surreal fashion, all of this was taking place in the presence of, and for the benefit of, that same media machine that had generated and amplified the inaccuracies that CACI was trying to correct. However, it was augmented now by a publicity-hungry politico.

An account in the *San Francisco Chronicle* mockingly likened the meeting to "a hostile interrogation," as Angelides repeatedly and rudely interrupted CACI's speakers.[380] But to the CACI team, it seemed that Johnson gave as good as he got. They thought he fared well in the sound-bite war with his pronouncement that the company's work in Iraq was saving soldiers' lives and CACI was proud of it. "What we do has to be done. It is vital to our country," Johnson, the West Point graduate, proclaimed. "We actually believe were it not for us or that support, that an additional guy or gal may have died."

Anson then asked, apparently for the benefit of the reporters he and his colleagues had assembled there, whether it was worth "the headline risk." It was clearly a calculated, insincere remark, since Angelides and the funds had actually created the current publicity and "headlines" over the entire issue by going to the press *before* contacting the company.

Johnson responded to Anson's question with, "it comes with the territory." In his mind, as in London's, when your military customers ask for

---

[380] Robert Collier, "Executive Grilled on Firm's Role in Iraq Torture," *San Francisco Chronicle*, August 3, 2004.

help in time of war, you stand up for duty. London and Johnson were both former military men who understood such matters, and they both knew that here they were addressing bureaucrats, and reporters apparently with scant knowledge, understanding, or even an appreciation for the uniform in a war zone. Johnson assured the California funds that any interrogator hired going forward would have to pass his personal top-level review.

Angelides was unmoved. His scripted performance continued as he read aloud from the oft-quoted and now infamous *illegally leaked* Taguba report. He repeated Taguba's suspicions about Stefanowicz, and then announced for the benefit the cameras that, "CACI needs to get out of this business or the pension funds need to get out of CACI." It was a crafty remark that the media in attendance featured prominently in their reports.[381] A week later, Angelides would repeat the comment in a televised interview on CNNfn. This was in sharp contrast to the view of some at CACI that the issue — essentially an investor relations question — should be resolved between the respective parties and not in the press.[382]

When London later heard of Angelides' statement about the funds needing to get out of CACI, his unruffled response was, "They know the business we're in and our good track record. If they can't accept CACI being in the intelligence-gathering interrogation business, they ought to get out of CACI. We have done nothing wrong as a business, or for our customers, or to anyone else, and we have done a lot right. And that includes value creation for our investors like the California funds."

Despite his own doubts and business advisor Burkhart's opposition to the idea, London had acquiesced to the meeting in California. London admitted that he held out a glimmer of hope that the meeting would, in fact, be conducted aboveboard. "A public company has an obligation to answer legitimate investor questions," London said.

---

[381] Ibid. The press who saw fit to mention their take on the CACI meeting with the California funds and Angelides included: Adam Tanner, "California Questions Firm Over Iraq Interrogators," Reuters, August 3, 2004; Michael M. Marois, "CACI Should be Dropped by Pensions, Angelides Says," Bloomberg, August 2, 2004; "Angelides Urges Pension Funds to Sell CACI Shares," *Los Angeles Times*, August 3, 2004; "In Brief," *Washington Post*, August 3, 2004.

[382] "Interview with Phil Angelides," *Street Sweep*, CNNfn., August 9, 2004.

But London had been concerned all along about the Californian's true motives, and his suspicions, it seemed, were confirmed by Angelides' theatrics and the media circus that took place there. The trip was primarily a waste of time and effort for CACI executives, who were taken away from more important business duties. Angelides had worked hard to set a booby trap for CACI. But the company was aware of his intentions, and decided to go to California anyway with the good faith intention of answering legitimate investor concerns for those who cared. Clearly the company had been asked to come to California not for the benefit of the state's investors, but for the underlying political agenda, so the politicians, shamefully, could admonish the management team in front of the media and strut on the political stage. It was a disgraceful misuse of public authority in London's view.

Surprisingly, the *Washington Post*, which had accomodated the political angle by quickly publishing Angelides' initial challenge to CACI in June, buried the story inside the business page with a brief wire service item that didn't even mention Angelides. The *Los Angeles Times* merely reprinted an edited version of the Bloomberg account. For major national news organizations, it was just another political press conference — and London and his team were delighted with their interpretations.

From across the country, CACI's leadership, however, was obliged to fire back at Angelides' political mockery. They had been willing to give the funds the benefit of the doubt going into the meeting in California. They had done this even knowing of Angelides' goal of solely advancing his own political agenda. London and his advisors saw the episode, as it played out, as an abuse of their goodwill and conscientious investor relations program, especially when the California State Treasurer's Office — a public office — had been used as a stage to mount such a disingenuous attack just to promote individual political aspirations.

London's opinion of Angelides was summed up in another favorite Churchill quote, "I expect the greatness of his office will find him out."[383]

The day after the Sacramento meeting, the CACI team issued a press release accusing Angelides of "political grandstanding." While

---

[383] Gretchen Rubin, *Forty Ways to Look at Winston Churchill*, op. cit. Quoted from a letter written by Sir Winston Churchill to his wife, Clementine, in 1935 referring to Anthony Eden on his appointment as Foreign Secretary under Prime Minister Stanley Baldwin.

promising to keep the California funds and all of its investors informed, the company called Angelides' conduct a disservice to California pensioners. "His posturing as a protector of the moral high ground in reality is a blatant quest for headlines to achieve personal political gain," CACI's press release said.[384]

Angelides' "sound bite," London later remembered, was exactly the kind of rhetoric London had expected but hoped would not emerge in the California meeting. Still miffed at the time and money that went into responding to CalPERS and CalSTRS, London recalled the warning he gave each member of his team as they headed west: "Mr. Angelides is not doing this to find out what happened." London had said, "He is in this for 'look at me, look at me' and his own personal gain. There won't be any 'high fives' at the end of the day, and nobody out there will say 'thanks for straightening us out.'"

Known for his personal touch and hands-on approach, London regularly stayed in direct contact with his clients and staff over the years, flying to various parts of the world to meet face to face with CACI's network of people. Although he had considered the trip to California, he was in strategic meetings in the U.K. with CACI executives, focusing his attention on the company's work and future growth that, ironically, would benefit the California funds investments in the long run.

Still annoyed months later, London said he should have gone with his initial gut instinct instead of going to the time and expense of the meeting. In the aftermath, although he did not regret responding to legitimate investor questions, he did regret having provided the pension funds with all the voluminous information they had requested, but did not appreciate. He believed that the agreement to attend a public meeting on Angelides' home turf had given the Californian exactly what he wanted — a sound bite in his local media to boost his next political campaign — at CACI's expense.

Even with London's misgivings, the team that went to California felt that they had held onto the high ground of the company's credibility. They felt they had underscored CACI's willingness to go into any legitimate forum and talk to shareholders about their concerns. While

---

[384] CACI Press Release, "CACI Meets With California Pension Funds About Work in Iraq, Company Challenges Politically Motivated Actions of California Treasurer Phil Angelides as Wrongly Rejecting Contractor's Support of Military," August 3, 2004.

Angelides was focused on his political aspirations, the CACI team believed that most others at the two funds were open to legitimate investor matters and to the company's update on current events.

But the CACI team was pleased that, at the end of their day in California after an amiable tour of the CalSTRS operation, they got a whispered vote of confidence from investment chief Ailman. Walking the CACI team to the door, Ailman didn't sound like a man who was ready to sell the fund's CACI holdings. Assuring his guests, he smiled, saying, "CACI's been a spectacular stock for us."

CHAPTER THIRTY-FIVE

CACI RISING

Mounting the offensive while waiting for more news

> "Thanks for the support you are providing in Iraq. I would
> hope that the American public will someday receive a
> clear, unbiased picture about our activities over there."
>
> ∾ LETTER FROM A RETIRED NAVY COMMANDER
> TO JACK LONDON, AUGUST 2004

AUGUST IS THE MONTH WHEN WASHINGTON, D.C., COLLECTIVELY heads to the beaches to escape the heavy sub-tropical air that, before air conditioning, won the city the designation as a hardship post for the diplomatic corps. But for CACI's people, August 2004 was not a time for vacation. Instead, it was a time of confidence reborn.

Though two major reports on prisoner abuse and Abu Ghraib were due for release near the month's close, CACI was reasonably confident that it had already seen the worst. The GSA inquiry had come and gone, and CACI was found to be responsible and fully qualified to continue doing business with the government. The army IG, though suggesting future adjustments in job requirements, had concluded that *every interrogator hired by CACI met the qualifications* spelled out in the army's statement of work. The potentially troublesome meeting with the California pension funds had wrapped up without any business impact and with only minimal negative coverage by the major media. And the company's business performance was nothing short of spectacular. The proverbial light was now streaming into the tunnel. Barring any unforeseen development, there was growing confidence that by the time the leaves turned for 2004, CACI might be back to business as usual.

When the CACI California team returned, there was good news waiting. On August 4, the army announced that it had awarded CACI a new contract, worth up to $23 million, to continue providing interrogation services in Iraq. More significant than the money, which remained small relative to the company's $1.5 billion in total revenue, was the army's endorsement of CACI's work. Taguba had raised questions about one of CACI's people, but a senior army contracting official now was telling inquiring reporters that the army was happy with the way the company was doing its job.

"The army said that coalition forces were 'satisfied' with CACI's performance, and that there had been no evidence to date that CACI itself was responsible for wrongdoing in connection with the scandal," the *Los Angeles Times* reported ironically under an incriminating headline.[385] With an opportunity to comment on good news, CACI happily delivered one of the company's core messages, telling the *Washington Post*: "Continuity in services to end the war on terrorism is essential, and the men and women of CACI are proud to support the army in doing so."[386] Not surprisingly, the *Post* published the CACI statement at the very end of the article, after several repeated criticisms. There seemed to be a consistent pattern of bias emerging from the *Post* in all of this.

In an internal announcement and a press release on the contract award, London stated: "We have a long and proud history of serving the U.S. military, and we are pleased once again to answer the call to assist our military's mission around the world. We have been criticized by some for providing interrogation services at the request of the U.S. Army, but we have been resolute in our position that in wartime we should respond when called. The interrogation of detainees, as part of overall intelli-

---

[385] T. Christian Miller, "Army Gives Contract to Company in Jail Scandal," *Los Angeles Times*, August 5, 2004.

[386] "CACI Gets New Interrogation Contract," *Washington Post*, August 5, 2004.

gence information gathering, is essential to protecting our troops, saving lives, and successfully completing the military mission."[387]

It was essentially the same message that Ken Johnson had delivered to Angelides. The Californian seemed indifferent but to the internal audience at a company with ranks full of military retirees and former servicemen and women, the words captured a shared sentiment of duty and pride.

Unfortunately, but perhaps not surprisingly, the good news of CACI's contract renewal was treated unfavorably by the press. Notwithstanding the positive reviews and praise that CACI was receiving about its employees' performance in Iraq from its military client there, headlines like "Army Gives Contract to Company in Jail Scandal" sent a negative message that would likely have increased the army's anxiety.[388] The army was already expressing concerns in its e-mails about the political pressure it was experiencing from its continued use of CACI interrogators in Iraq, apparently as a result of the negative publicity surrounding the Abu Ghraib ordeal. While keeping the company working in Iraq at Abu Ghraib would certainly send the message that the company's reputation was solid and its work there was satisfactory, the incessant media scrutiny and congressional inquiries would seem to eventually take its toll.

With London's guidance, following the media flurry around CACI's new contract in the late summer of 2004 for more work in Iraq, the company was now ready for an adjustment in its media approach. While uncommonly aggressive for a company in crisis in *responding* to events, CACI had largely avoided deliberate attempts to *make* news related to Abu Ghraib. While PR consultants will often advise companies to turn challenges into opportunities to tell their story, that strategy must be tailored to fit the situation. In May or June, attempts by CACI to initiate positive media would have been unsuccessful. By August, however, the media's declining interest in extending the CACI story on its own created an opening that the company could try to fill. London moved the company into the void with dispatch.

Within days of the Sacramento session with the pension funds, CACI fired off an extended response to Angelides in an op-ed signed by London

---

[387] CACI Press Release, "CACI Receives Contract Extension for U.S. Army Interrogation Support in Iraq," August 10, 2004.

[388] Miller, "Army Gives Contract to Company in Jail Scandal," op. cit.

to the *Sacramento Bee*.[389] The column cast the company in its role as a patriot supporting the troops in Iraq and defending the fundamental American principle of the presumption of innocence in the face of allegations. Those two values reflected London's deep-seated convictions and bridged the political spectrum. The call to duty would likely be seen as admirable to those who supported the war effort, and on principle it might also touch some who thought the war a mistake. Furthermore, even those who might think that the CACI team's patriotism was somehow misplaced would, at least, respect the idea that punishment for any individual misconduct in Iraq should be based on evidence and not media-driven speculation, hearsay and rumor. The op-ed succinctly summarized the company's view of itself and the way it had responded to the allegations about Abu Ghraib. And it conveyed London's core values and beliefs.[390]

CACI was unapologetic about its patriotism and duty to its government client, but Angelides "seemed to counsel CACI and all other businesses to turn our backs on soldiers when things get tough." The op-ed also aimed to separate Angelides from his pension fund colleagues with this suggestion: "While other pension fund board members focused on gathering information about a company they invest in, he seemed set on advancing his predetermined agenda." Angelides' political motivations, in CACI's view, took precedence over legitimate investor concerns, and this disservice to other company investors would be made known.

Although the newspaper delayed a few weeks in running the piece, its publication on August 19 produced elation and encouragement to those at CACI. After months on the receiving end, the company was building upon its confidence and proving its good standing.

---

[389] J.P. London, "Angelides takes wrong tack with CACI investment," op. cit. See Appendix I for the full text.

[390] The CACI leadership team had positioned the company over its four decades in business as an organization dedicated (in its U.S.-based operations) to loyal support of the federal government and the U.S. military armed services. This support and loyalty to the U.S. military was neither politically driven, nor politically motivated. Just as the U.S. military follows the direction of the Commanders-in-Chief, whomever they may be, CACI, in an analogous fashion has supported the direction and mission of the government and military since 1962 through nine presidential administrations with varying policies and agendas. The company has always endeavored to meet the legitimate needs and contract requirements set forth by the government and the military without political orientation of any sort.

Reader response to the op-ed was also highly positive. Among the many letters and e-mails CACI received was one from a retired navy commander who said, "Thanks for the support you are providing in Iraq. I would hope that the American public will someday receive a clear, unbiased, picture about our activities over there." An educator wrote to "convey to Mr. London my personal thanks for your organization's support of our troops and your work for our intelligence community." Another reader's comment was more succinct: "Keep up the good work and tell Angelides to 'jump in the lake.'"

That the op-ed ran on the very day that the company was receiving "hurrahs" on Wall Street for a stunning earnings performance meant there was a double dose of adrenaline working that day.

For an additional layer of good news, the company also had announced on August 18 that it had been awarded another contract from the Naval Sea Systems Command, this one worth $126 million over a several year period. That same week, *BusinessWeek* reporter Amy Tsao wrote that CACI seemed to be turning a corner and was looking like a good stock to buy.[391]

This was a rare respite for the CACI team. London was very proud of his employees all over the world who had, not only superbly carried out their daily jobs to support the company's business objectives, but had also responded courageously to the converging challenges presented by the negative media, attention-seeking politicians and opportunistic "experts."

London summed it up while briefing Wall Street analysts on the company's earnings:

"We have come through and come out the other side of this and feel very good about it, quite frankly. We're very proud of the way we've been able to be examined and come through with high credentials."

The earnings, released after the market close on August 18, had surpassed all market expectations and triggered a spectacular run up in share price that would last until early 2005. Despite the distraction of Abu Ghraib, the company's fourth quarter revenue had climbed 57 percent to $358.3 million, from $228.6 million in the same quarter the year before. And for the year as a whole, internal growth totaled 15 percent, at the very upper end of the company's 12–15 percent growth objective.

---

[391] Amy Tsao, "CACI: Wiping off Abu Ghraib's Taint," *BusinessWeek*, August 18, 2004.

Per share earnings were up from forty-five cents in fiscal 2003 to sixty-nine cents in fiscal 2004. The gain was significantly higher than the fifty-eight cents-a-share earnings predicted by Wall Street and the surprise drove the stock up $5.63 a share, a 14 percent gain, to $46.55. With that increase, the stock was now back to the pre-Abu Ghraib levels. For CalPERS and CalSTRS, who opted not to take Angelides' advice to "get out of CACI," the day's gain for the funds was worth more than $1.6 million.

"They had a blow-out quarter, and they've given us a very healthy outlook," Wall Street analyst Joseph Vafi told Reuters. Significantly, Vafi said anxiety about Iraq "is clearly in the rear view mirror at this point."[392]

The transcript of the earnings call makes clear that Vafi's opinion about Iraq was shared by his colleagues on Wall Street. The seventy-minute call dealt almost exclusively with financial matters. Iraq came up only twice — once with a question about the expenses associated with the investigation and, at the very end of the call, a second question about the possible effect of an army investigation due out the following week.

London noted that as a day-to-day matter, the Iraq issue was beginning to subside, and he was comfortable that the approaching report by Major General Fay would not have a significant impact.

"We've survived every possible deep examination, and I'm sure that we will survive very nicely whatever may come from the Fay report. I don't anticipate anything significant," London said. He noted that the company's own investigation had not produced any tangible evidence that CACI employees were involved in or were in any way responsible for the abuses and that whatever the Fay report might conclude, "we will be able to fare quite well beyond that."

In an additional display of the company's growing confidence as well as a bid to create news on its own terms, on August 12, CACI had finally issued a public statement about the results of its investigation conducted by external counsel Steptoe and Johnson.[393] This move, to release the

---

[392] "CACI Stock Surges Day After Profit Report," Reuters, August 19, 2004.

[393] CACI Press Release, "CACI Reports Preliminary Findings of Internal Investigation, Company Provides Information About Its Interrogator Support Personnel in Iraq, No Evidence of Abusive Wrongdoing Uncovered," August 12, 2004.

preliminary investigation's findings whatever they may be, had been recommended strongly by media advisor Claire Sanders Swift at a time when the media landscape was relatively tranquil.

After considerable discussion between the lawyers and the PR team about the release's language, the company issued "preliminary findings" that it could find no evidence that CACI employees had been involved in abuse. Other than the conclusion and a note about the constraints under which the lawyers operated, the press release provided no further information.

The release revealed that while some CACI interrogators had rotated out of their position for "routine reasons," several others had "left at the request of the army and are no longer with the company." The announcement said that the employees' departure "did *not* involve the abuse of detainees or any other inappropriate behavior that has been identified with the Abu Ghraib prison." (Some personnel turnover on services-type contracts is not at all that unusual, but it was an even greater challenge in Iraq due to the war zone environment, which was daunting to many who worked there.) For certain, it was a conscientious, yet carefully worded statement that was necessitated by the fact that other government investigations were still to be released.

The PR consultants at Prism worried that the lack of detail in the press release might attract a raft of probing and politically biased questions.

Sensitive to the media criticism of the army IG report just two weeks before, particularly the "whitewash" label, the PR consultants at Prism also feared that skeptical journalists might simply belittle the investigation. For one thing, any internal investigation faces an inherent credibility hurdle because of doubts that any institution, public or private, will voluntarily come clean if it finds wrongdoing. Indeed, internal and institutional bias or cover-up was among the very charges being tossed at the army IG. While the CACI investigation was handled exclusively by outside legal counsel at Steptoe & Johnson, not by CACI officials, the law firm did have a long-standing relationship with CACI.

In any case, London was still getting solid counsel from Swift that a press release on the internal investigation's findings should fare well. If something adverse had been found, she said, release it; if not, then say that nothing was found. "Let the chips fall where they may" was a slogan

London had used repeatedly. Swift recommended staying ahead of the story, whatever the case might be.

The investigation had faced some inherent limitations. Despite several requests, the army did not provide CACI with the Taguba annexes or any other documentation related to the abuse allegations. (Later, as time went by and most of the Annexes were declassified, the army provided them to the company's legal counsel). Access to Abu Ghraib prison and the people there was also limited, and the lawyers had no means or ability to question military personnel or detainees.

But what the lawyers did have was the company's blessings, a free hand to talk to CACI employees without oversight from company officials, and their own years of experience in sifting through bits and pieces of often contradictory evidence to reconstruct events and prepare a case for trial. They also possessed the ability, honed in the give-and-take of the courtroom and witness preparation, in framing questions and following up those questions in a way that coaxed information from even the most reluctant witnesses.

Using the skills at their disposal, the lawyers interviewed every CACI interrogator they could access, typically when the employees were outside Iraq for an R&R (rest and relaxation) break. Then, having established a relationship, they were able to follow up using satellite phone or e-mail once the CACI employees had returned to Iraq.

Beginning with Stefanowicz, whom the lawyers interviewed upon his departure from Iraq in early May, the lawyers conducted interviews with the majority of the CACI interrogators, as well as other CACI employees who served at Abu Ghraib. As interview built upon interview, the lawyers were able to make judgments about each witness's credibility, examine gaps or inconsistencies in the various accounts, and draw conclusions about the role of CACI's interrogators in events at Abu Ghraib.

Significantly, they could not confirm the suspicion of the Taguba Report about Stefanowicz or find any credible evidence of abuse by CACI interrogators.

The company's strategy of full disclosure was showing positive results. The journalists, who months earlier had cast a jaundiced eye on everything the company said and did, seemed to either have lost their interest in the story or came to the realization that the facts, as presented by the investigations and CACI, were telling a quite different

Abu Ghraib prison is a short distance west of Baghdad, about halfway to Fallujah on the Euphrates River. (CIA Factbook)

Overhead signs on an Iraqi highway show the route to Abu Ghraib.
(Spc. Joshua Dvirnak, U.S. Army)

An aerial view of Abu Ghraib in 2005. Detailed information about the prison is presented in Appendix G – Abu Ghraib Prison Profile and Record of Incidents. (GlobalSecurity.org and DigitalGlobe)

Civilian vehicles parked outside Abu Ghraib Prison in 2004. The exposed prison compound was vulnerable to mortar attacks and other hostilities, which occurred frequently during 2003. The prison had several guard towers and a barbed wire perimeter. (Awad Awad/AFP/Getty Images)

A soldier stands guard at a temporary holding facility inside Abu Ghraib prison in April 2004. (Norbert Schiller/epa/Corbis)

U.S. Marines hold their weapons ready as they guard Abu Ghraib prison outside Baghdad in May 2004. (Damir Sagolj/Reuters/Corbis)

U.S. troops secure the area outside Abu Ghraib prison where hundreds of Iraqis demonstrate, demanding the release of jailed relatives, in May 2004. (Faleh Kheiber/Reuters/Corbis)

Army soldiers place a sign for the Baghdad Central Correctional Facility, as Abu Ghraib was named by the Coalition Provisional Authority, in May of 2004. (Ceerwan Aziz/Reuters/Corbis)

U.S. soldiers maintain security at Abu Ghraib prison in May 2004. The Army faced many challenges at Abu Ghraib, including numerous escape attempts, fights, riots, and severe overcrowding. As part of the 800th Military Police Brigade that was in charge of several detention facilities in Iraq, Abu Ghraib was operated by one Military Police (MP) battalion, the 320th, with some 360 personnel. The 372nd MP company (also part of the 800th) was the unit whose soldiers were photographed committing the abuses. Estimates of detainee populations in the fall of 2003 vary, but between August 2003 and early 2004 the number of detainees rose from 3500 to over 7000. Some reports mention 10,000 detainees during this time. (Khampha Bouaphanh/Pool/Getty Images)

Photographers were given an opportunity to tour the prison, including the "Tier-1" hardsite at Abu Ghraib. These were concrete-walled, jail door-styled prison cells where the most dangerous detainees, or those believed to have the most useful intelligence information, were incarcerated. Less dangerous detainees were held in the tent camps and other open areas. (Anja Niedringhaus/AFP/Getty Images)

The notorious Abu Ghraib abuse photographs were taken at the "Tier-1" hardsite. The 372nd MP company of the 800th MP brigade took responsibility for the hardsite, Tier 1A and Tier 1B, by the middle of October 2003. (Anja Niedringhaus/AFP/Getty Images)

A panoramic view of a camp at Abu Ghraib in June 2004. Except for the hardsite, Abu Ghraib was mostly a tent compound. (Cris Bouroncle/AFP/Getty Images)

Detainees at Abu Ghraib wait to be relocated within the prison in June 2004. (Cris Bouroncle/AFP/Getty Images)

A U.S. Army sergeant oversees detainees moving into a cell as they wait to be processed for release in July 2004. (Joe Raedle/Getty Images)

Empty interrogation rooms ("booths") at Abu Ghraib prison in May 2004. Rooms featured a sitting area of several chairs and a table, overhead lighting, air conditioning and two-way mirrors for observation and security. (Stephanie Sinclair/Corbis)

Interrogation rooms were used by military and civilian contract interrogators along with contract linguists in questioning detainees at Abu Ghraib prison. Interrogation booth locations are shown in Appendix G – Abu Ghraib Prison Profile and Record of Incidents. (Stephanie Sinclair/Corbis)

The Reports: (Clockwise from top left) A cover of the Taguba report (SECRET/NO FOR-
EIGN DISSEMINATION) as later distributed. The Army Inspector General's July 2004
report. The April 2005 Government Accountability Office report on CACI's contract. The
August 2004 report from the investigation into detention operations led by the Honorable
James Schlesinger. Army Major General George R. Fay (R) and General Paul J. Kern (L),
members of a military panel to investigate cases of detainee abuse at Abu Ghraib prison
in Iraq, at a news briefing at the Pentagon in August 2004. Their Article 15-6 investigation
focused on intelligence activities, the 205th Military Intelligence Brigade, and facilities at
Abu Ghraib prison. The findings did not assign any overriding or major culpability to any
one person, nor did they ascribe any significant culpability to any contractor personnel.
The report's findings about contractors were considered of lesser significance. (Fay/Kern
briefing – Alex Wong/Getty Images) (Cover of Schlesinger report – GlobalSecurity.org)

The Investigators: (Top, left to right) Major General George R. Fay, General Paul J. Kern, Lieutenant General Anthony R. Jones, and Major General Antonio M. Taguba at a Senate Armed Services Committee hearing on September 8, 2004. The Article 15-6 investigative report by Kern, Jones and Fay focused on military intelligence, the events and people at Abu Ghraib, and the chain of command. Taguba's Article 15-6 (SECRET/ NO FOREIGN DISSEMINATION) investigative report on Military Police, which was illegally leaked in April of 2004, brought worldwide attention to the abuses at the prison. General Taguba later said in a 2007 interview with Seymour Hersh that he surmised that a senior military person may have (illegally) leaked his report. (Bottom, left to right) Former U.S. Army Inspector General Lieutenant General Paul T. Mikolashek, who authored the July 2004 Detainee Operations Inspection report, shown here on an earlier visit to Kuwait in 2000. James Schlesinger at a briefing on the August 2004 report that reviewed the Abu Ghraib abuses. Vice Admiral Albert T. Church III, who reviewed Department of Defense detention procedures, testifies at a March 2005 Senate Armed Services Committee Hearing. All testimony was given under oath. (Top: Alex Wong/ Getty Images) (Bottom row: Left – Stephanie McGehee/Reuters; Center – Alex Wong/ Getty Images; Right – Mark Wilson/Getty Images)

General John Abizaid and Major General Geoffrey Miller testify under oath before the Senate Armed Services Committee on Capitol Hill in May 2004 in Washington, D.C. Abizaid was the U.S. Central Command Commander from July 2003 to March 2007. Miller served as the Multi-National Force-Iraq Deputy Commander for detainee operations from August 2003 to November 2004. (Alex Wong/Getty Images)

Lieutenant General Ricardo Sanchez, who served as the commander of coalition forces in Iraq from June 2003 to June 2004, and former head of the Coalition Provision Authority Paul Bremer discuss the capture of Saddam Hussein at a Baghdad media briefing in December 2003. Hussein's capture was a result of intelligence derived from the interrogation of 5-10 of Hussein's former bodyguards and family members over a ten day period prior to his capture. (Steven Pearsall/US Air Force via Getty Images)

Secretary of Defense Donald Rumsfeld prepares to give sworn testimony on the Abu Ghraib abuse-related matters before the Senate Armed Services Committee in May 2004. (Stephen Jaffe/AFP/Getty Images)

Deputy Secretary of Defense Paul Wolfowitz testifies under oath during a May 2004 Senate Foreign Relations hearing on Iraq's future. In July 2004, Wolfowitz noted in an interview on MSNBC that Saddam Hussein's torture videos (including those made at Abu Ghraib) were receiving "zero coverage in the media." The videos depicted heinous acts, such as dismemberment, decapitation and murder carried out under Hussein's regime. At the time, Senators Rick Santorum and Joe Liebermann had held a press conference to show (Hussein's) real torture tapes from Abu Ghraib but it received little media interest. (Scott J. Ferrell/Congressional Quarterly/Getty Images)

(Left to right) Les Brownlee, giving a speech in October 2004, was acting Secretary of the Army at the time of the Abu Ghraib abuses in 2003. Brownlee gave sworn testimony to the Senate Armed Services Committee's May 2004 hearings on the abuses. (Matthew Cavanaugh/Getty Images) Stephen Cambone, Defense Undersecretary for Intelligence, also testified under oath before the Senate Armed Services Committee in May 2004 concerning Abu Ghraib. (Mark Wilson/Getty Images)

U.S President George W. Bush (center) speaks to the media after a classified briefing at the Pentagon on May 10, 2004. The briefing had been scheduled before the Abu Ghraib scandal made headlines. At the briefing were (L to R) U.S. Ambassador to Iraq John Negroponte, Secretary of State Colin Powell, Vice President Dick Cheney, Secretary of Defense Donald Rumsfeld, Joint Chiefs Chairman General Richard Myers and Joint Chiefs Vice Chairman General Peter Pace. (Mark Wilson/Getty Images)

Virginia Senator John Warner, Chairman of the Senate Armed Services Committee, addresses the media on conditions at Abu Ghraib prison in July 2004. Beginning in early May 2004, Warner spearheaded several inquiries into prison abuses with bipartisan support. (Mark Wilson/Getty Images)

Senators John McCain of Arizona and Lindsey Graham of South Carolina talk during a break in Senate Armed Services Committee hearings on Abu Ghraib in May 2004. McCain would introduce anti-torture legislation in 2005. (Scott J. Ferrell/Congressional Quarterly/Getty Images)

Sworn Testimony: (Left to right) Lt. General Lance Smith, Deputy Commander U.S. Central Command; Richard Myers, Chairman of the Joint Chiefs of Staff; U.S. Secretary of Defense Donald Rumsfeld; Les Brownlee, acting Secretary of the Army; and General Peter Schoomaker, Chief of Staff, U.S. Army, are sworn in to testify before the Senate Armed Services Committee about the Abu Ghraib abuses in May 2004. (Larry Downing/ Reuters/Corbis)

Testimony about Contractors: (Left) Lt. General Lance Smith was asked by Senator John McCain, "…what agencies or private contractors were in charge of interrogations? Did they have authority over the guards? And what were their instructions to the guards?" Smith duly replied that "They were not in charge. They were interrogators…. The brigade commander for the military intelligence brigade [was in charge of the interrogations.]" Another key statement in his sworn testimony was, "As stated, CACI employees are monitored and are under the supervision of U.S. Army personnel." (Right) Chairman of the Joint Chiefs of Staff Richard Myers' testimony highlighted the gravity of the allegations. "… I know we need to do things quickly and full disclosure and everything, but this 15-6 report, is what's called in the Army, the Taguba report, can result in administrative action such [as] relief from command and other administrative admonishments to military personnel. So it has to be very, very thorough." Myers also pointed out the potential detrimental impact to the war effort, "The story about the abuse was already public, but we were concerned that broadcasting the actual pictures would further inflame the tense situation that existed then in Iraq and further endanger the lives of coalition soldiers and hostages…." (Scott J. Ferrell/Congressional Quarterly/Getty Images)

U.S. Army officers at Abu Ghraib: (Clockwise from top left) Brigadier General Janis Karpinski, who had been in charge of the 800th Military Police Brigade, in Abu Ghraib prison in July 2003. (Oleg Popov/Reuters/Corbis) Colonel Thomas Pappas was commander of the 205th Military Intelligence Brigade at Abu Ghraib prison in 2003. (U.S. Army) Lt. Col. Steven Jordan, seen here leaving a July 2007 court martial proceeding, served as the director of the Joint Interrogation Debriefing Center at Abu Ghraib prison in 2003. (Paul J. Richards/AFP/Getty Images)

GSA: A corner view of the General Services Administration (GSA) building in Washington, D.C. GSA notified CACI by a faxed letter on May 7, 2004 that it would review CACI's interrogation contract for Abu Ghraib for possible suspension or debarment of the company. By July 7, 2004, the company's record had been cleared when GSA determined that no formal action would be taken. (U.S. General Services Administration)

GAO: The headquarters of the Government Accountability Office (GAO) in Washington, D.C. as seen from across an adjacent parking lot. GAO examined CACI's contract for interrogation work at Abu Ghraib and concluded that various administrative and procedural errors had been committed by the government and the contractor. CACI believed the GAO had not sufficiently weighed the exigent wartime contracting conditions that the Army faced with interrogator personnel shortages in Iraq, especially the unexpectedly high number of detainees at Abu Ghraib prison. In the fall of 2003, it had been estimated that the number of detainees at Abu Ghraib may have been as many as 7,000-10,000. (U.S. Government Accountability Office)

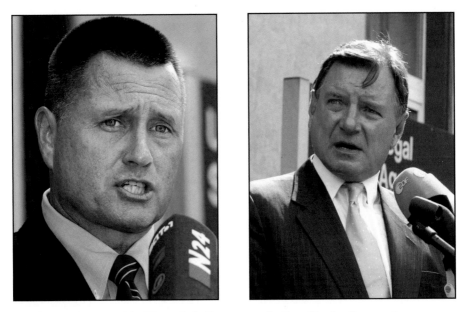

Soldiers' Attorneys: Guy Womack (left), attorney for Spc. Charles Graner, gives a statement after Graner's Abu Ghraib pre-trial hearing in August 2004. Attorney Gary R. Meyers (right) speaks to the press after the pre-trial hearing for Staff Sgt. Ivan "Chip" Frederick in August 2004. Also implicated (and later courts-martialed) were Spc. Megan Ambuhl, Sgt. Jamal Davis, PFC Lynndie England, Spc. Sabrina Harman, Spc. Roman Krol, and Spc. Jeremy Sivits, who were all seen committing the detainee abuses in the infamous Abu Ghraib prison photos. (Alex Grimm/Reuters/Corbis)

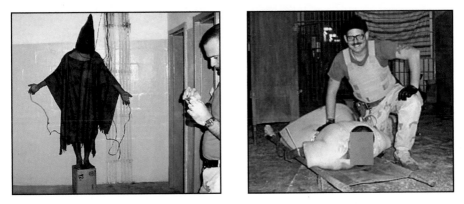

Abu Ghraib Photographs: The disturbing Abu Ghraib images catapulted the abuse story into a worldwide media frenzy. Frederick (left) took the highly publicized iconic picture now known as the 'hooded man'. This photo, with Frederick standing to the right, was taken just minutes later from another camera. Graner (right) poses atop a detainee that had been tied to a litter. As exemplified here, Graner is seen smiling in most photos taken of him.

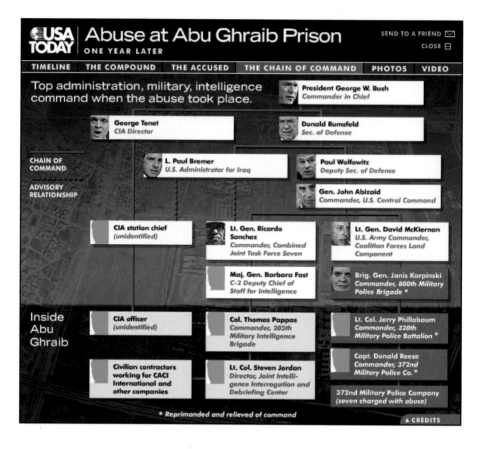

USA TODAY | Abuse at Abu Ghraib Prison
ONE YEAR LATER

TIMELINE | THE COMPOUND | THE ACCUSED | THE CHAIN OF COMMAND | PHOTOS | VIDEO

Top administration, military, intelligence command when the abuse took place.

President George W. Bush
Commander in Chief

George Tenet
CIA Director

Donald Rumsfeld
Sec. of Defense

CHAIN OF COMMAND

L. Paul Bremer
U.S. Administrator for Iraq

Paul Wolfowitz
Deputy Sec. of Defense

ADVISORY RELATIONSHIP

Gen. John Abizaid
Commander, U.S. Central Command

CIA station chief
(unidentified)

Lt. Gen. Ricardo Sanchez
Commander, Combined Joint Task Force Seven

Lt. Gen. David McKiernan
U.S. Army Commander, Coalition Forces Land Component

Maj. Gen. Barbara Fast
C-2 Deputy Chief of Staff for Intelligence

Brig. Gen. Janis Karpinski
*Commander, 800th Military Police Brigade ***

Inside Abu Ghraib

CIA officer
(unidentified)

Col. Thomas Pappas
Commander, 205th Military Intelligence Brigade

Lt. Col. Jerry Phillabaum
*Commander, 320th Military Police Battalion ***

Capt. Donald Reese
*Commander, 372nd Military Police Co. ***

Civilian contractors working for CACI International and other companies

Lt. Col. Steven Jordan
Director, Joint Intelligence Interrogation and Debriefing Center

372nd Military Police Company
(seven charged with abuse)

* Reprimanded and relieved of command

▲ CREDITS

Media Mistakes: A May 2004 USAToday.com chart originally showed CACI reporting to the CIA in the government's chain of command for work at Abu Ghraib prison in Iraq. There was a solid red line connecting CACI to the CIA box directly above it, despite the fact that the company only reported to the U.S. Army and had nothing to do with the CIA or any other organization at Abu Ghraib. The company informed the newspaper that CACI reported only to Lieutenant Colonel Steven Jordan, represented in the box next to CACI's on the right. The newspaper never contacted the company to inquire about the chain of command prior to publication. CACI discovered the error and had to contact the newspaper to insist the error be corrected. Only reluctantly did *USAToday* make the necessary corrections.

The Abu Ghraib chain of command is shown in red in the lower right corner. Brigadier General Janis Karpinski is shown as commander of the 800th Military Police Brigade. Specialist Charles Graner and Staff Sergeant Ivan "Chip" Frederick (as well as the other soldiers in the abuses photos) were assigned to the 372nd Military Police Company at Abu Ghraib. (*USA Today*)

HOW TO PROSECUTE CIVILIAN
CONTRACTORS FOR IRAQI ABUSE

NAS
15.12

HOW TO PROSECUTE CIVILIAN
CONTRACTORS FOR IRAQI ABUSE

S&P
6.36

Media Distortions: As shown by these still images from a TV broadcast, a major news network and other pundits were already discussing how to prosecute and punish contractors for Abu Ghraib abuses by May 8, 2004 – less than two weeks after the Taguba report and the abuse photos had been leaked. Although the several official investigation reports into intelligence gathering and interrogations would not come out for another two and half months, the media had already found CACI and other contractors guilty. CACI personnel do not appear in any of the infamous Abu Ghraib abuse photos and no hard evidence has ever been presented that demonstrates culpability for the scenes shown above or for any other alleged wrongdoing. (ITN Source)

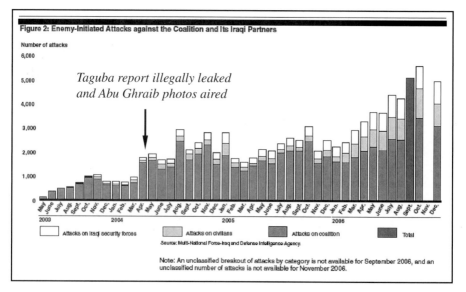

Figure 2: Enemy-Initiated Attacks against the Coalition and Its Iraqi Partners

Number of attacks

Taguba report illegally leaked and Abu Ghraib photos aired

Attacks on Iraqi security forces   Attacks on civilians   Attacks on coalition   Total

Source: Multi-National Force-Iraq and Defense Intelligence Agency.

Note: An unclassified breakout of attacks by category is not available for September 2006, and an unclassified number of attacks is not available for November 2006.

Abu Ghraib Impact: Enemy attacks on U.S.-led coalition forces surged after the abuses at Abu Ghraib prison were publicized internationally by *The New Yorker* magazine with the illegally leaked Taguba Report (SECRET/NO FOREIGN DISSEMINATION) and with the photos aired by CBS' *60 Minutes II* in April 2004. (U.S. Government Accountability Office)

A U.S. soldier looks at a CACI office in Iraq after it had been shelled in September 2004. A CACI employee was on R&R leave when his area was destroyed. No one was hurt in the attack. (CACI)

Iraq is a war zone. Three rockets hit a CACI employee compound during a mortar attack on January 23, 2007 in Iraq. While no CACI personnel were hurt, a contractor from another company was injured from one blast. Another rocket came through the roof and into a second floor room of another building, ending up undetonated in a closet. The unexploded rocket was removed. (CACI)

The *Washington Post*'s (CACI's hometown newspaper, above) coverage of CACI during the Abu Ghraib crisis included significant errors, distortions, and misinformation about the company. However, when CACI reached out to the newspaper to correct the mistakes and give the company's noticeably lacking side of the story, the *Post* dismissed CACI efforts. In particular, the *Post* rejected an op-ed piece submitted by CACI in response to an op-ed by Peter W. Singer that baselessly condemned the company. (Joe Raedle/Getty Images)

Donald Graham (left), the *Post*'s publisher and chairman of the board, was contacted by CEO J. P. London after several meetings with Post editors and letters to their reporters in attempt to get the paper to present balanced, fact-checked information when writing about CACI. Graham's response was that he did not oversee the information published in the *Post*, which he claimed was the job of the editors and their staff. (William Coupon/Corbis)

CACI's op-ed rebuttal that was declined by the *Washington Post* is presented in Appendix I.

Media Leaks in Washington Politics: While the Taguba report's illegal leak was never investigated, the Valerie Plame (above and left) leak case was a media and political sensation, resulting in a federal grand jury investigation, a criminal trial, and an ongoing civil suit. Plame's husband, Ambassador Joseph C. Wilson (left), had investigated the Bush administration's assertions that Iraq was buying uranium from Niger in 2002. He claimed the administration revealed his wife's identity as a covert CIA officer to the media as retribution for his series of op-eds questioning the facts used to justify invading Iraq, particularly a July 2003 *New York Times* piece entitled "What I Didn't Find in Africa." Federal records state that administration officials discussed Plame and her status with reporters in the summer of 2003, including syndicated columnist Robert Novak (below left) who disclosed Plame's name and status as a CIA "operative" working on the proliferation of weapons of mass destruction. (Chip Somodevilla/Getty Images; Matthew Cavanaugh/epa/Corbis)

Other critically important illegal leak cases include the revelation of the National Security Agency's Terrorist Surveillance Program and the government's Terrorist Finance Tracking Program to identify and monitor terrorist activity.

Robert Novak (left) speaks to reporters as he leaves U.S. District Court in Washington, D.C. after testifying in the I. Lewis 'Scooter' Libby trial in February 2007. Novak's column was the first to publicly disclose Plame's identity. Novak confirmed in a July 2006 column that White House political advisor Karl Rove was one of his sources. The *Washington Post*'s Bob Woodward's source, and one of Novak's other sources, was reported to be Deputy Secretary of State Richard Armitage. (Alex Wong, Getty Images)

New York Times reporter Judith Miller (left) speaks at a post-hearing news conference outside the U.S. District Court of Appeals for the District of Columbia in December 2004 as reporter Matthew Cooper of *TIME Magazine* (right) looks on. Cooper and Miller faced up to 18 months in prison for refusing a court order to testify about their contacts with confidential sources related to the Plame leak. (Shaun Heasley/Getty Images)

Duke Lacrosse Players' Media Tragedy: One of the three Duke University lacrosse players, falsely accused of rape in March 2006, proclaims his innocence to the media outside the Durham County Detention Center in May 2006. University faculty and students condemned the players in the school newspaper, while the media – without concrete evidence or proof – vilified members of the lacrosse team. The team's coach reportedly received death threats. (Sarah D. Davis/Getty Images)

The three Duke lacrosse players (seated) attend an April 2007 news conference in Raleigh, North Carolina after being cleared of all charges. The alleged victim's story quickly fell apart and no evidence was found during the investigation. Mike Nifong, the district attorney who pushed the case, was later fired and disbarred for misconduct during the investigation. (Grant Helverson/Getty Images)

The Newsweek Koran Media Tragedy: A May 2005 article in *Newsweek* claimed interrogators at Camp Delta at Guantanamo Naval Base in Cuba flushed a Koran down a toilet as a ploy to rattle detainees in August 2004. Although similar complaints had been previously made, the story was given credibility because the claims were reportedly confirmed by an anonymous government source. The story led to rioting and anti-American protests in several Islamic countries in which at least 17 people died. Under heavy criticism, *Newsweek* was forced to reevaluate its story and, this time, the anonymous source backed away from his initial claims. Deciding to acknowledge the error, *Newsweek* issued a statement that read, "Based on what we know now, we are retracting our original story that an internal military investigation had uncovered Koran abuse at Guantánamo Bay." A May 17, 2005 *New York Times* article declared that, "In the span of a few days, it has added a new dimension to the journalistic debate about anonymous sources..." (Mark Wilson/Pool/Reuters/Corbis)

White House Press Secretary Scott McClellan talks to the media about Newsweek's statement on the front lawn of the White House on May 16th, 2005. McClellan, puzzled by why *Newsweek* was so late in acknowledging that they got the facts wrong, stated, "I think there's a certain journalistic standard that should be met and in this instance it was not." (Paul J. Richards/AFP/Getty Images)

The company's headquarters sit just across Washington, D.C.'s Potomac River in Arlington, Virginia. The U.S. Capitol and the Washington Monument can be seen on the horizon. (CACI)

The sign in front of CACI's head-quarters displays the company's motto "Ever Vigilant." (CACI)

The graduation photo of Midshipman J. Phillip London, U.S. Naval Academy, Class of 1959, as it appears in the '59 "Lucky Bag," the Academy's yearbook. London took his oath of office and commission as an Ensign in the U.S. Navy on June 3, 1959. (CACI)

CACI Chairman, President and CEO Dr. J.P. (Jack) London served as the Presenting Sponsor of a CAUSE benefit fundraising gala held at the Women's Memorial building at Arlington National Cemetery in celebration of Armed Forces Day in 2006. CAUSE (Comfort for America's Uniformed Services) is a nonprofit volunteer organization that brings comfort and recreation into the lives of America's warfighters recuperating from wounds and injuries suffered in battle zones in Afghanistan and Iraq. CACI is a founding sponsor of the organization, which is supported as part of the company's Project Philanthropy program. (CACI)

In 2004, J.P. London was CACI CEO, President and Chairman of the Board when the Abu Ghraib crisis erupted. Prior to his career at CACI, London spent 12 years in the U.S. Navy (1959-71). While at CACI, and before, he also served 12 years in the Naval Reserve (1971-83) for a total of 24 years service. London is a U.S. Navy Captain, retired. (CACI)

A picture of the "Navy Jack" tie worn by CACI CEO J.P. London during the company's Abu Ghraib crisis. The tie represents the snake and motto of the navy jack flag, which was first used by the Continental Navy from 1775 to 1776. Since September 11, 2002, the flag has been flown by the United States Navy for the duration of the Global War on Terrorism.

A commemorative medallion, shown here, was presented to the team of CACI professionals and outside counselors who steered the company through the Abu Ghraib crisis at a dinner held at the Anderson House in Washington, D.C. in December 2004. The medallion represents the team's commitment and efforts to preserve the company's reputation and get the truth told. (CACI)

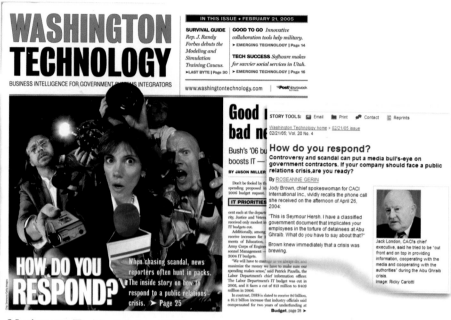

Moving on: (Top) In February 2005, a government contracting trade publication noted, as commented by Dan Goldberg of Washington, D.C.-based Qorvis Communications, that, "Many industry people were impressed with how CACI fought back and defended its employees." Goldberg added, "CACI made it clear it was going to correct the facts, and its aggressive strategy was pretty effective." (Reproduced with permission of *Washington Technology*, © 2008, 1105 Government Information Group. All rights reserved. Chip Simmons/Getty Images)

U.S. soldiers stand guard as freed Iraqi prisoners walk from Abu Ghraib prison in June 2006. The U.S. announced in March 2006 that it would close down operations at the prison and the facility would be transferred to the Iraqi Interior Ministry. (Wathiq Khuzaie/Pool/epa/Corbis)

In late 2007, CACI still had to reject lawsuit propaganda and the media's negative coverage. (CACI)

News Release

CACI International Inc - 1100 North Glebe Road - Arlington Virginia 22201

CACI Rejects Baseless Amendment to Iraq Detainee Lawsuit

Spurious Allegations Remain Unfounded in Rehash of Maliciously False Suit

Arlington, VA, December 20, 2007 - CACI International Inc (**NYSE:CAI**) announced today that it is responding vigorously to amendments to a malicious and unfounded lawsuit filed more than three and one-half years ago by the Center for Constitutional Rights (CCR). CACI totally rejects and denies all of the allegations and claims in this new legal filing. In the original lawsuit, CCR attempted to portray CACI as engaged in a conspiracy to abuse detainees at Abu Ghraib prison in 2004. In the amended lawsuit filed on December 17, CCR adds even more spurious claims against the company, accompanied by a slanderous press release on December 18 that confuses and obfuscates the facts. In their misleading news release, plaintiffs' counsels have erroneously claimed that scores of Iraqis have suddenly emerged to sue CACI. The plaintiff's news release talks so clearly that their amended complaint includes the addition of

story. Instead of skeptical questioning, the media reported mostly what the company said. The *New York Times, Washington Post*, CBS, Associated Press, and Reuters, among others, all reported the company's conclusion without challenge, other than noting that Taguba's report had suggested a different train of events.[394]

In effect, CACI's press release had slammed a home run by its favorable treatment, generating headlines that proclaimed the company had been cleared after months of suspicion. By announcing the results of its inquiry, the company had started to close the door on the suspicions of prisoner abuse by its employees.

Significant risk remained, however, in the form of the upcoming report by Major General George R. Fay. With the release of CACI's preliminary findings, the company had demonstrated credibility and a policy of full disclosure. These were main elements of CACI's Hypercrisis Management Model. But Fay's evaluation of the Abu Ghraib military intelligence organization might place CACI back in the spotlight.

---

[394] John Cushman, Jr., "The Reach of War: Inquiries; Private Company Finds No Evidence Its Interrogators Took Part in Prison Abuse," *New York Times*, August 13, 2004; "CACI Finds No Torture Involvement, Arlington Firm's Employee was Named in Army Report," *Washington Post*, August 13, 2004; Matt Andrejczak, "CACI says Army asked some interrogators to leave," *CBS MarketWarch*, August 12, 2004; "CACI says it will continue Iraq probe," Associated Press, August 12, 2004; "CACI internal probe finds no Iraq prisoner abuse," Reuters, August 13, 2004.

CHAPTER THIRTY-SIX

THE REPORTS OF AUGUST
Positive findings take CACI out of the spotlight

> "By October 2003, interrogation policy in
> Iraq had changed three times in less than
> thirty days and it became very confusing as
> to what techniques could be employed . . ."
> ∼ MAJOR GENERAL GEORGE R. FAY, AUGUST 25, 2004

A S THE SUMMER WOUND DOWN SO, TOO, DID THE PUBLIC examination of the Abu Ghraib abuses. Reports on August 24 by the Schlesinger panel (the Schlesinger report), and a day later by Generals Kern, Jones, and Fay (the Fay report) seemed to exhaust the media and generally satisfy public interest in Abu Ghraib. The military would proceed with additional inquiries, including examinations of interrogation practices at both Guantanamo Bay and Afghanistan, possible detainee abuse by special operations forces, and training for Reserve MI and MP soldiers. But those additional inquiries would take months more to produce reports and only portions would be released publicly. The two August reports were a mixed blessing. They briefly returned the company to the national spotlight, which was unpleasant. But the Fay report, notably, turned away in significant measure from Taguba's suggestion that CACI employee Stefanowicz had any broad responsibility for abuses at the prison. The reports appeared to serve as a welcome end to CACI's public ordeal.

Both reports appeared critical of senior military officers and the administration's civilian authorities in the Defense Department for failing to anticipate the challenges that the troops would face in Iraq, as well as for the manner in which certain aspects of post-major combat intelligence-gathering were handled. In somewhat different ways, both indicated that responsibility for detainee abuse, though not intended by any deliberate policy directives, was not solely the work of a handful of MPs on the night shift at Abu Ghraib. The reports documented more than a hundred cases of alleged or confirmed abuses in Afghanistan, Iraq and Guantanamo Bay, Cuba concerning the more than 50,000 detainees. Schlesinger noted, however, that from a statistical perspective in terms of the rate of reported abuse incidents per detainee, treatment of detainees in the overall war on terror was exemplary.[395] Nevertheless, the abuse issue triggered public debate that continued well into the following two years, through 2006 amid periodic media reports of additional alleged abuses beyond those alleged at Abu Ghraib.[396]

The Schlesinger panel, consisting of James R. Schlesinger, former defense secretary Harold Brown, former congresswoman Tillie Fowler, and retired air force general Charles Horner, found "institutional and personal responsibility at higher levels." It referred to Secretary of Defense Rumsfeld for interrogation policies set out in December of 2002 and revised in April 2003. "Had the secretary of defense had a wider range of legal opinions and a more robust debate regarding detainee policies and operations [in December 2002], his policy of April 16, 2003 might well have been developed and issued [sooner] in early December 2002," the panel said. The report stated that adjustments to the policies because of subsequent complaints from military attorneys "were one

---

[395] Hon. James R. Schlesinger, "Final Report of the Independent Panel to Review DoD Detainee Operations," August 2004.

[396] The debate became politically re-energized again in 2006, the mid-term election year.

element in contributing to uncertainties in the field as to which techniques were authorized." But the report also said, "Nonetheless, the secretary of state, secretary of defense, and the chairman of the joint chiefs of staff were all in agreement that treatment of detainees should be consistent with the Geneva Conventions. The president ordered accordingly that detainees were to be treated 'humanely' and . . . in a manner consistent with the principles of Geneva."[397]

The Jones report by Lt. Gen. Anthony R. Jones (of the Kern, Jones Fay report) also noted that neither DoD nor army doctrine caused abuse to occur and that "Abuses would not have occurred had doctrine been followed and mission training conducted." The Schlesinger panel had also noted that the government's civilian leadership had established different interrogation policies for Guantanamo Bay, Afghanistan, and Iraq. But Jones reported, "The extent of 'word of mouth' techniques that were passed to the interrogators at Abu Ghraib . . . due to prior assignments [at Afghanistan and Guantanamo Bay, Cuba] is unclear and likely impossible to definitively determine."[398]

Lt. Gen. Jones also noted that, "Policy memoranda promulgated by the CJTF-7 Commander [Lt. Gen. Sanchez] led indirectly to some of the non-violent and non-sexual abuses . . . allowed for interpretation in several areas, including use of dogs and removal of clothing. Particularly in light of the wide spectrum of interrogator qualifications, maturity and experiences (i.e., GTMO and Afghanistan), the memos did not set forth the limits on interrogations techniques."[399]

"We had interrogation operations in three different places with varying rules. That created ambiguity. Nonetheless, in the future such ambiguity is unacceptable," Schlesinger later wrote in a *Wall Street Journal* op-ed column. "A policy doctrine should be designed, so that soldiers are trained to observe the rules."[400]

The Schlesinger and Fay reports both supported the Taguba report's conclusion that lack of leadership contributed to the problems at the

---

[397] Schlesinger Report, op. cit.

[398] Fay Report, op. cit.

[399] Ibid.

[400] James Schlesinger, "The Truth About Our Soldiers," *Wall Street Journal*, September 11, 2004.

prison.[401] The Fay report observed that, "Leaders in key positions failed properly to supervise the interrogation operations at Abu Ghraib . . . Leaders also failed to react appropriately to those instances where detainee abuse was reported, either by other service members, contractors or by the International Red Cross."[402]

Schlesinger agreed with the Jones report's findings regarding the lack of proper supervision of prison operations and stated, "We concur with the Jones findings that LTG Sanchez and MG Wojdakowski failed to ensure proper staff oversight of detention and interrogations and operations."[403] Schlesinger further noted, "The aberrant behavior on the night shift in Cell Block 1 at Abu Ghraib would have been avoided with proper training, leadership and oversight," adding, "Had these noncommissioned officers behaved more like those on the day shift, these acts, which one participant [Spc. Lynndie England] described as 'just for the fun of it,' would not have taken place."[404]

Both investigations also noted that there was uncertainty created by frequent changes in interrogation policies in Iraq, including the adoption of techniques approved in an outdated 1987 army field manual instead of the most recent manual, which was last updated in 1992. The earlier manual indicated that the interrogator controls the prisoners' food, shelter, and clothing — language that was explicitly omitted in the 1992 version of the manual.

According to the Fay report, "Concepts for the non-doctrinal, non-field manual approaches and practices clearly came [to Abu Ghraib] from documents and personnel in Afghanistan and Guantanamo." These techniques included the use of stress positions, isolation, removal of clothing and use of dogs. Fay stated that, "Interrogators in Iraq, already familiar with the practice of some of these new ideas, implemented them even prior to any policy guidance from CJTF-7. These

---

401 "Abu Ghraib Accountability," *Wall Street Journal*, April 27, 2005. This was substantiated by the sworn statement of Specialist Jeremy C. Sivits, the first of the Abu Ghraib offenders to face a court martial who said of the photographed abuses: "Our command would have slammed us. They believe in doing the right thing. If they saw what was going on, there would be hell to pay."

402 Fay Report, op. cit.

403 Schlesinger Report, op. cit.

404 Ibid.

practices were accepted as SOP [standard operating procedure] by newly arrived interrogators."[405]

According to Fay, a September memo issued by OSJA [Office of Staff Judge Advocate] at CJTF-7 was changed within four days of drafting to reflect addition of techniques such as use of dogs, stress positions, loud music and light control with approval by LTG Sanchez. "In October 2003, the JIDC Interrogation Operations Officer, CPT Carolyn A. Wood, produced an "Interrogation Rules of Engagement" (IROE) chart as an aid for interrogators. Fay said, "The chart was confusing, however. It was not completely accurate and could be subject to various interpretations."[406]

"By October of 2003, interrogation policy in Iraq had changed three times in under thirty days, and it became very confusing as to what techniques could be employed and at what level non-doctrinal approach had to be approved," the Fay report stated.[407] Similarly, the Schlesinger panel observed that, "the existence of confusing and inconsistent interrogation technique policies contributed to the belief that additional interrogation techniques were condoned."[408]

Both reports also noted confusion over the role and responsibilities of the MP and MI at the prison and what the Schlesinger panel called "a series of tangled command relationships" at Abu Ghraib. The Fay report said, "A common observation was that MI knew what MI could do and what MI couldn't do; but MI did not know what the MPs could or could not do in their activities." He concluded that, "There was a distinct lack of experience in both camps."

Fay also noted: "In the past, the army conducted large EPW/Detainee exercises . . . that provided much of the training critical to MPs' and interrogators' understanding of their respective roles and responsibilities. These exercises were discontinued in the mid 1990s due to frequent deployments and force structure reductions, eliminating an excellent source of interoperability training."[409]

---

[405] Fay Report, op. cit.

[406] Ibid.

[407] Ibid.

[408] Schlesinger, "The Truth About Our Soldiers," op. cit.

[409] Fay Report, op. cit.

Both inquiries identified a range of complicating factors that raised stress at Abu Ghraib prison and which may have also contributed to abuses. Among these comments were that U.S. forces at Abu Ghraib were "under-strength, inadequately equipped, and weakly led." And, for the most part, they had not been trained for the mission they were assigned. At one point, there were seventy-five detainees to every single MP.[410]

The Fay report noted that, "Large quantities of detainees with little or no intelligence value swelled Abu Ghraib's population and led to a variety of overcrowding difficulties. Already scarce interrogator and analyst resources were pulled from interrogation operations to identify and screen increasing numbers of personnel whose capture documentation was incomplete or missing."

"To make matters worse, Abu Ghraib increasingly became the target of mortar attacks," the Fay report continued. "The prison is located in a hostile portion of Iraq, adjacent to several roads and highways, and near population centers."[411]

Mortar attacks were an almost daily occurrence, endangering detainees and U.S. troops alike. Five U.S. soldiers died as a result of mortar attacks on Abu Ghraib prison. In July 2003, Abu Ghraib was mortared twenty-five times. Five detainees died and more than sixty were wounded in a mortar attack in August of 2003.[412] On September 20, 2003 two U.S. soldiers were killed and fourteen wounded by mortars. In April of 2004, another twenty-two detainees were killed by mortars and approximately eighty others were wounded, some seriously.[413]

Fay's report called a late November 2003 shooting on Tier 1A at Abu Ghraib a "milestone event," triggering the use of military working dogs to both search cells and to intimidate the Iraqi police who were put under interrogation. Fay noted that, "There was a general understanding among the MI personnel present that LTG Sanchez had authorized suspending the existing ICRP [Interrogation and Counter Resistance Policies] (known by the Abu Ghraib personnel locally as the IROE) because of the shooting." But this was a false assumption. "Nobody is sure where

---

[410] Schlesinger Report, op. cit.

[411] Fay Report, op. cit.

[412] Schlesinger Report, op. cit.

[413] Fay Report, op. cit.

that information came from, but LTG Sanchez never gave such authorization," Fay said.[414]

Most significant among the reports' observations was that of Jones who stated that, *"The events at Abu Ghraib cannot be understood in a vacuum,"* adding that "interrelated aspects of the operational environment played important roles in the abuses that occurred at Abu Ghraib," including the fact that "the CJTF-7 headquarters lacked adequate personnel and equipment. In addition, the military police and military intelligence units at Abu Ghraib were severely under-resourced . . . opposition was robust and hostilities continued. . . . Therefore, CJTF-7 had to conduct tactical counter-insurgency operations while also executing its planned missions."[415]

Jones reported that in the fall of 2003, the number of detainees "rose exponentially due to tactical operations to capture counter-insurgents dangerous to U.S. forces and Iraqi civilians." And, according to Jones, "the CJTF-7 commander believed he had no choice but to use Abu Ghraib as a central detention facility," noting that, "in many cases, the situation, mission and environment dictated the decisions and the actions taken. . . ."[416]

Jones defined a number of events that led to the use of Abu Ghraib prison as a detention center. One was that Lt. General Sanchez and his V Corps staff quickly realized, "They were in a counter-insurgency operation with a complex, adaptive enemy that opposed the rule of law and ignored the Geneva Conventions." He noted, "This enemy opposed the transition of the new Iraqi governing councils that would enable self-rule . . ."[417] He added that, "As major counter-insurgency operations began in the July 2003 timeframe . . . [p]ressure increased to obtain operational intelligence . . . [and] the location of Saddam Hussein and information on WMD remained intelligence priorities." He further noted, ". . . battle damage, looting, pillaging, and criminal actions had decimated the government buildings and infrastructure necessary to detain prisoners of war or criminals."

---

[414] Ibid.

[415] Ibid.

[416] Ibid.

[417] Ibid.

Abu Ghraib had been envisioned by the U.S. Army as a temporary facility to be used until the new Iraqi government was in place and an Iraq prison was established at another site. However, Jones pointed out that, "Interrogating the detainees was a massive undertaking." And the Fay report highlighted the difficulty in processing and releasing detainees as the prison staff struggled to keep up. The Fay report stated that, "By February 2004, a standing board was established to deal with the ever increasing backlog."[418] The report added that, "As of late May 2004, over 8,500 detainees had been reviewed for release, with 5,300 plus being released."[419] The Fay report noted that "Interrogation operations in Abu Ghraib suffered from the effects of a broken detention operations system."[420]

Jones pointed out that the army had significantly reduced tactical interrogators since Desert Shield/Desert Storm and that creation of the Defense HUMINT Service and worldwide demands for these skills depleted the number of experienced interrogators. On the other hand, Jones credited the group's efforts, attributing Saddam Hussein's capture to HUMINT and the fusion of intelligence services.[421]

The Schlesinger and Fay reports provided significant new information about abuses at Abu Ghraib. Although separating the abuses seen in the photographs into a category that Schlesinger likened to the film *Animal House* and that were entirely unrelated to interrogation, the reports also identified new abuses involving MI personnel. They further separated abuses into those that were clearly criminal and others that may have resulted from confusion over rules.

The Jones report divided abuses into two categories: "intentional violent or sexual abuse" and "abusive actions taken based on misinterpretation or confusion about law or policy." Included in the second category were cases of clothing removal, some uses of dogs in interrogations, and the improper use of isolation (solitary confinement). Tellingly the reports noted that in a number of these instances, the alleged perpetrators ". . . may have honestly believed that their conduct was condoned"

---

[418] Ibid.

[419] Ibid.

[420] Ibid.

[421] Ibid.

and within the bounds of approved techniques. Jones suggested that some abuses fell between both categories and had elements of both, but suggested that, ". . . culpability in this area is best left to individual criminal or command investigations."[422]

Significantly, Jones said, "However, when reviewing the various reports on the number of abuses in the ITO [Iraq Theatre of Operations], it became clear there is no agreed upon definition of abuse among all legal, investigating and oversight agencies."[423] He added that most of the violent or sexual abuses occurred outside scheduled interrogations, and did not focus on intelligence-related prisoners.[424]

The Fay report provided the most complete list available up to that point of abuses at Abu Ghraib. It identified forty-four alleged incidents and said that involvement of MI personnel was alleged or proven in twenty-seven of these incidents. All told, it said that fifty-four individuals had "some degree of responsibility or complicity," a total that included the seven MPs who were already facing legal action by the army. Seventeen of the fifty-four were cited "for misunderstanding policy, regulation or law." Except for the MPs who had been previously identified and some senior officers, the report did not identify individuals by name, but by number and as "soldier" or "civilian" because the generals did not want to prejudice possible future judicial actions.

Fay told reporters that the abuses "range from the relatively minor abuses to the very significant abuses that everybody is familiar with in the pictures." But the report itself did not specifically distinguish between the categories in describing the abuses. And in discussing findings against specific individuals, it mixed the minor and the significant together, apparently leaving final judgments for other authorities.[425]

Both Schlesinger and Fay found that the facilities housed a significant number of "ghost" detainees under control of the Central Intelligence Agency, which was euphemistically referred to as "Other Government Agency." The presence and alleged mistreatment of the "ghosts," who

---

[422] Ibid.

[423] Ibid. See also Introduction and Glossary and Terms of Interest.

[424] Ibid.

[425] "Press briefing by General Paul Kern, Lieutenant General Anthony Jones and Major General George Fay." FDCH e-Media, Inc., August 25, 2004.

were reportedly never officially recorded as prisoners was asserted to have contributed to the abusive environment (according to the reports).

Fay stated, "While the FBI, JTF-121, Criminal Investigative Task Force, Iraq Survey Group and the CIA were all present at Abu Ghraib, the acronym "Other Government Agency" referred almost exclusively to the CIA. Lack of military control over OGA interrogator actions or lack of systematic accountability for detainees plagued detainee operations in Abu Ghraib almost from the start."[426]

CIA's activities, Fay said, "led to a loss of accountability, abuse, reduced interagency cooperation, and an unhealthy mystique that further poisoned the atmosphere at Abu Ghraib."[427] In subsequent Senate testimony, Fay said that at least two dozen ghost detainees existed, and his superior, General Kern, said there may have been as many as a hundred.[428] The release of the March 2005 Church report however, put the number of ghost detainees at thirty. The revelations about these detainees received considerable attention from both Congress and the news media for the next several weeks, further diminishing the spotlight on CACI.

The Fay report did raise concerns, however, about the army's management of civilian contractors and also identified alleged mistreatment by three CACI employees. Nevertheless, in a very positive development from CACI's perspective, Fay backed away completely from Taguba's sweeping suggestion that two civilians, Stefanowicz and Titan employee John Israel, were central figures in abuse. Indeed, in a stunning break with Taguba's words, Fay completely exonerated Israel of any misconduct and in significant measure fully discounted Taguba's allegations concerning Stefanowicz's role at Abu Ghraib.

Importantly, the Fay report stated that, "A direct comparison cannot be made of the abuses cited in the MG Taguba report and this one."

When a reporter suggested to Fay at a press conference that Stefanowicz had been "hung out to dry" for seven months, he seemed to avoid the question of whether Taguba had overreached. "In some instances, we verified what General Taguba said. In some instances, we were able to exonerate at least one of the individuals named in General

---

[426] Fay Report, op. cit.

[427] Ibid.

[428] "Press briefing by General Paul Kern," et al., op. cit.

Taguba's report. And we'll leave that for when the army decides that they're going to actually release names," Fay told the reporters.[429]

By now, CACI leadership had no doubts that Taguba had gone too far in his conclusions, and the company was quick to draw a line of demarcation between the Taguba report and Fay report.

"We were pleased to note that the Fay report clearly demonstrates that the responsibility for misconduct at Abu Ghraib was not that of the single CACI employee that had been vilified in the Taguba report," CACI said in a press release. The company also noted: "Nothing in the Fay report can be construed as CACI employees directing, participating in, or even observing anything close to what we have all seen in the dozens of horrendous photos."[430]

Indeed months later, in December 2004, the *Washington Post* conceded that the role of civilian contractors was "more limited" than initially reported.[431] It was a weak summation after what CACI had just been through because of the mountains of grossly distorted media reports.

But the Fay report released in August of 2004, which had expanded its focus to other individuals and other misbehaviors at the prison, also raised questions about some degree of possible misconduct on the part of two additional CACI employees. In the further assessment of additional individuals working at the prison, the Fay investigation (into MI activities) was clearly a much broader and more comprehensive effort than the earlier Taguba report that had focused primarily on the MPs.

A CACI employee identified in the report as "Civilian-05" was accused of grabbing a handcuffed detainee from a truck, pulling him to the ground, and dragging him to an interrogation booth. According to the report he also allegedly disobeyed regulations against drinking alcohol while at the prison. Civilian-05, who had received previous military interrogation training while on active duty, reportedly refused to take instructions from military trainers and, when confronted, he allegedly replied, "I have been doing this for twenty years and I do not need a twenty-year-old telling me how to do my job."

---

[429] Ibid.

[430] CACI Press Release, "CACI Says the Fay Report Clearly Shifts Focus of Blame Away From Its Employee Named in a Previous Report, Company Notes Employees Were Not Involved in Any Horrendous Acts," August 26, 2004.

[431] "Changes Behind the Barbed Wire," op. cit.

The Fay report recommended that this information on Civilian-05 be forwarded to the army general counsel for determination of whether he should be referred to the Department of Justice for prosecution. The information was also forwarded to the contracting officer for "appropriate contractual action."

Civilian-05 was not identified publicly, but CACI believed it recognized this employee as one who had left the company earlier in the summer at the army's request. Another former CACI interrogator, who had left the company at General Fay's request earlier in the summer, was also cited in the report.

During the chaotic round-up and questioning of Iraqi police (referred to thereafter at Abu Ghraib as the "IP Roundup") for possible involvement in the shooting of American soldiers on November 24, 2003, "Civilian-11" was allegedly said to have encouraged Staff Sergeant Chip Frederick to punish one of the Iraqi police. Frederick reportedly twisted the policeman's handcuffs allegedly causing pain. "Civilian-11" also allegedly failed to prevent Frederick from covering the policeman's mouth and nose. According to the report, "Civilian-11" was alleged to have later threatened to return the same policeman to Sergeant Frederick unless he answered questions, and to have threatened the improper use of a guard dog on the policeman by saying, "I'm going to get this dog on you," unless the man cooperated.

In another incident that occurred over a two-day period, Civilian-11, along with two soldiers, reportedly all participated in an interrogation in which all believed they had authority to use dogs from Col. Pappas or from Lt. Gen. Sanchez. The Fay report said, "It is probable that approval was granted by Col. Pappas without such authority." But it added, "LTG Sanchez stated he never approved use of dogs."[432]

In a separate incident previously shared with CACI by the army, "Civilian-11" was also accused of placing a detainee in an unauthorized stress position by having the detainee sit on the edge of a chair in a position where his back was exposed and, according to the Fay report, "where he might fall back and injure himself."[433] Civilian-11, who was

---

[432] Fay Report, op. cit.

[433] Ibid. CACI had the same incident reviewed by a panel of its in-house military retirees who returned a professional opinion that differed from the Fay report's conclusions that the detainee was placed in a position of stress.

photographed with a detainee and a translator, was cited as well for failing to prevent the detainee from being photographed. However, Civilian-11 stated that he was unaware that the group was being photographed.

Fay recommended that this information on Civilian-11 be forwarded to the army general counsel for determination of whether he should be referred to the Department of Justice for prosecution. The information was also forwarded to the contracting officer for "appropriate contractual action."

Notably, in another section of his report Fay stated that, "The fact these techniques were documented in the Interrogation Report suggests, however, that the interrogators believed they had the authority to use clothing as an incentive, as well as stress positions and were not attempting to hide their use. Stress positions were permissible with Commander, CJTF-7 approval at that time."[434]

Stefanowicz, referred to as "Civilian-21" in the report, was accused by unnamed sources of alleged inappropriate use of dogs and for allowing an unmuzzled dog in the room during an interrogation. According to the Fay report, ". . . circa 18 December 2003 . . . a 'high value' detainee . . . suspected to be involved with al Qaeda" was subjected to a "Military Working Dog Handler" in which the "dog is leashed but not muzzled" and Civilian-21 was alleged to have been present but "claimed to know nothing of this incident." Yet the Fay report also noted that an MI soldier was the lead interrogator for this detainee from December 18–21 (over the date of the incident) until the MI soldier departed Abu Ghraib on December 22. Stefanowicz then became the lead interrogator for this detainee. Even though Stefanowicz was apparently not the lead interrogator on the date of the alleged incident (around December 18, 2003), Fay surmised that it was "highly plausible that Civilian-21 used dogs without authorization. . . ." Fay referenced in this alleged incident two instances of hearsay; one being that the MI soldier reported to Fay that Stefanowicz had told him in December 2003 that the MPs had told Stefanowicz that the detainee's "bedding had been ripped apart by dogs," and the second being a report from another soldier that "she was told by SGT Frederick about dogs being used when Civilian-21 was there."[435]

---

[434] Ibid.

[435] Ibid.

In another situation Fay reported that Soldier-26, an MI soldier "was present during an interrogation of a detainee . . . suspected to have al Qaeda affiliations. Dogs were requested and approved about three days later," but according to Fay's account of this report the soldier "didn't know if the dog had to be muzzled or not, likely telling the dog handler to un-muzzle the dog . . . ICE [Interrogation and Control Element] stated that Civilian-21 used a dog during one of his interrogations and this is likely that occasion." Fay went on to describe the incident, "According to Soldier-14, Civilian-21 had the dog handler maintain control of the dog and did not make any threatening reference to the dog but apparently, 'felt just the presence of the dog would be unsettling to the detainee.'" Fay noted in this incident that, "Soldier-14 did not know who approved the procedure, but was verbally notified by Soldier-23 who supposedly received the approval from Col. Pappas." Fay, noting that Stefanowicz stated that he "once requested to use dogs, but it was never approved," cited this incident in concluding that, "Civilian-21 was deceitful in his statement."[436]

In another incident, an MI soldier alleged hearing dogs barking and saw a detainee on a mattress with a dog standing over him as Civilian-21, allegedly upstairs, yelled to Staff Sgt. Fredrick below to "take him back home" (possibly referring to returning the detainee, who was out of his cell and was assigned to Stefanowicz, back to his cell). This same soldier reported to Fay that it was "common knowledge that Civilian-21 used dogs" but Fay noted that this same soldier "could not identify anyone else specifically who knew of this common knowledge."[437]

Stefanowicz was also accused in the Fay report of pushing a detainee into a cell with his foot and failing to report abuse relayed by a third party when a soldier asked him to note a detainee's claim that he had been struck by an interpreter. Fay also faulted the soldier in this case for not reporting the detainee's allegation but Fay faulted Stefanowicz because the soldier claimed she told Stefanowicz, who reported that he did not hear the soldier's comments and therefore did not document it.

Stefanowicz also reportedly "bragged and laughed about shaving a detainee and forcing him to wear red women's underwear." Fay noted that it was overheard that an OGA was also "laughing about red panties

---

[436] Ibid.

[437] Ibid.

on detainees." But a similar case elsewhere in Fay's report where an individual joked and bragged about a particular situation of mistreatment was referred to as "boastful exaggeration." In that instance, Fay noted that a soldier told several people stories about MP abuse of detainees, but when interviewed, Fay noted the soldier "admitted that he and his friends would joke about noises they heard in the Hard Site," saying he "never thought anyone would take him seriously." In referring to this situation, Fay concluded, "This alleged abuse is likely an individual's boastful exaggeration . . . nothing more." Fay noted that, "Several alleged abuses were investigated and found to be unsubstantiated. Others turned out to be no more than general rumor or fabrication."[438]

Separately, however, Fay also noted that Stefanowicz had *reported* at least one instance of possible abuse, "On 16 November 2003, SOL-DIER-29 decided to strip a detainee in response to what she believed was uncooperative and physical recalcitrant behavior." He added, "CIVILIAN-21, a CACI contract interrogator, witnessed SOLDIER-29 and Soldier-10 escorting the scantily clad detainee from the Hard Site back to Camp Vigilant, wearing only his underwear and carrying his blanket. CIVILIAN-21 notified SGT Adams, who was SOLDIER-29's section chief, who in turn notified CPT Wood the ICE OIC [Interrogation Control Element, Officer in Charge]. SGT Adams immediately called SOLDIER-29 and SOLDIER-10 into her office, counseled them, and removed them from interrogation duties."[439]

Fay noted that, "The incident was relatively well known among JIDC personnel and appeared in several statements as second hand information when interviewees were asked if they knew of detainee abuse."[440]

The Fay report recommended that information on Civilian-21 be forwarded to the army general counsel for determination of whether he should be referred to the Department of Justice for prosecution. The information was also forwarded to the Contracting Officer for "appropriate contractual action."

The Fay report found that there was significant confusion about the rules and authority governing the use of dogs and whether the use of dogs required prior authorization from Lt. Gen. Ricardo Sanchez, then the

---

[438] Ibid.

[439] Ibid.

[440] Ibid.

senior commander in Iraq. There were also allegedly cases where Col. Pappas "authorized the use of dogs during interrogations" and "failed to properly supervise the use of dogs. . . ." In addition, the Fay report noted that a visiting military trainer from the army's intelligence school at Fort Huachuca reportedly suggested the use of dogs to Stefanowicz.

Fay also faulted the Fort Huachuca Interrogation Support to Counterterrorism Team (ISCT), stating that, "The ISCT team's lack of understanding of approved doctrine was a significant failure." Fay concluded the ISCT training was ineffective and "did nothing to prevent the abuses occurring at Abu Ghraib." Fay noted that while the ISCT Mobile Training Team (MTT) did offer several classes and formal training on the Geneva Conventions, they and the JIDC leadership "failed to include/require the contract personnel to attend the training."[441]

Fay's addition of alleged misconduct (though relatively minor, and which included actions that represented "misinterpretation or confusion regarding law or policy") by the two other CACI employees along with the details about Stefanowicz's alleged misconduct redirected media attention back to CACI. It also raised anew for CACI the question of possible company action against Stefanowicz, the only one of those mentioned in the Fay report who was still on the company's payroll (he had returned to the U.S. in May 2004).

Some critics among the media claimed Fay's report seemed to undercut CACI's own (albeit more limited) investigation, which said the company had not found, up to that date, "any credible or tangible evidence that substantiates the involvement of CACI personnel in the abuse of detainees at Abu Ghraib." The Associated Press, rather than noting the vast difference between "minor abuses' and "very significant abuses" (and the further differentiation between "abusive action taken based on misinterpretation or confusion regarding law or policy" and "intentional violent or sexual abuse"), not to mention the inherent constraints of the CACI internal investigation, announced that Fay's report contradicted CACI's investigation.[442] The *Financial Times* said in more

---

[441] Ibid. As noted earlier, training by the army was specified in the CACI SOW by the contract terms stating the government's commitment to provide the necessary training and indoctrination elements.

[442] Matthew Barakat, "CACI Employees Participated in Abu Ghraib Abuse: Army Report," Associated Press, August 25, 2004.

convoluted terms that Fay "appeared to reach a different conclusion."[443] Perhaps recognizing the greater reach exercised by the army in these more recent investigations, other media reports did not make a connection or draw a comparison between the two investigations.

In fact, Fay had cited fifty-four individuals in his report who represented a wide range of positions including MI, MP, medical soldiers, OGAs, and civilian contractors from both Titan and CACI. Twenty-seven of these individuals were cited for some degree of culpability and seventeen were cited for misunderstanding policy, regulation or law. Three MI soldiers who had previously received punishment under UCMJ were recommended for additional investigation. Seven MP soldiers identified in the Taguba report and who were currently under investigation and/or charges were also included in those numbers. Sixteen of these incidents of abuse by MP soldiers were alleged to have been "requested, encouraged, condoned or solicited" by MI personnel. In eleven instances, MI personnel were found to be directly linked to abuse.

However, the fact was, that as a result of the Fay report: No CACI personnel were cited for *any* major or malicious abuse and in at least one case a CACI employee, notably Stefanowicz, was recognized for reporting abuse. Nevertheless, information on all three CACI employees was forwarded to the army general counsel for determination of whether they should be referred to the Department of Justice for possible prosecution.

* * *

But in California, State Treasurer Phil Angelides predictably provided his own media spin with a press release that carried the army's conclusions in the Fay report to a greater extreme, saying — incredibly — that the reports confirmed that CACI interrogators were "deeply involved" in abuses. And he further urged CACI's management "to get out of denial."[444] However, the CACI team recognized that Angelides could not

---

[443] Joshua Chaffin, "Private Workers Found Central to Jail Abuse," *Financial Times*, August 27, 2004.

[444] California State Treasurer's Office Press Release, "CalSTRS, at Treasurer Angelides' urging, to call on CACI board to conduct full investigation and hold management responsible for interrogators' conduct at Iraq prison; CalSTRS schedules November vote to consider divesting its CACI holdings; Latest U.S. Army Investigation Found CACI Contract Interrogators Deeply Involved In 'Inhumane to Sadistic' Abuses," September 1, 2004.

possibly have arrived at his stated conclusion from an objective read of the Fay report — except with the intent to misrepresent Fay's findings. But London and his team took the politician's attack in stride and kept it all in perspective, knowing Angelides' only interest in CACI was to generate heavy-handed remarks that could attract public attention and votes.

The news coverage from the Fay and Schlesinger reports was the most substantial attention given to CACI since the release of the GSA report. In some ways, it was a replay of the first days of the crisis in that major news organizations were again highlighting CACI's connection to Abu Ghraib. But there were interesting differences as well. Most significantly, in contrast to May, the coverage of CACI was essentially a one-day event. In May, reporters had been so intrigued by the fact that interrogations were contracted to civilians that they worked hard to develop new angles and stories. In August, in light of a better educated public, increased congressional knowledge, and improved media awareness about the range of government contractor work in interrogation and other combat zone professional services, the new wave of articles about CACI would essentially end after a single day.

Perhaps, London reflected, CACI's unique hypercrisis media response strategy had worked well, too. There also may have been greater recognition now that the civilian interrogators were a relatively small part of the interrogation effort and the Abu Ghraib story.

More importantly, through the Fay report, the alleged link to CACI and its employees for significant responsibility or major culpability for the abuses at Abu Ghraib was essentially eliminated.

During the four months since the first news of the Taguba report leak, some media organizations seemed to have changed their perspective. They now appeared to recognize that the civilian contractor aspect was a small piece of a much larger story about interrogation methods overall.

According to Fay, the original number of interrogators at Abu Ghraib was only enough for several hundred detainees. "The number of interrogators initially assigned to the 205 MI BDE [Military Intelligence Brigade] was sufficient for a small detainee population of only several hundred. In late July 2003, only fourteen interrogation personnel were present in the 205 MI BDE to support interrogation operations at Abu Ghraib. All of these personnel were from one unit — A/519 MI BN

[Battalion]. By December 2003 Abu Ghraib (the JIDC) had approximately 160 205 MI personnel with forty-five interrogators and eighteen linguists/translators assigned to conduct interrogation operations. These personnel were from six different MI battalions and groups . . . interrogators from the U.S. Army Intelligence Center and School, Mobile Training Team (MTT) consisting of analysts and interrogators, and three interrogation teams consisting of six personnel from GTMO. . . ." Fay added that, "Still short of resources, the army hired contract interrogators from CACI International, and contract linguists from Titan Corporation in an attempt to address shortfalls."[445]

At another point in his report Fay stated that most of the units assigned to Abu Ghraib were incomplete and lacking their normal command structure, because MI units from all over the globe sent whatever interrogator and analyst support they could spare. "During October 2003, in addition to the elements of the already mentioned MI units and the Titan and CACI civilians, elements of the 470 MI GP [Group], 500 MI GP, and 66 MI GP appeared. These units were from Texas, Japan, and Germany and were part of the US Army Intelligence and Security Command (INSCOM), which tasked those subordinate units to send whatever interrogator and analyst support they had available."[446]

With this scenario in perspective, CACI interrogators clearly were a small piece of a much larger and more complex intelligence-gathering operation and organization.

Fay also made the point that: "The bringing together of so many parts of so many units, as well as civilians with very wide backgrounds

---

[445] Fay Report, op. cit. The first MI unit to arrive at Abu Ghraib was a detachment from the A/519 MI BN on July 25, 2003. Elements of the 325 MI BN arrived on September 10 followed by elements of the 323 MI BN at the end of September. CACI interrogators began to arrive in late September as well.

[446] Ibid. The Fay investigation found that the JIDC was not provided with adequate personnel resources to effectively operate as an interrogation center. The report stated, "The JIDC was established in an ad hoc manner without proper planning, personnel and logistical support for the missions it was intended to perform. Interrogation and analyst personnel were quickly kluged together from a half dozen units in an effort to meet personnel requirements. Even at its peak strength, interrogation and analyst manpower at the JIDC was too shorthanded to deal with the large number of detainees at hand."

and experience levels in a two-month time period, was a huge challenge from a command and control perspective."[447] This problem was compounded by the loss of leadership, as one officer rotated back to the U.S. in November 2003, another left on emergency leave in December and never returned and thus only one commissioned officer remained in the Operation Section to supervise this diverse operation.[448]

CACI interrogators began to arrive in Iraq in late September of 2003 and, in December, the company had six interrogators (about 13 percent of the interrogator workforce) who had primary interrogator duty at Abu Ghraib. In fact, CACI never had more than ten interrogators at the Abu Ghraib prison at any one time. With these numbers set in context, as such, it is hard to rationalize that the civilians were a driving force behind abuses or other events at the prison.

And, while the news coverage pertaining to CACI was significant following the official reports released in August, it consisted almost entirely of "sidebar" or secondary stories. The main stories covering the Fay report, though at times referring to issues surrounding contractors, rarely mentioned the company by name. CACI's absence from those reports was also indicative of the declining interest in CACI for many reporters and an increased acceptance of CACI's minimal presence and minor role.

The *Washington Post's* coverage was typical of this trend. Neither of the *Post's* two front-page stories on the Fay report mentioned CACI. But CACI was still included. The newspaper's report on CACI and Titan employees, however, was relegated to page A-18.[449]

---

[447] Ibid. Fay would include in his recommendations for the *future* that additional uniform training and background requirements be set for contract interrogators. Among these recommendations was the requirement for previous military interrogator training for contractor interrogators. The SOW for CACI contractor interrogators did not hold prior military interrogator training as a mandatory requirement although some two-thirds of CACI's personnel did have the aforementioned training and experience and the others had the requisite relevant training and experience with law enforcement organizations.

[448] Ibid.

[449] "6 Employees From CACI International, Titan Referred for Prosecution," *Washington Post*, August 26, 2004. An accurate headline would have read, "3 Employees from Titan and 3 from CACI . . ." Notwithstanding the *Post's* distorted and sensationalized headline, the actual allegations concerning 3 CACI employees in the Fay

The editorial writers also showed little interest in CACI or contractor issues, another distinction from the first month of the crisis when opinion pages were filled with discussion about the role of contract interrogators. In response to the August reports, the editorial page debate focused on the role of political leadership in Washington and in particular whether Defense Secretary Rumsfeld should resign. Unlike the report of the army IG, the Schlesinger and Fay reports were received more favorably by the media.

The *New York Times*, for example, commended the Kern-Jones-Fay triumvirate for "a painfully professional job" of dissecting the army's performance. On the other hand, the *New York Times* clearly held Rumsfeld accountable, and showed disappointment that Schlesinger's finding "was not going to produce a clear-eyed assessment of responsibility." The *Times* said not a word about CACI and the role of contractors.[450] The *Philadelphia Inquirer*, in an unusually long editorial on August 28, which continued to cling to old and increasingly irrelevant news, expressed concern that civilians who might have committed alleged abuses were outside the military justice system. But the reference was near the end of the editorial and CACI was never mentioned.[451]

The *Washington Post's* editorial writers also focused on accountability at the top of the administration, with particular attention given to memos from Rumsfeld and Lieutenant General Ricardo Sanchez for authorizing the use of dogs in interrogations.[452] In a subsequent news story, the *Post* declared that, "The issue of using military dogs illustrates how a blizzard of memos from senior officials sowed an impression of tolerance, if not approval, for aggressive interrogations."[453]

---

report did not appear to carry any charge of extremes. In reality, what Fay recommended was not that the employees be referred for prosecution, but that the information from his report be forwarded to the Army General Counsel for determination of whether specific contractors (individuals) should be referred to DOJ for prosecution. The *Post's* headline was a quantum leap far beyond the facts.

[450] "Abu Ghraib, The Next Step," *The New York Times*, August 27, 2004.

[451] "Failings Top to Bottom," *Philadelphia Inquirer*, August 28, 2004.

[452] "A Failure of Accountability," *Washington Post*, August 29, 2004.

[453] "Documents Helped Sow Abuse, Army Report Finds," *Washington Post*, August 30, 2004.

In the coming months, the media and critics would continue to repeat these exaggerations about the stated inappropriate use of military dogs in detainment and interrogation operations. This aspect of the military's operations was, indeed, overstated, as would later become obvious. During coverage of the 2007 court-martial proceedings of Lt. Col. Steven Jordan, a *Washington Post* article noted that "From October 2003 to May 2004, there were more than 4,060 interrogations at Abu Ghraib but only 48 requests to use techniques involving sleep manipulation, dogs, segregation and other harsh tactics, according to an internal military intelligence chart. [Military officials] Pappas and Sanchez had to approve such methods."[454]

This statement by the *Post* demonstrated that if only forty-eight requests for "harsher" techniques were made from over four thousand interrogations, then not only were these requests rare, but the interrogators knew their limits having had to justify to their chain of command if and why they needed to go beyond the standard techniques. This also demonstrated that there were rules and procedures within an organized command structure that were generally known and followed. It also showed that harsher techniques were typically unnecessary.[455]

CACI all along had pointed out that there was a chain of command and rules that their interrogators knew to follow. The company had also stressed that the severe actions in the abuse photos were not those that interrogators were trained to employ.

* * *

---

[454] Josh White, "Conflicting Portraits of Officer Charged Over Abu Ghraib," *Washington Post*, July 31, 2007.

[455] 48 out of 4,060 represents about 1%. The article did not reveal how many of these requests were approved, which may have been even less than the 48 requests.

Notice was taken of the *Post*'s "sources." The statistics were said to have come from "an internal military chart." The company tried to verify this data through publicly available sources as well as through CACI staff that had been in Iraq, but were not successful in finding the information. The company also contacted the article author through the *Post*'s Web site requesting information about the source of the data, but no response was ever received. The *Post* was apparently quoting an *anonymous* (or undisclosed) source.

Still, the Fay report had put back on the table for CACI the question of "what to do about Steve?" For months, the company had been saying that it would not rush to judgment, but that it would act promptly if evidence showed wrongdoing by any of its employees. For "Civilian-05" and "Civilian-11" the question was moot, as they had already left the company. But Stefanowicz, now in his fourth month of administrative time, required a decision.

London had waited patiently for four months while the official investigations were completed, paying Stefanowicz for administrative leave despite some reluctance from others within the company. But London saw the decision about Stefanowicz to be a complex issue. In his mind, the investigations' comments and supporting data on Stefanowicz had not been persuasive. Reading the Fay report, he saw a compilation of allegations which came largely from hearsay, primarily from a single source that seemingly lacked corroboration or substantiating evidence, and which involved a speculative interpretation of events.

It also appeared to London that the Fay report had catalogued accusations and given them equal weight for others to assess. For example, one soldier told Fay it was "common knowledge" that Stefanowicz liked to use dogs, but when pressed to explore who else shared that knowledge, the soldier could not point to any other second source, and neither did the Fay report. The same single soldier was the sole source for another cloudy incident in which Stefanowicz was said to have been present. This account was used to support a general statement that Civilian-21 had used dogs inappropriately.

To London, these alleged offenses were all primarily based on hearsay and, in any case, fell into what the Fay report had referred to as "minor abuses" or "abusive actions taken based on misinterpretation or confusion regarding law or policy." Fay also had noted the relative distinctions among the alleged violations when he talked to reporters.

But the Fay report, the document itself, did not draw that kind of distinction. The report tended to give an alleged rape (presumably by a translator) the same gravity (weighting) as pushing a detainee to the ground. These varying types of mistreatment and abuses were all listed together — the serious and the minor — and, according to the Fay report, were to be forwarded to the army general counsel for determination of whether they should be referred to the Justice Department for possible prosecution.

London was disturbed that any of CACI's people might have behaved inappropriately in any way. As he said in his public remarks, "We are disappointed and disheartened by the news that any of our employees or former employees are alleged to have engaged in any improper or inappropriate behavior." But he was also concerned by the failure of the reports to clearly distinguish between the widely varying degrees of alleged misconduct.

However, far more significant than the report's logging of allegations against Stefanowicz was Fay's withdrawal from Taguba's speculation that Stefanowicz had been among those most responsible for the abuses. Both Fay and Schlesinger concluded that the actions captured in the Abu Ghraib abuse photos were neither linked to interrogations *nor* prompted by interrogators.[456]

Taguba's allegation — suspicion — had exposed Stefanowicz (and CACI) to public retribution. The resulting turmoil sent CACI through months of accusations and anguish, and there were still lingering repercussions. Had Taguba's suspicion proven accurate, resulting difficulties for Stefanowicz could be considered justly deserved. But Fay, who apparently had presented the worst of the allegations against Stefanowicz, had *not* found evidence to substantiate Taguba's wide-reaching allegation.

While London believed the Fay report might have done a more succinct job in assessing and cataloging the information that was collected, he gave Fay and his staff plenty of credit for a thorough data collection job. In the material provided by Fay, there was no indication that Stefanowicz played the central role suggested by the Taguba report, nor that he engaged in the misconduct revealed by the photographs, which unfortunately were still being wrongfully and maliciously displayed next to CACI's name on various Web sites and in some news stories.

London's reluctance to fire Stefanowicz was also heavily influenced by the different army reactions to the three employees cited in Fay's report. Acting through Major Daniels, the army contracting officer's

---

[456] The Schlesinger report stated that, "The pictured abuses . . . were not part of authorized interrogations nor were they even directed at intelligence targets." Schlesinger, op. cit.

representative responsible for CACI's interrogation contract, Fay had said earlier that he wanted "Civilian-11" sent home and the army in Baghdad wanted "Civilian-05" sent home. Committed to responding promptly to its customer, CACI had removed both men. But curiously, neither Fay nor anybody else from the army had ever passed a similar message about Stefanowicz. In London's mind, the army's different reaction to the three interrogators spoke at least as loud as the official reports.

London, having refused to take any action that might suggest CACI would accept vague allegations about Stefanowicz in place of hard fact, believed the company had done the right thing by their employee. While always emphasizing that CACI would not tolerate wrongdoing by any employee, London stood firm in his belief in due process and the presumption of innocence. But he soon concluded that he could now release Stefanowicz with a clear conscience and he would tell his people to begin making the necessary arrangements for both parties to move on.

The Fay report also raised some specific concerns about the CACI contracting process as well as directing criticisms to the army for problems with its role with contract employees. It said that the army never attempted to fully educate military personnel about the management of contract employees. Like the Inspector General report, the Fay report was critical of the army's contract statement of work (SOW), which it said should have required some standardized training for contract interrogators (although the army's contract SOW for CACI *did* stipulate that the army would, in fact, provide certain specific training to contract employees). Both reports recommended future standardization of training for contract interrogators, and this would include prior military interrogation training as a hiring prerequisite.[457] This recommendation was aimed at providing greater uniformity in the background, experience, and training of interrogators for hire.

In any case, CACI would follow whatever new contract training requirements were specified, just as it had followed existing contract requirements all along. Army contract management policies, procedures or processes were not CACI's to debate or determine, but were the business of the U.S. government.

---

[457] See also Chapter 11 for details on CACI's SOW for Iraq interrogation support services.

Of greater concern to the CACI team, however, was Fay's declaration that a CACI employee *may* have violated the Federal Acquisition Regulation by helping draft the contract's SOW. CACI had earlier acknowledged the employee's involvement, which the company understood had been requested by the army. However, the company vigorously objected to the characterization that the employee's assistance violated federal rules since the rules prohibiting contractor involvement applied to competitive bid contracts. Because of the urgent need for interrogators, the Iraq intelligence support services contract was not put out to a lengthy competitive bid as that would have taken much longer. In a subsequent letter to Acting Army Secretary Brownlee, the company stated that Fay likely was not aware of CACI's situation as it applied to contracting rules in this particular instance.

In their letter to Brownlee, the CACI team also noted again, as a reminder of the context of the contracting situation, that the assistance was requested by the government "under urgent, wartime conditions" in order to quickly meet the needs of troops on the ground. CACI also noted that the SOW criteria were subject to review and approval by the government, and that the transaction had passed legal review by Major F. Abe Dymond, of the army's Judge Advocate General Corps.

The CACI team pointed out that federal rules bar contractor involvement in drafting an SOW *only* if it provides the contractor with an unfair competitive advantage. But the interrogator contract was a sole source award, i.e. one in which there were no other companies involved, and federal rules explicitly recognize that contractor assistance is allowed for these types of contract actions. Asked about this contract issue by *Government Executive*, Steve Schooner, the co-director of the Government Procurement Law Program at the George Washington University Law School indicated that Fay may have overlooked the distinction in CACI's case.

Historically, such collaboration wasn't always the case, Schooner said, but added that "'this is one of the most pervasive changes that came out of the 1990s [federal government contracting] acquisition reforms,' which gave the government more leeway to interact with industry. It's happening every day," Schooner told the media.[458]

---

[458] Shane Harris, "CACI Chief Defends Company's Interrogation Work," Govexec. com, September 2, 2004.

CACI leaders were also baffled by Fay's suggestion that some interrogators' lack of previous military interrogator training may have been correlated, in some way, with detainee mistreatment and abuses. This was clearly not the case with CACI people. For example, the CACI team noted that two of the three civilians whom the Fay report specifically cited, those known as "Civilian-11" and "Civilian-05," in fact, *did* possess prior military interrogation training. The third, Stefanowicz, from naval intelligence, was hired first as a screener, and was then advanced to interrogator with the army's agreement, because of the skills and experience he gained on the job, and that he had demonstrated to the army in Iraq.

Tellingly too, the Fay report noted, "The army has always stressed 'you train as you fight.'" He observed that no formal advanced interrogation training exists in the army and little to no training is given to MI leaders and supervisors. He further noted that there "were disparate elements of units and individuals including civilians that had never trained together. . . . There is no formal advanced interrogation training in the Army. Little, if any, formal training is provided to MI leaders and supervisors . . . in the management of interrogation and detainee operations. These skills can only be developed in the unit environment through assignments to an interrogation unit, involvement in interrogation training exercises, or on deployments. Unfortunately, unit training and exercises have become increasingly difficult to conduct due to the high pace of deployments of interrogation personnel and units." Fay added that, "Most interrogator training that occurred at Abu Ghraib was on-the-job-training," but also, "the fast-paced and austere environment limited the effectiveness of any training."[459]

In the company's view, the media's subsequent emphasis on observations and recommendations regarding military training of interrogators implied that CACI had fallen short of meeting its hiring responsibilities when, in fact, *every* official investigative review had found that *every* CACI employee met the contract requirements. Prior military interrogator training, as such, was *not* a mandatory requirement for hiring and staffing under the original August 2003 CACI contract. Obviously, if it were, individuals hired by CACI would have been required to have that experience. As noted before, relevant experience from organizations

---

[459] Fay Report, op. cit.

outside the military was deemed fully acceptable and appropriate under the SOW, if it had been gained through experience with the FBI, CIA, other federal law enforcement organizations, or state and local law enforcement departments.

The army IG, Lt. Gen. Mikolashek specifically stated, "In summary, contract interrogators in OIF [Operation Iraqi Freedom] met the requirements of the CJFT-7 C2 Interrogation Cell SOW. The SOW did not mandate military interrogation training as a perquisite for employment."

Mikolashek also stated that, "65 percent (twenty of thirty-one) of contract interrogators in OIF had previous experience as army or marine interrogators . . . where they received formal school training in military interrogation techniques and procedures. These individuals had received formal military interrogation training an average of nine and a half years prior to employment as interrogators in OIF."

Now, rather than getting credit for going above and beyond the basic requirements on its staffing, the company was being criticized for not predicting a future military IG report's recommendation beyond the original contract requirements. London and his advisors could only shake their heads in disbelief. They observed that a balanced media report would have noted that CACI had fully met *every* stated staffing specification of its contract, but the army had subsequently determined that it might have, in retrospect, set out different staffing requirements, and would do so in going forward.

In addition, London's team believed that CACI interrogators generally had more experience than some of the army's own interrogators as, indeed, the Schlesinger report noted. Specifically, Schlesinger pointed out that, "some of the older contractors had backgrounds as former military interrogators and were generally considered more effective than some of the junior enlisted personnel."[460]

The army IG's report had similarly noted that several of the soldiers it interviewed believed that CACI's interrogators did a better job than those supplied by the military.

And in March 2005, a third military inquiry, the Church report, would observe that "contract interrogators . . . on average were older and more experienced than military interrogators; many anecdotal reports indi-

---

[460] Schlesinger Report, op. cit.

cated that this gave contract interrogators additional credibility in the eyes of detainees, thus promoting successful interrogations."[461]

The team at CACI noted that it seemed curious to be focusing on the training considerations about interrogation, when it was the Geneva Conventions violation issues in the general treatment of prisoners that had been breached at Abu Ghraib. It was these basic moral behaviors, under the Geneva Conventions, or lack thereof, that pertained to all military and all contractors — regardless of their work or unit assignments — that was the central issue. Taken as a whole, the three published reports — by Schlesinger, the army Inspector General, and the later report by Admiral Church — indicate clearly that military interrogator training of contractors, though desirable, was *not* a defining factor in interrogator effectiveness *nor* in the abuse charges.

These government reports ran counter to the majority of the media's criticisms and assertions, which in fact distorted and misrepresented this recommendation among the numerous overall recommendations of the army, that military interrogator training should be a requirement for *future* contractor interrogator support services. Furthermore, the government reports did not claim that the lack of such training reduced interrogator effectiveness or results. Neither did these reports, in any way, demonstrate nor provide evidence that any of the abuses at Abu Ghraib were correlated or connected with any contracting process or procedure, or lack thereof.

However, the media's approach to covering this information left the erroneous impression that the lack of military training for contractor interrogators was, in actuality, a factor in the abuses at Abu Ghraib — and this was virtually proven not to be the case.

The matter of supervision had also irked the company's leadership for some time because of periodic erroneous news reports on this topic, including a July 28 article that first appeared on *Government Executive's* Web site stating that CACI personnel "were expected to oversee, monitor and manage security and intelligence-related activities, including the interrogation of detainees."[462] In a strongly worded letter to *Government Executive*, CACI's outside legal counsel Koegel replied that the

---

[461] Church Report, op. cit.

[462] Shane Harris, "Contractors were hired to oversee interrogations." *Government Executive*. July 27, 2004.

company was responsible only for administrative personnel management of its own employees. Moreover, he pointed out that as far as the company was concerned, "control over the interrogation operations at Abu Ghraib prison and elsewhere remained vested exclusively in the military chain of command." Koegel included a reminder that acting secretary of the army Brownlee and Secretary of Defense Rumsfeld, had both publicly testified before Congress under oath that the civilian contractor interrogators reported to the army.[463] All CACI interrogation support and services activity under the contract was *always solely* at the discretion and direction of the army.

Separately, the company issued a press release on July 29 spelling out the chain of command and quoting from the Rumsfeld, Brownlee, and Mikolashek testimony on Capitol Hill. It was an important contractual matter because assuming supervisory military (command) authority was something CACI would not do under any circumstances. While CACI fully accepted administrative responsibility for its own employees, it recognized that the army, both by contract and by fact, was the ultimate authority at Abu Ghraib.

To the company it seemed clear that all CACI interrogator personnel were unquestionably under the military chain of command. That the military approved or agreed to assignment of all interrogators was the first proof showing that the military was in control. The second was that the SOWs also specified that CACI personnel would be integrated with military personnel and that all CACI intelligence support personnel operated under the authority, control and direction of the military.

When CACI interrogators arrived in Iraq, they reported to their military supervisor. This supervisor assigned the interrogators their tasks, determined where the interrogators were placed, and created their work schedule. As to their work assignments, schedules, etc., contract interrogators were treated essentially the same as military interrogators with the exception that the CACI contractors wore civilian clothing as opposed to the military interrogators who were in uniform.

---

463 "U.S. Senate Armed Services Committee held a hearing on the treatment of Iraqi Prisoners Friday," op. cit. Secretary Rumsfeld and Secretary Brownlee both stated that civilian contractors were under supervision of the military, in response to a question posed by Senator Daniel Akaka (D-Hawaii).

At Abu Ghraib, all CACI interrogators were under the control and supervision of the Officer in Charge (OIC) of Interrogation Control, who at the time of the abuses at Abu Ghraib was army Captain Carolyn Wood. Both military and contract interrogators also reported to the Noncommissioned Officer in Charge (NOIC) who was also army personnel and who also reported to Captain Wood. These two officers and higher military authorities had exclusive authority over the interrogation rules of engagement (IROE) and any proposed deviation from them. Further, the interrogation teams were supervised by section leaders who also reported to the officers in charge. Given this strict chain of command, CACI interrogators could not in any way have had any legal, contractual, or decision authority or control over regulations, rules of engagement, operating procedures, or tasks.

Furthermore, CACI reported to the Contracting Officer's Representative (COR). The COR monitored CACI's compliance with the contract. The COR also assigned contract interrogators to various sites throughout Iraq and monitored how interrogators were deployed and supervised. (Upon arrival, the OIC of the unit to which the interrogator was assigned would be the supervising authority.)

The only supervisory positions held by CACI personnel were solely for internal (but important) company purposes, such as the country manager and site leads who provided administrative support to CACI personnel and interacted with army contract management personnel. These employees were also tasked by the contract to provide advisory services on general counter- and human-intelligence activities, but *never* had any interrogation rule making or policy or decision-making authority.

In its letter to Brownlee, CACI noted that its personnel had worked diligently to defend the integrity of the chain of command. Once, when a CACI employee who had served on civilian prison parole boards was listed by the army as Officer In Charge of a detainee assessment board at Abu Ghraib, the company pointed out the inappropriateness and improper nature of the assignment and asked the army to correct the organizational oversight, which it promptly did.

At CACI the army IG, Schlesinger and Fay reports were seen as important milestones. They were thorough, comprehensive and encompassing investigations, and of great service to the issue about the events and culpability at Abu Ghraib in late 2003.

As a defining event for CACI, the Fay report had clearly backed away from and in a sense repudiated the Taguba report's allegations that Stefanowicz was "directly or indirectly" responsible for the abuses at Abu Ghraib. Furthermore, the allegations in the Fay report against Civilian 21 simply didn't rise to the levels suggested earlier by Taguba and the media. The fact was, the Fay report had not found any CACI employees central to the abuses at Abu Ghraib. The case simply was not there.

Furthermore and despite their frustrations with some aspects of the Fay report, London and his advisors, though welcoming the thoroughness and rigor of the investigation, were cautiously optimistic that CACI's time in the spotlight might be coming to an end. There were no more reports about Abu Ghraib on the horizon and no more public meetings to attend. The stock share price had stabilized, trading within a narrow range as first the Schlesinger report and then the Fay report became public and closing up slightly for the week at $49.11. In fact, CACI's price was now up about half a dollar for the year as a whole, a positive indicator that business was returning to the pre-scandal level. It seemed that CACI's good name was being fully reaffirmed. The company appeared to be off the media radar screen — at least for the time being — and about to enjoy some well-deserved respite from it all.

But appearances are not always what they seem.

SECTION SIX

RIGHTING THE WRONGS

CHAPTER THIRTY-SEVEN

SINGING A DIFFERENT TUNE
Critiquing the critics

"How much easier it is to be critical than to be correct."
~ BENJAMIN DISRAELI

OR CACI, THE RELEASE OF THE FAY AND SCHLESINGER REPORTS brought with it a forgotten air of calm. After four months of waiting anxiously for the next bombshell, the next call from a reporter, or the next investigation to be concluded, the onslaught had slowed considerably. The story had moved on, but CACI soon discovered that some people would not let the opportunity pass to further assault CACI's good name.

The media continued its speculation about Rumsfeld's future and what, if any, part of Abu Ghraib was the responsibility of President Bush and his civilian leaders in Washington.[464] The Schlesinger panel members, as well as Generals Kern, Jones, and Fay, were summoned to Capitol Hill to publicly discuss their reports before both House and Senate Committees. The media continued to dig for information about the CIA's ghost detainees and reported on classified sections of Fay's

---

[464] It was becoming clear by the fall of 2004 that the Abu Ghraib abuses, detainee policy and treatment, and interrogation methods and rules would be a major political issue going forward.

inquiry. The daily news still included developments related to prisoner abuse, but on matters unrelated to CACI. Four Navy SEALs were charged with alleged abuses, including the alleged beating of a prisoner who later died at Abu Ghraib.[465] Human rights groups, backed by a group of eight retired generals and admirals, urged President Bush to appoint an independent inquiry into alleged abuses in Afghanistan, Guantanamo Bay, and Iraq.

At Abu Ghraib, Major General Geoffrey Miller, the former Guantanamo Bay detention center commander who had taken charge of the prisons in Iraq in April, launched a public relations offensive. Leading tours and granting interviews, Miller generated a series of upbeat news stories about how the team at Abu Ghraib was getting more information by treating prisoners by the rules. The *New York Times*, for example, reported on September 7, 2004, that General Miller's system "appears to mark a change in the chaotic and often coercive environment" that had prevailed before.[466] Similar reports were filed by the Associated Press and the *Los Angeles Times*, which headlined its article "Reforms in Place at Abu Ghraib."[467]

---

[465] The prisoner was later identified as Manadel al-Jamadi, who died after an intense interrogation while in U.S. custody at Abu Ghraib in November 2003. The SEALs had apprehended al-Jamadi because they had suspected him of supplying explosives in several attacks, including the October 2003 bombings of Red Cross offices in Baghdad that killed 12 people. The initial accounts stated that Al-Jamadi had been brought to Abu Ghraib by the SEALs and then interrogated by the CIA. Conflicting testimony recounts that al-Jamadi was fine when the SEALs brought him in and that he was allegedly beaten during the CIA interrogation. But at a May 2005 hearing, it was alleged that both the CIA and SEALs had beaten al-Jamadi at a Navy camp at Baghdad International Airport before he was taken to Abu Ghraib. At that hearing, one SEAL was acquitted of responsibility for the death, but the investigation remained open as of December 2006 (with no further information available by the end of 2007). After his death, al-Jamadi's body was wrapped in ice and stored in a shower for a day before being transferred from Abu Ghraib. Among the infamous abuse photos were shots of Specialists Sabrina Harman and Charles Graner each posing with the "thumbs up" gesture over al-Jamadi's corpse in the ice-filled body bag.

[466] Dexter Filkins, "General Says Less Coercion of Captives Yields Better Data," *New York Times*, September 7, 2004.

[467] Jim Krane, "General: Less Abuse Resulting in More Iraq Tips," Associated Press, September 6, 2004; Mark Mazzetti, "Reforms in Place at Abu Ghraib," *The Los Angeles Times*, September 4, 2004.

For CACI, the one break in the early September calm was a blast from California. Just as Burkhart had predicted and London had come to expect, Angelides resurfaced again. According to Burkhart, Angelides' previously successful attention-seeking forays that gave him headlines and sound bites reinforced the likelihood that he would persist. In her view, he was still after the potential gain it provided to his political aspirations.

Declaring that CACI "is going to be in jeopardy for quite some time," Angelides added a twist to his attack on CACI with a September 1 press release and a meeting with CalSTRS on September 2 to urge CACI's board to investigate management's performance.[468] Two weeks before, at Angelides' prodding, CalPERS had directed its investment committee to consider selling the fund's holdings in CACI. Of the media, only Reuters, which covers corporate news closely, and the *Sacramento Bee*, ostensibly the paper of record for news involving the California state government, paid notice.

In keeping with his instincts, London directed the communications team to ignore this latest move from Angelides, which was a significant deviation from the team's summer-long strategy of responding to every misstatement, but appropriate for dealing with Angelides' media-seeking antics.

* * *

However, CACI faced one last confrontation. Within weeks, after the Fay report clearly showed that the responsibility for misconduct at Abu Ghraib was not that of the single CACI employee named in the Taguba report, and after numerous efforts by CACI to clear the record on the company's work in Iraq, Peter W. Singer of the Brookings Institution launched his own caustic attack on the company.[469] Singer's abrupt assault left CACI observers wondering if he was somehow disturbed

---

[468] California State Treasurer's Office Press Release, September 1, 2004, op. cit. Angelides' release incorrectly referred to the contractors as "negotiators," when they were actually "interrogators" — two distinctly different roles and positions, not having anything in common with respect to their functions.

[469] The other individuals originally named by Taguba, Titan sub-contractor John Isreal, and Army Lt. Col. Steven Jordan and Col. Thomas Pappas, never drew Singer's ire.

that CACI came out relatively unscathed from the numerous official government investigations and the media's summer long onslaught.

These government investigative reports had made it clear: CACI's Stefanowicz was *not* the instigator of the difficulties and abuses at Abu Ghraib, and CACI was *not* involved in any significant Abu Ghraib abuse related issues.

Nonetheless, on Sunday, September 12, in a *Washington Post* opinion column, Peter W. Singer put forth his increasingly strident criticisms of the government and the government contracting industry. In the *Post's* Outlook section, Singer took aim at CACI in a 1,400-word piece entitled: "The Contract the Military Needs to Break."[470] It was a pointed attack on the government's use of contract interrogators, whom Singer alleged were operating "outside the military orbit" and who, he also insisted without proof or evidence, had long escaped scrutiny for their (alleged) misdeeds. The contract Singer chose to target and scuttle, however, was CACI's contract decision to honor the army's requirement for a small number of interrogators to supplement the army's own intelligence gathering efforts in Iraq.

In the first days after the Abu Ghraib photos appeared and before the media firestorm gained momentum, Singer had offered a few accurate and objective accounts or statements about CACI. He had noted that CACI did not have any unusual controversy in its past. But as the weeks went by, Singer became one of the most prolific of the media's self-proclaimed "expert" commentators speaking in opposition to the use of civilian contractors in the war. Despite his initial observation that Abu Ghraib was the first time the company had been "dragged into the public venue," he attempted to keep it there with his ongoing commentary, by splicing CACI's name into his criticisms of the government contracting process and the industry overall.

Seizing the opportunity to advance his apparent agenda for restructuring the military contracting process, Singer had written articles and op-eds, appeared on numerous radio and television talk shows, given speeches at conferences, and made himself readily available to reporters. He was indeed a widely recognized public figure with sharply drawn opinions that he openly and frequently shared with all the media. And his

---

[470] Peter W. Singer, "The Contract the Military Needs to Break," *Washington Post*, September 12, 2004.

remarks on government contractors grew more pointed and laden with accusations as time went by. He complained that the government was doing a poor job of monitoring contractor performance in Iraq. And within a week after the first allegations about Abu Ghraib, Singer proclaimed that, "we've let the contractors fall through a gap in the law."[471]

Singer's skeptical views about the government contracting industry predated Abu Ghraib going back to the publication of his book *Corporate Warriors* in 2003. Shortly after the news blitz about Abu Ghraib erupted, Singer wrote an op-ed titled "Outsourcing Interrogation: The Legal Vacuum" in which he attempted to lay the preponderance of the abuses at the feet of the contractors, listing as support for his argument, misbehaviors at the prison that were *never* attributed to contractors. Singer's op-ed stated that, "The interrogators have also indulged in depraved behavior such as making the prisoners perform simulated sex acts. . . ."[472] Even before the facts fully emerged from the official investigations, Singer had formulated unfavorable opinions about the contractors, which he continued to promulgate throughout the investigative phase by referencing inaccurate information. Further, Singer did not make clear in his accusations whether he referred to the interrogators (MI) and contractors or the Military Police (MP). Taguba's report had primarily investigated the role and activities of the MPs, not the MI interrogators. The Abu Ghraib abuse photos depicted MPs from the 372nd Military Police Company.

On September 10, following a September 8 appearance by Singer on CNN, CACI sent Singer a letter pointing out the false statements and inaccuracies in his remarks from that particular appearance and erroneous statements he had made over the previous months about the company's employees. Just a few days later, on September 12, Singer's *Post* op-ed appeared which made clear to CACI that Singer had ignored its letter and intended to persist in spreading misinformation.[473] That Singer wrote a critique venting his grievances against the contracting industry was not so surprising given his preconceived notions. And that was his

---

[471] Peter Singer, "Above the law, Above Decency; Private military contractors may escape punishment in the Iraqi prisoner abuse scandal," *Los Angeles Times*, May 2, 2004.

[472] Peter W. Singer, "Outsourcing Interrogation: the Legal Vacuum," op. cit.

[473] Peter W. Singer, "The Contract the Military Needs to Break," op. cit.

prerogative. But that Singer chose to single out and make sweeping over-generalizations about CACI was inappropriate. Singer continued to accuse the military of not dealing with contractors (implicitly CACI) harshly enough. While the findings in several official government investigations that had just been released contradicted Singer's claims, Singer ignored these conclusions and persisted in his assault. In his opinion article, Singer used CACI's name no less than nine times.[474] Titan was mentioned once, almost in passing. Clearly he was intent on targeting CACI.

Singer wrongly proclaimed, ". . . while two U.S. Army reports issued last month explored the question of military command responsibility, no one has demanded accountability from the corporate chain of command that played an *incontrovertible* [italics added] part in the Abu Ghraib abuses."[475] This statement defied explanation given that the contractors, and CACI in particular were the subject of, or part of, no less than nine official U.S. government investigations and inquiries. Singer's summary judgment of CACI's guilt was quite clear in his choice of the word "incontrovertible."[476]

Singer went on to make the exaggerated claim that CACI employees "made up more than half of all the analysts and interrogators at Abu Ghraib."[477] Yet the Fay report showed this claim to be factually wrong. Fay indicated that in December 2003 the JIDC at the prison had approximately 160 personnel with forty-five interrogators and eighteen translators (screeners were not a question in this regard). Since CACI only had six interrogators at Abu Ghraib in December 2003 and never had more than ten interrogators on site at any one time as the interrogation workforce increased, CACI interrogators represented, according to this data, closer to some 13 percent of the interrogators.

Singer also stated that, "Sixteen of the forty-four incidents of abuse . . . at Abu Ghraib *involved* [italics added] private contractors outside the domain of both the U.S. military and the U.S. government." But this was not the case either.

---

[474] Ibid.

[475] Ibid.

[476] "Incontrovertible" is defined as "not able to be denied or disputed" by *The New Oxford American Dictionary*, 2005 edition.

[477] Ibid.

The Fay report did discuss 44 incidents, of which 16 had the word "civilian" in the description. However, a detailed reading of the Fay report shows Singer's analysis to have been overly simplistic and misleading. Most importantly, CACI contractors clearly did *not* work outside the domain of the U.S. government or the military to which they were contracted.

The Fay report did not describe the 44 incidents as proven. In fact, a chart of the incidents was titled "Allegations of Abuse Incidents, the Nature of Reported Abuse, and Associated Personnel." "Allegations" and "Reported" do not equate to proven.

Of those sixteen incidents that included a reference to a "civilian," many did not even allege abuse. Singer's use of the word "involved," however, obviously implied participation in abuse. Yet, there were several examples where no involvement of any kind existed. Incident #2 in the Fay report described an assault on a female detainee by Military Intelligence personnel. The sole reference to a civilian contractor, regarding the incident according to the report, stated, "CIVILIAN-06 (Titan) was the assigned interpreter, but there is no indication he was present or involved." Similarly from the report, incident #5 stated that, "SOLDIER-25 claimed the detainee's allegation was made in the presence of CIVILIAN-21, Analyst/Interrogator, CACI, which CIVILIAN-21 denied hearing this report." According to another incident description in the Fay report, in which a CACI employee reported abuse, "CIVILIAN-21, a CACI contract interrogator, witnessed SOLDIER-29 and SOLDIER-10 escorting the scantily clad detainee from the Hard Site back to Camp Vigilant, wearing only his underwear and carrying his blanket. CIVILIAN-21 notified SGT Adams, who was SOLDIER-29's section chief, who in turn notified CPT Wood, the ICE OIC." Yet, Singer reported these incidents as "incontrovertible" evidence of abuse by contractors.

And Singer did not offer a description of the alleged abuses to let readers know that these were, in CACI's case, not anywhere near the type of abuses depicted in the notorious Abu Ghraib abuse photos, which were also listed among the 44 incidents. The other allegations made in the Fay report against CACI contractors were: (1) threatening a detainee with the presence of an intimidating soldier; (2) pulling a high-value detainee from a truck; (3) allowing a detainee to squat on a chair in an unauthorized stress position with another unidentified person having

photographed the prisoner; and (4) authorized and unauthorized presence and barking of dogs allegedly during interrogations. Furthermore,
although it was alleged that a CACI interrogator forced a detainee to
wear women's underwear, there was no mention of a detainee attributing any such role to a CACI interrogator. While inappropriate, these incidents, as described, were factually not commensurate with the other
abuses and humiliation mentioned in the Fay report, and which were
depicted in the publicized photos for which several soldiers were convicted. According to the Fay report's senior co-author, General Paul
Kern, such behavior represented primarily minor "abusive actions
taken based on misinterpretation or confusion about law or policy."[478]

Singer went on to say in the op-ed that: "Army investigators have
reported that six employees of private contractors were *involved* [italics
added] in incidents of abuse. . . ."[479] Not only was his choice of the
word "involved" an obvious overstatement but he failed to note that only
three of the six were associated with CACI (the other three were Titan
employees).[480]

Most egregious was Singer's broad follow-up claim about alleged contractor crimes: ". . . but potentially more [contractors] may have been *involved in other crimes* [italics added] in Iraq and elsewhere."[481] This
broad sweeping speculation and damning accusation, particularly referring to criminality in association with the mention of CACI, was unfounded, and misleading for several reasons. First, it gave readers the
impression that this was an actual finding of the official investigations
rather than a speculative notion put forth by Singer. Second, CACI was
never implicated for any misbehavior, or "crimes," elsewhere in Iraq or
anywhere else for that matter. CACI employees were limited mostly to

---

[478] "Press briefing by General Paul Kern, et al., op. cit.

[479] Peter W. Singer, "The Contract the Military Needs to Break," op. cit.

[480] This emphasis on all 6 employees in an op-ed which prominently named CACI
was strangely similar to the *Post*'s exaggerated headline, "6 Employees From
CACI International, Titan Referred for Prosecution." Both Singer and the *Post*
chose to minimize Titan, which employed half of the referenced employees,
while juxtaposing all 6 employees from both companies with CACI's name. There
were those at CACI who could not help but believe that this was not a coincidence in either case.

[481] Ibid.

the Green Zone around Baghdad and CACI had no interrogation services work anywhere else in the world outside of Iraq. Singer went on, however, to give as examples to support this speculative notion, the instance of an *unidentified* contractor accused of alleged rape, and another instance of a CIA contract employee in Afghanistan — *neither* of whom had anything to do with CACI.[482]

Singer noted in his *Post* op-ed that contractors were mentioned on thirty-eight pages of the Fay report but failed to separate comments on those thirty-eight pages according to the specific contractor, or to point out that *not* all of those thirty-eight pages carried negative or adverse remarks. Furthermore, Singer made no mention of any of the positive comments about CACI interrogators or the favorable findings of the recently released official reports that also demonstrably scaled back virtually all of the allegations in reference to Stefanowicz, the CACI employee, named in the Taguba report.

While postulating that the Fay report revealed "an outsourcing episode gone bad" Singer's follow-on statement actually provided the logical rationale for the CACI interrogation contract, which lent support to the fundamental fact that, far from being an outsourcing episode gone bad, it was a vital and necessary decision that provided valuable and timely services. The fact was that under the circumstances, as Singer himself stated, "when . . . the number of detainees rose, the Pentagon [the army] turned to private companies to hire additional help quickly."[483]

Further punching a hole in Singer's assessment of this outsourcing situation, were contradictory observations from all of the recently released official reports. The Army IG report stated that, "Contract interrogators were a force multiplier in OIF [Operation Iraqi Freedom], supplementing a shortage of military interrogators. Contract interrogators were used to perform screening and interrogation at collecting points (CPs) and in internment/resettlement (IR) facilities to free military

---

[482] The CIA contractor allegation would not apply to CACI as the company never had interrogator contracts with the CIA. And the Fay report indicated that "a review of all available records could not identify a translator [contractor] by name" given by the alleged victim, DETAINEE-05; and, CACI had no linguistics contracts with the army. The Fay report also noted that "DETAINEE-05's description of the interpreter partially matches CIVILIAN-17, Interpreter, Titan Corporation."

[483] Peter Singer, "The Contract the Military Needs to Break," op. cit.

interrogators and counterintelligence agents to perform tactical missions at point of capture."[484] The Fay report noted that, "Most Abu Ghraib interrogators performed their duties in a satisfactory manner without incident or violation of training standards." And the later Church report (released in March 2005) observed that, "Overall we found that contractors made a significant contribution to U.S. intelligence efforts. Contract interrogators . . . on average were older and more experienced than military interrogators; many anecdotal reports indicated that this gave contract interrogators additional credibility in the eyes of detainees, thus promoting successful interrogations. In addition, contract personnel often served longer tours than DoD personnel, creating continuity and enhancing corporate knowledge at their commands."[485]

Taking up the previously disputed points made by the media, Singer's op-ed harkened back to the oft misguided notion that there was a hidden agenda behind the fact that the interrogator contract was not opened up to competitive bid and that it utilized an existing IT BPA contract. The obvious rationale, and truth, was that this contract avenue offered the most expedient, quick-response solution to the army under the circumstances, which Singer had already acknowledged when he noted "the Pentagon turned to private companies to hire additional help quickly." Clearly this contract decision prevented any further delays from a lengthy bidding process and it allowed faster delivery by using a contract vehicle already in place.

Singer also stated, "contrary to federal acquisition regulations the contract was written by an employee of the firm," without accurately portraying Fay's qualifying comment that the contract "may" have violated the provisions of the Federal Acquisition Regulation. Furthermore this assertion by Singer neglected CACI's statements setting the record straight on the matter by pointing out that contractor involvement is a breach of Federal Regulations *only* when it gives a contractor a competitive advantage. And this was clearly not the case with the interrogator contract, which was a sole source contract issued in an emergency under the urgent war zone conditions.

---

[484] Department of Defense, Office of the Inspector General, "Contracts Awarded for the Coalition Provisional Authority by the Defense Contracting Command-Washington," op. cit.

[485] Church Report, op. cit.

Singer revealed his own convoluted interpretation of the official findings by stating that, "The process was so convoluted that months later, neither General Fay nor General Jones could figure out just who wanted private interrogators in the first place or why." Another inaccurate depiction of the Fay investigation, this misinterpretation by Singer was not a conclusion contained in the official report. Fay actually referred to the issue of Delivery Orders when noting, "While CJTF-7 is the requiring and funding activity for the Delivery Orders in question, it is not clear who, if anyone, in the army contracting or legal channels approved the use of the BPA, or why it was used." This is a reference to the fact that Fay had not yet determined who approved the use of the BPA contract vehicle or why it was used. But nothing in the Fay report supported Singer's statement, that Fay could not determine who wanted private interrogators at Abu Ghraib for CJTF-7 or why. In fact, the "who" and "why" were clear. Fay repeatedly pointed out in his report that CACI interrogators were sent to Abu Ghraib as part of a military decision along with several other military groups to help make up the shortfall in interrogators. This point couldn't possibly be missed by anyone doing a careful review of the Fay report. The army IG report also clearly pointed out that the purpose of contract interrogators was to supplement a shortage of military interrogators.

In another sweeping statement without basis in fact, Singer claimed that, "Hiring private contractors comes with another hidden price: corporate practices that would not pass military muster." The reality was that all of the CACI interrogators were qualified by the SOW, were U.S. citizens and held appropriate U.S. government security clearances at the Secret or higher levels. They were all also approved by the army or had obtained army agreement for their project assignments. And this damning statement by Singer neglected to note the conclusion by Schlesinger that, "The Naval Inspector General . . . found some of the older contractors had backgrounds as former military interrogators and were generally considered more effective than some of the junior enlisted military personnel."[486]

Singer's follow-up statement was that, "former employees [plural] of CACI had alleged that many of their fellow interrogators lacked proper experience or training. They asserted that in the rush to fill the billable

[486] Schlesinger Report, op. cit.

interrogator jobs, the firm had conducted five-minute phone interviews with applicants." Although Singer did not cite his source, it sounded very much like the already discredited media comments of Torin Nelson who, while initially complaining to the press following the media onslaught from the Abu Ghraib scandal that his interview was streamlined (due to his obvious qualifications), he later admitted that he did "not know about others," relative to their interview process. *All* CACI contract interrogators were hired with the approval or agreement of the army. And the army IG was clear on this matter stating, "In summary, contract interrogators in OIF [Operation Iraqi Freedom] met the requirements of the CJTF-7 C2 Interrogation Cell SOW."[487] But this point apparently did not factor into Singer's opinion article.

Singer went on to say that CACI "hadn't bothered to check their [applicants'] résumés, fingerprints or criminal records." This was a misrepresentation given CACI's thorough, painstaking screening of applicants who had, additionally, in most cases already been screened by the U.S. government for current and available security clearances and citizenship. CACI had repeatedly disclosed its rigorous recruiting and hiring process along with the fact that it met the army's requirements as set forth in the contracts' SOW. Out of 1,600 job applicants, fewer than 3 percent were pre-approved by CACI to be submitted to the U.S. Army for review and acceptance, and CACI had selectively hired only some three dozen out of that large original pool.

Despite all of this, Singer remarked that, ". . . army investigators found that 35 percent of the contract interrogators 'lacked formal military training as interrogators.'" Without a complete presentation of the facts, this statement implied that CACI's interrogators were inadequately equipped for their jobs. This was, of course, a gross misrepresentation of the situation since all (100 percent) of CACI hires met the SOW hiring requirements and were accepted for hire by the army. The army IG clearly stated, "The SOW did not mandate military interrogation training as a prerequisite for employment." The army IG noted, "Prior to May 2004, there was no CACI or CJTF-7 requirement for all contract interrogators to receive formal, comprehensive, military-specific interrogator training prior to performing interrogations." But the army IG report also pointed out that, "65 percent . . . of contract interrogators in OIF

---

[487] Army IG Report, op. cit.

had . . . training in military interrogation techniques and procedures. These individuals had received formal military interrogation training an average of 9.5 years prior to employment as interrogators in OIF." Besides failing to note that military training was not mandatory, Singer also failed to note that relevant civilian experience (from work with organizations such as the FBI, CIA, or other police or detective departments) fully met the interrogation qualifications and requirements as noted in the SOW. As stated in the army IG report, "These personnel [viz. the other 35 percent of CACI contract interrogators] conducted interrogations using skill sets obtained in previous occupational specialties such as civilian police interrogator or Military Intelligence (MI) officer."[488]

Singer neglected to specify that this reference to formal military interrogator training, as a "requirement" pertained to a *future* staffing suggestion as part of both the Fay reports and the army IG's recommendations.[489] Specifically, Fay said, "The key point would be agreement on some standardization of the training of contractor interrogators."[490] The army IG recommended, "The CFLCC contracting officer representative *modify* [italics added] the CJTF-7 C2 Interrogation Cell Statement of Work to require civilian interrogators to be former military interrogators trained in current interrogation policy and doctrine or receive formal training in current military interrogation policy and doctrine."[491]

The Schlesinger report and the army IG report not only noted that CACI interrogators met the contract requirements but *both* reports had said explicitly that the contractors provided valuable, effective support. Furthermore, none of the investigative reports, including the Fay report, claimed or concluded that the serious abuse problems at Abu Ghraib were directly connected to the training of contractors, or more importantly to the lack thereof. And the Schlesinger report had noted that a number of civilian contractors were *better* at their job than the military's own interrogators.

---

[488] Ibid.

[489] Singer, however, failed to note the Army IG finding that 2 out of the 4 interrogators supplied by Sytex, a subsidiary of Lockheed Martin based in Afghanistan reportedly did *not* have formal military interrogator training.

[490] Fay Report, op. cit.

[491] Department of Defense, Office of the Inspector General, "Detainee Operations Inspection," op. cit.

Singer stated that, "army investigators documented numerous instances in which contractors 'supervised' military officers," but he gave no specific examples of this. Nor did he note that CACI made a concerted effort to respect the chain of command and demonstrated this by having specifically asked on one occasion that the military correct a project chart to show that CACI employees did *not* supervise the military but, in fact, fell under the military chain of command.[492]

Singer added that there were "other instances in which contractors [plural] demonstrated disdain for uniformed clients" using as an example a (single) CACI employee alleged to have engaged in drinking alcohol at Abu Ghraib and who allegedly refused to take orders on one occasion. This one instance of insubordination by one person, even if true, could not possibly, nor credibly, support Singer's broad sweeping accusation. The only other allegation against this individual was dragging a handcuffed prisoner from a truck, which could not reasonably be construed as constituting anything close to torture.

*　*　*

However, Singer's most incendiary and reckless claim was in his assertion that *"The non-doctrinal use of contractors opened the door to making up other rules along the way, such as the non-doctrinal use of torture"*[493] [italics added]. This was an irresponsible allegation, as the CACI team saw it, that had no support in any of the official government investigative reports and had no basis in fact. Being presented in the context of a derogatory discussion about CACI, contractor interrogation services, and the Abu Ghraib abuses this statement could be posed as constituting a knowing effort to malign CACI and amounting to defamation *per se*.

The allegations against Stefanowicz or either of the other two CACI employees, as stated in the Fay report, certainly did not equate to anything close to being described as torture as that term has been properly used in these matters. Their actions as described in the official reports, if true, *may* have broken certain administrative or engagement rules, but by every common definition (and with common sense) these were not acts of

---

[492] Once when a CACI employee who had served on civilian prison parole boards was listed by the army as Officer-in-Charge of a detainee assessment board at Abu Ghraib, the company pointed out the inappropriateness of the assignment and asked the army to correct the organizational oversight.

[493] Peter Singer, "The Contract the Military Needs to Break," op. cit.

torture (The word "torture," as such, was not used or presented in any of the military personnel charges brought under UMCJ at courts martial).[494] Singer's assertions that, "The arrival of contract interrogators blurred lines of authority and obscured the differences between civilian and military tasks," and that, "This resembled the confused military command structure that investigators found at Abu Ghraib between military intelligence and military police units," point in fact, to the deficiencies in military command and organizational leadership that all of the official investigations — Taguba, Schlesinger and Fay — had found existed at Abu Ghraib.

The presence of contract workers who, contrary to Singer's assertions, were in fact under the military chain of command, did not contribute to the leadership confusion and problems that the official reports found within the military ranks at Abu Ghraib. To conclude otherwise seems to strain credible logic: it would be hard to argue convincingly or responsibly, that all would have gone "just fine" at Abu Ghraib if only the (CACI) contractors had not been there.

Singer's criticism (by virtue of Fay's observation) that the military was "unprepared for the arrival of contract interrogators and had no training to fall back on in the management, control, and discipline of these personnel," was a reflection of the various difficulties encountered by the army in meeting the challenges it faced in the war effort. These challenges were certainly numerous and daunting, but they clearly were not limited to, caused by, or the direct result of contractors being present who were obviously there to assist the army. In fact, Fay referred to the arrival of contractors as "another [but clearly not the only] complicating factor with respect to command and control," pointing out that there were a number of divergent units brought together to meet the interrogation needs at Abu Ghraib. This sudden infusion included personnel from six different MI battalions and groups from several different countries who "were part of the U.S. Army Intelligence and Security Command (INSCOM), which tasked those subordinate units to send

---

[494] According to the Schlesinger report, "In the summer of 2002, the Counsel of the President queried the Department of Justice Office of Legal Counsel (OLC) for an opinion on the standards of conduct for interrogation operations conducted by U.S. personnel outside of the U.S. and the applicability of the U.N. Convention Against Torture. The OLC responded in an August 1, 2002 opinion in which it held that in order to constitute torture, an act must be specifically intended to inflict severe physical or mental pain and suffering that is difficult to endure.

whatever interrogator and analyst support they had available." Fay pointed out too, that two supervisory officers soon left Abu Ghraib, one who rotated out in November and another who left on emergency leave in December and did not return. At this point, there was only one "commissioned officer remaining in the operations section."

Fay also noted that the Joint Interrogation and Debriefing Center (JIDC) had some challenges as it was being developed. His report relates these comments about JIDC: "The JIDC is a non-doctrinal organization. Initially, there was no joint manning document for JIDC. . . . There was no approval structure for JIDC. The manning document for JIDC was being created as the JIDC was already operating . . . procedures were ad hoc in nature . . . where possible, though, most processes and procedures were developed on the fly based upon the needs of the situation. The organization of the JIDC changed often . . . and contributed to the general turmoil at Abu Ghraib. Interrogators were not familiar with the new working arrangements . . . and were only slightly trained to conduct interrogations using translators. . . ." Fay noted that a re-organization within JIDC ". . . introduced another layer of complexity into an already stressed Abu Ghraib interrogation operations environment." But Fay also pointed out that, "In spite of this turmoil, lack of training and doctrine and shortages, the JIDC did mature over time and improved intelligence production derived from interrogations at Abu Ghraib." It, again, defies credibility to place all of these difficulties on the backs of the contractors, as Singer suggests. These problems would have existed as they did, even if no contractors had been present.

Singer's op-ed stated, "Despite all these dark findings [in the Fay and Schlesinger reports] . . . army investigators are at a loss over how to hold contractors accountable." Yet his next statement contradicted this claim by his own observation that, "the army referred individual employees' names to the Justice Department. . . ." Having already gone to great lengths to criticize how both the army and the contractors, namely CACI, were not doing *their* jobs Singer's complaints turned toward how the Department of Justice was not doing *its* job. Absent completion of the Justice Department's review and findings, including whether it would even pursue prosecution in the case of each individual contractor, Singer then lamented that contractor employees might not be charged.

He launched into further speculation about the various ways in which contractors could be convicted. This again revealed his presumption of guilt on the part of the contractors as well as his lack of confidence in the government's ability, in this case the Department of Justice, to make its own considered determination about whether prosecution would be warranted and, if so, what path that prosecution would take. It should be noted that the Department of Justice is not inclined toward indictments without probable cause, sufficient evidence, and a basis for believing a guilty verdict can be obtained.

Stating that "so far nothing official has actually been done," Singer signaled that he was entirely dismissive of all of the numerous and extensive official investigations and inquiries that had been conducted by the DoD (Schlesinger), the army (Taguba, Mikaloshek, Kern, Jones, Fay), Congress (House and Senate Hearings), GSA, DCAA, GAO, DOI, and CACI. This was further borne out in his statement, "But so far, the only formal investigation has been one conducted by the firm involved; CACI's investigation of CACI cleared CACI. Clearly, this is insufficient." This comment of "insufficient" of course was far from the truth and harkened back to the media's cries of "whitewash."

But Singer persisted: "One recourse could be to . . . punish bad corporate behavior by firing, or at least not rehiring the companies that have done wrong. But the army has not even exercised that minimal option." Singer had thus arrived at the punchline and purpose of his op-ed title, "The Contract the Military Needs to Break."

To the CACI team, Singer's attack on CACI as "The Contract the Military Needs to Break" seemed also to be a way of serving notice to army contracting officials that if they made any more contract awards for interrogation work to CACI, he would ensure that they would receive lots of public criticism, especially in the *Washington Post.*

Aside from this obvious lambasting of the manner in which the army was conducting its business along with his outright dismissal of the conclusions of the official government investigations, Singer's own interpretations and conclusions were wrong. The fact of the matter was that the allegations (after numerous comprehensive investigations were completed), against one CACI employee or even a total of three as alleged, did not equate to bad corporate behavior or justify dismissing an entire company of 9,500 employees. Moreover, all allegations against CACI employees were said to be among the "lesser" of the mistreatments, not those Fay deemed significant, and no employee had even been charged. If this kind of logic were applied, then it would follow that because a few soldiers within the MP unit at Abu Ghraib engaged in misconduct, the entire unit should be summarily convicted and cashiered from the service, without even the right to the court martial process.

Singer's op-ed was flawed primarily because, as the Fay report noted "Abu Ghraib *cannot* be understood in a vacuum [italics added]." The op-ed was a harsh, uninformed and unjustified attack on the U.S. military, the government, the justice system, the government contracting industry, and CACI.

In summary, Singer's op-ed was, without doubt, way off the mark. Opinion was one thing, even if unaware and uninformed, but this was opinion mixed with many flagrant inaccuracies and misrepresentations. Also disconcerting to many was that Singer's status supposedly represented a higher level of expertise and objectivity.[495] His public position gave him credibility with the media, but his analysis was, unfortunately for CACI, flawed.

Overall, the CACI team, in its opinion, felt that Singer's commentary in the article could only be described as misleading. He was "not one of those who in expressing opinions confine themselves to facts," London commented in quoting Mark Twain, as he described his own opinion of the op-ed.

London didn't object at all to Singer's personal opinion that civilian contractors should not be used to conduct interrogation if that was his view. That was a legitimate public policy issue and CACI had not involved itself in that debate. The company would simply provide the services if they were authorized, requested, and contractually sought — and would be proud as well to do so in support of an urgent wartime situation. But London could not abide any accusation from Singer or anyone else that CACI was consciously violating military doctrine or condoning *torture*. Singer's reference to torture in an article that also singled out CACI in such an unsupportable and incriminating fashion was entirely reprehensible.

---

[495] It is understood that views and opinions expressed by Mr. Peter W. Singer are his alone and not necessarily endorsed or sponsored by the Brookings Institution.

Though noting that Singer had written *Corporate Warriors* from his graduate studies research, a book on what Singer called the "privatized military industry," London had believed Singer's limited experience outside academia severely constrained his real-world knowledge and understanding.[496] CACI observers noted with irony that Singer even acknowledged in his book that after following and studying government contractors for weeks, he still did not have an understanding of contractors and how they operated. Singer had stated in his book that it should be read with the limitations of his knowledge in mind, but he did not provide the same cautions in his op-ed, which revealed several instances of such inadequacies. He had admitted his own lack of understanding of the contracting business in *Corporate Warriors* by stating that, "for all its growth, our understanding of it still remains greatly limited."

As some at CACI saw it, within a few years of writing his dissertation, Singer would curiously be called an expert apparently trying to challenge military decisions and even, arguably, giving orders to the military through the press. Besides making demands on what contracts it should break, he would also criticize the government on how it conducted its business dealings with government contractors. It was becoming apparent that the media, in its effort to find someone who could comment on government contractors had probably overestimated Singer's understanding of the industry and possibly underestimated his bias against it insofar as CACI was concerned.

Perhaps it was not a coincidence that the Singer op-ed came at a time when some army contracting people were circulating e-mail communications about "political" considerations associated with CACI interrogator services — and more importantly "breaking off" the CACI contract. But, if it was merely a coincidence, it was certainly an unfortunate one for CACI which had just come through a series of rigorous investigations with quite favorable findings and results overall.

Early on, Singer had been among those who speculated that by hiring CACI under an Interior Department contract, the government might be trying (consciously, covertly?) to hide the company's activities or shield its employees from prosecution. It was a baseless speculation that attacked and insulted the government, the U.S. Army, and knowingly and unfairly besmirched CACI's professional reputation.

---

[496] Peter W. Singer, *Corporate Warriors*, op. cit.

Singer had cast further doubts about the government and the contracting industry by stating to Minnesota Public Radio in June 2004, "There's the questions of accountability, the questions of who made the decision to use private contractors in the first place, whether it was in Afghanistan or in Abu Ghraib prison. . . . And then there's also the question of, how broad is this system: What companies were involved? That's something that wasn't identified today. Why was the decision made, who made it, etc.? There's a lot of broad questions that this raises." But tellingly Singer added, "So we're in the year that ends in '04, so you've got to expect this kind of stuff. Everything's going to be political these days."

Singer then commented further on his intent: "The big question is going to be whether we set up a system that doesn't respond to the politics of the day but actually a system that deals with contractors at large. Where they should be in these roles and how can *they* [italics added] be held accountable when things go bad?"

In *Corporate Warriors*, Singer had stated, "I have done my utmost to weed out the rumors from the facts and provide an objective analysis of the industry, indicating whenever appropriate what is confirmed and what is suspected." But Singer had not taken the same measures in his op-ed. As some people at CACI saw it, he had made connections between entirely unrelated circumstances, reported partial or unsubstantiated information, made inaccurate over-generalizations and then added his own embellishments to boost his largely unfounded arguments.

Given the tone of his op-ed, it is hard to believe that Singer had previously pointed out in his book that there was, "very little examination of the industry from an independent perspective. The topic is exceptionally controversial, with peoples' livelihoods, reputations, and even perhaps the industry's ultimate legality dependent on how academia and policymakers meld to understand it. Unfortunately, the small amount of the qualitative analysis that has been done is often highly polarized from the start, aimed at either extolling the firms to the extent of even comparing them to 'Messiahs' or condemning their mere existence."

Singer added to this, ". . . in turn, these biased findings are often misused by the firms *or by their opponents in pushing their own agendas.*" [Italics added].

Singer's op-ed, in his own words, had placed him among those who use "biased findings" from a "small amount of qualitative analysis" on government contractors to end up "pushing their own agendas" in "condemning their mere existence."

The lasting impression of Singer's op-ed and Singer's previous contradictory public statements was best summed up, it was thought, in another Churchill quote which London conveyed to his team at CACI, "Occasionally he stumbled over the truth but hastily picked himself up and hurried on as if nothing had happened."[497]

However, the most prophetic, cautionary note came from Singer himself, who, before he became an "expert" in the public spotlight, exclaimed in *Corporate Warriors* that "politics and warfare are fundamentally exciting stuff. Of greater significance, they are also matters far too important to be left to the ***so-called experts***." [bold italics added].[498]

---

[497] A reference by Sir Winston Churchill about Stanley Baldwin made in 1936.

[498] Peter W. Singer, *Corporate Warriors*, op. cit.

CHAPTER THIRTY-EIGHT

HOMETOWN HASSLE

CACI fights against an avalanche of bias

"I remain ever vigilant and as you might guess — ever defiant."

~ JACK LONDON E-MAIL TO A FRIEND, AUGUST 25, 2004

A T CACI, SINGER'S SEPTEMBER 12 WASHINGTON POST EDITORIAL blew the cap off a long simmering volcano. In addition to Singer, London held the *Post* accountable for the factual omissions, distortions, and misrepresentations in Singer's editorials.

CACI's response was multi-fold. First, London sent a personal letter to *Post* publisher Donald Graham, addressing the *Post's* failure to verify Singer's claims in his op-ed or check their accuracy with CACI. The CACI team believed the *Post* had failed in its obligation to check facts. They felt the paper had a responsibility to its readers as well as to the subject of the piece (in this case CACI) to verify its accuracy before publication. Attorney Koegel sent a second letter to Singer, pointing out the many gross errors and distortions and asking for retraction. A copy of that letter also went to Strobe Talbott, a former journalist and ambassador to Russia and now president of The Brookings Institution, the Washington, D.C. think tank where Singer was a fellow. Also copied on the letter were Brookings' chairman John L. Thornton and James B. Steinberg, director of Brookings' foreign policy studies. London himself wrote a personal letter to Talbott in which he said that Singer's misstatements reflected poorly on the Brookings Institution.

With Prism's assistance, in late September, London drafted his own editorial for submission to the *Post* to speak to the Singer misrepresentations, but also to make a positive case for the contracting industry and CACI's support of the U.S. Army in Iraq. With the title "Speaking up for Contractors and Our Good Work," London said he accepted the debate about contractors and whether the government was using them effectively. He reiterated his personal commitment to try always "to do the right thing" by honoring CACI's commitments to the army and by addressing and correcting any wrongdoing when it was proven and known to have occurred. However, his final words, the most important message of all, were: "We will not stand silent when facts are twisted to debase our good name."

Jody Brown's task was now to get the editorial published in the *Post*. A little over a week after Singer's piece, Brown and the *Post* Outlook section's Assistant Managing Editor Steve Luxenberg began a series of exchanges regarding publication of an op-ed by CACI's CEO in the Outlook section — where Singer's piece had been published.

To London's dismay, but not surprise, the *Post* turned down his op-ed piece.[499] To him and his colleagues at CACI, the rejection was proof that the *Post* held some significant biases as well. Why else would the *Post* not welcome the opportunity to print an op-ed response to Singer's prominently placed piece (with its bold headline at the top half of the Outlook section page)? Also, London reasoned, shouldn't an editorial by the chairman and CEO of a company accused of participation in the year's biggest and most salacious scandal, which was already covered extensively by major newspapers, be of interest to one of those newspapers and its readers? The only reasonable answer would appear to be yes. But the *Post*'s answer was "no." (In contrast, in the spirit of fairness and balanced reporting, London's original op-ed column was accepted and published by the *Register-Guard* newspaper in Eugene, Oregon, which had also printed the Singer column).[500]

---

[499] The full text of London's final op-ed is presented in Appendix I.

[500] Jack London, "Guest Viewpoint: Prison contractor defends itself," *Oregon Register-Guard*, September 27, 2004.

By now, London and Brown had grown increasingly incensed by the *Post*. They believed the newspaper's biases crept into its coverage of CACI and government contractors in general, many of whom were headquartered in the *Post's* own backyard and provided considerable business for their news coverage. The abuses at Abu Ghraib had seemed to crystallize the *Post's* and its reporters' not-so-subtle opposition to the U.S. and military involvement in the Iraq war.

Before Abu Ghraib, opposition to the war had been somewhat limited. But by providing a way to safely criticize the management of the war, Abu Ghraib became, it seemed, a convenient venue to express opposition to the war in Iraq and the Bush administration's policies.

London and Brown also believed that the *Post* tended to assign inexperienced reporters with insufficient knowledge and perhaps limited interest in government contracting, to cover CACI and its industry. They felt that many *Post* reporters saw the government contracting beat as a stepping stone and weren't truly interested in learning the details of the government contracting world.

The *Post* had assigned a reporter with relatively little experience in government contracting to cover the Abu Ghraib story. Her lack of familiarity with the complex government-contractor relationship was evident in the many errors her articles and their headlines contained, and she seemed to possess little ability to distinguish between facts and fabrications.

Some of CACI's discontent was the inevitable tension between a company that wanted the media to leave it alone or get its story straight, and an aggressive hometown newspaper that wanted to turn out dramatic politically oriented stories as one of the nation's most widely followed news outlets. For the *Post*, Abu Ghraib was both the largest international political story of the moment and also the most important local news story. In addition, it was an increasingly heated election year, in which CACI and Abu Ghraib were convenient political lightning rods. That meant tidbits about CACI that other news outlets might ignore or note only in passing got significant coverage from the *Post*. And because it was the newspaper that nearly every company executive, almost every employee, and a good many customers sat down with at the breakfast table in Washington, each word was likely to be scrutinized and every error hurt the company more.

The *Post's* initial story in June 2004 about CalPERS seemed to CACI to provide crystal-clear evidence of ill will from the newspaper.[501] Angelides had contacted the *Post* about CACI unbeknownst to the company. Most reputable newspapers would have contacted CACI to get the company's comment in order to provide balanced reporting. The story was prominently featured as one of the lead items in the *Post's* business section and ran at significant length. Nobody else had the news, yet the *Post* was pushing it hard. By giving the *Post* the exclusive first look at his letter, which he deviously designed to plant in the press before he had even sent it to CACI, Angelides converted a routine news item into a "scoop" and the *Post* jumped on it. For the newspaper and the "leaker," it was a "win-win." But for CACI, which was purposely put at a disadvantage, it was bad news at a time when the company was being hammered almost daily and was working relentlessly to retain its good name.

London had lost trust in the *Post* and its trickiness, but, even so, he did decide to extend the courtesy of taking its phone calls in hopes that if he told CACI's story often enough, it would ultimately be reflected in the paper's news coverage. However, in the space of five days in August, his view of the situation changed from annoyance to contempt, and a letter of complaint was sent to *Post* publisher Donald Graham.

On August 19, a *Post* reporter had joined others in the press corps with a glowing story on CACI's earnings.[502] But the *Post* article noted, alone among those reporting, that "despite scrutiny from the prison scandal," the company's fourth quarter profits were up 56 percent from the same period the year before. For CACI, the *Post's* continuing and repetitive reporting of the overly negative "old" news created concern that the newspaper's intent was to persist in dragging archaic, irrelevant and biased information into all of its current reporting about CACI.

And four days later on August 23, in a story that reflected an entirely different, yet negative angle, the *Post* featured CACI's acquisition of PTG as a deal gone sour.[503] While PTG was the source of the contract

[501] "Pension Funds Press CACI on Iraq Prison Role," op. cit. *Washington Post*, June 11, 2004.

[502] "Demand Helps CACI Profit Increase 56 percent," *Washington Post*, August 19, 2004.

[503] "Post 9/11 Mergers Brought Problems, Government Service Firms Often Leaped Before They Looked," *Washington Post*, August 23, 2004.

that evolved into interrogation services at Abu Ghraib, CACI considered the acquisition to be a positive one for the company and did not agree with the connection the *Post* was attempting to create. Not only had the acquisition brought in new revenue, as a strategic buyer CACI found that PTG also filled a requirement in the company's capabilities by adding field level intelligence services to CACI's already strong *in situ* strategic intelligence capabilities.

The sub-headline on the story noted that acquirers "often leaped before they looked," implying a lack of due diligence in the mergers and acquisitions process. On the contrary, CACI was (and is) known for conducting thorough and well-managed due diligence programs as one of the leading strategic consolidators in the industry.[504] The *Post* neglected another significant point about PTG, which was totally independent of the acquisition transaction. The fact was that interrogation services for Abu Ghraib were requested by the army in August of 2003, some three months *after* the acquisition closed in May of 2003. There was no way to know, or even predict a *future* contract in due diligence or the idea that the transaction would place CACI on the road to Abu Ghraib, *or* that subsequently providing such services could possibly involve the company with allegations in a controversy over prisoner abuse. Failing to perform due diligence — or "leaping before looking" in the *Post's* words — was not even relevant or remotely close to describing the facts about the CACI/PTG transaction. It was, as CACI people saw it, another of the *Post's* distortions of reality.

And while the *Post's* article noted that the other company featured in the article, ManTech International Inc., had just reported a money-losing quarter, it *failed* to mention CACI's record earnings. This was a stunning, yet obvious, omission considering CACI's earnings story was written just a few days before by the *Post* itself. The CACI team believed the *Post* intentionally omitted the earnings information because it would not support the premise of the article. Beyond being irresponsible, the omission may have actually misled readers, including those in the business community, by implying that CACI, too, was losing money, which could have posed an adverse business impact on the company and its shareholders.

---

[504] In acquiring 40 companies in the past 15 years, CACI's thorough review process is well known in the industry and has resulted in successful acquisitions in every case through December 2007.

The *Post* story also noted that CACI's interrogation contract had been placed under a GSA investigation. But in yet another significant and obvious omission, the *Post* did not inform readers that the inquiry had *ended* with the company being deemed responsible and fully qualified to do business with the government. A reader who did not follow CACI closely might assume from this article that GSA had not yet rendered a decision and might yet impose penalties on CACI that could put the company out of business.

Finally, the article failed to provide the reader with CACI's own assessment of the PTG acquisition even though the company had provided the *Post* with an eight-line statement from CACI's CEO about the deal. While London's statement acknowledged the challenges created by Abu Ghraib, he also observed that the abuse issue did not change the inherent strategic value of the transaction to the company.

"CACI made this investment for the long haul, and even now it is clear that we made a very good deal," London wrote. And he had evidence to back this up from a business perspective. But the *Post's* readers did not get the benefit of the CEO's statement.

London's statement also referenced CACI's record earnings and called PTG "a major driver that contributed significant revenue." *Not one* of London's words appeared in the *Post's* story.

At best, these were careless omissions. At worst, the story was purposefully slanted, and damaging reporting. Each of these failings by the *Washington Post* was recounted by London in an August 24 letter to *Post* publisher Donald Graham.

Initially, the newspaper's response was a *pro forma* dodge. Following London's letter outlining the inherent problems in the *Post's* article about CACI's alleged PTG merger difficulties, the newspaper's associate counsel, Eric Lieberman, offered a weak, evasive response. Instead of acknowledging their faulty reporting and taking responsibility for corrective action, the *Post* put the burden of responsibility on CACI itself for correcting the *Post's* own erroneous reporting on the company. At the same time the *Post* made sure it would control the outcome in terms of whether readers would actually see the corrections. Rather than offering to print a correction, Lieberman told CACI that the company could make its views known by writing to the newspaper's ombudsman or by submitting a letter to the editor or an op-ed for possible publication. Of course it would be the *Post's* decision as to whether a CACI letter to the editor or an op-ed would be printed in the paper (To that point, with Prism's assistance, London did, in fact, shortly thereafter in late September submit an op-ed that the *Post* refused to print).

By now fully aware of the *Post's* modus operandi, London e-mailed a friend on August 25, "I remain ever vigilant and, as you might guess — ever defiant."

A copy of London's letter to the editor was provided to the *Post's* reporter involved and the editors at the paper's business desk. Brown soon received a phone call from the *Post's* business editor, Jill Dutt, to explore the company's grievances. Dutt suggested that she meet personally with London to hear directly from the top about the company's concerns. And on September 6, the *Post* publicly acknowledged the shortcomings of its August 23 mergers article about the alleged problems with the PTG acquisition, as the newspaper had framed it. In a terse five-line correction, the paper reported that GSA "did not curtail CACI's eligibility" for government contracts and conceded: "An August 23 Business article should have included that information."[505]

All of this came off to those at CACI as being "too little too late." They wondered if the *Post* considered the impact that its reporting deficiencies had on the people who read the paper; not just CACI employees and shareholders but the disservice to the public in general who unknowingly consumed the *Post's* deficient and error-prone reporting as a result.

It was also not overlooked by the CACI team that the *Post* editors were probably aware of the pending Singer (September 12) op-ed piece at the time it was talking to CACI about the company's grievances.

Following the subsequent complaints to Graham about the September 12 Singer op-ed and submission of London's responding op-ed, Brown also received a highly unusual call from Luxenberg of the Outlook section, who explained at length why he would *not* publish London's article. What should have been a fairly routine submission turned out to be the exact opposite. First, Luxenberg lectured that the company's submission was not focused enough on the central issues pertaining to Iraq (as if matters related to detainee abuse at Abu Ghraib were not central

---

[505] Correction printed in *Washington Post* Financial Section, September 6, 2004.

to Iraq). He said the piece should not debate what CACI did or did not do, but that it should simply state the facts, which was what the *Post's* readers wanted to know (apparently the *Post* didn't feel that its readers were entitled to the "facts" that had not been accurately portrayed in Singer's op-ed). Luxenberg went on to say that London would have more credibility if he wrote about what happened in Iraq and not debate Peter Singer's piece (perhaps because the *Post* recognized that London's op-ed would likely raise tough questions about the credibility of Singer's op-ed). London and the CACI team found Luxenburg's comments to be wanting — certainly disingenuous. The *Post* allowed Singer to directly target CACI without sticking to the facts, but the newspaper didn't want — would not allow — CACI to respond to his malicious accusations and misrepresentations.

Luxenberg gave Brown two options: one, to resubmit a new piece with a broader perspective related to Iraq; or two, pare down what CACI had originally submitted and address it as a letter to the editor. The phone call from Luxenberg was an obvious signal that the newspaper had noted CACI's complaints but that it would not do anything about them.

Luxenberg's call may have also reflected CACI's decision to send its piece to Lieberman, the in-house lawyer, instead of the Outlook desk directly, and to ask Lieberman to coordinate publication. In a subsequent note, Lieberman told CACI that the decision about publication would be handled by the editors in the normal course of business. But he also noted that he had forwarded the piece and "explained the background of the submission."

On September 30, Brown submitted CACI's revised Outlook piece.[506] This version was an explanation of the contracting industry and CACI's role in Iraq. The piece briefly responded to general criticism the company had received, but avoided addressing Singer or his specific remarks. The CACI team felt confident that this new piece, as guided by the *Post*, ought to be accepted. Luxenberg responded in an e-mail that he would review the submission "to see if it works for Outlook. If not, I will let you know." He never did. The piece on which the CACI team had worked diligently in good faith and with the newspaper's guidance (even attempting to incorporate editor Luxem-

---

[506] See Appendix I.

berg's illogical and restrictive suggestions) would never be published by the *Post* in any form. The *Post* had orchestrated its predictable "runaround" and validated its reputation for pervasive editorial bias and arrogance.

One of the *Post's* principles, as laid down by founder Eugene Meyer, was that "The newspaper shall not be the ally of any special interest, but shall be fair and free and wholesome in its outlook on public affairs and public men."[507] This statement, if truly representative of the *Post*, would seem to have afforded the opportunity for the publication of CACI's op-ed. But CACI would not be given equal time in offering a response to Singer's "special interest" indictment and allegations.

Soon after, publisher Graham also placed a phone call to London. Graham declared that as a matter of policy, he did not interfere with the news operation or tell his people what to write. It came across as one more effort by the *Post* to make more excuses for itself. The phone call also signaled that London's mission to stand up for his company and push back on mischaracterizations and falsehoods about CACI had, at least, made the *Post* take some notice. London used the brief conversation to directly convey his belief that the newspaper's coverage was unbalanced and biased against CACI.

Whereas other corporate executives might have suffered in silence in homage to the dictum against taking issue with somebody "who buys ink by the barrel," London had lived by his personal commitment to set the record straight. And he was going to do it — no matter what.

Much less dramatically, the *Post* drew an important demarcation line in October 2004 when, for the first time since April, it wrote a Business section article about CACI that treated the company as it would any other contractor. In an October 28, 2004 report, the newspaper included CACI in a report about strong revenue growth among government contractors in the Washington, D.C. area. Most significantly, the article omitted what had become for the *Post* an obligatory reference to CACI's connection to Abu Ghraib.[508]

In an e-mail to Brown and others at CACI, Prism PR consultant Don Foley noted the absence of the "obligatory language." "The fact that

---

[507] Eugene Meyer's Principles for The Washington Post (http://www.washpost.com/gen_info/principles/index.shtml).

[508] "Washington Contractors' Sales Increase," *Washington Post*, October 28, 2004.

CACI is lumped with two other firms that are enjoying renewed success is heartening as well," Foley added.

While CACI continued to fight against unbalanced, untruthful, and factually inaccurate coverage from the media, the impact of the bad publicity — unjustified tarnish — on its relationship with its customers was beginning to be felt. CACI had remained highly regarded among the military on the ground and in the field, but some were becoming aware that communications within the army in Washington had been noting the "political" pressure on the army of "breaking off" with CACI.

Although the Department of the Army, still under an intense negative media attack, was believed and rumored to have looked at alternative contractor support to replace CACI in the fall of 2004, it did not do so. The company's reports received from the army in Baghdad consistently indicated that CACI was doing good work there. And from the way CACI saw the situation in Iraq, it was a vitally important matter to maintain the continuity of interrogator support services so as to not leave the army in the lurch on this critical aspect of its mission.

The fall of 2004 also saw major terrorist attacks in several important cities in Iraq, and CACI worked hard, and with considerable difficulty, in its effort to maintain its support team in the face of these increasing dangers. The task was formidable and not without serious challenges. In the fall of 2004, nevertheless, a decision was made by the army to put the CACI interrogator contract out for competitive bid (to be awarded in the middle of 2005).

As the cloud of crisis lifted somewhat, CACI also received some praise for its crisis management response.

SmartMoney, a personal business magazine published by Dow Jones Inc., noted in its October 1, 2004 issue that CACI's "vigorous defense and its clearance to continue doing government work suggest shareholders stay the course."[509] The UBS Investment house, in a report to investors on October 14, similarly lauded "the company's zealousness to disseminate the facts" and said "management's protection of its reputation should not be underestimated." UBS assigned a "buy" rating to CACI's stock and set a price target of $65.[510] In fact, as early as August,

---

[509] Eleanor Laise, "Street Smart: Update," *SmartMoney*, October 1, 2004.

[510] "CACI International: Sitting in the 'Sweet Spot' Initiated With Buy 1," UBS Investment Research, October 14, 2004.

Amy Tsao, writing in *Business Week*, saw signs that CACI troubles had run their course. "CACI has a proven track record and deep government connections. That probably bodes well for the future," she opined.[511]

The upbeat forecasts turned out to be prescient as CACI's shares had just begun a stunning ascent that would drive their price to $68.13 on the last day of 2004 — a gain of 41 percent for the year and an astonishing 83 percent increase from the year's low point on May 28, when the GSA's decision to investigate CACI was made public. London could rightly claim the CACI team had done their jobs — and then some — in justifiably defending and preserving CACI's "good name."

---

[511] Amy Tsao, "CACI: Wiping Off Abu Ghraib's Taint," op. cit.

CHAPTER THIRTY-NINE

CACI'S VIGILANCE PREVAILING

Back to business, but with lessons learned and questions lingering

"[CACI's] vigorous defense and its clearance to continue doing government work suggest shareholders stay the course."
〜 *SMART MONEY*, OCTOBER 1, 2004

WITHIN DAYS OF SINGER'S OP-ED COLUMN IN THE *WASHINGTON Post*, CACI encountered another flurry of media coverage when lawyers for the Center for Constitutional Rights asked a federal court to order CACI to provide sixteen weeks of interrogation training before it sent civilian interrogators to Iraq. CCR also asked for access to the personnel files of every CACI employee in Iraq. The injunction request attracted coverage from the Associated Press and Reuters, wire services whose stories were reprinted in newspapers worldwide. However, the judge declined an immediate ruling and, in fact, never did rule on the CCR request for injunctive relief. Then the press moved on — not just from the lawsuit, but from the issue of CACI and Abu Ghraib.

After nearly five months in the media's grip, CACI was being gradually released. In the months ahead, the company's name would turn up frequently in Abu Ghraib stories — usually, as a passing reference in a longer story or a brief item that soon vanished. The trend shifted to

CACI being referenced more often by those who used dated and often incorrect media reports, opinion articles and blogs to promote a particular (usually political, extremist, self-interest, or mean-spirited) viewpoint.

Still, the *Post's* local coverage had been unrelenting and unforgiving over that first year following the *New Yorker's* publication of its *illegally leaked* Taguba report article and the TV broadcast of the abuse photos on CBS's *60 Minutes II*. In fact, between the time the story broke in late April 2004 and the end of year, the *Post* had published over forty articles and items on CACI and Abu Ghraib. This figure seemed even more excessive considering that Abu Ghraib stories landed on the front page of the *Post* some five dozen times in the same period.

The issue of detainee abuse at Abu Ghraib, Guantanamo Bay, and in Afghanistan, would continue to pepper the news. Often, the new allegations were attributed to government documents or reports from government agencies. But *none* of the new abuse allegations touched on CACI, and the mainstream media mostly stopped bringing up CACI's name. As Abu Ghraib became less significant to the press, its interest in CACI apparently subsided as well.

The mainstream media's eventual disinterest in CACI was most evident when the names of former CACI interrogators surfaced at the court martial trial of U.S. Army Specialist Charles Graner, the alleged ringleader and much-photographed Abu Ghraib soldier among the military police. At this point, however, the media bypassed the opportunity to talk about CACI. At the start of the Abu Ghraib story, in May 2004 alone, the *Washington Post* had printed twenty stories that focused on CACI or contracting issues related to the company. But in January 2005, when a witness at Graner's court martial referenced CACI's employees, the *Post* did not name the company or the interrogators.[512] The *Los Angeles Times* and the *New York Times* also passed up the potential chance to draw CACI back into the scandal.[513] While satisfied in being passed over, the handling of the story raised a question to CACI leadership: if CACI was so significant in May 2004 when there was only a suspicion expressed and relevant investigations were incomplete, why did

[512] "Witness: Graner Ordered to Beat Prisoners," *Washington Post*, January 13, 2005.

[513] Richard A. Serrano, "Friendly Fire at Abu Ghraib Case,"*Los Angeles Times*, January 13, 2005; Kate Zernike, "Soldiers Testify on Orders to Soften Prisoners in Iraq," *New York Times*, January 13, 2005.

it matter so little less than a year later at the time the investigations were concluded and the truth was becoming more and more clear about its employees' limited role? Why was the early news on allegations of guilt so much more important than news now about the lack of proof for such allegations?

The shift may have reflected the short attention span of daily journalism. In the jargon of the trade, things that didn't happen today were "old news" and "yesterday's story." Or perhaps the *Washington Post* explained the difference on December 13 when it took a look at the year's events and concluded that "contractor employees played a more limited role in abusing prisoners at Abu Ghraib than initially suggested."[514] Getting to this truth had been CACI's driving purpose in its media response efforts, which had cost the company a tremendous amount of money and management effort. What's more, the unfortunate reality was not just that the company had been maligned by the media in its inaccurate and false reporting, but that the ordeal could have presented a considerable distraction to CACI from the critical work the company was performing for the nation's security. While this was not the case, it was the enduring commitment of CACI's dedicated professional and technical staff that continued to sustain the company's standard for excellence.

While far from a *mea culpa*, the *Post's* December 2004 retrospective carried concessions that the media may have omitted key context in its many early reports about CACI — an astonishing admission considering CACI's concerted effort to regularly inform the public. Journalists would likely say that they exercised "news judgment" when they decided to circulate news about CACI without supporting evidence.

And they would likely use the same argument when they decided that CACI wasn't really important when covering the Graner court martial. The lack of evidence against CACI's employees, apparently, was of no interest. But this is a weak argument given the emphasis that Graner's attorneys had put on the role of contractors in their client's defense during the story's early stages. The *Post's* December retrospective, in effect, publicly acknowledged the media's overexposure, if not obsession, with the Abu Ghraib contractor interrogation support topic when it was first leaked.

---

[514] "Changes Behind the Barbed Wire," op. cit.

Writing with months of hindsight, the *Post's* reporter observed that news articles about the Fay report focused on the graphic descriptions of abuse, but "little attention was paid to its conclusions about the military's failure to provide adequate oversight of contract workers." In recounting accusations that Stefanowicz had improperly allowed an unmuzzled dog in the room during an interrogation, the *Post* report noted Fay's observation that the civilian had been encouraged to take an assertive approach by a military training officer. That exculpatory fact was omitted in most of the initial media reporting about the Fay report. And in this latest story, the *Post* reporter quoted at length the conclusion of Stefanowicz's attorney, who said the Fay report "drastically back-pedaled" from Taguba's sweeping accusations about Stefanowicz's level of responsibility.[515]

The *Post's* December report, the only significant CACI-related Abu Ghraib story in the mainstream media after mid-September 2004, drew attention back to the company. But it also provided beneficial, if modest, concessions from the newspaper, which CACI could point to as evidence that the allegations against it were overblown. The company also felt it could credit its own tenacity for the story being published at all. It was believed that the retrospective was the fruit of an October 4 meeting between the *Post*, London, and Brown following the CEO's late summer complaints to *Post* publisher Graham about its slanted reporting. After the meeting, the *Post* representatives stated that it was probably time to "take another look" while also cautioning London that he "might not like the results."[516] Though the resulting article was not entirely satisfying to CACI in providing a comprehensive account of matters to fully set the record straight, the CACI team felt that without the company's persistence the *Post* article probably would not have been printed.

The muted concessions by the *Post* in December 2004, however, could never undo the hundreds of thousands of words in many hun-

---

[515] Ibid.

[516] London had noted to Brown immediately after the meeting that the *Post's* comments about CACI not liking the results of a coming article seemed to convey clearly the newspaper's anti-CACI bias. If the *Post* had approached the article idea objectively, why would it have felt compelled to warn London, Brown, and CACI ahead of time?

dreds (perhaps thousands) of news reports around the world from May to December 2004. But CACI's story was now on the record. The company's diligent presentation of the facts — the "Truth Will Out" — was now available to historians on the company's Web site and in its news releases.

* * *

As for CalPERS and CalSTRS, the company's stock proved to be a great performer. For all of 2004, the value of the two funds' holdings in CACI would climb steadily. Since the day of Angelides' first letter challenging the company's management because of Abu Ghraib, to the end of the year, the share price had risen almost 74 percent, adding $8.3 million to the value of the funds' portfolio. In an August interview on CNNfn, Angelides had tied his concerns about CACI to the decline in CACI's share price as a result of Abu Ghraib. But Angelides never publicly acknowledged the stock's strong resurgence when his doom-sayer predictions proved wrong.

The two funds continued to goad CACI publicly and privately over Abu Ghraib and persisted in challenging the company to consider managerial change. The funds linked their renewed agitation to the retirement of Ken Johnson, the company's president of U.S. operations, who had led the CACI team that met with the funds in Sacramento and who had assured them that he had assumed personal responsibility for the hiring of new interrogators. On September 30, Johnson, who was approaching retirement age, had announced that he would step down on November 1, to pursue personal interests and spend more time with his family.

On October 15, in a private letter to London, CalSTRS CEO Jack Ehnes claimed concern about Johnson's departure. Ehnes said Johnson's assumption of personal responsibility "allowed us to believe that the crisis described in the press and in the reports by General Fay and Jones was being handled at the highest level." It seemed preposterous to London and other senior managers that Ehnes would actually think Johnson was the only responsible CACI executive and that Johnson's departure would leave a vacuum. More telling, they found it hard to believe that Ehnes was still taking his cues from the press instead of talking to CACI. But Johnson's departure presented another opportunity for

CalSTRS to revive their protests, and Ehnes complained, "We remain unconvinced that the Company had conducted an adequate risk assessment associated with supplying interrogation services." Ehnes proposed a review by members of CACI's independent board of directors.

Continuing with their contrasting styles, CalPERS requested a review by the CACI Board of Directors in, not surprisingly, a *public* meeting at CalPERS three days later. Angelides promptly issued a press release taking credit for the CalPERS' action. "CACI's Board of Directors must independently investigate the breakdown of management, leadership and discipline at CACI. . . . It must fully and promptly get all the facts out into the open and reform the company's practices," Angelides said.[517] His references to a CACI "breakdown" left those in the company and on its board wondering how Angelides could possibly have failed to see the favorable comments reported about interrogators in the numerous investigations that had been recently completed. And his remarks about getting all the facts out in the open, left CACI wondering if he had ignored or totally missed the persistent efforts of the company to disseminate and make available as much information as possible. Puzzling, too, was the fact that the funds did not acknowledge that CACI had enhanced the fund's financial value during the year. But clearly this was simply more selective ignoring of the vital facts by Angelides and the California funds.

Ironically, the CalPERS action took place on the same day that a blistering editorial in the *Wall Street Journal*, "CalPERS and Cronyism," criticized the fund for its refusal to disclose its own investment management and advisory fees. Although stopping short of specific accusations, the editorial noted that some who benefited from CalPERS' investment decisions had contributed to either Angelides' or State Comptroller Steve Westly's political campaigns.[518] In its own press release responding to Angelides, CACI noted the *Journal's* editorial. And in a direct challenge, London invited the funds to sell their CACI stock.

---

[517] California State Treasurer's Office Press Release, "CalPERS, CalSTRS, at Treasurer Angelides' urging, to call on CACI board to conduct full investigation and hold management responsible for interrogators' conduct at Iraq prison; Latest U.S. Army Investigation Found CACI Contract Interrogators Deeply Involved In 'Inhumane to Sadistic' Abuses," op. cit.

[518] "CalPERS and Cronyism," *Wall Street Journal*, October 18, 2004.

"If Angelides and the fund want to walk away from a more than 50 percent return on their investment since August of this year in CACI, we fully support their decision," London stated.

In a private letter to Ehnes, CACI board member Dr. Warren R. Phillips, chairman of the board's corporate governance and nominating committee, firmly rebuffed Ehnes' request for board action. Phillips noted that the company had provided CalSTRS with voluminous written material and answered questions personally in Sacramento — "a level of attention from CACI that is disproportionate to your stock holdings and nearly unprecedented." He noted that CalSTRS representatives indicated at that time that they were satisfied with the company's response and that CalSTRS's silence between August 2 and October 15 seemed to confirm that satisfaction. He rejected the notion that Johnson's departure changed the situation in any way. And, as in the CACI public press release, Phillips observed matter of factly:

"At this point, if CalSTRS feels that the future risk of its investment in CACI is unacceptable, you are certainly welcome to sell your shares and take your gains."

Other exchanges, out of view of the media, occurred between the company and the funds for the balance of the year. CACI refused any more accommodation and, despite their complaints, the funds held onto their shares. The decision to retain the shares was explicitly confirmed by CalSTRS' Janice Hester-Amey in a Thanksgiving eve e-mail on November 24 in which she told Dave Dragics it was time "to try to lower the temperature a bit" and added, "First and foremost, we are a CACI shareholder and will remain a CACI shareholder so long as the current Investment Management Plan stays in place and we don't foresee a change." In the end, the funds listened not to Angelides' foreboding, but to their own financial interests.

Then, in the first week of December, CalPERS President Sean Harrigan was ousted from his post by the State Personnel Board on a three-to-two vote. One Democrat who had long supported Harrigan joined two Republicans in a move hailed by those who thought CalPERS was spending too much time on corporate governance activism. Though ostensibly the result of issues unrelated to the fracas with CACI, Harrigan's firing and the subsequent negative press directed to the funds was favorably received by those at CACI who had long restrained their frustrations while enduring the previous months of harassment from the funds.

But London's resolute efforts, at least, did not go unnoticed. The impression London apparently left on the investor community was summed up by one investor representative who, after CACI's January 25, 2005 earnings release conference call, was quoted in the feedback session as saying, "I would never want to be on Jack London's bad side. He's a man of unique words in this business. He says what's on his mind and it's refreshing. The best example of that is the clown at CalPERS, the government hack there, saying all kinds of horrible things about the company, trying to make himself look good. He's a poor Eliot Spitzer. The response from CACI was absolutely refreshing. I had never seen Jack London and I had this picture of George C. Scott, he has that voice. He is unique in our business as far as calling a spade a spade."[519]

* * *

Also moving on during the fall of 2004 was Steven Stefanowicz. By mutual agreement, Stefanowicz quietly departed CACI in late October 2004. On October 26, 2004, Stefanowicz submitted his resignation letter to a CACI senior project manager with whom he had coordinated throughout his time at the company. "While accomplishments are gratifying, the achievement drives us beyond our previous expectations," wrote Stefanowicz. "I thank you and CACI for an unparalleled opportunity to grow, which has allowed me to prepare for my next challenge." For six months after withdrawing him from Iraq, CACI had kept Stefanowicz on the payroll on administrative leave, without assigning him to contract project work. Convinced that CACI had done the honorable thing by providing support at a time that the Abu Ghraib controversy would have made it hard for Stefanowicz to find work, London was now comfortable with CACI severing the ties. Both company and employee felt it was time to close the chapter.

The company did not announce the departure publicly, though a notice was posted internally. Given the continuing investigation by the Department of Justice (DOJ), CACI did not want to say anything that might compromise that inquiry. After the fateful period in late 2003 at

---

[519] CACI Teleconference Feedback Report, Christensen & Associates, January 25, 2005.

Abu Ghraib, some four years later, as 2007 drew to a close, neither Stefanowicz nor any other CACI employee had been charged with wrongdoing by DOJ or any other legal body or jurisdiction. It was not known, however, whether DOJ would file charges or how it would ultimately conclude the matter. It was possible the former contractor employees could remain in the limbo of an "open investigation" for some time to come.

* * *

The two lawsuits against CACI and Titan continued with a series of legal maneuvers, including a bid by CCR to take over the second lawsuit. In the unique universe of legal posturing, CCR argued that the second suit on behalf of individual plaintiffs was a "copycat" suit that should be folded into its larger class action suit. In that instance, the legal alliances shifted temporarily as CACI's attorneys and the private lawyers who were suing the company both opposed the CCR motion. As 2004 came to a close and 2005 was emerging, the suits were proceeding separately. The courts weighed CCR's bid to enjoin the second detainee abuse lawsuit from proceeding, as well as CACI's motions for summary judgment. By their own admission, the plaintiffs were struggling to build their case. In a report sympathetic to CCR's suit, the left-leaning *New Standard* said, "[CCR] lawyers on the case admit they have yet to uncover a smoking gun connecting the private contractors to torture."[520]

Meanwhile, amid an ongoing public debate about the proper use of contract employees, CACI continued to provide a range of tactical support services, including intelligence and interrogation, to U.S. forces in Iraq. The risks of the enterprise were driven home in January of 2005 after several CACI employees narrowly escaped serious injury and death when a rocket attack killed two Americans at a contract office inside Baghdad's heavily guarded Green Zone. The rocket, which failed to explode, landed next to the desk of a CACI employee who was on leave to visit his family in the U.S.

Although the various official investigations had concluded that the abuses seen in the Abu Ghraib photos were unrelated to interrogation practices, there were concerns among some in the military that the backlash from the abuse scandal would make it harder to effectively gather information from detainees.

---

[520] Lisa Ashkenaz Croke, "Iraq Torture Investigators Reveal Scores of New Cases," *The New Standard*, December 31, 2004.

"Interrogators and detainees both know what the limits are. . . . They know that if the United States captures them, they will get a medical exam. They'll get their teeth fixed. They will get essentially a free physical and they will be released if they don't talk after a certain amount of time," one army officer told *World* magazine in January 2005.[521]

In February 2005, U.S. Army Provost Marshall General Donald Ryder, the major general whose own review (in fall 2003) of Abu Ghraib preceded Taguba's, said the army was changing the way it would train for, and conduct, detention operations. Ryder said the army wanted to address some of the problems that contributed to abuse. He also announced that the army had retooled its interrogation field manual for the first time since 1992. "It will be clearly laid out in policy . . . [to] clarify the rules and responsibilities of everyone who works inside the correctional facilities," Ryder told reporters.[522]

Also in a February 2005 column in the *Washington Post*, Republican Senator Lindsey Graham, a colonel in the U.S. Air Force Reserve, and Democratic Representative Jane Harman jointly called for a comprehensive review of interrogation techniques. After Abu Ghraib, many Americans seemed to erroneously consider interrogation to be a synonym for torture. This was most likely due to the loose use of the words "abuse" and "torture" by the media and other commentators without consideration or knowledge of their definitions and real meanings. This was further obfuscated by the oft-times inappropriate use of the word "interrogation" and "interrogator"; and further still by the inaccurate, less frequent use of the word "intelligence."[523] Graham and Harman noted that interrogation is a standard way to gain information in addressing domestic crime and in warfare as well. But they insisted that it must be done properly "to ensure that we gather needed information without giving America a black eye."[524]

---

[521] John Dawson, "Stunted Intelligence," *World*, January 29, 2005.

[522] "Army Revisiting Policies," *Washington Post*, February 24, 2005.

[523] It is important to note that according to *Webster's' New World Dictionary and Thesaurus* (2nd Edition), the terms "interrogate" and "torture" are *not* synonyms nor do they otherwise refer to each other in either the definition or the thesaurus sections therein. The term "abuse" also does not show the word "torture" as a synonym. See further: Glossary and Terms of Interest.

[524] Sen. Lindsey Graham and Rep. Jane Harman, "Clearing the Fog on Interrogations," *Washington Post*, February 19, 2005.

But it was not clear to everyone whether the corrective actions being instituted were properly balanced. Retired general Barry McCaffrey in early 2006 reflected and reported on the U.S. military's progress in Iraq and made note of the detention and interrogation policy situation. In discussing Abu Ghraib, he said, "We may be in danger of over-correcting. The AIF (al Qaeda Insurgent Force) are exploiting our overly restrictive procedure and are routinely defying the U.S. interrogators. . . . It is widely believed that the U.S. has a 'fourteen-day catch and release policy' and the AIF 'Suspect' will soon be back in action." He further commented, "This is an overstatement of reality, however, we do have a problem. Many of the AIF detainees routinely accuse U.S. soldiers of abuse under the silliest factual situations knowing it will trigger an automatic investigation."[525]

CACI's business, however, was constantly moving forward. Despite the loss of a small contract in the U.K. and the withdrawal from a few contract competitions while the company was in the process of addressing the Abu Ghraib issue, the company's business performance itself was largely unaffected in the first few months of the ordeal. In fact, CACI's fiscal 2004 earnings report (for fiscal year ending June 30, 2004) released in August 2004 was among its best ever.

From a business perspective, however, the most damaging political fallout for CACI would come in mid-2005 when the army's intelligence and interrogator support contract in Iraq, then valued at about $60 million a year, was awarded to another government contractor, L-3 Communications, a former subcontractor to CACI. The new contract to L-3 was valued in the range of $450 million over a five-year period. The overall amount of this award would far exceed the value of all the earlier interrogation contracts to CACI.[526]

---

[525] General Barry R. McCaffrey, USA (Ret), "Iraq and Kuwait, Observations from Iraqi Freedom," *West Point Academic Report*, April 2006.

[526] However, in December 2006 L-3 Communications lost its bid to continue the contract to provide translators in Iraq. This was reportedly the largest program for L-3 generating $600 million its last year representing 5 percent of the company's $12 billion revenue. CACI's former interrogator contract gave L-3 *both* the interrogator and linguistics contracts in Iraq that had been previously held, respectively, by CACI and Titan (which was acquired by L-3).

Those at CACI would recall the e-mails that had been circulating within army offices in the late summer of 2004 questioning the political necessity of "breaking" from CACI when the media was still applying intense pressure on the army for its decision, at the time, to continue with CACI's interrogation services contract.

It was not long afterward that Singer's September 12 op-ed in the *Post* (headlined "The Contract the Military Needs to Break") issued its overt admonition to the army not to contract again with CACI for these services. Yet all along, in the field, the army customers had been reporting to CACI management that the company's work was going well.

Of particular note and importance, the army's announced contracting decision in July of 2005 allowed for the new contractor, L-3, *to retain members of the CACI workforce in Iraq*. This was further *positive proof* that CACI's hiring plan had been successful and met the original requirements such that all its employees were obviously considered qualified to remain on site and continue their work in Iraq. The L-3 plans, including the hiring of CACI staff, CACI officials were told by the government, would rapidly meet the army's increased interrogation staffing needs in Iraq. This fact by itself immediately eliminated all of the earlier accusations stating that CACI had an untrained and unqualified staff. *Clearly CACI's interrogator staffing had not been a real issue in the first place and would not have drawn any public attention at all had it not been for the Abu Ghraib scandal.* But the media's wrongful damage to CACI was ultimately real *and* costly.

In September 2005, some members of the CACI team remained in Iraq, hired on by the new contractor, while others decided to move on. CACI continued to focus on and build its information technology and program support services to the army and to the intelligence community overall.

The people of CACI still felt good that they had stepped up and stood ready when called upon by the army in time of need during urgent wartime conditions in a combat zone. CACI and its executives would remember that it was their team that was there at the critical time in the very beginning — at the most undefined and challenging time when the foundation was first being laid. They had worked hard to fill the void and meet the need, and would always be proud of having done so.

* * *

Nevertheless, for CACI, the scars of wrongful media reporting would remain for quite some time. The private lawsuits would continue to run their course, and the company would continue to defend itself against those baseless claims vigorously and aggressively. CACI all along reported the suits to be without merit.

The company's name would continue to surface from time to time in a news story about Abu Ghraib, prisoner abuse, the Iraq war, or government contract matters. Because of a few unsubstantiated allegations in Major General Taguba's illegally leaked report, and the media's sensationalism, CACI would continue to be linked in some degree to Abu Ghraib even though CACI's work there is long finished and the prison is gone.[527]

For all of this, CACI would always have lingering questions.

How is it that the illegally leaked Taguba report documents did not result in an effort to discover the law-breaker who divulged classified information (SECRET/NO FOREIGN DISSEMINATION) that damaged America's image, threatened national security, and put Americans everywhere at risk?

Why weren't self-declared "expert commentators" challenged for their reckless speculations and inaccurate assertions? And why weren't individuals with personal political agendas called to task for their malicious and self-serving attacks?

Throughout the entire Abu Ghraib ordeal, there was no discussion about the person who had illegally leaked the Taguba report to Seymour Hersh in April of 2004. But despite the failure to pursue the Taguba report leak in 2004, in 2005 illegal leaks became big news. And this trend continued into 2006.

The first major publicized illegal leak was that of the identity of CIA operative Valerie Plame in June 2005 and how it related to her husband Joe Wilson, a U.S. foreign service diplomat who had been critical of the Bush administration and the Iraq war. The allegations of perjury and

---

[527] By December 2007, upon the completion of writing of this book, no government charges or indictments had been brought in any jurisdiction against any CACI employee or former employee.

cover-up resulted in the indictment of Scooter Libby, chief of staff to Vice President Dick Cheney.[528]

There would be more controversy about leaks in the months following the Plame case. In late December 2005, DOJ opened a criminal investigation into illegal leaks of classified information to the *New York Times* after the newspaper had reported on warrantless surveillance authorized by President George W. Bush and conducted by the National Security Agency since the September 11, 2001 terrorist attacks.[529] The surveillance program focused on international telephone calls by individuals in America communicating with suspected terrorists outside of the U.S. Editors at the *New York Times*, who were awarded a Pulitzer Prize for the story, indicated that they had sat on the story for nearly a year before releasing it. The release was viewed by some to be timed to coincide with the reauthorization of the Patriot Act and to upstage the Iraqi elections.[530]

In November of 2005, the Justice Department also initiated probes into leaks to the *Washington Post* of classified and unclassified information on alleged secret CIA prisons in Eastern Europe. The *Post's* Dana Priest was rewarded for reporting information based apparently on an illegal leak, by receiving a Pulitzer Prize on April 17, 2006 for her stories about secret U.S. detention centers in Europe. Her reports were reportedly derived from *illegally leaked* classified information or information that was provided by a CIA agent.[531]

Perhaps not coincidentally, a veteran CIA employee was fired in 2006 just ten days before her retirement for unauthorized contacts with

---

[528] The Plame leak was first revealed by reporter Bob Novak who confirmed in July 2006 that presidential advisor Karl Rove was one of his sources. Later, Richard Armitage, former Deputy Secretary of State to Colin Powell, was revealed publicly as one of the individuals who had named Ms. Plame. The disclosure was not the result of an investigation, but was reported publicly as a voluntary and inadvertent revelation by Armitage to reporters Bob Novak and Bob Woodward. Veteran journalists Michael Isikoff and David Corn write about these events in *Hubris: The Inside Story of Spin, Scandal, and the Selling of the Iraq War* (Crown, 2006).

[529] Toni Locy, "Justice Dept. Probing Domestic Spying Leak," Associated Press, December 30, 2005; Dan Eggen, "Justice Dept. Investigating Leak of NSA Wiretapping. Probe Seeks Source of Classified Data." *Washington Post*, December 31, 2005.

[530] Kelly Beaucar Vlahos, "Leaks Continued to Flow in 2006," FOXNews.com, January 2, 2007.

[531] David S. Broder, "Tension Over Press Leaks," *Washington Post*, April 27, 2006.

the press. It was suspected that she had leaked classified information to reporters, including allegations of secret CIA-run prisons in Eastern Europe to a *Washington Post* reporter.[532]

A few months later, in the summer of 2006, the *New York Times* revealed that it had information about how the U.S. government was monitoring banking and financial transactions in a highly secretive project in efforts to identify terrorist activity and plans. The DOJ again initiated an investigation.[533]

Leaks continued to gain momentum throughout 2006 likely fueled, at least in part, by the potential for being recognized with a prestigious award — in the form of a Pulitzer. FOX News stated, "The drip, drip, drip of government leaks continued to plunge the Bush administration into defense mode in 2006, dominating headlines and prompting calls from supporters to prosecute not only leakers but also the journalists."[534] In September 2006 findings from a classified intelligence report were *illegally leaked* to the *New York Times.* Included in the report's observations were that the war on terror in Iraq had increased the threat of violence there and the war was also being used as a recruiting tool for terrorists.[535]

In November 2006, ironically, a memo written by the National Security Advisor Stephen Hadley to the White House expressing concern about the ability of Iraq's prime minister to control Iraq's sectarian violence was leaked. The memo which continued the growing pattern of leaks to the *New York Times* was again timed to coincide with a key event in the government, the scheduled visit between President Bush and the Iraqi prime minister.[536]

In early December 2006, a letter that had been written by Secretary of Defense Donald Rumsfeld in November before his resignation was leaked. The letter, which was also predictably leaked to the *New York Times*, discussed Rumsfeld's concerns about the current Iraq war strategy.[537]

---

[532] Ibid.

[533] Kelly Beaucar Vlahos, "Leaks Continued to Flow in 2006," op. cit.

[534] Ibid.

[535] Ibid.

[536] Ibid.

[537] Ibid.

This slew of sensitive leaks drew immediate fire from several directions including the White House. President Bush reacted by stating, ". . . I do think that at some point in time it would be helpful if we can find somebody inside our government who is leaking materials — *clearly against the law* [italics added] — that they be held to account. Perhaps the best way to make sure people don't leak classified documents is that there be a consequence for doing so."[538]

Rep. Peter King (R-NY) the then-chairman of the House Homeland Security Committee called the leaks on bank transactions and the publication of their details "treasonous." King accused the *New York Times* of violating the 1917 Espionage Act and a Cold War-era law restricting publication of communications containing intelligence secrets. "The activities of the *New York Times* are shameful and irresponsible, and put Americans all over the world at risk by identifying sources and methods and warning our adversaries of our capabilities and techniques," King stated.

"It's just bad for the country," stated James Carafano, national security expert at the Heritage Foundation. "There are plenty of mechanisms for people to uncover others who are using secrecy to lie or conceal mistakes."[539] And while this is a true statement, it fails to recognize the primary, perhaps only, reason leaks are made to the media — for political impact.

Unfortunately, no one who made the illegal leaks in the Abu Ghraib case will likely ever be held accountable for breaking the law despite the many harmful repercussions. Abuses were already under investigation at Abu Ghraib and had been publicly reported to the press, so the whistleblower protections would seem to be inapplicable here. But more importantly, it begs the question, When such laws are broken, are there no consequences or penalties for the law-breakers?[540]

The leak did not seem to serve the purpose of revealing an unknown situation or exposing a "cover up." To the contrary, the premature and

---

[538] Ibid.

[539] "Little is Clear in Laws on Leaks," *Washington Post*, April 28, 2006

[540] It is reasonable to assume that whistleblower protections are not immunity from the criminal act (felony) of disclosing or making public, U.S. government-classified security documents. There are over fifty federal whistleblower disclosure laws (including some for the military), which protect workers from retaliation or other illegal treatment for *lawful* acts. They do not protect whistleblowers from willfully breaking the law themselves.

illegal release of partial investigation results through public dissemination of Taguba's report and the abuse photos (without the benefit of comprehensive conclusions drawn from the entire investigative process) created disastrous results.

As noted in a 2005 *Wall Street Journal* editorial, "The abuse reports went up the chain of command on January 13 last year; within a day an Army criminal probe had been started. Two days after that, Central Command issued a press release notifying the world of that investigation; on March 20 it was announced in Baghdad that criminal charges had been brought against six of the soldiers involved. A month earlier, meanwhile, Major General Antonio Taguba had completed an internal investigation of what had happened. This is all *before* the infamous photos were *leaked* to the press. . . . [italics added]"[541] The U.S. government and the military appears to have responded promptly to the abuse matter and responsibly notified the public through the press.

Inordinate and prolonged emphasis placed by the media on the Abu Ghraib scandal caused a nuclear chain reaction that would likely not have occurred if investigations could have unfolded uninterrupted by media overexposure. One can only speculate how better it would have been for investigators to arrive at their conclusions in a logical, objective manner with their proven findings announced at the end of the entire investigative process, after all of the facts, results and conclusions were established.

Many would argue that in the glare of the media's sensationalized, 24/7 obsession with every angle of the Abu Ghraib story which continued to drag on in the ensuing months of the investigation, the long term permanent damage was already done. There are those who might further argue that the damage done as a result of Abu Ghraib was disproportionate — to America's image, to the military's mission, to the U.S. government's efforts, to contractor reputations, and to Americans everywhere who were threatened, attacked and killed as a result.[542]

---

[541] "Abu Ghraib Accountability," op. cit.

[542] It is an irony that the Abu Ghraib abuse photographs depicting the tragic behavior of a relatively few rogue soldiers, who were part of a larger, noble mission to free a nation (Operation Iraqi Freedom), have been given such protracted worldwide exposure when the videotapes of the Abu Ghraib atrocities of Saddam Hussein, the dictator who enslaved and brutalized that same nation for some twenty-five years, remain unseen except by a very few.

While media sensationalism has waned, important questions linger: how is it that harsh uninformed accusations about CACI from all directions — the press, members of the government, including congressmen and military investigators, did not get corrected when nothing came to light to prove the alleged culpability with regard to the performance of the company's employee? Where was the media's obligation — responsibility — not to abuse freedom of the press, freedom of speech, or even the rule of law and the concept of due process, simply to get its sensational coverage?

Furthermore, how can the media — and even the U.S. government — level accusations through investigative reports against citizens or corporations, yet not routinely provide them a full, fair and judicial forum in which to confront their accusers? Clearly administrative hearings, audiences, and other such similar meetings are not the answer because they are laden with political trappings, partisan ideology, speech making, bureaucratic mechanisms, and further media sensationalism. Here again, the system urgently needs changes and improvements even while acknowledging the differing political viewpoints of those now struggling with these matters.

* * *

Many issues came to the surface for CACI during its media ordeal, and most were quite troubling. However, the CACI organization was able to move on from the scandal having learned some important lessons. These are summarized here:

Remember your culture. Most publicly responsible companies develop organizational philosophies, typically expressed in codes of ethics and conduct, mission statements, credos, etc., that establish a corporate culture and values structure. These philosophies should be the guide in times of crisis, just as they are for day-to-day operations. CACI has five value-defining documents in addition to its corporate ethics program.[543] The number one item on the company's "Top Ten Business Values" is "placing integrity and honesty above all else." This value, in addition to those that stressed "being accountable and taking responsi-

---

[543] See Appendix D: CACI Corporate Philosophy, the Company's Foundation Documents.

bility for what we do," gave CACI its sense of direction and the confidence to proceed. CACI would promptly acknowledge and address any mistakes or wrongdoing that was shown by the facts and evidence.

Be forthright. To CACI, this was not just a line from the corporate philosophy. Facts, especially in a crisis situation, can be scarce and difficult to discover. Uncertainty can create a void that will be filled by others' conjecture, opinions, and mistakes. Therefore, telling what you know, and when you know it for certain (apart from those items that should not be revealed due to security concerns), is essential in setting an accurate record and protecting the credibility of your company. Your stakeholders, including your customers, employees, investors, and the public, want to hear what you have to say and will listen to you. Moreover, your actions should equal your candor. Act appropriately and accordingly. For example, part of CACI's "Truth Will Out" strategy included fully cooperating with government investigations and launching its own investigation to get to the truth. But it also meant standing fast and pushing back against those who went way too far, such as the California pension funds, Phil Angelides, Peter W. Singer of the Brookings Institution, and the *Washington Post*.

Don't rush to judgment. There is enormous pressure on companies to act quickly and swiftly, which may work in some situations. Most of the time, however, not all of the needed information is available or known. Be patient. Take the time and make the effort to get all the facts and act only when appropriate. When the Abu Ghraib story broke, CACI was urged to immediately fire Steve Stefanowicz because of what was alleged in the Taguba report. But to date, no charges have ever been filed against him, and proof that he was "directly or indirectly responsible" — as Taguba "suspected" and asserted — has *never* come to light nor been supported by any facts. The subsequent Fay report cautioned that a direct comparison could not be made between abuses cited in the Fay report and the Taguba report. Significantly, Fay eliminated Taguba's Abu Ghraib culpability charge against Stefanowicz and scaled back other allegations, and — most significantly — exonerated John Israel altogether. Had CACI bowed to the pressure of the moment, it would have surely wrongfully fired Stefanowicz and unjustly damaged his reputation. The same caution applies to the media. The scoop-driven, sensationalizing media is quick to judge and neglects important facts and context, which can lead to severe mistakes and misjudgments. And there will always be opportunists who will want to take advantage of you at your most vulnerable moment. Avoid rash reactions and stick to your strategy.

Ask for help. Despite all of a company's capabilities, rarely does one organization have all the resources in place to react and deal with a crisis like Abu Ghraib. CACI had the people and processes to deal with the scandal, but not the experience and expertise in crisis management and government relations to minimize all the negative impacts. The company had never before needed a crisis management plan or engaged in any type of advocacy efforts with the government, so it called in those groups that had that specific know-how to counsel CACI leaders in their decision-making. Remember, you don't have to face it alone.

Acknowledge and move on. A company will need to do everything it can to confront and survive an ordeal like Abu Ghraib. But don't dwell on it. Manage the crisis, learn your lessons, recognize the people who helped you through, and keep going. Don't let a crisis define you. Let how you dealt with it be part of your company's experience — not its identity. Since Abu Ghraib, CACI has achieved significant levels of financial performance every quarter, acquired several companies, expanded its services, and has been awarded several billion dollars in multi-year competitive contracts from the federal government, particularly the military services. While a few might still associate CACI with Abu Ghraib, most link CACI to its continuing accomplishments and its remarkable record of over forty-five-years of excellent and dedicated work for its many customers, the U.S. government, the military and the American people.

CACI was confronted with many issues during the Abu Ghraib scandal and during its media ordeal. Analysis by PR experts of CACI's response to the media was a bit divided. Some have said the company's language was too strident at times. Others were convinced that the company deserved credit for accepting the challenge instead of shrinking from it.

"CACI made it clear it was going to correct the facts, and its aggressive strategy was pretty effective," suggested crisis counselor Don Goldberg, who as a White House staffer helped guide communications during President Clinton's impeachment trial in 1999.

But in some ways, the only verdict that mattered was the one reached by the people of CACI. Did their reputation and image with their customers and their shareholders come shining through?

Three years later, by late 2007, the following conclusions could be made:

CACI was not in any way to blame for Abu Ghraib.

- ☐ CACI's role was quite minimal, virtually negligible.
- ☐ Official military investigations (army IG, Schlesinger, Fay, and Church) showed that CACI interrogators met the army's contract SOW qualifications as interrogators.
- ☐ The absence of CACI's interrogator contractors from Abu Ghraib in 2003 and 2004 would *not* have prevented the abuse and humiliation that occurred at the prison. As noted in one official investigation, "The events at Abu Ghraib cannot be understood in a vacuum."
- ☐ No current or former CACI employee was charged with any wrong-doing (as of December 2007).
- ☐ CACI was thoroughly investigated and *was* cleared of any allegation of culpability in its contract/administrative and cost management matters; the company is and always has been a responsible and qualified government contractor.
- ☐ CACI fulfilled its commitment to its customer, the U.S. Army.

CACI handled the ordeal professionally and responsibly.

- ☐ CACI recognized and acknowledged that the tragedy of Abu Ghraib was harmful to all concerned; the Iraqi detainees and Iraqi government, the U.S. Army, its soldiers, the U.S. government and the American people and CACI.
- ☐ CACI understood and carried out its corporate responsibilities to everyone — customers, employees, shareholders and the public.
- ☐ CACI cooperated with every official investigation and even launched its own outside independent investigation to get to the facts and discover the truth.
- ☐ CACI followed the rule of law, the principle of due process, and held fast to the standard that a person is innocent until proven guilty.
- ☐ CACI followed a policy of open and honest communications with all stakeholders including its main customer the U.S. government.
- ☐ CACI followed the principles set forth in its corporate culture documents.

Finally, CACI is still highly respected and successful.

- □ CACI continues to win competitively bid contracts with an established and expanding customer base, including awards of prime contracts to support the U.S. Army's multiple-award, multi-year Strategic Services Sourcing (S3) effort and the Information Technology Enterprise Solutions 2 Services (ITES-2S) program, with a total estimated contract ceiling value of $19.25 and $20 billion, respectively.
- □ CACI continues an active mergers and acquisitions profile, acquiring National Security Research Inc. in 2005 and Information Systems Support Inc. and AlphaInsight Corp. in 2006 and the Institute for Quality Management and Wexford Group International in 2007.

As the ordeal of 2004 was coming to a close, London wanted his people to know how important their work had been and what they had accomplished. For their efforts and to achieve some closure, he planned a recognition and appreciation evening for the team.

At the end of its most trying year in CACI's history, on December 2, 2004, at the Anderson House near Washington, D.C.'s Embassy Row, Jack London gathered together most of those who had led the company through its toughest challenge. Noting that Anderson House was now headquarters to the Society of the Cincinnati, founded by Continental Army and Navy officers at the close of the American Revolution in 1783, and first headed personally by General George Washington, London opened the evening by saluting all the men and women, both military and civilian contractors, currently serving in Iraq. He also shared that he was thinking about all the American men and women, military and civilian contractors, who had served, as well as those who had fallen, in Iraq and Afghanistan fighting the global war on terror in defense of freedom.[544]

---

[544] The location of the dinner was especially poignant for London, whose ancestor kinsmen (collateral), four of whom had been original members of the Society of the Cincinnati. In addition to three Cincinnati kinsmen from the Continental Navy and one from the Continental Army, London had eight other direct lineage ancestors who served the patriot cause in the American Revolution. Although he was humble about this legacy, he was also proud of his heritage. The long history of his family's military service in America had given London further motivation to support his U.S. military customers. For London, honorably serving the U.S. Army at Abu Ghraib in Iraq would never have been an exception.

He acknowledged the CACI employees who were risking home, family, and personal safety in Iraq, and he showed the commemorative certificate and lapel pin he would present to every one of them on their return.

Then he turned to those assembled and thanked them, too.

He noted that there had been no book to guide the group through the challenge they faced in 2004 but the team prevailed in navigating the company successfully through the ordeal. He thanked his team for the energy, the time, the perspective, and the expertise they brought to the common effort. And then he delivered his firmly held bottom line:

"As we wrap up here tonight and as we look back on our efforts, always remember that we did the right thing. And when you do the right thing . . . **'the truth will out.'**"

EPILOGUE

CACI's comeback — Preserving CACI's good name

"We are made to persist. That's how we find out who we are."

∾ **TOBIAS WOLFF**

B Y THE TIME OF CACI'S ANDERSON HOUSE DINNER IN DECEMBER 2004, the Abu Ghraib story had begun to withdraw from the glare of the media's spotlight. Press coverage of CACI focused considerably more on its new business, contract awards, and financial performance. Also diminished was the unsettling anticipation that another surprise or ambush could appear at any minute. But none of this meant that the Abu Ghraib ordeal was over for CACI.

As of this writing, there are still unanswered questions about Abu Ghraib and continuing debate about interrogation methods and policies. But from a CACI perspective, some things appear relatively clear nearly four years after the initial call from Seymour Hersh.

By late 2005, CACI was being referred to as a model example of adherence to GSA rules. The company was now getting recognition for its efforts in 2003, when it was presented with the interrogation request from the army, to search for alternative contract vehicles.[545] Although the ensuing GSA inquiry had been a difficult ordeal for CACI, the

---

[545] Comments made by Tom Sisti, who performs law and policy work pertaining to government contracts for SAP, at the General Services Administration's Regulation Workshop, December 8 and 9, 2005, Washington, D.C.

finding made public was that CACI was a responsible, ethical company. And it was recognized that CACI had taken reasonable measures to suggest and consider alternatives before the blanket purchase agreement was adopted under the exigent wartime situation.

CACI continued to maintain its firm conviction that its prompt response to the U.S. Army's urgent request for interrogator support in August 2003 was the right thing to do. Moreover, the contract process used was validated by the actions taken by U.S. Army authorities, as well as the support and approval provided by the Interior Department's National Business Center at Ft. Huachuca, Arizona. The company continued to consider "scope" determination issues to be primarily the responsibility of the government, however, it also continued to emphasize its longstanding position that it would implement whatever changes were set forth in the rules to "get it right," and to properly support the government. (In 2004 CACI took administrative steps to enhance and adjust its contract oversight and review processes).

Media misrepresentations would continue periodically. The pattern of 24/7 news coverage during a major corporate crisis presents a unique and daunting challenge. It is virtually impossible to address the wrong aspects fast enough and make the corrections stick. The media's approach generally places the accused in the difficult position of having to prove their innocence. Subsequent reporting, repeated over and over, tends to focus on confirming the presumed guilt of the accused rather than investigating for the facts and unbiased truth. This disastrous inversion of the process can be fatal for individual reputations as well as entire organizations or populations — and must be resisted forcefully.[546]

The case of Abu Ghraib and the *illegally leaked* Taguba report (SECRET/NO FOREIGN DISSEMINATION) provides a crystal clear example of this process of distortion. The photos offered indisputable evidence that something had gone quite wrong. The media coverage of the allegations in the Taguba report, however, treated all aspects of this one report in a series of several ongoing investigations as the final conclusion, without noting the inconsistencies and waiting for further ex-

---

[546] This endless witch hunt proces, in the extreme, harkens back to the 1930s in Nazi Germany when the fascists' endless hate-filled propaganda messages about Communists and Jews — prejudices and lies repeated over and over — became a kind of "false reality" and led in large part to the horrors of World War II and the Holocaust.

ploration and validation. There was never a challenge or further scrutiny brought to the Taguba report allegations with respect to CACI. No probing questions were ever asked, despite the contrary findings from other investigations that followed, which provided conflicting testimony and the different results that were reported by other officials.

The concept of innocent until proven guilty is often stood on its head by the media, perhaps because accusations of guilt hold more intrigue. Speculation spins out of control about presumed guilt and what might have led to it, rather than exploring the validity of the accusations, and reserving conclusions until the results are released. Burkhart noted that this ongoing speculation fueled by the media builds into fixed assumptions. And in cases where investigations are not complete or "the jury is still out," this mounting presumption leads the media's audience, the public, to develop a preconceived idea about what the outcome will be.

As Burkhart observed with the Abu Ghraib ordeal, an outcome that does not match expectation, particularly expectation that is built up over months of constant media hype, is hard to accept. In fact, the resulting surprise to those who anticipate or support a certain outcome that does not meet their expectation leads to the emotions that occur from any shocking situation — denial, anger, and disappointment.

Upset by an unexpected outcome, some in the public question any reports that contradict their preconceived notion about what really happened based on the prior media hype and speculation. In many cases "conspiracy theories" emerge to explain the contradiction between expectation and outcome.[547] But this is not a recent phenomenon. Examples of public reaction to outcomes that did not meet media predictions are found throughout modern history. Sometimes errors and egos in the media have even caused this expectation-outcome gap.[548] In the case of Abu Ghraib, fictional conspiracy theories that evolved in the media

---

[547] The assassination of John F. Kennedy in Dallas, TX on November 22, 1963 to this day is surrounded by controversy and many conspiracy theories despite the Warren Commission conclusions.

[548] Most recently the nation's expectations took a roller coaster ride during the 2000 presidential election with George W. Bush opposing Al Gore. As NBC Anchor Brian Williams later stated, "I called Florida for Al Gore too. It was a horrible moment" referring to the 2000 election night debacle when networks prematurely awarded the presidency twice within two hours ("On Election Night, Networks Plan to Proceed with Caution," WashingtonPost.com, November 2, 2006). In another election

about CACI and government contractors were that: (1) contractors were hired ostensibly to carry out questionable tactics, avoid scrutiny, and/or evade potential prosecution; (2) the trip to Israel by CACI's CEO was somehow tied to acquiring knowledge of Israeli interrogation (or torture) methods; (3) CACI (and Titan) seemingly had unsavory "close ties to Israeli military and technology communities"; and (4) CACI and Titan had some sort of collaborative team arrangement devised to allegedly increase demand for their services. Of course, none of these theories were in any way true, and were an insult to everyone concerned.

The notorious Abu Ghraib abuse pictures and the sensationalized *illegally leaked* Taguba report were more emotionally charged and seemingly more powerful than the subsequent investigative reports and conclusions. None of the reports that followed (army IG, Schlesinger, and Kern, Jones, Fay) included any new graphic images or similarly strong accusatory language, nor did they greatly widen the sphere of culpability or deliver powerful new indictments. In fact, just the opposite could be argued with regard to Taguba's statement about the four individuals whom he suspected were "directly or indirectly responsible." The Titan contractor John Israel was exonerated, and allegations against CACI contractor Stefanowicz were either eliminated or dramatically scaled back. The two military officers, Pappas and Jordan ultimately faced lesser charges.[549]

---

example, the *Chicago Daily Tribune* newspaper on November 4, 1948 erroneously printed issues with the headline, "DEWEY DEFEATS TRUMAN." Many were predicting that incumbent Truman would lose his reelection bid because of splits in his (Democratic) party. During the election, much of the *Tribune's* composing room staff was on strike and early returns led the paper to believe that the Republican candidate Thomas Dewey would win. But Truman's aggressive and strategic campaign tactics led him to victory. Photos of the *Tribune's* mistaken headline displayed by Truman after his win have become famous.

[549] Col. Thomas Pappas was found guilty on two counts of dereliction of duty, fined $8,000, and relieved from command. In 2006, he received immunity for his testimony at the court-martial of an army dog handler where he stated that he gave permission to use military working dogs one time with one detainee. Lt. Col. Steven Jordan was court-martialed in 2007 and was found guilty of disobeying a general's command not to talk about the investigation but was acquitted of failing to control soldiers who had abused detainees. In 2008, the army dismissed Jordan's conviction outright. He received no jail time. See Appendix J–List of Abu Ghraib Verdicts, for further details.

The later investigative reports were comparatively anti-climactic and, for some, a letdown to what was expected or even advocated. The proverbial "other shoe" did not drop (because there wasn't one). And some in the media and the activist public, after months of unbridled hype and speculation, reacted with surprise, shock, denial, and, in some cases, anger.

Notably, Singer's September 2004 *Washington Post* op-ed is a clear example of the overt expression of these reactions, which Burkhart had noted came across as "an angry denial letter" carefully lacking the accurate portrayal of conclusions that had just been released by the official reports of August 2004 (viz. Schlesinger, and Kerns, Jones, Fay). Singer, reportedly, had long been critical of government outsourcing and government contractor oversight. He used the suspicions surrounding Abu Ghraib to espouse his views, pointing to CACI by way of example to support his premise. And while there was still uncertainty surrounding events at Abu Ghraib during the investigative process, he added his own speculation about CACI apparently to draw attention and support to his position about contractors in general.

The worldwide publicity of the Abu Ghraib scandal gave Singer a ready-made platform to distribute his opinions to a broad audience. When the conclusions of the official investigations took the focus and the accusations off CACI, it also took away a popular, credible example to support the cornerstone of Singer's views. Apparently unwilling to accept these recent investigative findings, Singer vented his feelings in his September *Post* op-ed. To bolster his position, he presented his argument as a challenge and demand to the military using incomplete information loosely held together by accusations, rather than fully referenced sources and detailed conclusions. The partial facts that he did include were taken out of context and patched in among sensationalized and misleading statements (as has been previously noted here).

The *Post's* publication of Singer's op-ed and its simultaneous refusal to publish London's counterpoints could be interpreted as an indication of the *Post's* own apparent disappointment and disagreement with the results of the official investigations that followed Taguba's earlier report.

* * *

From CACI's perspective, it seemed that the media and some critics were only interested in information that cast the company in an unfavorable light. For example, information that seemed to contradict the core story line, such as testimony that Stefanowicz had *reported* (*and documented*) some possible abuses, tended to be marginalized or ignored. News agencies generally gave passing notice when the Fay report contradicted Taguba's findings by sharply scaling back allegations about Stefanowicz and fully exonerating John Israel, *two* of the *four* men Taguba had suspected as having some major responsibility for the abuses. These significant discrepancies are important to those involved, but were barely addressed by the media and are not likely to ever be fully resolved in the minds of the readers who accepted the initial accounts as verified facts rather than the "suspicions" they were stated to be.

When official inquiries confirmed that CACI's interrogators met all of the army's contract SOW requirements, most news reports focused on the fact that about a third of the interrogators did not have previous *military* interrogator training, even though the army IG report stated that, "The SOW did not mandate military interrogation training as a prerequisite for employment."[550] This was because demonstrated equivalent civilian experience from major police departments, the CIA, FBI, DEA, was fully acceptable under the contract for hires who were also U.S. citizens with U.S. government security clearances.

Still, the media failed to note the more obvious and important fact that two-thirds of the people hired by CACI *did* have military interrogator training experience, proving that CACI had included this additional qualification for the majority of its hires before the army itself had decided to have it be a firm (mandatory) criterion in any future contract requirements. The reference to military training in the government reports had been taken out of context and treated as a point of deficiency by the media. In turn, this misleading point was used by self proclaimed "experts" as a basis for criticism, and by attorneys as a basis for lawsuits. But CACI had, in fact, *not only met but exceeded* all the staffing specifications for their contract. By emphasizing the converse facts about the military interrogator training aspects of the SOW, the media chose to define and report, not the picture presented — but the negative image of that picture.

---

[550] Army IG Report, op. cit.

The Schlesinger and Fay reports both brought up the issue of military interrogator training primarily as a future recommendation for a more uniform training program for contract interrogators. Recognizing the continued need for utilizing contractors for this vital work, their recommendations included suggestions on how to create a more consistent and, as Fay noted, a "standardized" system of training for contractors hired for interrogation support. This point never seemed to be fully grasped by the media.[551]

Nearly four years later some people remain in denial of the favorable outcome for CACI of the final official investigations. They continue to repeat previous suspicions and allegations and engage in further efforts to develop new theories and accusations rather than accepting the results of the official reports. And tragically by virtue of the fact that so much misinformation continues to abound and be repeated along with previous unproven allegations about CACI, many continue to believe the distortions rather than having the benefit of the truth. So strong has this misperception of CACI taken root that some in their own denial have suggested it is CACI that is in denial.

As noted in a *Wall Street Journal* opinion article following release of the Church report, "We'd have thought every American would be relieved to learn that ten major inquiries, sworn statements from thirty-seven high-level officials, and information gleaned from dozens of courts-martial and criminal investigations have cleared most senior civilian and military leaders of wrongdoing in the Abu Ghraib scandal and other Iraq prisoner abuses. Instead, the latest army report reaching this conclusion has induced further cries of whitewash." The *Journal* article further noted, "This wailing says more about the accusers than about any facts that have emerged in the year since the scandal broke. The media . . . flogged the Abu Ghraib story for months throughout . . . 2004. . . . But now that their worst chain of command conspiracy hypotheses have not panned out, they refuse to admit it."[552]

---

[551] The Schlesinger report noted that "continued use of contractors will be required, but contracts must specify the technical requirements and personnel qualifications, experience, and training needed." The Fay report stated, "The key point would be agreement on some *standardization* [italics added] of training of contractor interrogators."

[552] "Abu Ghraib Accountability," op. cit.

But there were other factors that besieged CACI. David Shaw, "Media Matters" columnist at the *Los Angeles Times*, in a column on media bias may have provided a clue to the mistakes and other flaws that dogged CACI. "Cynicism is the default position in the news media these days. Every politician is suspect. Reporters have become predators. 'Gotcha' journalism is the order of the day," Shaw said in May 2005.[553]

And if reporters happen to be wrong, they can move on to the next phase of the story and not be compelled to admit their mistakes or even defend them.

Instead of setting the record straight, most news organizations eventually reduced the attention they gave to CACI or just dropped the story altogether. The failure to update the earlier reports left intact the observer's first impression, which was based on incomplete investigations and the one inconsistent contradictory report from Taguba. This was further negatively embellished by the press through repetition of unverified information and even misinformation. When subsequent inquiries backed away from Taguba's conclusions, the media generally did not cover it. And when falsehoods were corrected, the media generally ignored it.

Also damaging to the company were the continuous links of CACI's name to the prison detainee abuse photographs where no CACI employee was depicted. The media repeatedly showed these Abu Ghraib photographs in articles where CACI's name was mentioned, discussed, or posted. The message and image planted in the observer's mind left the impression that CACI was, by proximity or association, a guilty accomplice in the photos. Yet this was nothing close to the truth.

However, this further strengthened the association of CACI to the detainee abuse scandal and helped keep this unjustified and false connection imprinted on the public's memory. In particular, the photograph of the hooded detainee with wires extended from his fingers was frequently and wrongfully shown in connection with CACI's name and logo despite the confession by one of the MPs for being responsible for this

---

[553] David Shaw, "For Journalists, Lessons in Conduct and Survival," *Los Angeles Times*, May 1, 2005.

particular act.[554] In fact, the company received several anonymously sent postcards depicting the cloaked and hooded detainee on a narrow box with cables hanging from his arms, with false accusatory messages well into 2006.

The images of Abu Ghraib were pivotal to the scandal. As *Time* noted within weeks of the *60 Minutes II* revelation of the first pictures, "Like a well-targeted attack-ad in a U.S. election campaign, the Abu Ghraib images make a visceral connection with an Arab audience, that no amount of contextualizing, apologies, reprimands, or school-painting can reverse. No ad agency could have produced a more effective al Qaeda recruitment tool. . . ."[555]

A few months later others in the press, citing the videotaped executions of Daniel Pearl, Nick Berg, Paul Johnson and army reservist Matt Maupin, noted that ". . . if recent developments are any indicator, we've entered a murkier, more troubling arena in the war on terror: visual warfare." Noting that "troubling questions abound," one such question posed was, ". . . shouldn't television journalists stop giving terrorists the forum they covet?" Further observations were that the media tends to portray inciteful imagery: "Network anchors lament global terrorism even as they become complicit partners," and "America's twenty-four hour news channels are essentially aiding the enemy. . . ." Former Washington, D.C. reporter David Broder wisely noted that, "the essential ingredient of any effective anti-terrorist

---

[554] Staff Sgt. Ivan Frederick II plead guilty for his involvement along with Spc. Sabrina Harman in placing wires on a detainee's hands and reportedly telling him he would be electrocuted if he fell off the box. The *New York Times* wrote a lengthy article in March 11, 2006 attributing the identity of the hooded detainee to Ali Shalal Qaissi who claimed to be that person, but shortly thereafter the *Times* issued a correction when it was shown that 2004 military reports named another detainee as the hooded individual. The paper stated, *"The Times did not adequately research Mr. Qaissi's insistence that he was the man in the photograph. Mr. Qaissi's account had already been broadcast and printed by other outlets, including PBS and Vanity Fair, without challenge."* [Italics added] Hassan H. Fattah, "Symbol of Abu Ghraib Seeks to Spare Others His Nightmare," *New York Times*, March 11, 2006. Ali Shalal Qaissi continues to claim to be the hooded figure and gives speeches at anti-war gatherings about "brutal methods of torture" he allegedly experienced at Abu Ghraib.

[555] Tony Karon, "How the Prison Scandal Sabotages the U.S. in Iraq," *Time*, May 4, 2004.

policy must be the denial to the terrorist of access to mass media outlets."[556]

On the other hand, the lack of coverage of the Saddam Hussein torture videos showed the media's lack of balance on Abu Ghraib. As Deborah Orin noted "these awful images didn't show up on American TV news. . . . But every TV network has endlessly shown photos of the humiliation of Iraqi prisoners by U.S. troops at Abu Ghraib. Why?" Her theory was, "In this era, a photo is everything. We highlight U.S. prisoner abuse because the photos aren't too offensive to show. We downplay Saddam's abuse precisely because it's far worse. . . . It's worse than creating moral equivalence between Saddam's tortures and prisoner abuse by U.S. troops. It's that we do far more to highlight our own wrongdoings precisely because they are less appalling." Orin added, "Terrorism is sometimes called asymmetric warfare. . . . Now it turns out that we also face asymmetric propaganda — where terrorists gain a P.R. advantage precisely because what they do is so horrific that our media aren't able to deal with it. . . . Reporters have to face up to the fact . . . . if we highlight the wrongs that Americans commit, but not . . . . the far worse horrors committed by others, we become propaganda tools for the other side."[557]

The *Wall Street Journal*'s solution to Orin's observation was to suggest that ". . . it doesn't seem that it would be that hard to provide context — to make sure that every story about American abuses at Abu Ghraib also included a graphic description of what went on there before Iraq's liberation," concluding, "Surely we have a right to demand better from the news media.[558]

Wall Street Journal columnist Robert Kaplan later put this unbalanced coverage in greater perspective. He noted the sparse media coverage of the first Medal of Honor recipient in the global war on terror, who was killed outside Baghdad airport in April 2003.[559] Kaplan pointed

[556] Mathew Felling, "Terrorists' visual warfare uses the media as a weapon," *Christian Science Monitor*, August 4, 2004.

[557] Deborah Orin, "Reporting for the Enemy; Media Won't Show Saddam's Evil," op. cit.

[558] James Taranto, "The Saddam Videos," *Wall Street Journal*, June 16, 2004.

[559] Sergeant First Class Paul R. Smith posthumously received the Medal of Honor in 2005 for his heroic actions in Operation Iraqi Freedom. His was the first Medal of Honor bestowed for service in action in Iraq. In April 2003, Smith engaged Iraqi troops at Baghdad International Airport to protect an aid station full of wounded Americans.

out that, "According to LexisNexis, by June 2005, two months after his posthumous award, his stirring story had drawn only 90 media mentions, compared with 4,677 for the supposed Quran abuse at Guantanamo Bay, and 5,159 for the court-martialed Abu Ghraib guard Lynndie England. While the exposure of wrongdoing by American troops is of the highest importance, it can become a tyranny of its own when taken to an extreme."[560]

For London and company, early suspicions about the fundamental flaws in the way the news media covers major news events were confirmed. London and others at CACI developed a strong belief that institutions or individuals under fire in crisis need to find alternative means for delivering information directly to key audiences. London said throughout the ordeal that organizational communication is like "speaking to a passing parade; you have to repeat yourself over and over, if you expect anyone to get your message."

CACI's "Truth Will Out" strategy was designed to try to fill the information void and counter falsifications through its own outreach program. It produced voluminous information and delivered it directly to key audiences such as customers, investors, employees, and members of Congress and their staffs. CACI created a special section on its Web site, issued numerous public statements, hosted public conference calls, and held direct conversations with individuals critical to the situation. The company also wrote directly to reporters on a regular basis with lengthy accounts of the facts at CACI's disposal, primarily through the targeted media response letters. Hundreds of these letters were sent out to every media source that stated something factually wrong or misleading about CACI.

Yet distorted news reports continued to espouse non-existent scenarios (viz. conspiracy theories). One example that lives on in cyberspace is the insinuated sinister association of CACI and John Israel. In May of 2004, CounterPunch.com, a political extremist news site, published an article claiming that John Israel, a Titan subcontractor mistakenly named as a CACI employee in the Taguba report (but who never worked for CACI), may not have held the required security clearance. It showed the job description for the interrogation position from CACI's

---

[560] Robert D. Kaplan, "Modern Heroes, Our soldiers like what they do. They want our respect, not our pity," *Wall Street Journal*, October 4, 2007.

Web site that included the requirement for Top Secret clearance. The report speculated that Israel was "an intelligence cover name [that] has fueled speculation whether this individual could have been one of a number of Israeli interrogators hired under a classified contract."[561] The article further claimed that CACI and Titan had "close ties to the Israeli military and technology communities."

London had visited the country of Israel only once in his life, in January 2004, to deliver the keynote address to the first annual Defense Aerospace Homeland Security Mission of Peace to Israel and Jordan, and to accept the Albert Einstein Technology Award from the Jerusalem Fund of Aish HaTorah in Israel. Other trip participants and award recipients included Homeland Security and Pentagon officials as well as several Congressional leaders — both Democrat (Evan Bayh and Ben Nelson) and Republican (John McHugh and John Linder).[562]

The CounterPunch piece was incredulous. Negating the credibility of the article at the outset, was the fact that John Israel was never a CACI employee, a fact the article obfuscated when it referred to Israel being named as both a CACI and Titan employee in the Taguba report. Furthermore, all CACI interrogators were U.S. citizens and CACI had no ties or connections to Israel — military, technical or otherwise. CACI never received any grants from any foundations of any nationality. And, CACI was not aware of any wrongdoing at Abu Ghraib prison until the story broke in April of 2004.

Sadly, another article cited the aforementioned piece verbatim in February 2005, nearly a year after the CounterPunch story was released and months after the official investigative reports were concluded and had established the actual facts regarding CACI employees.[563] Articles repeating and promoting these falsehoods continue to be

---

[561] "The Israeli Torture Template, Rape, Feces and Urine-Dipped Cloth Sacks," CounterPunch.org, May 10, 2004.

[562] Participants included Robert Liscouski, Assistant Secretary for Infrastructure Protection at the Department of Homeland Security, former Under Secretary of the army Joe Reeder, U.S. Senators Evan Bayh and Ben Nelson, Democrats from Indiana and Nebraska respectively, and U.S. Congressmen John Linder and John McHugh, both Republicans, from Georgia and New York, respectively.

[563] "The Israeli Traitors Running America's Invasion of Iraq," February 27, 2005 (http://www.geocities.com/carbonomics/MCtfirm/10tf26/10tf26me.html).

found in online searches for CACI and Abu Ghraib. For example, the Web site of a fringe 2008 presidential candidate penned a truly ghastly hallucination called "GSA gives CACI Green Light on Prison Sexual Torture."[564] The first line of the article described CACI as a company that "provides Israeli trained torture experts." It continued with a fictional conversation between GSA and CACI where the government agency approves the company's requests to develop nuclear bombs with Israel, massacre foreign troops, and crack security codes. One line even proclaims that CACI "could make one helluva lot of trouble for mankind." Another article reflective of those publications too raunchy and absurd to even acknowledge was called "Bush's POW Porn."[565]

Some news reports wrongly depicted CACI as a lobbying juggernaut, even though it had virtually no presence on Capitol Hill before Abu Ghraib. Another report discussed the impact of contributions supposedly funneled through the company's political action committee, a remarkable story because CACI has *never* had a political action committee and any nominal political campaign contributions come from individual employees, on their own, as private citizens.

Another totally false account occurred with the release of a May 2005 book published by the Penguin Group entitled *Inside the Wire* (about interrogations at Guantanamo Bay, Cuba), which stated that CACI provided interrogators in Cuba and implicitly linked the company to alleged abuse at that location. In fact, CACI had never provided interrogators to Guantanamo Bay. After a vigorous complaint was registered with Penguin by CACI (which was alerted to the error by an inquiry from a television news producer), the publisher, Penguin, and the authors, including a *Time* magazine reporter, acknowledged that they were wrong. Although erratum notices were placed in the book, thousands of books with false information remained available at bookstores and for online purchase, further perpetuating misinformation about CACI in the public domain.[566]

Through 2005 and well into 2006, CACI continued to receive flak from the media's exaggerated, misleading and false reporting. A *Los*

---

[564] "GSA gives CACI Green Light on Prison Sexual Torture," July 14, 2004 (http://www .randycrow.com/articles/071404.htm).

[565] Susan Block, "Bush's POW Porn," Counterpunch.org, May 14, 2004.

[566] *Inside the Wire* Erratum Notice, May 2, 2005.

Angeles Times op-ed column in March of 2005 claimed that CACI employees "were in the middle of the Abu Ghraib mess."[567] In May of 2005, Amnesty International USA's Web site again posted misleading statements about CACI. Their Web site asserted that "in *implicating* civilian contractors from CACI International and Titan Corporation, the army's reports on Abu Ghraib reminded us that it is even possible for private corporations to become *involved in torture and war crimes*"[568] [italics added]. No official U.S. government investigation of CACI had proven, verified, or even hinted at any such conclusion. Yet no report of the U.S. government, including the illegally leaked Taguba report, seemed beyond exaggeration or embellishment.

London would recall these unbelievable claims when he later read a quote by William James, who said, "There's nothing so absurd that if you repeat it often enough, people will believe it."[569]

* * *

The intensity of the Abu Ghraib scandal may have waned, but the problems and issues caused for CACI did not. In 2005 and well into 2006, CACI would continue to fight battles from the previous year and would have to deal with some new challenges.

One of those extended challenges was another report from the government. The Government Accountability Office (GAO) had reviewed the contracts under which CACI was asked to perform interrogation and intelligence-gathering services and had released its report at the end of April 2005.

The purpose of the GAO review was "to determine what breakdowns occurred in the process of procuring interrogation and other services and the contributing factors to the breakdowns."[570] After reviewing the contract, processes, and policies, the GAO report made specific recom-

---

[567] Max Boot, "The Iraq War's Outsourcing Snafu," Los Angeles Times, March 31, 2005.

[568] "Business and Human Rights," section on Amnesty International USA's Web site (http://www.amnestyusa.org/business/chippitts.html).

[569] Http://quotes.liberty-tree.ca.

[570] "Interagency Contracting Problems with DoD's and Interior's Orders to Support Military Operations," Government Accountability Office, GAO 05-201, April 2005 (http://www.gao.gov/new.items/d05201.pdf).

mendations that the Department of the Interior (DOI) and its National Business Center at Fort Huachuca (which had helped facilitate the interrogation contracts) improve their internal training and processes, and recommended that the Department of Defense (DoD) develop a mechanism to track the use of non-DoD contracts.

Before GAO released its final report, it had sent a draft to the involved parties, allowing them to respond to the findings and reply to anything they believed was wrong. The DOI and DoD sent brief responses concurring with the report and presenting their current efforts to fix problems.

CACI laid out its concerns in a nineteen-page response. First, CACI recommended that the final report more fully acknowledge and properly recognize the urgent, wartime circumstances when the army and the DOI initiated the contract. CACI acknowledged that the contracting policies and procedures on all sides had flaws, and the company had promptly begun upgrading its own processes. However, CACI viewed the excessive "after-the-fact" and apparent "second-guessing" of the war zone military contracting intentions and actions as inappropriate. Second, CACI reaffirmed its firm belief that the army and CACI, as well as the DOI, had acted reasonably, responsibly, and in good faith in accepting and performing the delivery orders for intelligence support services in Iraq given the conditions at the time. The company also reiterated that it was the army's in-country contracting personnel who had agreed to the use of the BPA (Blanket Purchase Agreement) for the intelligence support services. CACI had suggested the BPA when asked by the officials if the company already had an existing contract vehicle that might be used. And further, the DOI office at Ft. Huachuca had reviewed, approved and issued the contract order. Moreover, CACI had all along taken the clear and open position that the contract delivery orders were reasonably contracted for by Ft. Huachuca given the exigent wartime emergency circumstances. Even more to the point, the contract used in this case — a BPA developed around a GSA contract — *had earlier been approved for intelligence support services use by the GSA* in 1998, five years *before* CACI acquired PTG and its DOI BPA contract vehicle in May 2003.

The GAO report had also suggested that CACI inappropriately made contracting decisions, because CACI employees provided information and assistance to the army and DOI personnel involved in the contract acquisition. However, it did not note that this contract situation was unique, being executed during the critical stages of the war and that CACI did not — and could not — make contracting decisions or do anything beyond providing contract information and suggested work statements and requirements which was permissible under the prevailing regulations at the time.[571]

When the final report came out, however, GAO scarcely acknowledged CACI's concerns and summarily dismissed the evidence the company had provided in responding to those specific areas about CACI that were incorrect. It simply stated, "We did not find these [CACI's] arguments convincing."[572]

While CACI understood the justification and position of government agencies to make additional inquiries and delve further into the Abu Ghraib interrogation contract, though unusual by normal standards, the company was nevertheless stunned by the hard wire brushing it received in many cases. It was a harsh blow to the company that entered Iraq in 2003, proud to support, even in a small way, the U.S. Army and "Operation Iraqi Freedom" in liberating Iraq from a brutal dictatorship.

In early May 2005, CACI put out a press release acknowledging the inherent flaws in the government contracting procedures but reasserting its own specific differences with the report's company-specific findings. In any case, the media — particularly local and industry publications — made little or no mention of the GAO findings. This was a noteworthy and appropriate change in the mainstream media's stance from the saturated coverage of the year before.

★ ★ ★

More outrageous allegations about CACI would continue to emerge from new places. In August 2005, the radical extremist and outspoken radio talk show host Randi Rhodes, whose program aired daily on Air America, took aim at CACI. As part of a two day blast about the Abu Ghraib scandal, Rhodes accused CACI of heinous behavior, including the raping of young boys in Iraq, directing torture of detainees in Iraq,

---

[571] See Chapter 11 for CACI contract details and Chapter 18 for the FAR clauses that pertain.

[572] "Interagency Contracting Problems with DoD's and Interior's Orders to Support Military Operations," op. cit.

and importing techniques that the company was to have allegedly used in Guantanamo Bay and Afghanistan (where the company had never worked). With the worst of all possible accusations, she also referred to CACI as "hired killers." Rhodes claimed to have tried to contact CACI for comment but claimed that the company wasn't talking. All of her commentary was, of course, untrue.[573]

While no one from Rhodes' show or Air America had contacted CACI, they would hear from the company after the broadcasts. CACI's outside counsel, Bill Koegel, promptly sent a letter to Rhodes and Air America informing them that the comments were demonstrably false and defamatory and that they cast aspersions on CACI's integrity and reputation. The letter also demanded a written and broadcast retraction, pointing out that the company would take legal action if corrective measures were not taken on their part.

The Rhodes and Air America camp acknowledged receiving the letter but did nothing. Just as Koegel had warned, CACI filed a lawsuit in Virginia federal court at the end of September of 2005. CACI was serious about defending the integrity of its name and its business against such outright malicious lies. Recognizing its corporate responsibility toward its employees, customers and shareholders to defend its reputation, the company made a strong statement about the liability of defamatory statements. CACI submitted in its complaint that it would seek $1,000,000 in compensatory damages and $10,000,000 in punitive damages.

A couple of weeks after the suit had been filed, Rhodes finally responded. In a statement made during her show, she stated that, "in the course of my show, I may have mentioned CACI, a corporation. . . ."[574] She went on to claim that she prepared "thoroughly" before going on the air and relied on "reliable published materials." The sources she apparently selectively referenced were from those slanted toward radical, extremist, far left-wing, and like-minded Web sites — clearly avoiding any effort at balance and failing to confirm sources. Furthermore, she said she would fight the lawsuit and predicted that "during the discovery process, I anticipate that CACI will have to provide me with all information they have that disputes anything I said about CACI during my August 25 and 26 shows. And when that information is released, I

---

[573] Comments made during the *The Randi Rhodes Show* throughout August 2005.

[574] "Randi Rhodes Show," Air America, October 13, 2005.

believe that I, this company Piquant, and the truth will prevail."[575] Rhodes' assertions about herself and her company, whether prevailing or not, did not square with the truth. The CACI team would be resolute in its unwavering pursuit of a fair and factual conclusion.

On October 13, 2006 Air America and its corporate parent, Piquent, LLC, sought bankruptcy protection.[576] Its management was wrapped up in a series of financial problems and entangled in a web of legal challenges. Nevertheless, CACI continued its drive for the truth. In early 2007, CACI won court approval to proceed with its defamation lawsuit against Air America and Randi Rhodes despite the Chapter 11 bankruptcy protection.

While the Rhodes/Air America lawsuit proceeded, CACI was still in litigation with others. The two lawsuits filed in the summer of 2004 against CACI continued well into 2006. However, developments in both cases overwhelmingly favored CACI.

By August 2005, the suit brought on by Atlanta-based Edmond & Jones on behalf of clients they named the "Iraqi Torture Victims Group" (ITVG) was dealt several blows. The federal court judge presiding over the case had already dismissed most of the plaintiffs' claims. He also indicated that if the defendants, namely CACI and Titan, established through a summary judgment action that the companies had been under the supervision and direction of the military, then the rest of the claims would also be dismissed. The judge also reaffirmed a point that CACI had believed for a long time: "The plaintiffs apparently concede that they cannot sue the U.S. Government because of sovereign immunity."[577]

---

[575] Ibid.

[576] In September 2006, rumors that Air America was going to declare bankruptcy emerged when the network's star, Al Franken, publicly stated that he had not been paid. While Air America's spokeswoman denied the rumors, Franken stated on the air that the network was having cash flow problems. But he told listeners financial woes would not keep the network from staying on the air. Air America had financial issues since it began in 2004. The network also had other problems, including the departure of another celebrity host and an inquiry into a transfer of funds to start the network.

[577] United States District Court for the District of Columbia, Decision by Judge James Robertson re Ilham Nassir Ibrahim, et al v. Titan Corp., et al., Case 1:04-cv-01248-JR, Document 39, August 12, 2005.

And all the while there is ample evidence and sworn testimony available to show the supervisory and chain of command relationship of CACI employees. The only supervisory position held by CACI personnel was solely for internal company purposes, such as a country manager and site leads who provided administrative support to CACI personnel and liaised with Army contract personnel. These CACI personnel never had any decision-making authority for interrogator policy.

On the other hand, the lawsuit brought by CCR proceeded at a much slower pace. CACI succeeded in bringing the original suit that had been filed in California to the East Coast. Now, the U.S. Court of Appeals directed the District Court to reconsider the motion seeking to transfer the case from Virginia to D.C.[578]

The decisions from the ITVG case were of relevance and importance since many of the claims made in the CCR case were the same. In response to the ITVG decision, the CCR team drafted an amended complaint, which dropped several claims that were comparable to the claims dismissed in the other suit, and changed other allegations in an attempt to protect them from dismissal. The amended claim also added CACI Premier Technology and two other former Iraq-based employees to the suit. CACI was prepared to disprove these allegations, too.

In the midst of this legal jockeying, CCR also took some extreme and desperate measures to publicly promote itself in the case. In September 2005, CCR filed a news release that claimed that CCR was responsible for CACI leaving the Iraq interrogation contract. The release's title said, "The Center for Constitutional Rights Credits Pressure from Group and Public with CACI International Withdrawal from Iraq." The subtitle further claimed that CACI's "decision" came days after the amended claim was filed. This ludicrous pronouncement reinforced CACI's doubts about the competence of the CCR group both in terms of its ability to prosecute its case as well as its ability to understand the government contracting process.

The interrogation contract had been awarded to L-3 on a competitive award basis in July — two months before CCR even had the need to

---

[578] In late 2007, the Judge James Robertson of the U.S. District Court in the District of Columbia ruled on the summary judgment motions filed by both contractors. Robertson sustained Titan's (now a part of L-3 Communications Corp.) motion for summary judgment, but on a narrow issue denied CACI's motion for summary judgment pursuant to the question of supervision and direction.

draft an amended complaint and a month before the key decision in the
ITVG case. Clearly there was no relationship. But more importantly, the
CACI team questioned how CCR could have possibly missed the award
of the contract to another company for the work they had been suing
over. And how was it that well over a year after filing its suit, CCR remained unaware of the manner in which the government contract bidding process occurs?

As for the credibility of the CCR press release, why would CACI ac-
quiesce to an organization making unfounded claims against it with a
number of those claims already being dismissed as baseless? Quite simply, had CACI, rather than L-3, been awarded the contract, CACI
would still be in Iraq as long as they were needed by the customer. To
CACI, this was just another CCR publicity stunt to promote itself and
boost its weak case.

In 2005, another side of CCR was revealed when it became known
that CCR supported Lynne Stewart, the self-proclaimed radical attorney for Sheikh Omar Abdul Rahman who was convicted of masterminding the 1993 World Trade Center bombing. Stewart was convicted in
February 2005 for providing aid and support to Rahman and his "Islamic
Group," an Egypt-based terrorist organization with close links to the
al Qaeda network. Stewart met frequently with Rahman while he was in
jail and became, in effect, a messenger for him and his radical terrorist
group enabling Rahman to conduct business while behind bars.[579]

Ironically, as a "civil rights defender," Stewart made public Rahman's
instructions calling for the killing of those who did not subscribe to his
extremist interpretation of Islamic law and "a unanimous fatwah that
urges the Muslim nation to fight the Jews and to kill them wherever they
are."[580] Following the release of one particular Rahman message by
Stewart to Reuters in June 2003, instructing his group to withdraw from
a ceasefire, thirty-four people were killed at an Egyptian Sinai resort
and another sixty-four were killed at a Red Sea resort.[581]

[579] David Glovin "N.Y. Attorney Lynne Stewart Convicted of Aiding Terrorist Group,"
Bloomberg.com, February 10, 2005.

[580] Sherry Colb "Why Lynne Stewart, Attorney for a Terrorist, Is No Heroine: Crossing
the Line Between Advocate and Accomplice," FindLaw, July 30, 2003.

[581] Sharon Chadha "Lynne Stewart, Jihadi Lawyer," *Middle East Quarterly*, Winter,
2006.

After Stewart's indictment, CCR rallied to Stewart's defense, issuing a press release stating that her arrest was an "attack on attorneys who defend controversial figures."[582] But it seemed that CCR may have found another role in actively and directly helping those — Americans — who were linked to supporting, aiding, and abetting Islamic terrorist activity. Lynne Stewart reportedly stated that she considers terrorists "revolutionaries."[583]

* * *

Back in California, the pension funds and state officials were silent. After public proclamations of dissatisfaction and calls to divest, both CalPERS and CalSTRS demonstrated their private opinion of the value of CACI's stock.

On June 30, 2004 CalSTRS reportedly held 75,780 shares of CACI while CalPERS held 209,100 shares. A year later, on June 30, 2005, CalPERS had *increased* its investment to 216,300 shares of CACI. Halfway through 2005, the CalPERS investment had a market value of $13.6 million. CalSTRS, on the other hand, chose to take its profits. By the same date in 2005, CalSTRS had sold its nearly 76,000 shares with a value of approximately $4.7 million. Clearly, its investments in CACI had paid off.

And true to CACI's recognition that the posturing by the funds involved political motivations, both California State Treasurer Phil Angelides *and* State Controller Steve Westly threw their names into the 2006 gubernatorial race as Democratic candidates. Angelides beat Westly in the California Democratic primary in June 2006 but was defeated by incumbent Governor Arnold Schwarzenegger.

After his September 12, 2004 op-ed in the *Washington Post*, Peter Singer continued intermittently to give critical commentaries about government outsourcing and the roles of government contractors. He now began to take advantage of the extensive publicity of the Abu Ghraib scandal to insert CACI's name as an example among those he would refer to in the effort to support his arguments. It was becoming increasingly apparent that Abu Ghraib, and CACI's association with Abu

---

[582] Center for Constitutional Rights, "CCR's Additional Post-9/11 Cases."

[583] Michael Tremoglie "Who is Behind Lynne Stewart?" FrontPageMagazine.com, September 25, 2002.

Ghraib, would continue to provide convenient, emotionally charged examples for critics to point to even if it meant the risk of misconstruing the data.

Apparently, Singer may not have seen his own reflection in the criticism and advice he directed to the government, which he accused of being "woefully uninformed and ill-equipped in its relations with the [government contracting] industry." He chided that, "When mistakes are made, lessons are learned so that errors are not repeated." In a November 2004 speech in Geneva, Switzerland, Singer chastised the U.S. government proclaiming, "When it comes to the private military world, though, our government seems to be doing its utmost to learn nothing."[584] Yet Singer's continued repetition of inaccurate or incomplete information in relation to CACI has demonstrated, apparently, that the mistakes he has made in discussing the company have not resulted in lessons learned so that he does not repeat those errors.

In large part, Singer's commentaries have been criticisms about the government contracting industry overall, and his misstatements (knowing or otherwise) about CACI have been used to help support these views. Clearly by continuing his criticisms of the government, the Department of Justice, the military, the contracting industry and specific contractors including CACI, Singer has persisted in this disapproving and derogatory viewpoint. He has admitted but rarely emphasized the fact that in his words, "contractors are performing a role that if you took them out, the operation would collapse." Rather in describing what he called "some of the darkest and most controversial aspects of the war," he included "the role of CACI and Titan contractors working at the now infamous Abu Ghraib prison."[585]

These assertions by Singer about CACI contractors at Abu Ghraib demonstrate the pitfalls of not heeding Jones' important notation in the Fay report: "The events at Abu Ghraib cannot be understood in a vacuum." By extracting narrow aspects of the contractor situation from the overall picture of Abu Ghraib and then discussing them in a vacuum, the critical commentaries continue to contain faulty assumptions about

---

[584] Peter Singer, "The Private Military Industry and Iraq: What have we learned and where to next?" Geneva Centre for the Democratic Control of Armed Forces Policy Paper, November 2004 (http://www.dcaf.ch/_docs/pp04_private-military.pdf).

[585] Ibid.

CACI. Based on partial and misleading information, this has led, not surprisingly, to erroneous interpretations and conclusions.

Singer was also keen, it seems, on making flippant sound-bites such as, "In many ways, the private military [government contractor industry] sounds like something right out of an adventure novel or Hollywood movie."[586] But government contractors and the industry are very real, and reckless comments about punishing individuals and companies cannot be approached with a detached, and dismissive view toward due process and the concept of being innocent until *proven* guilty. Yet, Singer has even gone so far as to suggest that companies be labeled with "terrible repute" and even summarily "fired" for being investigated or as a consequence of being the target of allegations.[587] All of these scenarios indicate, it would seem, little concern for individuals or institutions, not to mention the rule of law. Singer's themes regarding CACI have continued to focus primarily on specific key areas that he has persisted in presenting inaccurately: (1) qualifications and training of CACI interrogators; (2) the role of interrogators at Abu Ghraib including level of assumed culpability; and (3) establishment of guilt and punishment as a foregone conclusion, including corporate responsibility and perceived government failure in not acting on his predetermined assumption about guilt.

Singer has continued to point to one aspect of the findings about CACI hires (viz. military training or lack thereof), as proof that CACI interrogators lacked sufficient background and training. This has been conveyed through public statements such as, "the rush for profits and mass numbers [in Iraq], have brought in a lesser crop of skills with potentially grave consequences," and "U.S. Army investigations of Abu Ghraib prison were *deeply concerned* [italics added] about the CACI contract, finding that 'approximately 35 percent of the contract interrogators lacked formal training as interrogators.'"[588] Factually and specifically, however: (1) as noted in the official investigations, formal military interrogator training was not a requirement at the time CACI was contracted but it was, instead, among the recommendations of the official investigations for *future* contractors; (2) all CACI interrogators

[586] Ibid.
[587] Ibid.
[588] Ibid.

were U.S. citizens who met or exceeded the army SOW requirements, including related experience from police work or FBI, DEA, ATF, etc.; (3) all CACI interrogators had appropriate security clearances, having met the background review and standards that those security clearances required; (4) all CACI interrogators were appropriately qualified and had been accepted, approved, or agreed to for service by the army; (5) the CACI contract SOW stipulated that the contract interrogators would receive further training by the army after they were hired; and (6) official investigations (army IG, Schlesinger, Fay and Church) have pointed out the important benefit of contract interrogators to the interrogation process. Moreover, the CACI interrogator contract represented less than 1 percent of overall revenue (sales, not profit) for the company — hardly a "rush for profits."

As to the roles and potential culpability of the CACI contractors, Singer has continually overstated the percentage of CACI interrogators at Abu Ghraib and the *potential* culpability of the three CACI contractors out of the fifty-four total individuals cited in the Fay report as having some alleged association with misconduct at Abu Ghraib. But even here the allegations were *relatively* minimal and insignificant. The official investigation findings of *alleged* mistreatment or abuse by the three CACI employees would clearly be in the category that Fay referred to as less significant or due to "misinterpretation or confusion regarding law or policy."[589] Yet Singer has gone so far as to state that, "The U.S. Army *found* that contractors were involved in 36 percent of the *proven* incidents . . ." of abuse at Abu Ghraib [italics added]. And he has repeatedly stated that "not one of these individuals has yet been indicted, prosecuted, or punished."[590] Certainly it would be the role and responsibility of the military and the Department of Justice, not Singer, to determine if contractor actions were chargeable offenses and to determine the punishment, if any. Singer's continuing mantra of a "free pass" has ignored the lengthy investigations into the Abu Ghraib crisis and the role of the Department of Justice in investigating abuse allegations.

As to the establishment of guilt and punishment, one must always be wary of those who subscribe to the philosophy "sentence first, verdict later."

---

[589] Fay report, op. cit.
[590] Peter W. Singer, "Outsourcing War," *Foreign Affairs*, March/April 2006.

Singer attempted to malign CACI, it would appear, with claims that the company was "rewarded with massive contract extensions for work in Iraq despite being in the midst of governmental investigations for their prior actions."[591] There is, however, another view: specifically, (1) the GSA review had already shown CACI to be a responsible company with business ethics and integrity worthy of continued contract awards; (2) CACI was receiving positive feedback on its performance from the army in the field during these investigations; (3) the army needed to maintain interrogator continuity to support its mission; (4) the SOW had originally contemplated a contract extension beyond the first year; (5) CACI was understandably a part of the official investigations that were being conducted along with the military and other contractors, OGA's etc., but certainly not "in the midst"; (6) no company should be penalized (or punished) simply for (only) being investigated; (7) "prior actions" if any, could be attributed at most to three employees out of 9,500 employees, who were never charged; and (8) the company itself has a long and recognized record for its fine reputation and ethical practices.

Singer's view and public commentary about CACI was simply inappropriate.

*　*　*

On Capitol Hill in July 2005, Arizona senator John McCain brought the detainee abuse issue back to prominence when he introduced two amendments to the 2006 DoD authorization bill. The first would require that the interrogation of all detainees in DoD custody conform to the Army's Field Manual on Intelligence Interrogation. The second would prohibit the use of torture and cruel, inhuman, and degrading treatment by U.S. government agencies.

These new measures were opposed by the Bush administration based upon the view that they were already covered by law. McCain had reintroduced them in October 2005 as an amendment to a military appropriations bill, and the measures passed with a 90 to 9 vote in the Senate that same month. The White House then revised its initial position, and in December 2005, McCain announced that a deal with the administration had been struck. The measure now also included a provision whereby civilian interrogators were given legal protections that were al-

---

[591] Peter Singer, "The Private Military Industry and Iraq: What have we learned and where to next?" op. cit.

ready held by their military counterparts. These amendments became known as the Detainee Treatment Act of 2005.

The political debate and controversy over interrogation methods, the Geneva Conventions, and the definition of "torture" continued, even becoming a campaign theme in the fall elections of 2006.

In September 2006 these same issues about interrogation methods and the treatment of non-military detainees would become the source of important debate between the White House and the Senate. That month, controversial legislation was introduced that supporters claimed would give the U.S. greater power in the Global War on Terror. This legislation, which became known as the Military Commission Act of 2006, gave the president authority to establish military commissions to try "unlawful enemy combatants."[592]

But Congress wasn't the only party interested in updating the rules. A year before, in October 2005, DoD had issued an "instruction" (or official policy) on the use of contractors in war zones. Entitled "Contractor Personnel Authorized to Accompany the U.S. Armed Forces," the instruction "establishes and implements policy and guidance, assigns responsibilities, and serves as a comprehensive source of DoD policy and procedures concerning DoD contractor personnel authorized to accompany the U.S. Armed Forces." It was intended to help everyone better understand their duties. This new policy not only included prime contractors but also all subcontractors, third-country nationals, and host nation personnel that are authorized by the Pentagon to accompany the U.S. military. With over 100,000 contractors (both U.S. citizens and other nationals) working on a wide array of contracts, projects and tasks along side U.S. troops in Iraq and Afghanistan, the government had been under some pressure to clarify the roles of civilian contractors and the extent of authority and protection they were afforded in the battlefield.

---

[592] The War Crimes Act of 1996 criminalized breaches of the Geneva Conventions so that the United States could prosecute war criminals. It was specifically geared to circumstances pertaining to North Vietnamese soldiers that tortured U.S. soldiers during the Vietnam War. The law defines a war crime to include a "grave breach of the Geneva Conventions," specifically noting that "grave breach" should have the meaning defined in any convention (related to the laws of war) to which the U.S. is a party. The law applies if either the victim or the perpetrator is a national of the United States or a member of the U.S. armed forces.

By December 2006, the army had also updated and released its Field Manual on Counterinsurgency that addressed the matter of detainee treatment and interrogation policy and doctrine.[593] However, these topics seemed destined to be debated well into the future.

The government also re-examined other areas. In October 2006, legislation was drafted to enable the General Services Administration (GSA) to revamp troubled operations and create a new purchasing service. Sponsors of the bill reportedly hoped that reorganization would "help improve the agency's financial controls and make for more efficient purchasing of services, equipment and supplies used by federal agencies."[594] The *Washington Post* stated, "In recent months, the GSA has been tagged as a problem agency. Its business began slumping in fiscal 2004, and its technology service began operating in the red. Some

---

[593] The U.S. Army and Marine Corps Counterinsurgency Field Manual (FM 3-24), dated December 15, 2006, provides guidelines on the treatment and interrogation of detainees, including reference to the Detainee Treatment Act of 2005 and Department of Defense Directive 2310.01E (see below). It states that, "No person . . . shall be subject to torture or cruel, or degrading treatment or punishment, in accordance with, and as defined in, U.S. Law." The manual, FM 3-24, was prepared under the direction of the Army's (then) Lt. General David H. Petraeus at the Combined Arms Center (Ft. Leavenworth, Kansas) and Marine Corps Deputy Commandant of Combat Development and Integration, Lt. General James F. Amos. In their foreword, Lt. Generals Petraeus and Amos called the manual an overdue effort to fill a "doctrinal gap" on counterinsurgency.

FM 3-24 makes further reference to the U.S. Army Field Manual on Intelligence Interrogation (FM 2-22.3) stipulating that, "No person . . . in detention . . . shall be subject to any treatment or technique of interrogation not authorized by and listed in . . . FM 2-22.3." FM 3-24 further references the Detainee Treatment Act of 2005, Section 1003, stating, ". . . 'cruel, inhuman, or degrading treatment or punishment' means the cruel, unusual, and inhumane treatment or punishment prohibited by the Fifth, Eighth, and Fourteenth Amendments to the Constitution of the United States, as defined in the United States Reservations, Declarations and Understandings to the United Nations Convention Against Torture and Other Forms of Cruel, Inhuman or Degrading Treatment or Punishment done at New York, December 10, 1984."

The Department of Defense Directive 2310.01E, *The Department of Defense Detainee Program*, reissued in 2006 the 1994 directive "to ensure compliance with the laws of the United States, the law of war, including the Geneva Conventions of 1949, and all applicable policies, directives, or other issuances . . ."

[594] "GSA Will Try to Fix Procurement Problems With a New Service," *Washington Post*, October 2, 2006.

field offices were investigated for improper contracting activities; some federal agencies became dissatisfied with GSA services and took their business elsewhere."[595] GSA, which receives most of its funding by contracting on behalf of federal agencies, projected a loss of $96–110 million for fiscal 2006. In an effort to break even in 2007, GSA announced that it had made a decision to drop some internal projects, cut back on travel and cancel some support projects.[596]

By December 2006, audits by the inspectors general of the Department of the Interior and the Department of Defense were being conducted on the contracting process of both departments. These audits examined forty-nine contracting deals, and concluded that 61 percent had evidence of "illegal contracts, ill advised contracts, and various failings of contract administration procedures."[597] The relationship between Interior and the DoD was established as a result of government and military cutbacks and procurement reform measures during the Clinton administration. These efforts were aimed at procurement streamlining and were intended to produce faster, cheaper, and smarter acquisitions. Auditors for the Deparment of Interior, one of several agencies designated to manage contracts for other agencies for a fee, stated, "These poor contracting practices have left DoD vulnerable to fraud, waste and abuse and DOI vulnerable to sanctions and the loss of the public trust."[598] But auditors of both DOD and DOI concluded that, "Interior did not follow through on oversight and collected $22.8 million in fees for work the Pentagon could have done itself."[599] Significantly, however, the Defense IG said that the Pentagon could have saved the $22.8 million in management fees paid to Interior had the DOD used GSA (instead of DOI) for their contracting needs.

Contracting officials were reportedly quoted in the Defense audit as stating that they went to Interior to save time. "'We used DOI because

---

[595] Ibid. At the time of the article, the president was expected to sign the bill.

[596] Several agencies, including GSA, had taken deep personnel cuts during the Clinton administration's procurement reform. Paul C. Light, "The True Size of Government," GovExec.com, January 1, 1999.

[597] "Interior, Pentagon Faulted in Audits; Efforts to Speed Defense Contracts Wasted Millions," *Washington Post*, December 25, 2006.

[598] Ibid.

[599] Ibid.

they are able to expedite the contracting process, one Defense official said. Another official stated that the Defense office 'did not have enough contracting people to handle the requirements.'" According to the findings of both audits, "More than half of the contracts examined were awarded without competition or without checks to determine that the prices were reasonable. . . . Ninety-two percent of the work reviewed was awarded without verifying that the contractors' cost estimates were accurate; 96 percent was inadequately monitored."[600]

Officials at both Defense and Interior said they had been working to fix the contracting problems cited in the audits. "We are currently reviewing the finding of the DoD IG . . ." stated an official at the Pentagon while Interior officials said they were adopting many of the auditor's recommendations and had made "giant strides."[601]

Meanwhile, back on Capitol Hill in December 2006, it was revealed that a provision to subject contractors to military courts martial was "slipped into a spending bill at the end of the last Congress."[602] Under military law known as the Uniform Code of Military Justice (UCMJ), commanders would have wide latitude in deciding who should be prosecuted. But critics noted that this would create constitutional challenges in that civilians prosecuted would receive a grand jury hearing rather than a hearing by a jury of their peers. The Supreme Court earlier had struck down civilian convictions under military law, and no civilian conviction under UCMJ has been upheld in over a century. Another complication of the bill would be in determining who the provision would "apply to," in that its broad interpretation could include other civilian workers, as well as reporters and other media personnel.

Commenting on the bill, Peter W. Singer stated, "Not one contractor of the entire military industry in Iraq has been charged with any crime over the last three and a half years let alone prosecuted or punished. Given the raw number of contractors, let alone the incidents we know about it boggles the mind." Singer did not specify or define the incidents he claimed "*we* know about."[603]

---

[600] Ibid.

[601] Ibid.

[602] "New Law Could Subject Civilians to Military Trial," *Washington Post*, January 15, 2007.

[603] Ibid.

As for the ongoing inquiries and reviews of abuse allegations, in January 2007 the *New York Times* reported that the Justice Department issued a letter in response to congressional inquiries into the status of those alleged abuse cases still under review by DOJ. The letter stated, ***"As with an American suspected of a crime, those Americans who are the subject of the referrals are innocent until proven guilty"*** [bold italics added]. The letter outlined the reasons no charges would be brought in most of the referred cases stating, "All were declined for insufficient evidence to warrant criminal prosecution for one or more of the following reasons: insufficient evidence of criminal conduct; insufficient evidence of the subject's involvement; insufficient evidence of criminal intent; low probability of conviction." The letter also stated, "When career prosecutors conclude that we cannot prove allegations of a crime beyond a reasonable doubt, the department — consistent with its longstanding practices and policies — will not prosecute."[604]

A government lawyer added, "We took these allegations very seriously. We tried hard to get the complete story, to get these cases to prosecution. A lot of effort has gone into this."[605]

The *Times* article noted that of ten cases referred to Justice by the inspector general of the CIA, one remained under investigation. The article also noted that one case stemming from an F.B.I. accusation of abuse at Guantanamo Bay also remained open.[606]

* * *

After two and a half years of silence and laying low, Spc. Joseph Darby, who had alerted army officials to the Abu Ghraib abuses, finally spoke out to the press about the photos in August 2006. In several media interviews, Darby confirmed the complex and confusing environment at Abu Ghraib. Asked if anyone besides soldiers were performing interrogations at Abu Ghraib, Darby stated, "Well, we have what we refer to as OGAs [Other Government Agencies]. And we didn't — you

---

[604] David Johnston, "Letter Tells of Difficulties in Prosecuting Detainee Abuse," *New York Times*, January 16, 2007.

[605] Ibid.

[606] Ibid.

know, I don't know who they worked for. But we did have civilians who were contractors on the installation who did interrogations."[607]

Darby also clarified in his interviews an important aspect of the abuse photographs and the interrogations stating, "Well, the thing about this is it wasn't being done for interrogation. The interrogators, when they actually wanted to speak to the prisoners, would come take them out of the tier and to a facility that they had where they sat down and talked to them. There was — the abuse wasn't being done for any kind of intelligence value at all."[608]

CACI people read Darby's comments as further evidence and clarification of their own internal investigation and findings. From reviews and findings by CACI's outside counsel, the company had concluded, based on all of the information, data and documents available to them that the outrageous behavior depicted in the abuse photos was not in any way related to interrogations conducted by CACI's civilian interrogators. While other investigation reports made the same observation, here was a primary witness providing further support by stating so himself.

Another Abu Ghraib figure that resurfaced in 2006 was Lt. Gen. Ricardo Sanchez, who had spent a year in command of all U.S. forces in Iraq. The man that Taguba had once called a "good friend" retired from the army in October, but apparently not willingly. Sanchez, who reportedly issued three memos authorizing use of stress positions, sleep deprivation, and dogs at Abu Ghraib with his written approval, said he was "forced to retire."[609] Although he was reported to be a candidate to become the next commander of U.S. Southern Command before the scandal broke, he apparently was passed over for the job. Even though an army investigation didn't find substantial evidence of criminal behavior during the Abu Ghraib scandal, Sanchez said, "I was essentially not offered another position in another three-star or four-star command."[610]

---

[607] Michelle Norris, "Whistleblower speaks out," *All Things Considered*, NPR, August 15, 2006. See also: David Johnston, "U.S. Inquiry Falters on Civilians Accused of Abusing Detainees," *New York Times*, December 19, 2006.

[608] Ibid.

[609] Kelly Kennedy, "Sanchez says he was 'forced to retire,'" *Army Times*, November 2, 2006.

[610] "Ex-Iraq commander 'forced' to retire, Ex-chief of U.S. forces in Iraq says military forced him to retire," Associated Press, November 2, 2006.

A year later, Sanchez had more to say. At a military reporters and editors association luncheon in October 2007, Sanchez admonished the media for their "unscrupulous reporting." Referring to the media's heckling of him, including jabs like "dictatorial and somewhat dense" and a "liar," Sanchez scolded, "In some cases I have never even met you, yet you feel qualified to make character judgments that are communicated to the world." He added that personal reputations had no value to the media and there was no regard for the "collateral damage" the press caused in their pursuit of front page stories.[611]

He further assailed the current state of the media. "Once reported, your assessments become conventional wisdom and nearly impossible to change. Other major challenges are your willingness to be manipulated by 'high level officials' who leak their stories and by lawyers who hyperbole to strengthen their arguments. Your unwillingness to accurately and prominently correct your mistakes and your agenda-driven biases contribute to this corrosive environment. All of these challenges combined create a media environment that does a tremendous disservice to America."[612]

Sanchez reminded the audience that the strength of American democracy and freedom was "linked to the ability to exercise freedom of the press" and that he had "completely supported the embedding of media into our formations up until my last day in uniform." But the essential problem as he saw it was one of maintaining ethical standards from within media institutions. Referencing the Society of Professional Journalists' Code of Ethics of seeking truth, providing fair and comprehensive accounts of events, and honesty in reporting, Sanchez declared, ". . . your profession, to some extent, has strayed from these ethical standards and allowed external agendas to manipulate what the American public sees on TV, what they read in our newspapers and what they see on the Web. For some of you, just like some of our politicians, the truth is of little to no value if it does not fit your own preconceived notions, biases, and agenda."[613]

---

[611] Military Reporters and Editors Luncheon Keynote Speech by Lt. Gen. Ricardo Sanchez (Ret.), October 12, 2007.

[612] Ibid.

[613] Ibid.

Noting that the media . . . "with total impunity and are rarely held accountable for unethical conduct," Sanchez asked, "Who is responsible for maintaining the ethical standards of the profession in order to ensure that our democracy does not continue to be threatened by this dangerous shift away from your sacred duty of public enlightenment?"[614]

Although Sanchez's candor may have shocked some, it was not surprising to those at CACI who had lived through the media-incited and propaganda-driven ordeal. Sanchez's observations and remarks echoed many of CACI's experiences, paralleled much of what CACI had endured, and reflected many of the company's own conclusions during the same media blitz.

Sanchez directed the second half of his address to national security with specific criticisms of failures in national leadership, partisan politics, and planning, proclaiming that, "overcoming this strategic failure is the first step toward achieving victory in Iraq — without bipartisan cooperation we are doomed to fail.[615] Sanchez warned, "As a Japanese proverb says, 'action without vision is a nightmare.' There is no question that America is living a nightmare with no end in sight."[616]

As if intended to prove him right, media reports virtually ignored his critical remarks and, instead, distorted Sanchez's comments by reporting that he had called the Iraq war a failure. That evening, Brian Williams on NBC's Nightly News declared ". . . Sanchez turned on the Bush administration, accusing it of failure in Iraq."[617] The headline on a front page story in the *New York Times* the next day ran, "Ex-Commander

---

[614] Ibid.

[615] Those criticisms included his belief that there was "incompetent strategic leadership within our national leaders." He blamed partisan politics for preventing "effective, executable, supportable solutions" and assigned Congress "significant responsibility for this failure since there has been no focused oversight of the nation's political and economic initiatives in this war." He also characterized the coalition effort as "hasty, unresourced, and often uncoordinated and unmanaged." Ibid.

[616] Ibid.

[617] Brent Baker, "Sanchez Blasts Media, But Media Only Highlight His Criticism of Bush," *NewsBusters*, October 15, 2007 (http://newsbusters.org/blogs/brent-baker/2007/10/15/sanchez-blasts-media-media-only-highlight-his-criticism-bush).

Says Iraq Effort is 'a Nightmare.'"[618] In addition to the twisting of his words, the article completely ignored Sanchez's media criticisms. Other media outlets also downplayed the general's media critique by either failing to mention those comments or trivializing them at the end of reports. The *Washington Post's* coverage of the speech relegated Sanchez's extensive critique to the last paragraph. In a dismissive and sarcarstic two-sentence summary, the *Post* characterized Sanchez's criticisms as simply that members of U.S. media "blow stories out of proportion and are unwilling to correct mistakes, and that the 'media environment is doing a great disservice to the nation.'"[619] It was no surprise to those at CACI that Sanchez's comments had largely fallen on deaf ears.

* * *

The last senior Abu Ghraib official to face charges over abuse allegations was Lieutenant Colonel Steven L. Jordan, who had briefly been the former director of the Joint Interrogation and Debriefing Center and the liaison officer to the 205th Military Intelligence Brigade. The Taguba report named Jordan as one of the four people "suspected" to be either "directly or indirectly responsible" for the abuses at Abu Ghraib. It was alleged in the Taguba report that Jordan had made misrepresentations to the investigation team, including his leadership role, and did not properly supervise the soldiers under his command. His military proceedings began in April of 2006 when the army announced that it would charge Jordan. In January of 2007, Jordan was arraigned on eight charges including cruelty and maltreatment, dereliction of duty, lying to investigators, and conduct unbecoming an officer, although four of the original charges were eventually dropped.

Jordan's court-martial was held in August of 2007. Prosecutors asserted that Jordan's failure as a leader during his brief assignment at Abu Ghraib encouraged detainee abuse. But Jordan's defense team argued that he was not in the chain of command that was responsible for training and supervising military intelligence or military police — including those soldiers already convicted for committing the abuses. In

---

[618] David S. Cloud, "Ex-Commander Says Iraq Effort is 'a Nightmare,'" *New York Times*, October 13, 2007.

[619] Josh White, 'Ex-Commander in Iraq Faults War Strategy, 'No End in Sight,' Says Retired General Sanchez," *Washington Post*, October 13, 2007.

a split verdict, Jordan was found guilty of disobeying a general's command not to talk about the investigation but was acquitted of failing to control soldiers who had abused detainees. The military jury issued Jordan a reprimand sparing him any jail time.[620]

Critics claimed that the prosecution efforts were disappointingly poor, but some still could not accept that no one in a senior leadership position was punished. Human Rights Watch senior researcher John Sifton complained that "the verdict was 'a disappointment but not a surprise,' given the meager case he said prosecutors presented to the jury of senior officers. Mr. Sifton said prosecutors completely failed to muster evidence, including military case law, to show that Colonel Jordan, even if he did not participate in or know about abuses, was, as a senior officer at Abu Ghraib, responsible for abuses that occurred there."[621] It seemed Jordan's trial was a referendum on Abu Ghraib for those who felt many higher up in the military chain of command escaped responsibility for the abuses. As could have been expected, the *Washington Post* could not help but pass judgment. The subheading to their article on the trial's results ran, "Verdict Means No One in Army's Upper Ranks Will be Imprisoned for the 2003 Mistreatment in Iraq."[622]

But the most important statement came from an insider. Apparently in response to the criticism, Jordan's lead defense counsel Samuel Spitzberg submitted a letter to the editor of his hometown newspaper, the Albany Times Union. Published two weeks after the Jordan verdict, Spitzberg's letter underscored his client's innocence. More importantly, it reemphasized a point CACI had been making for some time:

"Notwithstanding comments to the contrary, the famous pictures of Abu Ghraib that we all remember had nothing to do with the collection of military intelligence. The trial proved this point."[623]

---

[620] In January 2008, the army dismissed Jordan's conviction outright and gave him an administrative reprimand. See also Appendix J — List of Abu Ghraib Verdicts.

[621] Paul von Zielbauer, "Army Colonel Is Acquitted In Abu Ghraib Abuse Case," *New York Times*, August 29, 2007.

[622] Josh White, "Abu Ghraib Officer Cleared of Detainee Abuse; Verdict Means No One in Army's Upper Ranks Will Be Imprisoned for the 2003 Mistreatment in Iraq," *Washington Post*, August 29, 2007.

[623] Samuel Spitzberg, "Court-martial trial is a credit to justice system," *Albany Times Union*, September 12, 2007.

⋆ ⋆ ⋆

The man whose name became synonymous with the Abu Ghraib investigation, Major General Antonio Taguba, also reemerged after the ordeal. In the first half of 2007 Taguba sat down with the *New Yorker's* Seymour Hersh to discuss his perspective of the Abu Ghraib scandal. Hersh, who was the very same journalist who helped break the story on Taguba's *illegally leaked* report three years earlier, produced a sympathetic portrayal of Taguba. As the former military investigator described his discontent with the series of events that unfolded after his report was *leaked*, Taguba reiterated that he was ordered only to investigate the MPs and not the chain of command above them.

Taguba also expressed dismay with then secretary of defense Donald Rumsfeld and various senior officials who stated they knew nothing previously about the abuses and testified to that effect in front of the Senate Armed Services Committee in May 2004. During the interview, Taguba claimed that one of Rumsfeld's assistants received email confirming abuse in January 2004 and Taguba further contended that the investigation report had been disseminated through the appropriate chain of command.

Taguba also added now his own speculative thoughts. He stated his belief that his report was perhaps leaked by a senior military leader who knew about the investigation. Taguba's statement again raised the question of who leaked the report and why they did so.

Taguba and Hersh also discussed their speculations about the roles of the CIA and military intelligence in the affair. After Abu Ghraib, Taguba was pulled from transitioning to his next duty station in Georgia and was assigned to the U.S. Army Reserve Command for Transition and Transformation. Taguba said he believed he was reassigned to the Pentagon so he could be watched. In January 2006 Taguba was called by his superior officer and told he needed to retire by January 2007, which he did. Stating his opinion clearly, Taguba noted that no reason was given but that "they always shoot the messenger."[624]

As 2007 drew to a close, nearly four years *after* Taguba's report —neither the company nor any CACI employee had faced anything but allegation and innuendo. No charges were brought against Steve Stefanowicz or any other current or former employee for the Abu Ghraib abuses.

---

[624] Seymour Hersh, "The General's Report, How Antonio Taguba, who investigated the Abu Ghraib scandal, became one of its casualties," *New Yorker*, June 25, 2007.

The CACI team had reviewed all available reports and documents and could not find evidence to verify the allegations. The only documents not available to CACI were seven annexes from the Taguba report that the government had withheld. The rest of the 104 annexes, however, did not address Stefanowicz or CACI beyond Stefanowicz's and John Israel's interviews with Taguba. CACI could only assume that the lack of any other corroborating evidence in all the investigations meant those annexes did not contain information relevant or significant to CACI. In this regard, CACI remained prepared in case charges or indictments were brought up, but as time went on and reports from the DOJ referral investigations emerged, that possibility seemed less and less likely.

Still, by the end of 2007, there had been no media-driven inquiry or critical scrutiny focused on the Taguba report, which had set off the public relations crisis for CACI in the first place. The single sentence stating Taguba's "suspicion" that Stefanowicz and others were either "directly or indirectly responsible" in some way for the abuses at Abu Ghraib was the subject of many official investigations but was *not* itself subjected in any way to critical investigative reporting by the media.

Neither, it appears, was the "leaker" of the illegally leaked Taguba report sought out or investigated by government officials. No one in the press has either investigated or revealed the perpetrator.[625]

* * *

In the meantime, there would be changes at CACI. President Ken Johnson had retired from CACI in October 2004 and, after a thorough search, London hired former Computer Sciences Corporation executive Paul Cofoni as the new president of U.S. Operations in August 2005. [626] Also moving on was Senior Vice President Harry Thornsvard, a former PTG executive who had been at the heart of CACI's Iraq activities, accepting an offer to become a company president of RDR, a small Virginia-based, security-centric IT and systems engineering firm. Another key Iraq team member and CACI executive, John Hedrick, also retired in 2004. Looking to spend more time traveling and with his family, General Counsel Jeff Elefante retired in August 2005 after over twenty years with

---

[625] A list of convictions and reprimands stemming from the Abu Ghraib scandal can be found in Appendix J.

[626] Paul Cofoni was appointed President and Chief Executive Officer of CACI International Inc on July 1, 2007.

CACI. And in spring 2006, Sr. Vice President Chuck Mudd, a former PTG executive and line business manager at CACI who had made numerous and frequent trips to Iraq to monitor CACI's projects, also retired.

The makeup of the CACI response team changed slightly, but remained fully focused and determined as ever to preserve CACI's good name. To this day, the team continues to monitor the news and activist commentaries and Web sites, correcting errors and falsehoods in vigilantly guarding the company's reputation. Further, CACI's Web site section covering its business in Iraq which the communications team originally posted in 2004 remains active.[627] As CACI's communications officer Jody Brown put it, "Jack will never stand down on this matter. We will remain steadfast in our mission to preserve the company's good name, now and in the future."

New faces would come to the company in 2005 and 2006. They would be part of CACI's growth initiative, the "Alignment for Growth," which would realign the company's operations into four business groups, implemented to meet CACI's ambitious expansion goals, including industry "Tier 1" status and achieving $5 billion in revenue by fiscal year 2012. The "Alignment for Growth" was designed to position CACI for better client focus and help build the critical mass the company needed to pursue larger contracts and larger acquisitions in meeting its customer's needs.

With the largest acquisition in the company's history of the AMS division in April 2004, bigger business deals were also coming into the now larger CACI. Between January and September 2005, CACI announced nearly $1.2 billion in new contracts, including a five-year, estimated $150 million BPA with the General Services Administration, and the company was pursuing even more of the industry's biggest deals. Well-known for its aggressive mergers and acquisitions strategy, CACI was also working diligently, with Burkhart's assistance, to identify target companies that would add new expertise and business to the company. In October 2005, CACI announced the acquisition of National Security Research Inc., a strategic company specializing in solving defense and homeland security problems.[628] In 2006, CACI also acquired Information Systems Support Inc., and AlphaInsight Corp., two IT solutions providers to the federal

---

627 www.caci.com.

628 National Security Research Inc. was the last acquisition facilitated by Burkhart for CACI before she shifted her consulting into other business endeavors.

government. CACI was also continuing to report record growth and outstanding financial performance at the end of every quarter.

In early 2006, CACI made another business leap when it announced that it was awarded a contract, along with several other large firms, to support army work that could reach a total of $19.25 billion over the contract's five-year duration (plus a five-year option period) for engineering and logistics technology services. It was a new opportunity to serve the U.S. Army, and the award was greeted with much excitement at CACI.[629]

Overall, CACI's leaders believed that the company's success in 2005 and into 2006 validated the strategic decision they had made in May 2004 to recognize the national trauma from Abu Ghraib, to cooperate fully with every official government inquiry, to aggressively engage in its own investigative research, to distribute verified facts about the company and its employees, and to vigilantly correct misstatements and errors by the media and other third parties. Importantly and significantly, they would also acknowledge and address any wrongdoing when it was shown to be factual.

The company's leaders felt their effort benefited greatly from the foundation provided by a strong, pre-existing company standard of ethics memorialized over the years in CACI's written credo and mission statement and engrained in its culture. In hindsight, the senior executives also believed they would have benefited from a pre-existing crisis management plan and a stronger government relations program instead of starting those in the midst of crisis. But no one could have predicted the magnitude of events that unfolded in May 2004.

CACI was clearly moving on from Abu Ghraib. The success of CACI's comeback strategy became evident by 2008 when CACI placed second among *Fortune*'s Most Admired IT Services Companies and second among the Most Admired Companies in Virginia. And the Ethisphere Institute, in analyzing over 1000 federal contractors, named CACI one of the "Best Overall Ethics Programs." CACI received the highest rating of Excellent and ranked third among the 100 Largest Government Contractors. CACI also placed first in Best Ethics Training.

CEO Jack London was satisfied that he had made the right assessment of the Abu Ghraib situation when it broke open in the media. He

---

[629] CACI Press Release, "CACI Awarded Prime Contract on $19.25 Billion, Multiple-Award Services Program With U.S. Army, Strategic Services Sourcing (S3) Award to Support Defense C4ISR Community Largest Contract Award in CACI History," March 15, 2006.

had immediately taken charge to direct the creation of what would become CACI's own modern-day crisis management strategy and model. He was pleased it had worked so effectively overall, given the challenging and daunting circumstances facing the company at the time. He was also well aware that it was the whole team working together at CACI that had made it work so well.

As for the Abu Ghraib scandal, the debate about the causes of the abuses and photographs chronicled in the fall of 2003 may continue for years. And while no indisputable or widely agreed upon conclusion may ever be reached, there is a clear case that can be advanced. The case is that the record of fact shows that the Abu Ghraib abuses were *not* the failure of interrogation policies or techniques as such. Rather, they were largely the failure of army command leadership and control over the MPs of the 372nd MP Company and the lack of supervision, training and discipline within this unit. There were other significant issues as well; staffing shortages, a hostile environment, critical levels of overcrowding, inadequate logistics support (basing, rations, weapons, etc.) and personnel turnover. Nevertheless, a strong, focused, command-leadership regimen would, it seems, have mitigated the risks, if not favorably changed the outcome altogether. It would appear that no amount of finger-pointing, punditry, or media propaganda otherwise can alter these substantial and voluminous findings of fact as they have been determined from the multiple independent government investigations, testimonies given publicly under oath by numerous individuals, and various courts-martial, all that have addressed these matters in excruciating detail (to include: all records, memos, affidavits, depositions, sworn statements, digital photographs, videos, and considerable other documented evidence).

Business, then, would continue at a good pace as the company continued to march forward. There would surely be more challenges and triumphs. Just as the beginning of the Abu Ghraib ordeal had coincided with the birth of his first granddaughter by his daughter, CACI CEO Jack London would mark the last phases of the crisis in virtually the same way. In January 2006, his daughter and her husband welcomed their second child; this time a boy. And as this book was being completed, London's son and his wife announced the birth of their third son (London's fifth grandchild). CACI, its people, and their families were now all moving confidently towards the future.

THE CEO'S POSTSCRIPT

Reflections on Abu Ghraib, the media, and critically related issues by J.P. London.

> **"If it is not right, do not do it; if it is not true do not say it. For let thy efforts be."**
> ～ **MARCUS AURELIUS**

D URING 2004, I EXPERIENCED ONE OF THE MOST DIFFICULT—BUT also one of the most rewarding—years of my life.

In April of that year, a scandal erupted over allegations and photos of abuse at Abu Ghraib prison near Baghdad, Iraq. The world learned that during the late fall and early winter of 2003, a small number of American military police stationed at the prison had, tragically, participated in the abuse and humiliation of Iraqi detainees. Several official government investigations were soon launched into the events that had occurred at the prison at the time. The company I led, CACI, had placed a small group of employees in Iraq on a contract for our customer, the U.S. Army, in the early fall of 2003.[630] Stemming from what was later shown to be an *unsubstantiated* accusation in one of the initial reports about "responsibility" for those abuses, CACI would get pulled into the

---

[630] After twenty-three years in the position, J.P. London stepped aside as CEO and President of CACI International Inc on June 30, 2007. He remained Chairman of the Board.

controversy and embroiled in the subsequent media frenzy that ensued. And several more focused, in-depth investigations would follow.

During 2004 and into 2005, we faced numerous investigations and audits, a possible suspension from government contracting which could have put us out of business, egregious and outlandish lawsuits, despicable and vile accusations of various and numerous alleged misdeeds, and accusations from extremists in some of the most outrageous and vulgar language imaginable (none of which would be repeated in this book). We also experienced a constant onslaught of inaccurate and distorted news reporting that wrongly created a public perception of guilt on the part of our company. And we saw how some opportunistic third parties and so-called experts sought to use the media as a promotional tool to advance their own political or personal agendas. Unfortunately, these abuses of CACI continued through 2007.

Throughout this ordeal, CACI stood by the belief that the core values of fairness and due process do not vanish simply because someone is publicly and repeatedly accused in the media.

At *best*, the reporters and journalists of the media mostly got CACI's story wrong about Iraq and Abu Ghraib, despite all of our attempts to make the facts known. At *worst*, there were reported misrepresentations, exaggerations, fabrications, speculations, distortions, and in some cases, outright lies about our company that were, in my view, unforgivable.

During this ordeal, I had the honor of leading a dedicated team of CACI people and advisors, loyal Americans that vigorously withstood the tsunami effect of the news media barrage over Abu Ghraib. The media was relentless in its attempt to find someone guilty for what happened at Abu Ghraib. Many parties seemed eager to find "someone to hang" beyond the enlisted soldiers and the people clearly identified in the infamous Abu Ghraib abuse scandal photographs that came out that April along with the official investigations that followed.[631]

The public was also jumping to conclusions without evidence. Impatient for answers, as the investigations unfolded, in their uninformed eyes we were perceived to be guilty by association and accusation. This rush to judgment produced a reverberating and escalating

---

[631] No CACI employees appeared in any of the notorious Abu Ghraib detainee abuse photos.

effect. The media's hasty reporting was embellished by a coterie of self-styled "experts," opportunists, and speculators whose often baseless opinions and unfounded theorizing filled the void while information was still being gathered.

I am proud to say our team held firm through all of this, and stood up for the American concepts of justice, the rule of law, and the principle that a person (or a company) is innocent until proven guilty in a court of law. Witch hunts, lynch mobs, kangaroo courts, and trials by media are not the law of the land. We stood firm and pushed back against malicious unfounded attacks that were, for the most part, politically and personally motivated by those who loaded CACI onto their agendas. And we pushed back against a "scoop-driven" media that had apparently abandoned objectivity and fact-verification to get top billing for their stories. We would not allow any inaccurate statement or unwarranted accusation go unanswered, whether from the simply uninformed or the purely prejudiced. To do so would allow inaccuracies to persist and mushroom into larger more preposterous tales about CACI.

This book tells the story of our harrowing experience during the Abu Ghraib ordeal, its impact on our company, including the pressures of official investigations, questions from investors, inquiries from government leaders, and the harsh wire brushing we received from various government agencies. It also tells of the intense scrutiny from the media that led to incredibly negative publicity and harsh public criticism. And it tells of our success in resisting the avalanche of distorted media coverage, and misrepresentations in the numerous commentaries of so-called pundits to uphold our good name.

Ours is a story of how a company caught in the media's spotlight, under intense government examination, working in a war zone and swept up in a tragic, salacious scandal with international exposure, worked to pull itself out of the morass in order to sustain its fine reputation. I hope our story is considered both illuminating and thought-provoking.

Like all Americans, I was badly shaken by the photographs of the abuses. As a former naval officer, I was profoundly disturbed by the dishonor that anyone in our military could bring to the military uniform that I wore proudly for a dozen years of active duty beginning in 1959 and, then for twelve more years until 1983 as an active member of the

U.S. Naval Reserve.[632] I recognize along with everyone else that the Abu Ghraib abuses are a sad and deeply regrettable stain on our nation's military history. And we must all learn from it.

But in addition to seeing the photographs, I received a second sickening shock when I learned from a journalist that an employee of CACI had been accused of involvement in those abuses. The accusation appeared in an *illegally leaked* fifty-three-page summary report prepared by Major General Antonio M. Taguba as part of the U.S. Army's ongoing investigations into conditions at Abu Ghraib. Completed in February 2004, the report, based on an investigation of the military police (MP) at the prison, was classified and marked "SECRET/NO FOREIGN DISSEMINATION," and was not intended for public release. I can only imagine the shock and dismay that Major General Taguba must have endured as a result of these illegal leaks.

I was, of course, distressed to learn that one of our people might have had a role in those events and I prepared for the worst. But I was also upset to think that the classified Taguba report that this journalist possessed was an *illegally leaked* copy, the release of which *must* be viewed as both an illegal and an irresponsible act. In both my military and civilian careers, and as someone whose company performs professional and technical contract services for U.S. government agencies, I have sworn to respect document classifications and the U.S. government security laws that apply to them. To date, I have heard no comment, concern, or even curiosity expressed about who leaked that classified military report.[633] This also begs the question: Is breaking national security laws to be rewarded in this new society of apparent situational ethics? And if so, are all such security laws now open to discretionary observance?[634] And who now will make the decisions — to pursue or not pursue security violations — anyone?

---

[632] Captain London, USNR (Ret.) graduated from the U.S. Naval Academy in 1959 and retired from active naval reserve affiliation in 1983.

[633] December 2007.

[634] I wonder if the person who broke the law and illegally leaked the Taguba report had the good conscience even to consider the permanent and indelible harm that would surely follow releasing it to the media before all the abuse allegations were fully, completely, and thoroughly investigated. In addition, the image and reputation of America and its armed forces would be undoubtedly placed under months of constant intense, negative scrutiny while investigations were conducted and the situation was sorted out. Most importantly, the lives of everyone fighting for freedom in

Whether leaks occur, as commonly believed, because of ego or agenda, it has become more and more obvious that *illegal leaks* pose a danger to America and its citizens, as well as citizens of other countries. Leaks seriously undermine efforts to protect the country and those people acting in its service, especially those Americans in uniform in hostile or active combat zones. It seems appropriate and necessary that every person involved with the leak, from the "leaker" to the recipient, should be held accountable and punished if proven guilty of breaking the law. The damage that can be done by *illegal leaks* to the media should not be trivialized or rewarded. Nor should the debatable inadequacy of existing governing statutes be the determining factor in upholding the law.

These were just some of the many shocks that I would experience over the balance of 2004. Since then, CACI has fought to maintain its honorable reputation and its very survival because of the uncorroborated *suspicion* that one of our people *may* have had some degree of responsibility for what happened at Abu Ghraib. Throughout that first year, I felt like we were being buffeted by media tidal waves that had pounded us with inquiries and accusations day after day, all summer long.

The root of our crisis emerged from a few sentences on page forty-eight of the Major General's report, where Taguba wrote that Steven Stefanowicz, a CACI employee, was one of four people whom he "suspected" of being "either directly or indirectly responsible" for the abuses at Abu Ghraib.[635] The three other names cited in the report included two U.S. Army officers and another civilian contractor. At that time (April 2004), Mr. Stefanowicz was an interrogator at Abu Ghraib, in support of the U.S. Army.[636] He had gone to Iraq soon after our in-

---

Iraq were clearly put at risk by the backlash and by anything that further hampered important intelligence-gathering efforts. It was a ready made propaganda tool for al Qaeda and its Islamo-facist look-a-likes; and they would promptly make the most of it. In the near term, there would be wild speculation and gross exaggerations about the situation, and its causes and perpetrators. And the related and focused propaganda efforts would far outpace the investigations, the facts and the truth as far as CACI was concerned.

[635] Taguba Report, op. cit.

[636] Interrogation is the methodical, systematic inquiry and examination of an individual, typically by questioning (Cross examination, used in legal proceedings, is a term synonymous with interrogation.). *Webster's New World Dictionary and Thesaurus 2nd Ed.* (Wiley Publishing, Inc.: Cleveland: 2002). See also Glossary and Terms of Interest.

telligence support and interrogator services project had started in the fall of 2003, but in the capacity of a "screener," not interrogator.[637] He was soon advanced to interrogator with the agreement of the army because of his interpersonal skills and on-the-job experience and training.

Over time, I learned that there was no hard evidence to support Major General Taguba's speculative theory and "suspicions" about Mr. Stefanowicz. Subsequent investigative reports by the military backed away significantly from the sweeping and damaging allegations that Mr. Stefanowicz was involved or participated in any way with the kind of conduct shown in the photographs. In fact, *no* CACI employees appeared in any of the infamous Abu Ghraib abuse photos shown on international television in late April and May 2004.

A year later, in April 2005, I was shocked and dismayed by Major General Taguba's statement, in an interview with a California newspaper, that he really hadn't thought about which category of responsibility — "direct" or "indirect" — applied to the men he had singled out.[638] It saddened me greatly to see how little thought seemed to lay behind such momentous and severe accusations.[639]

And yet, to the date of this writing, no media critique or probing examination has ever been made by anyone into the Taguba report (*illegally leaked* to the hands of Seymour Hersh of the *New Yorker* magazine in April 2004). Notably too, the August 2004 investigative report by Major General Fay did not substantiate or provide any proof for Taguba's suspicions that Stefanowicz was "directly or indirectly" *responsible* for the abuses. Indeed the Fay report, for all intents and

---

637 Screeners were a different category than interrogators. Screeners duties do not include interrogation per se; they typically review detainees in the attempt to determine their status, e.g., enemy prisoner, criminal, terrorist, alien, citizen, etc. They do have frequent interaction with detainees. Screeners are also frequently assigned the task of evaluating the status or bona fides of personnel seeking employment by the government.

638 Leon Worden, "Taguba Interview: Sanchez 'Good Friend,'" *The Signal*, April 24, 2005.

639 Because Major General Taguba's report was classified SECRET/NO FOREIGN DISSEMINATION, and did not report firm conclusions, but instead referred matters, including those regarding Stefanowicz, *for further investigation*, it may be reasonably assumed that it was not drafted (nor intended) for public release and the resulting worldwide media coverage and public scrutiny.

purposes, exculpated the allegation of Stefanowicz's "direct or indirect" responsibility in the Taguba report.[640]

It is quite difficult to describe how I felt about the pain and turmoil that those ill-chosen words caused my company and the 9,500 people of CACI (in 2004), especially those who continued to risk their lives in Iraq to serve our country and our military customers every day.

I must add that I was also disappointed on many occasions by what I saw happening inside our government. CACI was to come under microscopic examination by a wide array of government agencies, understandably because of the Abu Ghraib ordeal, but in a larger part due to the overwhelmingly negative publicity surrounding the scandal. During all of this, I believed that we would be treated more even-handedly. But here, too, I was left with the impression that even in the government's view, we were considered guilty until and unless we could prove our innocence. Frankly, it also seemed to me that CACI was perhaps, regrettably, a convenient scapegoat for others' shortcomings or even personal political agendas.

* * *

Our most serious crisis as a company caught in the media whirlwind and the chaos of Abu Ghraib came from the General Services Administration (GSA), when on May 26, 2004, the company received a letter from the GSA's suspension and debarment official. Like a bomb dropped out of nowhere, the letter stated in cold harsh language that GSA was giving CACI just ten days to provide it with information as to why CACI should remain eligible for future government contracts. The basis of this request was not a question about the abuses at Abu Ghraib, but about the administrative propriety and procedural detail of the contract used by the U.S. Army to engage CACI to provide interrogator services. At worst, this GSA probe threatened to put CACI entirely out of business. At best, the outcome could possibly tarnish CACI's decades-long positive reputation as a responsible and trusted government contractor. And it was going to take lots of legal fees and senior management time and effort just to respond.

As a public corporation, we were also compelled to publicly disclose this threat to our business. On the morning of May 27, 2004, the company, with its board of directors' support, issued a press release concern-

---

[640] Fay Report, op. cit.

ing the GSA's inquiry. The stock market reacted harshly, sending the stock down twelve percent from $42.65 at the market's open on May 26 to $37.48 by the close of the very next day after CACI issued its release. CACI's stock price would stay below $39 until the end of June and hover around $40 until mid-August. At that point, the GSA inquiry and the government's official Abu Ghraib investigations had drawn to a close without concluding any culpability or direct responsibility on the part of any CACI employee or the company.

Our plight in responding to the GSA inquiry shows the trauma we went through in this respect, too. Ironically, this inquiry was due to the government's own concerns that somehow CACI had erred in its contract for professional interrogator services at Abu Ghraib prison in Iraq. This, of course, would not be consistent with CACI's long history of successful government work. As it would soon be shown, however, not only was the contracting process completely above-board and known by all the government parties, but the GSA itself in 1998 had set out the contracting precedents with PTG, Inc. (acquired by CACI in May 2003) that were used by the army and CACI for the interrogation contract out of Baghdad, Iraq, in the summer of 2003.

This intelligence support and interrogator services contract was born out of necessity during the escalating crisis over the huge, hostile detainee population being gathered up as the insurgency activity heightened that summer and fall. And this was when the U.S. military badly needed to obtain intelligence information as it fought to suppress the insurgency, find Saddam Hussein and his sons, and track down the al Qaeda and other Islamic terrorist fanatics and their leaders.

Our quick response to support the U.S. Army (which I felt a duty and honor-bound commitment to provide) during that brutal summer of 2003 cost CACI dearly in the avalanche of undeserved criticism and hateful attacks we endured that following year, and since, because of the news media's all-too-often misrepresentation and distortion of the facts.

Sometime later, I was told jokingly by a friend (and a ranking official in the government but with whom CACI has never had any business) that in Washington, D.C. you have to remember that famous cliché that "No good deed ever goes unpunished."

Yet for all our travails, as the reader has no doubt discovered, **I am very proud of the many fine CACI people that served in harm's**

way, did their job competently, and loyally supported their country.

In retrospect, there is an extreme irony about all of this. In late summer 2005, Hurricane Katrina's devastating effects in the U.S. Gulf States would quickly bring out the opposite view of government contracting in exigent and overwhelming emergency conditions. This time the media would criticize the government for *not* having the contracts to respond to the crisis. In Iraq in 2003 the government had a contract, used it, and took flak. Now the media and the critics were on the other side of the fence: having no contracts was viewed as the problem.[641]

As this book shows, CACI not only responded fully to the government review process, but we came out exceedingly well. I dare say we came through an unrelenting gauntlet of investigations and underwent intense scrutiny where very few companies (or people) would be able to endure nearly as well. Some companies I believe would not have survived this test.

---

[641] In the summer of 2004, the U.S. government had been severely criticized by the media and critics for outsourcing certain operating functions in Iraq and utilizing broad-based contracts to acquire interrogation and other services even though it was under exigent wartime circumstances. A year later, in September 2005, Hurricane Katrina hit the U.S. Gulf Coast, ravaging small towns and large cities like New Orleans. The Federal Emergency Management Agency (FEMA) and other federal and local organizations were put to the test and found themselves overwhelmed in dealing with the aftermath. This time, the media reported that the government was poorly utilizing contracts and failed to have sufficient procedures and resources in place to acquire outside help, thus preventing private companies from providing desperately needed assistance to the region. "'There were contracts in place. But obviously they were not adequate,' said Richard L. Skinner, the Homeland Security Department inspector general. 'I don't think the contracts in place ever contemplated anything this devastating. . . . They weren't prepared upfront to obtain the products and services they would need.'" ("Lack of contracts hampered FEMA, Dealing with disaster on the fly proved costly," *Washington Post*, October 10, 2005.) FEMA, for example, was forced to spend millions of dollars on last-minute, noncompetitive bid contracts that were made ineffective by the agency's own procurement shortcomings and voided altogether when Congress forced the agency to put out other contracts for competition.

While CACI and the government had been grilled for having used an existing contract to help in emergency wartime (combat: life and death) conditions in Iraq, the government was now taking the heat for not having the contracts and processes in place in the case of domestic emergencies like Hurricane Katrina.

This book has told the story of CACI and its people and how, as a team, they successfully stepped up to meet the challenges created by Abu Ghraib, Major General Taguba's report, release of the notorious abuse photos, intense public scrutiny, grueling news media examinations, and the extensive government investigations that were faced beginning late in April 2004. We endured a vigorous wire-brushing and came through intact.

Day after day for many months, we worked with little rest. Our challenge was enormous. The Abu Ghraib story was, arguably, one of the biggest scandals to hit the whole world in the last quarter century. What made it so large and dramatically different from all other international scandals lies in the very nature of the abuse story: it took place during a hotly debated war that was evolving into increasingly violent, guerilla-styled, asymmetric, urban warfare waged by al Qaeda, foreign intruders, suicidal terrorists, insurgents, and Baathist party remnants.[642]

In addition, the fact that the U.S. military was operating with contractors in the field, though not a new military practice, was news to the general public at the time.[643] Also new to the public was Abu Ghraib prison, the most notorious and hated "torture" prison in Iraq's history. It had been used by one of the most evil, murderous tyrants alive at the time — the despot Saddam Hussein.

The allegations coming out of the U.S. military's investigations of the Abu Ghraib abuses were wide-ranging, salacious and, in some cases bizarre, including sexual exploitation, nudity, and physical abuse. Murder and rape were also swept up in the wide-ranging allegations. In fact, those soldiers convicted of wrongdoing at Abu Ghraib were never even accused of any of the most extreme allegations of murder or rape. Also

---

[642] Published reports indicate such foreign intruders include people from Saudi Arabia, Algeria, Syria, Libya, Morocco, Oman, Tunisia, Yemen, Sudan, Egypt and even the United Kingdom. Iran is also accused of providing training, arms, and funding to Shiite militias.

[643] Patriot contractors have been used in support of our military operations as far back as the American Revolution and throughout our national history, including the Civil War, World Wars I and II, Korea, Vietnam, and the Gulf War of 1991. My direct ancestor, Michael Clardy of Halifax Country, Virginia, during the American Revolution was a government supplier to the Continental Line (Army) of at least "300 pounds of beef and four forages," as cited in the Virginia Public Service, Halifax County Court Book, 57, and Commission Book II, 264.

noteworthy is that no one associated with CACI was ever implicated of wrongdoing during those courts-martial. Some of these Abu Ghraib allegations were still under review during the time this book was being written, although neither CACI nor any of its employees (current or former) have ever been charged with any of these abuses.

But what made the story so awful was that there were hundreds, if not thousands, of vivid photographs of some of these aberrations and abuses being carried out by a few (relatively, quite few) U.S. service men and women. It was a small number, but they could be seen and counted in the graphic abuse photographs. Some of the scandalous abuse photos allegedly showed civilian contractors, but *none* were CACI employees. And on top of everything else, the story and the photos were broadcast around the world by an adrenaline-pumped media that was in an absolute state of frenzy in its frantic efforts to get its stories filed with every possible sensational detail included.

While the events of Abu Ghraib were unforgivably disgraceful, even worse were the dozens of ghastly kidnappings and beheadings carried out by al Qaeda and other terror groups in Iraq at the same time.[644] The

---

[644] In 2004, al Qaeda and other terror groups, desperate for success, focused on beheadings as a mechanism for heightening the terror and intimidation. An American businessman and contractor, 26-year-old Nicholas Berg, was the first to draw international attention with his tragic beheading by an al Qaeda operative, Jordanian Abu Musab Al Zarqawi, which was subsequently posted online. These acts all fit precisely and fully within the savagery of the Islamic-fascist al Qaeda movement. In October 2005, Al Zarqawi reaffirmed the *murder of innocent people* saying, "Islam does not differentiate between civilians and military, but rather distinguishes between Muslims and infidels [non-Muslims] . . . Muslim blood must be spared . . . but it is permissible to spill infidel blood." ("Zarqawi Justified Killing of Civilians," *Washington Times*, October 8, 2005.) Apparently he is referencing the Koran (Qur'an), which sets out specific perspectives on "beheadings" of those who "disbelieve" [and therefore are among the "infidels"]. Examples of this Islamic doctrine for beheadings are found in the Koran at 8:12 and 47:4. These passages read, in part, "So make those that believe stand firm. I will throw fear into the hearts of those who disbelieve. Then smite their necks and smite of them each finger." (8:12). And, "Now when ye meet in battle those who disbelieve, then it is smiting of their necks until, when ye have routed them, then making fast of bonds." (47:4), [M. Pickthall, trans., *The Koran* (New York: Campbell Publishers Ltd, 1992)]. From these perspectives, it also seems reasonable to conclude that the terrorists' war, in large part, is a religious war, a terrorist jihad, instigated and perpetuated by Islamic fanatics such as Al Zarqawi. Al Zarqawi was killed on June 7, 2006 by U.S. forces.

world news was saturated with coverage of the Abu Ghraib abuses, but the jihadists' kidnappings and beheadings of hostages (including several Americans) received little coverage in comparison, despite the fact that the beheadings were typically recorded and released on the terror groups' web sites and widely disseminated. Also virtually ignored by the media were videos of Saddam Hussein's tortures at Abu Ghraib which surfaced at the time. Senators Rick Santorum and Joe Lieberman held a press conference to show "the real torture tapes from Abu Ghraib" made by the Hussein regime.[645] The tapes showed graphic torture and murder of Iraqi victims, including dismemberment and decapitation. The Hussein videos prompted Cliff Kincaid of Accuracy in Media to observe, "This is far worse than making a prisoner wear women's panties which occurred under U.S. management of the prisoners."

Former Deputy Secretary of Defense Paul Wolfowitz complained in an interview on MSNBC, "there [was] . . . zero coverage of [the Saddam Hussein torture tapes] in the media."[646] Kincaid noted: "In fact, the [Saddam Hussein torture] video has been covered, by FOX News and a few other outlets . . . when FOX news broke the story of the Saddam torture videos, the [New York] Times ran five paragraphs back on page A14 with a small picture. That compares with 181 stories on American abuse of prisoners at Abu Ghraib, more than forty on the front page."[647]

Deborah Orin of the New York Post, who viewed the Saddam torture tapes, asked why no U.S. media "air[ed] the videos of Nick Berg and Wall Street Journal reporter Danny Pearl getting decapitated or of the U.S. contractors in Fallujah getting torn limb from limb by al Qaeda operatives," and yet still gave saturation coverage, including endless photos, of Iraq prisoners being abused by U.S. troops at Abu Ghraib. As the Wall Street Journal suggested, ". . . it doesn't seem that it would be that hard to provide context — to make sure that every story about American abuses at Abu Ghraib also included graphic descriptions of

---

[645] Santorum was a two-term Republican senator from Pennsylvania until he lost his reelection bid in 2006. Liebermann has been representing Connecticut in the Senate since 1988. Liebermann was a Democrat until 2006, when he lost the Democratic primary election. He subsequently ran and won as an Independent.

[646] Cliff Kincaid, "Hard Times for Hardball," Media Monitor, July 21, 2004.

[647] Ibid. As of July 2004.

what went on there before Iraq's liberation. . . . Surely we have a right to demand better from the news media."[648]

To subsequently hear some people compare Abu Ghraib and alleged events in Afghanistan and Guantanamo Bay to Nazi death camps, or to Soviet gulags or the killing fields of Pol Pot — or the horrors of Saddam Hussein — is totally unreasonable, and quite frankly, a deceit of the worst possible kind.[649] Most would surely believe the American people deserve more objective and factual observation, and certainly more honest reporting.

At CACI, we all clearly understood the gravity of the issue. We knew the abuse at Abu Ghraib was despicable and inexcusable in every way, including from the important fundamental viewpoint that our military (and its contractors) must always behave in a manner that fully reflects and maintains the high standards and values of our great free nation. The abuses at Abu Ghraib in late 2003 sadly fell far below any acceptable standard and are truly regrettable.

* * *

In light of all this, after the Abu Ghraib story broke, and throughout 2004, I was confronted with the management and public relations challenge of my career. Because of the enormity and weight of this crisis, the standard public relations crisis management response simply was not going to work for CACI.[650] Abu Ghraib was way too big a story. The scope of the scandal was daunting — and seemed endless.

Our first task was to assemble our team and try to determine for ourselves the truth of what happened at Abu Ghraib concerning the appalling abuses. It seemed to me impossible that our fine, proud company which had worked diligently for over 40 years to maintain the highest standards of ethics and integrity could be involved in any misconduct. But I know that mistakes can happen and things can go wrong, particu-

---

[648] Deborah Orin, "Reporting for the Enemy; Media Won't Show Saddam's Evil" op. cit.

[649] I know of these tragedies and their relative magnitudes. I have personally toured Nazi death camps in Poland and Germany, and have seen the "Killing Fields" of Pol Pot outside Phnom Penh, Cambodia, including the notorious "S-21" torture prison within the city.

[650] The CACI Hypercrisis Model is described in Appendix H.

larly during wartime situations, and especially in harsh chaotic combat zone conditions. My own military training has taught me that there are many examples of tragic and unforeseen consequences that occur during war. An example is the unfortunate occurrence of our own soldiers being accidentally or inadvertently killed by each other from so-called "friendly fire." Nonetheless, whatever our situation at CACI would turn out to be, my objective would be to get to the facts and get to the truth.

In that effort, all of us in senior management pledged to commit to the motto always "do the right thing" — to take responsibility and be account-able, to cooperate with the authorities, to seek and communicate the truth, to look for and publicize the facts, to tell the public what we learned, to ac-knowledge any mistakes, and to correct any problems. But we soon real-ized we also had to take up the defense of our people and our company's good name against the rising tide of false and unfounded accusations. The latter turned out to be by far our largest and most challenging task.

One good thing I was reminded of during this experience was the ability of determined and honest people to come together for a common cause, to face up to incredible public scrutiny, and with the help of a well-founded set of values, to meet and overcome the challenge of de-fending their work and their integrity from baseless and hateful accusa-tions. As I look back over three years later, I can readily say that I have never been prouder of any group of people than the fine team at CACI and the outside advisers who stood shoulder to shoulder with me during our Abu Ghraib ordeal in 2004.

CACI had an excellent reputation and positive image before Abu Ghraib and we still do, with our customers, our employees, and our share-holders. No single finding of any major consequence ensued from our or-deal; no culpability was found on any aspect of CACI's business operations. Where *relatively* minor administrative procedural or contractual mistakes were uncovered (and, in fact, there were some), we promptly corrected them. And I am *exceedingly* proud of the company and its people for this.

* * *

During our Abu Ghraib experience, I learned some troubling things, too. These lessons are retold in this book as well.

I learned that our society has become careless with words. We recklessly use terms and concepts interchangeably that have distinctly different definitions. The true meanings of words are often lost and confused. But this is a greater problem when the choice of words carries real consequences.

After the Abu Ghraib story broke, we quickly discovered that many of the pertinent terms were used inaccurately. Every objectionable action in the photographs was labeled as "torture," while most of it could be reasonably argued, was actually humiliation or physical and psychological "abuse." Many would ask, appropriately, is there any difference? There are those who would say there is and it is discernable. While I do not claim to be an expert in this field, I have found it most useful to frame some definitions and concepts, to better understand the subject and its important implications and these have been presented elsewhere in this book. (The public debate about these matters, the definitions, applications, and legality continued through the end of 2007. And this is for good reason when considering the intense emotions — and serious consequences — that such words carry.)

Torture as most commonly defined, is to intentionally inflict or cause severe or extreme, excruciating physical and mental pain and suffering or agony. While torture, as a method, can be used in the attempt to elicit specific results or responses, or can be used solely for cruel, sadistic, brutal and criminal ends, it is not synonymous with the other pertinent terms. For example, the definition of the word "abuse" can cover a range of actions, from simply abusing privileges to physically hurting or sexually assaulting someone. According to some interpretations or definitions, it does not necessarily entail the intentional and severe nature, or extreme, that torture does.[651]

Some may argue that such differentiation is mere semantics. But when there is a lack of consensus on meanings and applications of such terms, clarification is not some vocabulary exercise — it's the framework of the entire debate. And as we've seen, these terms, their definitions and their legal and statutory meanings and criminal penalties are the topics of vigorous ongoing debate.

We are fully aware of the wide array of allegations and accusations about abuse or torture at Abu Ghraib. Notably, however, to my knowledge and belief, there have been no charges brought against anyone including the court martialed MPs for committing "torture" at Abu

---

[651] See also the Introduction as well as the Glossary and Terms of Interest.

Ghraib and there have similarly been no convictions for "torture". Certainly there have been numerous convictions for abuse, assault, or other reprehensible offenses involving maltreatment of detainees. Yet the media continues to unabatedly and incorrectly use the word "torture" as a blanket description for everything that happened at Abu Ghraib. Sociologist Stjepan Mestrovic, who was both an expert witness and observer at some of the Abu Ghraib trials, concluded that the media portrayed an "inaccurate and misconstrued picture" of the scandal, obsessing over torture, even though the term was never used at trial.[652]

Another important mistake made was the connection of the terms torture and interrogation. Interrogation is the systemic questioning of a person to obtain specific useful information. It is similar to cross examination which is a synonymous term to interrogation.[653] The purpose of interrogation is to gain usable and reliable information. Many professional interrogators concur that torture is counterproductive in interrogations because the subject may say anything to stop the suffering. Clearly torture and interrogation are distinctly different.

Of particular note, army specialist Joe Darby, who submitted the infamous Abu Ghraib photos to his army superiors, stated in an important interview with the *Army Times* two years after the scandal broke that, "The soldiers involved at Abu Ghraib were not interrogating inmates." He added, "These guys were doing nothing but occupying themselves in very sick ways. It was never about the interrogations."[654]

Following the news break of abuses at Abu Ghraib, there were also questions as to why CACI was involved with interrogations. CACI is an information technology company that, among other capabilities, provides intelligence systems and IT solutions. Intelligence is the knowledge ascertained and assembled from the gathering, evaluation, and application of information that is actionable or usable for explicit decision-making, planning or action. CACI's professional offerings have included various services in these areas, including development of information management systems, collection and analysis systems, decision

---

652 Travis Measley, "Texas A&M Professor Calls Abu Ghraib Trials 'Complex Human Story'," op. cit.

653 Webster's New World Dictionary and Thesaurus, op. cit.

654 Kelly Kennedy, "A Different Kind of Hero; Some soldiers might think Joe Darby hurt the army, but the Abu Ghraib whistleblower says 'it had to be done,'" *Army Times*, September 18, 2006.

support tools and methodologies, as well as planning and support systems used as applications. So when the U.S. Army, which was using other contractors for interrogations in Afghanistan and Guantanamo Bay, approached CACI with the interrogation support request, the company concluded that putting together a team of professionals who would conduct intelligence gathering from interrogations was fully congruent with the company's existing services.

Many, perhaps, will view these discussions about definitions as insignificant semantics or that it's simply splitting hairs. But when the lives, livelihoods and reputations of so many people are involved, is it not crucial to be accurate in the definition and use of these words? Such inaccuracies, be it by innocent error or intentional misrepresentation, like propaganda, can have far-reaching consequences. And the backlash against the U.S. from the publicity over Abu Ghraib is proof that the consequences can be fatal. Beyond the several beheadings attributed to Abu Ghraib by the terrorists, a congressional hearing on November 17, 2005 revealed that average daily attacks on U.S. troops doubled following the media blitz of the Abu Ghraib abuses.[655]

* * *

There also needs to be more accountability in journalism. I also learned firsthand, in our unique experience, that "freedom of the press" is a double-edged sword that cuts in many directions. The first amendment to the U.S. Constitution secures the right of free speech and a free press. This great freedom is a pillar of our society and must always be preserved. But in our society, I believe every right has a corresponding responsibility. Like any right or privilege, it must not be misused to wrongfully harm the innocent. There is much abuse of first amendment rights these days, and we are all the less for it. Simply put, having the right to say something does not make it the right thing to do.

As detailed in the pages of this book, CACI was forced to spend an enormous amount of time and energy correcting repeated errors and

---

[655] Congressman John Murtha (D-PA) made calls for troop withdrawals from Iraq in late 2005. In an op-ed piece and news release on his congressional Web site, Murtha said that, "Since the revelation of Abu Ghraib, American casualties have doubled." He cited as proof that insurgent incidents had increased from about 150 per week to over 700 per week in 2004. Rep. John Murtha, "It's Time to Bring the Troops Home," www.wagingpeace.org, November 17, 2005.

inaccuracies in news report after news report. Some of the errors were small while others were quite significant, but collectively I noted over time that they provided a badly distorted picture to the public about CACI, our employees, and the service our people proudly provided to the United States military in Iraq.

I am not alone in my experience with the failures of the media. Tom Fenton, a CBS News senior foreign correspondent, sets it out clearly in his book, *Bad News, The Decline of Reporting, the Business of News, and the Danger to Us All.*[656] Fenton notes in his preface that writing his book was a sobering experience, as he examined news industry faults that have become so glaring. Fenton observes, "The networks are obsessed with the ratings race. Politicians and statesmen line up to appear on the ersatz news *Daily Show*, and bloggers seem to be breaking the real news." He continues his admonition: "Even as urgent problems of Iraq, Iran, North Korea and a resurgent Russia compete for our attention, the news media fiddles while Rome burns." And I must note he did not mention China, which now looms large on the world's stage of rising power players.

Among Fenton's major indictments is that the news industry is focused on profits. And he cites the decline of the industry's codes of standards, the obsession with ratings, and the packaging of news rather than gathering it.[657] This sentiment is echoed by journalist and *Frontline* producer Lowell Bergman, a former *60 Minutes* producer who is best known for his investigation of the tobacco industry, which was later made into the movie *The Insider.* Bergman said, "The reality is that if you talk to a network news executive, they'll tell you that they not only have to be worried about ratings but profits and that they don't have an

---

656 Tom Fenton, *Bad News, The Decline of Reporting, the Business of News, and the Danger to Us All* (Harper Collins Publishers, Inc., New York, 2005).

657 That the news media knows of its own lack of factual reporting is clearly publicized every day. If the news media reported all the facts accurately (and only the relevant, legitimate facts), then it would not be necessary for CNN to continually announce that it is, "the most trusted name in news," and for Fox News to constantly advertise its "fair and balanced" reporting. Perhaps it is necessary to promote a news organization's reputation because the viewers don't necessarily know whom to believe anymore. Prof. Philip Meyer postulated, "The values of journalism have been driven by a marketplace that assumes a scarcity of information. . . . [However] our age of information overload is putting that old equation under stress. Today, it is attention, not information that is the scarce good." (Philip Meyer, "Why Journalism Needs Ph.D.s," *The American Editor*, September 1996).

obligation anymore to follow what we used to call a fairness doctrine. Nor do they have to cover anything. They just need to put things on the air that look like they're real and call it news."[658]

As for Abu Ghraib, Fenton expressed particular concern for the media's coverage, noting the media's complete lack of attention to the subject before the infamous photos came out, in comparison to its "sensationalistic saturation coverage once the story broke." He laments, "Surely we can find a more balanced approach."

Too often, the first priority of the media seems to be to find the most sensational angle and to get it out first — even when the evidence is slim at best. Michael Kinsley, the editorial page editor of the *Los Angeles Times*, wrote that daily journalism is driven by a sensationalist mantra: "When a story is hot and competition is fierce, you go with the tiniest morsel before someone else does." I wasn't sure when I read the statement whether Mr. Kinsley thought that was a good or a bad approach, but I know I would feel better if there was something in there that emphasized getting the facts right. But let me be clear: I think Kinsley's comment sets forth an unsatisfactory criterion. That disturbing criterion seems off-the-mark, when the standard should be fairness, accuracy, or even just verified fact. Rather, it seems that virtually all the media and journalism itself is now subject to *sensationalism, speculation and spin* — becoming sadly, the "three 's'" of that once respectable profession.

One of the more pointed and skeptical critiques of the media came from Pulitzer-winning journalist, Peter R. Kahn, the chairman of Dow Jones. In a December 2006 *Wall Street Journal* Opinion page article, entitled "The Media in Need of Some Mending", Kahn points to disturbing trends in the media that have caused "public skepticism in America". The ten topics — problems — he writes of, all seem to have surfaced in CACI's experience with Abu Ghraib. He speaks of: (1) "The blurring lines between journalism and entertainment"; (2) "The blurring lines between news and opinion"; (3) "The blending of news and advertising"; (4) "The problems and pitfalls inherent in pack journalism" . . . and this is especially the case in scandal situations with the media's pack of hounds [wolves] in pursuit of prey and the loss of common sense and fairness; (5) "the issue of conflict and context" . . . where the public probably would want a middle of the road solution the media presents

---

[658] "Interview with Lowell Bergmann," JournalismJobs.com, January 2001.

the extremes; (6) "The exaggerated tendency toward pessimism"; (7) "The media's short attention span"; (8) "The growing media fascination with the bizarre, the perverse and the pathological — John Mark Karr journalism"; (9) "Social Orthodoxy, or political correctness"; and (10) "The matter of power".[659]

Kahn says that, "The press is at least partially responsible for greater public skepticism toward traditional institutions in America."[660] He makes a statement that we at CACI certainly recognized; that the ubiquitous media, including the press, Web sites and blogs, has become large and powerful, and increasingly and inappropriately influential in America's affairs. The phrase "inappropriate and undue influence" is not far off in describing the situation. And this is a trend of concern, even one to be guarded against as the CACI experience has clearly demonstrated.

Former CBS News insider, reporter, and producer Bernard Goldberg, winner of seven Emmy Awards, outlined his perspective on this subject in his book *Bias, A CBS Insider Exposes How the Media Distort the News.*[661]

In 1996, Goldberg wrote an op-ed in the *Wall Street Journal* on the media's "liberal bias" that created considerable reaction. In his subsequent statements, Goldberg elaborated that the liberal bias is derived from a media elite who are isolated from, and patronizing of other points of view. Goldberg further explains that reporters covering an issue "already have their take on these issues, and their take is overwhelmingly a liberal take on these issues."[662] Goldberg was criticized by many, including colleague Dan Rather, for his revelations.[663] Whether the media's bias is liberal or conservative or neither, it is hard to argue in

---

[659] Peter R. Kahn, "The Media In Need of Some Mending," *Wall Street Journal*, December 11, 2006.

[660] Ibid.

[661] Bernard Goldberg, *Bias, A CBS Insider Exposes How the Media Distort the News* (Regnery Publishing Inc., Washington, D.C., 2003).

[662] Renee Giachino, *"CFIF General Counsel Talks With Veteran CBS Reporter Bernard Goldberg About Media Bias,"* Center for Individual Freedom, August 12, 2004 (http://www.cfif.org/htdocs/freedomline/current/in_our_opinion/bernard_goldberg.htm).

[663] In contrast, Andy Rooney (of CBS's 60 Minutes) wrote Goldberg: "Bernie: In the future, if you have any derogatory remarks to make about CBS news or one of your co-workers . . . I hope you will do the same thing again." Goldberg, op. cit.

opposition that most media organizations, including both mainstream and bloggers, often seem to have a political view they are espousing. And this will always affect — negatively — the quality of fact-finding and journalistic reporting.

Another failure of modern journalism is that the reporters assigned to these stories often don't fully grasp their subjects. Reporters generally have a background only in journalism where they learn how to get, structure, and publish stories. It would appear that very few journalists have academic or professional backgrounds in other fields, like business, science, government, the military, political science or international relations. Yet these are the very topics on which they report. Many reporters who have been assigned to cover stories on CACI lack familiarity with government contracting, military activity, and sometimes even business in general. When the story is a brief reference to a contract award or some business development, the errors are usually minor and manageable, or immaterial. But when one of the biggest stories of the decade breaks, like Abu Ghraib, these same reporters are given front-page inputs with little or no exposure to, or experience with the relevant issues.[664] This can result in significant errors and misinterpretations that get reported and repeated before they can even be corrected. And by then, the mistakes are no longer manageable.

Skepticism about media also comes from how journalists get their stories. In many news reports, speculation by so-called "experts" and "unnamed sources" is given equal or greater weight than demonstrable facts. As this book was written, there was much concern on the part of the courts for these "unnamed and anonymous" sources. Norman Pearlstine's 2007 book *Off the Record* tells of his role as editor-in-chief of Time Inc., and his struggle with the courts and laws regarding anonymous (protected) sources, involved in leaks, whistle blower activity and the revealing of covert entities. Pearlstine's book describes the challenges he faced when Time Inc. was embroiled in the scandal surrounding the leaks which revealed the identity of CIA operative Valerie Plame. Special prosecutor Patrick Fitzgerald had subpoenaed documents pertaining to the sources for articles written for *Time* by reporter

---

[664] One of the *Washington Post's* reporters who consistently covered the Abu Ghraib scandal and CACI in 2004–2005 has subsequently covered entertainment stories for the paper.

Matthew Cooper (as well as Judith Miller from the *New York Times*). After losing lower court appeals and being denied a Supreme Court appeal, Pearlstine concluded *Time*'s role in the proceedings by providing Fitzgerald with the subpoenaed documents. (Miller eventually did the same after her source, former chief of staff to Vice President Dick Cheney, Lewis Libby, released her from their confidentiality agreement.)[665]

Pearlstine's decision was apparently based on his own belief that the sources' anonymity did not meet standards for protection and, in effect, the First Amendment issue did not override the underlying unlawful leaking activity. The case was illustrative of the growing concern about the media's integrity and reliability. "'We're in an era of judicial skepticism regarding the reliability and professionalism of the media generally,' said Rodney A. Smolla, dean of the University of Richmond School of Law, 'and that atmosphere, I think, makes courts reluctant to recognize any special First Amendment protection.'"[666]

As I look back on our experience of the Abu Ghraib ordeal, I am troubled by the stunning lack of accountability for such an important and powerful institution as the news media. There seems to be little penalty for mistakes and a high tolerance for careless work that would cost people their jobs in other businesses. The Society of Professional Journalists has an admirable Code of Ethics that divides journalists' responsibility into four categories: "Seek Truth and Report It," "Act Independently," "Minimize Harm," and "Be Accountable."[667] Sadly, it seems to me that many reporters, journalists, and publishers are unaware of, or forget that this code even exists. At times, they appear to fall quite short on the first responsibility — to find the truth.[668] It seems in the near future there

---

[665] On June 27, 2005, the U.S. Supreme Court announced that it would refuse to hear an appeal from a lower court decision ordering jail time for Judith Miller of the *New York Times* and Matthew Cooper of *Time* magazine for refusing to testify about their sources in an investigation into the media's disclosure of a CIA officer's identity.

[666] Adam Liptak, "Courts Grow Increasingly Skeptical of Any Special Protections for the Press," *The New York Times*, June 28, 2005.

[667] Society of Professional Journalists Code of Ethics, http://www.spj.org/ethicscode.asp.

[668] I believe journalists once had a higher regard for the truth, when there was a difference between what was news and what was just simply salacious and before journalists' opinions and biases became so prevalent and obvious. Television viewers had newsmen like Chet Huntley, David Brinkley, and Edward R. Murrow, whom they trusted and respected. These men went after the truth for the truth's sake, not for

will be even larger issues with the media. Particularly troubling is the frequency with which the media references classified information and anonymous sources. Our internet search of the phrase "according to a classified report" yielded nearly 8,500 results. And a search of the phrase "according to an anomymous source yielded nearly 10,300 results.[669]

The Plame case resurfaced calls for a federal shield law, which would protect the journalist-source relationship. Most states have shield laws or court decisions defining the level of protection. In an editorial by the *Washington Post* supporting legislation for a federal shield law, the paper claimed, "Many of the stories that expose government malfeasance, sear the nation's conscience, highlight violations of public trust or expose gross abuses of power come to light because people come forward to point journalists in the right direction or offer direct testimony on the condition that their names not be revealed. Protecting the identity of a source is a bedrock of American journalism. Unfortunately, recent history has shown that some federal prosecutors and civil litigants do not value this flow of information as much as those of us in the media and the public do."[670]

This viewpoint comes off as an arrogant and self-serving assertion. In fact, it seems the public, and the legal system to a greater extent,

---

ratings. Even during times of war, I remember journalists who stood out for their accurate reporting. There were hard-hitting cartoonists, too, like Bill Mauldin, who seemed to know just how to depict the real-life struggles of "GI Joe." During World War II, war correspondent Ernie Pyle went with the U.S. Army to North Africa, Sicily, Italy and accompanied Allied troops during the Normandy landings and witnessed the liberation of France. Instead of the movements of armies or the activities of generals, Pyle generally wrote from the perspective of the common soldier — a trademark of his intimate style of writing. By 1944 Pyle had established himself as one of the world's outstanding reporters and was hailed as America's most widely read war correspondent. In 1945, Pyle was awarded the Pulitzer Prize for journalism. Later that year he went with U.S. troops to Okinawa, where he was killed by a Japanese sniper while on a routine patrol. I had the experience of visiting his memorial in Okinawa on a visit to Japan in May of 2005. (From the Profile of Ernie Pyle by the Indiana Historical Society http://www.indianahistory.org/pop_hist/people/pyle.html.)

[669] Google search, October 8, 2007.

[670] "Shielding Sources, Journalists need protection at the federal level," *Washington Post*, August 1, 2007. The legislation would still compel disclosure of a source's identity if it was needed to prevent an act of terrorism against the U.S., prevent imminent death or bodily harm, or identity a person who unlawfully revealed a trade secret, private health information, or other nonpublic personal information.

would better recognize this 'value of the flow of information' if the information was accurate and verifiable. Anonymous or secret sources have in some cases led to important revelations, but these "leaks" can also turn out to be rumors, innuendo, or unsubstantiated accusations — even lies — by people with selfish motives or deceitful agendas. Great harm can come all too easily from a process that sponsors unaccountable "secret" sources.

For example, it's still not known who *illegally leaked* the Taguba report. The leak was an illegal act. Further, the report was preliminary and contained inaccuracies. Importantly, the report lacked substantiating factual evidence. As a result, CACI and its employees were publicly vilified because of this leak and the mistakes it contained. Our reputation and business — including the livelihoods of some 9,500 employees (in 2004) — were put at serious risk. Yet by late 2007 no charges had been filed against CACI or any employee. But the person who leaked the Taguba report has not been held accountable under the law.

Shield laws also highlight a double standard by the media that is seldom discussed. Journalists want protection for their sources and stories under the law, but a considerable number have broken the law to get those stories. Violations of laws on classified information by the media are well documented, like the Valerie Plame case previously cited. Despite the lack of prosecution (perhaps due to the risk of revealing even more sensitive information), unauthorized disclosure of classified information is still a crime and poses a serious threat to our national security. Yet it seems that journalists view the acquiring and use of such sensitive information as a praiseworthy accomplishment.

There also seems to be a belief among some journalists that it is acceptable to subvert the law. For example, the Reporters Committee for the Freedom of the Press promotes defying the law when a court upholds a subpoena. Their Web site even features a section on fighting subpoenas in all state and federal courts in order to protect "reporter's privilege." They define this privilege as "the right not to be compelled to testify or disclose sources and information in court."[671] Yet there is no such right under the law and such a "privilege" does not supersede the law.

---

[671] Reporters Committee for Freedom of the Press, *Privilege Compendium*, http://www.rcfp.org/privilege/index.php.

Patrick Fitzgerald, the special prosecutor in the Plame case, suggested that, "Any shield bill should require that a person seeking its protection first provide the subpoenaed information under seal to the court, to be released only if the court orders the information disclosed."[672] However, it seems doubtful that the media would agree to this quite reasonable compromise.

I can understand arguments for a federal shield law, like those made by Pearlstine, in which a shield law could protect attempts to stifle dissent, or those to create a uniform standard across the country. But it seems this "value" of information from anonymous sources that the *Post* speaks of is simply the desire by some in the media to say whatever they want without being held responsible for it. It seems to me that the media is looking to protect itself from the consequences of what it reports. The First Amendment allows for freedom of speech, but to my knowledge, not freedom from accountability. In my view, there is no need for shield laws or secret sources — bright sunshine on the media is better for all.

On the flip side, there is growing discussion about media accountability systems, which are "non-governmental means of inducing media and journalists to respect the ethical rules set by the profession . . . [aimed] at improving news media, using evaluation, monitoring, education or feedback."[673] Some methods are already commonplace, like a code of ethics, letters to the editor, ombudsman, and professional organizations, such as the Society of Professional Journalists. But other methods go further into monitoring, self-regulation, and press councils at regional and national levels. In my view, these all need reinforcement and formal oversight.

While some may say self regulation by the media is unrealistic or even a fantasy, there is a very real example said to be working effectively and efficiently today. Originating as the voluntary Press Council in 1953, the Press Complaints Commission (PCC) in the United Kingdom is "an independent body which deals with complaints from members of

---

[672] Patrick J. Fitzgerald, "Shield Law Perils . . . Bill Would Wreak Havoc on a System That Isn't Broken," *Washington Post*, October 4, 2007.

[673] Claude-Jean Bertand, "M°A°S, Media Accountability Systems — A list of "Media Accountability Systems" (M°A°S), non-governmental means of inciting news media to observe ethical rules," January 2003. http://www.media-accountability.org/html/frameset.php?page=library3.

the public about the editorial content of newspapers and magazines."[674] The PCC is charged with enforcing the media's Code of Practice which was framed by the newspaper and periodical industry itself
and binds all regional and national newspapers and magazines. The
Code states that all members of the press have a responsibility to uphold the highest professional standards. The code sets the benchmark
for ethical standards, protecting and balancing the rights of individuals
and the public's right to know. The PCC stresses that the Code "be ho-
noured not only to the letter but in the full spirit. There are sixteen sections within the code, including accuracy, opportunity to reply, and harassment by journalists.

The PCC states that, "It is the responsibility of editors and publishers to apply the Code to editorial material in both printed and online
versions of publications. They should take care to ensure it is observed
rigorously by all editorial staff and external contributors, including *non-
journalists* [italics added], in printed and online versions of publications.
Editors should cooperate swiftly with the PCC in the resolution of complaints. Any publication judged to have breached the Code must print
the adjudication in full and with due prominence, including headline
reference to the PCC."[675]

The PCC has no legal authority; it is completely voluntary. However,
the PCC is structured to ensure accountability and self regulation. There
are seventeen members of the Commission, all but five members coming
from outside the media. This majority of members with no connection to
the press ensures the PCC's independence from the newspaper industry.

The heart of the Commission's self regulation mechanism comes
from the Press Standards Board of Finance, modeled on the British
advertising industry self-regulatory system established in 1974. The
Board, made up of publishing executives, charges an annual levy on the
newspaper and periodical industries to finance the Press Complaints
Commission. "This arrangement ensures secure financial support for
the PCC, while its complete independence is at the same time guaranteed by a majority of lay members, and is a further sign of the industry's
commitment to effective self-regulation."[676]

---

[674] Press Complaints Commission, http://www.pcc.org.uk.

[675] Ibid.

[676] Ibid.

In 2006, the PCC received approximately 8,550 enquiries and 3,325 complaints were filed. Approximately two-thirds of the complaints specified under the Code of Practice dealt with accuracy in reporting and one-fifth dealt with privacy intrusion. Because the Commission's service is easy, free and fast (most complaints are addressed within just 35 working days), only 31 complaints had to be adjudicated in 2006. "All those which were critical of a newspaper were published in full and with due prominence by the publication concerned."[677]

The keys to PCC's success. I believe, are its stated "strengths of effective and independent self-regulation" and its accessibility to everyone along with its aim for a free and fair press.

Could such a concept work here in the U.S.? There are some industries that self regulate to some extent. The alcohol industry, for example, makes efforts to ensure advertising is not directed to an underage audience. The video game industry established the Entertainment Software Rating Board, which created a comprehensive labeling system that has rated over 8,000 games in over a decade. But would the publishing industry — perhaps even the media overall — be willing to instate some sort of self-regulation? Would the British model work here? This seems to be a question the American media should answer.

∗ ∗ ∗

The constant repetition of a consistent, but fallacious story line by news organizations has the effect of propaganda. I do not mean that the news media purposefully orchestrates propaganda campaigns, but simply that when the same false accusations are repeated day after day, frighteningly, they become accepted as true by large numbers of people — even before all of the evidence is collected or reviewed in a trial or other appropriate judicial proceeding. And this has the *collective effect of a propaganda assault.*[678]

---

[677] Ibid.

[678] **Propaganda** defined: "the deliberate (often media-based) dissemination of false or misleading information or ideas with specific intent to further one's cause or to damage an opposing cause by attempting to influence or convince with emotional emphasis, promote or oppose opinions, events, organizations or outcomes." Propaganda is a powerful communications and public opinion-influencing device. Joseph Goebbels, the Third Reich's Minister of Public Enlightenment and Propaganda, knew this when

As an example of how this "somebody high up did it" propaganda effect is recognized as having taken root, consider the commentary of a *Wall Street Journal* opinion article in April 2005 which stated: "We'd have thought every American would be relieved to learn that 10 major inquiries, sworn statements from 37 high-level officials, and information gleaned from dozens of courts-martial and criminal investigations have cleared most senior civilian and military leaders of wrongdoing in the Abu Ghraib scandal and other Iraq prisoner abuses. Instead, the latest army report reaching this conclusion has induced further cries of whitewash. . . . Sometimes we wonder if proponents of this torture-cum-whitewash accusation have ever stopped to consider the improbable nature of the cover-up they are now suggesting. Mr. Schlesinger and other investigators would all have to be lying. . . . There would have been a widespread outcry in the military if senior brass and civilians really were trying to shift blame for abuse onto the lower ranks."[679]

The *Journal* also noted that "there were abuses in Iraq . . . but abuses happen in war and in civilian prisons too. No hard evidence has been produced to support allegations that the abuses were "systematic" or that they were inspired, authorized or condoned by superiors up the chain of command. As Mr. Schlesinger also noted, by any statistical measure — such as the rate of reported abuse incidents per detainee — treatment of detainees in the overall war on terror has been exemplary. In short, the so-called "torture narrative" that was so hyped by the media last year was entirely false."[680]

The critical issue for those maligned by the media is this: When your reputation is wrongfully smeared or even ruined, how do you ever regain it?

In the case of Abu Ghraib, Major General Taguba's report was treated as gospel truth for months. And his "suspicion" about Steve Stefanowicz was repeated so often, as if it were proven fact, that I believe many Americans accepted it, without question, and continue to believe it as confirmed truth without the benefit of knowing the full results of

---

he was discussing the Nazi's propaganda efforts, "We do not talk to say something, but to obtain a certain effect." Harold D. Laswell, *Propaganda, The Formatting of Men's Attitudes*, ed. Jacques Ellul, (New York: Random House Inc., 1965).

[679] "Abu Ghraib Accountability," op. cit.

[680] Ibid.

the entire investigative process including findings from the later investigations. This is exactly how political propaganda works. When more comprehensive investigations subsequently *differed materially* with the Taguba report about CACI, contractors, and Steve Stefanowicz, it was virtually impossible to set the record straight. The damage of the persistent media coverage of the Taguba report had already been done. The propaganda effect was clearly demonstrated. And the propaganda approach continues to be used by some political activists who still cite false information and selective unsubstantiated aspects of CACI's Abu Ghraib experience for their own self-interest and actual (real) propaganda campaigns.

For the most part, this process has involved using the notorious abuse pictures (which show no CACI employees) in negative stories about the company to perpetuate the false association between the company and what is depicted in the pictures. This approach and its effects are similar to what I would call the "tabloid phenomenon" in which questionable images are used to support preposterous claims in order create sensationalism and sell stories.[681]

Another recent and famous example of this problem regarding the proliferation of misinformation and its persistent effects was when Richard Jewell was accused of planting a bomb at the 1996 Summer Olympics in Atlanta, Georgia.[682] A private security guard, Jewell had discovered a pipe bomb, alerted police, and helped to evacuate the area before it went off in Centennial Olympic Park, killing one woman and injuring over a hundred other people. Jewell was first hailed as a hero in the media. But when the *Atlanta Journal-Constitution* reported days later that the FBI was treating him as a possible suspect, based largely on the "lone bomber" profile, Jewell was subsequently and unconscionably pilloried in the media.

Though never officially charged, Jewell was consequently treated like a criminal. The ensuing media circus led to an aggressive and public search of his home by the FBI, questioning of his associates, and an investigation into his background. Two of the bombing victims even filed

---

[681] This particular technique is seen clearly in the 1930s' political and totalitarian poster art of Nazi Germany, Fascist Italy and the Communist Soviet Union.

[682] Elizabeth Farnsworth, "Olympic Park: Another Victim," *NewsHour with Jim Lehrer*, October 28, 1996 (http://www.pbs.org/newshour/bb/sports/jewell_10-28.html).

lawsuits against Jewell based on media reports (Ironically, litigious action was a similar experience to which CACI was subjected.) Jewell was cleared months later, in October 1996, when the Department of Justice released a letter saying he was no longer a target of their investigations. In a subsequent press conference, Jewell described how the FBI and the media had made his life a nightmare. After his exoneration, Jewell filed several libel lawsuits against the media outlets, including the Atlanta paper, the *New York Post*, and NBC News, which he considered to have maligned him, and insisted they should apologize to him. Jewell was finally exonerated in April of 2005, when Eric Rudolph pleaded guilty to carrying out the bombing attack at the Centennial Olympic Park, as well as three other attacks across the South.[683]

Another example of wrongful accusation sensationalized by the media came in March 2006 when three members of the Duke University lacrosse team were falsely accused of raping an African-American stripper during a team party. The local district attorney (DA), Mike Nifong, fervently pursued the case and the story became a media sensation. Within two months of the alleged raped, three players, Reade Seligmann, Collin Finnerty, and David Evans, were charged with first-degree forcible rape, sexual offense and kidnapping. Consequently, Duke University cancelled the rest of the lacrosse season and fired the team's coach. Fellow students and faculty denounced the accused players, including a full-page advertisement in the college newspaper taken out by eighty-eight faculty members condemning the players.[684] News crews and journalists flocked to North Carolina to cover the story. The three players were thrown to the media's gallows.

However, it turned out Nifong and the police were wrong. Not only had the police violated their own policies by allowing DA Nifong to lead the case, they had also not properly investigated the claims.[685]

---

[683] Richard Jewell died on August 29, 2007. At the time of his death, Jewell was still in litigation with the *Atlanta Journal-Constitution* to clear his name. In 2006, Georgia Governor Sonny Perdue honored Jewell for his rescue efforts at Atlanta's Olympic Park.

[684] "Presumed Guilty, A superb new book shows how trumped-up charges exposed faults in some of America's grandest institutions," *The Economist*, September 13, 2007.

[685] Matt Dees and Joseph Neff, "Ex-players seek $30 million settlement, Durham's insurance could cover $5 million," *The News & Observer*, September 8, 2007.

Moreover, while the three players had unimpeachable alibis, the accusers' story quickly fell apart. Her account of events often changed, including the number of assailants (ranging from 3 to 20), different timelines of events, as well as variations in the details of the supposed attack. The accuser also apparently had a "long record of alcohol and drug abuse, mental instability and making up far-fetched stories."[686] A second stripper at the party also refuted the accuser's claims.

Yet the media had no qualms about trying the Duke rape case in public. A later publication noted that, "The print media churned out headlines about 'a night of racial slurs, growing fear and finally sexual violence', and the TV talking heads reveled in the story line."[687] And an article on *Slate.com* contended that well into the collapse of the case, the *New York Times* "still seems bent on advancing its race-sex-class ideological agenda, even at the cost of ruining the lives of three young men who it has reason to know are very probably innocent."[688]

By December 2006, the case against the three young men had fallen apart and Nifong faced ethics charges brought by the North Carolina State Bar. The seventeen page complaint against the DA listed violations of "rules of professional conduct when speaking to reporters about the high-profile case. The complaint lists more than 100 examples of public statements Nifong made to the media . . . since March [2006]."[689] Nifong eventually lost his law license and was also found guilty of criminal contempt, serving a day in jail.

It wasn't until April 2007, however, that North Carolina Attorney General Roy Cooper dropped all charges against the three players. He even publicly declared them innocent and "the victims of a 'tragic rush to accuse' by a rogue prosecutor."[690] It was the media, however, that made the nationwide public damage to the young men's reputations possible in the first place.

---

[686] "Presumed Guilty, A superb new book shows how trumped-up charges exposed faults in some of America's grandest institutions," op. cit.

[687] Ibid.

[688] Stuart Taylor Jr., "Witness for the Prosecution? The New York Times is still victimizing innocent Dukies," *Slate.com*, August 29, 2006.

[689] Erin Coleman and Ken Smith, "State Bar Files Ethics Complaint Against Mike Nifong," *WRAL News*, December 28, 2006.

[690] Aaron Beard, "Prosecutors Drop Charges in Duke Case," *San Francisco Chronicle*, April 12, 2007.

Evans graduated in 2006, but Seligmann and Finnerty transferred to different schools. The ex-players were reportedly seeking $30 million over five years for the violation of their rights, as well as seeking new criminal justice reform laws in a federal civil-rights lawsuit against the city of Durham, North Carolina. Although the men were exonerated, their lives had been upended and their reputations (as well as that of the whole team) besmirched. And there is no venue for vindication that will restore their reputations on the scale that they were ruined. In the rush to political and media judgment, the lives of many were irrevocably harmed.

Jewell's name is now considered synonymous with false accusations of guilt, especially by the media. It's an experience the three Duke lacrosse players probably never thought they would have either. And unfortunately, CACI now appears to fall into the same category as far as Abu Ghraib is concerned: false accusations in the media that would wrongfully tarnish our good name.

The Richard Jewell and Duke rape cases are only two contemporary examples of accusations run amuck. While much damage is done just by those repeated allegations, it's also another slip down a dangerous slope. When the dissemination of allegations, misinformation, or even lies, becomes commonplace or — worse still — unchallenged, we risk accepting almost anything as fact. The most notorious example of this acceptance, of course, is the Nazi propaganda machine of the 1930's, which systematically stole Germany from its people and, in great part, made the Holocaust a gruesome reality throughout the 1930's and to its end in 1945.[691]

---

[691] While the Nazi example shows the effects of propaganda at its absolute worst, it also shows how propaganda is a cumulative process that, when unchecked, can lead to unimaginable consequences. When the Nazi party came to power in 1933, Adolf Hitler established the Reich Ministry of Public Enlightenment and Propaganda (headed by Joseph Goebbels) that instituted a comprehensive campaign to spread the Nazi message of "National Socialism" — including racism, anti-Semitism, and anti-Bolshevism. According to the U.S. Holocaust Memorial Museum, "The Nazi regime used propaganda effectively to mobilize the German population to support its wars of conquest until the very end of the regime. Nazi propaganda was likewise essential to motivating those who implemented the mass murder of the European Jews and of other victims of the Nazi regime. It also served to secure the acquiescence of millions of others — as bystanders — to racially targeted persecution and mass murder." Furthermore, it takes a massive

I have also seen during our Abu Ghraib experience how activist ideologue groups could manipulate information and take advantage of the media to make news organizations a tool for distributing their propaganda to the widest possible audience. An organization called the Center for Constitutional Rights (CCR) filed a lawsuit against CACI, which accused the company of conspiring with the U.S. government in a deliberate policy of torture, rape, and murder at Abu Ghraib. It was an absolutely preposterous and outrageous accusation with no support or merit whatsoever. And based on the questions asked by reporters at the news conference announcing the lawsuit at the time, even journalists seemed to sense that the accusations had little merit.

Still, because of the sensationalistic way journalism works, these ludicrous accusations received major press attention. And the CCR lawsuit along with the similar Iraqi Torture Victims lawsuit, continues to stoke the fires by using the media to repeat, not evidence, but allegations. In fact, it seems CCR is more interested in having its case aired in the media than in the courts. This too, smacks of a propaganda campaign.

* * *

While some in the media, as well as opponents of the war, seemed desperate to find some "higher ups" in the military chain of command,

---

response to stop propaganda and the resulting consequences when it becomes so destructive. In this case, it took a world war in which many Americans paid the ultimate price. As a student of WWII's European theater, I have visited the Nazi death camps and prisons in Poland at Auschwitz and Birkenau near Krakow, Treblinka near Warsaw, and in Germany in Sachsenhausen near Berlin and Dachau near Munich. My kinsman cousin, Lawrence A. London, of the Oklahoma 45th Infantry Division in World War II, was with the unit that liberated Dachau, outside Munich on April 29, 1945. At Dachau, I saw the commemoration plaque of the 45th Division liberation assault in which Lawrence had participated. (His personal photographs of this despicable death hole are now in the Jewish Holocaust Museum's files in Dallas, Texas.) I also lost an uncle and a cousin fighting Germany in WWII: 2nd Lt. Gordon L. Phillips, USA, 83rd Infantry Division, was killed in combat July 9th, 1944 near St. Lô, France in Normandy; and 2nd Lt. James M. Scott, Jr., USA, 548th Bomber Squadron 8th Air Force (U.S. Army Air Force) bombardier, was killed April 8, 1944 in a B-17 raid over Germany. (He is buried in the U.S. National Cemetery, Cambridge, England, which I visited in January 2006.)

or the (political) administration, guilty of directing the abuses at Abu Ghraib, there were no findings of fact from the publicly available investigative reports that supported such views.

In addition, from the official government investigations, the public testimony provided under oath, the individual courts-martial, and all other facts verified, acknowledged or reported, it seems that a case might be convincingly argued that the Abu Ghraib abuses (such as appeared in the notorious photographs) would have happened even if contractors (CACI and Titan) had *not* been present. Further, some might argue that the abuses might *not* have happened if court-martialed soldiers Charles Graner and Ivan "Chip" Frederick had been stationed somewhere else in the fall of 2003.

At the same time, from another perspective, psychologist and expert witness, Philip Zimbardo, in commenting about Sgt. Frederick's trial, stated that, "The team of military investigators and prosecutors invested considerable zeal in preparing the case against each of the seven accused MPs. (*Had the military command responsible for Abu Ghraib invested a fraction of that attention, concern, and resources in oversight and maintenance of discipline, there would have likely been no need for these trials.*) [italics added]"[692] This viewpoint further supports the official reports' findings that the notorious Abu Ghraib abuses happened because 'good order and discipline' were sorely lacking and the rogue MPs carried out their unauthorized and malicious actions unchecked.[693]

* * *

Stories have been produced about CACI that have had far-reaching impact and these stories were still appearing in 2007. And in today's Internet-driven world, once a claim is made, however false or wrong it

---

[692] Phillip Zimbardo, *The Lucifer Effect, Understanding How Good People Turn Evil* (New York; Random House, 2007).

[693] As Schlesinger made note in his report (cited earlier), "The aberrant behavior on the night shift in Cell Block 1 at Abu Ghraib would have been avoided with proper training, leadership and oversight." He further remarked that, "Had these noncommissioned officers behaved more like those on the day shift, these acts, which one participant [Lynndie England] described as 'just for the fun of it,' would not have taken place." (Schlesinger report, op. cit.)

may be, it becomes part of a lasting and indelible record that resides on Web sites and in databases all around the world. Our job became one of constantly correcting this record, but preventing and righting this propaganda effect is daunting.

Included among those who propagated misinformation, were so-called experts who came into the discussion of Abu Ghraib with misconceptions or biased agendas. Even without Lieutenant General Jones' warning that Abu Ghraib could not be understood in a vacuum, it is surprising that someone in the position of Peter W. Singer of the Brookings Institution — or anyone who wished to do a scholarly review and discussion of the role of contractors at Abu Ghraib — would, apparently, attempt to do so in a vacuum. Yet, Singer's persistent presentations, specifically his damning commentary about CACI, seemed to be a contradiction to the basic tenants of research, that data should be collected in an unbiased fashion. Thorough investigations must be conducted to allow relevant data to yield non-prejudiced results and the formulation of a defensible conclusion. Singer has ostensibly taken an adversarial position (i.e., that of a proactive advocate) of selecting and emphasizing those data and facts that fit his hypothesis, and deriving conclusions that fit his predetermined theory. And while he may do as he pleases and is entitled to do so, we may similarly critique openly and express freely our disagreement with his approach or his opinions, or both.

The Abu Ghraib scandal demanded investigation and appropriate recommendations. And the government contracting industry also could benefit from further study and understanding. Both government and industry deserve objective study by scholars and government researchers who are not activists, who will conduct thorough research, and who are interested in fully understanding the industry. While critical analysis is important, balanced assessment also involves grasping the industry's value proposition for the government and the American people.

Further review and future research should be constructive and acknowledge the current contribution and role of contractors, and not simply be a "witch hunt" in pursuit of a damning indictment that points only to shortcomings that are frequently based on incomplete or incorrect information. The American people deserve better.

As we have seen, the repetition of unfounded allegations can create a destructive propaganda effect, leading people to believe that conjecture and innuendo are the truth. Such manipulation of information not only misleads the public, it can undermine the rule of law. Specifically, it can reverse one of America's most important and revered legal principles — the presumption of innocence. How can someone be innocent until proven guilty in a court of law if the accused party has already been tried and convicted by a reckless media machine and a misinformed court of public opinion?

In our American system, an accused person, or institution, is presumed innocent until the evidence proves otherwise. At trial, the prosecution must prove guilt beyond a reasonable doubt to a jury of peers. But today's saturated media coverage seems to promote, in some cases, a club-wielding, lynch mob mentality that demands instant punishment before the accusation is fully investigated, tried and proven. In today's climate, the accused are now often presumed guilty and unjustifiably put in the desperate position of having to prove their innocence.

I had no idea how serious this frightening deviation from the rule of law had become — as a result of the *media's inappropriate and undue influence* — until CACI was put through it.

In fact, I have given it much thought over the past few years, and I think free societies face a great danger from the lack of checks and balances when the press and public activist groups (of any persuasion) get carried away on these kinds of frenzied rampages. It doesn't happen every day, of course, but when it does it is quite damaging to our democracy. The old newspaper adage, "If it bleeds, it leads," has been taken to a new extreme in this modern era of worldwide 24/7 television and Internet news coverage.

Indeed, it strikes me that one way to get a cause, even propaganda, into the news is to make a sensational accusation — the more salacious and heinous the better. No matter how thin the evidence, sensational and emotionally charged accusations seem to get a lot more press coverage than information that demonstrates the accusations are baseless. Recent examples include CBS and Dan Rather's debacle over falsified documents about George W. Bush's National Guard service, and *Newsweek* magazine's fiasco over false and exaggerated claims of Koran abuse at Guantanamo Bay.[694] These news organizations made serious claims and substantial accusations that turned out to be completely false.

Moreover, it seems the mere appearance of sensational accusations in a news story by itself adds at least a veneer of credibility. Thanks to the Internet, these false news reports can then be delivered directly to millions of people — some quite gullible — almost everywhere in the world. Accusations originating from one source can be repeated over and over again, and embellished in a way that can make them appear to come from multiple and independent sources.

There is a darker side to this extremism, too, as I see it. At CACI, we received a full hate-filled blast from a wide realm of political radicals, extremists and spiteful opportunists. From crass (and sometimes threatening) e-mails sent to the company, to malicious diatribes posted on blogs and alternative news sites, CACI became a convenient target for everything some people thought was wrong with politics, government, the military, contractors, the Iraq war, and America itself. We were labeled "kings of pain" and called "torturers" and these outrageous accusations couldn't possibly be further from the truth.

Instead of allowing the facts to unfold or contributing to a healthy debate about legitimate issues, the far-fetched, unsubstantiated speculation, sordid insults and malicious attacks from this commentary only worked to undermine the legitimate search for the truth.

There is a militant and intolerant demagoguery about all of this that is quite disturbing and, in my opinion, a trend that is increasing, not waning. A media out of control with no self-control can be a frightening thing — dangerous and abusive — as we have seen here in our situation.

On the larger media integrity question the serious concerns remain and urgently need attention. They should be dealt with, of course, directly by the media leadership itself. And as a start, I urge members of the news media and especially its leadership, to take a

---

[694] Howard Kurtz, "Rather Admits 'Mistake in Judgment,' CBS Was Misled About Bush National Guard Documents, Anchor Says," September 21, 2004; Howard Kurtz, "Newsweek Retracts Guantanamo Story, Item on Koran Sparked Deadly Protests," *Washington Post*, May 17, 2005.

closer look at how they do their work and the values that guide their work. I think that "getting the facts right" must be given the highest value and importance. I think reporters need to remember that freedom of the press gives them great power to do good, but also to do great harm. When they accept this power and freedom of the press, they also must accept the responsibility — laid out in their own code of ethics — to minimize undeserved harm and to be accountable at the highest standard.

Terrorist organizations also know that the media can be an effective tool for their use in furthering their cause. "Al Qaeda is keenly aware that the battle is ultimately for the 'hearts and minds of the ummah.'"[695] Ayman al-Zawahri (Osama bin Laden's deputy), admitted in 2005 ". . . that most 'of this battle is taking place in the battlefield of the media.'" Ayman al-Zawahiri has been a frequent and out-front al Qaeda spokesman, playing to international Muslim and Arab audiences with the party line of resisting the "Great Satan," killing infidels and "defending" the cause of Islam.[696]

The media is seen as an effective recruitment, fundraising, and propaganda tool. For example, al Qaeda intentionally films every violent attack it can. Some footage is used in training videos, but many end up as well-produced promotional videos, complete with soundtracks, and posted on the Internet. "For some Arab viewers who don't regularly view Western media, the overwhelming impression from the videos could be that militants are winning. The benefit for militants is to turn a single attack into a larger strategic weapon."[697]

One scholar wrote that the media's manipulation by terrorists and their tactics are well-known: "Terrorists also force their target audiences to ask why they are at the receiving end of violence. The media are the most likely sources of this information — often by offering terrorists or their supporters the opportunity to directly communicate their grievances, interests, causes, and objectives. Unwittingly, the mass media thus accommodate terrorists' desire to advertise the reasons behind their violence."[698]

---

695 Jim Michaels, "U.S. pulls plug on 6 al-Qaeda media outlets," *USAToday*, October 5, 2007. The term 'ummah' refers to the community of Muslim believers.

696 Ibid.

697 Ibid.

698 Brigitte L. Nacos, "Accomplice or Witness? The Media's Role in Terrorism," *Current History*, April 2000.

The U.S. government and military are also quite aware of this. In his September 2007 testimony to Congress, the U.S. commander in Iraq Army General David Petraeus stated, ". . . in recognition of the fact that this war is not only being fought on the ground in Iraq, but also in cyberspace, [the report of recommendations] also notes the need to contest the enemy's growing use of that important medium to spread extremism."[699] In October 2007, it was reported that the U.S. military had captured at least six al Qaeda media outlets and twenty suspected propaganda leaders since June of the same year.

In addition to studying American counter-terrorism tactics in order to develop new ways to strike at the U.S. and other targets, the Islamic terrorist movement has also consciously and intentionally used the American media and American people, recognizing the media is a tool that can be used to weaken the will of the American people in time of war. In an article on the Al-Ansar Web site, purported al Qaeda activist Abu-Ubayd Al-Qurashi wrote, "Al Qaeda has studied North Vietnam's victory over the United States, and found that Hanoi had 'fully understood that America's center of gravity lay in the American people,' and by killing America's 'dearest ones' . . . the war ended with victory on the Vietnamese side."[700]

This Vietnam-like propaganda strategy and result should be heeded and not be allowed to be repeated by the Islamo-fascist movement. The effect can be enduring. I found, for instance, that the Vietnam propaganda precedent is regrettably still operating. I was in Vietnam in the fall of 2003 and found that, even then, the Communists were still publicizing their propagandized "triumph" over the U.S. and the American military in various museums and cultural centers in Saigon (Ho Chi Minh City), Hue, Hanoi, and Haiphong where I visited. In Hanoi, people of all ages, but particularly the very young and the elderly tugged at my jacket, pressing me to buy paperback books by former secretary of defense Robert S. McNamara, setting forth his public "confessions" for his (and supposedly

---

[699] Ashley Phillips, "Experts: Iraq War Being Fought in Cyberspace, General Petraeus Says Extremists Use the Internet as a Tool in Battle," *ABC News*, September 11, 2007.

[700] Michael Scheuer, *Imperial Hubris, Why the West is Losing the War on Terror* (Washington, D.C.: Potomac Books, 2005). Also see "A Lesson on War" from December 19, 2002 on Al-Ansar's Web site.

America's) transgressions against the Vietnamese people in the 1960s.[701] Even those on the streets of Hanoi, when I was there, seemed to understand the power and influence of propaganda targeted at the U.S.

All of this reminds me of something said by former British Prime Minister Margaret Thatcher: "And we must try to find ways to starve the terrorist and the hijacker of the oxygen of publicity on which they depend."[702]

In the years ahead, I fear that our nation and our Western culture may see large-scale and worldwide, hate-filled challenges, like has not been seen in centuries. The trendlines are clear. To prevail in all of this, we must be able to communicate with each other — honestly and factually — so that our actions and responses to the threats are effective, and above all, successful. For our part, CACI's experience, as laid out in this book, demonstrates that the public at large needs to develop a much more skeptical and healthy disbelief about what it reads and hears from the profit-driven and politically motivated side of the media. The public needs to demand accuracy and critically question the media, its sources, its claims, its biases, and its motivations.

Take the Taguba report, as we have said, no one — media or public — raised even one critical comment or inquiry seeking evidence or validation of his statements and suspicions. Nor did they exercise restraint with the knowledge that Taguba's investigation was not directed at interrogators (even though he offered his opinions and "suspicions"

---

701 I believe McNamara was guilty of falling into the Communist propaganda trap when he presented his critique (interpreted by many as an "apology") of the U.S.'s actions in Vietnam in his later writings, the two most well known titles being *In Retrospect: The Tragedy and Lessons of Vietnam* by Brian VanDeMark and Robert S. McNamara (New York: Times Books, 1996) and *Argument Without End: In Search of Answers to the Vietnam Tragedy* by Robert S. McNamara, et al. (Washington, D.C.: Public Affairs Press, 2000). While McNamara may have been trying to explain his actions, these publications have served to reinforce the terrorist enemies' viewpoint that the way to undermine American military objectives is to dishearten and prey upon the impatience and anxiety of the American public — just as Ho Chi Minh and North Vietnam clearly did in the 1960s and early '70s.

702 Margaret Thatcher Foundation. This is a famous line from a speech that Thatcher gave to the American Bar Association in Albert Hall (London) in July 15, 1985. (http://www.margaretthatcher.org/speeches/displaydocument.asp?docid=106096).

about them), but rather its focus was on the MPs. They also failed to preface their reports with the acknowledgement that the investigation of interrogators would follow with its own set of conclusions.

The media has traditionally been the institution to question and rigorously investigate, but, in this case it did not. In fact, Taguba's report continues to be discussed in a vacuum without recognition of, or reference to, the several other official investigations conducted at the time. And quotes from Taguba's report continue to be disseminated including the incorrect, unsubstantiated aspects that were addressed in those other subsequent and important investigations.

★ ★ ★

While I do not have any final answers to these issues involving the ethics, standards and integrity of the news media and its *modus operandi*, I *do* know what companies (or any organization) can do when they find themselves caught in a media firestorm and in the middle of a great public controversy. To the issue itself, we have set forth several principles and our own crisis response model in this book. They are presented here to serve as guideposts for others who find themselves on similarly treacherous terrain.

I believe strongly that when under fire, companies owe it to themselves, to their employees, to their shareholders and to their customers as well as to their community and to their country, to seek out the truth, and to stand up for what is right — to do the right thing. They need to get the facts and tell people what those facts are, as soon as they are known, and even if they hurt. They need to tell those facts over and over at every opportunity to keep the record straight. They need to communicate to the news media, but also challenge it to get and keep the story right — in every detail. Indeed, they must *insist* that the media report the story accurately. They need to correct journalists directly and to push back firmly when reporters are wrong. And they must also take these proactive steps when any other individuals or organizations persist in propagating erroneous material, distortions or misinformation.

This is the position we took at CACI — to resist the injustices, to get the facts out and insist they be told accurately — to do the right thing so that "the truth will out." This is the story relayed in the pages of this book.

I believe it's an important story; that is why I wanted it told, and why the team at CACI wanted it published. I also think you will find it timely and relevant, and that it holds considerable value and meaning — today — for our free and open society.

J.P. London
December 31, 2007

> **"The opinion of honest men, friends to freedom and well-wishers to mankind, where ever they may happen to be born or reside, is the only kind of reputation a wise man could ever desire."**
> ~ **GEORGE WASHINGTON, JUNE 20, 1788**

APPENDIX A

Setting the Record Straight

THE EXAMPLES BELOW SHOW SOME OF THE MOST COMMON FALSEHOODS and fallacious media or pundit errors made about CACI, followed by the truth about CACI's work and conduct throughout the investigations about Abu Ghraib.

ERROR — The use of government contractors for military support in a war zone was first introduced with the Iraq war. FALSE.

TRUTH — Contractors have been used throughout American history to support the military going back to the Revolutionary War (1775–1783). The Pinkerton detective agency was a primary source of intelligence during the Civil War. Since the Gulf War of 1991 contractors have played a vital role in every major U.S. military engagement. The Clinton administration turned to private firms to provide a variety of field services in the Balkan conflict rather than call up military reserve units.

* * *

ERROR — Abu Ghraib was the first time and place that the U.S. government used civilian contractors for interrogation of detainees. FALSE.

TRUTH — Government contractors were already being used for interrogation in Guantanamo Bay, Cuba and in Afghanistan, before the U.S. Army contracted with CACI to provide interrogators in Iraq.

* * *

ERROR — There was no investigation into the abuses at Abu Ghraib before Taguba's report. FALSE.

TRUTH — According to Gen. Richard B. Myers, Chairman, Joint Chiefs of Staff, ". . . the commander of the CJTF-7, General Sanchez back in August said 'I want to look at our detention operations and our interrogation operations.' And he had the provost marshal of the army, Major General Ryder appointed to do that investigation."

* * *

ERROR — The Taguba report was released to the public by the army in April 2004. FALSE.

TRUTH — The Taguba report was a classified document (SECRET/NO FOREIGN DISSEMINATION) that was *illegally leaked* to the press before the army and DoD had had a full opportunity to review and act on the report. As stated by Secretary of Defense Rumsfeld in his sworn testimony to the Senate Armed Services Committee, "We did not release the Taguba report to the press. That was done by someone to release against the law a secret document." He added, "All I know is when it was made public, when somebody took a secret document out of prosecutorial channels and released it to the press, I do not believe it was yet anywhere in the Pentagon. Certainly, I had not been given it or seen it."

* * *

ERROR — The source who broke the law by *illegally looking* the classified military document written by Gen. Antonio Taguba (known as the Taguba report) to the press in the middle of an ongoing military investigation and legal proceedings has been prosecuted. FALSE.

TRUTH — The person who broke the law by *illegally leaking* the classified Taguba report to the press alleging abuse by members of the military (who were entitled to due process without influence) and CACI and its employee (before all evidence was gathered and investigations concluded), and exposing U.S. military and U.S. citizens to increased danger and violence, has never been identified or brought to justice.

* * *

ERROR — The Taguba report is based on an in depth and detailed investigation into the intelligence gathering and interrogation practices at Abu Ghraib. FALSE.

TRUTH — The Taguba report was *not* based on an investigation of interrogators, interrogation practices, or intelligence gathering at Abu Ghraib. The Taguba report was based on the investigation of Military Police (MP) activity at Abu Ghraib.

* * *

ERROR — The Taguba report was the final investigative report on abuse allegations at Abu Ghraib in 2003 and early 2004. FALSE.

TRUTH — The Taguba report was *one of several* investigations into abuse allegations at Abu Ghraib and it was directed specifically at investigating Military Police (MPs). Other investigations followed that specifically examined other aspects of the prison, including intelligence gathering, interrogations and interrogators. In several cases these later reports came to different conclusions than Taguba, including his conclusions about interrogators. At the time the Taguba report was *illegally leaked* to the press and being quoted widely, Secretary of Defense Donald Rumsfeld stated in his sworn testimony under oath to the Senate Armed Services Committee (June, 7, 2004), "In addition to the Taguba report, there are other investigations under way. . . . And because all the facts are not in hand, there will be corrections and clarifications to the record as more information is learned."

* * *

ERROR — All of Taguba's recommendations were implemented by the military and the government at the conclusion of his report. FALSE.

TRUTH — According to Lt. Gen. Lance L. Smith, in his testimony to the House Armed Services Committee on May 7, 2004, "I would say seventy-five percent [75%] of the recommendations have already been implemented. And the ones that have not are either in the process of being implemented or being evaluated as to whether that's the best course or another course might be better."

* * *

ERROR — CACI and its employees were "involved in," "participated in," or have been "charged" with abusing detainees or "directing the abuse" of detainees at Abu Ghraib. FALSE.

TRUTH — Neither CACI nor any of its employees have been found or proven to be "involved in" or "participated in" or "charged" with abuse nor have they been indicted for "directing abuse". Several investigations resulted from the abuse allegations at Abu Ghraib. The first, the Ryder report, made no mention of CACI. The second, the Taguba report, which was based on an investigation of Military Police (*not* military intelligence, including interrogators) stated a *suspicion* about *one* CACI employee and misidentified another suspected individual as a CACI employee. Several other official investigations followed (including specific investigations of interrogators and intelligence gathering at Abu Ghraib) which did not result in anyone from CACI being indicted or charged with any abuses at Abu Ghraib. In his report, Taguba urged that CACI employee Steven Stefanowicz be removed from his job, reprimanded, and denied his security clearance for allegedly lying to the investigating team and allegedly allowing or ordering MPs, who were not trained in interrogation techniques, to facilitate interrogations by setting conditions that Taguba said were neither authorized nor in accordance with Army regulations. All of Taguba's allegations remain unsupported based on all of the evidence made available to date.

* * *

ERROR — The Taguba report provided "evidence" that two CACI employees were "either indirectly or directly" responsible for the abuses at Abu Ghraib prison. FALSE.

TRUTH — Only one of the two people listed in Taguba's report as being employed by CACI was a CACI employee. John Israel was never employed by CACI. The Taguba report was also *not* an investigation of CACI employees or of interrogators at Abu Ghraib. The generalized conclusion of the Taguba report (based on an investigation of Military Police) as it related to the one employee of CACI (Steven Stefanowicz) remains completely unsupported by any of the documents and evidence made available to date. The Taguba report is also contradicted in important respects by the army's subsequent Kern/Jones/Fay report that investigated Military Intelligence and interrogators.

* * *

ERROR — John Israel worked for CACI as a "secret agent". FALSE.

TRUTH — John Israel was incorrectly identified as a CACI employee in the Taguba report. Israel was employed by a Titan (Corp.) subcontractor as a translator and never worked for CACI. CACI has no knowledge of the circumstances of John Israel's employment.

* * *

ERROR — Taguba "found" that Steven Stefanowicz engaged in or directed abuse of detainees at Abu Ghraib. FALSE.

TRUTH — Taguba did not "find" Stefanowicz to have engaged in abuse but stated his *"suspicion"* that Stefanowicz, along with three other individuals (two U.S. Army officers and one civilian contractor), was either *"directly or indirectly"* responsible, an allegation that was not specifically defined, verified or elaborated upon with regard to Stefanowicz.

* * *

ERROR — Taguba provided "back up support and evidence" for his statement that CACI interrogator, Steven Stefanowicz, was either *"directly or indirectly"* responsible for the abuses at Abu Ghraib (along with 3 other individuals, one of whom Taguba also listed as a CACI employee). FALSE.

TRUTH — Neither the Taguba report itself, nor any of the annexes of the report (released to date) provided any evidence to support the *"suspicion"* that Steve Stefanowicz, a CACI employee was *"directly or indirectly"* responsible for abuses at Abu Ghraib. In a 2005 interview, Taguba himself stated that he had not given much thought to what he meant by "direct" or "indirect." Later investigations and reports did not validate Taguba's statement in this regard and one of the other 3 individuals named, another civilian, John Israel, was later fully exonerated.

* * *

ERROR — CACI provided mercenaries or armed private security personnel or physical security services. FALSE.

TRUTH — CACI does not and never has provided "mercenary" war-fighter combatant forces or services, armed private security personnel, para-military, or any physical security services; nor has CACI ever engaged in any such business activity requiring or involving employees' regular occupational combatant use of arms/weapons.

* * *

ERROR — CACI engaged in spy activities. FALSE.

TRUTH — CACI has never performed any spy work or engaged in any similar espionage activities.

* * *

ERROR — CACI knew of assassinations. FALSE.

TRUTH — CACI has never had any knowledge of assassinations, murders, or any other similar unlawful activities.

* * *

ERROR — CACI provided translation and/or interpreter services. CACI employees could not speak or read English. FALSE.

TRUTH — CACI did not provide translator or interpreter services in Iraq or Afghanistan in the 2003–2004 period. All of CACI's interrogators in Iraq were U.S. citizens who held appropriate current U.S. government security clearances and were native English speakers.

* * *

ERROR — CACI solicited the U.S. Army for interrogation work at Abu Ghraib. FALSE.

TRUTH — Prior to its acquisition by CACI, Premier Technology Group (PTG) provided intelligence services to the U.S. Army in Europe, which were later deployed to Baghdad in support of the army in Iraq. CACI was aware of the army's stretched resources in Iraq and worked with the U.S. Army in contracting for the needed additional intelligence and interrogation support.

CACI had approached army contracting offices in Iraq and Kuwait to provide additional work that might be needed, including intelligence support services. Those offices lacked the resources to contract directly for needed services, and encouraged CACI PTG to consider existing contractual vehicles as an alternative. Subsequently, Army intelligence in Baghdad made a decision to sole-source to CACI PTG certain intelligence support services, including the interrogation support services. That was accomplished through the BPA and DOI delivery orders issued under the GSA IT schedule contract.

* * *

ERROR — Interrogation services were a significant part of CACI's revenue. FALSE.

TRUTH — CACI's interrogation support and analysis work for the U.S. Army in Iraq was less than 1 percent of the company's total worldwide business.

* * *

ERROR — CACI provided interrogators at Guantanamo Bay, Cuba and Afghanistan. FALSE.

TRUTH — CACI never had interrogators at Guantanamo Bay or Afghanistan. CACI interrogation services were provided only in Iraq. Civilian interrogators at Guantanamo Bay and Afghanistan were provided by other government contractors.

* * *

ERROR — CACI contract interrogators made up "half" of or the "majority" of interrogators at Abu Ghraib. FALSE.

TRUTH — CACI did not have more than 10 interrogators assigned and working at Abu Ghraib prison at any one time. During that same period, CACI employed approximately 140 other people for a wide range of intelligence, technical, logistics and project support work throughout Iraq.

* * *

ERROR — CACI was under pressure to fill interrogator slots quickly and faced financial penalties for not filling quotas on time, which would have looked bad on the company's record. FALSE.

TRUTH — CACI's contract, as is standard, contained manning requirements specifying the type and number of positions. The Army was critically short handed and the company held weekly updates with the customer to advise them about the arrival of personnel. Staff at the prison was desperately needed. However, CACI could only send employees which fully met the standards established by the contract. None of the official or publicly disclosed investigations have produced any evidence of any conditions set to improperly manipulate quotas.

* * *

ERROR — CACI employees were not U.S. citizens, nor did they have the required security clearances. FALSE.

TRUTH — All CACI employees in Iraq were U.S. citizens and held appropriate and current U.S government security clearances. Nor was there ever any condition set to increase quotas and none of the official and publicly disclosed investigations have produced any evidence of this.

* * *

ERROR — CACI shortcut its hiring process by not fully interviewing and qualifying applicants. In its haste to fill interrogator positions CACI hired "cooks and truck drivers." CACI employed individuals who did not meet the hiring criteria and were not qualified to do interrogations. FALSE.

TRUTH — CACI was rigorous and selective in its hiring process carefully screening and qualifying all potential interrogators presented to the U.S. Army for the army's review or acceptance. Out of approximately 1600 job applications, only 3 percent met the statement of work requirements and qualifications and were interviewed. CACI streamlined its interview process for applicants who were clearly qualified based on background and experience, but did not shortcut its hiring process.

All CACI interrogators met the qualifications set forth in the army's Statement of Work for the contract. Hiring selections were made by staff with expertise in the contract and job requirements. Fewer than 2 percent of applicants were employed as CACI interrogators in Iraq. All interrogators were U.S. citizens. All interrogators had appropriate U.S. government security clearances, which require government background checks. All interrogators hired for work in Iraq were approved or accepted by the army.

The Statement of Work further specified that the army would provide CACI employees with readiness training and briefings on rules of engagement and general orders applicable to U.S. Armed Forces, DoD civilians and U.S. contractors.

The Army Inspector General concluded that every one of CACI's interrogators satisfied the qualification criteria established by the government and set forth in the contract. Furthermore, the Church report stated, "On average, contractors were more experienced than military interrogators and this advantage enhanced their credibility with detainees and promoted successful interrogations. There is no link between approved interrogation techniques and detainee abuse." The Schlesinger report stated, "some of the older contractors had backgrounds as former military interrogators and were generally considered more effective than some of the junior enlisted personnel."

* * *

ERROR — CACI interrogators reported to the CIA. FALSE.

TRUTH — CACI interrogators never reported to the CIA; CACI employees only reported to U.S. military and CACI chains of command. At all times, CACI employees were subject to the supervision, direction and control of the military in performing their duties. The CACI chain of command was for administrative and personnel management requirements and not for control or management of the interrogator support project's activities.

* * *

ERROR — CACI interrogators lacked military training. FALSE.

TRUTH — Two thirds of CACI interrogators had previous military interrogator specialist training and the rest had equivalent experience from work in, or employment by, other agencies, such as, the FBI, CIA, DEA or major police departments. Military training, per se, was *not* a requirement in the army's Statement of Work for interrogators, in as much as the appropriate equivalent experiences may be obtained in other organizations as noted. CACI interrogators met all the requirements for the job set out in the army Statement of Work and were approved or agreed to for service by the army. Three official military reports based on Abu Ghraib investigations indicated that military training, though desirable, had not been mandatory in CACI's contract and was neither a defining factor in interrogator effectiveness, nor in the abuse charges.

* * *

ERROR — CACI interrogators worked under little or no supervision. FALSE.

TRUTH — The performance of CACI employees was monitored by both U.S. military and CACI chains of command. CACI recruited individuals who possessed the maturity and experience needed for the job, since the positions, by their nature, did not require continuous supervision. When CACI interrogators arrived in Iraq, they reported to their military supervisor. This supervisor assigned the interrogators their tasks, determined where the interrogators were placed and created their work schedules. All interrogators were under the control and supervision of the officer-in-charge of interrogation control.

⋆ ⋆ ⋆

ERROR — CACI personnel supervised and/or directed the actions of military personnel. FALSE.

TRUTH — CACI employees operated under the direct monitoring, supervision and control of the U.S. military. At no time did CACI employees have "chain of command" or supervisory authority over military personnel. At all times the U.S. government had oversight of CACI's employees reporting to work and this fact was supported in the Senate Armed Services hearings in May 2004. Secretary of Defense Donald Rumsfeld stated under oath in response to the question of what the roles of contractors were and who supervised them that the contractors are, "responsible to military intelligence who hire them and have the responsibility for supervising them." Acting Secretary of Army Les Brownlee under oath added, "in the theatre we have employed civilian contract interrogators and linguists, the central command has done this, and these people have no supervisory capabilities at all. They work under the supervision of officers-in-charge or noncommissioned officers-in-charge of whatever team or unit they are on. And they, most of them, are retired military and they are usually of the skill that they retired in and that is what they are employed for, and they assist in these processes. But they are not in a supervisory role." Maj. Gen. Geoffrey Miller under oath further stated, "no civilian contractors had a supervisory position. It's the military . . . who sets the priorities and ensures that we meet our standards."

⋆ ⋆ ⋆

ERROR — CACI and the company's personnel were in charge of interrogations at Abu Ghraib. FALSE.

TRUTH — Neither CACI nor any of its interrogators were ever in charge of interrogations or of U.S. military personnel, but were reported to the military chain of command. This is borne out in the testimony of key military leaders at the Senate Armed Services Committee hearings on May 7, 2004 when Senator McCain asked, "I'd like to know who was in charge of the — what agencies or private contractors were in charge of interrogations? Did they have authority over the guards?" "I'm asking who was in charge of the interrogations?" Lt. Gen.

Smith under oath responded, "They were not in charge. They were interrogators." Senator McCain rephrased, "My question is who was in charge of the interrogations?" and Lt. Gen. Smith answered, "The brigade commander for the military intelligence brigade."

Secretary of Defense, Donald Rumsfeld also stated "The answer is that the civilian contractors . . . they're responsible to military intelligence who hire them, and have the responsibility over them."

* * *

ERROR — CACI interrogators instructed the military police to "soften up" the prisoners for interrogation. FALSE.

TRUTH — There is no credible evidence that has been made available at any time to support allegations that any CACI interrogators directed any abuse of any detainee at any time, nor that they even had any authority whatsoever to have done so. The abuse of detainees at Abu Ghraib had nothing to do with interrogations, and this has been amply demonstrated by government investigations and reports as well as in related testimony under oath.

Interrogators did not direct the actions of military police and military police did not report to interrogators. According to Senator Roberts, during the Armed Services Committee hearings on May 7, 2004, "They [military intelligence and CIA representatives] indicated that at that particular time they did not know — had no evidence of any direction on the part of intelligence personnel at this prison suggesting that they commit these abuses at the behest of the military interrogators who asked the military police to, quote, "soften up" the detainees to prepare them for the interrogation."

Joseph Darby, the soldier who submitted the Abu Ghraib pictures to his army supervisors in January 2004, stated, "These guys [MPs] were doing nothing but occupying themselves in very sick ways. It was never about interrogations."

* * *

ERROR — Abuse at Abu Ghraib occurred as a result of detainee interrogations by CACI. FALSE.

TRUTH — Abuse at Abu Ghraib was not a function of interrogation practices. Furthermore, at all times CACI interrogator personnel were under the supervision of the U.S. military. As Joseph Darby, the soldier who submitted the Abu Ghraib pictures to his army supervisors stated, "The soldiers involved at Abu Ghraib [abuses] were not interrogating inmates." "These guys [MPs] were doing nothing but occupying themselves in very sick ways. It was never about interrogations." The Church report also stated, "There is no link between approved interrogation techniques and detainee abuse."

* * *

ERROR — CACI CEO's trip to Israel in January 2004 was made to investigate interrogation operations and torture methods. FALSE.

TRUTH — The CEO's trip to Israel was part of a delegation to attend a conference titled "Defense Aerospace Homeland Security Mission of Peace". In addition to CACI's CEO (Dr. London) attendees included Dr. Rodney Leibowitz, Chairman of First Responder Inc., Dr. Sergio Magistri, President of Invision Technologies, Inc., Robert Liscouski, Assistant Secretary for Information Analysis & Infrastructure Protection for Homeland Security, Joe Reeder, former Undersecretary of the Army, Senator Evan Bayh (D-Indiana), Senator Ben Nelson (D-Kansas), Congressman John Linder (R-Georgia) and Congressman John McHugh (R-New York). The delegation included numerous other government leaders and businessmen. CACI's CEO received the Albert Einstein Lifetime Achievement Award along with certain other attendees. The delegation included neither trips to prisons nor any research into interrogation. Previous attendees to the conference have included Senator John Kerry (D-Massachusetts), Former U.S. President Bill Clinton, former Prime Minister Margaret Thatcher, and news people Barbra Walters and Tom Brokaw.

* * *

ERROR — CACI was involved or responsible for torture and/or detainee abuse in Iraq and elsewhere in the world. FALSE.

TRUTH — CACI has never engaged in any activities that fit or in any way whatsoever resemble torture, in Iraq, or anywhere else in the world at any time.

* * *

ERROR — CACI relied on interrogation work for revenue growth. CACI engaged in illegal acts in its interrogation practices to increase its profits. CACI devised and condoned torture so as to increase profits and revenue. FALSE.

TRUTH — CACI did not seek interrogation work but responded to a need for such services by the U.S. Army for this work. CACI's interrogation work was nominal, representing less than 1% of the company's total business. CACI does not condone and has never engaged in any business activities that may be characterized in any way as "torture." CACI has never done business that would condone, use, or promote any harm (intentional or otherwise) to anyone. CACI's revenue is derived solely from respectable, legitimate and lawful business operations.

* * *

ERROR — CACI and Titan (Corp.) "teamed up" to conspire with members of the U.S. government or Army to increase demand for their services in order to increase revenues. FALSE.

TRUTH — CACI and Titan had no partnership or contractual arrangement in Iraq at any time. CACI's interrogation contract work represented less than 1% of its overall business. CACI did not engage in any activity that could be described in any way as an effort to increase interrogation demand. In fact, as a result of the company's rigorous hiring process aimed at providing qualified interrogators, some authorized positions were unfilled because of the difficulty of getting qualified applicants in service in Iraq under hostile warzone conditions.

* * *

ERROR — Images of CACI employees appear in the horrific detainee abuse photos taken at Abu Ghraib prison. FALSE.

TRUTH — No CACI employee is depicted or seen in any of the notorious detainee abuse photos from Abu Ghraib prison.

* * *

ERROR — Iraq detainees have identified specific CACI employees as abusing them. FALSE.

TRUTH — Some Iraq detainees who allege being abused at Abu Ghraib have reportedly stated that they were aware that contract employees were at the prison but no detainees have identified any specific CACI employee as abusing them. Nor has any verifiable evidence been provided substantiating or proving such allegations.

* * *

ERROR — Brigadier General Karpinski has stated that she saw CACI interrogators abuse detainees. FALSE.

TRUTH — Brigadier General Karpinski has never claimed that she saw any CACI employee abuse any detainee. General Karpinski has stated that she was aware of CACI interrogators being present at the prison but has neither identified any specific CACI interrogators as engaging in any abuse nor provided verifiable evidence of any CACI interrogator being involved in detainee abuse.

* * *

ERROR — None of CACI's employees have been investigated for alleged involvement in abuse at Abu Ghraib. FALSE.

TRUTH — The Department of the Army conducted multiple investigations regarding potential abuse by any civilian contract employee at Abu Ghraib, including those of CACI. Maj. Gen. Fay referred 3 CACI employees to the Department of the Army for further investigation and possible referral to the Department of Justice, but to date no one from CACI has been charged or indicted for any wrongdoing.

* * *

ERROR — CACI and the army purposely hid the interrogator contract work under the Department of the Interior's Blanket Purchase Agreement (BPA) to conduct illegal contracts or business activities. The CACI interrogation contract was issued through the Department of Interior in order to shelter its employees from potential prosecution within the military structure. FALSE.

TRUTH — CACI did not hide its contract or project work and did not engage in any illegal activities. The goal in using an existing BPA contract was speed, not to support any secret agenda. CACI's project work in Iraq was always public (unclassified) information. Blanket Purchase Agreements (BPA's) have been in use since 1998 and federal government procurement regulations provide for BPA's to enable the contracting agency (in this case, located at Ft. Huachuca, AZ) to increase efficiency. Issued initially by the contracting office at Ft. Huachuca (then an Army contracting office), administration of the contract was transferred by the government to the Interior Department (DOI). The existing DOI Blanket Purchase Agreement, which was already in place at Ft. Huachuca, was used simply for expediency rather than going through the time consuming process of pursuing another contract vehicle to fulfill the army's critical need for interrogators during an urgent and exigent war time situation. BPA's were important for the army, as it has worked to add resources in Iraq at a time of extreme need and urgency.

* * *

ERROR — CACI used an existing Information Technology (IT) Blanket Purchase Agreement contract to get around the administrative details of a contract specific to interrogation work. CACI used an existing blanket purchase agreement to avoid a competitive bid of the interrogation contract. FALSE.

TRUTH — Given the urgent and compelling circumstances of the Iraq war, the U.S. Army determined to have CACI provide intelligence support services on a sole-source basis. An existing Blanket Purchase Agreement for IT services was used for the purpose of expediency with the open agreement of the army and Department of Interior due to the army's critical need during urgent war time conditions in which interrogators were needed. The interrogation work was seen as an extension of the work that CACI was conducting under the contract, which called for tactical intelligence information collection, data analysis and decision support. According to Frank Quimby, spokesman for the Department of the Interior (DOI) approved the interrogation work under the IT Blanket Purchase Agreement because it included "information technology aspects". CACI acquired the GSA schedule contract as part of the assets it acquired when it bought Premier Technology Group, Inc. (PTG) in May 2003. As background, the U.S. Army Directorate of Contracting, Fort Huachuca, Arizona had previously awarded a Blanket Purchase Agreement to PTG against GSA Schedule Group 70 (Information Technology). The same contract (BPA GSA IT schedule 70) was also used initially by Lockheed Martin for interrogation services at Guantanamo Bay, Cuba.

* * *

ERROR — Using a contract with CACI for services to the army, but which was administered by the Department of Interior, made it difficult and confusing to determine who was accountable for the contract. FALSE.

TRUTH — According to Frank Quimby of the Department of the Interior, all three parties, contractor, Army and Interior, have legal responsibilities. "'CACI's responsibility is to provide the services at a (negotiated) price,' he said. 'The Interior Department is responsible for administering the contract,' which includes issuing checks and contract forms." "The Army is to provide the specifications, (determine the) pay, and supervise the contract work and contract workers." "They have the legal responsibility to provide the supervision of the contractors by the Army officers, who report up the chain of command."

Quimby also reported at the time the Taguba report was *illegally leaked* to the press that he had asked the army if it was satisfied with CACI's work and the response he received was "yes."

* * *

ERROR — CACI's contract was a "cost-plus" contract that provided commissions (fees) to the company for add-on service and cost overruns. FALSE.

TRUTH — CACI's contract was not a cost-plus contract. The U.S. government does not engage in cost-plus "percentage (of cost) fee" contracts; only reimbursable *fixed* fee, or incentive, or award fee contracts are in current use. Contractor fees, based on a percentage of cost, on "cost plus" contracts have not been utilized by the government since, at least, the 1950's (if ever). CACI's DOI BPA IT contract was what is commonly known as a Time and Material (T&M) contract, where a fixed number of hours are worked per week per employee and so charged on an hourly rate basis. Material costs, if any, or other approved and necessary costs associated with the work are charged at cost as approved by the government customer.

* * *

ERROR — CACI violated federal regulations by allowing its civilian project manager to assist in the contract process by helping to draft the initial statement of work language. FALSE.

TRUTH — The Federal Acquisition Regulation (FAR) bars contractor involvement in drafting a statement of work *only* if it provides the contractor a competitive advantage. But the CACI interrogator contract was initiated as a sole source award issued under urgent wartime conditions, and the FAR at section 9.505-2(b) allows for a contractor to assist in preparing the statement of work when it is a sole source award. The government always makes all its final contract decisions. Federal contracting rules, which were changed in the 1990's government acquisition reform, explicitly recognize that contractor assistance is allowed for these types of contract actions, as in CACI's contracting case. In the context of this contracting situation the assistance was agreed and accepted by the U.S. government during urgent wartime conditions in order to quickly meet the needs of the U.S. military. This process was also subject to review and approval by the government at every step and the contract transaction passed legal review by the army's Judge Advocate General Corps, before it was awarded to CACI.

* * *

ERROR — The GSA investigation and correspondence regarding CACI meant the contractor was barred from federal contracts. FALSE.

TRUTH — GSA's initial letter requested a response from CACI on several contract issues and a final letter said GSA saw no reason to suspend/debar CACI. The company was neither barred nor suspended from government contracts.

* * *

ERROR — CACI's debt rating was downgraded. FALSE.

TRUTH — Standard & Poor's briefly placed CACI on "watch status" during the initial Iraq crisis, but the company's debt ratings were never downgraded.

* * *

ERROR — CACI's interrogation business put shareholder investments at risk. FALSE.

TRUTH — CACI's interrogation work in Iraq never placed investments in the company at risk. The company's work in Iraq, though quite important to CACI and the U.S. Army, was a small part of CACI's overall portfolio of contracts (less then 1%) and was not pursued as a major line of business. The GSA's review of CACI's BPA contract with the DOI at Ft. Huachuca was promptly completed without business interruption.

* * *

ERROR — The Calvert Group of mutual funds concluded that CACI violated human rights and was a weapons-maker. FALSE.

TRUTH — CACI is a recognized industry leader in corporate ethics and has never committed or been a party to any human rights abuses. CACI does not condone such behavior. Such charges have no basis in fact and are totally without merit. CACI has never been a weapons maker or weapons merchant. The Calvert Group determined to divest itself of stock in CACI because of the allegations in the Taguba Report. To CACI's knowledge, the Calvert Group made no evidence-based determination itself regarding CACI's conduct in Iraq.

* * *

ERROR — CACI has no corporate policy on ethics and human rights. FALSE.

TRUTH — For several decades, CACI has had established policies on ethics and corporate values. CACI provides, as a standard part of its business practice, several documents, which are published by the company on ethics, the rights of others, and the process for reporting wrongdoing by employees. Every CACI employee receives ethics training and annually recertifies their understanding of, and commitment to abide by, CACI's Code of Ethics and Business Conduct Standards. In addition, every CACI employee deployed to work in Iraq also reviewed and signed an additional document, the CACI Code of Conduct in Iraq.

* * *

ERROR — CACI did a poor job of due diligence when acquiring PTG. FALSE.

TRUTH — A thorough due diligence was performed when CACI bought out PTG, which is a regular and routine part of the CACI mergers and acquisition program. There were no significant defects discovered at the time of the transaction (which closed in May of 2003).

* * *

ERROR — California State Treasurer Phil Angelides, along with CalPERS and CalSTRS, contacted CACI to answer questions about the company's work at Abu Ghraib without success before notifying the *Washington Post* that they wanted to talk to CACI. FALSE.

TRUTH — CACI participated in several investor conferences on May 20th, June 2nd, and June 8th to provide the investor community with the verified facts and information that the company had on the Abu Ghraib situation and to answer questions. However, the company found no record of anyone from the California funds participating on the calls or the webcast of those calls. No one from the California funds contacted CACI seeking information about its Iraq business or to ask questions *prior* to notifying the *Post*. CACI subsequently found no issues raised by the California State Treasurer's Office that the company had not already addressed fully in its public information releases.

* * *

ERROR — CACI was in "denial" about its Abu Ghraib work. FALSE.

TRUTH — CACI frequently distributed information to the public about issues regarding its work at Abu Ghraib through several channels, including numerous press releases. CACI also posted information on an Iraq section of its website as it became known. At the same time, CACI followed the rule of law, especially the principle that an individual is innocent until proven guilty. There were no CACI "denials" about any facts or truths about the company's interrogator work at Abu Ghraib prison. CACI did not and would not come to judgment unless and until all the relevant facts are set forth.

* * *

ERROR — CACI was not forthcoming in telling the public what it knew about Abu Ghraib at the time the scandal broke. CACI was not forthcoming with information on the crisis as it unfolded. FALSE.

TRUTH — CACI became aware of the Abu Ghraib abuses at the same time as the public. CACI was forthcoming with all constituencies regarding CACI's business in Iraq and disseminated information that the company became aware of through official investigations that were being conducted at the time. CACI practiced open and honest communications in every aspect of the Iraq Abu Ghraib case, as demonstrated by its numerous press releases, extensive investor and employee outreach activities, and cooperation with all U.S. government investigations. CACI also launched its own internal investigation and announced its preliminary findings to the public, even before other investigations were concluded. CACI was diligent in correcting erroneous media reports as soon as possible both directly to the source and in its posting of 42 Frequently Asked Questions (FAQ's) about CACI in Iraq on the company's website beginning on May 20, 2004. CACI has continued to update the site and to respond to erroneous information as needed.

* * *

ERROR — CACI's Army client was unsatisfied with the interrogation services being performed. FALSE.

TRUTH — Client correspondence to CACI expressed a high level of satisfaction and gratitude — CACI's initial interrogation contract was replaced by a new contract with the company in August of 2004. CACI did have some challenges in meeting staffing levels for Iraq in the fall of 2004 due to the intensity of warzone dangers at the time but there were never any significant problems with CACI's work expressed by the army in Iraq. Frank Quimby, spokesman for DOI reported at the time the Taguba report was *illegally leaked* that he had inquired of the army if it was satisfied with CACI's work and the response he received was "yes."

*   *   *

ERROR — CACI Board members are selected for the purpose of exerting influence to gain favor for CACI business and contract awards. Current and past CACI board members had roles/influence in CACI's Abu Ghraib work/contract "cover up." FALSE.

TRUTH — CACI has a strict conflict of interest policy for Board members, which operate as an independent body consistent with the Sarbanes-Oxley Act and New York Stock Exchange rules. As a public company CACI Board members are all publicly elected by the shareholders every year. CACI's Board represents leaders in the industry because they have the expertise to provide industry advice and direction. There has never been any CACI "cover up". No current or former CACI board member has ever used any influence or engaged in inappropriate activities whatsoever with regard to the Iraq crisis or any other matter at any time.

*   *   *

ERROR — CACI and its CEO, in particular, made excessive profits from the company's work in Iraq. FALSE.

TRUTH — The profit margins of government services contractors have historically been lower than commercial business, so much so that Wall St. analysts and investors have often ignored these companies in the past. With the decline of the "dot-com" industry in early 2001, government contracting stock values began to rise as they became more attractive to investors who saw the solid business opportunity and history of service they represented. Following the "9-11" terrorist attacks, some government contractors, like CACI, that provided high-tech defense and security related services, particularly in homeland security and intelligence, saw their stock values increase. As demand for services increased, revenue and profits also increased. CACI implemented a stock split in December 2001, some 18 months prior to the Iraq War. Moreover, CACI's work in Iraq represented less than 1% of the company's overall business. In addition, CACI's acquisition program added increased revenue and profit to the company, particularly with the AMS acquisition in May 2004.

Further, CACI's CEO during the Abu Ghraib crisis (J. P. London) has purchased and accumulated CACI stock for nearly 35 years, the value of which has increased during that time. Approaching the age of 70, he began several years ago to sell his stock for retirement. Some have confused (perhaps intentionally) his stock sales as salary or "profit", which is not true. The annual salary of CACI's CEO had been below other industry leaders and the stock he has sold represents the result of a lifetime of work — not profit or pay made during the Iraq war. Moreover, during this period thousands of American investors, pensioners and working people have seen their investment in CACI appreciate as well.

* * *

ERROR — CACI used large sums of money from political donations and its political action committees (PACs) to lobby Congress and influence legislation including the defeat of a bill sponsored by Sen. Chris Dodd that would bar civilian contractors from certain kinds of military work. FALSE.

TRUTH — CACI has no PAC, and has never been involved with a PAC, never lobbied Congress about legislation, and had no role whatsoever regarding the Dodd bill. Any political contributions coming from CACI employees are made solely on a private individual basis at the employees' choice and have represented contributions to both Democratic and Republican members and parties.

* * *

ERROR — CACI has leveraged business with the government through its connections with members of Congress and people of influence. FALSE.

TRUTH — CACI does not have a history of close relationships or connections with members of Congress or people connected to those in Congress, nor has the company traditionally used the service of lobbyists. When CACI found itself under attack in the media after the Abu Ghraib events became public, the company had to familiarize itself to those on Capital Hill and this was done primarily through staffers rather than getting direct meetings with members of Congress. Publicly televised Congressional hearings on May 7, 2004 showed that Congressional leaders were not familiar with CACI.

* * *

ERROR — CACI has used the services of lobbyists, like the Livingston Group, to gain influence on Capital Hill. FALSE.

TRUTH — CACI does not have a history of lobbying. The Livingston Group was used in the Louisiana region for marketing support and business development assistance from 1999–2001. The firm of Clark and Weinstock was engaged by CACI in the summer of 2004 during the company's Abu Ghraib ordeal to assist in its government relations efforts to familiarize those on Capital Hill with the company.

★ ★ ★

ERROR — The Center for Constitutional Rights (CCR) successfully pressured CACI into dropping its interrogation contract in Iraq. FALSE.

TRUTH — CCR has had no bearing at any time on CACI contract work or any other business issue for that matter. CACI was not successful in its re-bid for the Iraq interrogator contract, which was awarded to L-3 Corp. at the army's choosing in 2005. A significant number of CACI's interrogators took employment with the new company and remained in Iraq to support the U.S. Army. This is further evidence that CACI interrogators met the experience and professional qualifications required by the army contract.

★ ★ ★

ERROR — Private government contracting is a recent phenomenon of the war on terrorism that is costly to taxpayers. FALSE.

TRUTH — The growth of the private government contracting sector was due to military downsizing in the early 1990s aimed at reducing military personnel levels. The system of private contracting was set up to save taxpayer money by using contractors on an "as needed" basis rather than maintaining military salaries and benefits year round, year after year, on through retirement (and costs) for non-military kinds of work. When contractor services are no longer required they can be cut back quickly. High technology has also driven the shift toward contractors who possess professional computer and technical skills that are not readily available in an all-volunteer force in the numbers and skill categories required. Contractor support remains readily available for years at a time without training reinvestment by the government. Furthermore, there was a very substantial increase in 2003 in civilian contractors supporting forces on the battlefield in Iraq versus the 1991 Gulf War. Of course, the magnitude and duration of the 2003 Iraq War has been substantially greater than the 1991 Gulf War.

APPENDIX B
The CACI's Abu Ghraib Experience — Who's Who

CACI INTERNATIONAL INC

Dr. J. Phillip ("Jack") London — is Chairman of the Board of CACI International Inc. He also held the positions of President and Chief Executive Officer until July 2007. London joined the company in 1972. He was elected to the Board of Directors in 1981, was appointed President and CEO in 1984 and became Chairman of the Board in 1990. He is considered by many in the industry as the founder of modern day CACI. London directed the CACI management team and advisors during the Abu Ghraib crisis from April through December of 2004. He is the primary designer of CACI's hypercrisis management strategy in response to the allegations of the *illegally leaked* army report (SECRET/NO FOREIGN DISSEMINATION) authored by Major General Anthony M. Taguba. London led all of CACI's responses and initiatives for investor relations, public relations, legal affairs, and operations. London's many honors include being selected by the Association of the United States Army (AUSA) in October 2003 to receive its John W. Dixon Award, an honor given annually to a distinguished industry leader who has made outstanding contributions to America's defense; and having an Ethics in Business Award presented in his name each year by the Human Resource Leadership Awards of Greater Washington. In March 2007 London received the Navy League of the United States Fleet Admiral Chester W. Nimitz Award for exemplary leadership in the maritime defense industry. London is a 1959 graduate of the U.S. Naval Academy at Annapolis. He is a graduate of the U.S. Naval Postgraduate School (Monterey, CA) where he received a master of science degree in operations research. He also holds a doctorate in business administration (with distinction) from the George Washington University. A Naval Aviator and a carrier helicopter pilot in his early military career, London is a retired captain in the U.S. Navy Reserves with 24 years total service.

Ken Johnson — joined CACI in 1999 as the President of U.S. Operations for CACI. With more than 27 years of industry experience, Johnson ensured that CACI's operations continued unaffected during the Abu Ghraib crisis. A 1969 graduate of the U.S. Military Academy at West Point, Johnson served with the U.S. Army Infantry in Vietnam as a military advisor. He retired from CACI in November of 2004.

Greg Bradford — is President of CACI's United Kingdom (UK) organization. Bradford managed client, government, and media relations in the UK during the Abu Ghraib crisis. He joined CACI in 1979. He served with the U.S. Army in Vietnam and later received his juris doctor degree from the University of San Diego.

Jeff Elefante — served as CACI's General Counsel. A member of CACI's Legal Division since 1983, Elefante managed the company's legal matters in the Abu Ghraib crisis, including responding to government requests for internal records, contracts and policies, developing strategies, document control, and security. He received his juris doctor degree from Georgetown University. Elefante retired from CACI in September of 2005.

Jody Brown — is Executive Vice President of Business Communications and Public Relations at CACI. She is responsible for all media affairs, directing and implementing the company's business and public relations, marketing communications, employee communications, recognition and incentive, and community outreach programs. During the Abu Ghraib crisis, Brown, then a senior vice president, working with the CEO, was instrumental in leading and managing CACI's media relations, developing public outreach and public affairs strategies, and implementing employee and company communications. She began her career at CACI in 1984 as a graphic designer. Brown received a bachelor's degree in visual communications from the University of Maryland, with advanced coursework in public ralations and crisis communications.

Ron Schneider — is Executive Vice President of Business Development for CACI. During the Abu Ghraib crisis, Schneider, then a senior vice president, working directly with the CEO, was executive lead on managing the operational side of CACI's response to government inquiries, including directing tasks, developing project strategies, and reviewing internal processes. He directed CACI's Iraq contract staffing and requirements reviews. He served as the CEO's project coordinator for CACI's Iraq Steering Group. Schneider obtained a degree in applied behavioral science from National Lewis University.

David Dragics — is Senior Vice President of Investor Relations. During the Abu Ghraib crisis, Dragics was the company's day-to-day interface with financial markets and shareholders, informing them of CACI's cooperation with government investigations. A retired colonel in the U.S. Army Reserve that included service in Vietnam and the 1991 Gulf War, he has over 25 years of experience in investor relations and finance in the technology industry. Dragics holds a master of business administration from the University of Pittsburgh.

John Hedrick — was Executive Vice President of the CACI business unit that absorbed the Premier Technology Group (PTG). He has over three decades experience in information technology, operations, and project management. He retired from the Army obtaining the rank of Brigadier General and then later retired from CACI in 2004. Hedrick holds a master of business administration from Tulane University and attended the Army War College.

Harry Thornsvard — was Senior Vice President with CACI Premier Technology, Inc. He was in charge of the division that initially hired the interrogators. Thornsvard has over two decades experience in Army logistics. He holds a master of arts from the University of Texas at Austin. In 2004, Thornsvard left CACI to become president of RDR, a Virginia-based, security-centric IT and systems engineering firm.

Chuck Mudd — was Vice President of the Operational Support Division of CACI Premier Technology, Inc. until March of 2006. His responsibilities included managing CACI employees in Iraq, supporting the Multi-National Forces-Iraq, and making monthly trips to Iraq to meet with employees and the military command. Mudd is a retired U.S. Army Colonel with over 30 years of Army acquisitions experience, both military and private. He holds a master's degree in public administration from Western Kentucky University and a master of science in computer science from George Washington University. He is a graduate of the Army War College, the Defense Systems Management College and the Armed Forces Staff College.

Mark Billings — is a senior director with CACI Premier Technology, Inc. who was one of the leads on CACI's intelligence projects in Iraq. Billings has over 30 years of information technology and program management experience with the U.S. Army and defense industry. He holds a master's degree in information sciences from the Florida Institute of Technology.

Scott Northrop — was a project manager within CACI's Operations & Intelligence Division. During the Abu Ghraib crisis, Northrop, then Deputy Project Manager and In-Country Manager in Iraq, managed on-the-ground operations and was instrumental in obtaining and providing critical information and documentation to CACI headquarters. He obtained a master of business administration from City University. Northrop left CACI in April of 2006.

Dan Porvaznik — was a project manager with CACI Premier Technology, Inc. and was a site lead in Iraq on the C2 and C4 intelligence and logistics contracts. Porvaznik also held several intelligence management and analysis positions with the company in Iraq and Germany. Prior to joining PTG, he spent over two decades in the U.S. Marine Corps, focusing on military intelligence. Porvaznik resigned from CACI Premier Technology, Inc. in 2006.

Terry Raney — is Senior Vice President and Division Manager of the Business Management Division of CACI and a recognized expert in procurement, acquisition policy, contract management, and defense economics. Raney has over 17 years of DoD acquisition experience, including service as the Acting Associate Deputy Assistant Secretary (Contracting) for the Air Force. He had also previously been Chief of Contract Policy for the Air Force, a professor and department chairman at the Defense Systems Management College, and Deputy Department Head of the Department of Economics and Geography at the Air Force Academy, where he was an assistant professor of economics. Raney holds a doctorate in economics from Georgetown University.

Mike Gray — was Senior Vice President and Director of Contracts for CACI. During the Iraq crisis, Gray led all contract review efforts for various investigations, including negotiating extensions for inquiries from the Defense Contract Audit Agency. Gray has over 30 years of experience in operations and contract management in the technology and defense sectors. He received his bachelor's degree in marketing from Cansinius College. Gray left CACI in 2007.

Thomas Horrigan — is Vice President of Corporate Strategic Proposals for CACI Federal. He is responsible for corporate level unclassified proposals on recompete and new business opportunities and participates in bid process milestone reviews and strategic opportunity reviews associated with unclassified bids. Horrigan was a member of the team that scrutinized the qualifications of CACI contract interrogators. Horrigan also spent six years active duty as a U.S. Naval officer. Horrigan graduated from the U.S. Naval Academy with a bachelor's degree in engineering.

Amy Monahan — is a Senior Project Manager within CACI Premier Technology, Inc. She supervises project managers responsible for daily operations in Europe and Afghanistan. Monahan was Senior Project Manager responsible for the overall administration of the Intelligence Support Services contract in Iraq, including deliverables, funding, and employee relations. Monahan holds a bachelor's degree in English from George Mason University.

Steven Stefanowicz — was initially hired by CACI as a screener, and was later promoted to an interrogator with CACI at Abu Ghraib prison in Iraq. He had been singled out along with three other individuals (two Army officers and one other civilian) in the Taguba report for suspicion of being directly or indirectly responsible for prisoner abuses, but evidence has never materialized to support these allegations. Stefanowicz graduated from the University of Maryland and then joined the navy reserve. He subsequently held various business positions in the U.S. and Australia. After September 11, 2001, Stefanowicz returned to service as an intelligence specialist in Oman. He was employed by CACI between September of 2003 and October of 2004. As of December 2007, no charges had been filed against Stefanowicz in any jurisdiction.

Daniel Johnson — was a CACI contract interrogator at Abu Ghraib prison from the end of 2003 through July 2004. At that time, Johnson had approximately 10 years experience in linguistics, human intelligence collection, screening and interrogation, including assignments with the U.S. Army and Military Intelligence.

Timothy Dugan — was a CACI contract interrogator at Abu Ghraib prison from the end of 2003 through July 2004. Dugan possessed over two decades experience, including interrogation and linguistics in the U.S. Army as well as corporate investigations. Dugan holds a bachelors degree in political science and history from Heidelberg College and attended the Defense Language Institiute in Monterey, CA for Russian Linguistics.

Z. Selin Hur — is a management consultant to Dr. London, having joined CACI in April of 2004. She created and maintained CACI's knowledge repository during the Abu Ghraib crisis, also providing research and communications support. She contributed significantly to the preparation of this book with organization, extensive writing, research, fact-checking, and editing. Hur's background in business and technology consulting includes positions at EDS and the World Bank. She holds a master of business administration and master's degree in public and international affairs from the University of Pittsburgh.

Lillian Brannon — was Executive Administrator and trusted advisor to Dr. London for over 25 years until her retirement in December 2007. She managed Dr. London's schedule, correspondence, and relations with his executive staff and clients and industry colleagues. She was instrumental in organizing and managing and coordinating London's schedule for communications and operations during the Abu Ghraib crisis.

Steptoe & Johnson

J. William Koegel — is a partner in the Washington, D.C.-based law firm of Steptoe & Johnson LLP, serving as legal counsel and professional responsibility advisor to the firm. He specializes in litigation. Koegel acted as the outside counsel to CACI, advising the company on a variety of Abu Ghraib litigation and crisis-related issues. He led the team for CACI's internal investigation of the prisoner abuse allegations and was instrumental in developing the company's response to the General Services Administration's inquiry into the company's contract work for the U.S. Army in Iraq. Koegel received his juris doctor degree from Boston College.

John O'Connor — is a partner at Steptoe & Johnson, where he specializes in civil litigation and insurance disputes. O'Connor served three years as a judge advocate in the U.S. Marine Corps. He worked with Bill Koegel to advise the company on Abu Ghraib-related issues. O'Connor received his juris doctor degree from the University of Maryland.

Prism Public Affairs

Don Foley — a veteran public relations advisor, was the lead public relations crisis management advisor to CACI during the Abu Ghraib crisis. After 20 years on Capitol Hill, he spent four years as vice president of worldwide corporate communications for Northwest Airlines and two years as chief operating officer at Powell Tate, a Washington, D.C. public affairs firm, before becoming a founding partner of Prism Public Affairs. Foley joined the X PRIZE Foundation as a Senior Director of the Automotive X PRIZE in June 2007 and was promoted to Executive Director shortly thereafter. Foley received a bachelor's degree in political science and urban affairs from St. Louis University.

Michael Gelb — provided strategic and crisis counsel, issue management, press relations, and writing services for CACI during the Abu Ghraib crisis. Gelb also provided the basic foundation and scope for this book with interviewing, writing, research, and content organization. He prepared the first full draft of this book and was a major initial contributor. As a journalist, Gelb had previously covered the White House, public policy, and politics for a decade at Reuters. He was a founding member of Powell Tate, a Washington, D.C. public relations firm, where he was executive vice president before founding Gelb Strategies in 2001. Gelb received a bachelor of arts in history from Penn State University.

Clark & Weinstock

David Berteau — is a government relations consultant with over 30 years of experience in public and private sector management, including more than 15 years of experience in senior defense management positions. During the Abu Ghraib ordeal, Berteau advised London on CACI's relations with Congress and other government agencies. He is also a faculty member of Syracuse University's Maxwell School and holds a master of public affairs degree from the University of Texas at Austin.

Arent Fox

Craig King — is head of Arent Fox's Government Contractor Services Group, where he provides legal advice and representation pertaining to aspects of doing business with federal and state governments. As a leading expert in public contract law, King directed CACI's response to the General Services Administration's inquiry about the company's contract work for the U.S. Army for work in Iraq. He received his juris doctor from Georgetown University.

Burkhart Enterprises, LLC

Dr. Jennifer Burkhart — is president of Burkhart Enterprises, LLC, providing business development and mergers and acquisition (M&A) advisory services. She began M&A development with CACI in 1999 as an outside consultant researching and developing acquisition candidates for the company, successfully facilitating the close of several acquisitions with annual revenues totaling $200 million. By mid-2004, Burkhart's role with CACI also included that of outside business consultant providing analytical support, behavioral insights and recommendations to management. These efforts focused on the psychological aspects of company communication and public messaging in addressing company perception and image as it related to CACI's work at Abu Ghraib. Burkhart also was a key reviewer and major contributor to the book during the final stages of preparation, providing strategic editorial recommendations. Dr. Burkhart holds a doctorate in psychology from the Ohio State University and conducted postdoctoral training in marketing at the University of Pittsburgh.

ClaireMedia LLC

Claire Sanders Swift — is a national media consultant and president of ClaireMedia LLC in Washington, DC. She spent 15 years as a television producer working on TV shows such as PrimeTime Live, Dateline, ABC News, NBC News, CBS News, MSNBC, PBS, HBO, CNN, Good Morning America, Washington Post, Wall Street Journal, New York Times, Associated Press and UPI. In 2001, she started her own strategic media development company. Swift has been the recipient of two Emmy awards and a National Headliner Award. Swift graduated from Hollins College.

U.S. Government Officials

Donald H. Rumsfeld — was the 21st Secretary of Defense. The former Navy pilot had also served as the 13th Secretary of Defense, White House Chief of Staff, U.S. Ambassador to NATO, U.S. Congressman, and chief executive officer of two Fortune 500 companies. He served in the U.S. Navy as an aviator and flight instructor, then spent over three decades in the Reserves. In 1977, Rumsfeld was awarded the nation's highest civilian honor, the Presidential Medal of Freedom. Rumsfeld announced he would step down as the Secretary of Defense in November of 2006. He had served in the position longer than any previous Secretary of Defense.

General Richard B. Myers — is a former U.S. Air Force general who served as the fifteenth Chairman of the Joint Chiefs of Staff between October 2001 and September 2005 when he retired from active duty. His Air Force career included operational command and leadership positions in a variety of Air Force and Joint assignments, including the North American Aerospace Defense Command and U.S. Space Command. Myers holds a masters in business administration from Auburn University. He also attended the Air Command and Staff College as well as the U.S. Army War College.

Les Brownlee — was the Acting Secretary of the Army between May 2003 and December 2004, a period that included the Abu Ghraib abuses and scandal. He had also been the Undersecretary of the Army since 2001. Prior to this, Brownlee held positions with the Senate Armed Services Committee and is a retired Army colonel.

Dr. Stephen Cambone — was the Under Secretary of Defense for Intelligence. Cambone was previously the Director, Program Analysis and Evaluation, Office of the Secretary of Defense and the Principal Deputy Under Secretary of Defense for Policy. Cambone graduated from the Claremont Graduate School with a Ph.D. in Political Science.

General Peter J. Schoomaker — was the 35th Chief of Staff, United States Army. General Schoomaker spent 31 years in a variety of command and staff assignments with both conventional and special operations forces around the world, including Operation Desert Shield/ Storm. Schoomaker holds a masters in Management from Central Michigan University. His military education includes the United States Army Command and General Staff College and the National War College.

Major General Donald Ryder — was an officer and military lawyer who, as Provost Marshall, was the most senior officer in the Criminal Investigation Division. In 2003 Ryder conducted an inquiry (the Ryder report) into detention facilities and abuse of prisoners in Iraq, cited in the Taguba Report. He was commissioned in 1971 through the Army Reserve Officer Training Corps. Ryder's major duty assignments included command positions of Military Police units and centers in the U.S. and Germany. He retired from active duty in the fall of 2006.

Major General Anthony M. Taguba — was the author of the Article 15-6 Investigation of the 800th Military Police Brigade, also known as the Taguba report. His report (SECRET/NO FOREIGN DISSEMINATION) was *illegally leaked* to Seymour Hersh of the *New Yorker* magazine and was made public on April 30, 2004. After the investigation, Taguba served as deputy chief, Army Reserve/Deputy Commander, in the U.S. Army Reserve Command for Transition and Transformation. Taguba retired from the military in January 2007.

Major General George W. Fay — was a co-author of the Article 15-6 Investigation of the Abu Ghraib Prison and 205th Military Intelligence Brigade, an Army inquiry on the role of military intelligence personnel in prisoner abuse at the Abu Ghraib facility in Iraq, also known as the Fay report.

Lieutenant General Anthony R. Jones — was a co-author, along with Major General Fay and General Paul J. Kern, of the Article 15-6 Investigation of the Abu Ghraib Prison and 205th Military Intelligence Brigade (the Fay report). He subsequently served as Deputy Commanding General and Chief of Staff of the U.S. Army Training and Doctrine Command.

General Paul J. Kern — was the senior officer and third co-author of the Article 15-6 Investigation of the Abu Ghraib Prison and 205th Military Intelligence Brigade (the Fay report). In November 2004, Kern retired from the Army where he last served as the Commanding General of Army Materiel Command.

James R. Schlesinger — led the investigation and report on the causes of detainee abuse, interrogation policy, and command responsibilities. Schlesinger was Director of the CIA in 1973, Secretary of Defense from 1973 to 1975, and the first Secretary of Energy. Schlesinger is currently on the board of directors of several companies.

Lieutenant General Paul Mikolashek — was the Department of the Army's 61st Inspector General and a retired three-star general. He served in Vietnam, Europe, and the United States as he rose through the ranks. Before assuming his role as Inspector General, he commanded the 3rd U.S. Army/U.S. Army Forces Central Command and Coalition/Joint Forces Land Component Command, which controlled all ground forces in Afghanistan in Operation Enduring Freedom.

Major General Geoffrey Miller — was the warden of the prison at Guantanamo Bay, Cuba, and was later appointed the deputy commanding general for detainee operations for Multi-National Forces-Iraq. He took over for suspended Brigadier General Janis Karpinski in March 2004. The Taguba report noted that Miller's recommendations of using military police in support of interrogation at Abu Ghraib was a breach of official policy. Miller denied that he specifically ordered guards to humiliate and torture prisoners to obtain confessions. He vowed to reduce the number of prisoners in Abu Ghraib, adhere to military laws as well as the Geneva Convention, investigate allegations of abuse, and reform the Iraqi prison system. In 2006, Miller invoked his right to avoid self-incrimination (under military law) and refused to tesitify at the trial of an Abu Ghraib dog handler. A 2006 report by Army Inspector General Lieutenant Stanley Green stated that there was no evidence to support allegations against Miller of deriliction and lying to Congress about his part at Abu Ghraib. The Senate Armed Services Committee, however, continued to investigate Miller's role in the scandal. Miller retired from the Army on July 30, 2006 after assuring members of the committee that he would make himself available to them if requested.

Lieutenant General Ricardo Sanchez — was the commander of U.S. ground forces in Iraq. During his command tenure in Iraq, Sanchez oversaw the targeting of Uday and Qusay Hussein and the capture of Saddam Hussein. It was during his command that the abuses occurred at Abu Ghraib prison. In his role as commander of allied ground forces in Iraq, Sanchez was succeeded by the four-star general, former Army Vice Chief of Staff George Casey. Sanchez then served on active duty in Germany, relinquishing command of the U.S. Army's V Corps on Sept. 6, 2006. Sanchez retired from active duty in November 2006. Sanchez claimed he was forced to retire because of his alleged affiliation with the Abu Ghraib abuse scandal. Although an Army investigation found no evidence to substantiate the allegations, Sanchez reportedly was not offered another senior level command, which he had expected after leaving Iraq.

Major General Barbara Fast — was the senior military intelligence officer in Iraq during the time of the Abu Ghraib abuses. While the Fay report found that changes she put in place "improved the intelligence process and saved the lives of Coalition Forces and Iraqi civilians," the Schlesinger report concluded that Fast should have better advised her superior, Lt. Gen. Ricardo Sanchez, on the right way to run intelligence operations. Although never charged or officially reprimanded for wrongdoing, critics believed she should have been held partly accountable for the abuse. Fast subsequently became the commanding general of the U.S. Army Intelligence Center at Fort Huachuca, Arizona, and the last commander of the 66th Military Intelligence Group in Augsburg, Germany. Fast holds a master of business administration degree from Boston University. She is also a graduate of the Military Intelligence Officer Basic and Advanced Courses, the Armed Forces Staff College and the Army War College.

Major Eugene Anthony Daniels — was military intelligence Contracting Officer Representative (COR) of the Multi-National Forces Iraq/Coalition Force in Iraq from February 2004 to February 2005. Daniels monitored CACI's contract and employees in Iraq, reporting the Army's satisfaction with CACI employees back to the company. Major Daniels redeployed from Iraq with III Corps back to Ft. Hood, Texas, and he was scheduled to redeploy to Iraq in November 2005 with the 1st Calvary Division.

Joseph A. Neurauter — was the Director of the General Services Agency's (GSA) Acquisition Integrity Office and the organization's suspension and debarment official. He was the key official at GSA in reviewing CACI's contracts with the U.S. Army as administered by the Department of the Interior at Ft. Huachuca, Arizona.

Captain Carolyn Wood — was a U.S. Army military intelligence officer who served in both Afghanistan and Iraq and was alleged to be centrally involved in prisoner abuse cases. In 2002 Wood was in command of an intelligence unit in Afghanistan where she expanded the interrogation procedures to the use of stress positions, extended isolation, removal of clothing, and the use of dogs. Military Police who were charged in the deaths of two detainees there tried to mitigate their responsibility by attempting to link the expanded interrogation procedures to the abuses. Wood then went to Abu Ghraib in August 2003 and recommended the establishment of the Hard Site in Abu Ghraib based on her experience in Afghanistan. Wood also played a key role in drafting the interrogation rules that were issued from General Ricardo Sanchez's office in September 2003. An Army inquiry concluded there was confusion under Captain Wood's leadership and some interrogation techniques continued to be used without the required authorization. Wood testified at the pretrial hearing against Lynndie England that the conduct went far beyond the intelligence orders she had given to the MPs at Abu Ghraib. As of November 2005, Wood was reported to still be an interrogation instructor at the Army's military intelligence instruction centre at Fort Huachuca. Wood previously served ten years as an enlisted soldier in the U.S. Army, rising to the rank of Staff Sergeant, prior to being commissioned as an officer.

Others

John Israel — is an Iraqi-American who worked for a Titan Corporation subcontractor as an Arabic translator with the 205th Military Intelligence Brigade in Abu Ghraib. He was mistakenly identified in the Taguba report as a CACI employee. Israel was also named in the Taguba report as one of the people either directly or indirectly responsible for the detainee abuse but has never been charged with anything in relation to Abu Ghraib. He was exonerated by the Fay report of any allegations stemming from the Taguba report.

Henry E. Hockeimer — is a partner at the Philadelphia law firm of Ballard, Spahr, Andrews and Ingersoll LLP. Hockeimer represented Steven Stefanowicz but also focuses his practice on white collar litigation. Hockeimer received his juris doctor from the Catholic University of America.

APPENDIX C

Timeline: CACI and Abu Ghraib Key Events and Milestones

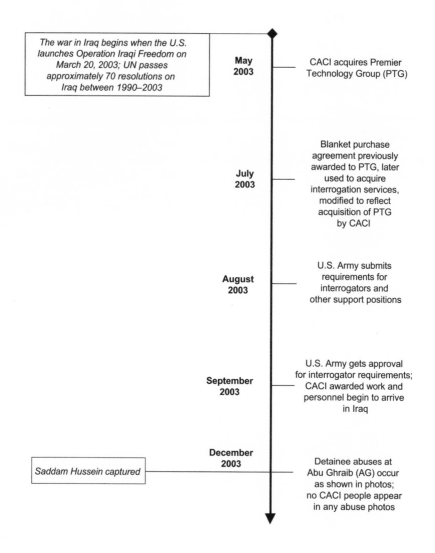

The war in Iraq begins when the U.S. launches Operation Iraqi Freedom on March 20, 2003; UN passes approximately 70 resolutions on Iraq between 1990–2003

May 2003

CACI acquires Premier Technology Group (PTG)

July 2003

Blanket purchase agreement previously awarded to PTG, later used to acquire interrogation services, modified to reflect acquisition of PTG by CACI

August 2003

U.S. Army submits requirements for interrogators and other support positions

September 2003

U.S. Army gets approval for interrogator requirements; CACI awarded work and personnel begin to arrive in Iraq

December 2003

Saddam Hussein captured

Detainee abuses at Abu Ghraib (AG) occur as shown in photos; no CACI people appear in any abuse photos

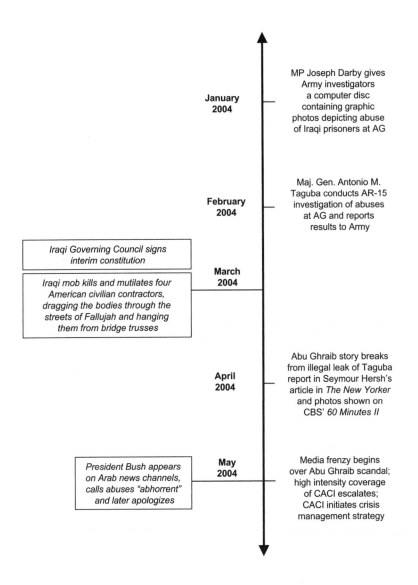

January
2004

MP Joseph Darby gives
Army investigators
a computer disc
containing graphic
photos depicting abuse
of Iraqi prisoners at AG

February
2004

Maj. Gen. Antonio M.
Taguba conducts AR-15
investigation of abuses
at AG and reports
results to Army

*Iraqi Governing Council signs
interim constitution*

March
2004

*Iraqi mob kills and mutilates four
American civilian contractors,
dragging the bodies through the
streets of Fallujah and hanging
them from bridge trusses*

April
2004

Abu Ghraib story breaks
from illegal leak of Taguba
report in Seymour Hersh's
article in *The New Yorker*
and photos shown on
CBS' *60 Minutes II*

May
2004

*President Bush appears
on Arab news channels,
calls abuses "abhorrent"
and later apologizes*

Media frenzy begins
over Abu Ghraib scandal;
high intensity coverage
of CACI escalates;
CACI initiates crisis
management strategy

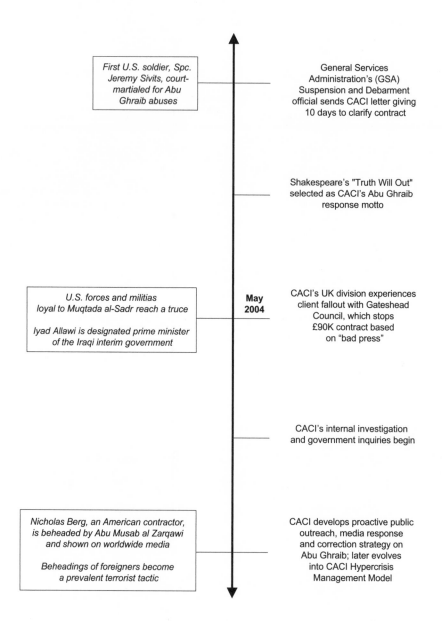

First U.S. soldier, Spc. Jeremy Sivits, court-martialed for Abu Ghraib abuses

General Services Administration's (GSA) Suspension and Debarment official sends CACI letter giving 10 days to clarify contract

Shakespeare's "Truth Will Out" selected as CACI's Abu Ghraib response motto

U.S. forces and militias loyal to Muqtada al-Sadr reach a truce

Iyad Allawi is designated prime minister of the Iraqi interim government

May 2004

CACI's UK division experiences client fallout with Gateshead Council, which stops £90K contract based on "bad press"

CACI's internal investigation and government inquiries begin

Nicholas Berg, an American contractor, is beheaded by Abu Musab al Zarqawi and shown on worldwide media

Beheadings of foreigners become a prevalent terrorist tactic

CACI develops proactive public outreach, media response and correction strategy on Abu Ghraib; later evolves into CACI Hypercrisis Management Model

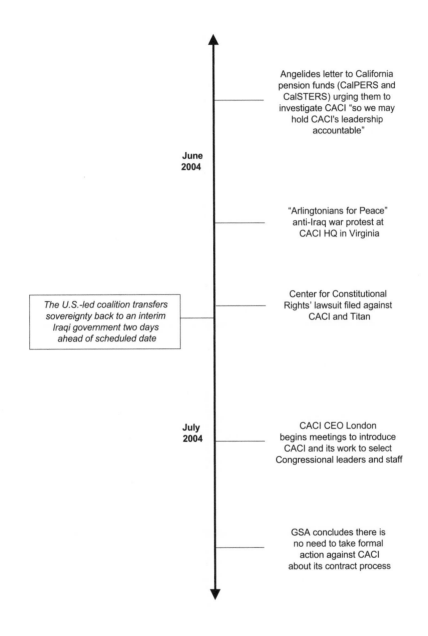

Angelides letter to California
pension funds (CalPERS and
CalSTERS) urging them to
investigate CACI "so we may
hold CACI's leadership
accountable"

June
2004

"Arlingtonians for Peace"
anti-Iraq war protest at
CACI HQ in Virginia

The U.S.-led coalition transfers
sovereignty back to an interim
Iraqi government two days
ahead of scheduled date

Center for Constitutional
Rights' lawsuit filed against
CACI and Titan

July
2004

CACI CEO London
begins meetings to introduce
CACI and its work to select
Congressional leaders and staff

GSA concludes there is
no need to take formal
action against CACI
about its contract process

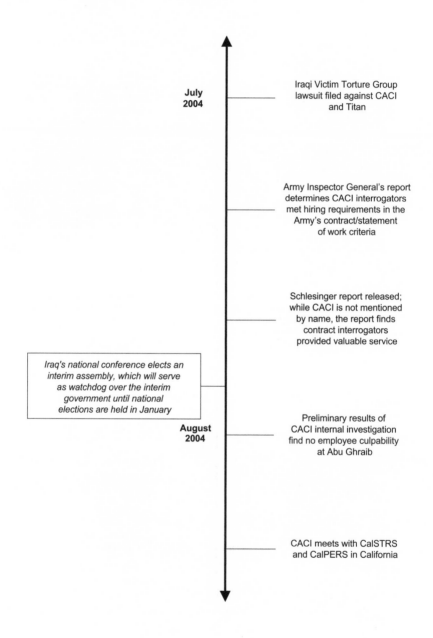

July
2004

Iraqi Victim Torture Group
lawsuit filed against CACI
and Titan

Army Inspector General's report
determines CACI interrogators
met hiring requirements in the
Army's contract/statement
of work criteria

Schlesinger report released;
while CACI is not mentioned
by name, the report finds
contract interrogators
provided valuable service

*Iraq's national conference elects an
interim assembly, which will serve
as watchdog over the interim
government until national
elections are held in January*

August
2004

Preliminary results of
CACI internal investigation
find no employee culpability
at Abu Ghraib

CACI meets with CalSTRS
and CalPERS in California

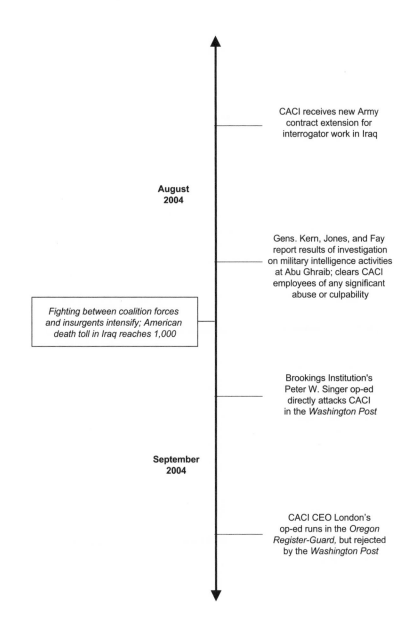

CACI receives new Army
contract extension for
interrogator work in Iraq

**August
2004**

Gens. Kern, Jones, and Fay
report results of investigation
on military intelligence activities
at Abu Ghraib; clears CACI
employees of any significant
abuse or culpability

Fighting between coalition forces
and insurgents intensify; American
death toll in Iraq reaches 1,000

Brookings Institution's
Peter W. Singer op-ed
directly attacks CACI
in the *Washington Post*

**September
2004**

CACI CEO London's
op-ed runs in the *Oregon
Register-Guard,* but rejected
by the *Washington Post*

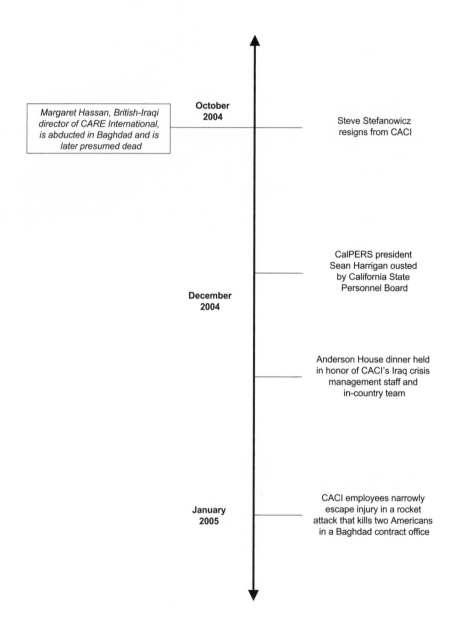

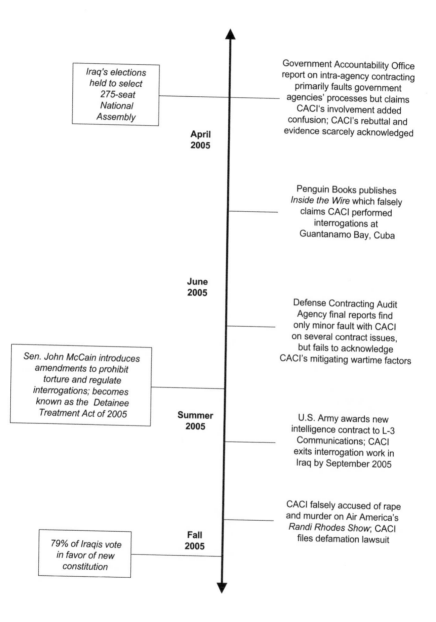

Iraq's elections held to select 275-seat National Assembly

Government Accountability Office report on intra-agency contracting primarily faults government agencies' processes but claims CACI's involvement added confusion; CACI's rebuttal and evidence scarcely acknowledged

April 2005

Penguin Books publishes *Inside the Wire* which falsely claims CACI performed interrogations at Guantanamo Bay, Cuba

June 2005

Defense Contracting Audit Agency final reports find only minor fault with CACI on several contract issues, but fails to acknowledge CACI's mitigating wartime factors

Sen. John McCain introduces amendments to prohibit torture and regulate interrogations; becomes known as the Detainee Treatment Act of 2005

Summer 2005

U.S. Army awards new intelligence contract to L-3 Communications; CACI exits interrogation work in Iraq by September 2005

CACI falsely accused of rape and murder on Air America's *Randi Rhodes Show*; CACI files defamation lawsuit

Fall 2005

79% of Iraqis vote in favor of new constitution

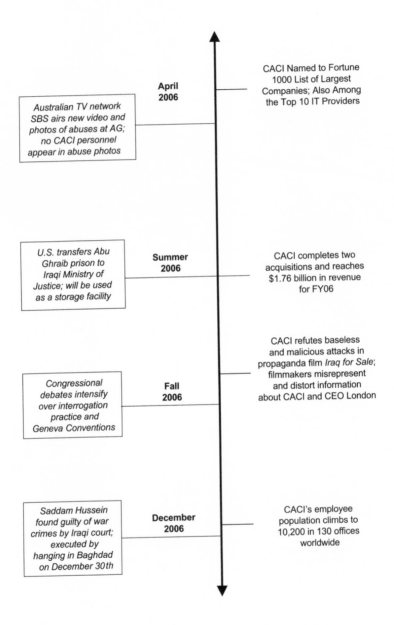

April 2006

Australian TV network SBS airs new video and photos of abuses at AG; no CACI personnel appear in abuse photos

CACI Named to Fortune 1000 List of Largest Companies; Also Among the Top 10 IT Providers

Summer 2006

U.S. transfers Abu Ghraib prison to Iraqi Ministry of Justice; will be used as a storage facility

CACI completes two acquisitions and reaches $1.76 billion in revenue for FY06

Fall 2006

Congressional debates intensify over interrogation practice and Geneva Conventions

CACI refutes baseless and malicious attacks in propaganda film *Iraq for Sale*; filmmakers misrepresent and distort information about CACI and CEO London

December 2006

Saddam Hussein found guilty of war crimes by Iraqi court; executed by hanging in Baghdad on December 30th

CACI's employee population climbs to 10,200 in 130 offices worldwide

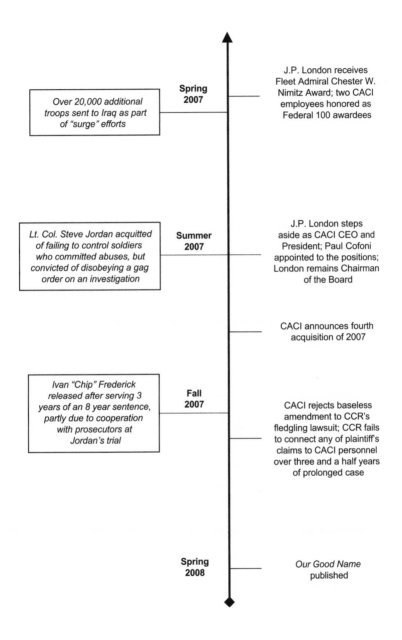

Over 20,000 additional troops sent to Iraq as part of "surge" efforts

Spring 2007

J.P. London receives Fleet Admiral Chester W. Nimitz Award; two CACI employees honored as Federal 100 awardees

Lt. Col. Steve Jordan acquitted of failing to control soldiers who committed abuses, but convicted of disobeying a gag order on an investigation

Summer 2007

J.P. London steps aside as CACI CEO and President; Paul Cofoni appointed to the positions; London remains Chairman of the Board

CACI announces fourth acquisition of 2007

Ivan "Chip" Frederick released after serving 3 years of an 8 year sentence, partly due to cooperation with prosecutors at Jordan's trial

Fall 2007

CACI rejects baseless amendment to CCR's fledgling lawsuit; CCR fails to connect any of plaintiff's claims to CACI personnel over three and a half years of prolonged case

Spring 2008

Our Good Name published

APPENDIX D

CACI Corporate Philosophy: The Company's Foundation Documents

EVER VIGILANT

Our Ten Business Values*

1 Placing integrity and honesty above all else.

2 Putting clients first.

3 Creating value for clients and delivering quality.

4 Fostering career opportunities for our people.

5 Maintaining a value-oriented culture, where people enjoy working.

6 Growing our business and making good profits, year after year.

7 Creating and enhancing shareholder value, year after year.

8 Being accountable and taking responsibility for what we do.

9 Treating each other fairly and with mutual respect, including our business partners, vendors, suppliers and the public at large.

10 Maintaining a high-quality reputation for CACI and its people.

*CACI's Ten Business Values reflect the ethics, goals, and standards that the company and its people aspire to operate by — to achieve and sustain.

Credo

Although changes may occur in our marketplace, or in our technologies, we believe certain fundamental attitudes set CACI people apart from the rest. At CACI we take pride in our commitment to:

- *Quality service* and *best value* for our clients,

- *Individual opportunity* and *respect* for each other,

- *Integrity* and *excellence* in our work, and

- *Distinction* and the *competitive edge* in our markets.

CACI
EVER VIGILANT

Operational Philosophy

1. Our Clients...Number One

At CACI the client is ... Number One! We are a client service-oriented company. We are in business to provide quality services and products to our clients. Their needs are our opportunities. Our goal is complete client satisfaction. Once we have a client, our goal is to keep that client forever. Our "Ten Commandments of Client Consulting" are our continuing road map for service.

2. Our Quality...Top-Notch

At CACI our motto is "Quality Client Service and Best Value" (QCS/BV). Our "good name," our reputation, is paramount. We strive always to be "top-notch"... quality is everything. We are the "best value" company. We perform valuable project services and provide quality products. In everything we do our goal is quality, distinction, and excellence.

3. Our People...The Best

At CACI people are the most important asset. Our people bring distinction to all we do; they are the best. Our people are "team players." They are flexible and can adapt quickly as business conditions and technology changes occur. At CACI we offer virtually unlimited equal opportunity for growth, recognition, and reward for all capable people. Our people are fiercely proud of their legacy of the "CACI entrepreneurial spirit." They are determined to succeed and refuse to fail.

4. Our Responsibilities...Fully Accountable

At CACI we insist on taking full responsibility for ourselves as individuals. We are fully accountable for what we do. Our published Code of Ethics delineates our uncompromising policies on compliance with the laws and regulations of the jurisdictions where we conduct business. We reward legitimate success and forgive understandable failure (no one is perfect!), but we always learn from our mistakes.

5. Our Productivity...The Highest

At CACI high productivity is our constant goal. We are always competitive. We use time and resources efficiently; we waste nothing. We constantly strive to reduce costs in order to price effectively and make good profits. We are resourceful and innovative. We are information technology-oriented. We apply modern methods and technology expertly for our clients and for ourselves in "meeting the challenge of change." We develop cost-effective solutions; we are the "problem solvers."

6. Our Value...The Bottom Line

Our business purpose is to increase the net worth of our stockholders. On behalf of our stockholders, we constantly seek opportunities to develop our lines of business and sustain high value for our stockholders and our people. We continue to focus on enhancing the value of CACI in everything we do.

APPENDIX E

Select CACI News Releases Concerning Abu Ghraib[703]

CACI STATES POSITION ABOUT REPORTED ALLEGATIONS CONCERNING EMPLOYEES IN IRAQ

No Information on Improper Behavior Reported to Company by U.S. Government; Company Does Not Tolerate Illegal Behavior by Employees

Arlington, Va., May 3, 2004 — CACI International Inc. (NYSE: CAI) said today that with respect to the alleged improper employee behavior toward prisoners in Iraq recently reported in the media, despite inquiries, the company thus far has received no information on the matter from the U.S. Government. The company continues to support the army's mission in Iraq and around the world.

"CACI does not condone, tolerate, or in any way endorse illegal behavior on the part of its employees or those with whom it works while conducting CACI business in any circumstance at any time. In the event there is wrongdoing on the part of any CACI employee, we will take swift action to correct it immediately, but at this time we have no information from the U.S. Government of any violations or wrongful behavior," said CACI Chairman, President, and CEO Dr. J.P. (Jack) London. London continued, "At the same time, it is also important to note that

---

[703] All CACI news releases are archived and available at www.caci.com

our country is at war, and we recognize that many of our employees have put themselves in harm's way along with the thousands of other brave men and women. They have dedicated their lives to supporting our military in the effort to protect our freedom and to help gain freedom for others. We commend their bravery, their loyalty, and their hard work." London added, "For security reasons, we do not disclose or discuss the assignments or locations of our employees around the world. We are mindful of the recent unfortunate deaths, mutilations, and abductions of contractors in areas of conflict. In this regard, we are highly sensitive to their well being and to their families."

CACI said it has never seen nor has it been provided a copy of an apparent 53-page confidential study presumably written by Major General Antonio M. Taguba in late February and apparently obtained and reported on by The New Yorker magazine. The company said it is aware of the study only from the extracts reported in the media. CACI said it had formally requested a copy of the confidential report from the U.S. Department of Defense, since the report was apparently leaked to the media. Further, CACI said that in its experience, the U.S. Army has always been prompt to inform the company of any questions or issues. CACI reiterated that it had received no information of any pending actions against any CACI employee's performance relating to prisoner abuse matters.

The company further stated that one of the people reported to be an employee in the New Yorker article about the Taguba report is not and never has been a CACI employee.

The company stated that its employees, many of whom are former military personnel, are experienced individuals who have received relevant professional training. The company has supported the U.S. Army's investigation since it began several months ago, at which time CACI personnel in Iraq volunteered to be interviewed by army officials in connection with that investigation. CACI said it has received no information of any pending actions against any CACI employee.

CACI stated that it has retained outside counsel to investigate actions of company employees in connection with the allegations reported in the media. In addition, the company reported that it is currently reviewing its worldwide operations to assure the public and its customers that CACI continues to maintain its high ethical standards of conduct and quality service.

CACI RESPONDS TO ALLEGATIONS IN THE MEDIA ABOUT ITS EMPLOYEES IN IRAQ AND TO FINANCIAL COMMUNITY INTERESTS

Arlington Va., May 5, 2004 — CACI International Inc. (NYSE: CAI) announced that its Chairman, President, and CEO Dr. J.P. (Jack) London issued the following statement in a conference call to the investment community earlier today:

"First, I want to share our expression of disappointment, outrage, and disgust on behalf of all of the employees at CACI regarding the allegations of abuse at the Abu Ghraib prison.

"In being responsive to our investors and the public, two of the biggest challenges we're facing are the lack of information that has been provided from the U.S. Government to our company in these matters and the fact that we are dealing with significant amounts of classified information. We are also dealing with the security and safety of CACI people in the theater at-large. We have received no information from the Department of Defense and the U.S. Government on this matter.

"The information that we have been getting comes from the news media. They are, in turn, quoting from a leaked classified document. We have also formally requested a copy of the Taguba report that was reported and discussed in the article in *The New Yorker* magazine. We are intending to follow up with our own investigations as previously indicated. That report, however, remains a classified document. It has not been declassified and has not been provided to us despite the fact that we've requested it. It is also true that the report has been published widely, is on the Internet, and is available otherwise. We have taken advantage of that fact and have become familiar with the document, and have read it in detail. We know what is in the report even though it has not been provided to us in a formal way.

"The fact remains that we are simply not able to confirm in any fashion that any CACI employee was involved in prisoner abuse at Abu Ghraib prison, notwithstanding allegations reported through the media. Because of our relationship as a contractor for the

Department of Defense, we must rely on formal communications from the department in this matter in terms of our work activity, the scope of work, the continuation of work, and the quality of our performance. We have no reports of any adverse nature.

"At present, all CACI employees continue to work on site providing the contracted-for services to our clients in that location and around the world.

"CACI does not condone or tolerate or endorse in any fashion any illegal, inappropriate behavior on the part of any of its employees in any circumstance at any time anywhere. If, regrettably, any CACI employee was involved in any way at any time in any of the alleged behavior that occurred in Iraq and has been reported in the media and elsewhere, for those employees I will certainly personally take immediate, appropriate action. We will be relentless in identifying and punishing any improper behavior that damages this company's image and reputation, which is significant in our marketplace, or impugns the reputation of any of its hardworking, honorable employees. If there is illegal behavior on the part of any employee, it is not indicative of the mode of operation of this corporation or of the patriotic service of thousands of CACI's honorable, hardworking people diligently pursuing their assignments.

"I must report that we have not received any information to stop any of our work, to terminate or suspend any of our employees, or otherwise show cause for any inability to perform in any fashion regarding the alleged, discussed and repeated issues in the press. We are eager to find out as soon as possible what has happened, and we have taken steps to inquire.

"Furthermore, CACI employees have volunteered and were interviewed at the beginning of the investigations months ago. As a result of some of these alleged activities, we have launched our own independent investigation, supported by competent, outside legal counsel. And our Board of Directors has been informed. If we are asked to participate in any investigations by the U.S. Government, you must be assured that we will fully cooperate.

"Meanwhile, CACI continues to support the Army's mission in Iraq and around the world, as well as our other military service clients. There has been no immediate economic impact on CACI as a result of any of these allegations in terms of contracts or ongoing business in any form whatsoever. We are still aggressively recruiting to fill urgent and important assignments and requirements on our contracts based throughout the world. To date we have received no communication from the Defense Department concerning termination of any contracts, any delivery orders, any activities, any where in the world. And we do not expect any.

"CACI employees are supporting our efforts in Iraq, and they provide valuable skill augmentations in important critical areas in support of the U.S. military's wartime mission activities in this critical combat zone. As I have said many times before, the government is shorthanded in some of these critical skill set areas, and relies on qualified contractors to provide a wide variety of competent, professional services related to the global war on terrorism. We have been proud to support those initiatives and requirements. The people we have recruited have been competent and capable. Their credentials meet the professional expectations of the assignments to which they are dedicated. CACI people in Iraq meet or exceed those qualifications in all cases.

"The fact is that the majority of our work is providing information technology and technology solutions to the U.S. government. The interrogation services fit within the portfolio of our service offerings within the intelligence community that includes equipment-sensing devices, communications needs and requirements, maintenance and training, as well as data collection, evaluation, analysis, product development, and decision support tools. Interrogation services are simply one small element of that portfolio broadly categorized as data collection. They are much less than one percent of our entire business base. Our work throughout the intelligence community spans many of these other areas, as I have indicated. This support is from the tactical level all the way to the national and strategic level.

"We are all appalled by the reported actions of a few — and actually grieved — when so many professional and patriotic Americans are sacrificing so much to defend our country against terror and to support the freedom of Iraq."

CACI REJECTS LAWSUIT AS SLANDEROUS AND MALICIOUS

Frivolous Suit Based on False Statements, Conjecture and Speculation

Arlington, Va., June 10, 2004 — CACI International Inc. (NYSE: CAI) today issued the following statement: Yesterday, a New York-based human rights activist group filed a lawsuit in San Diego federal court. The suit accuses CACI, Titan Corporation of San Diego, and several named individuals of conspiring with the U.S. government to carry out various crimes against detainees at detention centers in Iraq.

CACI rejects and denies the allegations of the suit as being a malicious recitation of false statements and intentional distortions. CACI does not have and has never had any agreement with Titan Corporation or anyone else pertaining to conspiring with the government, or to perpetrate abuses of any kind on anyone. CACI has never entered into a conspiracy with the government, or anyone else, to perpetrate abuses of any kind.

The suit alleges a plethora of heinous acts that the company rejects and denies in their totality.

The company has not, nor have any of its employees, been charged with any wrongdoing or illegal acts relating to any work in Iraq. The lawsuit filed against CACI falsely alleges that CACI had contracts for interrogation work in Guantanamo Bay, Cuba. Similarly, named defendant John Israel is not, and has never been, an employee of CACI. These falsehoods and inaccuracies simply demonstrate the utter lack of investigation prior to filing suit by the entities ultimately behind this lawsuit.

The company has stated repeatedly that it will not condone, tolerate or endorse any illegal behavior at any time. The company will act forcefully and promptly if evidence is discovered showing that its employees acted in violation of the law or of CACI's policies. At the same time, the company will not rush to judgment on the basis of slander, distortion, false claims, partial reports, or any incomplete investigations. The company supports the concepts of the rule of law, due process, and the presumption of innocence.

In light of the frivolous and malicious nature of this lawsuit, as well as the apparent lack of any pre-filing investigation of the facts, the company stated it is examining its options for sanctions against the lawyers who participated in the filing of this lawsuit.

CACI CLARIFIES INFORMATION ABOUT
INTERROGATOR SERVICES IN IRAQ

Company Corrects Inaccurate and False Information Being Widely Disseminated

Arlington, Va., June 28, 2004 — CACI International Inc. (NYSE: CAI) today stated that due to the erroneous, inaccurate and false information being widely disseminated and repeated, it has again become necessary to clarify various aspects of its contract arrangements with the U.S. Army to provide interrogator services (an intelligence information gathering function) in Iraq.

For more than 42 years, CACI has proudly provided information technology (IT) services to its U.S. government customers to meet their mission and systems goals. For over four decades the company has successfully provided IT services during nine U.S. Presidential administrations that have had varying policies and objectives. CACI's steadfast objective in its government contracting has always been to support the country's future through quality service.

With over 9,400 employees, operating from over 100 office locations in the U.S.A. and around the world, CACI takes pride in satisfying its customers and in complying with the highest ethical standards. CACI's advanced information technology solutions and intelligence support services in Iraq enhance military effectiveness. Our efforts also free up the troops for other critical military missions. The company has been commended for its performance from its U.S. military customers in Iraq.

While CACI provides services around the world for the U.S. government, its recent work in Iraq has received attention because of widely disseminated media reports of abuse at the Abu Ghraib prison near Baghdad.

Unfortunately, various media reports have included erroneous, inaccurate and false information, which the company intends to correct. Additional information on this matter is available on CACI's website, www.caci.com.

The company stated the following facts:

☐ CACI does not now provide, and never has provided, interrogator services to any U.S. government entity at Guantanamo Bay, Cuba, or in Afghanistan. CACI's limited role in providing interrogators in support of the U.S. Army has been confined to Iraq. Allegations to the contrary are totally false.

☐ CACI's contract arrangements with the U.S. military have not been fashioned in a manner intended to mislead or to otherwise deceive anyone at any time and any such allegations are totally false. CACI's contracts are a natural outgrowth of the contracting arrangements pursuant to which CACI and its acquired predecessor, Premier Technology Group Inc., provided support to its U.S. Army clients for a number of years. All arrangements have been fully visible at all times to U.S. government contracting authorities.

☐ CACI acquired its General Services Administration (GSA) Schedule Contract and Blanket Purchase Agreement (BPA) under which the interrogation (an intelligence information gathering function) services are being provided as part of the assets it acquired from Premier Technology Group, Inc. in May 2003. The subject GSA Schedule Group 70 (Information Technology) contract was awarded to Premier Technology Group in 1998. The then U.S. Army Directorate of Contracting, Fort Huachuca, Arizona, awarded the subject BPA to Premier Technology Group under that GSA Schedule Group 70 contract in September 1998. Administration of the BPA was transferred from the U.S. Army at Fort Huachuca to the National Business Center (NBC), Department of Interior at Fort Huachuca on January 14, 2001 as part of a government reorganization that saw the Army contracting office become part of the Department of the Interior when army operations at Fort Huachuca were substantially reduced. The subject BPA was extended for an additional five years by the NBC, and modified on July 31, 2003, as is customary, to reflect the acquisition by CACI. When the U.S. Army required interrogator support after deploying to Iraq, and contracting offices in Iraq and Kuwait said they were unable to take on the added administrative effort, the U.S. Army contracted for needed support in Iraq through the Fort Huachuca BPA. The U.S. Army continues to convey its satisfaction with the services being provided by CACI on these projects and has requested CACI's continued support.

☐ CACI's contract with the U.S. military requires the company to provide interrogators (for intelligence information gathering) who have had training and/or experience in one or more related fields specified by the government. Those candidates who have been determined to meet the government-specified qualifications and hired are assigned to work in Iraq under the direct project supervision of the U.S. Army. These are the requirements of CACI's contract, and CACI has performed in accordance with the requirements.

☐ CACI's Statement of Work for interrogators requires individuals with specified information-gathering and analysis experience at the tactical and operational levels who possess at a minimum a Department of Defense Secret-level security clearance, which requires U.S. government background checks on the individuals. The Statement of Work further specifies that the U.S. military will provide readiness training and briefings on rules of engagement and general orders applicable to coalition armed forces, DoD civilians and U.S. contractors, including the provisions of the Geneva Conventions.

☐ CACI's contract requires that employees work under the monitoring and supervision of the U.S. military chain-of-command in Iraq. CACI personnel have no responsibility for management, supervisory or command authority over any non-CACI personnel. CACI operates a full-time, in-country administrative chain-of-command over all of its employees in Iraq.

☐ CACI has recruited qualified candidates with the capability to perform their assignment with moderate to minimal supervision in order to ensure that the candidates have sufficient experience and maturity to be responsible and accountable. Employees are responsible for their actions and work performance regardless of the environment into which they are placed.

☐ As to widely repeated employee misinformation, CACI has never employed Mr. John Israel. Mr. John Israel was incorrectly identified as a CACI employee in the **illegally** released, "leaked" sections of the classified (SECRET/NO FOREIGN DISSEMINATION) report issued by Major General Antonio M. Taguba regarding allegations of abuse of detainees at Abu Ghraib prison. Mr. Israel is not now and never has been an employee of CACI.

☐ CACI employee Steven A. Stefanowicz was the only CACI employee identified in the Taguba report. The report alleges culpable wrongdoing on the part of Mr. Stefanowicz; however, Henry Hockeimer, Jr., a partner in Hangley Aronchick Segal & Pudlin in Philadelphia, attorney for Mr. Stefanowicz, has stated, "Any meaningful review of the facts will inevitably lead to the conclusion that Mr. Stefanowicz's conduct was both appropriate and authorized."

☐ CACI does not condone or tolerate illegal acts or behavior on the part of its employees. It is the company's clear and unambiguous policy that all its activities shall comply with all applicable laws at all times. In the unfortunate event that a CACI employee acted improperly or illegally, CACI will take immediate and appropriate action. To date, however, no CACI employee has been formally charged or indicted by the U.S. government with any wrongdoing, and the company has not discovered any evidence confirming allegations of culpable behavior despite active investigation into the matter. Reflecting CACI's commitment to individual rights and civil rights, as well as the rule of law and due process, the company will not condemn an individual on the basis of unsubstantiated and unproven allegations.

☐ CACI's interrogation (an intelligence information gathering function) support and analysis work for the U.S. Army in Iraq is a very small fraction, less than 1 percent, of the company's total worldwide business. Nonetheless, CACI is proud of its people for the work and the service they have provided for the U.S. military and their country under hazardous conditions in Iraq.

☐ CACI is not now and never has been involved in political activist pursuits of any kind for its own individual corporate benefit.

☐ CACI does not now have and never has had a political action committee (PAC). The Company makes no effort whatsoever to influence or interfere with the rights of its officers and employees to participate as they see fit in supporting any candidate for office through a private donation.

Additional information, news releases and FAQs on CACI's Iraq business and these matters is up on CACI's website, www.caci.com.

CACI MEETS WITH CALIFORNIA PENSION FUNDS ABOUT WORK IN IRAQ

Company Challenges Politically Motivated Actions of California Treasurer Phil Angelides as Wrongly Rejecting Contractor's Support of Military

Arlington, Va., August 3, 2004 — CACI International Inc. (NYSE: CAI) reported today that members of the company's management met with representatives of the California State Teachers Retirement Fund (CalSTRS) and the California Public Employees Retirement System (CalPERS) in Sacramento to provide information about the company's work in Iraq. Even though CalSTRS and CalPERS hold only about one-half percent of CACI shares, the company met with the funds to respond to questions raised by the funds. CACI recognizes that consideration of investment potential is always a *bona fide* subject for shareholder evaluation. CACI welcomed the opportunity to engage in a dialogue with the funds on that and related subjects. CACI believes that it has fully responded to the funds' questions with regard to its operational and fiduciary responsibilities in performing its contract work to support the U.S. military mission in Iraq.

California Treasurer Phil Angelides, however, chose to use this meeting for political grandstanding. By taking the position that CACI should get out of its interrogation line of business or the funds should get out of CACI stock, Mr. Angelides has expressed his willingness to turn his back on solid investments and the companies that support America's military mission and troops deployed in harm's way. CACI, however, has no intention of abandoning the fine people who serve the country or our customer's vital mission to protect America's future and to project the war against terrorism. CACI regrets that, rather than participating in responsibly evaluating investment potential to California fund participants, Mr. Angelides chose to pursue his own political agenda. With little or no knowledge of the requirements surrounding the interrogation process, Mr. Angelides rejects CACI as an investment opportunity by arbitrarily assigning a disproportionate significance to this one area of intelligence collection and analysis.

The meeting was intended to be informative and clear up any questions about the company's work in Iraq. CACI has since the beginning of

May, and will continue to provide information about these matters to keep shareholders, customers and employees fully informed. CACI finds Mr. Angelides' behavior to be a disservice to its California investors. His posturing as a protector of the moral high ground in reality is a blatant quest for headlines to achieve personal political gain.

In the meeting, CACI also reiterated that it does not condone, tolerate or in any way endorse illegal behavior by its employees and said it would take swift action if the evidence demonstrates wrongdoing by any of its employees. But it also emphasized that its strong commitment to the fundamental American principle that presumes people are innocent until proven guilty.

CACI noted that it has provided shareholders with a continuous flow of information about its Iraq work, including interrogation services, over the past several months — hosting conference calls that have been webcast, presenting at investor conferences, filing frequent press releases, and posting information on its web site on a regular basis.

"We will not rush to take punitive action against any person without reasonable confirming evidence," the company told the funds' representatives in a 15-page written response to questions previously submitted by the two funds.

CACI continues to provide professional interrogation and analyst support services (an intelligence information gathering function) to the U.S. Army in Iraq. Since 1962, the company has successfully provided IT services during nine U.S. Presidential administrations that have had varying policies and objectives. With more than 9,400 employees operating from over 100 office locations in the USA and around the world, CACI takes pride in satisfying its customers and in complying with the highest ethical standards.

CACI's advanced information technology solutions and intelligence support services in Iraq enhance military effectiveness. The company's efforts also free troops to concentrate on other critical military missions. Its U.S. military customers in Iraq have commended the company for its performance.

Additional information, news releases, and FAQs on CACI's Iraq business and these related matters is available on CACI's website: www.caci.com.

CACI SAYS CHURCH REPORT UNDERSCORES CRITICAL VALUE OF INTERROGATION SERVICES TO SAVING MILITARY LIVES AND NATIONAL SECURITY

Report Says Civilian Interrogators Often Had More Experience and Served Longer Than Military Counterparts

Arlington, Va., March 10, 2005 — CACI International Inc. (NYSE: CAI) announced today that it was pleased that a new review of interrogation practices by Navy Inspector General and Vice Admiral Albert T. Church recognized the value and diligent service of civilian interrogators provided by CACI and other private contractors. Since August 2003, CACI has supported military intelligence gathering efforts by providing interrogation and other information and intelligence analysis services in Iraq. CACI does not and never has provided interrogators in either Afghanistan or Guantanamo Bay, Cuba.

"Today's report makes clear that civilian interrogation services are essential to the war against terrorism," CACI Chairman and CEO Jack London said. "As one senior military official noted, 'interrogation operations in Afghanistan, Iraq and Guantanamo cannot be reasonably accomplished without contractor support.'"

"We are tremendously proud of every CACI employee who is supporting U.S. efforts in Iraq and elsewhere to fight terror and spread freedom," London added. "Despite the controversy of the past year, they have stayed the course, braved danger, and conducted themselves with the highest ethics to support our country."

"I am very pleased that their contribution has been recognized by Vice Admiral Church and those who worked with him on this report. I believe that our work in Iraq was instrumental in helping to save American lives and will help bring this operation to a successful conclusion," London also said.

During Senate testimony and in the unclassified Executive Summary of his report released today, Vice Admiral Church concluded:

□ "Contractors made a significant contribution to U.S. intelligence efforts."

□ On average, contractors were more experienced than military interrogators and that this advantage enhanced their credibility with detainees and promoted successful interrogations."

□ "Interrogation techniques were not a causal factor in the abuses of detainees."

□ "Contract personnel often served longer tours than DoD personnel, creating continuity and enhancing corporate knowledge of their commands," and

□ Despite the publicity surrounding Abu Ghraib, "we found very few instances of abuse involving contractors."

London reiterated that CACI expects all of its employees to fully comply with the military's rules of engagement and international laws regarding the treatment of prisoners. He also noted that the company has cooperated fully and will continue to cooperate with all official inquiries regarding interrogation and detention policies.

CACI also reiterated emphatically that it does not condone, tolerate or in any way endorse illegal behavior by its employees and said it would take swift action if the evidence demonstrates culpable wrongdoing by any of its employees. But, CACI also emphasized its strong commitment to the fundamental American principle that people are presumed innocent until proven guilty.

London said that CACI only has access to the 21-page executive summary of the Church Report and does not know if the "very few instances" of contractor abuses involve CACI employees. He said the company will seek further information from the government. To date, no CACI employee has been formally charged with misconduct at Abu Ghraib or elsewhere in Iraq.

London observed that the Church report, like the Fay Report released last August, does not suggest in any way that CACI employees bore substantial responsibility for the widely reported abuses at Abu Ghraib.

"The conclusions of the Church and Fay reports differ significantly with some of the suggestions made by Major General Taguba about

responsibility for abuses at Abu Ghraib. These reports have fully exonerated at least one of the civilians assigned responsibility by Major General Taguba and greatly scaled back allegations about a CACI employee
named in the Taguba report," London said.

London also noted Vice Admiral Church's conclusion that only a
small number of substantiated abuses in Iraq "could in any way be considered related to interrogation."

APPENDIX F

List of U.S. Military and Government Investigations Related to CACI and its Work in Iraq

Date	Investigation	Reason
March 2004 (*illegally leaked* to media)	Taguba Investigation and Report: Article 15-6 Investigation of the 800th Military Police Brigade	To investigate the conduct of operations within the 800th Military Police (MP) Brigade for reports of detainee abuse
May 26, 2004	General Services Administration (GSA) Investigation	To determine whether the GSA schedule was misused in the issuance of task orders with the knowledge and consent of CACI
June 9, 2004	Defense Contracting Audit Agency (DCAA) Investigation	To review the potential misuse by CACI of the GSA schedule on this Department of Interior contract that is funded by the Army, since "interrogator" type effort is not a function normally provided by CACI in its GSA schedule
July 2004	Department of the Interior — Inspector General Investigation and Report	To review 12 procurements placed under GSA Federal Supply Schedules 70 and 871 by the National Business Center to CACI
July 21, 2004	Department of the Army — Inspector General Investigation and Report	To conduct an assessment of detainee operations in Afghanistan and Iraq.
August 2004	Fay/Jones/Kern Investigation and Report: AR 15-6 Investigation of the Abu Ghraib Detention Facility and 205th Military Intelligence Brigade	To investigate allegations that members of the 205th Military Intelligence (MI) Brigade were involved in detainee abuse at the Abu Ghraib
August 23, 2004	Schlesinger Investigation Report: Final Report of the Independent Panel to Review DoD Detainee Operations	To review Department of Defense detention operations
March 10, 2005	Church Investigation and Report: Unclassified Executive Summary of Report	To conduct a comprehensive review of Department of Defense interrogation operations
April 2005	Government Accountability Office (GAO) Investigation and Report	To determine what breakdowns occurred in the process of procuring interrogation and other services and the contributing factors to the breakdowns. Report any interagency contracting problems with DoD's and Interior's orders to support military operations

Conducted by	Results/CACI Perspective
Major General Antonio M. Taguba, U.S. Army	CACI employee "suspected" for responsibility in Abu Ghraib abuses; one contractor named who was not a CACI employee
GSA Suspension and Debarment Official Joseph A. Neurauter	CACI cleared; no action deemed necessary by government to protect its interests
DCAA Herndon Branch Office	DCAA found minor fault with CACI on several contract issues, although it did not acknowledge evidence provided to the agency showing CACI's course of action/rationale
U.S. Department of the Interior — Inspector General, Federal Technology Service	11 out of 12 procurements were determined to be out of scope under the schedule, but no further action necessary
U.S. Department of the Army, Office of the Inspector General	All CACI contract employees met the requirements of the contract's statement of work/criteria for hiring
Major General George R. Fay, General Paul J. Kern, Lieutenant General Anthony R. Jones	Conclusion that no CACI employee was responsible for abuses at Abu Ghraib, but several other relatively minor incidents were asserted
Hon. James R. Schlesinger [Hon. Harold Brown, Hon. Tillie K. Fowler, Gen. Charles A. Horner (USAF, Ret.)]	One observation stated was that some older contractors were more effective than some younger military personnel
Vice Admiral Albert T. Church, III	Contractors were bridging gaps in military resources but a few were found to be marginally involved in lesser incidents
U.S. Government Accountability Office	Found fault primarily with involved government agencies' contracting processes but claimed CACI involvement added confusion; report scarcely acknowledged CACI's evidence or responses otherwise

APPENDIX G

Abu Ghraib Prison Profile and Record of Incidents

HISTORY

Built by British contractors in the 1960s about 20 miles/32 km west of Baghdad, Abu Ghraib covered 280 acres (1.15 km²). Under the Ba'athist government, the prison had developed a reputation as a place of torture, sometimes referred to in the western media as "Saddam's Torture Central." According to reports by the State Department, "Under Saddam Hussein's orders, the security apparatus in Iraq routinely and systematically torture[d] its citizens."[704] Methods of brutality included a wide range of both physical and mental torture, including beatings, rape, dismemberment and decapitations. Conservative estimates of the scale of the depravity included the execution of nearly 4,000 prisoners in 1984, and several other mass executions between 1994 and 2001. There have also been several press reports of mass graves within the perimeter or near the prison.

By 2001, the prison was thought to have held as many as 15,000 inmates. The prison was divided into five separate walled compounds for different types of prisoners. These compounds were designated for foreign prisoners, long sentences, short sentences, capital crimes, and "special" crimes. The "special" crimes division (used primarily for political prisoners) included "open" and "closed" wings; the closed wing housed only Shi'ites, who were not permitted visitors or outside contact.

---

[704] U.S. Department of State International Information Programs, "Silence Through Torture: Iraq, A Population Silenced," February 2003.

In October 2002, Hussein announced a general amnesty for prisoners at Abu Ghraib and freed its inmates. Unconfirmed reports claimed that 13,000 inmates were released. The prison was reported to have been deserted following the amnesty. When Hussein's government fell, the prison compound was looted by former prisoners.

ABU GHRAIB: 2003–2004

Abu Ghraib was renamed the Baghdad Central Detention Center (also called the Baghdad Central Correctional Facility or BCCF) after U.S.-led forces expelled the former Iraqi government, although the former name of the facility was more commonly used. Initially designated by coalition administrator Paul Bremer to hold Iraqi criminals under the control of Iraqi police, the prison's role was expanded to include detention of U.S. military enemy prisoners. Abu Ghraib served as both a forward operating base and a detention facility.

Abu Ghraib prison was a vast-compound, consisting of several separate facilities; the "hard site," Camp Vigilant and Camp Ganci (the two

GlobalSecurity.org & DigitalGlobe

The layout of Abu Ghraib

camps were later replaced by Camp Redemption in the summer of 2004). Except for Tier-1, the hard site was under the control of Iraqi prison guards, while the rest was under U.S. control. The area of the facility known as the hard site was where the most dangerous prisoners and those most valuable in terms of intelligence value were held. This is also the part of the prison in which the abuses of Iraqi detainees described in the government reports took place and where the infamous abuse photos were taken by MP's.

Abu Ghraib was dangerously overcrowded. The detainee population at Abu Ghraib in the period from August 2003 to early 2004 is reported variously as 3,500 rising to some 10,000 by late autumn. One estimate had nearly 7,000 detainees by October with another counting 6,000 in early December 2003.

At its peak in early 2004, the prison held more than 7,000 people. As of February 2005, Abu Ghraib's population fell to 3,060 prisoners. That number rose again to 3,446 by April of the same year. The facility was operated by only one battalion, even though Army doctrine called for one battalion per 4,000 enemy soldiers.

Abu Ghraib also presented significant security challenges. Located in a hostile urban area not far from Baghdad, the prison was spread out over a flat landscape and surrounded by main roadways on all sides. It was subjected almost daily to mortar attacks by insurgent forces, exposing soldiers, contractors and detainees to constant danger. This also greatly exacerbated the ability of U.S. forces to maintain order and discipline in the generally overcrowded facility.

* * *

The Fay report described the situation that evolved at Abu Ghraib during the Iraq War.[705] Before the war, planners estimated 30,000–100,000 enemy prisoners of war would need to be secured, segregated, detained, and interrogated. The 800th MP Brigade was given the mission to establish as many as 12 detention centers, to be run by subordinate battalion units. As of May 2003, only an estimated 600 detainees

---

[705] Major General George R. Fay, Investigating Officer, *AR 15-6 Investigation of the Abu Ghraib Detention Facility and 205th Military Intelligence Brigade*, Sections 5 and 6.

were being held, a combination of enemy prisoners and criminals. As a result, additional military police units previously identified for deployment were demobilized back to the U.S. The original plan also envisioned that only the prisoners remaining from the initial major combat operations would require detention facilities, and they would eventually be released or turned over to the Iraqi authorities once justice departments and criminal detention facilities were re-established.

In the fall of 2003, the number of detainees rose rapidly due to tactical operations to capture dangerous counter-insurgents. The prison population consisting of criminals, insurgents, security detainees, and detainees with potential intelligence value grew to an estimated 4,000–5,000 personnel. At that time, the Combined Joint Task Force-7 (CJTF-7) commander believed he had no choice but to use Abu Ghraib as the central detention facility.

In June 2003, when the CJTF-7 organization was established, a joint manning document (JMD) was developed to delineate the specific skill sets of personnel needed to perform the increased roles and functions of this new headquarters. It was formally approved for 1,400 personnel in December 2003. Of the 1,400 personnel required by the JMD, the V Corps staff transitioned only 495.

Disparate support from the CJTF-7 staff and the lack of aggressive oversight resulted in a lower priority for meeting resource needs of detention facilities. During the time period of the Abu Ghraib abuses (late 2003), the intelligence focus was on Saddam Hussein's capture and exploitation of documents related to Saddam Hussein, preparation for Ramadan, and large-scale enemy activity at Fallujah and Najaf. The effort to expand the intelligence organization, obtain operational intelligence about the counter-insurgency, and support the Coalition Provisional Authority (CPA) consumed the efforts of the CJTF-7 staff. The army had significantly reduced tactical interrogators since operations Desert Storm/Desert Shield, and creation of the Defense HUMINT Service and worldwide demands for these skills depleted the number of experienced interrogators. Responsibilities for oversight of tactical interrogation procedures, intelligence analysis and reporting at Abu Ghraib and elsewhere were entrusted to the commanders in the field.

The 320th MP battalion was specifically charged by the 800th MP Brigade with operating the Abu Ghraib detainee facility. Initially, the

Commander of the 205th Military Intelligence (MI) Brigade, who was designated by CJTF-7 as the commander of the forward operating base Abu Ghraib in November 2003, did not specify an MI unit or organization for interrogation operations at Abu Ghraib. But the military did not have the necessary personnel available for screening and questioning the increasing number of detainees. Interrogators, analysts, and linguists arrived at Abu Ghraib from multiple units and locations within the 205th MI Brigade. As the need to address intelligence gathering continued, contractor personnel were also later used to augment interrogation, analyst, and linguist personnel at Abu Ghraib.

There are conflicting statements regarding who had the responsibilities to implement and oversee the Joint Interrogation and Debriefing Center (JIDC) at Abu Ghraib. No defined organization existed to implement the JIDC concept. A JIDC was established at Abu Ghraib based on the assessment and recommendations of Major General Geoffrey Miller. At the time, Abu Ghraib had only a few hundred detainees. Lt. Colonel Steve Jordan was sent to Abu Ghraib to oversee the establishment of the JIDC. In November of 2003, Colonel Thomas Pappas assumed the role of commander of the forward operating base and directed activities of the JIDC. Lieutenant Colonel Jordan became the deputy director of the JIDC. A portion of the approved CJTF-7 JMD earmarked 169 personnel for the interrogation operations and analysis cells in the JIDC. Major General Barbara Fast's staff provided priority intelligence requirements for the interrogators and analysts. Due to shortages, many of these positions were filled with contractor personnel. The situation was also complicated by the lack of an organizational MI unit and chain of command at Abu Ghraib solely responsible for MI personnel and intelligence operations.

According to the testimony of soldiers interviewed during the investigation conducted by Major General Antonio M. Taguba, "There seemed little interest from the top brass in providing the prison facility with what it needed to get the job done. None of the top commanders wanted to hear about the lack of prison guards, lack of guns for MPs or floodlights to bathe the compounds at night and prevent escapes, almost a constant threat at Abu Ghraib. Soldiers complained that there were not enough of them to properly man guard towers or patrol perimeters. The detainees were often separated from freedom by little more than a few strands of wire and were always on edge because of the dismal living conditions and the shortage of edible food."[706]

Others reported that, the problems at Abu Ghraib seemed to have "had their roots months earlier at another U.S.-run detention center in southern Iraq called Camp Bucca. Evidence showed that MPs viciously attacked prisoners there, including one who [reportedly] had his nose smashed in. Four soldiers were given less than honorable discharges but were not prosecuted." One officer who worked at Abu Ghraib told General Taguba that he was convinced that had Camp Bucca cases been prosecuted, Abu Ghraib would never have happened.[707]

CLOSING ABU GHRAIB

In March 2006, the U.S. military announced it intended to permanently shut down all operations at Abu Ghraib within three months. The facility would then be turned over to the Iraqi government to be potentially transformed into an Iraqi military base. The 4,500 prisoners housed at Abu Ghraib would be transferred to other facilities, including Camp Cropper, the high-security prison near the Baghdad airport.[708] Ironically, Camp Cropper is where Abu Ghraib despot, Saddam Hussein, was being held at the time.

On September 1, 2006, the U.S. Army turned control of Abu Ghraib prison over to the Iraqi Army.

RECORD OF INCIDENTS

Date	Incident
June 12, 2003	Two prisoners attempted to escape detention at Baghdad International Airport.

---

[706] Edward T. Pound and Kit. R. Roane, "Hell on Earth," by *US News & World Report*, July 19, 2004.

[707] Ibid.

[708] Jake Tapper and Sonia Gallego, "U.S. to Close Infamous Abu Ghraib Prison," *ABCNews*, March 9, 2006.

Date	Incident
June 13, 2003	There was an escape and recapture of a detainee and the shooting of eight detainees. One guard was injured and the tower guards fired lethal rounds at the rioters, injuring seven and killing one detainee. The same day, 30–40 detainees rioted and pelted three interior MP guards with rocks.
August 16, 2003	Three mortar rounds were fired into the prison, killing six Iraqi detainees and injuring many more.
August 17, 2003	Coalition forces engaged an individual in the vicinity of the prison who was later identified as a reporter. The individual was evacuated to a hospital but was pronounced dead on arrival.
November 5, 2003	At least two detainees escaped.
November 7, 2003	One detainee escaped.
November 8, 2003	Six detainees escaped.
November 24, 2003	There was a riot and shooting of 12 detainees. Several detainees allegedly began to riot in one of the encampments in apparent protest of their living conditions. This resulted in the shooting deaths of three detainees, nine wounded detainees, and nine injured U.S. soldiers.
November 24, 2003	A detainee allegedly had a pistol in his cell and an extraction team shot him with non-lethal rounds in the process of recovering the weapon. An investigation concluded that one of the detainees had gotten a pistol and knives from an Iraqi guard working in the encampment.
December 13, 2003	There were three separate incidences of detainee-on-detainee fights, which resulted in the shooting by non-lethal means into crowd in each case.
December 17, 2003	Several detainees allegedly assaulted an MP inside one of the encampments, resulting in a shooting by non-lethal means of a detainee.
January 14, 2004	An Iraqi guard assisted a detainee to escape by signing him out on a work detail and disappearing with him.

Date	Incident
April 2 & 3, 2004	The prison was attacked by 40–60 insurgents, who detonated car bombs and fired rocket-propelled grenades. Between 20 and 44 Americans and 12 Iraqi prisoners were injured in the attack. A second assault was also carried out about a day later, and it is believed that several insurgents were killed and more than 40 U.S. soldiers and at least 13 Iraqi prisoners injured. According to the U.S. military, about 50 insurgents were injured and a few others killed. Al Qaeda has claimed responsibility for both of the strikes.
April 21, 2004	At least 21 prisoners were killed and more than 100 wounded when suspected anti-coalition rebels shelled the prison in what may have been a botched attempt to free insurgents detained for taking part in the uprising against coalition forces.
Late April 2004	Photographs which depicted abuse and torture of Iraqi prisoners held at the Abu Ghraib prison while in U.S. custody were published in the U.S.
January 14, 2005	28 detainees escape while being transported from Abu Ghraib to another Baghdad area facility.
April 2, 2005	Between 40 and 60 insurgents said to be lead by Abu Musab Al Zarqawi's organization attack using mortars, rockets, ground assaults and a car bomb. 44 Americans and 13 Iraqi prisoners were injured in the attack.
May 26, 2005	Three detainees escaped sneaking through two holes in the perimeter fence before dawn.
June 7, 2005	Rioting erupted after a detainee tried to escape during a heavy sandstorm. After the detainee was caught, other detainees in several compounds threw rocks at guards and the portable light generators. Four guards and six detainees were injured and treated at the scene.
August 28, 2005	Three detainees escaped.

APPENDIX H
The CACI Hypercrisis Management Model

IN OVER FOUR DECADES, CACI HAD NEVER EXPERIENCED AN ORDEAL anything like the media crisis and government investigations resulting from Abu Ghraib prison scandal. CACI had kept a relatively low profile and was therefore little known beyond its industry. The company's reputation was virtually untarnished.

When the scandal broke in April of 2004, CACI was unjustly put on the defensive. Not only were the size and scope of the crisis yet to be determined, but so were the implications. This uncertainty put CACI initially in a reactive posture; the company could only respond to what confronted it. But as the crisis progressed during the first couple of weeks, the company became increasingly aware that: (1) the issue was going to be a long-term ordeal; (2) it would require a comprehensive, proactive approach; and (3) outside specialists' support and legal counsel would be needed.

During the first few weeks, CACI was bombarded by media and government inquiries that required immediate attention. At the same time, the company wanted to keep the public, its clients, employees and its investors informed. While CACI had not developed formalized crisis management procedures, it did have established culture, policies and practices on which to base its actions.

First and foremost, for direction CACI could reference its company value statements. The longstanding company credo stating the company's intentions and beliefs called for:

- ☐ Quality service and best value for our clients,
- ☐ Individual opportunity and respect for each other,

☐ Integrity and excellence in our work, and

☐ Distinction and the competitive edge in our markets.

CACI had also developed a Credo and Operational Philosophy as part of the company's culture. But it was the Ten Business Values that set CACI's culture apart from other companies. This document states that CACI focuses on:

1. Placing integrity and honesty above all else.
2. Putting clients first.
3. Creating value for clients and delivering quality.
4. Fostering career opportunities for our people.
5. Maintaining a value-oriented culture, where people enjoy working.
6. Growing our business and making good profits, year after year.
7. Creating and enhancing shareholder value, year after year.
8. Being accountable and taking responsibility for what we do.
9. Treating each other fairly and with mutual respect, including our business partners, vendors, suppliers and the public at large.
10. Maintaining a high-quality reputation for CACI and its people.

The company's culture called for fostering integrity, meeting client needs, and looking out for the best interests of the company's stakeholders. This existing foundation was the basis from which CACI drew its decisions. As a result, CACI knew that doing its own investigation while supporting the official government investigations was vital in order to get answers. CACI also emphasized being forthright and accountable when facts emerged. At the same time, the company found it necessary to address the emergence and persistence of non-factual, unsubstantiated and inaccurate information.

The crisis management model that characterized CACI in the first few weeks, and that most companies respond with in the beginning of a crisis, was undeveloped and *ad hoc*. While CACI had business continuity procedures, they did not cover crises of this nature or this magnitude. CACI began by reacting to the developments of the Abu Ghraib crisis before it began to act upon them.

In this early crisis management model, as shown in Exhibit 1, CACI responded to internal and external parties as the events of the crisis un-

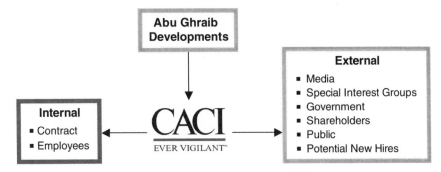

Exhibit 1: Early CACI Crisis Management Model

folded. Internal responses were geared to reassuring employees while re-examining the company's Iraq contract. External responses were aimed at informing the public of CACI's position and activities. Examples of these external responses included conducting interviews with the print media, providing answers to government requests for contract details, holding conference calls with the investment community, and developing standardized letters of response to inquiries received from the public and from the media.

CACI successfully implemented the first two steps in crisis management: acceptance of responsibility and accountability, and a willingness to take positive steps. The company stated from the beginning that it took the allegations seriously, would investigate the matter and cooperate with other investigations, and act accordingly if anyone within the company was found culpable of any wrongdoing.

However, as the scandal grew, CACI knew it had to develop a more comprehensive approach that would meet both short-term and long-term needs. While crisis communications had begun with press releases, conference calls, and media interviews, other areas like risk mitigation, operations, and maintaining the company's favorable reputation had to be addressed.

PHASE I: CACI CRISIS MANAGEMENT

The CACI Crisis Management phase dealt with immediate concerns raised by the crisis created by the *illegally leaked* Taguba report in conjunction with the publication of the infamous Abu Ghraib pictures. Both incidents created a great deal of sensationalism at a time when there was still a considerable lack of information. And this information would be slow in coming because other investigations were just beginning or still underway and would not be completed for several more months.

CACI had to monitor and manage the message about the company. This entailed reviewing information that was made publicly available to ensure accuracy. At the same time, it required gathering further information, correcting erroneous reports, and distributing confirmed facts. It was necessary to sustain the process of monitoring and managing the message until other investigations yielded verified findings and validated conclusions. During this time the media, "experts", activists and other interested parties began to fill the void where information was not yet available and was lacking or where questions were raised that did not have ready answers. This void was filled quickly by speculation, exaggeration and allegations — and in some cases "conspiracy theories."

In responding to inaccurate information *CACI's goal was to keep the message clear, concise and consistent.* This would make the information provided by the company easier to repeat and help increase the likelihood that its accuracy would be maintained. Complicated or complex communication from the company could lead to misinterpretation and additional inaccuracies in its further distribution. *CACI's focus was to clarify, not confuse.* In order to achieve this, the CACI team developed "fact file" which served as a repository for the known information that would be used to address questions, issues or mistakes that remained constant themes throughout the crisis. Examples included how CACI did not hire "mercenaries", the definition of "minimum supervision" in CACI recruiting ads, reporting and supervisory chain for civilian interrogators, etc. The fact file kept CACI's response messages consistent, clear and concise by keeping the language the same throughout while also tailoring it to the specific issue or question raised along the way.

The efforts of Phase I were directed to broad audiences simultaneously: the public, employees and their families, customers, investors, key government officials (e.g., Congress, those heading up the official investigations, CACI's military client on the Abu Ghraib matter), and interest groups (activists, bloggers, politicos, etc.). But the central audience was the media, which supplied information to all of these groups.

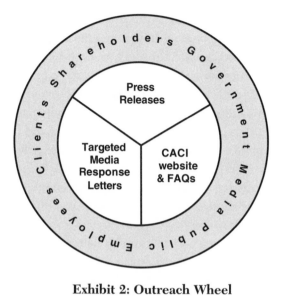

Exhibit 2: Outreach Wheel

While the company was correcting and distributing information, CACI's audience was also the media's audience. The diverse media, which was feeding information to the public at the same time in larger volumes and at greater rates than CACI, was a constant focus for the company in its overall hypercrisis management efforts.

For the media, a tactical three pronged approach was developed which would draw from the company's fact file. These three prongs which formed CACI's Outreach Wheel (Exhibit 2) were made up of (1) press releases, (2) targeted media response letters (emails), and (3) an FAQ (frequently asked questions) section on the CACI website. While press releases were traditional tools for addressing crisis situations in the press, London hit upon a multidimensional proactive strategy with his ideas of both targeted media response letters and the FAQ's to add further to the company's communications arsenal. This strategic and tactical approach is summarized below:

Frequent press releases. London broadened the use of the press releases to make them more comprehensive and to distribute these more frequently, even when there were no triggering events within the crisis. This was aimed at getting CACI's own message out in order to stay abreast of and, if possible, ahead of the constant wave of media reports. These media reports were coming from a number of different sources (a 24 hour, worldwide media machine) which made the task enormous.

Targeted media response letters. The goal of the targeted media response letters was to address specific issues, questions and errors on a direct, immediate and individual basis to the media in a manner that a press release could not. Targeted media response letters could be sent regularly, frequently, and could be repeated as often as necessary (although the company developed a timing strategy to avoid a "junk mail" effect when it was necessary to send additional letters to the same source).

Web site FAQ section. The FAQ section of the CACI Web site provided a 24/7 (twenty-four hours a day, seven days a week) public display of issues (questions) raised and the known facts (answers). The FAQs added an even more constant and robust repository for CACI's message to ensure that the verifiable facts and validated information was available to all of the company's key audiences. CACI also regularly invited the press to view the FAQ section on the company's Web site.

All three prongs of CACI's media response wheel helped the company achieve ***accuracy, consistency and constancy*** in its response to the media matters. These three prongs supported and reinforced each other. For example, the media response letters that were triggered in response to a media event (e.g. speculative articles on possible legal treatment of civilian interrogators) that in turn created an issue (question) could be drawn upon for postings to the FAQ section of the company Web site along with the response (answer) which was also addressed in the media response letters (e.g., no evidence had been produced to charge civilian interrogators). And when employees or clients posed questions (issues) that were posted to the FAQ Web site along with the answer (response), these could be added to the targeted response letters where necessary and appropriate in responding to specific media articles. Further, when press releases were prepared, pertinent information that the CACI team found necessary to repeat in a public forum, could be pulled from both the media response letters and FAQs. This circular, multifaceted three-pronged process augmented the way in which CACI dealt with the massive media machine on an ongoing basis throughout the crisis and it further facilitated the company's internal coordination efforts as well.

Operationally, what did this approach entail?

In all, it meant gathering as much information as possible on the interrogation contract, the news stories, and the individuals involved. The CACI leadership team needed to know the details of every aspect of the contract work, including individuals named in the Taguba report and all others at the prison site.

It meant monitoring news reports for developments in the story in addition to what was being said about the company. It also meant fielding questions from external parties, such as the media, government, and private citizens. CACI would respond to media inquiries as well as cooperate with government investigations, but would also respond to feedback from the public. This feedback sometimes took the form of notes of support, but more often consisted of negative reaction including hate mail that could also pose a security threat.

Importantly, all of this would be done while maintaining daily business operations. That would include keeping clients, shareholders, the investment community, and employees up-to-date with the crisis itself and what aspects of the crisis were at hand (e.g., GSA inquiry) and the management activities the company was undertaking (e.g., internal investigation). CACI believed that a company must not shut down communications or avoid the public during a crisis.

In most corporate crises, there are *five threats to the organization: operational viability, financial stability, legal action, reputation and credibility.*

CACI needed to ensure that the crisis didn't affect its *operational viability* by keeping a steady focus on daily business operations. CACI decided immediately to work with clients in keeping them apprised of the company's crisis management activities and reassuring those clients that their projects would be unaffected. CACI employees were also a high priority and were informed regularly through internal conference calls, corporate publications, and an Iraq section on the internal corporate intranet that allowed employees to read communications about the crisis from CACI management as well as post questions to CACI leadership. In addition, an Iraq section was created on the company's external public website that included the FAQ section which was also available to the media and public providing a centralized source about CACI in Iraq.

Financial stability was a two-pronged approach. On one hand, CACI's financial team continued to maintain its normal business operations. CACI's acquisition of the Defense and Intelligence Group from American Management Systems, Inc. had just taken place on May 1, 2004 and the final financial details were being completed at that time. On the other hand, at the same time, the costs of crisis management had to be calculated and managed. This included the internal investigation, additional man-hours from within CACI, fees for consultants hired specifically for the project and analysis of the costs associated with the interrogation contract. Beyond this, the company maintained its focus on investor relations to keep financial markets and shareholders informed of CACI's cooperation with government investigations and provide them with verified factual information as it emerged.

Two lawsuits illustrate the *legal action* threat CACI would confront in the crisis. In addition to spearheading the company's internal investigation, the law firm of Steptoe & Johnson, CACI's longstanding outside counsel, would take the lead in responding to the lawsuits and correspondence about Abu Ghraib that required legal consideration. This would allow CACI's own legal team to focus on Iraq contract issues, although an attorney specializing in government contracts was also brought in to support CACI's legal efforts as well.

Reputation and credibility threats were ongoing throughout the crisis, primarily through erroneous and damaging information that was being disseminated through various channels including the media, internet blogs, protests and the lawsuits. CACI's positive reputation and credibility were demonstrated and maintained through numerous avenues. The company's commitment to the "truth will out" approach of seeking and distributing the known facts demonstrated the company's commitment to finding and reporting the truth. CACI's commitment to its mission statement and credo demonstrated its long established principles and values. CACI's commitment to holding to the standards of the rule of law and the concept that an accused person is "innocent until proven guilty" demonstrated that the company supported what was right and just. Similarly, CACI's commitment to being accountable and that it would take action if evidence emerged of someone breaking the law demonstrated corporate responsibility. The company's credibility and its positive reputation had already been established over the past four decades and this could be pointed to as well in support of its efforts during the crisis.

Who would implement all of the aspects of this comprehensive strategy?

Tactically, CACI's entire team focused on media response efforts (detailed above) and outreach to employees, clients, shareholders and the general public.

CACI soon realized that some facets of the crisis were beyond its expertise and available personnel. Although the company had taken an open communications approach, the scale and scope of the public relations crisis response was well beyond the company's experience. Therefore, CACI turned to additional *consultants* to assist its efforts.

The firm of Prism Public Affairs was brought in for its expertise on government relations and crisis communications. Not only did they provide the additional manpower and necessary skills, Prism had the prior experience of guiding companies in CACI's industry through crises. In addition, the expertise of Claire Sanders Swift of Claire Media, LLC, was drawn upon to specifically provide input into ways to deal with the media's treatment of Steve Stefanowicz who was at the heart of the Abu Ghraib scandal for CACI. Beyond these consultants and the CACI communications team, London recognized the value of tapping into the additional skills of individuals already serving the company in other capacities. To this end, he expanded the role of Jody Brown, Senior Vice President for Business Communications and PR at CACI to lead and manage CACI's media relations, public outreach, public affairs and implementation of employee and company communications. London also tapped Ron Schneider (Senior Vice President of Business Strategy) to take a leadership role in CACI's customer outreach by making sure that senior people in the military and civilian agencies who did business with CACI received firsthand briefings about he company's work in Iraq. Schneider's focus was on how CACI was addressing customer concerns about Abu Ghraib, to reassure them that CACI was probing for answers and would reveal information that was uncovered. Schneider also was the internal project coordinator for the review of CACI's hiring and staffing for the army's intelligence and interrogator support contract in Iraq. London also engaged the efforts of Dr. Jennifer Burkhart (an outside business advisor to CACI), from the company's M&A search program, to assist in providing analytical support and recommendations dealing with the psychological aspects of company communications and public messaging in addressing company perception and image related to Abu Ghraib. Burkhart provided background research on specific individuals and took the lead in drafting the media response letters. And London tapped consultant, Z. Selin Hur, to support the media response efforts, create and maintain CACI's knowledge repository, and provide additional communications support.

Another aspect of crisis management in which CACI had little experience was dealing with Capitol Hill. While CACI's clients had always been the government, it predominantly dealt with the various government departments and agencies on specific contracts. CACI had never lobbied the U.S. Congress and had chosen to refrain from doing so. But now with Congressional interest in the Abu Ghraib scandal, CACI realized it needed to familiarize those on Capitol Hill with the company. CACI could not let the Abu Ghraib scandal define the company or be its only image. And the company needed to make sure any inaccurate information going to Congress was corrected so that the facts would stand on the record. The consulting firm of Clark and Weinstock was brought in to help the CACI CEO arrange meetings with key Congressional members and their staffs. CACI would increase its profile on the Hill without crossing over to the more typical advocacy-driven lobbying efforts. The CEO's goal was to make the company known, tell what CACI knew about the crisis and answer questions. This process was conducted with great caution and care, as the company did not want in any way to give the appearance of trying to influence the government inquiries at hand.

It was immediately and abundantly evident, however, that virtually *no one*, anywhere, had much experience dealing with a public relations crisis the magnitude of the Abu Ghraib scandal. For CACI, it became clear it was dealing with a *hypercrisis*.

What began as a reactive, *ad hoc* approach to crisis management, evolved into a multi-faceted, proactive strategy. A new CACI hypercrisis management model was created. It is illustrated in Exhibit 3.

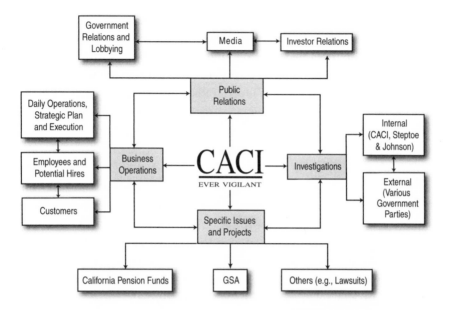

Exhibit 3: CACI Hypercrisis Management Model

PHASE II: CACI COMEBACK

The CACI Comeback phase of CACI's Hypercrisis Management Model was initiated alongside the Crisis Management phase at the outset. From the beginning, CACI was mindful of its responsibility to all of its stakeholders — clients, employees and investors, not only to acknowledge the crisis and accept appropriate accountability for its role as an employer, but also to communicate reassurance to them that the company would meet its obligations. Another aspect of this phase was rebounding from the tarnish of the crisis, upholding the company's good name and retaining the company's positive image that it had enjoyed before the crisis.

Phase II overlapped with Phase I in that it involved engaging in the necessary activities outlined in the Phase I pushback aspect of crisis management but with the additional recognition that these efforts had to be heightened and re-doubled. This meant not just attention to questions and concerns, but amplification of the answers and findings.

It meant not just being reactive, but also being pre-emptive and proactive. It also meant maintaining continuity of business operations at the same high standards that the company had sustained in the past, not allowing the crisis to become a distraction, or to compromise in any way the quality of CACI's service. During the crisis London frequently reminded his team of the company motto: "Quality service and best value for our clients" and "Integrity and excellence in our work" with the additional reminder that they also had the responsibility not to let the crisis distract or define CACI.

Phase II efforts meant reaching out beyond the immediate crisis to do additional outreach. For example, the customer outreach process spearheaded by Ron Schneider was a very important aspect of the CACI comeback plan, which was initiated in the middle of the crisis. This outreach was directed to 100 key client industry leaders to keep them apprised of the crisis by answering questions and letting them know the team would remain available to them to address future concerns. Schneider was successful in reaching 75% of the individuals he had identified to meet with, and the overall feedback from this effort was positive. Outreach efforts were also implemented with investors to provide accurate feedback in order to maintain investor confidence based on solid business principles, rather than reaction to negative, premature or inaccurate news. The long-term benefit of this outreach approach was quite valuable.

While the focus of Phase I (CACI Crisis Management) was to manage the immediate crisis and mitigate damage, the focus of Phase II (CACI Comeback) was to uphold CACI's solid footing and retain its positive image. Phase II planning also meant recognizing the process would be a long term effort to continue preserving CACI's good name and maintain its favorable reputation. CACI's four decades of solid performance and its good reputation remained important throughout the crisis as both the measure of the company's past performance and the benchmark for its future efforts. Besides managing the crisis, finding the truth, taking responsibility and doing the right thing, CACI endeavored to preserve the company's good name regardless of what the investigations might reveal about one or few of its 9,600 employees. CACI's straightforward approach of full and frequent disclosure transcended both Phase I and Phase II of the Hypercrisis Management model to become a staple part of CACI's ongoing public relations and communications strategy.

CACI's approach to crisis management may have matured, but was it successful? How well did CACI fare?

As of the summer of 2005, CACI was still dealing with the lingering effects of the Abu Ghraib scandal, but by every measure the company continued to maintain positive momentum and ongoing business success. Despite the loss of a small contract in the U.K., the company's business performance was largely unaffected after the first few months of the ordeal. Indeed, CACI's fiscal 2004 earnings report released in August of 2004 was among its best ever and triggered the start of a major run-up in its share price that lasted until the end of the year. And by August of 2005, CACI was able to announce another year of record financial results, reporting a record $1.62 billion in revenue (for its fiscal year ending June 30, 2005).

Also, in late 2005 CACI was being referred to as a model example of adherence to GSA rules. The company was cited for its efforts to search for an alternative contract vehicle, when it had initially been requested by the Army in 2003 to provide interrogators under an existing contract.[709] Although the GSA inquiry had been difficult for CACI, it clearly demonstrated to both the public and the federal community that CACI had been and continued to be a responsible company.

CACI also recorded a number of lessons learned. Some lessons taught CACI the intensity and unfairness of public scrutiny in the midst of a worldwide scandal and this helped the company identify its own unique approach in navigating a treacherous media terrain. Importantly, the CACI team recognized that the media was not their friend. Other lessons resulted in the tightening of some internal procedures, and delivering the operational benefits of better business practices.

Perhaps most importantly, the company's trust in its corporate culture was strongly reaffirmed. The values and principles that had guided the company through more than 40 years of ethical practices and quality

---

[709] Comments made by Tom Sisti, who performs law and policy work pertaining to government contracts for SAP, at the General Services Administration's Regulation Workshop, December 8 and 9, 2005, Washington, D.C.

client service would also form the foundation for CACI's successful response to an unprecedented crisis.

At the foundation of CACI's hypercrisis management model were key principles that the team adhered to throughout:

- ☐ Establish clear priorities early on.
- ☐ Trust in core values, "do the right thing," and tell the truth.
- ☐ Look to the company credo and mission statement to help focus on doing the right thing.
- ☐ Get the facts and keep them straight.
- ☐ Honor the public record and seek to set it straight whenever it strays.
- ☐ Cooperate fully with all official investigations.
- ☐ Publicly and clearly commit to correct problems quickly.
- ☐ Make clear that the company supports the rule of law, including due process and the presumption of innocence; no "kangaroo courts" and no rush to judgment.
- ☐ Emphasize that the company will take firm action upon confirmed evidence of wrongdoing.
- ☐ Push back against *every* instance of false or erroneous news reports or other public statements.
- ☐ Recognize that the media is not an ally and cannot be relied upon to get the story and facts straight.
- ☐ Recognize that the media will go after "bad news" before "good news," but will seldom — if ever — correct its errors.
- ☐ Be aware of the "negative propaganda effect" created by a media rampaging over a "bad news" issue.
- ☐ Seek and insist on public corrections for errors or distortions.
- ☐ Understand that the media is a worldwide, 24/7 operation in which stories get caught in a non-stop feeding frenzy, creating a tsunami effect that can overwhelm, damage — even destroy — people and institutions in its path.
- ☐ Tell the company's story over and over again in every available forum—state it clearly and firmly in plain English.
- ☐ Communicate directly, fully, and frequently with customers, employees, shareholders, and the public.

□ Accept that things may get worse before they get better
□ Resist "lynch mob" and "witch hunt" pressures to find a scapegoat
□ Work to defend CACI's *good name* by doing whatever is proper and appropriate to preserve the company's reputation

CACI has now, through 2007, instituted its Hypercrisis Management Model procedures into the company's business continuity plans. CACI's leadership is hopeful the company will not have to face a crisis like Abu Ghraib again, but with this model in place, CACI is better equipped to remain prepared in the future and ***ever vigilant*** in preserving its good name.

APPENDIX I

Op-Ed Piece by J.P. London Rejected by the Washington Post

In the Spotlight's Glare, Contractors Soldier on in Iraq
DR. J.P. ("JACK") LONDON, CACI CHAIRMAN, PRESIDENT, AND CEO

AMID THE BROAD DEBATE ABOUT U.S. POLICY IN IRAQ, NEWSPAPER headlines periodically draw attention to the role of private contractors who seem to be wherever the soldiers are. Some contractors have died tragic deaths, murdered by insurgent forces. Others have faced intense scrutiny for possible misconduct at Abu Ghraib. With the visibility have come new questions as Americans ask what jobs contractors have been assigned, how they are performing, and how the contractor-military relationship works.

These are fair questions. Periodic reviews of key strategies are certainly appropriate in response to changing circumstances, including the need to find the best ways to combat global terrorism.

Although events in Iraq may have alerted many Americans about contracting of federal government services for the first time, reliance on the private sector for a wide range of tasks has been a proven policy throughout the government since the 1960s, and in some instances before that. Our space and nuclear programs, for example, have partnered with the private sector from their beginnings. For the military, partnering with contractors has been a core of planning since the early 1990s and gained momentum during the Clinton administration.

To provide benefit, review of the contracting process requires perspective. Human nature being what it is, critics in these debates tend to dominate the platform. Pointing to missteps as evidence that a strategy or program isn't working is far easier than demonstrating the routine competence of people doing their jobs correctly every day. So, as the discussion proceeds, it is important to balance the ledger — to speak up for the thousands of private employees who are helping U.S. troops do their job in Iraq and also to explain how contractors, including my company, CACI, contribute to America's national security by enhancing military effectiveness.

Military planners, including the Defense Department's top civilians in the last two administrations, point to a number of benefits from the collaboration between the armed forces and private contractors.

The use of private contractors enables the military to concentrate on its core competencies, while obtaining a range of critical skills and expertise from civilian specialists. The increasing reliance on high-tech weaponry to help reduce casualties and give American troops control of the battlefield has created a new need for technical capabilities that are often in short supply among the young soldiers that make up the bulk of the military. Intelligence work, which can involve sophisticated computer analysis, can also benefit from private sector expertise developed over many years of specialized work in the civilian world.

Contractors also can handle a range of routine logistical and support tasks, including property management, computer networking, engineering, maintenance and even trash removal, that do not require military personnel.

Using private contractors for non-combat assignments frees troops for critical military missions and makes it possible to meet America's security needs with an all-volunteer force. For example, the Army's force reduction from more than 700,000 at the end of the Persian Gulf War to fewer than 500,000 today would simply not have been possible without the shift of many non-military tasks to the private sector. Simply put, the use of contractors for non-combat assignments allows a greater percentage of troops to focus on purely military tasks, which in turn allows the armed forces to protect our national security with a smaller, permanent force. Conversely, assigning fewer jobs to contractors increases the number of soldiers needed to accomplish the military's mission.

"The Army must focus its energies and talents on our core competencies — functions we perform better than anyone else — and seek to obtain other needed products or services from the private sector where it makes sense," a former Defense official previously explained of the military's relationship with private contractors.

There also is significant evidence that the availability of private contractors through competitive sourcing has saved money and enabled the military to shift dollars to areas of greatest need. The Defense Department has estimated a savings of $5.5 billion since 2000 by opening about 72,000 jobs to commercial competition. A recent study by Jacques Gansler, Pentagon acquisition chief during the final years of the Clinton administration, shows average savings of 33 percent from competitive sourcing of Defense Department contracts.

Many argue, however, that the use of contractors has gone too far and that the military has wrongly shifted to the private sector some jobs that should be done only by those in uniform. For example, there are critics who say that security work performed in some instances by private contractors should be a military job. Others have focused on interrogation services provided by CACI.

For a few critics of the contracting system, the presence of CACI interrogators at Abu Ghraib has been held out as an example. Some have tried to equate the very function of interrogation with the abuse of personal liberties. But the taking of prisoners and the act of interrogation is a necessary part of every battlefield, including the fight against terrorism. In a combat zone, good information is literally a matter of life and death. Done properly, intelligence gathering can help our troops achieve their mission, shorten the conflict, and reduce the loss of life on all sides.

That is the context in which we considered the Army's request for interrogators. Facing a shortage of available interrogators and a vital need to collect intelligence that can change the course of battle, the Army turned to CACI for help in August 2003. We believed then and believe today that saying "yes" to that request was the right and only answer to give under those circumstances. When doing public work, certain obligations come with the job.

In considering the value of contracting, the reliability of the contractor is key. Absent a commitment to quality work and quality ethics, the arrangement won't work.

At CACI, we sum up the contractors' obligations with the simple mantra: "Do the right thing." As a good partner with the military, the "right thing" in current circumstances includes keeping our commitments to provide a range of logistical, tactical, intelligence, and information services to assist our troops in Iraq and around the world. It also means sticking with the tough jobs, including interrogation, as long as the Army needs those services.

The right thing means full cooperation with inquiries when our performance is questioned. That is why from the first word of abuses, CACI has cooperated with every inquiry, responded to all requests for information, launched its own investigation, shared its own findings with the government, and reported to the public on a regular basis. CACI has been reviewed by several governing bodies, including the General Services Administration, which concluded that CACI is a "responsible" company worthy of continuing its contract work with the government without penalty or sanctions, and by the U.S. Army Inspector General, who determined that *all* of CACI's contract interrogators in Iraq met the military statement of work for their job requirements in performing assigned responsibilities. CACI also made public its own rigorous selection process for recruiting and hiring interrogators to ensure that its contractors met the military's requirements, were U.S. citizens, had security clearances and were trained in the Geneva Conventions. CACI has a strong commitment to the fundamental American principle that people are presumed innocent until proven guilty. If the evidence confirms misconduct by a CACI employee, the right thing means decisive action against those who have done wrong.

Doing the right thing also means defending our name and reputation when we are wrongly maligned. In some forums, CACI has been falsely and maliciously accused of outrageous actions, including a deliberate policy of murder and torture. Others have cited the unfortunate events at Abu Ghraib as a basis for condemning the contracting process itself — broadly blaming the military's use of contractors for "the non-doctrinal use of torture" and asserting, without a shred of evidence, that contractors may have committed other crimes as well. These allegations are flat wrong — across the board — and are not legitimate facts for the discussion of the military-contractor relationship.

Like every human endeavor, the military's use of private contractors is not perfect. The military and contractors alike have a responsibility to learn from experience in Iraq to fix problems as they arise and make the contracting process as effective as possible in meeting national security needs. But repairs, not dismantling, should be the order of the day. While it is useful to discuss "lessons learned," we think it is equally important to advance the dialogue on the vast number of good and right things that contractors have provided over the past decades and today in a world that needs agile, flexible, and seamless operations for critical and vital missions. On balance, we believe the system has worked extraordinarily well to meet the military's needs for special skills and expertise, to reduce defense costs, to allow America's soldiers to do the exclusively military jobs they do best, and to enable the military to develop the flexible response necessary to fulfill a wide range of missions in a time of terrorism.

APPENDIX J
Abu Ghraib Verdicts

LIST OF ABU GHRAIB VERDICTS
(in alphabetical order)

Specialist Megan Ambuhl, of Centreville, VA, pleaded guilty in October 2004 to charges of dereliction of duty for failing to prevent or report maltreatment of prisoners. Ambuhl was sentenced to reduction in rank to private and loss of a half-month's pay without serving prison time in her plea bargain. She also received an "other than honorable" discharge from the army. In 2005, Ambuhl married Charles Graner, Jr., who was convicted and is serving time for his role in the Abu Ghraib abuses. By 2006, Ambuhl had returned to Northern Virginia, where she reportedly works as a histology lab technician.

Sergeant Santos A. Cardona, of Fullerton, CA, was convicted in June 2006 on counts of dereliction of duty and aggravated assault for allowing his dog to bark in the face of a kneeling detainee as requested by another soldier who was not an interrogator. Cardona was sentenced to 90 days' hard labor and a reduction in rank to specialist. He was also ordered to forfeit $600 a month in pay for 12 months. Cardona was acquitted of unlawfully having his dog bite a detainee and conspiring with another dog handler to frighten prisoners as a game.

Specialist Armin Cruz, of Plano, TX, was sentenced to eight months in prison in September 2004 after pleading guilty to conspiracy and mistreating prisoners. He also received a bad conduct discharge from the army. Cruz was accused of forcing naked prisoners to crawl along the floor and handcuffing men together.

Sergeant Javal Davis, of Roselle, NJ, received a six-month prison sentence after pleading guilty in February of 2005 to assault, dereliction of duty, and lying to army investigators. He received a bad conduct discharge from the army as well. Davis admitted stepping on the hands and feet of handcuffed detainees and falling with his full weight on top of them.

Private First Class Lynndie England, of Ft. Ashby, WV, pleaded not guilty when the army reopened her court-martial in the summer of 2005 on charges of mistreating Iraqi prisoners. Earlier in 2005, England had agreed to plead guilty to several charges in return for reduced prison time. But an army judge threw out her plea, saying the confession she had worked out with army prosecutors was not believable. She was convicted in September 2005 of one count of conspiracy, four counts of maltreating detainees, and one count of committing an indecent act. She was acquitted on a second conspiracy count. England was sentenced to three years in prison and given a dishonorable discharge.

Staff Sergeant Ivan Frederick, of Buckingham, VA, was sentenced to 8½ years in prison in October 2004 after pleading guilty to conspiracy, dereliction of duty, maltreatment of detainees, assault, and committing an indecent act. Frederick admitted he helped place wires on a detainee's hands and told the detainee he would be electrocuted if he fell off a box. In October 2007, Frederick was paroled from Ft. Leavenworth after serving approximately 3 years of an 8-year sentence in exchange for his cooperation and testimony in the 2007 court-martial of Lt. Col. Steven Jordan.

Specialist Charles Graner, Jr., of Uniontown, PA, is serving a 10-year prison sentence at Fort Leavenworth, KS, after he was found guilty in January 2005 of conspiracy to maltreat detainees, failing to protect detainees from abuse, cruelty, and maltreatment, as well as charges of assault, indecency, adultery, and obstruction of justice. Graner was also given a dishonorable discharge. Prosecutors described Graner, who was said to be Lyndie England's ex-boyfriend, as the ringleader of a group of Abu Ghraib military prison guards who mistreated Iraqi detainees. He was photographed giving the thumbs-up sign behind a pile of naked detainees and having ordered them to masturbate.

Specialist Sabrina Harman, of Lorton, VA, was convicted on six of seven counts of conspiracy and dereliction of duty in May 2005, and was acquitted of one maltreatment charge. Harman was sentenced to six months in prison, with credit for 51 days already served, and was given a bad conduct discharge.

Lieutenant Colonel Steven L. Jordan — is the former director of the Joint Interrogation Debriefing Center and the liaison officer to the 205th Military Intelligence Brigade. The Taguba report named Jordan as one of the four people "suspected" to be either "directly or indirectly" responsible for the abuses at Abu Ghraib. Jordan was determined to have made misrepresentations to the investigation team, including his leadership role, and did not properly supervise the soldiers under his command. In April 2006, the army announced that it planned to charge Jordan for dereliction of duty, lying to investigators, and conduct unbecoming an officer. In January 2007, Jordan was arraigned on eight charges including cruelty and maltreatment as well as dereliction of duty, although four of the original charges were eventually dropped. Jordan's court-martial was held in August 2007. In a split verdict, Jordan was found guilty of disobeying a general's command not to talk about the investigation, but was acquitted of failing to control soldiers who had abused detainees. The military jury issued Jordan a reprimand sparing him any jail time. But in January 2008, the army dismissed the conviction outright. Jordan's attorney had argued that a federal criminal conviction [for disobeying Major General Fay's gag order] was "unjust" and the army found that evidence presented by the defense at trial and post-trial supported this claim. Jordan was instead given an administrative reprimand that cited his disobeying of Fay's order but cleared him of criminal responsibility.

Brigadier General Janis Karpinski was head of the 800th Military Police Brigade at Abu Ghraib. She was demoted from Brigadier General to Colonel in June of 2004 in the aftermath of the Abu Ghraib abuse scandal. The demotion meant her career in the military was effectively over and she subsequently retired. Karpinski's unit was in charge of the prison compound when Iraqi detainees were physically abused and sexually humiliated by military police soldiers in the fall of 2003. She wrote *One Woman's Army: The Commanding General of Abu Ghraib Tells Her Story*, which was released in October 2005.

Specialist Roman Krol, of Randolph, MA, pleaded guilty to charges of conspiracy to abuse and two counts of abusing detainees. He was sentenced in February 2005 to 10 months in prison. He pleaded not guilty to a charge of slapping a detainee in the face. He admitted pouring water on naked detainees and forcing them to crawl around the floor at Abu Ghraib, and throwing a foam football at them while they were handcuffed.

Colonel Thomas M. Pappas — was brigade commander of the 205th Military Intelligence Brigade. He was in charge of military intelligence personnel at Abu Ghraib prison and was subsequently found guilty of two counts of dereliction of duty for his role in the Abu Ghraib prisoner abuse scandal, for allowing dogs to be present during interrogations, and for not supplying his troops with sufficient training. He was fined $8000 for the offenses and relieved from command. In 2006, he testified under immunity at the court-martial of an Army dog handler that he gave permission to use military working dogs one time with one detainee.

Specialist Jeremy Sivits, of Hyndman, PA, pleaded guilty in May 2004 to four counts, including alleging conspiracy to maltreat detainees, and dereliction of duty for negligently failing to protect detainees from abuse, cruelty, and maltreatment, and for taking pictures of naked Iraqi prisoners being humiliated, including some of the photographs that triggered the scandal. The former military guard was sentenced to a year in prison.

Sergeant Michael J. Smith, of Ft. Lauderdale, FL, in March 2006 was found guilty of five of 13 counts, including the maltreatment of prisoners and conspiring with another dog handler in a contest to try to frighten detainees. He was sentenced to six months' confinement, demoted to the rank of private, and had his monthly pay reduced by $750 for three months. After serving time, he was discharged for bad conduct.

APPENDIX K

Unacceptable or Unimaginable?

Putting the Media's Coverage of Abu Ghraib in
Perspective with Terrorist Acts and Historical
Atrocities of the 20th Century

T HE PHOTOGRAPHS OF THE ABUSES IN ABU GHRAIB PRISON WERE A
shock to the American psyche and a considerable setback to America's reputation in the rest of the world. There is a belief that the U.S. military and its partners, particularly in the Iraq war zone, should hold themselves to a higher standard. But harsh realizations about the unacceptably abusive conduct of a few American soldiers towards detainees had far reaching consequences.

The Abu Ghraib story had different implications for different people. For the military, it was a matter of culpability and character. As for the media, it now had a new scintillating angle to an already contentious war story. Anti-war activists embraced the images for their own agendas. The naming of two U.S. corporations, including CACI, also introduced many Americans to the military's outsourcing of certain tasks to government contractors. Abu Ghraib justifiably raised many questions and calls by the public and government for answers and accountability. But for U.S. politicians of all persuasions, Abu Ghraib was a political powder keg — and it blew sky high.

Had the Abu Ghraib photos not been taken or leaked, perhaps the abuses and investigations would have never made it into public interest. Allegations of abuse had already appeared in a few short articles early in 2004, but did not receive much attention. Journalists assert the story's impact and duration in the media would have been much less without the accompanying photos.

However unacceptable, the behavior depicted in the photos was far from the worst of human crimes. By some arguments (and definitions), it was not even torture, although the various abuses were routinely and erroneously called as such by the media, and subsequently, the public.

Meanwhile, the Abu Ghraib events overshadowed the slaughter of innocent Americans and foreigners at the hands of extremist terror groups in Iraq, many linked to al Qaeda; and to events that can easily be called more heinous, more horrendous, than the abuses at Abu Ghraib. And these atrocities certainly were criminal acts that warranted justice. By the end of October 2004, more than 150 foreigners (mainly contractors and aid workers) as well as many Iraqis had been kidnapped, held hostage, even murdered — sometimes beheaded — by insurgents in Iraq.[710] And with regard to beheadings, the insurgent terrorists clearly appeared to have been following their radical interpretations of the Koran, the Islamic holy book.[711] Figure 1 presents a list of these atrocities that includes American victims.

The best-known example at the time was Nicholas Berg, a 26 year-old businessman, who was condemned and beheaded on May 8, 2004 by captors who videotaped and enabled the media to broadcast the event. The two most striking images from the Berg murder were the blurry still

---

[710] "Iraq: Contractors, Aid Workers, Journalists — More Than 150 Kidnapped," *The Associated Press*, October 22, 2004.

[711] Apropos of the radical terrorists' interpretations: A complete reading of the Koran (Qu'ran) 47:4 for the beheading of disbelievers (infidels) says: "Now when ye meet in battle those who disbelieve, then it is smiting of the necks until, when ye have routed them, their making fast of bonds; and afterward either grace or ransom till the war lay down its burdens. That (is the ordinance). And if Allah willed He could have punished them (without you) but (thus it is ordained) that He may try some of you by means of others. And those who are slain in the way of Allah, He rendereth not their actions vain."

A similar "beheading" quote from the Koran for "disbelievers" (infidels) is found in the Koran [8:12]: "When the Lord inspired the angels, (saying:) I am with you. So make those who believe stand firm. I will throw fear into the hearts of those who disbelieve. Then smite the necks and smite of them each finger." [M. Pickthall, trans., *The Koran* (New York: Campbell Publishers Ltd, 1992)].

Figure 1: Partial list of terrorist beheadings and killings September 2001–August 2006[1]

Date	Victim(s)[2]	Suspected/Confirmed Perpetrators
06/25/06	Four Russian embassy workers are kidnapped and killed	Mujahedeen Shura Council
06/19/06	Pfc. **Kristian Menchaca** and Pfc. **Thomas Turner** killed, their bodies desecrated, then booby-trapped	Mujahedeen Shura Council
05/13/06	Four humanitarian workers kidnapped and killed	Unknown assailants
03/10/06	**Tom Fox** killed and apparently tortured	Swords of Righteousness Brigades
12/10/05	Egyptian engineer Ibrahim Sayed Hilali killed	Unknown assailants
12/08/05	American security consultant **Ronald Schulz** killed	Islamic Army in Iraq
07/02/05	Egyptian diplomat Ihab al-Sherif killed	Al Qaeda in Iraq
05/09/05	Japanese security guard Akihiko Saito killed	Ansar al-Sunna Army
04/28/05	Six unidentified Sudanese killed	Ansar al-Sunna Army
01/16/05	Egyptian driver Ibrahim Mohammed Ismail beheaded	Abu Musab al-Zarqawi[3]
12/16/05	Italian photographer Salvatore Santoro killed	Unidentified group
11/15/04	British-Iraqi aid worker Margaret Hassan kidnapped and presumed dead	Unidentified group
11/02/04	Unidentified Jordanian hostage	Unknown assailants
10/30/04	Japanese backpacker Shosei Koda beheaded	Abu Musab al-Zarqawi
10/23/04	Iraqi Seif Kanaan beheaded	Ansar al-Sunna Army
10/22/04	Macedonian workers Dalibor Lazarevski, Zoran Naskovski, Dragan Markovic killed	Islamic Army in Iraq
10/15/04	Iraqi Ala al-Maliki killed	Jaysh Ansar al-Sunna
10/14/04	Turkish driver Ramazan Elbu beheaded	Ansar al-Sunna Army
10/11/04	Turkish contractor Maher Kemal beheaded	Ansar al-Sunna Army
10/08/04	American **Kenneth Bigley** beheaded	Abu Musab al-Zarqawi
10/04/04	Turkish hostage, Yilmaz Dabca, killed	Abu Bakar al-Sidiq
10/02/04	Iraqi Barie Nafie Dawoud Ibrahim beheaded	Ansar al-Sunna Army
10/02/04	Iraqi-Italian Iyad Anwar Wali killed	Abu Bakar al-Sidiq
09/28/04	Iraqis Fadhek Ibrahim and Firas Imeyyel killed	Abu Bakar al-Sidiq

Figure 1: (continued)

Date	Victim(s)[2]	Suspected/Confirmed Perpetrators
09/21/04	American hostage **Jack Hensley** beheaded	Abu Musab al-Zarqawi
09/21/04	Turkish driver Akar Besir killed	Unknown assailants
09/20/04	American hostage **Eugene Armstrong** beheaded	Abu Musab al-Zarqawi
09/13/04	Turkish hostage Durmus Kumdereli beheaded	Tawhid wal Jihad
09/08/04	Three Muslim "informants," Kalu Din, Mishri Gujjar, and Ghulam Shah, beheaded	Unknown assailants
09/05/04	Egyptian Nasser Juma killed	Unknown assailants
09/03/04	Three Iraqi Kurdish militia men killed	Unknown assailants
08/31/04	12 Nepalese hostages killed, 1 by beheading	Ansar al-Sunna Army
08/26/04	Italian journalist Enzo Baldoni killed	Islamic Army
08/10/04	Suspected Egyptian "spy" Mohammed Mutawalli beheaded	Tawhid wal Jihad
08/06/04	Unnamed Bulgarian hostage beheaded	Unknown assailants
08/02/04	Turkish hostage Murat Yuce beheaded	Tawhid wal Jihad
07/28/04	Unnamed Bulgarian hostage beheaded	Unknown assailants
07/28/04	Pakistanis Raja Azad and Sajad Naeem killed	Islamic Army in Iraq
07/27/04	American hostage **Paul Johnson** beheaded	Al Qaeda
07/13/04	Bulgarian truck drivers Georgi Lazov and Ivaylo Kepov beheaded	Abu Musab al-Zarqawi
06/22/04	South Korean interpreter Kim Sun Il beheaded	Abu Musab al-Zarqawi
06/21/04	Lebanese construction worker Hussein Ali Alyan tortured and killed	Unknown assailants
05/08/04	American hostage **Nicholas Berg** beheaded	Abu Musab al-Zarqawi
04/14/04	Italian security guard Fabrizio Quattrocchi killed	Green Battalion
04/14/04	Dane Henrik Frandsen abducted and killed	Not stated
01/31/02	American reporter **Daniel Pearl** (Pakistan)[4] killed	Al Qaeda

[1] Compiled from various reference and news sources

[2] American victims are in bolded typeface

[3] Abu Musab al-Zarqawi was the al Qaeda leader in Iraq at the time

[4] Al Qaeda leader Khalid Sheikh Mohammed, known as the principle architect of the 9/11 attacks, is alleged to have ordered Pearl's murder. Some reports state that Mohammed confessed under CIA interrogation in 2006 that he personally committed the crime. However, in 2002, a British national originally from Pakistan, Ahmed Omar Saeed Sheikh, who had affiliations with terror groups including al Qaeda, was convicted and sentenced to death by a Pakistani court for the abduction and death of Daniel Pearl.

shot from the video of Berg in an orange jumpsuit — intentionally shown to mimic the ones worn by Abu Ghraib detainees — kneeling down before his captors and the picture of Berg's father sitting on his front lawn bowing his head in his hands in grief. Berg's murder gained considerable media attention. In fact, when released, the video of Berg's brutal decapitation was the most popular search item on the Internet.[712] The videos of the various beheadings were even made available online and sold to extremists as "entertainment" in Iraq and in the rest of the Arab world.[713]

The capture and beheading of at least 60 foreigners and other Americans in the following years also garnered media coverage but to a much lesser extent than Berg's. "It seems that it's no longer automatic front page news when an American is beheaded on camera by terrorists," said CBS's Dick Meyer.[714] Here, then, are two comparative stories. Both were acts of wrongdoing in the same war zone. But the Abu Ghraib detainee abuse story clearly was given more media, political, and public attention in the U.S. and around the world, than the more heinous kidnappings and murders of American, foreign, and Iraqi civilians. It should not be ignored that considerable effort has been made to investigate and prosecute those found responsible for the Abu Ghraib abuses while the numerous kidnappings and brutal murders by terrorists have received little to no such effort. Why is that?

There are several theories that attempt to answer this question. One is that the Abu Ghraib story was more widely covered, particularly by the U.S. media, because an anti-war finger could be pointed to America. Another is that the U.S. military and the accused companies were more visible and accessible than the terrorist groups in Iraq. It has also been argued that the Abu Ghraib photos were easier to stomach than the beheading videos. Some have also asserted that Americans simply became preoccupied with the 2004 presidential election and Abu Ghraib was one of the anti-war centerpieces. And there was speculation that Americans became numbed to the terrorist beheading stories— maybe it was just old news?

---

[712] Matthew McAllester, "Iraqi Beheading Now Fueling New Global 'Snuff' Film Market," *Newsday*, October 17, 2004.

[713] Ibrahim al-Marashi, "Iraq's Hostage Crisis: Kidnappings, Mass Media and The Iraqi Insurgency" *Middle East Review of International Affairs*, Vol. 8, No. 4 (December 2004).

[714] Dick Meyer, "Benumbed by Beheadings?" cbsnews.com, September 29, 2004.

Did the frequency of the beheadings cause them to lose their shock impact? One theory posits, "If it starts happening three times a week they're not going to get the attention as the other ones did."[715]

There have been arguments stating the benefits of not over-publicizing beheadings in the media. First, the videos would give the terrorist groups an opportunity to display their name and symbols to promote themselves. Second, it would give the terrorist groups an opportunity to attempt to intimidate Western audiences, influence politics and inspire potential recruits.[716] One viewpoint even argues that the "amount of media coverage the beheadings attract guarantees there will be many more."[717]

It must be stated, however, that *not* focusing media attention on these atrocities in fear of giving exposure to terrorists hinders Americans from telling and knowing the truth. Allowing terror groups to dictate what our media reports, for whatever proposed reasons, is not acceptable. It can be argued that this lack of coverage led to a loss of perspective and the value of what is really important. But why should a story that was easier to report outweigh another story that was arguably much more significant? The abuses at Abu Ghraib were clearly wrong and unacceptable but the abuses could be stopped, procedures improved, and the culpable parties held accountable. However, would there be any justice — any focus of investigation — for the innocent victims, so brutally murdered by terrorists?

Importantly, the kidnapping, murder, and beheading of innocent victims demonstrated the high ongoing risks of the work performed by contractors, aid workers — and even journalists — to rebuild the country of Iraq. It also fully revealed the barbaric savagery embedded in the extremist, terrorist movement. These were crimes (war crimes?) against people trying to help the country. The atrocities even led some companies and coalition partners to retreat from Iraq altogether, thus undermining the hard-earned progress made there. Yet, it seemed, all of this was far less important than Abu Ghraib.

One terrorism expert explained, "What we lose is a glimpse of the truth, unadulterated and clear. It is absolutely fair to judge America by

---

[715] Susan Taylor Martin, "Horror is the Point of Recent Beheadings," *St. Petersburg Times*, September 23, 2004.

[716] al-Marashi, op. cit.

[717] "Beheadings: Terrorism is a Symptom of a Bigger Problem," *JihadWatch.org*, July 7, 2004.

its misconduct at the Abu Ghraib prison in Baghdad, for we are not a nation willing to torture an enemy to death; it is also absolutely fair to judge our Islamic enemies by a public beheading, for it clarifies how primitive and cruel it is within their nature to be."[718]

Unfortunately, human history is full of cruelty far worse than detainee abuse or a single beheading. We only need to go a century back to find numerous examples. Figure 2 lists examples of these atrocities.

Unsurprisingly, images of these events in the early twentieth century were not as abundant or readily available for distribution. And certainly the worldwide availability provided by 24/7 news operations and the Internet have changed everything. But as those pictures (and sometimes even film) emerged, we saw what torture and other abuse crimes looked like. Even those images barely captured the enormous scale and scope of suffering. Perhaps these countries were too far away and times were too long ago to affect many Americans. Perhaps the number of victims was beyond imagination. It was not until the 2004 movie *Hotel Rwanda*, for example, that most of the American people realized that nearly a million people died in less than a year during the Rwandan genocide. And this was an event that occurred only 10 years before, and during the modern age of mass communications.

Even acts of terror against Americans have not held as much of the public's attention as Abu Ghraib. Figure 3 presents a list of these tragic events.

Other than the indelible September 11 images, how many of these events have stayed in the American psyche to the extent that Abu Ghraib has? Yet these events are far more vicious and many are part of an overall long-term strategy to harm the U.S. politically, economically and socially. Even the October 2002 sniper attacks on the greater Washington, D.C. area, which took ten lives, have become a faint memory for most.

Images of terror are not new either. From last will and testament (statement) videos of suicide bombers to photographs of Nazi death chambers to museum-hung paintings depicting historical atrocities, the recording or portrayal of violent acts has always been a part of human history. In the present era of mass communications and geopolitical upheaval, such imagery takes on new forms, new channels, and new meanings.

---

[718] Harvey Kushner with Bart Davis, *Holy War on the Home Front, The Secret Islamic Terror Network in the United States*, (New York: Sentinel, 2004).

Figure 2: Notable Atrocities of the 20th century*

Date	Event	Description	Victims
1921–1939	Stalin's Purges ("the Great Terror"), Soviet Union	Stalin-orchestrated Bolshevik campaign of persecution and political repression aimed at removal of potential rival Communist leaders and party members whose loyalty he doubted, and other social groups	Approximately 1 million dead, 400,000 sentenced to labor camps, 200,000 exiled or deported
1937–1938	"Rape of Nanking" Nanking, China	Imperial Japanese Army capture of Nanking is followed by rape, looting, arson and execution of prisoners of war and civilians, including children, under pretext of eliminating Chinese soldiers disguised as civilians	150,000–300,000 killed
1942	Bataan Death March, Philippines	Nearly 2/3 of 75,000 Filipino and American soldiers who surrendered to Japanese army are forced to walk up to 90 miles over several days to internment camps, during which many were beaten, tortured, killed or died	Approximately 5,000–10,000 Filipino and 600–650 American prisoners of war killed or died
1942–1943	River Kwai ("Death Railway"), Thailand	200,000 Asian laborers and 60,000 Allied prisoners of war forced to build several bridges for Burma Railway and many die from overwork, malnutrition, and disease	100,000 Asian laborers and 16,000 Allied POWs died
1942–1945	Holocaust, Germany, Poland, Belarus	Known as deliberate extermination of Jews by Adolph Hitler-led Nazi regime, victims also included gays, disabled people, Roma, and political prisoners	9–11 million killed (6 millions Jews)
1975–1979	"Killing Fields," Cambodia	Pol Pot-led Communist Khmer Rouge regime tortured and killed nearly everyone suspected of 'pre-revolutionary' acts; mass burial sat sites known as Killing Fields	1.7–2.3 million killed
1994	Rwandan Genocide, Rwanda	Hutu militias attack and kill ethnic Tutsis and moderate Hutu sympathizers during Rwandan civil war	800,000–1 million killed
1995	Srebrenica Massacre, Bosnia and Herzogovinia	Army of Republika Srpska (Serbs) units killed Bosniak males in Srebrenica region during the Bosnian War; other mass killings, rapes, detentions, destruction and deportation committed by Serbian groups	8,000 killed
2003–present	Darfur Genocide, Darfur Sudan	Groups of African Muslims rebelled against the Khartoum government for chronic inequalities between Africans and the ruling Arab Muslim elite. In retaliation, the government armed local militias known as "Janjaweed," who terrorize Africans by destroying villages, killing and maiming men, ransacking food supplies, blocking international assistance, and raping African women to humiliate them and weaken tribal ethnic lines.	200,000–400,000 killed, 2.5 million displaced

*Compiled from various reference and news sources.

Figure 3: Notable terrorist acts of the modern era*

Date	Event	Victims
02/14/79	U.S. Ambassador to Afghanistan Adolph Dubs kidnapped and killed in gunfire between police and captors	1 killed
11/04/79	American diplomats held hostage up to 14 months in Tehran, Iran	66 hostages
11/20/79	Islamic fundamentalists temporarily seize the Grand Mosque in Mecca, Saudi Arabia	254 killed, 600 wounded
10/06/81	Egyptian President Anwar Sadat assassinated by Muslim extremists in Cairo, Egypt	1 killed
01/18/82	Lt. Col. Charles Ray, USA, military attaché to the U.S. embassy in Paris, is killed by the Lebanese Armed Revolutionary Faction	1 killed
08/01/82	Pan Am Flight 830 to Hawaii bombed by Palestinian terrorists while preparing for descent	1 killed, 15 wounded
04/18/83	Hezbollah bombs U.S. embassy in Beirut	63 killed, 120 injured
10/23/83	Hezbollah bombs U.S. Marines HQ and French paratrooper base in Beirut	307 killed, 75 injured
12/12/83	Iranian-sponsored bomb attack on U.S. embassy in Kuwait	6 killed, 80 wounded
1982–1992	Hezbollah kidnaps and murders numerous U.S. officials in Lebanon	30 kidnapped, several killed
01/18/84	Hezbollah murders American University of Beirut president Malcolm Kerr	1 killed
09/20/84	Hezbollah bombs U.S. embassy annex in Aukar, Lebanon	9 killed, 58 injured
04/12/85	Restaurant near USAF base in Madrid, Spain bombed, authorities blame Hezbollah but the case was never solved	18 killed, 82 wounded
06/14/85	Hezbollah hijacks TWA 847 and diverts it to Beirut, singling out a U.S. navy diver and killing him	1 killed
08/08/85	Car bomb detonated at main USAF base in Germany by Palestine-trained radical left-wing German terror group	3 killed, 20 wounded
10/07/85	Palestinian terrorists attack cruise ship Achille Lauro	1 killed
11/23/85	Abu Nidal Organization hijacks Egypt Air flight 648	65 killed

*Compiled from various reference and news sources.

Figure 3: (continued)

Date	Event	Victims
12/27/85	Abu Nidal Organization attacks American and Israeli airline counters in Rome and Vienna	24 killed, 110 wounded
04/02/86	Arab Revolutionary cell detonates bomb on TWA flight 840 during descent	4 killed, 5 injured
04/05/86	Abu Nidal, helped by Libya, bombs West Berlin disco	3 killed, 200+ injured
09/05/86	Abu Nidal hijacks Pan Am 73 in Karachi and detonates hand grenades hours after landing	21 killed, 100 injured
04/14/88	Japanese Red Army, under the direction of Popular Front for the Liberation of Palestine terror group, detonate car bomb outside USO club in Naples	5 killed, 15 injured
12/21/88	Popular Front for the Liberation of Palestine, helped by Libya, detonate bomb on Pan Am 103 over Lockerbie, Scotland	270 killed
01/18–19/91	Iraqi agents attempt bombings of Americans in Indonesia, Philippines and Thailand	n/a
12/29/92	Al Qaeda bomb detonated in a hotel in Aden, Yemen	2 killed
01/25/93	Gunman attacks CIA headquarters in Northern Virginia	2 killed, 3 wounded
02/26/93	First World Trade Center bombing	7 killed, 1040 wounded
04/14/93	Iraqi intelligence agents attempt assassination of George H. W. Bush in Kuwait	None
04/03–04/93	"Black Hawk Down," Mogadishu, Somalia, U.S. military helicopters attacked	18 killed, 84 wounded
12/08/94	Operation Bojinka (Philippines), precursor to 9/11 attacks, foiled by Philippine police	None
03/08/95	Al Qaeda-affiliated terrorists murder U.S. diplomats in Pakistan	2 killed, 1 wounded
11/13/95	bin Laden-connected terrorists bomb U.S. military training complex in Saudi Arabia	7 killed, 50 wounded
06/25/96	Hezbollah bombs Khobar Towers at Dhahran Air Base, Saudi Arabia	19 killed, 500 wounded
02/23/97	Palestinian gunman opens fire on tourists atop Empire State Building	1 killed, 6 wounded
11/12/97	Two Islamic terrorist groups kill American oil company workers and driver	5 killed

Figure 3: (continued)

Date	Event	Victims
02/23/98	bin Laden and al Zawahiri reunite and join forces against U.S.	n/a
08/07/98	Al Qaeda bombs U.S. embassies in Nairobi and Dar es Salaam	224 killed, 5000 wounded
12/98	Iraqi intelligence plots to bomb Radio Free Europe in Prague	None
12/28/98	Yemeni terrorists kidnap and murder western tourists	16 kidnapped, 4 killed
11/12/99	Rocket attacks target U.S. installation in Islamabad	None
08/12/00	4 American mountain climbers kidnapped by Islamic Movement of Uzbekistan, but escape six days later	4 kidnapped
10/12/00	Terrorists bomb the USS *Cole* docked in Aden, Yemen	17 killed, 29 injured
12/20/00	Jemaah Islamiyah set off bombs throughout Manila, including U.S. embassy	22 killed
09/11/01	Al Qaeda hijacks 4 planes and crashes two into the WTC towers, one into the Pentagon, and the fourth crashes in rural western Pennsylvania	2974 killed
09/01	Anthrax sent to U.S. Congress and New York State Government offices, and to several media outlets	5 killed, 17 infected
12/22/01	Richard Reid attempts to destroy American Airlines 63 by detonating shoe bomb	None
07/04/02	Egyptian gunman opens fire at an El Al ticket counter at Los Angeles International Airport	3 killed
11/15/03	Suicide attackers drive truck bombs into two synagogues in Istanbul	25 killed, 300 injured
11/20/03	Suicide bombers detonate truck bombs at the HSBC Bank and the British Consulate in Istanbul.	30 killed, 400 wounded
03/11/04	Series of coordinated bombs explode on four commuter trains during morning rush hour in Madrid, Spain.	191 killed, 1,755 wounded
07/07/05	A series of coordinated terrorist bomb blasts hit London's public transport system during the morning rush hour. Two weeks later, on July 21, there were four more attempted attacks on the public transport system	52 killed, 700 injured

Figure 3: (continued)

Date	Event	Victims
08/10/06	A major anti-terrorist operation disrupts an alleged bomb plot targeting multiple airplanes bound for the United States flying through London's Heathrow Airport.	None
05/07/07	Six men, inspired by Jihadist videos, plotting to kill U.S. soldiers at Fort Dix, are arrested	None
12/27/07	Former Pakistani Prime Minister Benazir Bhutto is assassinated in an Al-Qaeda-linked bombing after speaking at a political rally in Rawalpindi	20 killed

During the Abu Ghraib scandal and in the years before and since, thousands of innocent civilians and heroic coalition forces have lost their lives in the struggle to liberate and rebuild Iraq. Terrorist groups continue to kidnap and slaughter their hostages. Suicide bombers still injure and murder on an all too frequent basis. In October 2005, terrorist and Iraq al Qaeda leader Abu Musab al-Zarqawi was reported to have reaffirmed the slaughter of innocent people, "Islam does not differentiate between civilians and military, but rather distinguishes between Muslims and infidels . . . Muslim blood must be spared . . . but it is permissible to spill infidel blood."[719]

Soldiers make the ultimate sacrifice for the hope of democracy in Iraq. It is easy to get swept up in a story like Abu Ghraib, but it should not be done at the expense of greater offenses — ones that lead to death, violence, bloodshed and chaos. "It is worth noting one of the great lessons of the twentieth century: averting our eyes from evil is easy and perilous."[720] No one should be permitted to look away, especially the media — the shared venue — that allows Americans to see what is happening in the world. They should *not* diminish or suppress the truth of even the hardest of things to observe. Similarly, they should not go to excess in publishing and displaying events in a fashion that distorts or exaggerates perspective and reality.

Abu Ghraib was unacceptable, but it is nowhere near being in the same category as those truly horrendous atrocities — the unimaginable.

---

[719] "Zarqawi Justifies Killing of Civilians," *Washington Times*, October 8, 2005. Zarqawi was killed in an attack on his hiding place on June 7, 2006 in Baqubah, 30 miles north of Baghdad.

[720] Meyer, op. cit.

LIST OF ABBREVIATIONS & ACRONYMS

ALS — American Legal Systems
AMS — American Management Systems
ATF — (Bureau of) Alcohol, Tobacco and Firearms
BCCF — Baghdad Central Correctional Facility
BDE — Brigade
BN — Battalion
BPA — Blanket Purchase Agreement
C2 — (Coalition Task Force) Intelligence Support
C4 — (Coalition Task Force) Logistics Support
CalPERS — California Public Employees' Retirement System
CalSTRS — California State Teachers' Retirement System
CCR — Center for Constitutional Rights
CENTCOM — U.S. Central Command
CEO — Chief Executive Officer
CFLCC — Coalition Forces Land Component Command
CFO — Chief Financial Officer
CI — Counterintelligence
CIA — Central Intelligence Agency
CISG — CACI Iraq Steering Group
CPT — Captain
COL — Colonel
COO — Chief Operating Officer
COR — Contracting Officer Representative
DA — District Attorney
DAIG — Department of the Army Inspector General

DCAA — Defense Contract Audit Agency
DEA — Drug Enforcement Administration
DIA — Defense Intelligence Agency
DOD — Department of Defense
DOI — Department of Interior
DOJ — Department of Justice
EPW — Enemy Prisoner of War
FAQ — Frequently Asked Questions
FAR — Federal Acquisition Regulation
FBI — Federal Bureau of Investigation
FEMA — Federal Emergency Management Agency
G2 — U.S. Army, Intelligence Staff at Corps & Division
G3 — U.S. Army, Operations, Plans, & Training Staff at Corps & Division
G4 — U.S. Army, Logistics Staff at Corps & Division
GAO — Government Accountability Office (formerly known as the
    General Accounting Office)
GP — General Purpose
GSA — General Services Administration
GTMO — Guantanamo Bay, Cuba
HUMINT — Human Intelligence
ICE — Interrogation and Control Element
ICRP — Interrogation and Counter-Resistance Policies
IED — Improvised Explosive Devices
IG — Inspector General
INS — Immigration and Naturalization Services
IO — Investigating Officer
IR — Investor Relations
IROE — Interrogation Rules of Engagement
ISCT — Interrogation Support to Counterterrorism Team
IT — Information Technology
ITO — Iraq Theatre of Operations
J&J — Johnson and Johnson
JIDC — Joint Interrogation and Debriefing Center
JTF — Joint Task Force
LTG — Lieutenant General
M&A — Mergers and Acquisitions
MEJA — Military Extraterritorial Jurisdiction Act

MG — Major General
MI — Military Intelligence
MP — Military Police
MOS — Military Occupational Specialty
MTT — Mobile Training Team
NOIC — Non-commissioned Officer-in-Charge
OGA — Other Government Agency
OIC — Officer-in-Charge
OIF — Operation Iraqi Freedom
OSJA — Office of Staff Judge Advocate
PTG — Premier Technology Group
POGO — Project on Government Oversight
PMF — Private Military Firms
PR — Public Relations
Regulation FD — Regulation Fair Disclosure
RFP — Request for Proposal
ROTC — Reserve Officer Training Corps
R & R — Rest and Relaxation
S&P — Standard & Poor's
SEC — Securities & Exchange Commission
SGT — Sergeant
SJA — Staff Judge Advocate
SST — Staff Sergeant
SOW — Statement of Work
TS/SCI — Top Secret/Sensitive Compartmented Information
UK — United Kingdom
USAREUR — United States Army, European Command

GLOSSARY & TERMS OF INTEREST CONCERNING ISLAM AND THE MIDDLE EAST

97E Military Occupational Specialty (MOS) — was the U.S. Army's classification code (at the time of the occurrences of the Abu Ghraib abuses) for a human intelligence collector, also known as an interrogator.

Abu Ghraib — is a prison located a short distance west of Baghdad, Iraq used by American forces to house detainees. It was previously used by Saddam Hussein for holding and often torturing prisoners. CACI provided the U.S. Army with interrogation, analyst and screener services at the prison from 2003 to 2005. In March 2006, the U.S. announced that it would end operations at Abu Ghraib and transfer the facility to the Iraqi government in June.

Abuse — is the maltreatment or excessive or improper treatment of something or someone. Abuse is typically cruel or detrimental in manner, taking a verbal, physical, and even sexual form.

Army Field Manual 2-22.3, *Human Intelligence Collector Operations* — provides doctrinal guidance, techniques, and procedures governing the employment of human intelligence (HUMINT) collection and analytical assets in support of intelligence needs, including HUMINT operations, the roles and responsibilities of HUMINT collectors, and the roles of those providing command, control, and technical support of HUMINT collection operations. In accordance with the Detainee Treatment Act of 2005, the manual lists the only interrogation approaches and

techniques authorized for use against any detainee, and specifies that some
may also require additional approval before implementation. This manual
is intended for use by military, civilian, and civilian contractor HUMINT
collectors, as well as commanders, staff officers, and military intelligence
(MI) personnel charged with HUMINT collection effort responsibilities.

**Army Field Manual (and Marine Corps Reference Publica-
tion) 3-24, *Counterinsurgency Field Manual*** — is a joint Army and
Marine Corps effort that establishes doctrine (fundamental principles)
for military operations in a counterinsurgence environment. It provides
guidance to ground forces to achieve success in counterinsurgency operations, discusses historical approaches to counterinsurgency taken by
American forces, and highlights the importance of continually evaluating the circumstances of a counterinsurgency campaign so forces can
adapt their actions. The manual is intentionally broad in scope and involves principles applicable to various areas of operation, such as extending the military's responsibilities to include tasks like nation-build-
ing, aiding the rebuilding of infrastructure, and facilitating the
establishment of local governance and the rule of law.

Article 15-6 Investigation — is a military inquiry into the facts surrounding offenses allegedly committed by a member of a command; part
of the Uniform Code of Military Justice procedures.

The Brookings Institution — is an independent, nonpartisan organization devoted to research, analysis, and public education with an
emphasis on economics, foreign policy, governance, and metropolitan
policy. Journalists sometimes describe Brookings as "centrist" or "liberal," though some critics on the left view it as conservative. At the same
time, staunch conservatives have been vocal in their criticism of Brookings as a liberal institution. Other observers have also noted the organization's leftist leanings. Although the think tank has received funding
from such libertarian groups as The Bradley Foundation, known for its
advocacy of laissez-faire capitalism, prominent center-left figures such
as Teresa Heinz Kerry are also supporters. The current president is
Strobe Talbott, who previously was the Deputy Secretary of State during
the Clinton administration and is a former editor at Time Magazine.
Brookings currently has over 200 resident and nonresident scholars.

CACI International Inc (CACI) — is a publicly owned, Delaware-
chartered corporation traded on the New York Stock Exchange (NYSE:

CAI). Founded in 1962, CACI is headquartered in Arlington, VA and provides information technology and network solutions to the federal government. CACI has approximately 11,500 employees in over 100 offices around the world (December 2007). The company's revenue was approximately $1.94 billion in its fiscal year 2007 (ended June 30, 2007).

Center for Constitutional Rights (CCR) — describes itself as a non-profit legal and educational organization dedicated to protecting and advancing the rights guaranteed by the U.S. Constitution and the Universal Declaration of Human Rights. Critics argue CCR is a "legal left" organization founded and led by radical, far left-wing lawyers who have exploited high-profile events, like the Abu Ghraib scandal, to promote their own political views and agenda, most recently against U.S. foreign policy.

Church Report — is the March 2005 report by Vice Admiral Albert T. Church, III on Department of Defense interrogation operations, particulary on the development of approved interrogation policy, the actual employment of interrogation techniques, and what role, if any, these played in the detainee abuses. Also investigated was the use of civilian contractors in interrogation operations, the support or participation of the DoD in interrogation activities of other government agencies, and medical issues relating to interrogations. It reported that contractors were bridging gaps in military resources, although it concluded that a few were alleged to be marginally involved in lesser incidents of mistreatment.

Civilian Contractors — are companies and their employees who provide services and/or products in performance of a legal government contractual obligation. The contracts for services and/or products are usually part of a negotiated contractual process that binds the government and the contracted party to specific obligations, services, and stipulations covered by federal acquisition regulations. These companies and their employees may be deployed in theaters of war.

Classification — is the determination that official information requires, in the interests of national security, a specific degree of protection against unauthorized disclosure, coupled with a designation signifying that such a determination has been made. It is also the category to which national security information and material is assigned to denote the degree of damage that unauthorized disclosure would cause to national defense or foreign relations of the United States and to denote the degree of protection required. The three most common classifications are:

Top Secret — National security information or material that requires the highest degree of protection and the unauthorized disclosure of which could reasonably be expected to cause exceptionally grave damage to the national security.

Secret — National security information or material that requires a substantial degree of protection and the unauthorized disclosure of which could reasonably be expected to cause serious damage to the national security.

Confidential — National security information or material that requires protection and the unauthorized disclosure of which could reasonably be expected to cause damage to the national security.

Conservative — refers to the political philosophy of conservatism, traditionalism, or belonging to a conservative party, group, or movement. Conservatism is a political philosophy or attitude emphasizing respect for individual rights, traditional institutions, social customs, and the rule of law. It also entails distrust of entrenched government and judicial activism, large paternalistic government, and opposition to sudden, radical and disorderly change in the established order and social system. This includes the inclination toward a more strict interpretation of the U.S. Constitution and the Bill of Rights. The Republican Party is typically associated with conservatism.

Contracting Officer (CO) — is a U.S. military officer or civilian employee who has the authority to enter into and administer contracts and determinations as well as findings about such contracts. This individual is appointed under the provisions of the Federal Acquisition Regulation.

Contract Officer's Representative (COR) — is an individual designated by a contracting officer in accordance with subsection 201.602-2 of the Defense Federal Acquisition Regulation Supplement and authorized in writing by the contracting officer to perform specific technical or administrative functions.

Counterintelligence (CI) — is information gathered and activities conducted to protect against espionage, other adversarial or enemy intelligence activities, sabotage, or assassinations conducted by or on behalf of foreign governments or elements thereof, foreign organizations, individual foreigners, or international terrorist activities.

Court(s) Martial — is (are) a military court that determines guilt or non-guilt, and proper punishments for members of the military subject to military law, known as the Uniform Code of Military Justice (UMCJ). They are generally found in all countries with militaries to try members of the military for breaches of military discipline. In addition, they may be used to try enemy prisoners of war for war crimes, and the Geneva Conventions require that POWs who are on trial for war crimes be subject to the same procedures as the holding army's own soldiers would be.

DD Form 489 — is a Geneva Convention Identity Card for civilians who accompany the Armed Forces.

DD Form 1173 — is a tan colored ID Card for active duty family members and military retirees and their dependents, which authorize access to commissary exchange and certain morale, welfare and recreation privileges.

Defense Contract Audit Agency (DCAA) — was established by a Department of Defense (DoD) directive to perform all contract auditing for the agency and provide accounting and financial advisory services for DoD procurement and contract administration activities.

Department of Defense Directive 2310.01E — reissued a 1994 directive to revise policy and responsibilities within the Department of Defense for a Detainee Program to ensure compliance with the laws of the United States, the laws of war, including Geneva Conventions of 1949, and all applicable policies, directives, or other issuances.

Detainee — is a person held in custody for questioning or interrogation; sometimes defined as being held for a political offense. In the Global War on Terror, a detainee may be held in confinement pending a final determination of status. A detainee may be a terrorist, insurgent or enemy combatant/collaborator, spy or informant, and can include persons questioned for terrorist and terror-related activities.

Detainee Treatment Act of 2005 — was an amendment to the 2006 United States Senate Department of Defense Appropriations Act introduced by Arizona Senator John McCain. It became the Detainee Treatment Act of 2005 as Title X of the Department of Defense Authorization bill. The amendment prohibits inhumane treatment of prisoners, including prisoners at Guantanamo Bay, Cuba, by confining interrogations to the techniques in FM 34-52 Intelligence Interrogation. (See also Army Field Manual FM2-22.3).

"Do the Right Thing" — is CACI's basic business ethic, brought to bear with added emphasis during the company's Abu Ghraib ordeal of 2004.

Espionage — is the act of obtaining, delivering, transmitting, communicating, or receiving information about national defense with an intent, or reason to believe, that the information may be used to the injury of the United States or to the advantage of any foreign nation. Espionage is a violation of 18 United States Code 792-798 and Article 106, Uniform Code of Military Justice.

Fay Report — is the August 2004 report by Major General George W. Fay, Lieutenant General Anthony R. Jones, and General Paul J. Kern of the AR 15-6 investigation of the Abu Ghraib prison and 205th Military Intelligence Brigade, an Army inquiry on the role of military intelligence personnel in prisoner abuse at the Abu Ghraib facility in Iraq.

Federal Acquisition Regulation (FAR) — is the primary regulation for use by all federal executive agencies in their contracting and acquisition of supplies and services with U.S. government-appropriated funds.

Geneva Conventions — consist of multilateral treaties formulated in Geneva, Switzerland that set the standards for international law for humanitarian concerns, particularly to protect the victims of conflicts. The conventions consist of four treaties that cover topics including the treatment of casualties, civilians, prisoners of war, and medical personnel. The first convention was established in 1863, with three more added and revised in 1949. In 1977 and 2005 three separate amendments, called protocols, were made part of the Conventions. Nearly all 200 countries of the world are "signatory" nations, meaning that they have ratified these conventions and enacted national laws to make grave violations of the Conventions a punishable criminal offense. However, nonstate and terrorist organizations are not signatories to the Conventions.

Get it Right — is a July 2004 plan by the General Services Administration (GSA) to ensure the proper use of GSA contracting vehicles and services in order to be in full compliance with the Federal Acquisition Regulation and best practices.

GI — is an enlisted person in or a veteran of any of the U.S. armed forces, especially a person enlisted in the army; GI actually is G1 ("gee one," using the Roman numeral I). G1 is a standard regular fighting soldier, military personnel section. G2 is the staff intelligence section.

Many incorrectly believe that GI stands for 'Government Issue' or 'General Inductee'.

Government Contracting — refers to the practice of the government (federal, state, and local) acquiring a vast array goods and services from suppliers. Contracts are awarded to responsible companies offering commercial items (or special purpose items uniquely required by the government) at fair and reasonable prices, as determined by a Contracting Officer. While there are several other contracting methods not addressed here, the three primary types of contracts are:

Fixed Price Contracts — aim to control or reduce costs and perform efficiently. The contractor assumes maximum risk and full responsibility for all costs and resulting profit, but it also provides maximum incentive for the contractor to control costs and perform effectively. Firm Fixed Price contracts are the government's preferred method of contracting and are used when a sealed bid is involved and for acquiring fully specified supplies and services and/or for acquiring commercial items. Government management flexibility over Fixed Price Contracts is minimal or negligible.

Cost Reimbursement Contracts — provide for payment of allowable incurred costs, to the extent prescribed in the contract. These contracts establish an estimate of total costs for the purpose of obligating funds and also establish a ceiling that the contractor may not exceed, except at their own risk. Cost reimbursement contracts place the least cost and performance risk on the contractor. Cost reimbursement contracts are suitable for use only when uncertainties involved in contract performance do not permit costs to be estimated with sufficient accuracy to use any type of fixed price contract. They are generally used for research and development contracts or when maximum government management flexibility over contract implementation is required. They are generally prohibited for the acquisition of commercial items.

Time and Material Contracts — are used only when it is not possible to estimate accurately the extent or duration of the work or to anticipate costs with any reasonable degree of confidence. Therefore, the contractors bill direct labor hours at specified hourly rates and charges any required and pre-approved materials at cost. Time and material contracts are often used for services, supplies and materials. CACI's intelligence and interrogator support services contracts for the U.S. Army in Iraq and at Abu Ghraib were of this type.

Guantanamo Bay — is a U.S. Navy base located on the south side of Cuba serving as the cornerstone of U.S. military operations in the Caribbean Theater. It provides logistics support to both U.S. Navy and Coast Guard vessels and aircraft. The base also houses the Joint Task Force Guantanamo, which conducts detention and interrogation operations, coordinates and implements detainee screening operations, and supports law enforcement and war crimes investigations.

Habeas Corpus — is a court order addressed to a prison official (or other custodian) ordering that a prisoner be brought before the court for determination of whether that person is serving a lawful sentence and/or whether he or she should be released from custody. The writ of habeas corpus in common law countries is an important instrument for the safeguarding of individual freedom against arbitrary state action.

Human Intelligence (HUMINT) — is the intelligence derived from the intelligence collection discipline that uses human beings as both sources and collectors, and where the human being is the primary collection instrument. Sources may be informants or spies. Information and intelligence may be obtained through interrogation of detainees or prisoners.

Humiliation — is to hurt the pride or dignity of a person or group. While humiliation can be self-inflicted, humiliation of one person by another is often used as a way of asserting power over others, and is a common form of intimidation, oppression or abuse.

Information Technology (IT) — is broadly defined as the development, installation, and implementation of computer systems, networks and applications.

Insurgent — is a person who rises in forcible, militant opposition to lawful authority, especially a person who engages in armed resistance to a government or to the execution of its laws. An insurgent, also known as a rebel, seditionist, anarchist, can be a member of a section of a political party that revolts against the methods or policies of that party. Insurgents' motivations can vary widely, and can include factors such as ideology, politics, economics, religion, morality, culture, ethnicity, society or a combination of these factors.

Intelligence — is the product resulting from the collection, processing, analysis, evaluation and interpretation of available information and knowledge obtained through covert or overt observation, investigation, analysis, or understanding. It is typically gathered and prepared concerning a foreign government, individual, or organizational adversaries, enemies, combatants or terrorists and collected from people (i.e., prisoners, informants, or spies) or from a wide variety of technological collection or listening means (Also see HUMINT).

Interrogation — is the methodical, systematic examination of an individual, typically by questioning, in a formal or official manner to obtain specific useful information and intelligence. Interrogations are typically used to derive such information from detained persons, including criminal suspects, prisoners of war, terrorists or insurgents.

Interrogator — is someone who conducts interrogations on a professional basis.

KUBARK — was a cryptonym for the CIA's counterintelligence collections operation in the early 1960's. The operation also produced a Counterintelligence Interrogation Manual in 1963 (declassified in 1997) that is considered symbolic of the sometimes clandestine, coercive and brutal nature of the Cold War.

Left wing — refers to the liberal or socialist section of a political party or system. Also known as liberals, seculars, progressives, socialists, the more extreme elements can include radical, far left-wing, totalitarian, or communist factions.

Liberal — refers to the political philosophy of liberalism, progressivism, or belonging to a liberal party, group, or movement. Liberalism is a political theory founded on the belief in the natural goodness of humans and the autonomy of the individual and favoring civil and political liberties, government by law with the consent of the governed, and protection from arbitrary authority. The Democratic Party is commonly associated with liberalism.

Media — is a means of mass communication, such as print, radio and television broadcast, Internet, and wireless transmission. It also refers to the group of journalists and others who constitute the public communications industry and profession.

Mercenary — is a paid soldier who serves in a foreign army (but not in a war directly involving his own country). In most cases, the term 'mercenary' refers to a soldier who is fighting or engaging in warfare essentially for private gain, usually with little regard for ideological, national, or political considerations. As a result of the assumption that a mercenary is normally motivated by money, the term "mercenary" sometimes carries negative connotations.

Military Commission Act of 2006 — authorizes the President to establish military commissions to try "unlawful enemy combatants". The act prohibits these combatants from invoking the Geneva Conventions as a source of rights during commission proceedings and filing *habeas corpus* petitions in federal court. The commissions are also authorized to impose any punishment not forbidden by the Uniform Code of Military Justice, including the death penalty. Under the Act, each commission must have at least five members, who are any commissioned officer on active duty in the Armed Forces. Each commission is also assigned a military judge trial and defense counsel, court reporters and interpreters.

Military Extraterritorial Jurisdiction Act (MEJA) — provides for federal jurisdiction over crimes committed abroad by civilians who are accompanying or employed by the U.S. military. Enacted in 2000, the statute covers all civilian employees of the military, as well as civilian contractors (and subcontractors), employees of contractors (and subcontractors), and dependents residing with these workers. MEJA covers both citizens and non-citizens, except for those who are nationals of, or ordinarily resident in, the host country. MEJA also covers discharged and, in some cases, active duty members of the armed services. MEJA creates no new substantive offenses, but incorporates a range of existing federal criminal offenses that may be used to prosecute defense contractors, media and others who commit crimes outside U.S. territory.

Patriot Act — is the name by which *The Uniting and Strengthening America by Providing Appropriate Tools Required to Intercept and Obstruct Terrorism Act of 2001* (Public Law 107-56) is known. The act was signed into law in October 2001 and renewed in March of 2006. Although the bill received Congressional and Presidential support, it is a controversial piece of federal legislation. The act was a response to the terrorist attacks against the United States and dramatically expanded the authority of American law enforcement for the stated purpose of fighting terrorism in the United States and abroad. The Act increased the authority of law enforcement agencies to search telephone and email communications, as well as financial, medical and other records. The Act also amended immigration, banking, and money laundering laws as well as the Foreign Intelligence Surveillance Act. It has also been used to detect and prosecute other alleged potential crimes, such as providing false information on terrorism. Federal courts declared some sections of the act unconstitutional because they encroached upon civil liberties. The act also extended the definition of those involved in terrorism to include domestic terrorism.

Prisoner of War (POW) — also known as an Enemy Prisoner of War (EPW), is a person who is captured and held as an enemy during war, especially a member of the enemy armed forces. U.S. policy determined that those individuals that belong to terrorist organizations or promote such activities are excluded from the POW/EPW categories. Al Qaeda members are an example of this exclusion.

Private Military Company (PMC) — is a for-profit enterprise, sometimes a corporation or a limited liability partnership, which provides specialized services and expertise related to activites formerly associated with the government. The services and expertise include defense functions, military training, force protection, and security tasks. While PMCs often provide services to supplement operations involving official armed forces, they also are used to undertake security tasks where no state actor is involved, such as personal security details. PMCs tend to be concentrated in areas of low intensity conflict, where deploying traditional armed forces might be too politically, diplomatically, or economically risky. However, they also collaborate with strong states providing military training and in endeavors associated with the enhancement of homeland security. PMCs are also known as "private security companies" or "security contractors," although the latter term usually refers to individuals employed or contracted by PMCs. Services are mainly rendered for other business corporations, international and non-governmental organizations, and state forces. Private military companies are sometimes grouped into the general category of defense contractors. However, most defense contractors supply specialized hardware and weaponry and sometimes personnel to support and service such equipment, whereas PMCs supply personnel with specialized operational and tactical skills, which often include combat experience.

Propaganda — is the deliberate (often media-based) dissemination of false or misleading information or ideas with specific intent to further one's cause or to damage an opposing cause by attempting to influence or convince with emotional emphasis, promote or oppose opinions, events, organizations or outcomes.

Right wing — refers to the conservative section of a political party or system. Also called conservative or reactionary, the more extreme elements can include radical, ultra-conservative, far right-wing, totalitarian, or facist groups.

Rule of Law — is an authoritative legal doctrine, principle, or precept applied to the facts of an appropriate case; the "rule of law" is generally associated with concepts such as *Nullum crimen, nulla poena sine praevia lege poenali* (there can be no crime committed, and no punishment meted out, without a violation of penal law as it existed at the time), no *ex post facto* laws; also includes the concepts of presumption of innocence, double jeopardy, legal equality, and *habeas corpus*.

Due Process — is the administration of justice according to established rules and principles. It is based on the principle that a person cannot be deprived of life, liberty or property without appropriate legal procedures and safeguards.

Innocent Until Proven Guilty — is the principle that no person shall be considered guilty until convicted by a court of law in which the prosecution has the burden of proof to convince the court that the accused is guilty beyond a reasonable doubt (also known as "presumption of innocence).

Ryder Report — is a November 2003 report of the investigation by former Provost General Maj. Gen. Donald Ryder to conduct an assessment of detainee operations in Afghanistan and Iraq. Recommendations included that the duties of the Military Police troops who guard detainees should be kept strictly separated from those of the Military Intelligence troops who interrogate them.

Schlesinger Report — is an August 2004 report of an independent panel lead by the Hon. James R. Schlesinger to review Department of Defense detention operations.

Screener — is someone who is responsible for reviewing and managing select security programs and classifying detainees, local service contractor employees, etc., and who provides support to military police and interrogators.

Secret/No Foreign Dissemination — is a security classification for government and military documents. "Secret" refers to national security information or material that requires a substantial degree of protection and the unauthorized disclosure of which could reasonably be expected to cause serious damage to the national security. Examples of "serious damage" include disruption of foreign relations significantly affecting the national security; significant impairment of a program or policy directly related to the national security; revelation of significant military plans or intelligence operations; and compromise of significant scientific or technological developments relating to national security. "No foreign" means that foreigners may not see nor be provided any knowledge about the document or information.

Security Clearance — is an administrative determination by a competent authority that an individual is eligible, from a security standpoint, for access to classified information. Basic clearances start with Confidential, Secret and Top Secret. More advanced clearances include Top Secret/SCI (Sensitive Compartmented Information) or SAP (Special Access Programs).

Spy — is a person employed by a government (or any organization) to obtain secret information or intelligence about the activities, plans, methods of another person, organization or (usually) hostile country, especially with reference to military or government affairs.

Statement of Work (SOW) — is a document primarily for use in procurement, which specifies the work requirements for a project or program. It is used in conjunction with specifications and standards as a basis for a contract. It is also used to determine whether the contractor meets stated performance requirements.

Taguba Report — is the *illegally leaked* (SECRET/NO FOREIGN DISSEMINATION) Article 15-6 Investigation report prepared by Maj. Gen. Antonio M. Taguba in March 2004 on alleged abuse of prisoners by members of the 800th Military Police Brigade at the Abu Ghraib Prison in Baghdad. It was ordered by Lt. Gen. Ricardo Sanchez, Commander of Joint Task Force-7, the senior U.S. military official in Iraq, following persistent allegations of human rights abuses at the prison.

Terrorist — is a term used to describe violence or other harmful (particularly murderous) acts and the persons who perpetrate them, committed (or threatened) against innocent civilians by individuals or groups for political, ideological, nationalist, or religious goals. Using a type of unconventional, asymmetric or irregular warfare, terrorists attempts to weaken or supplant existing political landscapes through capitulation, acquiescence, or radicalization, as opposed to solely using acts of aggressive subversion, rebellion or direct military action.

Terrorism — is the calculated use of unlawful violence or threat of unlawful violence to instill fear. It is intended to coerce or to intimidate persons, governments or societies in the pursuit of goals that are generally political, religious, or ideological, and often seditionist or anarchist in intent.

"The Truth Will Out" — is a phrase used in the play *The Merchant of Venice* by William Shakespeare. In Act 2, Scene 2, a character named Launcelot says, "Well, old man, I will tell you news of your son, give me your blessing, truth will come to light, murder cannot be hid long, a man's son may, but in the end truth will out." It was the project title chosen for CACI's efforts to manage the allegations and accusations stemming from the company's interrogation work at Abu Ghraib prison.

Torture — is to intentionally inflict or cause severe, extreme physical and mental pain and suffering, excruciating agony for coercion or punishment, intimidation, obtaining information or confession, or for intentional cruelty.

Traitor — is someone who betrays one's country, a cause, or a trust, especially one who commits treason. It also refers generally to a person who says one thing and deceitfully does another.

Treason — is a violation of allegiance toward one's country or sovereign, especially the betrayal of one's country by waging war against it or by consciously and purposely acting to aid its enemies as defined by the Constitution. It also refers generally to a betrayal of trust or confidence.

"Tylenol Case" — refers to the 1982 public relations and product tampering crisis when seven people in Chicago died after they had ingested Extra-Strength Tylenol capsules, which were later determined to have been laced with cyanide. The deaths made national news and caused a massive, nationwide panic. The poisonings made it necessary for Tylenol maker Johnson & Johnson to immediately launch a public relations program in order to save the integrity of both their product and their corporation as a whole.

Uniform Code of Military Justice — is the foundation of U.S. military law. Passed into law in 1950, the UCMJ is found in Title 10, Subtitle A, Part II, Chapter 47 of the United States Code. UCMJ is a federal law created by Congress which applies to all members of the uniformed services of the U.S.

V Corps — is the army's contingency force for European and Central Command missions with more than 42,000 soldiers and civilians. Based in Heidelburg, Germany, the V Corps serves in the European Command and is the U.S. Army's only forward-deployed corps headquarters.

Vigilance — is the process of paying close and continuous attention, and to be alert and watchful, especially to avoid danger.

War Crimes Act of 1996 — defines a war crime to include a "grave breach of the Geneva Conventions," specifically noting that "grave breach" should have the meaning defined in any convention (related to the laws of war) to which the U.S. is a party. The definition of "grave breach" in some of the Geneva Conventions has text that extend additional protections, but all the Conventions share the following text in common: ". . . committed against persons or property protected by the Convention: wilful killing, torture or inhuman treatment, including biological experiments, willfully causing great suffering or serious injury to body or health." The law applies if either the victim or the perpetrator is a national of the United States or a member of the U.S. armed forces. The penalty may be life imprisonment or death. The death penalty is only invoked if the conduct resulted in the death of one or more victims.

Whistleblower — is a current or former member of an organization, usually a business or government agency, who reports misconduct to people or entities (often the media) that have the power and presumed willingness to take corrective action. The reported misconduct is generally illegal or a threat to public interest, i.e., fraud, health, safety violations, or corruption. There are over fifty federal laws and numerous state statutes that govern whistleblowing and retaliation against the whistleblower. Some major statutes include the Whistleblower Protection Act (5 U.S.C. § 1221(e)), Military Whistleblower Protection Act (10 U.S.C. § 1034), and protections are offered in other legislation, including the 2002 Sarbanes-Oxley Act.

Terms of Interest Concerning Islam and the Middle East

Abu Ayyub al-Masri (possibly also identified as Abu Hamza al-Muhajer) — is an Egyptian Islamic Jihad militant and member of al Qaeda in Iraq. He was a senior aide to former leader Abu Musab al-Zarqawi, who was killed in a U.S. airstrike on June 7, 2006. He reportedly succeeded al-Zarqawi as the leader of al Qaeda in Iraq.

Abu Hamza al-Masri — was a Muslim cleric and the former imam of London mosque. Hamza, who has publicly expressed support for al Qaeda and Osama bin Laden, also led the "Supporters of Sharia", a group dedicated to the rule of Islamic law. He has been linked to bomb plots in Yemen, attempts to establish a terrorist training camp in Oregon, and providing aid to al Qaeda. In October 2004, Hamza, who denounced the U.K.'s involvement in the War in Iraq, was charged with 16 crimes under the provisions of various U.K. anti-terror statutes. He was convicted of eleven charges in February 2006 and is currently serving a seven year prison term for soliciting murder and inciting racial hatred. Hamza is also notable for having lost both his hands and the use of his left eye and currently uses a hook as his right hand.

Abu Musab Al-Zarqawi — was a Jordanian jihadi commander who was the purported leader of al Qaeda in Iraq. He was killed in an air attack on his hiding place on June 7, 2006 in Baqubah, 30 miles north of Baghdad. His terror network has been active in Europe, Afghanistan, Iraq, and Africa. Zarqawi's terror group is considered the main source of kidnappings, bombings, and assassination attempts in Iraq. Although he was thought to have had links with the global al Qaeda network, some terrorism experts regarded his group as autonomous — perhaps even a rival to Osama bin Laden's organization — although this has been debated by some.

Abu Ubayd al-Qurashi — is believed to be a top aide of Osama bin Laden and an al Qaeda strategist.

Al-Ansar — is an Arab language publication purportedly published by al Qaeda.

Al-Gama'a al-Islamiyya (The Islamic Group) — is a militant Egyptian Islamist movement, led by blind cleric Omar Abdel-Rahman, that is considered to be a terrorist organization by the United States, European Union and Egyptian governments. The group is dedicated to overthrowing the Egyptian government and replacing it with an Islamic state.

Al Jazeera — meaning "The Island," is an Arabic-language television channel based in Doha, Qatar. Its willingness to broadcast dissenting views, including those on call-in shows, created controversies in the autocratic Persian Gulf Arab States. The station gained worldwide attention following the September 11, 2001 attacks, when it broadcast video statements by Osama bin Laden and other al Qaeda leaders. Al Jazeera operates several specialized channels including Al Jazeera Sports, Al Jazeera Live (conferences in real time without editing or commentary), and the Al Jazeera Children's Channel. Al Jazeera International, an English-language channel was launched in November 2006. In addition to its TV channels, Al Jazeera operates Arabic and English-language Web sites.

Al Qaeda — or "The Base," was formed in 1988 by Osama bin Laden and his associate Mohammed Atef to bring together Arabs who fought in Afghanistan against the Soviet invasion. It serves as a focal point or umbrella entity for a global network that includes terrorist cells in various — currently estimated at over 60 — countries. A common factor in all these groups is the use of terror (including suicide bombings, murders, etc.) for the attainment of their goal of overthrowing what they perceive to be "heretic" regimes and the establishment of an Islamist regime in such countries. Al Qaeda sees the United States as providing support to the various "heretic" regimes of the world, including Saudi Arabia, Egypt, Israel and the United Nations. Al Qaeda was also responsible for the attacks on the U.S. on September 11, 2001, which killed nearly 3,000 innocent civilian victims.

Ayatollah — is a title among Shi'ites in the religious hierarchy achieved by scholars who have demonstrated highly advanced knowledge of Islamic law and religion; also used as a formal title for such leader.

Ayman al-Zawahri — is the second in charge of al Qaeda. Zawahri gave up the affluent life of a Cairo doctor to dedicate himself to the Islamist underground. In the 1960s he joined Egypt's Muslim Brotherhood, the Arab world's oldest and largest Islamist group. He was tried, along with many others, for links to the 1981 assassination of Egyptian President Anwar Sadat but was acquitted of the main charges and only served a three-year jail term for illegal arms possession. In 1985, Zawahri left Egypt for Pakistan, where he worked as a doctor treating fighters wounded in battles against Soviet forces occupying neighboring Afghanistan. In 1993, he took over the leadership of Jihad, Egypt's second largest Islamic armed group. Zawahri joined forces with bin Ladin in 1998. He has been indicted in connection with the 1998 bombings of the U.S. embassies in Kenya and Tanzania. A military court in Egypt sentenced Zawahri to death "in absentia" in 1999 for militant activities.

Baath Party — (also known as the Arab Socialist Baath Party) was founded in 1947 as a radical, secular Arab nationalist political party. It functioned as a pan-Arab party with branches in different Arab countries, but was strongest in Syria and Iraq, coming to power in both countries in 1963. In 1966 the Syrian and Iraqi parties split into two rival organizations. Both Baath parties retained the same name, and maintain parallel structures in the Arab world. The Baathists ruled Iraq briefly in 1963, and then again from July 1968 until 2003. After the *de facto* deposition of President Saddam Hussein's Baathist regime in the course of the 2003 Iraq war, the government authorities banned the Iraqi Baath Party in June 2003.

Caliph (Caliphate) — is a male leader of an Islamic polity, regarded as a successor of Muhammad and was used to refer to any of the former Muslim rulers of Baghdad (until 1258) and of the Ottoman Empire (from 1571 until 1924). The office or jurisdiction of a caliph is called a *caliphate*. Ottoman Turkish sultans held the last caliphate until it was abolished by Mustafa Kemal Atatürk in 1924.

Dawah — means "to invite" in Arabic, but is also translated as "the call to Islam." The word's use in the religion means an invitation to the submission and surrender to Allah (God) and Islam. Muslims are considered to have an obligation to invite (or convert) others to Islam. Dawah is sometimes referred to as the act of preaching (proselytizing) Islam.

Dhimmi — was a "free" (non-slave), non-Muslim subject of a state governed in accordance with sharia (Islamic law). The word means "protected" or "guilty" in Arabic. A *dhimmi* is a person of the *dhimma*, a term in Islamic law which refers to a "pact" contracted between non-Muslims and authorities from their ruling Islamic government. This status was originally only made available to non-Muslims who were "People of the Book," (specifically Jews and Christians), but later was extended to other conquered or subjagated peoples. The dhimma, as a protected minority, were allowed religious freedoms, subject to certain social restrictions and legal limitations, and were provided protection in exchange for subservience and loyalty to the Islamic order and a poll tax known as *jizya*. Some Muslim scholars express opinions justifying the imposition of the jizya on non-Muslims living under Muslim rule, based on Sura 9:29 of the Koran: "You shall fight back against those who do not believe in Allah, nor in the Last Day, nor do they prohibit what Allah and His messenger have prohibited, nor do they abide by the religion of truth — among those who received the scripture — until they pay the due tax, willingly or unwillingly." [Note: There are slight variations in other translation of the Arabic text.]

Fatwa — is a legal opinion or ruling issued by an Islamic scholar or Imam. It is frequently associated with a judicial-styled pronouncement and may be about a person, a government, or a social custom. A fatwa may declare and call for the death or execution of an individual or group. The most widely known "execution" fatwa was the one pronounced against *The Satanic Verses* author Salman Rushdie in 1989 by the Ayatollah Khomeini. The fatwa caused the attacks, injuries, and even murders of several dozen people — both Muslim and non-Muslims — many of whom were associated with the translation or publishing of the book. In 1999, an Iranian foundation reportedly put a $2.8 million bounty on killing Rushdie.

Hadith — are sacred sayings attributed to Muhammed, which were originally handed down by oral tradition, but later written down. While the Koran is the primary scripture in Islam, the Hadith exist as an additional or secondary form of scripture and consists of anecdotes about Muhammed's statements, actions, or his affirmations of other's actions, as this was all held to be with the inspiration of Allah (God). Around the 9th century scholars began to assemble those writings regarded as authentic. There are now six such collections, each consisting of several thousand anecdotes, sayings, and traditions that have now been established as a canonical repository (*the Hadith*) for use in deciding various points of Islamic law (Sharia) and related theological doctrines.

Hamas — or "Islamic Resistance Movement" (the Arabic acronym means "zeal") is a Palestinian Sunni Islamist organization that currently (since January 2006) forms the majority party of the Palestinian National Authority. Created in 1987 by the Gaza wing of the Muslim Brotherhood at the beginning of the First Intifada, Hamas is known outside of the Palestinian territories chiefly for its targeted suicide bombings and other attacks directed against Israeli civilians, as well as against military and security forces. Hamas is listed as a terrorist organization by many nations, including the U.S., but Hamas' supporters see it as a legitimate resistance movement fighting the Israeli occupation of the Palestinian territories. Hamas has gained further popularity by establishing extensive welfare programs, funding schools, orphanages, and healthcare clinics, throughout the West Bank and Gaza Strip.

Hezbollah — meaning "party of God," is a Shi'a Islamist militant and political organization based in Lebanon with reported links to the Iranian government (The Islamic Republic of Iran). It follows a distinct version of Islamic Shia ideology developed by Ayatollah Ruhollah Khomeini, leader of the 1979 Islamic Revolution in Iran.

Imam — is an Arabic word meaning "leader," often being the head of a congregation who leads them in prayer. The Shia Muslims believe that an Imam is someone who is able to lead mankind in all aspects of life whereas for Sunni Muslims the term is also used for a recognized religious leader or teacher in Islam.

Islam — is a monotheistic religion founded in Arabia in the early part of the 7th century. It is characterized by the doctrine of submission to Allah (God) and recognition of Muhammed (570–632) as the final prophet. Muhammed is known as the founder of Islam and called the messenger of God. He was a religious, political and warrior leader of Arabs in and around Medina and Mecca up to circa 630 A.D., with an army said at one point to be as many as 10,000 strong (reports vary with some saying much less). Followers of Islam are referred to as Muslims (those who submit to Allah). Muslim is also a commonly used as a term that refers to the people or nations that practice Islam and, in general, to the Muslim world. The early expansion of Islam — the Muslim world — came in the 7th to 9th centuries, spreading throughout the Middle East, North Africa, and east toward India. Islam's first major foray into Europe was through the Iberian Peninsula, but was halted in 732 A.D. at the Battle of Tours where the Franks, led by Charles Martel, defeated the Umayyad Caliphate army. The next significant Islamic move into

Europe was the conquests of the Ottoman Empire, which were stymied during the siege of Vienna in 1529. Most of the Islamic world today is found in the Middle East, North Africa, parts of sub-Saharan Africa, and extends east through Afghanistan, Pakistan and parts of India. There is also a large Muslim population in South East Asia. In 2007, there were some 1.5 billion Muslims in the world.

Jihad — refers to a 'holy war' undertaken by Muslims against unbelievers. In Arabic, its literal meaning is "to strive" or "effort," but is also expressed as a sacred duty by Muslims to "struggle in the way of Allah (God)." Jihad can also mean the protection and expansion of an Islamic state, as jihad is the only form of warfare permissible under Islamic law. When interpreted as a 'holy war,' jihad can include overthrowing governments that fail to enforce the Sharia, or Islamic law. (See Sharia) Historically, jihad has been viewed as a holy war fought as a sacred duty by Muslims, but also broadly refers to any vigorous or emotional support for an idea or principle. *Jihadi* is one who undertakes a jihad.

Jizya — is the poll tax formerly paid by minority religious groups within the Muslim empire. (See Dhimmi)

Kafir — is an Arabic word meaning "ingrate," although it is most often translated into English as "infidel." In Islam it refers to a person who does not recognize Allah (as the one true God) or Muhammed as his prophet; a person who hides, denies or covers the truth. It is also used as a derogatory term to describe non-believers, non-Muslims, apostates from Islam and sometimes between different sects of Muslims.

Khalid Sheikh Mohammed — is a former al Qaeda commander in Kuwait and self-admitted mastermind behind the September 11, 2001 terror attacks. Captured in Pakistan in March 2003, Mohammed spent four years in U.S. custody. By March 2007, he had confessed to masterminding the September 11 attacks, the Richard Reid shoe bombing attempt to blow up an airliner over the Atlantic Ocean, the Bali nightclub bombing in Indonesia, the 1993 World Trade Center bombing and various other failed terrorist attacks. He also admitted to have personally beheaded Wall Street Journal reporter Daniel Pearl in 2002.

Koran (Qu'ran) — is the sacred text of Islam, divided into 114 chapters, or suras: revered as the word of God, dictated to Muhammad by the archangel Gabriel, and accepted as the foundation of Islamic law, religion, culture, and politics.

Madrasah — is the Arabic word for school. A typical madrasah usually offers two courses of study: a "hifz" course that is memorization of the Koran (the person who commits the entire Koran to memory is called a hafiz); and an "alim" course leading the candidate to become an accepted scholar in the community.

Mohammed Omar — also known as Mullah Mohammad Omar, or simply Mullah Omar, is the reclusive leader of the Taliban in Afghanistan and was Afghanistan's de facto head of state from 1996 to 2001. Omar is also known as Emir al-Momineen (Commander of the Faithful), as declared by his followers in 1994. Since the 2001 war in Afghanistan began he has been in hiding and is wanted by U.S. authorities for harboring Osama bin Laden and his al Qaeda organization. In 2006, Omar made two statements; the first noting the death of Abu Musab al-Zarqawi and the second, a declaration that foreign forces would be driven out of Afghanistan.

Mujahideen — is an Islamic-Arabic term for Muslims fighting in a war or involved in any other struggle. Mujahid, and its plural, mujahideen, come from the same Arabic linguistic root as *jihad* ("struggle"). In the late 20th century and early 21st century, the term "mujahideen" became the name of various armed fighters who subscribe to militant Islamic ideologies, although there is not always an explicit "holy" or "warrior" meaning of the word. The best-known mujahideen were the various loosely aligned Afghan opposition groups that fought against the Soviet invasion of Afghanistan during the 1980s and then fought against each other after 1988 in the subsequent Afghan Civil War.

Muslim — pertains to the religion, law, or civilization of Islam, or a person that is an adherent to Islam. Literally meaning "one who submits to Allah (God)," a Muslim who is a follower of the Islamic prophet Mohammed.

Omar Abdel-Rahman — is the spiritual leader of Al-Gama'a al-Islamiyya (The Islamic Group). He was accused of conspiring to bomb the World Trade Center in 1993, but was convicted and sentenced to life imprisonment for his advocacy of a subsequent conspiracy to bomb New York landmarks, including the United Nations and FBI offices. The Islamic Group has publicly threatened to retaliate against the United States unless Rahman is released from prison. Al-Gama'a al-Islamiyya militants are also responsible for the November 17, 1997 attack at the

Temple of Hatshepsut in Luxor, in which a band of six men machine-gunned and hacked to death with knives 58 foreign tourists and four Egyptians, killing 71 people altogether. The organization may have also been indirectly involved in the assassination of president Anwar Sadat in 1981, for which the group later expressed remorse. Although al-Islamiyya reportedly renounced bloodshed in 1998 and vehemently denied having joined forces with al Qaeda, the group continued to be listed on the U.S. Department of State's List of Designated Foreign Terrorist Organizations in 2007.

Osama bin Laden — is the presumed founder and leader of the terrorist organization al Qaeda that was created around 1988 to consolidate an international terror network established during the Afghan-Soviet War of the 1980s. Afterward, bin Laden's followers joined other foreign conflicts, including Somalia, the Balkans, and Chechnya, which contributed to al Qaeda's global reach and helped recruit additional members. Following an ineffectual attempt to depose the Saudi royal family and impose Islamic rule on the Arabian Peninsula, bin Laden was deported from Saudi Arabia. He found refuge in Sudan where he operated until 1996, establishing connections with other Islamic terrorist groups. When ousted from Sudan under U.S. pressure, he returned to Afghanistan where he allied himself with the Taliban, the radical Islamic fascist regime of the 1990s. Bin Laden's al Qaeda masterminded the barbaric attacks of September 11, 2001 that killed some 3,000 innocent civilians. Both bin Laden and al Qaeda have been directly linked to the August 7, 1998 bombing of the U.S. embassies in Nairobi, Kenya, and Dar es Salaam, Tanzania, which killed 224 people. They are also linked to the October 2000 bombing attack on the U.S.S. *Cole* in Yemen that killed 17 U.S. Navy personnel. (See al Qaeda)

Saddam Hussein (Abd al-Majid al-Tikriti) — was the dictator president of Iraq from July 16, 1979 until April 9, 2003. Hussein, who led Iraq as head of the Ba'ath Party, practiced one-party rule and censorship, while also instigating violence and mass killings against Iraq's Shia, Kurdish, and Marsh Arab populations. In his rise to power, he espoused secular pan-Arabism, economic modernization, and Arab socialism. Hussein is best known for ruling Iraq as a dictator and committing atrocities against his own people to maintain control of the country. He was captured by U.S. forces on December 13, 2003. On November

5, 2006, he was convicted of crimes against humanity by the Iraq Special Tribunal and was sentenced to death by hanging. Hussein was executed on December 30, 2006.

Salafism — is an orthodox fundamentalist movement within Sunni Islam. "Salafi" is an umbrella term for adherents of a particular form of Islamic revivalism who vary amongst themselves as to its definition, but share a rejection of contemporary Islamic teachings in favor of a return to the Salaf, as Islam was practiced by the first three generations of Muslims. Salafism is a commonly used term for the Sunni Islamic school of thinking that considers the pious ancestors (Salaf) of the earliest period of Islam to be an example of how Islam should be practiced. It is a return to sharia-minded orthodoxy that would purify Islam from unwarranted changes since the religion's inception, the criteria for judging which would be the Qur'an and hadith. Salafis generally reject violence and terrorist acts, but those committed to jihad — jihadist Salafis — are extremists who are willing to use violence and terror to advance their cause. There is an extended Salafi jihadist movement, which has attracted rootless or committed internationalist militants to fight the jihad in areas such as Kashmir, Bosnia, Chechnya, Afghanistan, and the Philippines.

Sayyid Qutb — was an Egyptian Islamist, author, and the leading intellectual of the Egyptian Muslim Brotherhood in the 1950s and 60s. In the Muslim world he is best known for his work on Islamic fundamentalism, extensive Quranic commentary, and contributions to modern perceptions of Islamic concepts of jihad and ummah. In the West, Qutb is identified as the man whose ideas would shape al Qaeda. Qutb's brother, Muhammad, a professor of Islamic Studies and publisher of his works based in Saudi Arabia, helped spread Qutb's influence. One of Muhammad Qutb's students and later follower was Ayman Zawahiri, who became a member of the Egyptian Islamic Jihad terror group, mentor of Osama bin Laden and a leading member of al Qaeda. Bin Laden regularly attended weekly public university lectures by Muhammad Qutb and read Sayyid Qutb's writings. In 1954, Qutb was imprisoned for his opposition to government policies after the attempted assassination of Gamal Abdel Nasser, who had led a coup of Egypt's pro-Western monarchist government two years earlier. Qutb and the Muslim Brotherhood welcomed the coup and expected Nasser to establish an Islamic government, but Nasser's secular nationalist ideology was incompatible with the Brotherhood's totalitarian Islamism. Qutb was released from prison in 1964 but was rearrested 8 months later, accused of plotting to overthrow the state and subjected to what many considered a show trial. Many of the charges against Qutb in court were taken directly from his anti-secular and anti-Western writings during his imprisonment and he steadfastly supported the statements in court. Qutb was convicted and executed in August 1966.

Shahid — sometimes known as a Muslim martyr, is a religious term in Islam that literally means "witness". It is a title that is given to a Muslim after his death if he died during fulfillment of a religious commandment, or during a war for the religion.

Sharia — meaning "way" or "path" in Arabic, refers to the body of Islamic law. It is the legal framework within which public and some private aspects of life are regulated for those living in a legal system based on Islamic principles of jurisprudence. Sharia deals with many aspects of day-to-day life, including politics, economics, banking, business law, contract law, sexuality, and social issues. Some Islamic scholars accept Sharia as the body of precedent and legal theory established before the 19th century, while other scholars view Sharia as a changing body, and include Islamic legal theory from the contemporary period.

Shia (or Shiites) — is a member of the branch of Islam that regards Ali ibn Abi Talib (Muhammad's cousin and son-in-law) and his descendants as the legitimate successors to Muhammad and rejects the first three caliphs. The majority of the population in Iraq and Iran is Shia.

Sufism — is a mystic tradition of Islam encompassing a diverse range of beliefs and practices dedicated to Allah/God, divine love and sometimes to help a fellow man.

Sunni — is the branch of Islam that accepts the first four caliphs as rightful successors of Muhammad. The Sunni are a minority in Iraq, but were affiliated with Saddam Hussein's regime since he was Sunni. Sunni Islam is the dominant and majority sect in the Muslim world.

Taliban — is a Sunni Islamist fundamentalist movement, which by and large ruled most of Afghanistan from 1996 until 2001, and is currently engaged in a protracted guerilla war against NATO-led coalition forces within Afghanistan. (See Osama bin Laden)

Umma — refers to the Muslim community or people, considered to extend from Mauritania to Pakistan.

Wahhabi — is an 18th century Orthodox Sunni Islamic movement, based on the teachings of Muhammad ibn Abd al Wahhab. It is the dominant form of Islam in the Arabian Peninsula (especially within Saudi Arabia and Qatar), small areas in Africa, and in western Iraq. The primary doctrine of Wahhabism is Tawhid (the uniqueness and unity of God). It treats the Koran and Hadith as fundamental texts, as interpreted upon the understanding of the first three generations of Islam, and is further explained by commentaries, like al Wahhab's. Wahhabism is the term given to the movement by its opponents and is the term most widely used and recognized today as describing this branch of Islam. However, its followers call themselves Muwahhidun ("unitarians," or unifiers of the Islamic practice). The term "Wahhabi" is often considered derogatory and rarely used by the people it is used to describe. The terms "Wahhabism" and "Salafism" are often used interchangeably, but Wahhabism is considered to be a particular, ultra-conservative orientation, within Salafism. Most puritanical groups in the Muslim world are Salafi in orientation, but not necessarily Wahhabi. The appeal of Wahhabism reportedly stems from Arab nationalism, reformism and control of the two Muslim holy cities of Mecca and Medina (thus greatly influencing Muslim culture and thinking). The discovery of the Persian Gulf oil fields has allowed Wahhabis to promote their interpretations of Islam using billions of dollars from oil export revenue. It is estimated that these revenues have funded about 90 percent of the expenses of the entire faith, paying for books, scholarships, fellowships, and mosques — including expansion into the United States

BIBLIOGRAPHY

All references and links to Web sites were correct and current during the preparation of this book. The authors recognize that the information presented on those sites may change, thus altering the content and meanings therein.

Newspapers & Magazines

"3 Prisoners Escape from Iraq's Abu Ghraib jail; Search under way for inmates who fled through holes in fence." *Reuters*. May 26, 2005 http://www.msnbc.msn.com/id/7992499/.

"A Failure of Accountability." *Washington Post*. August 29, 2004.

Aboul-Enein, Youssef H. "Ayman Al-Zawahiri's Knights under the Prophet's Banner: the Al-Qaeda Manifesto." *Military Review*. January–February 2005.

"Abu Ghraib Accountability." *Wall Street Journal*. April 27, 2005.

"Abu Ghraib Dog Handler Gets 6 Months, Sergeant Convicted Of Using Dog To Terrify Detainees" *CBS/Associated Press*. March 22, 2006 http://www.cbsnews.com/stories/2006/03/22/iraq/main1430842.shtml.

"Abu Ghraib, The Next Step." *New York Times*. August 27, 2004.

"Abu Ghraib, Whitewashed." *New York Times*. July 24, 2004.

Abunimah, Ali. "Israeli Link Possible in U.S. Torture Techniques." *Daily Star*. May 11, 2004.

"Abuse of Iraqis POWs by GIs Probed, 60 Minutes II has Exclusive Report on Alleged Mistreatment." *CBS*. April 27, 2004 www.cbsnews.com/stories/2004/04/27/60II/main614063.shtml.

"Air America acknowledges some layoffs." *USAToday*. September 14, 2006 http://www.usatoday.com/life/2006-09-14-air-america_x.htm. Viewed September 21, 2006.

"Air Force Streamlines Acquisition Process." *Air Force Link*. August 14, 2002.

al-Marashi, Ibrahim. "Iraq's Hostage Crisis: Kidnappings, Mass Media and The Iraqi Insurgency." *Middle East Review of International Affairs*. Vol. 8, No. 4 (December 2004) http://meria.idc.ac.il/journal/2004/issue4/jv8no4a1.html.

"An Army Whitewash." *Washington Post*. July 25, 2004.

Anderson, Tania. "Survival of the Fittest. Jack London is hunting down deals that could turn CACI International into a major player in homeland security," *Washington Business Journal*. January 3, 2003.

Andrejczak, Matt. "CACI says Army asked some interrogators to leave." *CBS MarketWarch*. August 12, 2004.

"Angelides Urges Pension Funds to Sell CACI Shares." *Los Angeles Times*. August 3, 2004.

"Arabs Outraged By Photos of U.S. Forces Humiliating Iraqis," *USAToday*, May 2, 2004 www.usatoday.com/news/world/iraq/2004-05-01-prisoner-abuse_x.htm.

"Army Inspector General Reports 94 Cases of Prisoner Abuse." *Associated Press*. July 22, 2004.

"Army to Charge Officer in Iraq Prison Abuse." *Los Angeles Times*. April 26, 2006.

Ashkenaz Croke, Lisa. "Iraq Torture Investigators Reveal Scores of New Cases." *New Standard*. December 31, 2004.

Asser, Martin. "Abu Ghraib: Dark Stain on Iraq's Past," *BBC News*. May 25, 2004.

Avant, Deborah. "What Are Those Contractors Doing in Iraq?" *Washington Post*. May 7, 2004.

———. "Think again: Mercenaries." *Foreign Policy*. July/August 2004.

Baker, Brent. "Sanchez Blasts Media, But Media Only Highlight His Criticism of Bush." *NewsBusters*. October 15, 2007 http://newsbusters.org/blogs/brent-baker/2007/10/15/sanchez-blasts-media-media-only-highlight-his-criticism-bush.

Barakat, Matthew. "Contractor: Army happy with interrogators." *Guardian Unlimited*. May 11, 2004.

———. "CACI Employees Participated in Abu Ghraib Abuse: Army Report." *Associated Press*. August 25, 2004.

Barr, Stephen. "GSA Will Try to Fix Procurement Problems With a New Service." *Washington Post*. October 2, 2006.

Beaudette, Marie. "Seeking Payback; Money for Abused Iraqis Won't Come Easily nor Without Some Creative Legal Argument." *Legal Times*. June 28, 2004.

"Beheadings: Terrorism is a Symptom of a Bigger Problem." *JihadWatch* *.org*. July 7, 2004 http://www.jihadwatch.org/archives/002425.php.

Behn, Sharon. "U.S. addresses control of security companies." *Washington Times*. May 5, 2004 http://www.washtimes.com/world/20040505-122432-9701r. htm.

Berry, Kate. "The CalPERS Machine." *Los Angeles Business Journal*. May 10, 2004.

———. "Battle for better corporate governance earns cheers for fund." *Los Angeles Business Journal*. May 10, 2004.

Bliss, Jeff, and Tony Capaccio. "U.S. Army Says No Systemic Failure in Iraq Prisons." *Bloomberg News Service*. July 22, 2004

Block, Susan. "Bush's POW Porn." *Counterpunch.org*. May 14, 2004.

Boot, Max. "The Iraq War's Outsourcing Snafu." *Los Angeles Times*. March 31, 2005.

Borger, Julian. "Cooks and Drivers Were Working as Interrogators." "Private contractor lifts the lid on systematic failures at Abu Ghraib jail." *The Guardian*. May 7, 2004 http://www.guardian.co.uk/international/story/ 0,3604,1211351,00.html.

———. "The Danger of Market Forces." *The Guardian*. May 6, 2004 http://www.guardian.co.uk/elsewhere/journalist/story/0,1210696,00.html.

———. "U.S. Military in Torture Scandal," *The Guardian*. April 30, 2004 http://www.guardian.co.uk/Iraq/Story/0,2763,1206725,00.html.

Bowles, Abby. "CACI Under Investigation by GSA, DOD, Interior for Role in Iraqi Prisoner Abuse." *Federal Contract Report*. June 1, 2004.

Breed, Allen G. "Soldier who turned over abuse photo says he agonized before reporting." *Associated Press*. August 7, 2004.

Brewster, Deborah, and Simon London. "CalPERS Chief Relaxes in the Eye of the Storm." *Financial Times*. June 2, 2004.

Broder, John M. and James Risen, "Contractor Deaths in Iraq Soar to Record," New York Times, May 19, 2007.

Brinkley, Joel. "9/11 Sent Army Contractor on Path to Abu Ghraib." *New York Times*. May 19, 2004.

Brinkley, Joel, and James Glanz. "Contractors in Sensitive Roles, Unchecked." *New York Times*. May 7, 2004.

———. "The Struggle for Iraq: Civilian Employees; Contract Workers Implicated in February Army Report on Prison Abuse Remain on the Job." *New York Times*. May 4, 2004.

Broder, David S. "Tension Over Press Leaks." *Washington Post*. April 27, 2006.

Buchanan, Kirsty. "Block British Firm's Iraq Deals, says Plaid MP." *Western Mail*. May 22, 2004.

Buffaloe, David L. "Defining Asymmetric Warfare." *Land Warfare Papers No. 58*. September 2006.

Burnett, Victoria et al. "From Building Camps to Gathering Intelligence, Dozens of Tasks Once in the Hands of Soldiers are Now Carried out by Contractors." *Financial Times*. August 11, 2003.

Burns, Robert. "Army Demotes a One-Star General Accused of Dereliction in Prisoner Abuse Scandal." *Associated Press*. May 5, 2005.

Bybee, Jay S. "Memorandum for Alberto R. Gonzales, Counsel to the President, and William J. Haynes II, General Counsel of the Department of Defense." January 22, 2002 http://www.washingtonpost.com/wp-srv/nation/documents/012202bybee.pdf.

"CACI internal probe finds no Iraq prisoner abuse." *Reuters*. August 13, 2004.

"CACI rejects lawsuit as frivolous." *Associated Press*. July 27, 2004.

"CACI says it will continue Iraq probe." *Associated Press*. August 12, 2004.

"CACI stock surges day after profit report." *Reuters*. August 19, 2004.

"CalPERS and Cronyism," *Wall Street Journal*. October 18, 2004.

Castaneda, Antonio. "50 Insurgents Hurt in Attack at Abu Ghraib, U.S. Military Says About 50 Insurgents Wounded in Attack on Abu Ghraib Prison." *Associated Press*. April 3, 2005 http://abcnews.go.com/International/wireStory?id=638677.

Chadha, Sharon. "Lynne Stewart, Jihadi Lawyer." *Middle East Quarterly*. Winter 2006 http://www.meforum.org/article/887 (viewed December 22, 2006).

Chaffin, Joshua. "Private Workers Found Central to Jail Abuse." *Financial Times*. August 27, 2004.

————. "Contractors Face Class Action Suit." *Financial Times*. June 10, 2004.

————. "Contract Interrogators Hired to Avoid Supervision." *Financial Times*. May 21, 2004 http://search.ft.com/searchArticle?id=040521001384& query=contract+interrogators&vsc_appId=totalSearch&state=Form.

————. "U.S. Turns to Private Sector for Spies." *Financial Times*. May 17, 2004.

————. "Dismay and Surprise that U.S. Army Outsources Interrogation." *Financial Times*. May 7, 2004.

————. "Prison Torture Scandal Throws Spotlight on Private Contractors." *Financial Times*. May 4, 2004 http://search.ft.com/searchArticle?queryText= steven+schooner&javascriptEnabled=true&id=040504000815.

Chatterjee, Pratap. "An Interrogator Speaks Out." *CorpWatch.org*. May 7, 2005.

Chatterjee, Pratap, and A.C. Thompson. "Private Contractors and Torture at Abu Ghraib." *CorpWatch.org*. May 7, 2004 http://search.corpwatch.org/search? cs=&q=Contractors+Abu+Ghraib++site:+corpwatch.org&ch=http:%2F% 2Fcorpwatch.org%2Farticle.php%3Fid=10828&fm=off.

Clabaugh, Jeff. "CACI calls new lawsuit farcical," *Washington Business Journal*, July 27, 2004

————. "AES and CACI Struck from Social Index." *Washington Business Journal*. June 14, 2004.

————. "Calvert Fund May Drop CACI." *Washington Business Journal*. May 13, 2004.

Cloud, David S. "Ex-Commander Says Iraq Effort is 'a Nightmare.'" *New York Times*. October 13, 2007.

Colb, Sherry. "Why Lynne Stewart, Attorney for a Terrorist, Is No Heroine: Crossing the Line Between Advocate and Accomplice." *FindLaw*. July 30, 2003.

Collier, Robert. "Executive Grilled on Firm's Role in Iraq Torture." *San Francisco Chronicle*. August 3, 2004 http://sfgate.com/cgi-bin/article.cgi?file= /c/a/2004/08/03/BAG5781RDQ1.DTL.

"Company Mann." *Harper's Magazine*. July 1, 2004.

Cooper, Christopher, and Greg Jaffe. "Iraq Prison Rules Seen as Too Harsh for Guantanamo." *Wall Street Journal*. June 15, 2005.

"Correction." *Washington Post*. September 6, 2004.

Crock, Stan. "Homeland Security Is CACI's Domain; Specializing in IT work for the intelligence community, this Beltway company has zoomed to a higher profile since September 11 attacks." *BusinessWeek*. November 25, 2002 http://www.businessweek.com/magazine/content/02_47/b3809101.htm.

Crow, Randy. "GSA Gives CACI Green Light on Prison Sexual Torture." July 14, 2004 http://www.randycrow.com/articles/071404.htm.

Cushman, Jr., John. "The Reach of War: Inquiries; Private Company Finds No Evidence Its Interrogators Took Part in Prison Abuse." *New York Times*, August 13, 2004.

Darmiento, Laurence. "Content Below the Radar, No. 3 CalSTRS Exerts its Influence." *Los Angeles Business Journal*. May 10, 2004.

Dart, Bob. "Prison Abuse Allegations Put Pentagon's Use of Private Contractors Under Scrutiny." *Cox News Service*. May 7, 2004.

Dawson, John. "Stunted Intelligence." *World Magazine*. January 29, 2005.

"Deadliest Attack On U.S. Base Insurgents, Previously Attacked Flimsy American Dining Hall Tents." *CBS/Associated Press*. December 22, 2004 http://www.cbsnews.com/stories/2004/12/22/iraq/main662421.shtml (viewed October 30, 2006).

Diamond, John. "Senate Votes to Ban Torture of Terrorism Detainees." *USAToday*. November 15, 2005 http://www.usatoday.com/news/washington/2005-11-15-detainees_x.htm.

———. "Prewar intelligence predicted Iraqi insurgency." *USAToday*. October 24, 2004 http://www.usatoday.com/news/washington/2004-10-24-insurgence-intel_x.htm

Dimanno, Rosie. "Abu Ghraib Prison: Nowhere in Iraq Was Butchery More Rife." *Toronto Star*. April 13, 2003.

Dishneau, David. "Officer seeks dismissal of Abu Ghraib charges, Defense shows documents that accused officer wasn't in the chain of command." *Richmond Times-Dispatch*. January 31, 2007 http://www.timesdispatch.com/servlet/Satellite?pagename=RTD%2FMGArticle%2FRTD_BasicArticle&c=MGArticle&cid=1149192937284&path=%21news&s=1045855934842 (viewed February 1, 2007).

———. "Abu Ghraib Dog Handler Sentenced, Sgt. Santos Cardona Gets 90 Days Hard Labor And Reduction In Rank." *CBS/Associated Press*. June 2, 2006 http://www.cbsnews.com/stories/2006/06/02/iraq/main1676792.shtml.

———. "Army says colonel lacked authority to allow dog use." *Associated Press*. March 13, 2006.

Debusmann, Bernd. "In Iraq, contractor deaths near 650, legal fog thickens." *Reuters*. October 10, 2006 http://today.reuters.com/News/CrisesArticle.aspx?storyId=N10275842 (viewed December 12, 2006).

D'Souza, Dinesh. "The Far Enemy." *American Legion Magazine*. June 2007.

Eggen, Dan. "Justice Dept. Investigating Leak of NSA Wiretapping, Probe Seeks Source of Classified Data." *Washington Post*. December 31, 2005 http://www.washingtonpost.com/wp-dyn/content/article/2005/12/30/AR2005 123000538.html (viewed March 20, 2006).

―――. "Little is Clear in Laws on Leaks." *Washington Post*. April 28, 2006.

Einholf, Christopher J. "The Fall and Rise of Torture: A Comparative and Historical Analysis." *Sociological Theory* 25:2. June 2007 http://www.asanet.org/galleries/default-file/June07STFeature.pdf.

Eunjung Cha, Ariana, and Renae Merle. "Line Increasingly Blurred Between Soldiers and Civilian Contractors." *Washington Post*. May 13, 2004.

"Ex-Iraq commander 'forced' to retire, Ex-chief of U.S. forces in Iraq says military forced him to retire." *Associated Press*. November 2, 2006 http://www.msnbc.com/id/15523964 (viewed November 2, 2006).

"Ex-workers testify about Halliburton, Responsibility questioned at Hill hearing." *Washington Post*. September 19, 2006 http://www.washingtonpost.com/wp-dyn/content/article/2006/09/18/AR2006091801154.html.

"Failings Top to Bottom." *Philadelphia Inquirer*. August 28, 2004.

Falksohn, Rudiger, Siegesmund von Ilsemann, Susanne Koelbl, Gerhard Sporl, Volkhard Windfuhr, and Bernhard Zand. "Excesses of Sex and Violence." *Der Spiegel*. May 10, 2004 http://service.spiegel.de/cache/international/spiegel/0,1518,299193,00.html.

Fattah, Hassan H. "Symbol of Abu Ghraib Seeks to Spare Others His Nightmare." *New York Times*. March 11, 2006 http://www.nytimes.com/2006/03/11/international/middleeast/11ghraib.html?pagewanted=1&ei=5088&en=28375a62dd419d60&ex=1299733200&partner=rssnyt&emc=rss (viewed October 26, 2006).

Felling, Matthew. "Terrorists' visual warfare uses the media as a weapon." *Christian Science Monitor*. August 4, 2004 http://www.csmonitor.com/2004/0804/p09s02-coop.htm (viewed January 26, 2007).

Filkins, Dexter. "General Says Less Coercion of Captives Yields Better Data." *New York Times*. September 7, 2004

Fitzgerald, Patrick J. "Shield Law Perils . . . Bill Would Wreak Havoc on a System That Isn't Broken." *Washington Post*. October 4, 2007.

Fleming, Sue. "U.S. Contractor Looks Into Iraq Prison Abuses." *Reuters*. May 3, 2004.

Foster, Lawrence G. "The Johnson & Johnson Credo and the Tylenol Crisis." *New Jersey Bell Journal* Vol. 6 No. 1, 1983.

French, Matthew. "CACI Caught in Iraqi Prison Scandal." *Federal Computer Week*. June 7, 2004.

Fulton, Ben. "The Interrogator; After Abu Ghraib and Gitmo, Torin Nelson has some questions about the War on Terror." *Salt Lake City Weekly*. March 10, 2005.

Gaither, Chris. "Investing with an Agenda." *Boston Globe*. April 20, 2003.

Galloway, Joseph L. "U.S. General Defends His Adherence to Geneva Conventions in Iraq." *San Jose Mercury News*. May 5, 2005 http://www.mercury news.com/mld/mercurynews/news/politics/14512695.htm (viewed May 9, 2006).

Galuszka, Peter. "Brains Behind the Brawn: in the complex world of privatized defense, three firms are giving the military its best weapon — technology." *Chief Executive*. June 1, 2004.

Gerin, Roseanne. "Report: CACI interrogators lacked training, but met contract." *Washington Technology*. July 26, 2004 http://www.washingtontech nology.com/news/1_1/daily_news/24099-1.html.

———. "CACI leaps GSA debarment hurdle." *Washington Technology*. July 8, 2004 http://www.washingtontechnology.com/news/1_1/daily_news/ 23948-1.html.

———. "Contractors caught under a microscope, Iraq prison scandal raises questions about outsourcing." *Washington Technology*. May 24, 2004 http:// www.washingtontechnology.com/news/19_4/resellers-distributors/23555-1.html.

Gibson, Gail and Scott Shane. "Contractors act as interrogators, Control: The Pentagon's hiring of civilians to question prisoners raises accountability issues." *Baltimore Sun*. May 4, 2004 http://www.baltimoresun.com/news/nation world/bal-te.contractors04may04,0,6476999.story?coll=bal-nationworld-headlines.

Glovin, David. "N.Y. Attorney Lynne Stewart Convicted of Aiding Terrorist Group." *Bloomberg*. February 10, 2005.

Graham, Sen. Lindsey, and Rep. Jane Harman. "Clearing the Fog on Interrogations." *Washington Post*. February 19, 2005.

Groner, Jonathan. "Untested Law Key in Iraqi Abuse Scandal." *Legal Times*. May 10, 2004.

Grossman, Elaine M. "Possible Interrogation Contractor Influence Cited In Senate Vote." *Inside The Pentagon*. June 24, 2004.

"GSA reviews CACI contract." *Washington Technology*. June 7, 2004.

Hanson, Christopher. "Tortured Logic, CBS held the Abu Ghraib photos on principle, right?" *Columbia Journalism Review* July/August 2004 http:// www.cjr.org/issues/2004/4/voices-hanson.asp.

Hardy, Michael. "CACI faces potential debarment." *Federal Computer Week*. May 28, 2004 http://www.fcw.com/article83034-05-28-04-Web.

Harris, Shane. "Contractors were hired to oversee interrogations." *Government Executive*. July 27, 2004.

———. "CACI chief defends company's interrogation work." *Government Executive*. September 2, 2004.

———. "GSA queries Lockheed Martin on interrogation contracts." *Government Executive*. July 29, 2004 http://www.govexec.com/dailyfed/0704/0702904h1.htm.

———. "CACI Chief Defends Company's Interrogation Work." *Government Executive*. September 2, 2004 http://www.govexec.com/dailyfed/0904/090204h1.htm.

Hersh, Seymour. "The General's Report, How Antonio Taguba, who investigated the Abu Ghraib scandal, became one of its casualties," *New Yorker*. June 25, 2007.

———. "Torture at Abu Ghraib." *New Yorker*. May 10, 2004 (posted online April 30, 2004) http://www.newyorker.com/fact/content/?040510fa_fact.

———. "Smashing Camelot; What's Left of the Kennedy Myth Takes a Hit From a Big Bucks Expose." *Time Magazine*. November 17, 1997.

Higham, Scott, Josh White, and Christian Davenport. "A Prison on the Brink; Usual Military Checks and Balances Went Missing." *Washington Post*. May 9, 2004 http://www.washingtonpost.com/wp-dyn/articles/A11413-2004May8.html.

Hoffman, Lisa. "Prison Scandal Spotlights Role of Civilian Intelligence Operatives," *Scripps Howard News Service*. May 3, 2004.

Hoffman, Trish. "Abu Ghraib Dog Handler Gets Six Months." *Army News Service*. March 23, 2006 http://www4.army.mil/ocpa/read.php?story_id_key=8720 (viewed May 9, 2006).

Howell, Deborah. "A Dilemma Within Quotation Marks." *Washington Post*. August 19, 2007.

Howell, Deborah. "Quote, Unquote." *Washington Post*. August 12, 2007.

"In Brief." *Washington Post*. August 3, 2004.

"Inside the Wire Erratum Notice." *PRNewswire*. May 1, 2005 http://biz.yahoo.com/prnews/050501/nysu019.html?.v=6.

"Iraq: Contractors, Aid Workers, Journalists — More Than 150 Kidnapped." *Associated Press*. October 22, 2004 www.corpwatch.org/article.php?id=11601.

"Iraq Prison Staff Seen as Issue; Lawyer for a U.S. Soldier Accused of Abuse Alleges Contractors Are Used to Question Inmates There." *Los Angeles Times*. April 30, 2004.

"Iraqi PM Says Detainees May Have Been Tortured, 'Concerned' Pentagon Officials Say Raided Prison Is not Run by U.S. forces." *Associated Press*. November 15, 2005 http://www.msnbc.msn.com/id/10051259/.

"The Israeli Traitors Running America's Invasion of Iraq." February 27, 2005 http://www.geocities.com/carbonomics/MCtfirm/10tf26/10tf26me.html.

Jaffe, Greg, David S. Cloud and Gary Fields Wall. "Legal Loophole Arises in Iraq." *Wall Street Journal*. May 4, 2004.

Jehl, Douglas, and Eric Schmitt. "In Abuse, a Portrayal of Ill—Prepared, Overwhelmed G.I.s." *New York Times*. May 9, 2004 http://www.nytimes.com/2004/05/09/international/middleeast/09PRIS.html?ex=1165381200&en=09902169ae61c043&ei=5070.

Johnston, David. "Letter Tells of Difficulties in Prosecuting Detainee Abuse. *New York Times*. January 17, 2007.

———. "U.S. Inquiry Falters on Civilians Accused of Abusing Detainees." *New York Times*. December 19, 2006

Kahn, Peter R. "The Media In Need of Some Mending." *Wall Street Journal*. December 11, 2006.

Kaplan, Robert D. "Modern Heroes, Our soldiers like what they do. They want our respect, not our pity." *Wall Street Journal*. October 4, 2007.

Karon, Tony. "How the Prison Scandal Sabotages the U.S. in Iraq." *Time*. May 4, 2004.

Keller, Josh. "Reporter Recounts Years Behind the D.C. Scenes, Seymour Hersh Wrote on Abu Ghraib Scandal." *Daily Californian*. October 11, 2004.

Kelly, Susanne. "Richmond march wants troops home." *Worker's World*. July 15, 2004 http://www.workers.org/ww/2004/richmond0715.php.

Kelley, Matt. "Pentagon Memo Warned on Army Contractors." *Associated Press*. May 7, 2004.

———. "Pentagon Memo Warned in 2002 About Lax Oversight of Army Contractors." *Associated Press*. May 7, 2004.

Kennedy, Kelly. "Sanchez says he was 'forced to retire.'" *Army Times*. November 2, 2006 http://www.armytimes.com/story.php?f=1-292925-2329877.php (viewed November 6, 2006).

———. "A Different Kind of Hero; Some soldiers might think Joe Darby hurt the Army, but the Abu Ghraib whistleblower says 'it had to be done.'" *Army Times*. September 18, 2006.

Kerr, Richard, Thomas Wolfe, Rebecca Donegan, and Aris Pappas. "Issues for the US Intelligence Community." *Studies in Intelligence*. Vol. 49, No. 3, 2005.

Kincaid, Cliff. "Hard Times for Hardball." *Media Monitor*, July 21, 2004 http://www.aim.org/media_monitor/A1753_0_2_0_C/ (viewed January 30, 2007).

Kissel, Mary, Christopher Cooper, and Jonathan Karp. "Two Contractors Accused of Role in Iraq Jail Abuse." *Wall Street Journal*. June 10, 2004.

Knight, Jerry. "Tylenol's Maker Shows How to Respond to Crisis, Johnson & Johnson Sets Example in Crisis." *Washington Post*. October 11, 1982.

Krane, Jim. "General: Less Abuse Resulting in More Iraq Tips." *Associated Press*. September 6, 2004.

———. "Iraq Prison Report Details Lax Discipline." *Associated Press*. May 8, 2004.

Krauthammer, Charles. "The Abu Ghraib Panic." *Washington Post*. May 14, 2004.

Kupelian, David. "New video reveals real torture scandal; Saddam's daily horrors make America's Abu Ghraib abuses seem almost trivial." *WorldNet Daily.com*. June 21, 2004.

Kurtz, Howard. "On Election Night, Networks Plan to Proceed With Caution." *Washington Post*. November 2, 2006.

———. "Newsweek Retracts Guantanamo Story, Item on Koran Sparked Deadly Protests." *Washington Post*. May 17, 2005 http://www.washingtonpost.com/wp-dyn/content/article/2005/05/16/AR2005051601262.html (viewed December 4, 2006).

———. "USA Today Reporter Resigns, Tom Squitieri Used Other Papers' Quotes." *Washington Post*. May 6, 2005 http://www.washingtonpost.com/wp-dyn/content/article/2005/05/05/AR2005050501876.html.

———. "Rather Admits 'Mistake in Judgment,' CBS Was Misled About Bush National Guard Documents, Anchor Says." *Washington Post*. September 21, 2004 http://www.washingtonpost.com/wp-dyn/articles/A35531-2004 Sep20.html (viewed December 4, 2006).

Lacquement, Richard. "Book Review of Peter Singer's *Corporate Warriors*." *Naval War College Review*. Autumn 2004 http://www.nwc.navy.mil/PRESS/Review/2004/SummerAutumn/br6-sa04.htm.

Laise, Eleanor. "Street Smart: Update." *SmartMoney*. October 1, 2004.

Larson, Sarah. "Former soldier in abuse case defended." *phillyburbs.com*. May 11, 2004.

Leiby, Richard. "Rangers Lead the Way in Exposing Author as a Fraud." *Washington Post*. May 2, 2004.

————. "The Gadflier." *Washington Post*. July 6, 2003.

Lewis, Neil A., "The Reach of War: The Memorandums; Documents Build a Case for Working Outside the Laws on Interrogating Prisoners," New York Times, June 9, 2004.

Lichtblau, Eric and James Risen. "Bank Data is Sifted by U.S. in Secret to Block Terror." *New York Times*. June 23, 2006.

Light, Paul C. "The True Size of Government." *GovExec.com*. January 1, 1999.

Liptak, Adam. "17 ex-P.O.W.'s set back again in claim against Iraq." *New York Times*. June 5, 2004.

————. "Courts grow increasingly skeptical of any special protections for the press." *New York Times*. June 28, 2005.

Liptak, Adam, and Michael Janofsky. "Scrappy Group of Lawyers Shows Way for Big Firms." *New York Times*. June 30, 2004.

Lococo, Edmond. "Fund May Dump Firms Linked to Iraq Prison Scandal." *Bloomberg News*. May 14, 2004.

Locy, Toni. "Justice Dept. Probing Domestic Spying Leak." *Associated Press*. December 30, 2005 http://news.yahoo.com/s/ap/20051230/ap_on_go_ca_st_pe/domestic_spying_probe.

Lombino, David. "Air America faces a Cash Crunch, Its Star Host Says." *New York Sun*. September 14, 2006 http://www.nysun.com/pf/php?id=39678. Viewed September 21, 2006.

London, Jack. "Guest Viewpoint: Prison contractor defends itself." *Oregon Register-Guard*. September 27, 2004.

————. "Angelides Takes Wrong Tack With CACI Investment." *Sacramento Bee*. August 19, 2004.

Loney, Jim. "Abu Ghraib was hell, U.S. soldier tells abuse hearing." *Reuters*. August 6, 2004.

Madsen, Wayne. "The Israeli Torture Template, Rape, Feces, and Urine-dripped Cloth Sacks." *CounterPunch.org*. May 10, 2004.

Marois, Michael M. "CACI Should be Dropped by Pensions, Angelides Says." *Bloomberg*. August 2, 2004.

Martin, Susan Taylor. "Horror Is the Point of Recent Beheadings." *St. Petersburg Times*. September 23, 2004 http://www.sptimes.com/2004/09/23/news_pf/Worldandnation/Horror_is_the_point_o.shtml.

Mayer, Jane. "A Deadly Interrogation; Can the C.I.A. legally kill a prisoner?" *New Yorker*. November 7, 2006.

Mazzetti, Mark. "Reforms in Place at Abu Ghraib." *Los Angeles Times*. September 4, 2004.

———. "Army Calls Abuses of Detainees 'Aberrations'." *Los Angeles Times*. July 23, 2004.

McAllester, Matthew. "Iraqi Beheading Now Fueling New Global 'Snuff' Film Market." *Newsday*. October 17, 2004.

McCaffrey USA (Ret), General Barry R. "Iraq and Kuwait, Observations from Iraqi Freedom." *West Point Academic Report*. April 2006.

McCarthy, Ellen. "Changes Behind the Barbed Wire." *Washington Post*. December 13, 2004.

———. "Washington Contractors' Sales Increase." *Washington Post*. October 28, 2004.

———. "Post 9/11 Mergers Brought Problems, Government Service Firms Often Leaped Before They Looked." *Washington Post*. August 23, 2004.

———. "Demand Helps CACI Profit Increase 56%." *Washington Post*. August 19, 2004.

———. "CACI Finds No Torture Involvement, Arlington Firm's Employee was Named in Army Report." August 13, 2004.

———. "CACI Gets New Interrogation Contract." *Washington Post*. August 5, 2004.

———. "Interior Dept. Inquiry Faults Procurement." *Washington Post*. July 14, 2004.

———. "Government Clears CACI for Contracts, GSA Decides Not to Bar Firm Over Work for Army in Iraq." *Washington Post*. July 8, 2004.

———. "Pension Funds Press CACI on Iraq Prison Role." *Washington Post*. June 11, 2004.

———. "Contractors Sometimes Stretch Their Deals." *Washington Post*. May 31, 2004.

———. "CACI Faces New Probe of Contract." *Washington Post*. May 28, 2004.

———. "CACI Contracts Blocked; Current Work Can Continue." *Washington Post*. May 26, 2004 http://www.washingtonpost.com/wp-dyn/articles/A55758-2004May25.html.

———. "CACI Contract: From Supplies to Interrogation." *Washington Post*. May 17, 2004.

McCarthy, Ellen, and Frank Ahrens. "Family and Friends Close Ranks Around Civilian Interrogator." *Washington Post*. May 14, 2004.

McCoy, Kevin. "U.S. Missed Need for Prison Personnel in War Plans." *USAToday*. June 15, 2004 http://www.usatoday.com/news/world/iraq/2004-06-14-military-police-shortage_x.htm.

McDonald, Heather. "How to Interrogate Terrorists." *City Journal*. Winter 2005 http://www.city-journal.org/html/15_1_terrorists.html.

McDonald, R. Robin. "New Suit Over Abu Ghraib Abuse Claims Filed." *Legal Intelligencer*. July 29, 2004.

———. "Contractors Face New Suit Over Abu Ghraib Abuse Claims," *Fulton County Daily Report*. July 28, 2004.

Measley, Travis. "Texas A&M professor calls Abu Ghraib trials 'complex human story'." *University Wire*. September 11, 2007.

Melloan, George. "Wishing Won't Make Terrorism Go Away." *Wall Street Journal*. May 18, 2004.

Merle, Renae. "Census Counts 100,000 Contractors in Iraq, Civilian Number; Duties are Issues." *Washington Post*. December 5, 2006 http://www.washingtonpost.com/wp-dyn/content/article/2006/12/04/AR2006120401311.html (viewed December 12, 2006).

———. "Titan Admits Bribery In Africa, Contractor Will Pay $28.5 Million to Settle Criminal, SEC Cases." *Washington Post*. March 2, 2005 http://www.washingtonpost.com/wp-dyn/articles/A64554-2005Mar1.html.

Merle, Renae and Ellen McCarthy. "6 Employees From CACI International, Titan Referred for Prosecution." *Washington Post*. August 26, 2004.

Merle, Renae and Griff Witte. "Lack of Contracts Hampered FEMA, Dealing with Disaster on the Fly Proved Costly." *Washington Post*. October 10, 2005.

Meyer, Dick. "Benumbed by Beheadings?" *cbsnews.com*. September 29, 2004 http://www.cbsnews.com/stories/2004/09/24/opinion/meyer/main645410.shtml.

Meyer, Philip. "Why Journalism Needs Ph.D.s." *The American Editor*. September 1996 http://www.asne.org/kiosk/editor/september/meyer.htm.

Michaels, Jim. "U.S. pulls plug on 6 al-Qaeda media outlets." *USAToday*. October 5, 2007.

"Military Contractors Take the Heat." *Daily Dispatch (South Africa)*. May 7, 2004 http://www.dispatch.co.za/2004/05/07/Foreign/contract.html (viewed January 4, 2007).

Miller, T. Christian. "Army Gives Contract to Company in Jail Scandal." *Los Angeles Times*. August 5, 2004.

————. "Contractors Fall Through Legal Crack." *Los Angeles Times*. May 4, 2004.

Moreno Gonzales, John and Arnold Abrams. "Families of accused soldiers blame civilians." *Newsday.com*. April 30, 2004.

Murtha, Rep. John. "It's Time to Bring the Troops Home." *www.waging peace.org*. November 17, 2005 http://www.wagingpeace.org/articles/2005/11/17_murtha-its-time-to-bring-the-troops-home.htm.

Myers, Lisa. "Climate at Abu Ghraib distressed former interrogator." *NBC News*. May 10, 2004.

Nacos, Brigitte L. "Accomplice or Witness? The Media's Role in Terrorism," *Current History*. April 2000 http://www.currenthistory.com/org_pdf_files/99/636/99_636_174.pdf (viewed January 3, 2006).

Nadler, David M. "The Pendulum Swings Back." *Federal Computer Week*. August 16, 2004.

"N.Y. Lawyer Convicted of Aiding Terrorists," *Associated Press*. February 11, 2005.

O'Brien, Susie. "My Life With an Accused Torturer." *Herald Sun*. May 10, 2004.

O'Harrow, Jr., Robert and Scott Higham. "Interior, Pentagon Faulted in Audits; Efforts to Speed Defense Contracts Wasted Millions." *Washington Post*. December 25, 2006 http://www.washingtonpost.com/wp-dyn/content/article/2006/12/24/AR2006122400916.html (viewed January 12, 2007).

O'Reilly, Bill. "Is the Abu Ghraib Ruling Dangerous?" *The O'Reilly Factor*, *Fox News*. September 29, 2005.

"Officer charged in Abu Ghraib to be court-martialed." *Associated Press*. January 26, 2007.

Orin, Deborah. "Reporting for the Enemy; Media Won't Show Saddam's Evil." *New York Post*. June 16, 2004.

Palmeri, Christopher. "Up Front: Taking a Firm Swipe at CalPERS." *BusinessWeek*. August 16, 2004 http://www.businessweek.com/magazine/content/04_33/c3896016_mz003.htm.

Penenberg, Adam. "Searching for *The New York Times*." *Wired News*. July 14, 2004 http://www.wired.com/news/culture/0,1284,64110,00.html (viewed December 18, 2006).

"Pentagon folly." *Arizona Daily Star*. May 8, 2004.

Perazzo, John. "CCR: Fifth Column Law Factory." *Front Page Magazine*. July 31, 2002 http://www.frontpagemag.com/Articles/ReadArticle.asp?id=2155.

Phillips, Ashley. "Experts: Iraq War Being Fought in Cyberspace, General Petraeus Says Extremists Use the Internet as a Tool in Battle." *ABC News*. September 11, 2007 http://abcnews.go.com/Technology/story?id=3583106&page=1.

Phinney, David. "Torture for Profit." *Guerilla News Network*. September 21, 2004 http://gnn.tv/articles/110/Torture_for_Profit.

———. "Firm's Work at Guantanamo Prison Under Review." *Federal Times*. July 19, 2004.

———. "Contractors' Improper Billing Plagues Iraq Effort." *Federal Times*. June 21, 2004.

———. "DoD Tightening Contracting Rules After Iraq Prison Scandals." *Federal Times*. June 8, 2004.

Piptak, Adam. "17 Ex-P.O.W's Set Back Again in Claim Against Iraq." *New York Times*. June 5, 2004.

Pound, Edward T., and Kit R. Roane. "Hell on Earth." *U.S. News & World Report*. July 19, 2004.

Priest, Dana and R. Jeffrey Smith. "Memo Offered Justification for Use of Torture, Justice Dept. Gave Advice in 2002." *Washington Post*. June 8, 2004.

"Private Warriors: New PBS Doc Questions Role of Military Contractors in Iraq." *DemocracyNow.org*. June 21, 2005 http://www.democracynow.org/article.pl?sid=05/06/21/1335238 (viewed January 26, 2007).

Reddy, Anitha. "CACI in the Dark on Reports of Abuse." *Washington Post*. May 6, 2004.

———. "At CACI, Concerns About Growth; Some Worry AMS Will Drag Revenue." *Washington Post*. March 15, 2004.

———. "Local, Canadian Firms to Buy and Split AMS." *Washington Post*. March 11, 2004.

———. "CACI Hungers to Reach the Top Tier." *Washington Post*. October 20, 2003.

Reid, T.R. "Witness: Graner Ordered to Beat Prisoners." *Washington Post*. January 13, 2005.

Repsher Emery, Gail. "Numerous Iraq Task Orders Fall Outside the Scope of Their Contracts." *Washington Technology Report*. June 16, 2004.

Ricchiardi, Sherry. "Missed Signals." *American Journalism Review*. August/September 2004 http://www.ajr.org/Article.asp?id=3716.

"Rushing off a cliff." *New York Times*. September 28, 2006 http://www.nytimes.com/2006/09/28/opinion/28thu1.html?ex=1317096000&en=3eb3ba3410944ff9&ei=5090&partner=rssuserland&emc=rss (viewed January 12, 2007).

Saransohn, Judy. "Special Interests." *Washington Post*. July 7, 2005 http://www.washingtonpost.com/wp-yn/content/article/2005/07/06/AR2005070602153_2.html.

Savage, Charlie. "McCain Fights Exception to Torture Ban, ex-POW Assails Bid to Exempt CIA." *Boston Globe*. October 26, 2005 http://www.boston.com/news/nation/washington/articles/2005/10/26/mccain_fights_exception_to_torture_ban/.

———. "Bush Could Bypass New Torture Ban, Waiver Right Is Reserved." *Boston Globe*. January 4, 2006 http://www.boston.com/news/nation/washington/articles/2006/01/04/bush_could_bypass_new_torture_ban/ (viewed January 5, 2006).

Scarborough, Rowan. "Interrogators pressured to make inmates talk." *Washington Times*. May 5, 2004.

Schaff, William. "Taking Stock: Enterprise Software: Let's Make a Deal." *InformationWeek*. March 22, 2004.

Scheer, Peter. "Press freedom undermined by prosecutions." *San Jose Mercury News*. March 13, 2006 http://www.mercurynews.com/mld/mercurynews/news/opinion/14086762.htm (Viewed March 20, 2006).

Schmidt, Susan, "Ashcroft Refuses to Release '02 Memo; Document Details Suffering Alowed in Interrogations," Washington Post, June 9, 2004.

Schmitt, Eric. "Army Report Says Flaws in Detention Did Not Cause the Abuses at Abu Ghraib." *New York Times*. July 23, 2004.

Schlesinger, James. "The Truth About Our Soldiers." *Wall Street Journal*. September 11, 2004.

Schudson, Michael. "For a few dollars more never mind morality, objectivity or contextuality." *Financial Times*. July 31, 2004.

Schwartz, Nelson D. "The Pentagon's Private Army." *Fortune Magazine*. March 17, 2003 http://money.cnn.com/magazines/fortune/fortune_archive/2003/03/17/339252/index.htm.

Serrano, Richard A. "Friendly Fire at Abu Ghraib Case." *Los Angeles Times*. January 13, 2005.

Schudson, Michael. "For a few dollars more, Never mind morality, objectivity or contextuality—the truth is that sometimes journalists in pursuit of their least noble instincts produce their most noble work." *Financial Times (Weekend Magazine)*. July 31, 2004.

Shaw, David. "For Journalists, Lessons in Conduct and Survival." *Los Angeles Times*. May 1, 2005.

Shawl, Jeannie. "Bush signs Military Commissions Act." *Jurist*. October 17, 2006 http://jurist.law.pitt.edu/paperchase/2006/10/bush-signs-military-commissions-act.php (viewed January 8, 2007).

Sherker, Michael. "Intelligence Ethics and Non-coercive Interrogation." *Defense Intelligence Journal*. v. 16 no. 1 2007.

Sherman, Jason. "New DOD Policy to Guide Role of Contractors on the Battlefield." *InsideDefense.com*. October 21, 2005 http://defense.iwpnewsstand. com/insider.asp?issue=10202005.

Singer, Peter W. "Outsourcing War," *Foreign Affairs*. March/April 2005. Http://www.foreignaffairs.org/2005030/faessay84211/p-w-singer/outsourcing-war.html.

Singer, Peter W. "The Private Military Industry and Iraq: What have we learned and where to next?" *Geneva Centre for the Democratic Control of Armed Forces Policy Paper*. November 2004 http://www.dcaf.ch/_docs/pp04_private-military.pdf (viewed January 23, 2007).

―――. "The Contract the Military Needs to Break." *Washington Post*. September 12, 2004.

―――. "Outsourcing Interrogation: the Legal Vacuum." *Pakistan Daily Times*. May 11, 2004.

―――. "Above Law, Above Decency; Private military contractors may escape punishment in the Iraqi prisoner abuse scandal." *Los Angeles Times*. May 2, 2004.

Smith, R. Jeffrey. "Documents Helped Sow Abuse, Army Report Finds." *Washington Post*. August 30, 2004.

Smith, R. Jeffrey, and Josh White. "General Granted Latitude at Prison." *Washington Post*. June 12, 2004.

Spagot, Elliot. "Lockheed effectively scuttles merger with Titan." *SanLouisObispo.com*. June 24, 2004.

Spitzberg, Samuel. "Court-martial trial is a credit to justice system." *Albany Times Union*. September 12, 2007.

Squitieri, Tom and Dave Moniz. "U.S. Army re-examines deaths of Iraqi prisoners." *USAToday*. June 28, 2004.

Stanley, Trevor. "Profile of Abu Musab al-Zarqawi." *Perspectives on World History and Current Events*. Accessed July 2005 http://www.pwhce.org/zarqawi.html.

Stanton, John. "United Kingdom, United States and Israel: Kings of Pain." *Dissident Voice*. May 13, 2004 http://www.dissidentvoice.org/May2004/Stanton0513.htm.

Starr, Barbara. "Soldiers charges with abusing Iraqi prisoners." *CNN.com*. March 20, 2004.

Stockman, Farah. "Army Finds 49 Abuse Cases." *Boston Globe.* July 23, 2004.

————. "Civilians Identified in Abuse May Face No Charges." *Boston Globe.* May 4, 2004 http://www.boston.com/news/nation/articles/2004/05/04/civilians_idd_in_abuse_may_face_no_charges/.

Strupp, Joe. "Supreme Court Will Not Hear Miller/Cooper Case." *Editor & Publisher.* June 27, 2005 http://www.editorandpublisher.com/eandp/news/article_display.jsp?vnu_content_id=1000968809.

Tanner, Adam. "California Questions Firm Over Iraq Interrogators." *Reuters.* August 3, 2004.

Tapper, Jake, and Sonia Gallego. "U.S. to Close Infamous Abu Ghraib Prison." *ABC News.* March 9, 2006 http://abcnews.go.com/WNT/print?id+1707023 (viewed May 10, 2006).

Taranto, James. "The Saddam Torture Videos." *Wall Street Journal.* June 16, 2004 http://www.opinionjournal.com/best/?id=11000 5224.

"Torture Profiteers! Lawsuit Charges Two U.S. Corporations Conspired with U.S. Officials to Torture and Abuse Detainees in Iraq." June 9, 2004 http://www.iwantchange.org/corp_rule.php?id=181.

Tremoglie, Michael. "Who is Behind Lynne Stewart?" *FrontPageMagazine.com.* September 25, 2002.

Tsao, Amy. "CACI: Wiping off Abu Ghraib's Taint." *BusinessWeek.* August 18, 2004 http://www.businessweek.com/technology/content/aug2004/tc20040818_0593_tc055.htm.

Tyson, Anne Scott. "Private Security Workers Living on Edge in Iraq." *Washington Post.* April 23, 2005 http://www.washingtonpost.com/wp-dyn/articles/A10547-2005Apr22.html.

"Unit Says It Gave Earlier Warning of Abuse in Iraq." *Gainesville Sun.* June 14, 2004.

"U.S. soldiers charged with abusing detainees, 5 accused of allegedly kicking, punching prisoners in Iraq on Sept. 7." *Associated Press.* November 7, 2005 http://www.msnbc.msn.com/id/9958811.

Vedantam, Shankar. "Why Torture Keeps Pace With Enlightenment." *Washington Post.* June 11, 2007 http://www.washingtonpost.com/wp-dyn/content/article/2007/06/10/AR2007061001216.html?sub=AR

Vest, Jason. "Haunted by Abu Ghraib—Having helped reveal abuses at the notorious prison, former interrogator Torin Nelson opens up about why it happened and how is has wrecked his career." *GovExec.com.* October 3, 2005.

Vlahos, Kelly Beaucar, "Leaks Continued to Flow in 2006," *FoxNews.com*, January 2, 2007 http://www.foxnews.com/story/0,2933,240377,00.html (viewed January 5, 2007).

von Zielbauer, Paul. "Army Colonel Is Acquitted In Abu Ghraib Abuse Case." *New York Times*. August 29, 2007.

Wakeman, Nick. "9th Annual Top 100 Federal Prime Contractors." *Washington Technology*. May 6, 2002 http://www.washingtontechnology.com/news/17_3/features/18213-1.html.

Washburn, David. "San Diego-based Titan hit with lawsuit over Iraqi prisoner abuse." *San Diego Union-Tribune*, July 28, 2004.

Washburn, David, and Bruce V. Bigelow. "Debate on Military Contractors Heats Up." *San Diego Union Tribune*. May 7, 2004 http://www.signonsandiego.com/news/military/20040507-9999-1n7contract.html.

Washington Post Principles. http://www.washpost.com/gen_info/principles/index.shtml.

Weil, Jonathan, and Joann S. Lublin. "Gadfly Activism at CalPERS Leads to Possible Ouster of President." *Wall Street Journal*. December 1, 2004.

Weinburg, Neil "Sanctimonious in Sacramento." *Forbes.com*. May 10, 2004 http://www.forbes.com/home/free_forbes/2004/0510/052.html.

Whalen, Sarah. "What Might Sharon Know About CACI?" *Arab News*. May 14, 2004.

White, Josh. "Army Officer is Cleared in Abu Ghraib Scandal." *Washington Post*. January 10, 2008.

———. 'Ex-Commander in Iraq Faults War Strategy, 'No End in Sight,' Says Retired General Sanchez." *Washington Post*. October 13, 2007.

———. "Abu Ghraib Officer Cleared of Detainee Abuse; Verdict Means No One in Army's Upper Ranks Will Be Imprisoned for the 2003 Mistreatment in Iraq." *Washington Pos*. August 29, 2007.

———. "Conflicting Portraits of Officer Charged Over Abu Ghraib." *Washington Post*. July 31, 2007.

———. "General Who Ran Guantanamo Bay Retires." *Washington Post*. August 1, 2006.

———. "Abu Ghraib Dog Tactics Came From Guantanamo, Testimony Further Links Procedures at 2 Facilities." *Washington Post*. July 27, 2005.

———. "Army Revisiting Policies and Training for Prison Guards." *Washington Post*. February 24, 2005.

White, Josh, and Scott Higham. "Army Calls Abuses 'Aberrations.'" *Washington Post*. July 23, 2004.

"White House Looks to Weaken Abuse Ban." *CBS and Associated Press*. October 25, 2005 http://www.cbsnews.com/stories/2005/10/25/politics/main 979430.shtml.

Williams, David. "Private US military contractors face heat." *Manila Times*. May 7, 2004 http://www.manilatimes.net/national/2004/may/07/yehey/world/ 20040507wor3.html.

Witte, Griff. "New Law Could Subject Civilians to Military Trial." *Washington Post*. January 15, 2007.

"Who's Who on Abu Ghraib Conviction List." *Associated Press*. May 4, 2005 http://www.msnbc.msn.com/id/7709487/.

Worden, Leon. "Taguba Interview: Sanchez 'Good Friend.'" *Signal*. April 24, 2005.

———. "State Controller, Treasurer Question Investments in CACI." *Signal*. July 10, 2004 http://www.scvhistory.com/scvhistory/signal/iraq/sg071004b. htm.

———. "Interrogator: Chaos Reigned at Abu Ghraib; Veteran of Guantanamo Bay encountered dramatic differences when he checked in for work at Iraq prison." *Signal*. June 20, 2004.

———. "Army May Be Misusing Contractors." *Signal*. June 15, 2004.

———. "Interior: Army Never Reported Abuse; Agency responsible for dealing with intelligence firm hasn't taken action because no problems were ever reported, official says." *Signal*. June 9, 2004.

Zagorin, Adam, and Sally B. Donnelly. "Gitmo Goat or Hero?" *Time*. March 27, 2006 http://www.time.com/time/archive/preview/0,10987,1174697,00.html (viewed May 9, 2006).

"Zarqawi Justifies Killing of Civilians." *Washington Times*. October 8, 2005.

Zernike, Kate. "At abuse hearing, no testimony that G.I.'s acted on orders." *New York Times*. August 6, 2004.

———. "Soldiers Testify on Orders to Soften Prisoners in Iraq." *New York Times*. January 13, 2005.

Zernike, Kate, and David Rohde. "Forced Nudity of Iraqi Prisoners is Seen as a Pervasive Pattern, Not Isolated Incidents." *New York Times*. June 8, 2004.

Books

Ahmed, Akbar S. *Islam Today, A Short Introduction to the Muslim World* (London: I.B. Tauris & Co., 1999).

Alvarez, Jr., Everett, and Anthony S. Pitch. *Chained Eagle, The Heroic Story of the First American Shot Down over North Vietnam.* (Washington, D.C.: Potomac Books, Inc., 2005).

Ankerberg, John and John Weldon. *Fast Facts on Islam, What You Need to Know Now* (Eugene: Harvest House, 2001).

Anonymous. *Through Our Enemies Eyes, Osama bin Laden, Radical Islam, and the Future of America.* (Dulles: Brassey's, Inc., 2002).

Armstrong, Karen. *Holy War, the Crusades and Their Impact on Today's World.* (New York: Anchor, 2001).

Barnett, Roger W. *Asymmetrical Warfare, Today's Challenge to U.S. Military Power* (Dulles: Brassey's, Inc., 2003).

Beck, MD, Aaron T. *Prisoners of Hate, The Cognitive Basis of Anger, Hostility, and Violence.* (New York: Perennial HarperCollins, 1999).

Bergen, Peter L. *Holy War Inc., Inside the Secret World of Osama bin Laden.* (New York: Touchstone, 2002).

Binnendijk, Hans, and Richard L. Kugler. *Seeing the Elephant, The U.S. Role in Global Security.* (Washington, D.C.: Potomac Books, Inc., 2006).

Bozell III, L. Brent. *Weapons of Mass Distortion, The Coming Meltdown of the Liberal Media.* (New York: Crown Forum, 2004).

Brennan, Joseph Gerard. *Foundations of Moral Obligation, A Practical Guide to Ethics and Morality.* (Novato: Presidio, 1992).

Burke, Jason. *Al Qaeda, The True Story of Radical Islam.* (New York: Penguin, 2003).

Chatterjee, Pratap. *Iraq, Inc. A Profitable Occupation.* (New York: Seven Stories Press, 2004).

Clarke, Richard A. *Against All Enemies, Inside America's War on Terror* (New York: Free Press, 2004).

Coll, Steve. *Ghost War, The Secret History of the CIA, Afghanistan and bin Laden, from the Sovier Invasion to September 11, 2001* (New York: Penguin, 2004).

Corum, James S. *Fighting the War on Terror, A Counterinsurgency Strategy.* (St. Paul: Zenith Press, 2007).

Crile, George. *Charlie Wilson's War, The Extraordinary Story of How the Wildest Man in Congress and a Rogue CIA Agent Changed the History of Our Time.* (New York: Grove Press, 2003).

Danner Mark. *Torture and Truth: America, Abu Ghraib, and the War on Terror*. (New York: New York Review Books, 2004).

Ellul, Jacques. *Propaganda, The Formatting of Men's Attitudes*. (New York: Vintage Books, Random House Inc., 1973).

El-Nawawy, Mohammed, and Adel Iskandar. *Al Jazeera: The Story of the Network That Is Rattling Governments and Redefining Modern Journalism*. (Boulder: Westview, 2003).

Fenton, Tom. *Bad News, The Decline of Reporting, the Business of News, and the Danger to Us All*. (New York: HarperCollins Publishers, Inc., 2005).

Fram, David and Richard Perle. *An End to Evil, How to Win the War on Terror*. (New York: Random House, 2003).

Friedman, Norman. *Terrorism, Afghanistan and America's New Way of War*. (Annapolis; Naval Institute Press, 2003).

Gabrieli, Francesco. *Arab Historians of the Crusades*. (New York: Barnes & Noble, 1993).

Gaffney, Frank J. and colleagues. *War Fighting, 10 Steps America Must Take to Prevail in the War for the Free World*. (Annapolis; Naval Institute Press, 2006).

Gerges, Fawaz. *Journey of the Jihadist, Inside Muslim Militancy*. (New York: Harcourt, 2006).

Granot, Hayim and Jay Levinson. *Terror Bombings, The New Urban Threat, Practical Approaches for Response Agencies and Security*. (Tel Aviv: Dekel, 2002).

Goldberg, Bernard. *Bias, A CBS Insider Exposes How the Media Distort the News* (Washington, DC: Regnery Publishing Inc., 2003).

Hafez, Mohammed M. *Suicide Bombers in Iraq: The Strategy and Ideology of Martyrdom* (Washington, D.C.: United States Institute of Peace Press, 2007).

Heffelfinger, Christopher, editor. *Unmasking Terror, A Global Review of Terrorist Activities*. (Washington, D.C.: Jamestown Foundation, 2005).

Hess, Stephen and Marvin Kolb, editors. *The Media and the War on Terror*. (Washington D.C.: Brookings Institution Press, 2003).

Holy Koran (New York: Knopf, 1992).

Hosseini, Khalid. *The Kite Runner*. (New York: Penguin, 2003).

Huntington, Samuel P. *The Clash of Civilizations and the Remaking of World Order* (New York: Touchstone, 1997).

Intelligence Science Board, *Educing Information, Interrogations: Science and Art, Foundation for the Future, Phase 1 Report*. (Washington, DC: National Defense Intelligence College, 2006).

Karpinski, Janis. *One Woman's Army, The Commanding General at Abu Ghraib Tells Her Story* (New York: Hyperion, 2005).

Kepel, Gilles. *The War for Muslim Minds*. (Cambridge: Harvard University Press, 2004).

Kushner, Harvey with Bart Davis. *Holy War on the Home Front, The Secret Islamic Terror Network in the United States*. (New York: Sentinel, 2004).

Lacquier, Walter, editor. *Voices of Terror, Manifestos, Writings and Manuals of al Qaeda, Hammas and other Terrorists from Around the World and Throughout the Ages*. (New York: Reed Press, 2004).

Lanning, Michael Lee. *Mercenaries: Soldiers of Fortune, from Ancient Greece to Today's Private Military Companies*. (New York: Ballantine, 2005).

Lewis, Bernard. *The Crisis of Islam, Holy War and Unholy Terror*. (New York: Random House, 2003).

Mackey, Chris, and Greg Miller. *The Interrogators: Inside the Secret War Against al Qaeda*. (New York: Little, Brown and Company, 2004).

Mahmud, S.F. *A Short History of Islam* (Karachi: Oxford University Press, 1988).

Malkin, Michelle. *Invasion, How America Still Welcomes Terrorists, Criminals and Other Foreign Menances to Our Shores*. (Washington, D.C.; Regnery, 2002).

Mansfield, Laura. *His Own Words, A Translation of the Writings of Dr. Ayman al Zawahiri*. (Old Tappan: TLG Publications, 2006).

Masr, Vali. *The Shia Revival, How Conflicts within Islam Will Shape the Future*. (New York: W.W. Norton, 2006).

McCain, John. *Faith of My Fathers, A Family Memoir* (New York: Random House, 1999).

McKelvey, Tara. *Monstering, Inside America's Policy of Secret Interrogations and Torture in the Terror War*. (New York: Carroll & Graf, 2007).

McNamara, Robert S. *Argument Without End: In Search of Answers to the Vietnam Tragedy* (New York: Persues, 1999).

McNamara, Robert S. *In Retrospect*. (New York: Random House, 1997).

Mestrovic, S.G. *The Trials of Abu Ghraib, An Expert Witness Account of Shame and Honor*. (Boulder: Paradigm, 2007).

Miles MD, Steven H. *Oath Betrayed, Torture, Medical Complicity and the War on Terror* (New York: Random House, 2006).

Miniter, Richard. *Disinformation, 22 Media Myths that Undermine the War on Terror* (Washington, DC: Regnery Publishing, 2005).

Nacos, Brigitte. *Mass-Mediated Terrorism: The Central Role of the Media in Terrorism and Counterterrorism.* (Lanham: Rowman & Littlefield, 2007).

Nacos, Brigitte. *Terrorism and the Media.* (New York: Columbia University Press, 1996).

National Commission on Terrorist Attacks. *The 9/11 Commission Report: Final Report of the National Commission on Terrorist Attacks Upon the United States.* (New York: W.W. Norton & Company, 2004).

Norris, Piper, and Marion R. Rust, editors. *Framing Terrorism: The News Media, the Government and the Public.* (New York: Routledge, 2003).

O'Neill, Bard E. *Insurgency and Terrorism, Inside Modern Revolutionary Warfare.* (Dulles: Brassey's, 1990).

The Oxford American Desk Dictionary and Thesaurus, 2nd Ed. (New York: Berkley Publishing Group, 2001).

Palmer, Nancy, editor. *Terrorism, War, and the Press.* (Cambridge: Joan Shorenstein Center, 2003).

Patterson USAF (Ret.), Lt. Col. Robert "Buzz." *War Crimes, The Left's Campaign to Destroy Our Military and Lose the War on Terror.* (New York: Crown, 2007).

Perry, John. *Torture, Religious Ethics and National Security* (Ottawa: Novalis, 2005).

Phares, Walid. *Future Jihad, Terrorist Strategies Against the West.* (New York: Palgrave Macmillan, 2005).

Pipes, Daniel. *Militant Islam Reaches America.* (New York: W.W. Norton, 2002).

Pollack, Kenneth M. *The Threatening Storm.* (New York: Random House, 2002).

Riley-Smith, Jonathan, editor. *The Oxford History of the Crusades.* (Oxford: Oxford University Press, 1999).

Rhodes, Anthony. *Propaganda—The Art of Persuasion: World War II; An Allied and Axis Visual Record, 1933–1945.* (Leicester: The Wellington Press, 1987).

Rubin, Gretchen. *Forty Ways to Look at Winston Churchill.* (New York: Random House Trade Paperback, 2003).

Ryan, Mike. *Special Operations in Iraq.* (Barnsley: Pen and Sword Military, 2004).

Runciman, Steve. *A History of the Crusade, Vol. I The First Crusade.* (Cambridge: Cambridge University Press, 1999).

Runciman, Steve. *A History of the Crusade, Vol. II The Kingdom of Jerusalem.* (Cambridge: Cambridge University Press, 1999).

Runciman, Steve. *A History of the Crusade, Vol. III The Kingdom of Acre.* (Cambridge: Cambridge University Press, 1999).

Saar, Erik and Viveca Novak. *Inside the Wire: A Military Intelligence Soldier's Eyewitness Account of Life at Guantanamo.* (New York: Penguin Press, 2005).

Scahill, Jeremy. *Blackwater, The Rise of the World's Most Powerful Mercenary Army.* (New York: Nation Books, 2007).

Schumacher, Col. Gerald. *A Bloody Business, America's War Zone Contractors and the Occupation of Iraq* (St. Paul: Zenith Press, 2006).

Schweikart, Larry. *America's Victories, Why the U.S. Wins Wars and Will Win the War on Terror.* (New York: Sentinel, 2006).

Selb, Philip. *Beyond the Front Lines: How the News Media Cover a World Shaped by War.* (New York: Palgrave Macmillan, 2006).

Shah, Sirdir Ikbal Ali. *Muhammed: The Prophet* (Paris: Tractus Books, 1996).

Singer, Peter. *Corporate Warriors: The Rise of the Privatized Military Industry.* (Ithaca: Cornell University Press, 2003).

Spencer, Robert. *The Politically Incorrect Guide to Islam (and the Crusades).* (Washington: D.C.: Regnery Publishing Inc., 2005).

Spencer, Robert. *Islam Unveiled,Disturbing Questions about the World's Fastest-growing Faith.* (Washington: D.C.: Regnery, 2002).

Steyn, Mark. *America Alone, The End of the World As We Know It.* (Washington, D.C.: Regnery Publishing Inc., 2006).

Tyerman, Christopher. *God's War, A History of the Crusades.* (London: Penguin, 2006).

U.S. Army and U.S. Marine Corps. *Counterinsurgency Field Manual, Army Field Manual No.3-24 and Marine Corps Warfighting Publication No.3-33.5* (Chicago: University of Chicago Press, 2007).

Walzer, Michael. *Just and Unjust Wars, A Moral Argument with Historical Illustrations.* (New York: Basic Books, 1977).

The War in Iraq, The Illustrated Story. (New York: Life Books, 2003).

Webster's New World Dictionary and Thesaurus 2nd Ed. (Cleveland: Wiley Publishing, Inc., 2002).

Wright, Lawrence. *Looming Tower, Al Qaeda and The Road to 9/11.* (New York: Vintage Books, 2006).

Wright, Micah Ian. *You Back the Attack, We'll Bomb Who We Want, Remixed War Propaganda*. (New York: Seven Stories Press, 2003).

Yoo, John. *War by Other Means, An Insider's Account of the War on Terror*. (New York: Atlantic Monthly Press, 2006).

Zimbardo, Phillip. *The Lucifer Effect: Understanding How Good People Turn Evil*. (Random House: New York, 2007).

Television and Radio

"Accounting for Abuse." *PBS Online NewsHour* (a NewsHour with Jim Lehrer online transcript). August 24, 2004 http://www.pbs.org/newshour/bb/military/july-dec04/abughraib_8-25.html.

Farnsworth, Elizabeth. "Olympic Park: Another Victim." *NewsHour with Jim Lehrer*. October 28, 1996 http://www.pbs.org/newshour/bb/sports/jewell_10-28.html.

"Interview with Brian Williams." *CNN*. December 4, 2006 http://transcripts.cnn.com/TRANSCRIPTS/0512/04/rs.01.html (viewed December 11, 2006).

"Interview with Chris Mackey." *Fresh Air — National Public Radio*. July 20, 2004.

"Interview with Chris Mackey." *American Morning — CNN*. July 19, 2004 http://transcripts.cnn.com/TRANSCRIPTS/0407/19/ltm.04.html.

"Interview with Peter Singer (Transcript #090801 cb.k01)." *Insight — CNN International*. September 8, 2004.

"Interview with Peter Singer." *Marketplace — Minnesota Public Radio*. August 26, 2004 http://marketplace.publicradio.org/shows/2004/08/26_mpp.html.

"Interview with Peter Singer." *Marketplace — Minnesota Public Radio*. June 17, 2004.

"Interview with Peter W. Singer." *Fresh Air — National Public Radio*. May 11, 2004.

"Interview with Ron Daniels." *NOW with Bill Moyers — PBS*. June 11, 2004.

"Interview with Torin Nelson." *Deborah Norville Tonight — MSNBC*. May 11, 2004.

"Interview with Torin Nelson." *NBC Nightly News*. May 10, 2004.

Jennings, Peter. "Inside Iraq's Notorious Abu Ghraib Prison," transcript of report filed on ABC News. January 31, 2005 http://www.abcnews.go.com/WNT/print?id=451784.

Norris, Michelle. "Whistleblower speaks out." *All Things Considered. NPR*. August 15, 2006.

Phillips, Kyra. "Abu Ghraib Whistleblower Shares Story." *Interview with Joseph Darby. CNN.* August 15, 2006.

Other (Reports, Press Releases, Etc.)

Army Field Manual 34-52. *Intelligence Operations.* September 1992, http://www.fas.org/irp/doddir/army/fm34-52.pdf.

Army Field Manual 2-22.3 (FM 34-52). *Human Intelligence Collector Operations.* December 2006. Http://www.fas.org/irp/doddir/army.fm2-22-3.pdf.

"Briefing on Investigations into Military Intelligence." August 25, 2004.

CACI Annual Report 2004. http://www.shareholder.com/caci/annual.cfm.

"CACI Denies Allegations Made in Abu Ghraib Abuse Case." *Dow Jones News Service.* July 27, 2004.

CACI investor teleconference call. May 27, 2004 http://www.shareholder.com/caci/MediaRegister.cfm?MediaID=12011.

CACI Press Release. "CACI States Position About Reported Allegations Concerning Employees in Iraq." May 3, 2004 http://www.caci.com/about/news/news2004/05_03_04_2_NR.html.

———. "CACI Emphasizes Facts Presented During Congressional Testimony on Iraq Prison Investigation and Requirements Related to Company's U.S. Military Contract, No information on improper behavior reported to company by U.S. Government; Company does not tolerate illegal behavior by employees." May 9, 2004 http://www.caci.com/about/news/news2004/05_09_04_NR.html.

———. "CACI to Provide Information to GSA Regarding Department of Interior ContractWork Performed for U.S. Army in Iraq." May 26, 2004 http://www.caci.com/about/news/news2004/05_27_04_2_NR.html.

———. "CACI Continues to Inform Investment Community and Public at Large About CACI's Business In Iraq, The Company Seeks to Correct Inaccurate Reports." June 13, 2004 http://www.caci.com/about/news/news2004/06_13_04_NR.html

———. "GSA Determines That No Suspension or Debarment of CACI Is Necessary." July 7, 2004 http://www.caci.com/about/news/news2004/07_07_04_2_NR.html.

———. "CACI Corrects Public Information about its Services Contract for U.S. Army Interrogation Support in Iraq." July 20, 2004 http://www.caci.com/about/news/news2004/07_20_04_NR.html.

———. "Army Inspector General Report Determines CACI Interrogators Met Army Statement of Work Criteria." July 22, 2004 http://www.caci.com/about/news/news2004/07_22_04_2_NR.html.

———. "CACI Rejects Lawsuit as Slanderous and Ludicrous, Frivolous Suit Based on False Statements Without Merit." July 27, 2004 http://www.caci.com/about/news/news2004/07_27_04_NR.html.

———. "CACI Meets With California Pension Funds About Work in Iraq, Company Challenges Politically Motivated Actions of California Treasurer Phil Angelides as Wrongly Rejecting Contractor's Support of Military." August 3, 2004 http://www.caci.com/about/news/news2004/08_03_04_NR.html.

———. "CACI Receives Contract Extension for U.S. Army Interrogation Support in Iraq." August 10, 2004 http://www.caci.com/about/news/news2004/08_10_04_NR.html.

———. "CACI Reports Preliminary Findings of Internal Investigation, Company Provides Information About Its Interrogator Support Personnel in Iraq, No Evidence of Abusive Wrongdoing Uncovered." August 12, 2004 http://www.caci.com/about/news/news2004/08_12_04_NR.html.

———. "CACI Says the Fay Report Clearly Shifts Focus of Blame Away From Its Employee Named in a Previous Report, Company Notes Employees Were Not Involved in Any Horrendous Acts." August 26, 2004 http://www.caci.com/about/news/news2004/08_26_04_NR.html.

———. "CACI Says GAO Report on Interagency Contracting Fails to Acknowledge Urgent Impact of Wartime Circumstances on Contracting Practices." May 2, 2005 www.caci.com/about/news/news2005/05_05_05_NR.html.

———. "CACI Awarded Prime Contract on $19.25 Billion, Multiple-Award Services Program With U.S. Army, Strategic Services Sourcing (S3) Award to Support Defense C4ISR Community Largest Contract Award in CACI History," March 15, 2006. http://www.caci.com/about/news/news2006/03_15_06_NR.html.

California State Controller's Office Press Release. "Westly Seeks Anti-Torture Investment Policy." July 6, 2004.

California State Treasurer's Office Press Release. "CalPERS, CalSTRS, at Treasurer Angelides' urging, to call on CACI board to conduct full investigation and hold management responsible for interrogators' conduct at Iraq prison; Latest U.S. Army Investigation Found CACI Contract Interrogators Deeply Involved In 'Inhumane to Sadistic' Abuses." October 18, 2004 http://www.treasurer.ca.gov/news/releases/2004/101804_iraq.pdf (viewed December 22, 2006).

————. "CalSTRS, at Treasurer Angelides' urging, to call on CACI board to conduct full investigation and hold management responsible for interrogators' conduct at Iraq prison; CalSTRS schedules November vote to consider divesting its CACI holdings, Latest U.S. Army Investigation Found CACI Contract Negotiators.

Deeply Involved In 'Inhumane to Sadistic' Abuses." September 1, 2004 http://www.treasurer.ca.gov/news/releases/2004/090104_cacistrs.pdf (viewed December 21, 2006).

CalPERS Investment Report 2004 http://www.calpers.ca.gov/invest/invest mentreport-2004/toc.asp.

CalSTRS Stock Portfolio 2004 http://www.calstrs.com/Investments/usStock. aspx.

Calvert Online. "Issue Brief, Weapons." http://www.calvert.com/sri_ib_21. html?

————. "Social Analysis Criteria." http://www.calvert.com/sri_647.html.

Center for Constitutional Rights. "CCR's Additional Post-9/11 Cases." http://www.ccr-ny.org/v2/rasul_v_bush/911cases.asp (viewed December 22, 2006).

"CCR Collaborates on New Book 'You Back The Attack!' May 12, 2003 http://www.ccr-ny.org/v2/reports/report.asp?ObjID=94YJF1MzCb&Content =242.

————. "It's Time to Stand Up and Break the Silence About Bush's War Against Iraq." 2002 http://www.ccr-ny.org/v2/viewpoints/docs/no_war_pam phlet.pdf.

Church, III, Vice Admiral Albert T. "Unclassified Executive Summary of report by Vice Admiral Albert T. Church, III." March 10, 2005 http://www. defenselink.mil/news/Mar2005/d20050310exe.pdf.

Defense Contract Audit Agency. *DCAA Contract Audit Manual, Vol. 1 of 2, Chapters 1–8*. Washington, DC: U.S. Government Printing Office, January 2005.

Edmond & Jones Press Release. "Iraqis Civilians File Claim Against Private U.S. Firms Murder, Torture and Abuse.," July 27, 2004.

Fay, Major General George R., Lieutenant General Anthony R. Jones, General Paul Kern. *AR 15-6 Investigation of Abu Ghraib Detention Facility and 205th Military Intelligence Brigade*. August 23, 2004 http://www4.army. mil/ocpa/reports/ar15-6/AR15-6.pdf.

Giachino, Renee. "CFIF General Counsel Talks With Veteran CBS Reporter Bernard Goldberg About Media Bias." Center for Individual Freedom. August 12, 2004 http://www.cfif.org/htdocs/freedomline/current/in_our_opinion/bernard_goldberg.htm.

Hugman, Bruce. "A Presentation by a Consultant to the Uppsala Monitoring Centre. Pretoria." September 2004 http://www.who.int/medicines/organization/qsm/activities/drugsafety/updatepresentations/19b_Crisis_management.ppt.

International Alliance for Justice. "Report on the Conference of Iraqi Women." October 4, 2002.

"Interview with Lowell Bergman" JournalismJobs.com. January 2001 http://www.journalismjobs.com/interview_bergman.cfm.

Joint Chiefs of Staff. *Department of Defense Dictionary of Military and Associated Terms, Joint Publication 1-02*. May 2005 http://www.dtic.mil/doctrine/jel/doddict/data/i/02679.html.

Letter from Joseph Neurauter, GSA Suspension and Debarment Official, to CACI CEO J.P. London, July 7, 2004.

Lockheed Martin Press Release, "Lockheed Martin Terminates Merger Agreement with the Titan Corporation." June 26, 2004 http://www.lockheedmartin.com/wms/findPage.do?dsp=fec&ci=15290&rsbci=0&fti=112&ti=0&sc=400 (viewed December 29, 2006).

London, Jack. "Keynote Address to Century Club of George Mason University." November 5, 2003 http://www.caci.com/speeches/jpl_GMU_11-5-03_speech.shtml.

"McCain Statement on Detainee Amendments." Press Release from the office of Senator John McCain. October 5, 2005 http://www.mccain.senate.gov/index.cfm?fuseaction=Newscenter. ViewPressRelease&Content_id=1611.

Military Reporters and Editors Luncheon Keynote Speech by Lt. Gen. Ricardo Sanchez (Ret.). October 12, 2007 http://www.militaryreporters.org/sanchez_101207.html (viewed October 17, 2007).

"The Nuclear Arms Race." http://academic.brooklyn.cuny.edu/physics/sobel/Nucphys/race.html.

Pitts, Chip. "Business and Human Rights." *Amnesty International USA*. http://www.amnestyusa.org/business/chippitts.html.

"Press briefing by General Paul Kern, Lieutenant General Anthony Jones and Major General George Fay." FDCH e-Media, Inc. August 25, 2004.

Profile of Ayman al-Zawahri. *Al Jazeera*. February 21, 2005. http://english.aljazeera.net/NR/exeres/78446020-E13D-48EE-962F-98E0E08E543B.htm.

"Profile of Ernie Pyle." Indiana Historical Society http://www.indianahistory.org/pop_hist/people/pyle.html.

Profile of J. P. "Jack" London for the 2004 Federal 100 Winners. *Federal Computer Week*. March 16, 2004. http://fcw.com/events/fed100/2004/London.asp.

Project on Government Oversight. "Federal Contractor Misconduct: Failures of the Suspension and Debarment System." May 10, 2002 http://www.pogo.org/p/contracts/co-020505-contractors.html.

Ratner, Michael "Making Us Less Free: War on Terrorism or War on Liberty?" Center for Constitutional Rights. May 2002 http://www.ccr-ny.org/v2/viewpoints/viewpoint.asp?ObjID=YLhsqUx1eu&Content=143.

"Remarks of U.S. Rep. Curt Weldon (D-PA) at Hearing of House Armed Services Committee." May 7, 2004 http://commdocs.house.gov/committees/security/has128000.000/has128000_0f.htm.

Rigby, Ken. *Technical Management — a Pragmatic Approach*. http://sparc.airtime.co.uk/users/wysywig/gloss.htm.

Schlesinger, James. "Final Report of the Independent Panel to Review DoD Detainee Operations." August 23, 2004 http://www.pentagon.mil/news/Aug2004/d20040824finalreport.pdf.

Shakespeare, William. *The Merchant of Venice*. http://www.online-literature.com/shakespeare/merchant/.

Standard & Poor's Press Release. "S&P Revises CACI Intl Outlook to Negative from Stable." *Dow Jones Newswire*. June 1, 2004.

"Statement by Rep. Henry Waxman on H.R. 627." May 6, 2004 http://www.henrywaxman.house.gov/news_files/news_statements_res_iraq_05_06_04.htm.

"Statement of Mr. William H. Reed, Director, Defense Contract Audit Agency, House Committee on Government Reform." June 9, 2004 http://www.halliburtonwatch.org/news/DCAA_testimony.pdf.

"Sworn Statement of Torin Nelson." Deposition taken by Susan Burke, Burke Pyle, LLC. filed in the United States District Court, For the District of Columbia. September 9, 2006.

"Sworn Statement by Steven Anthony Stefanowicz as Released by Atty. Henry Hockeimer." June 14, 2004.

Taguba, Major General Antonio M. *Article 15-6 Investigation of the 800th Military Police Brigade*. March 2004 http://www.npr.org/iraq/2004/prison_abuse_report.pdf.

Taguba Annex # 90 Testimony of [Mr. Steve Stephanowicz-Redacted] US civilian contract interrogator, CACI, 205th MI Brigade. http://www.aclu.org/torturefoia/released/a90.pdf.

"Testimony of Major General Antonio M. Taguba; Stephen A. Cambone, Undersecretary of Defense for Intelligence; and Lt. General Lance Smith, Deputy Commander of Central Command before the Senate Armed Services Committee." May 11, 2004 http://wid.ap.org/transcripts/040511iraq_senate. html.

UBS Investment Research. "CACI International: Sitting in the 'Sweet Spot;' Initiated With Buy 1." October 14, 2004.

U.S. Code, Title 18. http://caselaw.lp.findlaw.com/casecode/uscodes/18/parts/i/chapters/113c/sections/section_2340.html.

U.S. Department of the Army, Office of the Inspector General, Lieutenant General Paul T. Mikolashek. "Detainee Operations Inspection." July 21, 2004 http://www4.army.mil/ocpa/reports/ArmyIGDetaineeAbuse/index. html.

U.S. Department of Defense. "Detainee Operations Briefing by Major General Geoffrey Miller." May 4, 2004 http://www.defenselink.mil/transcripts/2004/tr20040504-1424.html.

U.S. Department of Defense, Office of the Inspector General. "Contracts Awarded for the Coalition Provisional Authority by the Defense Contracting Command-Washington." March 18, 2004 http://www.dodig.osd.mil/Audit/reports/FY04/04057sum.htm.

U.S. Department of Defense, Office of the Inspector General. "Review of DoD-Directed investigations of Detainee Abuse (U)." August 25, 2006 http://www.dodig.osd.mil/Inspections/IPO/reports/r_IPO2004C005.pdf.

U.S. Department of Defense. "2001 Quadrennial Defense Review Report." September 30, 2001 http://www.defenselink.mil/pubs/qdr2001.pdf.

U.S. Department of the Interior. *Blanket Purchase Agreements Handbooks*. September 2000. http://www.usbr.gov/pmts/acquisitions/bpahandbook. html.

U.S. Department of the Interior — National Business Center, Contract Number NBCHA010005.

U.S. Department of the Interior, Office of the Inspector General. "Review of 12 Procurements Placed Under General Services Administration Federal Supply Schedules 70 and 871 by the National Business Center." July 16, 2004 http://www.oig.doi.gov/upload/CACI%20LETTER3.pdf.

U.S. Department of State International Information Programs. "Silence Through Torture: Iraq, A Population Silenced." February 2003 http://usinfo. state.gov/products/pubs/silenced/torture.htm.

U.S. Government Accountability Office. "Interagency Contracting Problems with DOD's and Interior's Orders to Support Military Operations." GAO 05-201, April 2005 http://www.gao.gov/new.items/d05201.pdf.

U.S. General Accountability Office. "Rebuilding Iraq: Fiscal Years 2003 Contract Award Procedures and Management Challenges." June 2004 http://www.gao.gov/new.items/d04605.pdf.

U.S. Government Accountability Office. "Military Operations: Contractors Provide Vital Services to Deployed Forces but Are Not Adequately Addressed in DOD Plans, GAO-03-695." June 24, 2003 http://www.gao.gov/new.items/d03695.pdf.

U.S. General Services Administration. "Audit of Federal Technology Service's Client Support Centers (Report Number A020144/T/5/Z04002)." January 8, 2004.

U.S. Senate Armed Services Committee. "Hearing on the treatment of Iraqi Prisoners." May 6, 2004 http://www.washingtonpost.com/wp-dyn/articles/A8575-2004May7.html.

Whaley's Bibliography of Counterdeception, Second Edition, May 2006 (CD-ROM).

Websites

Al Jazeera (profile of Ayman al-Zawahiri) http://english.aljazeera.net/NR/exeres/78446020-E13D-48EE-962F-98E0E08E543B.htm

Answers.com http://www.answers.com/topic/abu-ghraib-prison

Anti-Defamation League. "About Osama bin Laden." http://www.adl.org/terrorism_america/bin_l.asp.

BrainyQuote.com http://www.brainyquote.com/quotes/quotes/m/margaretth162424.html

The Brookings Institution http://www.brookings.edu/index/about.htm

CalSTRS http://www.calstrs.com/Investments/usStock.aspx

Canadian Broadcasting Corp http.www.cbc.ca/news/background/iraq/abu ghraib_timeline.html

Center for Constitutional Rights http://www.ccr-ny.org/v2/about/mission_vision.asp

CounterPunch.com http://www.counterpunch.com

Counterterrorism Blog http://www.counterterrorismblog.org

Dictionary http://www.websters.com, http://www.dictionary.com

Dictionary of Military and Associated Terms http://www.dtic.mil/doctrine/jel/doddict/

Digger History http://www.diggerhistory.info/pages-help/faq4.htm#gi

Federal Acquisition Regulation http://www.acquisition.gov/far/loadmainre.html

Geneva Conventions http://www.genevaconventions.org/, http://www.law-ref.org/GENEVA/kw-torture.html (viewed December 16, 2005), http://www.ohchr.org/english/law/cat.htm

Global Security.com http://www.globalsecurity.org/intell/world/iraq/abu-ghurayb-prison-investigation.htm

Guantanamo Bay Naval Base http://www.nsgtmo.navy.mil/

Human Rights First http://www.humanrightsfirst.org/us_law/detainees/us_torture_laws.htm

InfoPlease http://www.infoplease.com/spot/iraqtimeline1.html

Liberty Quotes http://quotes.liberty-tree.ca/quotes.nsf/QuotesHistory?ReadForm&Start=1&Count=1000&ExpandView

The Literature Network http://www.online-literature.com/shakespeare/merchant/

Managing Standards version 4.6 http://sparc.airtime.co.uk/users/wysywig/gloss.htm

Margaret Thatcher Foundation http://www.margaretthatcher.org/speeches/displaydocument.asp?docid=106096

Miriam-Webster Online Dictionary http://www.m-w.com/dicitonary/torture/

NavAir Training Systems Division http://www.ntsc.navy.mil/Resources/Library/Acqguide/cor.htm

Office of UK Prime Minister Tony Blair http://www.number-10.gov.uk/output/page4.asp

Proverbia http://en.proverbia.net/citasautor.asp?autor=16497&page=5

Red Cross http://www.redcross.lv/en/conventions.htm

Reporters Committee for Freedom of the Press. *Privilege Compendium.* http://www.rcfp.org/privilege/index.php.

Society of Professional Journalists. *Code of Ethics.* http://www.spj.org/ethics_code.asp.

South Asia Terrorism Portal. http://www.satp.org/satporgtp/usa/Al_Queda.htm.

Spartacus http://www.spartacus.schoolnet.co.uk/

ThinkExist Quotes http://en.thinkexist.com/quotes/top/

United Nations Conventions on Torture. http://www.ohchr.org/english/law/cat.htm.

U.S. Code http://caselaw.lp.findlaw.com/casecode/uscodes/18/parts/i/chapters/113c/sections/section_2340.html

U.S. Government Services Administration http://www.gsa.gov/Portal/gsa/ep/contentView.do?contentId=17028&contentType=GSA_OVERVIEW

U.S. Marine Corps http://www.usmc.mil/maradmins/maradmin2000.nsf/0/df5f5be5ceb9b41e85256e54006c4c90?OpenDocument

V Corps http://www.vcorps.army.mil/organization/default.htm

ACKNOWLEDGMENTS

BY THE END OF 2007, I HAD BEEN WITH CACI FOR OVER THIRTY-five years. During this time, I have had the good fortune and pleasure of working with some of the most talented and dedicated people in the national security and information technology industry. Because of their hard work and loyalty, I was even more determined to ensure that CACI's fine reputation was maintained. And this book needed a team just as talented and dedicated to ensure that our story was told well. The Abu Ghraib ordeal demonstrated that 'Ever Vigilant' is more than our company motto. This book is the story of CACI's vigilance.

First, I want to acknowledge and thank Michael Gelb who prepared our book's initial structure and an early draft version of the text. Michael was also there during the crisis as part of our external public relations team and personally knew many of the details and facts of the story. He interviewed most of the CACI team that worked on the Abu Ghraib crisis. His proximity to the situation as well as his professional objectivity gave CACI's story unique candor and perspective. I also want to thank CACI's Executive Vice President of Corporate Communications, Jody Brown, who was instrumental in coordinating this book project and its many reviews. A key member of our strategy development team, Jody was on the front line of the crisis every day from the very beginning, managing our media relations and public outreach efforts. She was also the key staff support person on our employee communications efforts. I also thank Jody's communications staff who provided editorial back up through Michael Pino and many of the graphic and photo layout designs through Stan Poczatek. Thanks also go to Z. Selin Hur for her many contributions to this book and her arduous research efforts and support of our media response process throughout the ordeal. Selin's efforts were essential to the compilation of this book; researching, writing, editing and organizing its contents every step of the way. My gratitude also goes to Dr. Jennifer Burkhart whose invaluable analytical input, behavioral insights and recommendations on our corporate messaging and image were fundamental to CACI's "push back" efforts. Jennifer also provided important review and feedback as a major contributor in the development of this book and was most helpful in the editorial critique of the final copy.

I would also like to acknowledge and thank other vital CACI team members who lived through and helped CACI weather the storm of the crisis. Without their expertise and hard work, their late nights and long weekends, we would not have prevailed as thoroughly and forcefully as we did. Ron Schneider, our Executive Vice President of Corporate Strategic Business Development, was indispensable in guiding and managing our Iraq response team through their review of CACI's business process and for adeptly leading the implementation of our customer outreach.

I want to thank our Iraq contract project team. They include Mark Billings, Chuck Mudd, Dave Norton, and Scott Northrop, who were all critical in determining the facts, keeping morale high with our employees there, and maintaining CACI's positive relationship with the U.S. Army in Iraq. Former President of U.S. Operations, Ken Johnson, along with former executives Jon Hendrick and Harry Thornsvard, supported the CACI team while making sure that CACI's daily operations continued uninterrupted. Terry Raney's role was key in the review of our contract procedures; providing valuable perspective, advice and judgment. We appreciate the work and efforts of all.

Thanks also go to Mike Gray who led our CACI contracts team in overcoming numerous challenges, including the negotiation of the extension of some of our responses to government inquiries. Our audit group also worked tirelessly with the various government agency personnel to answer their many inquiries. Additional CACI people who were major contributors to our efforts included Tom Horrigan, for his expertise in reviewing and organizing voluminous and complicated information, and Amy Monahan, who diligently supported the recruiting and management of employees during that critical time. David Dragics, CACI's Investor Relations manager advanced our efforts to get the facts and information, once verified, through to our investors and the financial markets. Former General Counsel Jeff Elefante and CACI's legal team contributed extensively to our efforts with contracts, government investigations and lawsuits. We are grateful for the support and contributions of all of these fine CACI people.

Outside Counsel Bill Koegel, with assistance from his associates at Steptoe and Johnson, worked diligently as a key member of our team, from directing CACI's internal investigation to providing recommendations to the company on important legal matters. Attorney Craig King at Arent Fox was invaluable in supporting us with the GSA inquiry. I also thank Don Foley and the team at Prism Public Affairs for their assistance; from screening the daily press to contributing to CACI's outreach strategies. David Berteau at Clark & Weinstock is acknowledged for his valuable help with our approach and efforts in getting our message and the facts about our work in Iraq to lawmakers.

Most importantly, my Executive Administrator of 26 years, Lillian Brannon, is warmly thanked for all her help in facilitating the organization, preparation and momentum of our book project as well as maintaining support for our ongoing business and operational needs.

It is with deep gratitude that I also thank the 9,500 men and women of CACI (at the time we confronted the crisis) for their hard work and dedication to our customers and our company. They kept the business growing and helped maintain our good name. Throughout the crisis, they held their heads high and assured everyone around them that CACI remained an outstanding and highly reputable company that provided top quality service to its customers in the U.S. military and government. I thank the members of our board of directors at the time, who all supported and encouraged the approach we took in responding to the crisis and its media-driven excess. My sincere appreciation also goes out to the numerous shareholders and business associates of CACI who provided a steady stream of support and encouragement throughout the ordeal and who continue to do so. I also want to thank the professional staff at Regnery, especially Kate Frantz, for providing valuable input and editorial expertise.

It would be an incomplete "acknowledgment" if I did not thank my many family members, friends and colleagues. During our ordeal, I had dozens upon dozens of close friends, relatives, customers, classmates, and military and government colleagues, who took the time to express their confidence and support to me and my company while we were under assault. I thank each one of them with all humility.

I owe a very special appreciation to my children and their spouses, my grandchildren, and my wife for all their support and confidence in our determination to always do the right thing. I am also grateful to my wife for sharing my every value and belief in life's basic principles; always with such courage, resolve, integrity and faith. On matters of faith, integrity, loyalty and patriotism, I have with me forever the spirit and example of my mother and father.

Finally, I would like to extend my thanks to you, the readers. CACI could only publicize the facts as they became known. Unfortunately, verified information and conclusions were slow in coming and, once established, have often been ignored or even dismissed—intentionally in some cases. Your interest in our story and your openness to learn the facts for yourself are vital to our "Truth will out" commitment to preserve our good name. For this I will always be grateful.

J.P. London
December 2007

ABOUT J. PHILLIP LONDON

Dr. J. Phillip ("Jack") London is the Executive Chairman and Chairman of the Board of CACI International Inc, a New York Stock Exchange-listed company. For twenty-three years, from July 1984 through June 2007, he served as President and CEO of CACI. London joined CACI in 1972 as a project manager. By 1984 London had become Chief Executive Officer. He was elected to the board in 1981 and was elected Chairman in 1990 upon the passing of the company's chairman and co-founder. Through this period, London developed and directed CACI's growth from a small professional services consulting firm to a leading information technology company with over 11,500 employees in over 100 offices worldwide (December 2007). As part of this growth, Dr. London designed and developed CACI's highly successful mergers and acquisitions program and negotiated or oversaw thirty-seven transactions as CEO. Today the company serves as a trusted national security asset to the U.S. government in the fields of information technology and network communications services.

In 2004, London led CACI successfully through its media-exaggerated entanglement in the Abu Ghraib scandal. London, an Oklahoma native, is a graduate of the U.S. Naval Academy with the class of 1959. He retired as a U.S. Navy Captain after serving 12 years as a U.S. naval officer and aviator, and another 12 years with the reserves. His navy career includes participation on the airborne recovery team for Colonel John Glenn's Mercury project space flight in *Friendship 7* in February 1962 and service during the Cuban Missile Crisis in the fall of 1962.

London was awarded a masters degree in operations research from U.S. Naval Postgraduate School and received a doctorate in business administration "with distinction" from the George Washington University. Dr. London's industry recognition includes being named CEO of the Year by the George Washington University and Entrepreneur of the Year by Ernst & Young. He has received the distinguished John W. Dixon Award from the Association of the United States Army for outstanding industry leadership. He was the 2007 recipient of the Navy League of the United States' prestigious Fleet Admiral Chester W. Nimitz Award for outstanding leadership and commitment to maritime industry. Each year since 2002, the Human Resources Leadership Awards of Greater Washington presents its annual Ethics in Business Award in Dr. London's name. He is active in industry and community affairs and leads many of CACI's philanthropy and public service affiliations.

INDEX